According to appearances they [flirtatious house guests at Monticello] had many nibbles and bites, but whether the hooks took firm hold of any particular subject or not, is a secret not communicated to me. If not, we shall know it by a return to their angling grounds, for here they fix them until they catch something to their palate.

EDWIN MORRIS BETTS (1892–1958), whose interest in Thomas Jefferson's domestic concerns produced editions of the *Farm Book* and the *Garden Book,* began the editing of these letters in 1956 under a grant from the American Philosophical Society. He invited James Adam Bear, Jr., Curator of Monticello, to assist him in his work, and during Dr. Betts's illness and following his death, Mr. Bear continued the project and carried it to its completion.

JAMES ADAM BEAR, JR., has brought special interests and training (B.A. and M.A. in History, 1943 and 1952, the University of Virginia; M.A. in Library Science, Simmons College, 1954, and a number of years as Assistant Curator of Manuscripts at the University of Virginia Library) to the editing of President Jefferson's family letters. In addition to discharging his curatorial duties at Monticello, Mr. Bear has produced other works concerning Virginia history, Monticello, and Jefferson's domestic life: *A Checklist of Virginia Almanacs* (1962), *Old Pictures of Monticello,* and *Jefferson Advises His Children and Grandchildren on Their Reading.* He is co-author of the *Monticello Handbook* and is presently editing *Memoirs of a Monticello Slave* and Edmund Bacon's *Life at Monticello.* As unpublished works he has completed an index of the Jefferson account books and a medical chronology of the third president. He is presently compiling a bibliography of Jefferson's writings and printed material dealing with his unofficial activities.

THE FAMILY LETTERS OF THOMAS JEFFERSON

EDITED BY

EDWIN MORRIS BETTS AND JAMES ADAM BEAR, JR.

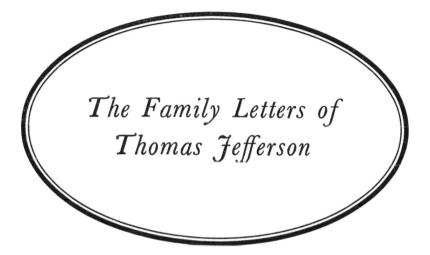

The Family Letters of
Thomas Jefferson

UNIVERSITY OF MISSOURI PRESS
COLUMBIA • MISSOURI

Preface

Thomas Jefferson was a prolific letter writer in a great letter-writing age: it has been estimated that he wrote and received as many as fifty thousand letters. Writing these was a great burden, especially in his later years when old age and rheumatism rendered writing slow and difficult. He then complained that to fill a single page was the work of almost an entire day. Correspondence with his children and grandchildren, however, could at no time of his life have been considered anything but pleasant. For, next to being with his family, hearing from and about them was his delight.

The family letters are not limited to family matters, but deal with local affairs in Paris, Philadelphia, New York, Washington, and Albemarle County, Virginia, or wherever the correspondents happened to be. They are also concerned with farm problems, the construction of the house and gardens at Monticello, and innumerable other subjects, including the perils of ennui, the fine arts, and poignant suggestions on how to get along with one's neighbors. It is the family relationship, however, that commands the interest and makes the letters as entertaining to the general reader as they are instructive to the scholar.

Jefferson could write with facility and authority on subjects ranging from agriculture to architecture, from philosophy to history, but it was in the role of parent and grandparent that he wrote with most assurance and pleasure. As such he believed in telling his correspondents something worth while, and he ran the gamut of parental prerogatives by proposing stern regimens of occupation and improvement while confidently advising on how to ensure happiness in the married state or on the nursing of children. Amid such parental dicta one does not lose sight of the fact that Jefferson was a loving and excellent father, if a possessive and precise one.

In addition to giving an admirable picture of Jefferson as a parent and grandparent, these manuscripts depict him in the unfamiliar role of "parent-in-law." It is one he played to the hilt, and the reader must be left to form his own conclusions of this side of the man. It may be observed, however, that, in spite of all of his benevolence to Messrs. Thomas Mann Randolph, Jr., and John Wayles Eppes, his sons-in-law, he was sometimes difficult.

The letters reiterate Jefferson's desire for the ineffable pleasures of family society as opposed to the hated occupation of politics. Too, they represent him as intimately as possible, since not a single letter between him and Mrs. Jefferson is known to survive. It is believed he destroyed them after her death. This other side can be perceived only through this family correspondence, which was no more intended for public perusal than the letter to Joseph Priestley on the question of his religious beliefs. In sum, these letters present Jefferson's portrait as a family man, painted chiefly by himself, but with the assistance of his fourteen children and grandchildren.

The editorial work was begun by the late Jeffersonian scholar, Dr. Edwin Morris Betts, in 1956 under a grant from the American Philosophical Society. Dr. Betts had previously edited the *Farm Book* and *Garden Book* and seemed a natural choice to continue the exploration of Jefferson's domestic side. During his first months on the project, Dr. Betts asked me to assist him, which I was delighted to do. The work was progressing satisfactorily when he suffered the first of several illnesses that incapacitated him for many months and eventually led to his death.

When I assumed the editorship, I reviewed the existing plans carefully and decided to modify the policy so as to make it conform in general with the editorial method of *The Papers of Thomas Jefferson*, edited by Dr. Julian P. Boyd. It is not to be inferred, however, that these few letters will be treated as those in that definitive work.

Since all letters are either from or to Jefferson, they are headed by the name of the other correspondent, as, "From Ellen Wayles Randolph" or "To Martha Jefferson Randolph." The date line, salutation, and complimentary close remain in their original form. The date line has been placed at the head of the letter. Commas and capitals have been inserted here and there. The first letter of each sentence is capitalized, and the prefixes of address, such as *mr, mrs,* and *miss,* are altered to *Mr., Mrs.,* and *Miss.* The ampersand is expanded to *and* in all cases except when used with the names of business firms, as, *Farrel & Jones.* No attempt has been made to alter spelling, even with respect to proper names. Punctuation is maintained as far as possible as it appears in the original, but periods are inserted where needed and dashes removed. No attempt has been made to identify or distinguish between a recipient's copy and a file draft, the present purpose being only to use a complete and legible text when available.

The locations of the 570 manuscripts included in this correspondence are not given; these may be found by consulting the photocopies of the Alphabetical and Chronological Checklists of Jefferson Manuscripts (including letters to him) prepared by The Jefferson Office, Princeton University, Princeton, New Jersey, and those placed in a number of research centers throughout the United States. I wish, however, to acknowledge permission to use these letters as having been granted by the Alderman Library of the University of Virginia, Charlottesville, Virginia (ViU); Colonial Williamsburg, Inc., Williamsburg, Virginia (ViWC); the Henry E. Huntington Library and Art Gallery, San Marino, California (CSmH); The Jefferson Office, Jervis Library, Rome, New York; The Library of Congress, Washington, D.C. (DLC); Massachusetts Historical Society, Boston, Massachusetts (MHi); The Pierpont Morgan Library, New York, New York (NNP); Princeton University Library, Princeton, New Jersey; The University of North Carolina, Chapel Hill, North Carolina; and Gordon Trist Burke, Omaha, Nebraska; John Randolph Burke, Bryn Mawr, Pennsylvania; Harold Jefferson Coolidge, Washington, D. C.; James H. Eddy, New Canaan, Connecticut; Mrs. Robert Graham, Alexandria, Virginia; Robert H. Kean, Charlottesville, Virginia; Mrs. Page Taylor Kirk, Charlottesville, Virginia; Mrs. A. Slater Lamond, Alexandria, Virginia; Cecil Eppes Shine, Jr., Miami, Florida; Walter C. Stearns, Ridgefield, Connecticut; Miss Olivia Taylor, Charlottesville, Virginia; and Mrs. Harold M. Wilson, Miami, Florida. The texts of a number of letters are from Sarah Nicholas Randolph, *The Domestic Life of Thomas Jefferson* (New York, 1871); this is also an excellent account of the personal side of Jefferson.

I wish to express my sincere appreciation to those persons who very kindly have assisted in a greater or lesser degree in the editing of these letters: Francis L. Berkeley, Jr., Mrs. Edwin M. Betts, Miss Anne E. H. Freudenberg, Donald R. Haynes, Herbert Gantner.

Morrison H. Heckscher, E. L. Inabinett, John M. Jennings, Mrs. Mary Dillard Kenny, Dumas Malone, Howard C. Rice, Jr., William H. Runge, Miss Mary Elizabeth Ryall, John M. Shaw, Roger E. Stoddard, Kendon L. Stubbs, Mrs. Mabel Apple Talley, The Jefferson Office, Princeton, New Jersey, d'Alte Welch, Mr. and Mrs. Walter Muir Whitehill, and John Cook Wyllie.

J.A.B.

Charlottesville, Virginia
December, 1965

Contents

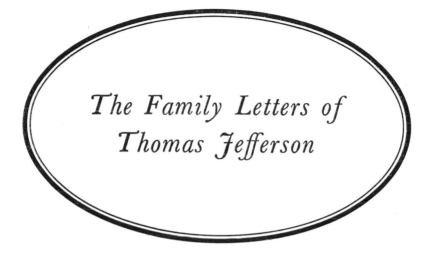

*The Family Letters of
Thomas Jefferson*

Introduction

Monticello was the place beyond all others where Jefferson could enjoy the supreme satisfaction of family associations. Often while burdened with public office he found it difficult to believe that existence could be a blessing, except when something called to mind his family and farm. Of the two, it was the "ineffable pleasures . . . of family society" which always came first in his affections.[1]

During his happiest years, his daughters Martha and Mary,[2] with his wife, the former Martha Wayles Skelton, made the contented household at Monticello where literary and agricultural projects were eagerly pursued. This contentment was shattered by the tragic death of Mrs. Jefferson on September 6, 1782, a few months after the birth of their daughter Lucy Elizabeth. The bereavement welded an enduring bond between ten-year-old Martha and her father, while it caused Mary, aged four, and the infant Lucy to be sent to live at Eppington[3] with Aunt Elizabeth and Uncle Francis Eppes — the only early home and parents these children were ever to know. Little Lucy was not to know them long, for she died at two, while her father was abroad.

Besides inducing him to resume the chores of public life sooner

1. Thomas Jefferson to Martha Jefferson Randolph, June 8, 1797, Coolidge Collection, Massachusetts Historical Society. Hereafter cited as MHi. Jefferson will be referred to as TJ.

2. Since these children were called by different names at different times during their lives, they will be referred to in this work by their given names, Martha and Mary. Martha, named for her mother, was sometimes called Patsy and especially so as a child. Mary, in the family, was Pol or Polly, in France, Marie or Mademoiselle Polie, and after returning home, Maria. They addressed each other as Sister Patsy or Polly and their father as Papa. As Martha grew older she used the more conventional Father, but Mary was no more consistent in addressing her father than in corresponding with him.

3. Elizabeth Wayles Eppes and Martha Wayles Jefferson were half sisters; John Wayles of The Forest, Charles City County, was their father. Eppington, the Eppes home, was located on the Appomattox River in southern Chesterfield County.

3

than he otherwise might have, the loss of his wife cast Jefferson into a role he intensely regretted, that of a "vagrant" father. Despite his aversion to bringing up children *in absentia*, as a labor of love he undertook maternal as well as paternal duties that might have defeated a less dedicated parent. Presently, inclination combined with habit to make him willing as well as capable, for he possessed, as Randall notes,[4] a feminine dexterity of manipulation, also patience and a knack of anticipating the children's many wants. For example, to the purchase of a frock for Martha or of a doll for Mary he would devote as much detailed care as he would expend in outlining a course of study for his nephew Peter Carr. By giving thoughtful consideration to trifling as well as to serious questions he won the children's confidence so that they found no problem too trite or too delicate for discussion with him.

The correspondence with his children began while Jefferson was in Annapolis in 1783. His first letter set the tone with the telling of something worth while, even as he ran the course of parental prerogatives by recommending strict regimens for personal conduct, appearance, and study habits. Such admonitions, written without realistic appreciation of the ages of his little charges, must have puzzled them at times. Doubtless he was attempting to produce a lasting impression and, above all, to enable them to avoid the pitfalls of ennui, the perils of indolence! The nature of his approach, didactic and moralistic as it may seem to us, did but prove he was a dedicated father, seriously concerned over rearing his daughters.

Jefferson received the notification of his appointment as diplomatic representative to the French government while he was in the Maryland capital, and he left the city with such dispatch that there was no time for a farewell visit to his younger children. Consequently, he never saw little Lucy again. En route to New England, he picked up Martha in Philadelphia, where she was at school. They arrived in Boston on June 18, and on July 5, 1784, the two sailed aboard the *Ceres* for England, landing at Cowes on the 26th. Nineteen days later, father and daughter reached Paris and took temporary quarters at the Hotel d'Orleans.[5]

The ensuing busy weeks were a shakedown period for the Jeffersons. Martha, who had to be outfitted as a diplomat's daugh-

4. Henry S. Randall, *The Life of Thomas Jefferson* (New York, 1858), I, 481–82. Hereafter cited as Randall.
5. Dumas Malone, *Jefferson and the Rights of Man* (Boston, 1951), 4–6.

ter, wrote that her father always accompanied her on the rather hectic visits to the mantuamaker, the staymaker, and the dressmaker. For the convent school, Abbaye Royale de Panthemont, which she entered prior to August 24, she required a uniform that she described as "crimson made like a frock, laced behind, with the tail, like a robe de cour, hooked on, muslin cuffs and tuckers." This sounds like a formal costume for a child not yet twelve, but the tone of the convent was not so pompous as to prevent her sixty schoolmates from calling Martha "Jeff" or "Jeffy."

The Jeffersons had not been more than a month in France when Lucy, Mary, and several of the Eppes children in Virginia contracted the whooping cough to which Lucy succumbed. She died about October 13, 1784, but Mrs. Eppes's letter informing her brother-in-law of his loss did not reach him until May 6, 1785.[6] Jefferson, already anxious to reunite his family, began to accelerate plans to have Mary sent to France as soon as possible.

After apprising the Eppeses of his wishes, Jefferson instructed Francis Eppes relative to the conditions to be met before Mary could undertake the voyage. First, on account of the equinoctial storms, she must sail from Virginia only "in the months of April, May, June or July." Next, a responsible person must attend her, "A careful negro woman, as Isabel . . . if she has had the smallpox, would suffice under the patronage of a gentleman." Finally, a safe vessel, one that should have made one voyage and be no more than five years old, must be found.[7]

In writing to Mary, her father said, "I wish so much to see you that I have desired your uncle and aunt to send you to me . . . you shall have as many dolls and playthings as you want." To this, Mary, now nearly nine, realizing that her secure position in the Eppes family was threatened, responded with a truthfulness and tenacity reminiscent of her father: "I don't want to go to France, I had rather stay with Aunt Eppes."[8]

One by one the obstacles that must at times have seemed insurmountable to the anxious father were removed, albeit with difficulty. The danger from Algerine pirates was to be avoided by sending Mary only in a ship that, being English or French, would be immune from attack. Elizabeth Eppes, having little desire to send her niece on such a trip, wrote her brother-in-law that she

6. Julian P. Boyd and others, editors, *The Papers of Thomas Jefferson* (Princeton, 1950——), VII, 441–42. Hereafter cited as *Papers*.

7. TJ to Francis Eppes [August 30, 1785], *Papers*, VIII, 451.

8. September 20, 1785, *Papers:* VIII, 532–33; [ca. May 22, 1786], IX, 560–61. 560–61.

was "in hopes of your countermanding your orders with regard to dear Polly [Mary]." [9] After months of trying negotiations, little Mary was taken aboard (ostensibly to play with her cousins and become accustomed to the ship), and then, exhausted from play, she fell asleep. Quietly the others were taken off, and Mary was left with Sally Hemings, a fourteen-year-old slave girl, as her companion on the journey. [10] The master, Captain Ramsay, took such care for her comfort that they soon became fast friends.

In April of 1787 Jefferson informed Martha that "our dear Polly will certainly . . . come this summer. . . . When she arrives, she will become a precious charge on your hands. . . ." Mrs. John Adams, to whom Captain Ramsay delivered Mary on their arrival in London, experienced the excitement of the little girl's first reaching Europe and notified the anxious father: "I have to congratulate you upon the safe arrival of your little Daughter. . . . She is in fine Health and a Lovely little girl." [11] Mrs. Adams had as difficult a time in persuading her to leave Captain Ramsay as Petit, [12] Jefferson's trusted servant, had in coaxing her to take leave of Mrs. Adams. So attached was she to her new friend that Petit needed several days to gain her confidence. When the two finally arrived at the Hotel de Langeac, Jefferson was overjoyed, but Mary no doubt was confused and probably failed to recognize her father.

During the first week, Martha came home and stayed with her sister, "leading her from time to time to the convent, til she became familiarized to it." [13] Soon after Mary had joined Martha at school, Jefferson proudly informed Mrs. Eppes of her progress: "This [French] she begins to speak easily enough and to read as well as English. She will begin Spanish in a few days, and has lately begun the harpsichord and drawing." [14] Never again would he have the opportunity of rendering such an excellent report, for Mary was not readily attracted to her books.

At this stage neither of the children displayed signs of having inherited their father's brilliance. Dumas Malone writes of Martha at this time, "If not a talented girl she was on her way to becoming a cultivated young woman." [15] Unusually dutiful, she was as tran-

9. March 31, 1787, *Papers*, XI, 260.
10. Malone, *Jefferson and the Rights of Man*, 134–35, and *Papers*, XI, 502.
11. June 26 and 27, 1787, *Papers*, XI, 501–3.
12. Adrien Petit was TJ's maître d'hôtel and a trusted servant.
13. TJ to Elizabeth Wayles Eppes, July 28, 1787, *Papers*, XI, 634. He reviews for Mrs. Eppes Mary's first day at school.
14. July 12, 1788, *Papers*, XIII, 347.
15. Malone, *Jefferson and the Rights of Man*, 131.

quil, sturdy, and self-reliant as her father, and like him was distinguished-looking rather than handsome. Martha's granddaughter Sarah Nicholas Randolph wrote of her as "a sweet girl, delicacy and sensibility are read in her every gesture, and her manners are in unison with all that is amiable and lovely," and although "not handsome at twelve she was tall and aristocratic looking."

Mary, unlike Martha in physical appearance as in temperament, was timid and clinging and often forgetful of her father's stern directions respecting the studies he urged her to master and report on to him. She has been described as singularly beautiful and delicate physically; in this no doubt she resembled her mother. Miss Randolph's description, based on family tradition, noted her great-aunt as having been "rather a querulous little beauty."[16]

After the return voyage to America the family disembarked at Norfolk on November 23, 1789. Mary was now a child of eleven and Martha a grownup of seventeen. If the younger was not entertaining thoughts of the opposite sex, apparently the elder was, and probably during the trip to Monticello the spark of love was ignited. When and where she and young Thomas Mann Randolph, Jr., her third cousin, met and courted remains something of a mystery. Jefferson's account book, which listed the itinerary to Monticello, failed to record a visit to Tuckahoe, Randolph's Goochland County home. They could have met while Jefferson was in Richmond, or it is possible, as Malone suggests, that they might have spent several days at Tuckahoe on a side trip from Richmond. William Gaines, in his fine dissertation on Randolph, expresses the opinion that Thomas Mann began to court Martha during the Christmas season of 1789–1790, and this would have been their first meeting since his childhood at Edgehill, his father's Albemarle County farm, several miles east of Monticello.

Despite the lack of details, we know that they were impressed with each other, and by January 30, 1790, they had become engaged.[17] Jefferson did not attempt to influence the romance, since in the case of young Randolph, his fears were groundless that his

16. Sarah Nicholas Randolph, "Mrs. Thomas Mann Randolph," in Mrs. O. J. Wister and Miss Agnes Irwin, editors, *Worthy Women of Our First Century* (Philadelphia, 1877), 16, 17, 23.

17. William H. Gaines, "Thomas Mann Randolph" (unpublished dissertation, University of Virginia, 1950), 60. Hereafter cited as "Gaines."

The trip up country took nearly a month from Norfolk. They arrived at Monticello December 24, 1789. It is interesting to note that family tradition maintains that the two met in Paris; however, neither Gaines nor Dr. Boyd in the *Papers* shows evidence to support the tradition. See Account Book 1789 for their itinerary from Norfolk to Monticello.

daughter might marry a Virginia blockhead (he quoted the odds at 14 to 1). The future father-in-law showed his thorough approval of the match by writing of the groom as "a young gentleman of genius, science, and honorable mind." [18]

Once the couple were engaged, their marriage date was soon settled. The ceremony was held at Monticello on February 23 (possibly a little earlier than would normally have been the case), allowing Jefferson time to reach his post as Secretary of State in New York City by late March. Little has been recorded about the wedding or the festivities that followed. The event, however, was duly put down in Jefferson's account book: "My daughter Martha is this day married to Thos. Mann Randolph, junr."

On March 1 Jefferson departed for New York, leaving Mary in the charge of the honeymoon pair at Monticello. The next several months found the newlyweds leading a sort of "ambulatory life at various places in Virginia: at Richmond, Varina and Eppington, accompanied, of course, by Mary." The family was united for a month in the early fall of 1790 at Monticello, at which time a home for the Randolphs was discussed.

Eager for them to settle at Edgehill, Jefferson, with his son-in-law's approval, undertook preliminary negotiations with the senior Randolph. Disagreement between father and son over a minor point, however, delayed the desired result so that for some time the Randolphs were without a home of their own.[19]

The expected arrival of a grandchild thoroughly excited Jefferson, who upon learning of it wrote Martha how to take care of herself. This granddaughter was born at Monticello, January 23, 1791. On hearing the news, Grandfather Jefferson acknowledged that such events were the "arch of matrimonial happiness."[20] No doubt acting upon a suggestion by his wife, Thomas Mann Randolph, Jr., asked Jefferson to select a name. He complied by choosing "Anne Cary" because, as he rationalized it, the name belonged

18. TJ to Barbé-Marbois, December 5, 1783, Papers, VI, 374, and "Autobiography," in Andrew A. Lipscomb and Albert Ellery Bergh, editors, The Writings of Thomas Jefferson, Memorial Edition (Washington, 1903), I, 161. 19. "Gaines," 62–63.

20. TJ to Martha Jefferson Randolph, February 9, 1791, Pierpont Morgan Library, New York City. Hereafter cited as NNP.

Jefferson kept a record of births and deaths of the grandchildren in his Book of Common Prayer (Oxford, 1752), which is now in the Alderman Library at University of Virginia. Hereafter cited as ViU. The twelve pages containing these data are reproduced in Thomas Jefferson's Prayer Book (Charlottesville, n.d.), cited later as Jefferson's Prayer Book.

to both sides of the family.[21] Grandpapa, as he was soon to be called, first saw the baby at Monticello in September, when she was eight months old.

On October 12, 1791, Jefferson left Monticello for Philadelphia, taking Mary with him so she could be placed in school. Until his resignation as Secretary of State in 1793, Jefferson, sometimes accompanied by Mary, commuted between Albemarle and the capital several times a year. During his Philadelphia residence additional grandchildren were being born at Monticello. The second, Thomas Jefferson Randolph, arrived September 12, 1792, and on August 30, 1794, came Ellen Wayles Randolph, Martha's only child to die in infancy. The second of this name was born October 13, 1796.[22]

The year 1797 was important for the Monticello family. For Jefferson it brought his return to public life as Vice-President,[23] and for Mary it was the time of her marriage to John Wayles Eppes, the eldest of Uncle and Aunt Eppes's children, her half first cousin and childhood playmate at Eppington. Jefferson hailed the union with "inexpressible pleasure," for he had known "Jack" from infancy and superintended his schooling when the boy was in Philadelphia. He confided to Martha that Jack "could not have been more to my wishes if I had had the whole free earth to have chosen a partner for her."[24]

The happy father, as possessive of Mary as of Martha, prophesied, "I now see our fireside formed into a group, no one member of which has a fibre in their composition which can ever produce any jarring or jealousies among us. . . . In order to keep us all together . . . I think to open and resettle the plantation of Pantops for them." He then advised Mary that "harmony in the marriage state is the very first object to be aimed at . . . that a husband finds his affections wearied out by a constant string of little checks and obstacles."[25] The ceremony took place at Monticello on October 13, 1797, and was perfunctorily noted in the account book: "My daughter Maria married this day."[26]

Unlike the Randolphs, the Eppeses did not remain in Albemarle

21. TJ to Martha Jefferson Randolph, March 17, 1791. Edgehill Randolph Papers, University of Virginia. Hereafter cited as EHR.

22. *Jefferson's Prayer Book*, vii.

23. His Vice-Presidential term began Saturday, March 4, 1797.

24. June 8, 1797. MHi.

25. January 7, 1798. MHi.

26. Malone, *Jefferson and the Ordeal of Liberty* (Boston, 1962), 239–40, gives the best account of the wedding.

for any extended period after their marriage. At some time prior to December 2, they proceeded down country to Eppington and Mount Blanco, near Petersburg, where they stayed for nearly a year. They decided, much to Jefferson's chagrin, not to accept his offer of the Pantops farm, preferring instead the Tidewater site at Bermuda Hundred on the south side of the James River in Chesterfield County given them by Father Eppes.[27] Consequently, neither John Wayles nor his children became as integral a part of the Monticello family as did the Randolphs.

Mary, a shy and diffident child, grew into a retiring adult, lacking vigor and inclination for society. In her teens she had exhibited a "gentle sweetness of character,"[28] bearing out the promise she had shown as a child. Her family role was almost negative, and she never rid herself of self-distrust and deprecation, not possessing her sister's self-assurance, gained from the knowledge that she was the talented daughter of a great man.

To deserve and retain their father's love had been the aim implanted in both daughters from their early youth. In the case of Martha, Jefferson's helper and companion ever since the dark days following Mrs. Jefferson's death, the bond with her father was so strong that her husband never completely displaced her father, and the dearest wish of her heart was to be with Jefferson under any and all circumstances. Apparently, she would have borne almost any privation rather than fail in the duties of this relationship, which she had taken upon herself as a sacred obligation. Mary, on the other hand, conscious that her father was more congenial with Martha than with herself, never outgrew her fear of not having her proportionate share in his affections. She could not endure independence. She clung to those she loved and after her marriage transferred to the husband she called "the most beloved of my heart"[29] the first place in her love. Although both girls were unquestionably devoted daughters, Martha's almost lyrical protestations that her marriage could not disturb her intense feelings for her father contrast with Mary's quieter expressions of affection.

Mary enjoyed only seven years with the most beloved of her

27. The indenture between Francis and Elizabeth Eppes and Thomas Jefferson, in which they devised to Mary and John Wayles Eppes the Pantops farm near Monticello, the tract at Bermuda Hundred in Chesterfield County, and the Angola tract in Cumberland County, is in the Henry E. Huntington Library, San Marino, California. Hereafter cited as CSmH.
28. Randall, II, 223.
29. Mary Jefferson Eppes to John Wayles Eppes, December 10 [1801]. ViU.

heart, dying in 1804 at twenty-six[30] and leaving two children, Francis, aged three, and an infant, Maria Jefferson, who did not survive many months. Mary Eppes's death, indeed, as that of Mrs. Jefferson, was caused by complications following the birth of a daughter. Mary had become an Eppes by association in 1782, and one in name in 1797. Of the "happy family" dispersed in 1782, she was the second to return after death to Monticello, where she was buried near her mother in the family cemetery on the lonely slope of the mountain.

From 1797 to 1809, during Jefferson's terms as Vice-President and President, his chief communication with his relations was by the post to and from Monticello, Edgehill, or Bermuda Hundred Often he complained of its irregularity and of the long intervals between letters. Besides maintaining a large, burdensome official correspondence, he wrote regularly to the Eppes and Randolph families and later to those grandchildren who could read and write. By the time Jefferson left Washington for all time, his grandchildren included seven young Randolphs — Anne Cary, Thomas Jefferson, Ellen Wayles, Cornelia, Virginia, Mary, Benjamin Franklin, and James Madison.

Retirement meant happy days at Monticello for Jefferson and for Martha, who experienced infinite pleasure at seeing herself and her children established under the kindly and benevolent influence of her father. These were good years for the children also, as they now had someone to fill the void in their lives caused by their father's prolonged absences and apparent lack of interest in their welfare.

As the six older Randolphs passed from childhood others arrived to take their places: Meriwether Lewis in 1810, Septimia Anne or "Tim" in 1814, and George Wythe in 1818. Jefferson's living grandchildren now numbered eleven Randolphs and one Eppes. Her grandfather's influence in naming Septimia is not so easily discernible as in the cases of the other Randolph children. However, family tradition has it that by the time she was born, no girls' names having immediately sprung to mind, as the seventh granddaughter she was called Septimia, perhaps at Jefferson's suggestion.[31]

The children at Monticello provided constant pleasure and in-

30. She died at Monticello on "April 17. 1804 between 8. and 9. A.M." Account Book 1804.

31. "Mrs. Septimia R. Meikleham, Jefferson's Granddaughter," an undated clipping (probably from a Washington, D. C., newspaper) in the Septimia Randolph Meikleham Folder at Monticello.

terest for Jefferson, who willingly paid for their food, clothing, and education, even though by so doing he further burdened his already straitened finances. Typical of his relations with his son-in-law and with his grandchildren was his request that the cost and care of educating Meriwether Lewis, Ben, and George — "the boys" as he called them — should be assigned to him. And it was also characteristic of his generosity that he should conclude by writing, "I will send them to any schools you should prefer, and direct any course you may desire."[32] The father consented, and the boys went to various neighborhood schools and, eventually, to the University of Virginia.

Not only did Grandpapa, as he was known in the family, provide the essentials of living and the education for his descendants, but he also defrayed such incidental expenses as the cost for James and Ben to attend the dinner honoring Lafayette at the University in 1824.[33] A few account-book entries reveal these activities in detail:

> June 2, 1825. Jas. M. Randolph to pay for a book 1.87½
> June 18, 1825. Gave Ellen Coolidge for pocket money 100 D.
> October 1, 1825. Cornelia pocket money 2.25
> January 3, 1826. Mary R. pocket money 2. D . . .
> February 8, 1826. Drew on Raphael in favr. of B. F. Randolph
> for 30. D. and M. Lewis Randolph for 60. D.
> tuition fees at University . . .

Although his day-to-day relations with Francis Eppes were not so close as with Martha's children, Jefferson never lost sight of Francis's well-being and was particularly concerned over his education. The letters between them attest to a happy rapport. This was somewhat shaken, however, when an eager Francis, not having finished his studies, informed his grandfather of his marriage plans. Jefferson, who had hoped Francis would finish his formal education before assuming the responsibilities of a family, expressed his anxiety to the young man's father. Doubtless recalling his own past and possibly that of Martha's, he said he believed that the European concept of coming of age at twenty-five was "more conformable with the natural maturity of the body and mind of man than ours of twenty-one," and furthermore he saw that "the

32. TJ used the expression "the boys" in his account books when referring to his younger grandsons. TJ to Thomas Mann Randolph, Jr., October 8, 1820. MHi.

33. Account Book 1825, August 20: "James and Ben. dinner to Fayette 5.50 D."

interruption of studies and filling our houses with children are consequences of early marriage." [34] His grandson married the girl anyway; notwithstanding the objections of his father and grand-father, Francis Eppes at twenty-one married Mary Elizabeth Cleland Randolph, a fourth cousin, on November 28, 1822.[35]

Jefferson's last year opened badly for him. He was oppressed "with disease, debility, age and embarrassed affairs." [36] Indeed, his pecuniary difficulties had by now reached such a state that an appeal was made to the state legislature for permission to hold a lottery to dispose of certain lands. After permission had been granted by a very reluctant legislature, the family decided to seek succor from a public subscription; however, as encouraging as the results were for the moment, this device fell far, far short of the need.

In March Jefferson made his will, leaving Poplar Forest to Francis Eppes and, after several small bequests, devising the remainder of his estate in trust to Jefferson Randolph, Nicholas P. Trist, a grandson-in-law, and Alexander P. Garrett, for the sole benefit of Martha and her children. Jefferson's one desire was to prevent Randolph's creditors from laying claim to an inheritance Martha might have to share with her husband; he was not moved by antipathy to a son-in-law who by his own acts had set himself apart from his family. In this same month, Jefferson's financial situation had become so distressing that he wrote an old schoolmate that he would "welcome the hour which shall once more reassemble our antient class." [37]

The hour was not long in coming. On July 4, at fifty minutes past the meridian, Jefferson died in his bedroom at Monticello. His death was caused by the complications of old age. Jefferson Randolph, Trist, his trusted body-servant Burwell, and Dr. Robley Dunglison had maintained the bedside vigil since the venerable patriot had lapsed into a stupor on July 2. When it became apparent that he was dying, other members of the household were called in to pay their last respects. During the immediate forenoon

34. TJ to John Wayles Eppes, July 28, 1822. CSmH.
35. Walter Lewis Zorn, *The Descendants of the Presidents of the United States of America* (Monroe, Michigan, 1955), 58.
The bride was the daughter of Jane Cary Randolph, Thomas Mann Randolph, Jr.'s sister, and Thomas Eston Randolph, a cousin. Randolph was a merchant and postmaster at Milton and resided at Ashton, across the Rivanna River from Milton.
36. Joseph C. Vance, "Thomas Jefferson Randolph" (unpublished dissertation, University of Virginia, 1957), 94–106. Also, Randall, III, 527–29.
37. To Thomas Walker Maury, March 3, 1826. ViU.

of the fourth, Jefferson sank into total unconsciousness and was oblivious to everything around him. His languid circulation and laborious breathing told those assembled that the end was not far off, and soon the spark of life passed quietly out of his body. Jefferson Randolph then stepped toward his grandfather and closed his eyes.[38]

The following day Jefferson was carried in a simple coffin, undoubtedly made by John Hemings the slave cabinetmaker, down the tree-lined "Walk to the Graveyard," where he was interred without pomp or circumstance, except for the rites of the Episcopal Church as read by the Reverend Mr. Hatch. He was placed next to his beloved wife and close by his own dear Mary.

38. Jefferson's death is described in detail in Randall, III, 543–52. Included are the accounts by Thomas Jefferson Randolph, Nicholas P. Trist, and Dr. Robley Dunglison.

Peter Jefferson
(1707/8-1757) m
Jane Randolph
(1720-1776)

Jane
(1740-1755)

Mary
(1741-1817) m
Col. John Bolling

Thomas
(1743-1826) m
Martha Wayles Skelton
(1748-1782)

Elizabeth
(1744-1774)

Martha
(1746-1811) m
Dabney Carr
(1743-1773)

Peter Feild
(1748-1748)

Son
(1750-1750)

Lucy
(1752-1784) m
Charles L. Lewis

Anna Scott
(1755-1805) m
Hastings Marks

Randolph
(1755-1815) m
(1) Anne J. Lewis and
(2) Mitchie B. Pryor.

Martha
(1772-1836) m
Thomas Mann Randolph
(1768-1828)

Son
(1777-1777)

Mary
(1778-1804) m
John Wayles Eppes
(1773-1823)

Daughter
(1780-1781)

Lucy Elizabeth
(1782-1784)

Jane Barbara
(1766-1840) m
Wilson Cary
(1760-1793)

Lucy
(1768-1803) m
Richard Terrell

Peter
(1770-1815) m
Hester (Smith) Stevenson
(1767-1834)

Col. Samuel
(1771-1855) m
(1) Barbara Carr
and (2) Maria Dabney Watson

Dabney
(1773-1837) m
Elizabeth Carr
(1780-1838)

Mary (Polly)
(ch. 1768)

Infant (1800-1800)
Francis Wayles Eppes
(1801-1881)
Maria Jefferson Eppes
(1804-1807)

Anne Cary
(1791-1826) m
Charles Lewis Bankhead
(1788-1835)

Thomas Jefferson
(1792-1875) m
Jane Hollins Nicholas
(1798-1871)

Ellen Wayles
(1794-1795)

Ellen Wayles
(1796-1876) m
Joseph Coolidge
(1798-1879)

Cornelia Jefferson
(1799-1871)

Virginia Jefferson
(1801-1882) m
Nicholas Philip Trist
(1800-1874)

Mary Jefferson
(1803-1876)

James Madison
(1806-1834)

Benjamin Franklin
(1808-1871) m
Sarah Champe Carter
(1810-1897)

Meriwether Lewis
(1810-1837) m
Elizabeth Martin

Septimia Anne
(1814-1887) m
David Scott Meikleham
(1804-1849)

George Wythe
(1818-1867) m
Mary E. (Adams) Pope
(1830-1871)

Martha Jefferson Trist
(1826-1915)

Member of Congress

TO MARTHA JEFFERSON

Annapolis Nov. 28. 1783

MY DEAR PATSY

After four days journey I arrived here without any accident and in as good health as when I left Philadelphia. The conviction that you would be more improved in the situation I have placed you than if still with me, has solaced me on my parting with you, which my love for you has rendered a difficult thing. The acquirements which I hope you will make under the tutors I have provided for you will render you more worthy of my love, and if they cannot increase it they will prevent it's diminution. Consider the good lady [1] who has taken you under her roof, who has undertaken to see that you perform all your exercises, and to admonish you in all those wanderings from what is right or what is clever to which your inexperience would expose you, consider her I say as your mother, as the only person to whom, since the loss with which heaven has been pleased to afflict you, you can now look up; and that her displeasure or disapprobation on any occasion will be an immense misfortune which should you be so unhappy as to incur by any unguarded act, think no concession too much to regain her good will. With respect to the distribution of your time the following is what I should approve.

from 8. to 10 o'clock practise music.
from 10. to 1. dance one day and draw another
from 1. to 2. draw on the day you dance, and write a letter the next day.
from 3. to 4. read French.
from 4. to 5. exercise yourself in music.
from 5. till bedtime read English, write &c.

Communicate this plan to Mrs. Hopkinson and if she approves of it pursue it. As long as Mrs. Trist [2] remains in Philadelphia cultivate her affections. She has been a valuable friend to you and her good sense and good heart make her valued by all who know her and by nobody on earth more than by me. I expect you will write to me by every post. Inform me what books you read, what tunes

19

you learn, and inclose me your best copy of every lesson in drawing. Write also one letter every week either to your aunt Eppes,[3] your aunt Skipwith,[4] your aunt Carr,[5] or the little lady[6] from whom I now inclose a letter, and always put the letter you so write under cover to me. Take care that you never spell a word wrong. Always before you write a word consider how it is spelt, and if you do not remember it, turn to a dictionary. It produces great praise to a lady to spell well. I have placed my happiness on seeing you good and accomplished, and no distress which this world can now bring on me could equal that of your disappointing my hopes. If you love me then, strive to be good under every situation and to all living creatures, and to acquire those accomplishments which I have put in your power, and which will go far towards ensuring you the warmest love of your affectionate father,

TH: JEFFERSON

P. S. Keep my letters and read them at times that you may always have present in your mind those things which will endear you to me.

1. Mrs. Thomas Hopkinson was the mother of TJ's friend Francis Hopkinson, a prominent Philadelphian and a signer of the Declaration of Independence. *Papers,* VI, 361.

2. Eliza House Trist (Mrs. Nicholas) was a sister of Samuel House of Philadelphia. TJ lodged with their parent Mrs. Mary House at her boardinghouse in 1782. *Papers,* VI, 226.

3. Elizabeth Wayles Eppes (Mrs. Francis) was a half sister of Martha Wayles Skelton Jefferson (Mrs. Thomas) and the wife of Francis Eppes of Eppington in Chesterfield County. See George Green Shackelford, "William Short, Jefferson's Adopted Son, 1758–1849" (unpublished dissertation, University of Virginia), for excellent genealogical charts on those members of the Wayles and Skipwith families who are met with in these letters; for the Eppes family, see Eva Turner Clark, *Francis Epes His Ancestors and Descendants* (New York, 1942).

4. Tabitha Wayles Skipwith (Mrs. Robert) or Anne Wayles Skipwith (Mrs. Henry) were also half sisters of Martha Wayles Jefferson.

5. Martha Jefferson Carr (Mrs. Dabney) was TJ's sister.

6. Probably Polly Floyd, a daughter of William Floyd of New York. *Papers,* VI, 240, 361.

To MARTHA JEFFERSON

Annapolis Dec. 11. 1783

MY DEAR PATSY

I wrote you by the post this day fortnight, since which I have received two letters from you. I am afraid that you may not have sent to the post office and therefore that my letter may be still lying there. Tho' my business here may not let me write to you every week yet it will not be amiss for you to enquire at the office every week. I wrote to Mr. House[1] by the last post. Perhaps his letter may still be in the office. I hope you will have good sense enough to disregard those foolish predictions that the world is to be at an end soon. The almighty has never made known to any body at what time he created it, nor will he tell any body when he means to put an end to it, if ever he means to do it. As to preparations for that event, the best way is for you to be always prepared for it. The only way to be so is never to do nor say a bad thing. If ever you are about to say any thing amiss or to do any thing wrong, consider before hand. You will feel something within you which will tell you it is wrong and ought not to be said or done: this is your conscience, and be sure to obey it. Our maker has given us all, this faithful internal Monitor, and if you always obey it, you will always be prepared for the end of the world: or for a much more certain event which is death. This must happen to all: it puts an end to the world as to us, and the way to be ready for it is never to do a wrong act. I am glad you are proceeding regularly under your tutors. You must not let the sickness of your French master interrupt your reading French, because you are able to do that with the help of your dictionary. Remember I desired you to send me the best copy you should make of every lesson Mr. Cimitiere[2] should set you. In this I hope you will be punctual because it will let me see how you are going on. Always let me know too what tunes you play. Present my compliments to Mrs Hopkinson, Mrs. House and Mrs. Trist. I had a letter from your uncle Eppes[3] last week informing me that Polly is very well, and Lucy[4] recovered from an indisposition. I am my dear Patsy your affectionate father,   TH: JEFFERSON

1. Samuel House of Philadelphia.
2. Pierre Eugène du Simitière was Martha's art tutor. Note the various spellings of his name used by TJ: Cimitiere, Simetiere.
3. Francis Eppes.
4. Mary and Lucy Elizabeth Jefferson were TJ's younger daughters.

To Martha Jefferson

Annapolis Dec. 22. 1783

MY DEAR PATSY

I hoped before this to have received letters from you regularly and weekly by the post, and also to have had a letter to forward from you to one of your aunts as I desired in my letter of November 27th. I am afraid you do not comply with my desires expressed in that letter. Your not writing to me every week is one instance, and your having never sent me any of your copies of Mr. Simitiere's lessons is another. I shall be very much mortified and disappointed if you become inattentive to my wishes and particularly to the directions of that letter which I meant for your principal guide. I omitted in that to advise you on the subject of dress, which I know you are a little apt to neglect. I do not wish you to be gayly clothed at this time of life, but that what you wear should be fine of it's kind; but above all things, and at all times let your clothes be clean, whole, and properly put on. Do not fancy you must wear them till the dirt is visible to the eye. You will be the last who will be sensible of this. Some ladies think they may under the privileges of the dishabille be loose and negligent of their dress in the morning. But be you from the moment you rise till you go to bed as cleanly and properly dressed as at the hours of dinner or tea. A lady who has been seen as a sloven or slut in the morning, will never efface the impression she then made with all the dress and pageantry she can afterwards involve herself in. Nothing is so disgusting to our sex as a want of cleanliness and delicacy in yours. I hope therefore the moment you rise from bed, your first work will be to dress yourself in such a stile as that you may be seen by any gentleman without his being able to discover a pin amiss, or any other circumstance of neatness wanting.

By a letter from Mr. Short[1] I learn that your sisters are well. I hope I shall soon receive a letter from you informing me you are so. I wrote a letter to Polly lately, which I supposed her aunt would read to her. I dare say it pleased her, as would a letter from you. I am sorry Mrs. Trist has determined to go at so inclement a season, as I fear she will suffer much more than she expects. Present my compliments to her and the good family there, as also very particularly to Mrs. Hopkinson whose health and happiness I have much at heart. I hope you are obedient and respectful to her in every circumstance and that your manners will be such as to engage her affections. I am my Dear Patsy Yours sincerely and affectionately,   TH: JEFFERSON

1. William Short was TJ's secretary in Paris and a good friend.

To Martha Jefferson

Annapolis Jan. 15. 1784.

MY DEAR PATSY

Your letter by the post is not yet come to hand, that by Mr. Beresford[1] I received this morning. Your long silence had induced me almost to suspect you had forgotten me and the more so as I had desired you to write to me every week. I am anxious to know what books you read, what tunes you can play, and to receive specimens of your drawing. With respect to your meeting Mr. Simitiere at Mr. Rittenhouse's,[2] nothing could give me more pleasure than your being much with that worthy family wherein you will see the best examples of rational life and learn to esteem and copy them. But I should be very tender of obtruding you on the family as it might perhaps be not always convenient to them for you to be there at your hours of attending Mr. Simitiere. I can only say then that if it has been desired by Mr. and Mrs. Rittenhouse in such a way as that Mrs. Hopkinson shall be satisfied they will not consider it as inconvenient, I would have you thankfully accept it and conduct yourself with so much attention to the family as that they may never feel themselves incommoded by it. I hope Mrs. Hopkinson will be so good as to act for you in this matter with that delicacy and prudence of which she is so capable. I have so much at heart your learning to draw, and should be uneasy at your losing this opportunity which probably is your last. But I remind you to inclose me every week a copy of all your lessons in drawing that I may judge how you come on. I have had very ill health since I came here.[3] I have been just able to attend my duty in the state house, but not to go out on any other occasion. I am however considerably better. Present my highest esteem to Mrs. Hopkinson and accept yourself assurances of the sincere love with which I am my dear Patsy Yours affectionately,

TH: JEFFERSON

1. Possibly a delegate to the Continental Congress from Maryland. See *Papers*, VI, 437, 465.

2. David Rittenhouse was the celebrated Philadelphia scientist, patriot, and friend of TJ's.

3. TJ wrote to James Madison on January 1, 1784: "I have had very ill health since I have been here and am getting rather lower than otherwise." (*Papers*, VI, 438.) He is not explicit in alluding to his ailment; however, about March 1 he suffered an attack of the periodical headache, which was probably migraine. Whatever the causes of his illnesses, he was restricted in reading and writing as well as in public pursuits until about mid-April. See "Medical Chronology of Thomas Jefferson," a typescript in the Monticello Files of excerpts from Jefferson manuscripts and other sources relating to his health; hereafter cited as "Medical Chronology."

To Martha Jefferson

Annapolis Feb. 18. 1784.

DEAR PATSY

I have received two or three letters from you since I wrote last. Indeed my health has been so bad that I have been able scarcely to read, write or do any thing else. Your letters to your aunt and the others shall be forwarded. I hope you will continue to inclose to me every week one for some of your friends in Virginia. I am sorry Mr. Cimitiere cannot attend you, because it is probable you will never have another opportunity of learning to draw, and it is a pretty and pleasing accomplishment. With respect to the paiment of the guinea, I would wish him to receive it, because if there is to be a doubt between him and me, which of us acts rightly, I would chuse to remove it clearly off my own shoulders. You must thank Mrs. Hopkinson for me for the trouble she gave herself in this matter, from which she will be relieved by paying Mr. Cimitiere his demand. Perhaps when the season becomes milder he will consent to attend you. I am sorry your French master cannot be more punctual. I hope you nevertheless read French every day as I advised you. Your letter to me in French gave me great satisfaction and I wish you to exercise yourself in the same way frequently. Your sisters are well. I am in hopes the money I had placed in the bank subject to Mrs. Hopkinson's order had not failed. Lest it should have done so, inform her that I have now sent there a further supply. Deliver my most respectful compliments to her and be assured of the love with which I am My dear Patsy Your's affectionately,   TH: JEFFERSON

To Martha Jefferson

Annapolis Mar. 19. 1784.

DEAR PATSY

It is now very long since I have had a letter from you. I hope you continue in good health, and attention to the several objects for which I placed you in Philadelphia. I take for granted you go on with your music and dancing, that when your French master can attend, you receive his instructions, and read by yourself when he cannot. Let me know what books you have read since I left you, and what tunes you can play. Have you been able to coax Cimitiere to continue? Letters by yesterday's post inform me your sisters are well. I inclose you a letter I received from Dear Polly.

I send herewith Mr. Zane's[1] present of the looking glass which I dare say he intended for you. Wait upon Mrs. House and let her know, if she should not have heard from Mrs. Trist lately, that we have received a letter from her by a gentleman immediately from Fort Pitt. She is very well and expects to leave that place about the first of April.[2] Present me in the most friendly terms to your patroness Mrs. Hopkinson and be assured of the love with which I am Dr. Patsy yours affectionately,

TH: JEFFERSON

Mr. Maury[3] will deliver you this, who is lately from Virginia and is my particular friend.

1. Isaac Zane, a friend of TJ's, was proprietor of the Marlboro Iron Works in Frederick County, Maryland.
2. Mrs. Trist was traveling from Philadelphia to New Orleans. The late Gordon Trist Burke, a Trist and Jefferson descendant who lived in Omaha, Nebraska, owned the manuscript diary of her trip.
3. James Maury was the son of the Reverend Mr. James Maury and a classmate of TJ's at the Reverend Mr. Maury's classical school in Albemarle County. TJ was three years older than his friend. Malone, *Jefferson the Virginian* (Boston, 1948), 40–44.

From Mary Jefferson

Eppington April 1. 1784.

MY DEAR PATSY

I want to know what day you are going to come and see me, and if you will bring Sister Patsy, and my baby[1] with you. I was mighty glad of my sash's, and gave Cousin Booling[2] one. I can almost read. Your affectionate daughter,

POLLY JEFFERSON

1. Possibly a doll.
2. Martha Bolling Eppes was a daughter of Elizabeth and Francis Eppes.

To Martha Jefferson

Annapolis Apr. 4. 1784.

MY DEAR PATSY

This will be handed you by Genl. Gates,[1] who going to Philadelphia furnishes me with the opportunity of writing to you. I am again getting my health, and have some expectations of going to Philadelphia ere long; but of this am not certain. I have had no letters from Eppington since I wrote you last, and have not received one from you I think these two months. I wish to know what you read, what tunes you play, how you come on in your writing, whether you have been able to persuade Simetiere to continue, how you do, and how Mrs. Hopkinson does. These are articles of intelligence which will always be pleasing to me. Present my compliments respectfully to Mrs. Hopkinson, give her occasion always to be pleased with your grateful returns for the kind care she takes of you, and be assured of the love with which I am Dr. Patsy Yours affectionately, TH: JEFFERSON

1. General Horatio Gates, the Revolutionary War commander.

TO MARTHA JEFFERSON

Annapolis Apr. 17. 1784.

MY DEAR PATSY

I have not received a letter from you since early in February. This is far short of my injunctions to write once a week by post. I wish this for my own gratification as well as for your improvement. I received yesterday letters from Eppington by which I learn that the families there and at Hors du monde[1] are well, and that your cousin Cary[2] has a son. Lucy has been unwell during the winter but is got better. I am in hopes the approaching mild season will reestablish my health perfectly, in which case I shall probably take a trip to Philadelphia. I wish much to know what books you have read since I left you, and what tunes you can play. Present my compliments affectionately to Mrs. Hopkinson. I inclose you a letter which I suppose to be from your aunt Eppes. I am my dear Patsy Your's affectionately, TH: JEFFERSON

1. Colonel Henry Skipwith's home in Cumberland County.
2. Wilson Jefferson Cary was a son of Jane Barbara Carr, TJ's niece, and Wilson Cary of Richneck, his 4,000-acre estate in Warwick County. Edson I. Carr, *The Carr Family Records* (Rockton, Illinois, 1894), is the only published work on this family; it is hereafter cited as *Carr Family*. See also *The Virginia Carys* (New York, 1919), a particularly useful study.

Minister to France

From Mary Jefferson

[Eppington ca. 13 Sep. 1785?] [1]

DEAR PAPA

I want to see you and sister Patsy, but you must come to Uncle
Eppes's house.   POLLY JEFFERSON

1. Date from *Papers,* VIII, 517.

To Mary Jefferson

Paris Sep. 20. 1785.

MY DEAR POLLY

I have not received a letter from you since I came to France.
If you knew how much I love you and what pleasure the receipt
of your letters gave me at Philadelphia, you would have written
to me, or at least have told your aunt what to write, and her goodness would have induced her to take the trouble of writing it. I
wish so much to see you that I have desired your uncle and aunt
to send you to me. I know, my dear Polly, how sorry you will be,
and ought to be, to leave them and your cousins but your [sister
and m]yself cannot live without you, and after a while we will
carry you back again to see your friends in Virginia. In the meantime you shall be taught here to play on the harpsichord, to draw,
to dance, to read and talk French and such other things as will
make you more worthy of the love of your friends. But above all
things, by our care and love of you, we will teach you to love us
more than you will do if you stay so far from us. I have had no
opportunity since Colo. LeMaire [1] went, to send you any thing:
but when you come here you shall have as many dolls and playthings as you want for yourself, or to send to your cousins whenever you shall have opportunities. I hope you are a very good girl,
that you love your uncle and aunt very much, and are very thank-
ful to them for all their goodness to you; that you never suffer
yourself to be angry with any body, that you give your playthings
to those who want them, that you do whatever any body desires

29

of you that is right, that you never tell stories, never beg for any thing, mind your book and your work when your aunt tells you, never play but when she permits you, nor go where she forbids you. Remember too as a constant charge not to go out without your bonnet because it will make you very ugly and then we should not love you so much. If you will always practise these lessons we shall continue to love you as we do now, and it is impossible to love you more. We shall hope to have you with us next summer, to find you a very good girl, and to [assure you of the truth] of our affection to you. Adieu my dear child! Your's affectionately,

TH: JEFFERSON

1. Colonel Jacques Le Maire was a representative of the State of Virginia in Europe for the purpose of purchasing arms and supplies. *Papers*, III, 124n.

TO MARTHA JEFFERSON

Paris Mar. 6. 1786.

MY DEAR PATSY

I shall be absent so short a time that any letter you would write to me would hardly get to London[1] before I should be coming away; and it is the more discouraging to write as they open all letters in the post office. Should however sickness or any other circumstance render a letter to me necessary, send it here to Mr. Short and he will direct and forward it. I shall defer engaging your drawing master till I return. I hope then to find you much advanced in your music. I need not tell you what pleasure it gives me to see you improve in every thing agreeable and useful. The more you learn the more I love you, and I rest the happiness of my life on seeing you beloved by all the world, which you will be sure to be if to a good heart you join those accomplishments so peculiarly pleasing in your sex. Adieu my dear child; lose no moment in improving your head, nor any opportunity of exercising your heart in benevolence. Your's affectionately,

TH: JEFFERSON

1. TJ made his only trip to England at this time. He arrived in London on March 11, departed the country on April 26, and returned to Paris on April 30. For his itinerary while there, consult the Account Book 1786. See also Edward Dumbauld, *Thomas Jefferson American Tourist* (Norman, Oklahoma, 1946), 69–82.

FROM MARY JEFFERSON

[ca. 22 May 1786?][1]

DEAR PAPA

I long to see you, and hope that you and sister Patsy are well; give my love to her and tell her that I long to see her, and hope that you and she will come very soon to see us. I hope you will send me a doll. I am very sorry that you have sent for me. I don't want to go to France, I had rather stay with Aunt Eppes. Aunt Carr, Aunt Nancy[2] and Cousin Polly Carr[3] are here. Your most happy and dutiful daughter,   POLLY JEFFERSON

1. Date from *Papers*, IX, 560–61.
2. Anna Scott Jefferson Marks (Mrs. Hastings) was TJ's youngest sister and the twin of Randolph, his only brother. She was known in the family as Nancy. Malone, *Jefferson the Virginian*, [426]–31.
3. Mary or Polly Carr was TJ's niece and daughter of Martha Jefferson Carr.

TO MARTHA JEFFERSON

[Nov. 1786]

I will call for you today, my dear between twelve and one. You must be dressed, because we drink tea with Mrs. Montgomery.[1] Bring your music and drawings. Adieu my dear Patsy.

1. Mrs. Dorcas Montgomery was a Philadelphian who went to France in 1780/1. See *Papers*, X, 282–83.

TO MARTHA JEFFERSON

Saturday Nov. 4. [1786]

MY DEAR PATSY

Two of your country-women, Mrs. Barrett[1] and Mrs. Montgomery, will dine with me tomorrow. I wish you could come and dine with them. If you can obtain leave let me know in the morning and I will come for you between one and two o'clock. You must come dressed. Adieu my dear Patsy your's affectionately,

TH: J.

1. Mrs. Nathaniel Barrett was the wife of a commercial agent representing a group of Boston merchants in France. Lester J. Cappon, *The Adams-Jefferson Letters* (Chapel Hill, 1959), I, 73.

FROM MARTHA JEFFERSON

Panthemont[1] february [i.e. March] 8 1787[2]

Being disapointed in my expectation of receiving a letter from my dear papa, I have resolved to break so painful a silence by giving you an example that I hope you will follow, particularly as you know how much pleasure your letters give me. I hope your wrist[3] is better and I am inclined to think that your voyage is rather for your pleasure than for your health. However I hope it will answer both purposes. I will now tell you how I go on with my masters. I have began a beautiful tune with balbastre,[4] done a very pretty landskip with Pariseau, a little man playing on the violin, and began another beautiful landskape. I go on very slowly with my tite live,[5] its being in such ancient italian that I can not read with out my master and very little with him even. As for the dansing master I intend to leave him off as soon as my month is finished. Tell me if you are still determined that I shall dine at the abesse's table.[6] If you are I shall at the end of my quarter. The kings speach[7] and that of the eveque de Narbone[8] has been copied all over the convent. As for Monseur he rose up to speak but set down again with out daring to open his lips. I know no news but supose Mr. Short will write you enough for him and me too. Mde. Thaubenen[9] desires her compliments to you. Adieu my dear papa. I am afraid you will not be able to read my scrawl but I have not the time of coppying it over again. Therefore I must beg your indulgence and assure [you] of the tender affection of yours,

M JEFFERSON

Pray write often and long letters.

1. Date from *Papers*, XI, 203.

2. Martha entered the Abbaye Royale de Panthemont (Pentemont is an older spelling) sometime prior to August 24, 1784, for on this day she wrote from there to Eliza House Trist in Philadelphia and her father noted in his accounts on August 26th: "Pd. at . . . Panthemont for Patsy 1500 f."

The school was located at the corner of the Rue de Grenelle and Rue de Bellechasse in the Faubourg Saint-Germain in Paris. See *Papers:* VII, 410–11; XIV, illustration opposite p. 360, and xl–xli for a commentary on the school.

The reason for this letter and the several that followed between February 28 and June 10 was TJ's absence from Paris on his tour of southern France and Italy. See Dumbauld, *Thomas Jefferson American Tourist*, 83–109.

3. TJ's right wrist was broken on September 18, 1786, presumably while on a stroll in the Cours la Reine with Maria Cosway. It was improperly attended to by his physicians and troubled him a great deal for the next several months, also later in life. Consult "Medical Chronology" for treatment, etc., also Malone, *Jefferson and the Rights of Man*, 73, and *Papers*, X, 432n.

4. Claude Louis Balbastre was a composer, teacher, and organist of the Church of St. Roch in Paris. For one month's instruction on the harpsichord

he charged TJ 144 livres. See Account Book 1789, May 2, and Arthur Loesser, *Men, Women and Pianos* (New York, 1954), 317.

5. Titus Livius, *History of the Roman People*. This is possibly the Jacopo Nardi translation of 1562. See E. Millicent Sowerby, *Catalogue of the Library of Thomas Jefferson* (Washington, 1952–1959), Number 53; hereafter cited as Sowerby. The Sowerby editions are not always those mentioned in these letters.

6. Madame de Béthisy de Mézières was abbess from 1743 until 1790. It is presumed Martha sat at her table.

7. Reference is to the speech of Louis XVI to the Assembly of Notables wherein he expressed an inclination to consult with them on affairs of the kingdom.

8. Arthur Richard de Dillon, Bishop of Narbonne.

9. Sister Jeanne-Louise de Stendt de Taubenheim, who had taken the veil at the Abbaye Royale de Panthemont in 1750, was the Maîtresse des Pensionnaires, or Mistress of Boarding Pupils, when the Jefferson girls were at the convent. She was of Saxon origin. Although her name is variously spelled by the correspondents here, the correct spelling is Taubenheim. Information through the courtesy of Howard C. Rice, Jr., of the Princeton University Library, a scholar well versed in the history of this school.

From Martha Jefferson

March 25th, 1787.

My dear Papa

Though the knowledge of your health gave me the greatest pleasure, yet I own I was not a little disappointed in not receiving a letter from you. However, I console myself with the thought of having one very soon, as you promised to write to me every week. Until now you have not kept your word the least in the world, but I hope you will make up for your silence by writing me a fine, long letter by the first opportunity. *Titus Livius* puts me out of my wits. I can not read a word by myself, and I read of it very seldom with my master; however, I hope I shall soon be able to take it up again. All my other masters go on much the same, perhaps better. Every body here is very well, particularly Madame L'Abbesse, who has visited almost a quarter of the new building, a thing that she has not done for two or three years before now. I have not heard any thing of my harpsichord,[1] and I am afraid it will not come before your arrival. They make every day some new history on the Assemblée des Notables. I will not tell you any, for fear of taking a trip to the Bastile for my pains, which I am by no means disposed to do at this moment. I go on pretty well with Thucydides, and hope I shall very soon finish it. I expect Mr. Short every instant for my letter, therefore I must leave you.

Adieu, my dear papa; be assured you are never a moment absent from my thoughts, and believe me to be, your most affectionate child,   M. JEFFERSON

1. The harpsichord was purchased from Jacob Kirchmann (Kirkman), a German working in England, at a cost of approximately 59 livres. It arrived in Paris on November 20, 1787. See TJ to John Paradise, May 25, 1786, *Papers*, IX, 579; John Trumbull to TJ, September 17, 1787, *Papers*, XII, 138; TJ to R. & A. Garvey, November 21, 1787, *Papers*, XII, 374, and Account Book 1787, entries for November 14 and December 1.

TO MARTHA JEFFERSON

Aix en Provence March. 28. 1787.

I was happy, my dear Patsy, to receive, on my arrival here, your letter informing me of your health and occupations. I have not written to you sooner because I have been almost constantly on the road. My journey hitherto has been a very pleasing one. It was undertaken with the hope that the mineral waters of this place might restore strength to my wrist. Other considerations also concurred. Instruction, amusement, and abstraction from business, of which I had too much at Paris. I am glad to learn that you are employed in things new and good in your music and drawing. You know what have been my fears for some time past; that you do not employ yourself so closely as I could wish. You have promised me a more assiduous attention, and I have great confidence in what you promise. It is your future happiness which interests me, and nothing can contribute more to it (moral rectitude always excepted) than the contracting a habit of industry and activity. Of all the cankers of human happiness, none corrodes it with so silent, yet so baneful a tooth, as indolence. Body and mind both unemployed, our being becomes a burthen, and every object about us loathsome, even the dearest. Idleness begets ennui, ennui the hypochondria, and that a diseased body. No laborious person was ever yet hysterical. Exercise and application produce order in our affairs, health of body, chearfulness of mind, and these make us precious to our friends. It is while we are young that the habit of industry is formed. If not then, it never is afterwards. The fortune of our lives therefore depends on employing well the short period of youth. If at any moment, my dear, you catch yourself in idleness, start from it as you would from the precipice of a gulph. You are not however to consider yourself as unemployed while taking exercise. That is necessary for your health, and health is the first of all objects. For this reason if you leave your dancing

master for the summer, you must increase your other exercise. I
do not like your saying that you are unable to read the antient
print of your Livy, but with the aid of your master. We are always
equal to what we undertake with resolution. A little degree of
this will enable you to decypher your Livy. If you always lean
on your master, you will never be able to proceed without him.
It is a part of the American character to consider nothing as desperate; to surmount every difficulty by resolution and contrivance.
In Europe there are shops for every want. It's inhabitants therefore have no idea that their wants can be furnished otherwise.
Remote from all other aid, we are obliged to invent and to execute; to find means within ourselves, and not to lean on others.
Consider therefore the conquering your Livy as an exercise in the
habit of surmounting difficulties, a habit which will be necessary
to you in the country where you are to live, and without which
you will be thought a very helpless animal, and less esteemed.
Music, drawing, books, invention and exercise will be so many
resources to you against ennui. But there are others which to this
object add that of utility. These are the needle, and domestic
oeconomy. The latter you cannot learn here, but the former you
may. In the country life of America there are many moments when
a woman can have recourse to nothing but her needle for employment. In a dull company and in dull weather for instance.
It is ill manners to read; it is ill manners to leave them; no card-
playing there among genteel people; that is abandoned to black-
guards. The needle is then a valuable resource. Besides without
knowing to use it herself, how can the mistress of a family direct
the works of her servants? You ask me to write you long letters.
I will do it my dear, on condition you will read them from time
to time, and practice what they will inculcate. Their precepts will
be dictated by experience, by a perfect knowledge of the situation
in which you will be placed, and by the fondest love for you. This
it is which makes me wish to see you more qualified than common.
My expectations from you are high: yet not higher than you may
attain. Industry and resolution are all that are wanting. No body
in this world can make me so happy, or so miserable as you. Retirement from public life will ere long become necessary for me.
To your sister and yourself I look to render the evening of my
life serene and contented. It's morning has been clouded by loss
after loss till I have nothing left but you. I do not doubt either
your affection or dispositions. But great exertions are necessary,
and you have little time left to make them. Be industrious then,

my dear child. Think nothing unsurmountable by resolution and application, and you will be all that I wish you to be. You ask me if it is my desire you should dine at the abbess's table? It is. Propose it as such to Madame de Traubenheim with my respectful compliments and thanks for her care of you. Continue to love me with all the warmth with which you are beloved by, my dear Patsy, yours affectionately,   TH: JEFFERSON

FROM MARY JEFFERSON

[ca. 31 Mch. 1787][1]

DEAR PAPA,

I should be very happy to see you, but I can not go to France, and hope that you and sister Patsy are well. Your affectionate daughter. Adieu.   MARY JEFFERSON

1. Date from *Papers,* XI, 260.

TO MARTHA JEFFERSON

Toulon April 7. 1787.

MY DEAR PATSY

I received yesterday at Marseilles your letter of March 25. and I received it with pleasure because it announced to me that you were well. Experience learns us to be always anxious about the health of those whom we love. I have not been able to write to you so often as I expected, because I am generally on the road; and when I stop any where, I am occupied in seeing what is to be seen. It will be some time now, perhaps three weeks before I shall be able to write to you again. But this need not slacken your writing to me, because you have leisure, and your letters come regularly to me. I have received letters which inform me that our dear Polly will certainly come to us this summer. By the time I return it will be time to expect her. When she arrives, she will become a precious charge on your hands. The difference of your age, and your common loss of a mother, will put that office on you. Teach her above all things to be good: because without that we can neither be valued by others, nor set any value on ourselves. Teach her to be always true. No vice is so mean as the want of truth, and at the same time so useless. Teach her never to be angry. Anger only serves to torment ourselves, to divert others, and alienate their esteem. And teach her industry and application to useful pursuits. I will venture to assure you that if you inculcate this in her mind you will make her a happy being in herself, a most inestimable friend to you, and precious to all the world. In teaching her these dispositions of mind, you will be more fixed in them yourself, and render yourself dear to all your acquaintance. Practice them then, my dear, without ceasing. If ever you find yourself in difficulty and doubt how to extricate yourself, do what is right, and you will find it the easiest way of getting out of the difficulty. Do it for the additional incitement of increasing the happiness of him who loves you infinitely, and who is my dear Patsy your's affectionately,

TH: JEFFERSON

FROM MARTHA JEFFERSON

Panthemont, April 9th, 1787.

MY DEAR PAPA

I am very glad that the beginning of your voyage has been so pleasing, and I hope that the rest will not be less so, as it is a great consolation for me, being deprived of the pleasure of seeing you, to know at least that you are happy. I hope your resolution of returning in the end of April is always the same. I do not doubt but what Mr. Short has written you word that my sister sets off with Fulwar Skipwith[1] in the month of May, and she will be here in July. Then, indeed, shall I be the happiest of mortals; united to what I have the dearest in the world, nothing more will be requisite to render my happiness complete. I am not so industrious as you or I would wish, but I hope that in taking pains I very soon shall be. I have already begun to study more. I have not heard any news of my harpsichord; it will be really very disagreeable if it is not here before your arrival. I am learning a very pretty thing now, but it is very hard. I have drawn several little flowers, all alone, that the master even has not seen; indeed, he advised me to draw as much alone as possible, for that is of more use than all I could do with him. I shall take up my Livy, as you desire it. I shall begin it again, as I have lost the thread of the history. As for the hysterics, you may be quiet on that head, as I am not lazy enough to fear them. Mrs. Barett has wanted me out, but Mr. Short told her that you had forgotten to tell Madame L'Abbesse to let me go out with her. There was a gentleman, a few days ago, that killed himself because he thought his wife did not love him. They had been married ten years. I believe that if every husband in Paris was to do as much, there would be nothing but widows left. I shall speak to Madame Thaubeneu [Taubenheim] about dining at the Abbess's table. As for needlework, the only kind that I could learn here would be embroidery, indeed netting also; but I could not do much of those in America, because of the impossibility of having proper silks; however, they will not be totally useless. You say your expectations for me are high, yet not higher than I can attain. Then be assured, my dear papa, that you shall be satisfied in that, as well as in any thing else that lies in my power; for what I hold most precious is your satisfaction, indeed I should be miserable without it. You wrote me a long letter, as I asked you; however, it would have been much more so without so wide a margin. Adieu, my dear papa. Be assured of the tenderest affection of your loving daughter,

M. JEFFERSON

Pray answer me very soon — a long letter, without a margin. I will try to follow the advice they contain with the most scrupulous exactitude.

1. Fulwar Skipwith was an uncle of Henry Skipwith. Mary did not accompany him to France; instead, she was attended by a Mr. John Amonit, "a young man of character," according to Francis Eppes, who was going to France to receive a legacy. See Francis Eppes to TJ, April 24, 1787, *Papers*, XV, 636. It is worth noting again that Mary, the principal in this action, had no desire to leave Aunt Eppes and Eppington for her father and Paris.

FROM MARTHA JEFFERSON

Paris May 3 1787

MY DEAR PAPA

I was very sorry to see by your letter To Mr. Short that your return would be put off however I hope of not much, as you must be here for the arival of my sister. I wish I was my self all that you tell me to make her however I will try to be as near like it as I can. I have another landskape since I wrote to you last and began another peice of music. I have not been able to do more having been confined some time to my bed with a violent head ake and a pain in my side which afterwards blistered up and made me suffer a great deal. But I am now much better. I have seen a phisician who has just drawn two of my companions out of a most dreadful situation which gave me a great deal of trust in him but the most disagreable is that I have been obliged to discontinue all my masters and am able now to take only some of them, those that are the least fatiguing.[1] However I hope soon to take them all very soon. Mde. L'abesse has just had a fluxion de poitrine and has been at the last extremity but now is better. The pays bas[2] have revolted against the emperor who is gone to Prussia to join with the empress and the venitians to war against the turcs. The plague is in spain. A virginia ship comming to spain met with a corser of the same strength. They fought And the battle lasted an hour and a quarter. The Americans gained and boarded the corser where they found chains that had been prepared for them. They took them and made use of them for the algerians them selves. They returned to virginia from whence they are to go back to algers to change the prisoners to which if the algerians will not consent the poor creatures will be sold as slaves. Good god have we not enough? I wish with all my soul that the poor negroes were all freed. It grieves my heart when I think that these our fellow creatures should be treated so teribly as they are by many of our country men. A coach and six well shut up was seen to go to the bastille and the baron de Breteuil[3] went two hours before to prepare an apartment. They supose it to be Mde. De Polignac[4] and her sister, however no one knows. The king asked Mr. D'harcourt how much a year was necessary for the Dauphin.[5] M. D'harcourt [aft]er having looked over the accounts told [him] two millions upon which the king could [not] help expressing his astonishement because each of his daughters cost him nine, so Mde. de Polignac has pocketed the rest. Mr. Smith[6] is at Paris. That is all the news I know. They told me a great deal more but I have forgot it. Adieu my dear papa believe me to be for life your most tender and affectionate child,

M. JEFFERSON

1. Since Martha was well on April 9, she must have become ill between then and May 3. William Short wrote TJ on May 8 (*Papers*, XI, 357) that she had been only "indisposed" but recovered; on the 14th he reported her perfectly recovered (*Papers*, XI, 362). An article by D. P. Thompson, "A Talk with Jefferson," *Harper's New Monthly Magazine*, XXVI, 833–35, suggests "a typhus fever" as her ailment, but this is unsupported by any evidence. The physician is believed to have been Dr. Richard Gem, an eminent Parisian practitioner.

2. The Low Countries, that is, the Netherlands.

3. Louis-Charles-Auguste Le Tonnelier, Baron de Breteuil, a minister in the King's household.

4. Governess of the children of the royal household and close friend of Marie Antoinette.

5. Eldest son of the King of France. M. d'Harcourt was his tutor.

6. William Stephens Smith.

To Martha Jefferson

Marseilles May 5. 1787.

My dear Patsy

I got back to Aix the day before yesterday, and found there your letter of the 9th. of April, from which I presume you to be well tho' you do not say so. In order to exercise your geography I will give you a detail of my journey. You must therefore take your map and trace out the following places. Dijon, Lyons, Pont St. Esprit, Nismes, Arles, St. Remis, Aix, Marseilles, Toulon, Hieres, Frejus, Antibes, Nice, Col de Tende, Coni, Turin, Vercelli, Milan, Pavia, Tortona, Novi, Genoa, by sea to Albenga, by land to Monaco, Nice, Antibes, Frejus, Brignolles, Aix, and Marseille. The day after tomorrow I set out hence for Aix, Avignon, Pont du Gard, Nismes, Montpelier, Narbonne, along the Canal of Languedoc to Toulouse, Bordeaux, Rochefort, Rochelle, Nantes, Lorient, Nantes, Tours, Orleans, and Paris where I shall arrive about the middle of June, after having travelled something of a thousand leagues. From Genoa to Aix was very fatiguing, the first two days having been at sea, and mortally sick, two more clambering the cliffs of the Appennine, sometimes on foot, sometimes on a mule according as the path was more or less difficult, and two others travelling thro' the night as well as day, without sleep. I am not yet rested, and shall therefore shortly give you rest by closing my letter, after mentioning that I have received a letter from your sister, which tho a year old, gave me great pleasure. I inclose it for your perusal, as I think it will be pleasing to you also. But take care of it, and return it to me when I shall get back to Paris, for trifling as it seems, it is precious to me. When I left Paris, I wrote to London to desire that your harpsichord might be sent during the months of April and May, so that I am in hopes it will arrive a little before I shall, and give me an opportunity of judging whether you have got the better of that want of industry which I had began to fear would be the rock on which you would split. Determine never to be idle. No person will have occasion to complain of the want of time, who never loses any. It is wonderful how much may be done, if we are always doing. And that you may be always doing good, my dear, is the ardent prayer of yours affectionately,   TH: JEFFERSON

To Martha Jefferson

May 21. 1787.

I write to you, my dear Patsy, from the Canal of Languedoc, on which I am at present sailing, as I have been for a week past, cloudless skies above, limpid waters below, and find on each hand a row of nightingales in full chorus. This delightful bird had given me a rich treat before at the fountain of Vaucluse. After visiting the tomb of Laura at Avignon, I went to see this fountain, a noble one of itself, and rendered for ever famous by the songs of Petrarch who lived near it. I arrived there somewhat fatigued, and sat down by the fountain to repose myself. It gushes, of the size of a river, from a secluded valley of the mountain, the ruins of Petrarch's chateau being perched on a rock 200 feet perpendicular above. To add to the enchantment of the scene, every tree and bush was filled with nightingales in full song. I think you told me you had not yet noticed this bird. As you have trees in the garden of the convent, there must be nightingales in them, and this is the season of their song. Endeavor my dear, to make yourself acquainted with the music of this bird, that when you return to your own country you may be able to estimate it's merit in comparison with that of the mocking bird. The latter has the advantage of singing thro' a great part of the year, whereas the nightingale sings but about 5. or 6 weeks in the spring, and a still shorter term and with a more feeble voice in the fall. I expect to be at Paris about the middle of next month. By that time we may begin to expect our dear Polly. It will be a circumstance of inexpressible comfort to me to have you both with me once more. The object most interesting to me for the residue of my life, will be to see you both developing daily those principles of virtue and goodness which will make you valuable to others and happy in yourselves, and acquiring those talents and that degree of science which will guard you at all times against ennui, the most dangerous poison of life. A mind always employed is always happy. This is the true secret, the grand recipe for felicity. The idle are the only wretched. In a world which furnishes so many emploiments which are useful, and so many which are amusing, it is our own fault if we ever know what ennui is, or if we are ever driven to the miserable resource of gaming, which corrupts our dispositions, and teaches us a habit of hostility against all mankind. We are now entering the port of Toulouse, where I quit my bark; and of course must conclude my letter. Be good and be industrious, and you will be what I shall most love in this world. Adieu my dear child. Yours affectionately,   TH: JEFFERSON

FROM MARTHA JEFFERSON

Paris, May 27th, 1787.

MY DEAR PAPA

I was very glad to see by your letter that you were on your return, and I hope that I shall very soon have the pleasure of seeing you. My sister's letter gave me a great deal of happiness. I wish she would write to me; but as I shall enjoy her presence very soon, it will make up for a neglect that I own gives me the greatest pain. I still remember enough of geography to know where the places marked in your letter are. I intend to copy over my extracts and learn them by heart. I have learnt several new pieces on the harpsichord, drawn five landscapes and three flowers, and hope to have done something more by the time you come. I go on pretty well with my history, and as for *Tite Live* I have begun it three or four times, and go on so slowly with it that I believe I never shall finish it. It was in vain that I took courage; it serves to little good in the execution of a thing almost impossible. I read a little of it with my master who tells me almost all the words, and, in fine, it makes me lose my time. I begin to have really great difficulty to write English; I wish I had some pretty letters to form my style. Pray tell me if it is certain that my sister comes in the month of July, because if it is, Madame De Taubenheim will keep a bed for her. My harpsichord is not come yet. Madame L'Abbesse is better, but she still keeps her bed. Madame De Taubenheim sends her compliments to you. Pray how does your arm go? I am very well now. Adieu, my dear papa; as I do not know any news, I must finish in assuring you of the sincerest affection of your loving child,   M. JEFFERSON

TO MARTHA JEFFERSON

Nantes June 1. 1787.

MY DEAR PATSY

Your letter of May 3. came to me at this place. Since this I hear nothing from you; but I hope your health is reestablished. I have received letters from America as late as March assuring me that your sister shall be sent this summer. At that time however they did not know certainly by what occasion she could come. There was a hope of getting her under care of the French Consul and his lady, who thought of coming to France. The moment and place of her arrival therefore are still incertain. I forgot in my last letter to desire you to learn all your old tunes over again perfectly, that I may hear them on your harpsichord on it's arrival. I have no news of it however since I left Paris, tho' presume it will arrive immediately as I had ordered. Learn some slow movements of simple melody, for the Celestini stop,[1] as it suits such only. I am just setting out for Lorient, and shall have the happiness of seeing you at Paris about the 12th. or 15th. of this month, and of assuring you in person of the sincere love of Your's affectionately,   TH: JEFFERSON

1. A mechanism that produces different levels of tonal quality and is operated by a set of knobs on the front board of the harpsichord. See Loesser, *Men, Women and Pianos,* 13–14, and for the operation of this particular stop, see Adam Walker to TJ, August 20, 1787, *Papers,* XII, 47–49.

To Martha Jefferson

Paris June 14. 1787.

I send you, my dear Patsy, the 15 livres you desired.[1] You propose this to me as an anticipation of five weeks allowance. But do you not see my dear how imprudent it is to lay out in one moment what should accomodate you for five weeks? That this is a departure from that rule which I wish to see you governed by, thro' your whole life, of never buying any thing which you have not money in your pocket to pay for? Be assured that it gives much more pain to the mind to be in debt, than to do without any article whatever which we may seem to want. The purchase you have made is one of those I am always ready to make for you, because it is my wish to see you dressed always cleanly and a little more than decently. But apply to me first for the money before you make a purchase, were it only to avoid breaking thro' your rule. Learn yourself the habit of adhering vigorously to the rules you lay down for yourself. I will come for you about eleven o'clock on Saturday. Hurry the making your gown, and also your redingcote. You will go with me some day next week to dine at the Marquis Fayette's. Adieu my dear daughter. Your's affectionately,

TH: JEFFERSON

1. As a general rule TJ was very generous in giving his children as well as grandchildren gifts of money.

To MARTHA JEFFERSON

Thursday June 28. [1787]

MY DEAR PATSY

Madame de Traubenheim wrote me word yesterday you were unwell. I shall come to Panthemont to-day to pay her a visit, and to bring you to dine, if well enough. Let me know by the bearer if you are well enough to come out. Make it a rule hereafter to come dressed otherwise than in your uniform. Our dear Polly was to sail certainly the 1st. of May. She must therefore be arrived in England now.[1] Adieu, my dear, Yours affectionately,

TH: J.

1. She arrived there on June 26. *Papers,* XI, 501.

To MARTHA JEFFERSON

Friday July 6. [1787]

I shall with the greatest pleasure, my dear Patsy, participate with you of the honour of Miss Annesley's[1] company in our ride this afternoon. Assure her of my thankfulness for it as well as your own. The day being warm, I shall not be with you till between five and six o'clock. Adieu, my dear Your's affectionately,

TH: J.

1. Julia Annesley was a schoolmate. See *Report of the Curator to the Board of The Thomas Jefferson Memorial Foundation April 13, 1960* (Charlottesville, 1961) for a reproduction of Martha Jefferson's manuscript list of schoolmates at Panthemont.

To MARTHA JEFFERSON

June 16, 1788

Madame de Corney[1] proposes, my Dear to carry you to the Opera tomorrow evening. I will therefore call for you precisely at five oclock. Be ready without fail before that hour. Know exactly at what hour they will shut your doors in the evening, and as you come down to the carriage see exactly what oclock it is by the Convent clock that we may not be deceived as to the time. Adieu. Yours' affectionately,   Tн: J.

Kisses to Polly. She will keep your supper for you till you return tomorrow night.

1. Second wife of Dominique-Louis Ethis de Corny, a *Commissaire des guerres* for the French army in America. On his return to France he married Marguerite Victoire de Palerne, a widow. The De Cornys became acquainted with Jefferson during his stay in France, and Madame de Corny corresponded with him for many years after his return to America.

According to the *Journal de Paris*, Martha attended *La Toison d'Or*, also known as *Médée à Colchis* (Medea in Colchis), which was performed in the Académie Royale de Musique.

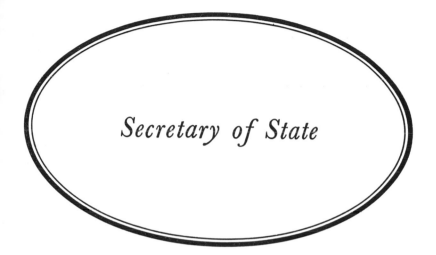

Secretary of State

MARRIAGE SETTLEMENT FOR MARTHA JEFFERSON

This indenture made on the 21st. day of Feb. in the year of our lord 1790. between Thos. Jefferson of the 1st. part, Martha Jefferson daughter of the said Thos. of the 2d. part Thos. Mann Randolph the elder of the 3d. part and Thos. Mann Randolph the younger, son of the said T. M. R. the elder of the 4th. part witnesseth that forasmuch as a marriage is shortly to be had between the said Thos. M. R. the younger and the said M. J. and the said T. M. R. the elder hath undertaken to convey in feesimple to the said T. M. the younger and did convey by deed indentured bearing date the 15th. day of this present month for his advancement a certain tract of land in the county of Henrico called Varina and containing 950. acres with 40. negroes then on and belonging to the same tract and the stocks and utensils thereto also belonging, now the said T. J. in consideration of the said undertaking and conveyance of the said T. M. the elder and also of the marriage so proposed to be had and of the natural love and affection which he the said Thos. bears to his daughter Martha, and for her advancement in life, and for the further sum of 5/ to him in hand paid by the said M. and another like sum of 5/ to him in hand paid by the said T. M. the elder, and yet another like sum of 5/ to him in hand paid by the said T. M. the younger, hath given granted bargained sold and appointed unto the said Martha and her heirs, and by these presents doth give grant bargain sell and according to powers in him legally vested doth appoint unto the said M. and her heirs a parcel of land in the county of Bedford containing 1000. as. be the same more or less, part of the tract of land called the Poplar Forest and at the Westernmost end thereof to be laid off and separated from the residue of the said tract by a line to begin at a red oak sapling expressed in the patent to be at the intersection of the two lines No. 21. W. 145. poles and N. 53½ E. 40. po. and to run thence across the said tract directly to the line expressed in the said patent to bear S. 60. E. 420. po. and to the point thereof which shall be 230. po. from a white oak expressed in the same patent to be at the Westernmost end of the said line: together with the following slaves to wit, Jack, Patty, Betty and Judy forming one family, Tom, Lucy, Polly and Davy forming another family, Jeffery, Joan, Scilla and Nancy forming another family, Lundy and Betty being husband and wife, Jupiter, Phyllis the elder, Phyllis the younger, Sandy, John and Sam forming a 5th. family which said five families are now on or belonging to the premisses, and also one other family of seven persons at the old plantation to wit Billy, Sarah, Peg, Louis, Abby, Patty and Harry, and also all the stock of work horses, cattle, hogs and sheep and the plantation utensils now on or belonging to the plantation called Wingo's where the said five families first mentioned are employed: to have and to hold the said parcel of lands with it's appurtenances and the said slaves and stocks to her the said M. and her heirs free of every incumbrance in law or equity. In witness whereof the said T. J. hath hereto set his hand and seal the day and year first above written.   TH: JEFFERSON

Signed sealed and delivered in
presence of (the words 'and appointed'
19th line being first interlined)
    NICHOLAS LEWIS
    NICHOLAS LEWIS, JR.
    ROBERT LEWIS

1. For the Jefferson-Randolph family consultations, dowry, and date of the marriage, see Thomas Mann Randolph, Sr., to TJ of January 30, 1790; TJ to Randolph, February 4, 1790, and TJ to James Madison, February 14, 1790, *Papers*, XVI, 135, 154–55; also, footnote on 155.

The elder Randolph executed a deed conveying Varina, an estate of 950 acres in Henrico County, Virginia, to the young couple. TJ matched this by giving 1,000 acres in the Poplar Forest tract in Bedford County, Virginia, to Martha and her heirs, not to her husband. Slaves were included in each gift.

Martha and Thomas Mann Randolph, Jr., were married at Monticello on February 23, 1790, by the Reverend Mr. James Maury, Sr. The occasion was a small affair, with only the immediate families in attendance. See Malone, *Jefferson and the Rights of Man*, 250–53, for the best account of the marriage. The marriage bond is on file in the Albemarle County Courthouse in Charlottesville, Virginia.

TO MARTHA JEFFERSON RANDOLPH

New York April 4. 1790.

MY DEAR DAUGHTER

I saw in Philadelphia your friends Mrs. Trist and Miss Rittenhouse. Both complained of your not writing. In Baltimore I inquired after Mrs. Buchanan[1] and Miss Holliday. The latter is lately turned methodist, the former was married the evening I was there to a Mr. Turnbull[2] of Petersburg in Virginia. Of course you will see her there. I find it difficult to procure a tolerable house here. It seems it is a practice to let all the houses the 1st. of February, and to enter into them the 1st of May. Of course I was too late to engage one, at least in the Broadway, where all my business lies. I have taken an indifferent one nearly opposite Mrs. Elsworth's[3] which may give me time to look about me and provide a better before the arrival of my furniture. I am anxious to hear from you, of your health, your occupations, where you are etc. Do not neglect your music. It will be a companion which will sweeten many hours of life to you. I assure you mine here is triste enough. Having had yourself and dear Poll to live with me so long, to exercise my affections and chear me in the intervals of business, I feel heavily these separations from you. It is a circumstance of consolation to know that you are happier; and to see a prospect of it's continuance in the prudence and even temper both of Mr. Randolph and yourself. Your new condition will call for abundance of little sacrifices but they will be greatly overpaid by the measure of affection they will secure to you. The happiness of your life depends now on the continuing to please a single person. To this all other objects must be secondary; even your love to me, were it possible that that could ever be an obstacle. But this it can never be. Neither of you can ever have a more faithful friend than my self, nor one on whom you can count for more sacrifices. My own is become a secondary object to the happiness of you both. Cherish then for me, my dear child, the affection of your husband, and continue to love me as you have done, and to render my life a blessing by the prospect it may hold up to me of seeing you happy. Kiss Maria for me if she is with you, and present me cordially to Mr. Randolph: assuring yourself of the constant and unchangeable love of your's affectionately,

TH: JEFFERSON

1. Rachel Buchanan was a Philadelphia schoolmistress who resided on Cedar Street between Fifth and Sixth streets. James Hardee, *The Philadelphia Directory and Register* (Philadelphia, 1793).

2. The marriage was between Sarah Buchanan of Baltimore and Robert Turnbull of Prince George County, Virginia, and took place in March, 1791. Sarah being unable to consummate the marriage, Turnbull later sued for divorce. Reported in William Waller Hening, *The Statutes at Large; Being a Collection of All the Laws of Virginia* (Richmond, 1823), XIII, 301-2.

3. The house was located at 57 Maiden Lane. Mrs. Oliver Ellsworth was the wife of Chief Justice Oliver Ellsworth. Malone, *Jefferson and the Rights of Man*, 257.

To Mary Jefferson

New York Apr. 11. 1790.

Where are you, my dear Maria? How do you do? How are you occupied? Write me a letter by the first post and answer me all these questions. Tell me whether you see the sun rise every day? How many pages a day you read in Don Quixot? How far you are advanced in him? Whether you repeat a Grammar lesson every day? What else you read? How many hours a day you sew? Whether you have an opportunity of continuing your music? Whether you know how to make a pudding yet, to cut out a beef stake, to sow spinach or to set a hen? Be good my dear, as I have always found you, never be angry with any body, nor speak harm of them, try to let every body's faults be forgotten, as you would wish yours to be; take more pleasure in giving what is best to another than in having it yourself, and then all the world will love you, and I more than all the world. If your sister is with you kiss her and tell her how much I love her also, and present my affections to Mr. Randolph. Love your Aunt and Uncle and be dutiful and obliging to them for all their kindness to you. What would you do without them, and with such a vagrant for a father? Say to both of them a thousand affectionate things for me: and Adieu my dear Maria.   TH: JEFFERSON

FROM MARTHA JEFFERSON RANDOLPH

Richmond April 25 1790

I recieved yours My Dearest Father with more pleasure than is possible for me to express and am happy to hear that you are at last settled at New York as I am in hopes we shall now hear from you often. We are just returned from a visit up the country to Aunt Carr's and Mrs. Flemming's.[1] It has not been possible as yet to carry dear Pol to Eppington for want of horses as Mr. Randolph was unwilling to borrow his father's for so long a time but I expect certainly to be there in ten days at latest. I intend writing to Mrs. Trist and Holly[2] by the next post and promise you not to leave Richmond without writing also to my friends in Europe. I hope you have not given over comming to Virginia this fall as I assure you My dear papa my happiness can never be compleat without your company. Mr. Randolph omits nothing that can in the least contribute to it. I have made it my study to

please him in every *thing* and do consider all other objects as
secondary to that *except* my love for you. I do not know where
we are to spend the summer. Mr. Randolph has some thoughts
of settling at Varina[3] for a little while till he can buy a part of
Edgehill. I am much averse to it my self but shall certainly comply if he thinks it necessary. My health is perfectly good as also
dear Polly's. I have recieved a letter from Mrs. Curson[4] who
informs me that the Duke of Dorset and Lady Caroline[5] are
both going to be married, the former to a Miss Cope.[6] Adieu My
Dear Pappa. I am with the tenderest affection yours,

                                                    M RANDOLPH

1. Mary Randolph Fleming (Mrs. Tarlton) was Thomas Mann Randolph,
Jr.'s aunt. Fleming owned land on both sides of the James River, his home
Rockcastle being in Powhatan County opposite the present-day Rockcastle,
Goochland County, site of the St. Emma Military School.
2. Possibly the Miss Holliday of TJ to Martha Jefferson Randolph, April 4,
1790.
3. A Randolph estate of 950 acres in Henrico County. Martha and Thomas
Mann Randolph, Jr., resided there briefly in 1790.
4. Mrs. B. Carson; possibly the married name of a former classmate.
5. Lady Caroline Tufton was a particular friend of Martha's at school in
Paris.
6. Arabella Diana Cope, daughter of Sir Charles Cope, married John Frederick Sackville, the third Duke of Dorset, British Ambassador-Extraordinary
and Plenipotentiary to the Court of France from December 26, 1783, until
August 8, 1790.

FROM MARY JEFFERSON

                                        Richmond, April 25th. 1790.
MY DEAR PAPA

I am afraid you will be displeased in knowing where I am, but
I hope you will not, as Mr. Randolph certainly had some good
reason, though I do not know it. I have not been able to read in
Don Quixote every day, as I have been traveling ever since I saw
you last, and the dictionary is too large to go in the pocket of the
chariot, nor have I yet had an opportunity of continuing my
music. I am now reading Robertson's Amcrica.[1] I thank you for
the advice you were so good as to give me, and will try to follow
it. Adieu, my dear papa, I am your affectionate daughter,

                                                    MARY JEFFERSON

1. Probably Book I of William Robertson's *History of America*. The first
edition was printed in London in 1777. This work, in all editions, contained a
brief history of Virginia to 1652. Sowerby 468, 469.

To Martha Jefferson Randolph

New York Apr. 26. 1790.

MY DEAR PATSY

I wrote you last on the 4th. instant. In my letter of the 19th. to Mr. Randolph I inclosed one to you from England. I now send a packet from France, which comes from Botidour.[1] I have now been seven weeks from you my dear and have never heard one tittle from you. I write regularly once a week to Mr. Randolph, yourself, or Polly, in hopes it may induce a letter from one of you every week also. If each would answer by the first post my letter to them, I should receive it within the three weeks so as to keep up a regular correspondence with each. I hope there are letters on the way for me. What I mentioned to Mr. Randolph in my letter of last week relative to Mr. Bedford[2] is not confirmed. Some deny the fact. I inclose for Mr. Randolph Fenno's paper.[3] He promises henceforward to give his foreign news from the Leyden gazette, so that it will be worth reading. I long to hear how you pass your time. I think both Mr. Randolph and yourself will suffer with ennui at Richmond. Interesting occupations are essential to happiness: indeed the whole art of being happy consists in the art of finding emploiment. I know none so interesting, and which croud upon us as much, as those of a domestic nature. I look forward therefore to your commencing housekeepers on your own farm, with some anxiety. Till then you will not know how to fill up your time, and your weariness of the things around you will assume the form of a weariness of one another. I hope Mr. Randolph's idea of settling near Monticello will gain strength; and that no other settlement will in the mean time be fixed on. I wish some expedient may be devised for settling him at Edgehill.[4] No circumstance ever made me feel so strongly the thraldom of Mr. Wayles's debt.[5] Were I liberated from that, I should not fear but that Colo. Randolph and myself, by making it a joint contribution, could effect the fixing you there, without interfering with what he otherwise proposes to give to Mr. Randolph. I shall hope when I return to Virginia in the fall that some means may be found of effecting all our wishes. Present me affectionately to Mr. Randolph and Polly, and my friendly respects to Colo. Randolph. Adieu my dear. Your's affectionately, TH: JEFFERSON

1. Marie Jacinthe de Botidoux was a schoolmate and close friend. Her miniature is now at Monticello.
2. A Delaware judge. TJ was reporting the story that the Judge had killed

his wife's adulterer "with the same shot" that wounded her. TJ to Thomas Mann Randolph, Jr., April 18, 1790. *Papers,* XVI, 351.

3. *The Gazette of the United States,* a Federalist paper, edited by John Fenno.

4. A very desirable tract of about 1,152½ acres in Albemarle County, on the north side of the Rivanna River and adjacent to the Southwest Mountains, a few miles east of Monticello. It had come into the Randolph family as part of a grant of 2,400 acres to William Randolph, Thomas Mann Randolph, Jr.'s grandfather. (The remainder of the tract was sold to John Harvie, Jr., on January 1, 1792.) William Randolph devised this tract to his only son Thomas Mann Randolph, Sr., by will probated March 18, 1745. Thomas Mann, Sr., then by deed dated April 12, 1793, conveyed it with a general warranty to his son in consideration of 2,000£. This deed, although executed in the presence of three witnesses, was never proven by them and consequently was not entered on the county records until August 10, 1822. For a complete record of these proceedings, see "Abstract of Title to the Shadwell Properties," "Abstract #II," drawn by Mr. Venable Minor, a distinguished member of the Albemarle bar. Copies may be seen in the Manuscripts Division at the Alderman Library and at Monticello.

TJ was very anxious to have Martha and Thomas Mann settle in Albemarle and so wrote to his son-in-law: "It . . . is essential to my happiness, our living near together." (March 4, 1792. ViU.) He did not relinquish his efforts until this wish had been realized. See also TJ to Thomas Mann Randolph, Jr., May 30, 1790. *Papers,* XVI, 449.

5. The Wayles debt was inherited through his wife, Martha Wayles Skelton. For a comprehensive explanation, see *Papers,* XV, 642 ff., and Malone, *Jefferson the Virginian,* 441–46.

To Mary Jefferson

New York May 2. 1790.

MY DEAR MARIA

I wrote to you three weeks ago, and have not yet received an answer. I hope however that one is on the way and that I shall receive it by the first post. I think it very long to have been absent from Virginia two months and not to have received a line either from yourself, your sister or Mr. Randolph, and I am very uneasy at it. As I write once a week to one of the other of you in turn, if you would answer my letter the day or day after you receive it, it would always come to my hands before I write the next to you. We had two days of snow about the beginning of last week. Let me know if it snowed where you are. I send you some prints of a new kind for your amusement. I send several to enable you to be generous to your friends. I want much to hear how you employ yourself. Present my best affections to your uncle, aunt and cousins, if you are with them, or Mr. Randolph and your sister, if with them: be assured of my tender love to you, and continue yours to your affectionate,   TH: JEFFERSON

To Martha Jefferson Randolph

New York May 16. 1790.

MY DEAR PATSY

Your's of the 25th. of April came to hand ten days ago, and yesterday I received Mr. Randolph's of the 3d. instant. When I wrote to him last week, I hoped to have been soon rid of the periodical headach which had attacked me. It has indeed been remarkeably slight since that, but I am not yet quite clear of it. I expect every fit to be the last.[1] I inclose the newspapers for Mr. Randolph. He will probably judge, as the world does, from the stile and subject of the discourses on Davila,[2] that they are the production of the Vice-president. On Monday last the President was taken with a peripneumony of threatening appearance. Yesterday (which was the 5th. day) he was thought by the physicians to be dying. However about 4. oclock in the evening a copious sweat came on, his expectoration which had been thin and ichorous, began to assume a well digested form, his articulation became distinct, and in the course of two hours it was evident he had gone thro' a favorable crisis. He continues mending to-day, and from total despair we are now in good hopes of him. Indeed he is thought quite safe. My head does not permit me to add more than the affectionate love to you all of Yours,

TH: JEFFERSON

1. His headache began about May 1 and continued until July 4. He wrote Peter Carr on June 13: ". . . an attack of the periodical headach which came on me the 1st of May, has not yet quitted me. The first week was violent, the rest has been moderate and for these 10 days past I have been able to do business." (ViU.) See also "Medical Chronology."

2. "Discourses on Davila," a series of weekly newspaper articles in which John Adams expressed the antirevolutionary spirit in America and supported the British system of government. They began to appear in the *Gazette of the United States* in 1790.

From Mary Jefferson

Eppington May 23 [1790]

DEAR PAPA

I received your affectionate letter when I was at presqu'isle[1] but was not able to answer it before I came here as the next day we went to uncle Bolings[2] and then came here. I thank you for the pictures you was so kind as to send me and will try that your advise shall not be thrown away. I read in don quixote every day to my aunt and say my grammer in spanish and english and write and read in robertson's america. After I am done that I work till dinner and a little more after. It did not snow at all last month. My cousin Boling and myself made a pudding the other day. My aunt has given us a hen and chickens. Adieu my Dear papa. Believe me to be your ever dutiful and affetionate daughter,

MARIA JEFFERSON

1. David Meade Randolph was a cousin of TJ's who resided at Presqu'ile, in Chesterfield County.

2. John Bolling was married to TJ's sister Mary Jefferson, who was known in the family as Aunt Bolling. They resided at Chestnut Grove, also in Chesterfield County. For the Bolling family genealogy, see Robert A. Brock and Wyndham Robertson, *Pochontas, alias Matoaka, and Descendants* (Richmond, 1887).

TO MARY JEFFERSON

New York May 23. 1790.

MY DEAR MARIA

I was glad to receive your letter of April 25. because I had been near two months without hearing from any of you. I hope you will now always write immediately on receiving a letter from me. Your last told me what you were not doing: that you were not reading Don Quixot, not applying to your music. I hope your next will tell me what you are doing. Tell your Uncle that the President after having been so ill as at one time to be thought dying, is now quite recovered. I have been these three weeks confined by a periodical headach. It has been the most moderate I ever had: but it has not yet left me. Present my best affections to your Uncle and aunt. Tell the latter I shall never have thanks enough for her kindness to you, and that you will repay her in love and duty. Adieu my dear Maria. Your's affectionately,

TH: JEFFERSON

TO MARTHA JEFFERSON RANDOLPH

New York June 6. 1790.

MY DEAR DAUGHTER

Your favor of May 28. from Eppington came to me yesterday, with the welcome which accompanies ever the tidings I recieve from you. Your resolution to go to housekeeping is a good one, tho' I think it had better be postponed till the fall. You are not yet seasoned to the climate, and it would therefore be prudent not to go to a sickly position till the sickly season is over. My former letters to Mr. Randolph and yourself will have apprised you of the pleasure it will give me to see you fixed in Albemarle; and the wish to co-operate in this, and to effect it, will determine me to come to Virginia in September or October at all events. Till then I should think it better that you should take no measures for Varina which might be inconvenient. The lower house of Congress have voted to remove to Philadelphia. It is thought the Senate will be equally divided on the question, and consequently that the decision will rest with the Vice-President. Were we to be removed there, I should be so much nearer to you. I had an attack of my periodical head-ach, very violent for a few days. It soon subsided so as to be very slight. I am not quite clear of it now, tho I have been able to resume business for this week past. It can hardly be called a pain now, but only a disagreeable sensation of the head every morning. I am going tomorrow on a sailing party of three or four days with the President. Should we meet sea enough to make me sick I shall hope it will carry off the remains of my headach. Assure Mr. Randolph of my affectionate remembrance. I suppose Maria is not with you. Adieu my dear Daughter. Your's affectionately,   TH: JEFFERSON

To Mary Jefferson

New York June 13. 1790.

My dear Maria

I have recieved your letter of May 23. which was in answer to mine of May 2. but I wrote you also on the 23d. of May, so that you still owe me an answer to that, which I hope is now on the road. In matters of correspondence as well as of money you must never be in debt. I am much pleased with the account you give me of your occupations, and the making the pudding is as good an article of them as any. When I come to Virginia I shall insist on eating a pudding of your own making, as well as on trying other specimens of your skill. You must make the most of your time while you are with so good an aunt who can learn you every thing. We had not peas nor strawberries here till the 8th. day of this month. On the same day I heard the first Whip-poor-will whistle. Swallows and martins appeared here on the 21st. of April. When did they appear with you? And when had you peas, strawberries,

and whip-poor-wills in Virginia? Take notice hereafter whether
the whip-poor-wills always come with the strawberries and peas.
Send me a copy of the maxims I gave you, also a list of the books
I promised you. I have had a long touch of my periodical head-
ach, but a very moderate one. It has not quite left me yet. Adieu,
my dear, love your uncle, aunt and cousins, and me more than all.
Your's affectionately,   TH: JEFFERSON

To Martha Jefferson Randolph

New York June 27. 1790.

MY DEAR MARTHA

My last news from you were conveyed in your letter of May 28.
I ascribe this to your present ambulatory life. I hope when you are
more in the way of the post, I shall receive letters regularly once
a week from one or the other of you, as I write regularly once a
week myself. In my letter of the last week to Mr. Randolph I mentioned the appearances of a war between England and Spain. We
have nothing newer on that subject. There is a report indeed that
there are three British frigates off our cost; but I know not on
what it is founded. I think it probable that Congress will pass a
bill for removing to Philadelphia for ten years, and then to
Georgetown. The question will be brought on tomorrow and it's
fate be determined probably in the course of the ensuing week.
I shall not be able to decide the time of my coming to Virginia till
Congress shall have adjourned. The moment I can fix it I will inform you of it. I inclosed you the last week a letter from some
of your English acquaintance. I now inclose you an engraving of
the President done by Wright[1] who drew the picture of him which
I have at Paris. My tender affections attend you all. Adieu, my dear.
Your's affectionately,   TH: JEFFERSON

1. Joseph Wright, the American portraitist, who worked in Philadelphia
and New York City. TJ, in his draft copy of his "Catalogue of Paintings &c.
at Monticello" (ViU), made this very interesting notation: "When Genl. Washington attended the meeting of the Cincinnati in Philadelphia May. 1784. then
passing through that city on my way from Annapolis to Boston to embark
for Europe I could only allow Wright time to finish the head and face, and
sketch the outlines of the body. These and the drapery were afterwards finished
at Paris by Trumbull." From a manuscript owned by Mrs. Page Kirk of
Charlottesville, Virginia, now on loan to the University of Virginia.
    The portrait is now in the Massachusetts Historical Society and is repro-
duced in *Papers*, VII, facing page 133, with a descriptive note on page xxvii.

To Mary Jefferson

New York July 4. 1790.

I have written you, my dear Maria, four letters since I have been here, and I have received from you only two. You owe me two then, and the present will make three. This is a kind of debt I will not give up. You may ask how I will help myself? By petitioning your aunt, as soon as you receive a letter to make you go without your dinner till you have answered it. How goes on the Spanish? How many chickens have you raised this summer? Send me a list of the books I have promised you at different times. Tell me what sort of weather you have had, what sort of crops are likely to be made, how your uncle and aunt, and the family do, and how you do yourself. I shall see you in September for a short time. Adieu, my dear Poll. Your's affectionately,   TH: JEFFERSON

To Martha Jefferson Randolph

New York July 17. 1790.

MY DEAR PATSY

I recieved two days ago your's of July 2. with Mr. Randolph's of July 3. Mine of the 11th. to Mr. Randolph will have informed you that I expect to set out from hence for Monticello about the 1st. of September. As this depends on the adjournment of Congress and they begin to be impatient it is more probable I may set out sooner than later. However my letters will keep you better informed as the time approaches. Colo. Randolph's marriage[1] was to be expected. All his amusements depending on society, he cannot live alone. The settlement spoken of may be liable to objections in point of prudence and justice. However I hope it will not be the cause of any diminution of affection between him and Mr. Randolph and yourself. That cannot remedy the evil, and may make it a great deal worse. Besides your interests which might be injured by a misunderstanding be assured that your happiness would be infinitely affected. It would be a canker-worm corroding eternally on your minds. Therefore, my dear child, redouble your assiduities to keep the affections of Colo. Randolph and his lady (if he is to have one) in proportion as the difficulties increase. He is an excellent good man, to whose temper nothing can be objected but too much facility, too much milk. Avail yourself of this softness then to obtain his attachment. If the lady has any thing difficult in her dispositions, avoid what is rough, and attach her good qualities to you. Consider what are otherwise as a bad stop in your harpsichord. Do not touch on it, but make yourself happy with the good ones. Every human being, my dear, must thus be viewed according to what it is good for, for none of us, no not one, is perfect; and were we to love none who had imperfections, this world would be a desart for our love. All we can do is to make the best of our friends: love and cherish what is good in them, and keep out of the way of what is bad: but no more think of rejecting them for it than of throwing away a piece of music for a flat passage or two. Your situation will require peculiar attentions and respects to both parties. Let no proof be too much for either your patience or acquiescence. Be you my dear, the link of love, union, and peace for the whole family. The world will give you the more credit for it, in proportion to the difficulty of the task. And your own happiness will be the greater as you percieve that you promote that of others. Former acquaintance, and equality of age, will render it the easier for you to cultivate and gain the love of the lady. The mother too becomes a very necessary object of attentions. This marriage renders it doubtful with me whether it will be better to direct our overtures to Colo. R. or Mr. H. for a farm for Mr. Randolph. Mr. H. has a good tract of land on the other side Edgehill, and it may not be unadvisable to begin by buying out a dangerous neighbor. I wish Mr. Randolph could have him sounded to see if he will sell, and at what price; but sounded thro' such a channel as would excite no suspicion that it comes from Mr. Randolph or myself. Colo. Monroe would be a good and unsuspected hand as he once thought of buying the same lands. Adieu my dear child. Present my warm attachment to Mr. Randolph. Your's affectionately,   Th: Jefferson

1. Thomas Mann Randolph, Sr., married Gabriella Harvie, the daughter of John Harvie of Richmond. She was less than half his age. See Malone, *Jefferson the Virginian*, 428, and *Jefferson and the Rights of Man*, 320.

From Mary Jefferson

Eppington july 20, [1790]

Dear Papa

I hope you will excuse my not writing to you before tho I have none for myself. I am very sorry to hear that you have been sick but flatter myself that it is over. My aunt skipwith has been very

sick but she is better now. We have been to see her two or three
times. You tell me in your last letter that you will see me in september but I have received a letter from my Brother[1] that says
you will not be here before February. As his is later than yours
I am afraid you have changed your mind. The books that you
have promised me are Anacharsis[2] gibbons roman empire. If
you are coming in september I hope you will not forget your
promise of buying new jacks for the pianoforte that is at monticello. Adieu my dear Papa. I am your affectionate Daughter,

MARY JEFFERSON

My Uncle and Aunt desire to be affectionately remembered to you.

MJ

1. Thomas Mann Randolph, Jr., her brother-in-law, whom Mary generally
referred to as "brother."
2. Jean-Jacques Barthèlemy, *Voyage du jeune Anacharsis en Grèce* (Paris,
1789). Sowerby 41.

TO MARY JEFFERSON

New York July 25. 1790.

No letter from you yet, my dear Maria. You now owe me four,
and I insist on your writing me one every week till you shall have
paid the debt. I write to you every three weeks, and I think you
have quite as little to do as I have, so that I may expect letter for
letter. The account stands at present as follows.

Maria Jefferson	Dr.	to Th: Jefferson	Cr.
April. 11. To letter of this date 1.		April 25. By letter of this date 1.	
May. 2. To do. of this date 1.		May. 23. By do. of this date 1.	
23. To do. of this date 1.		Balance due T. J.	4.
June 13. To do. of this date 1.			6.
July 4. To do. of this date 1.			
25. To do. of this date 1.			
6.			

I am in hopes of seeing you at Monticello early in September, and
that your aunt and uncle will find it convenient to come and
rough it with us awhile, and to partake of the pudding you are
to make for us by way of shewing your skill. However good, be
assured it will be a great additional gratification to see that you are
improved in Spanish, in writing, in needle work, in good humor,
and kind and generous dispositions; and that you grow daily more
and more worthy the love of, dear Maria, Your's affectionately,

TH: JEFFERSON

To Martha Jefferson Randolph

New York Aug. 8. 1790.

Congress being certainly to rise the day after tomorrow, I can now, my dear Patsy, be more certain of the time at which I can be at Monticello, and which I think will be from the 8th. to the 15th. of September: more likely to be sooner than later. I shall leave this about a fortnight hence, but must stay some days to have arrangements taken for my future residence in Philadelphia. I hope to be able to pass a month at least with you at Monticello. I am in hopes Mr. Randolph will take dear Poll in his pocket. Tell him I have sent him the model of the mould-board[1] by Mr. David Randolph who left this place yesterday. I must trouble you to give notice to Martin[2] to be at Monticello by the 1st. of September that he may have things prepared. If you know any thing of Bob,[3] I should be glad of the same notice to him, tho' I suppose him to be in the neighborhood of Fredericksbg, and in that case I will have him notified thro' Mr. Fitzhugh. I have written to Mr. Brown[4] for some necessaries to be sent to Monticello, and to send on some chairs which will go hence to the care of Mr. D. Randolph at the Hundred,[5] to be forwarded to Mr. Brown at Richmond. If Mr. Randolph can give a little attention to the forwarding these articles we shall be the more comfortable. Present me to him and Maria affectionately, and continue to love me as I do you, my dear, most sincerely, TH: JEFFERSON

1. The exact date TJ fashioned his first mouldboard for a plough is not established. In the *Farm Book,* 47–49, Betts states it was not until after his return from Paris in 1789 that the idea was discussed with Thomas Mann Randolph, Jr. The model herein mentioned was completed sometime between that date and August, 1790, and sent on to his son-in-law. In recognition of his work on the mouldboard, TJ in 1810 was made a foreign associate of the French Society of Agriculture.

2. It was a practice when speaking of slaves, as Martin, to use their first names, which in most instances was the only one they had, several exceptions being the Hemingses and Joe Fosset. A white servant or employee was generally addressed as "Mr." or simply by his last name.

3. Robert Hemings (usually the "Bob" of these letters) was a member of the able slave family at Monticello who were extended many liberties and opportunities not available to others in bondage. Betty Hemings, a light-colored Negress, had twelve children, one of whom was Bob Hemings, by several individuals, at least one of whom was white. The name Hemings is believed to have come from an English sea captain, her father. The family came to Monticello as a part of Martha Jefferson's patrimony from her father John Wayles. For additional information on this family as well as on slaves in general at Monticello and other Jefferson farms, see the *Farm Book; Memoirs of a Monticello Slave;* Hamilton W. Pierson, *Jefferson at Monticello, The Private Life of Thomas Jefferson* (New York, 1862), this being chiefly the reminiscences of Edmund Bacon, the overseer at Monticello for twenty years

during Jefferson's lifetime; and Malone, *Jefferson and the Rights of Man.* John Cook Wyllie, Librarian of the Alderman Library at the University of Virginia, is a well-versed scholar on the slave hierarchy at Monticello. Mrs. Pearl Graham of Sunset Beach, California, has also made an extensive study of the Hemings family.

4. John Brown was a Richmond factor.

5. Bermuda Hundred was an Eppes estate on the Appomattox River in Chesterfield County. It was deeded to John Wayles Eppes on the occasion of his marriage to Mary Jefferson.

TO MARTHA JEFFERSON RANDOLPH

New York Aug. 22. 1790.

MY DEAR DAUGHTER

The last letter I recieved from you was of the 2d. July. In mine of the 14th. inst. to Mr. Randolph I informed him I should set out the next day to Rhode island with the President. I did so, and returned yesterday, after a very pleasant sail of two days going and two days returning thro the Sound. We visited Newport and Providence, where the President was received with great cordiality. He expects to leave this place the 30th. My letter of about that date will inform Mr. Randolph of the day I shall set out from hence, which will probably be about the 1st. of Sep. and allowing for my necessary detention at Philadelphia I shall in that case be at Monticello between the 14th. and 20th. of September, where I shall hope the pleasure of passing a month with you. I am afraid you will suffer inconvenience from the detention of your harness; but without it I could not have used my carriage till I recieve my own harness from France which I hardly expect now till September. I think you understood Lady Caroline Tufton was about to be married. But in a London paper put into my hands by Mr. Rutledge[1] I saw her attendance at court mentioned and under the name you knew her by. We have no news yet whether the war between England and Spain has commenced. Kiss dear Poll for me, and remember me to Mr. Randolph. Adieu my dear. Your's affectionately,   TH: JEFFERSON

1. John Rutledge of South Carolina.

FROM MARY JEFFERSON

recd. Aug. 28. [1790]

DEAR PAPA

I have just received your last favour of july 25 and am determined to write to you every day till I have discharged my debt.

When we were in Cumberland[1] we went to Church and heard some singing Masters that sang very well. They are to come here to learn my cousins to sing and as I know you have no objections to my learning any thing I am to be a scholar and hope to give you the pleasure of hearing an anthem. We had pease the 14 of may and strawberries the 17 of the same month tho not in that abundance we are accustomed to in consequence of a frost this spring. As for the martins swallows and whippoorwills I was so taken up with my chickens that I never attended to them and therefore cannot tell you when they came tho I was so unfortunate as to lose half of them for my cousin Bolling and myself have raised but 13 between us. Adieu my Dear Papa.

Believe me to be your affectionate daughter,

MARY JEFFERSON

1. Mary was at Hors du Monde.

To MARTHA JEFFERSON RANDOLPH

Philadelphia Dec. 1. 1790.

MY DEAR DAUGHTER

In my letter of last week to Mr. Randolph I mentioned that I should write every Wednesday to him, yourself and Polly alternately, and that my letters arriving at Monticello the Saturday and the answer being sent off on Sunday I should receive it the day before I should have to write again to the same person, so as that the correspondence with each would be exactly kept up. I hope you will do it on your part. I delivered the fan and note to your friend Mrs. Waters (Miss Rittenhouse that was)[1] she being now married to a Doctr. Waters. They live in the house with her father. She complained of the petit format of your letter, and Mrs. Trist of no letter. I inclose you the Magasin des Modes of July. My furniture is arrived from Paris: but it will be long before I can open the packages,[2] as my house will not be ready to recieve them for some weeks. As soon as they are the mattrasses &c. shall be sent on. News for Mr. Randolph. The letters from Paris inform that as yet all is safe there. They are emitting great sums of paper money. They rather believe there will be no war between Spain and England: but the letters from London count on a war, and it seems rather probable. A general peace is established in the North of Europe, except between Russia and Turkey. It is expected between them also. Wheat here is a French crown the bushel. Kiss dear Poll for me. Remember me to Mr. Randolph. I do not know yet how the Edgehill negociation has terminated. Adieu my dear, Your's affectionately,　　　TH: JEFFERSON

1. Esther Rittenhouse Waters (Mrs. Nicholas Baker) was the daughter of David Rittenhouse.

2. When TJ departed France in 1789 he expected to return to his post in Paris, and consequently none of his household and few personal possessions accompanied him to America. These were packed by Petit under William Short's direction (see TJ to Short, March 12 and April 6, 1790, *Papers*, XVI, 228–30, 318–20) and sent on under a long packing list or invoice entitled: "Memorandum of the objects made and furnished by me Grévin master box maker for Mr. de Jefferson Minister of the United States of North America July 17, 1790." (DLC.) There were eighty-six packing cases: fifteen contained books, nine wine, and the remainder household and personal possessions. Some were sent to Philadelphia, others to Monticello via Norfolk. It was about these boxes that TJ was writing to Martha.

TO MARY JEFFERSON

Philadelphia Dec. 7. 1790

MY DEAR POLL

This week I write to you, and if you answer my letter as soon as you recieve it, and send it to Colo. Bell[1] at Charlottesville I shall recieve it the day before I write to you again, which will be three weeks hence: and this I shall expect you to do always so that by the correspondence of Mr. Randolph, your sister and yourself I may hear from home once a week. Mr. Randolph's letter from Richmond came to me about five days ago. How do you all do? Tell me that in your letter, also what is going forward with you, how you employ yourself, what weather you have had. We have already had two or three snows here. The workmen are so slow in finishing the house I have rented here that I know not when I shall have it ready except one room which they promise me this week, and which will be my bedroom, study, dining room and parlour. I am not able to give any later news about peace or war than of October 16. which I mentioned in my last to your sister. Wheat has fallen a few pence, and will I think continue to fall, slowly at first and rapidly after a while. Adieu my dear Maria. Kiss your sister for me, and assure Mr. Randolph of my affection. I will not tell you how much I love you, lest by rendering you vain, it might render you less worthy of my love. Encore Adieu.

TH: J.

1. Colonel Thomas Bell, a resident of Charlottesville and friend of TJ's.

To Martha Jefferson Randolph

Philadelphia Dec. 23. 1790.

MY DEAR DAUGHTER

This is a scolding letter for you all. I have not recieved a scrip of a pen from home since I left it which is now eleven weeks. I think it so easy for you to write me one letter every week, which will be but once in three weeks for each of you, when I write one every week who have not one moment's repose from business from the first to the last moment of the week. Perhaps you think you have nothing to say to me. It is a great deal to say you are all well, or that one has a cold, another a fever &c., besides that there is not a sprig of grass that shoots uninteresting to me, nor any thing that moves, from yourself down to Bergere or Grizzle.[1] Write then my dear daughter punctually on your day, and Mr. Randolph and Polly on theirs. I suspect you may have news to tell me of yourself of the most tender interest to me. Why silent then?

I am still without a house, and consequently without a place to open my furniture. This has prevented my sending you what I was to send for Monticello. In the mean time the river is frozen up so as that no vessel can get out, nor probably will these two months: so that you will be much longer without them than I had hoped. I know how inconvenient this will be and am distressed at it; but there is no help. I send a pamphlet for Mr. Randolph. My best affections to him, Polly and yourself. Adieu my dear,

TH: JEFFERSON

1. TJ's highly prized sheep dogs. Bergere was purchased in Le Havre October 7, 1789. The Account Book reads: "Pd. for a chienne bergere big with pup. 36ᴴ." For information regarding the actual purchase of this dog, see *Papers*, XV, 509n., and for a report on the dog population at Monticello several years later, consult Martha Jefferson Randolph to TJ, May 27, 1792.

To Mary Jefferson

Philadelphia Jan. 5. 1790 [1791][1]

I did not write to you, my dear Poll, the last week, because I was really angry at recieving no letter. I have now been near nine weeks from home, and have never had a scrip of a pen, when by the regularity of the post, I might recieve your letters as frequently and as exactly as if I were at Charlottesville. I ascribed it at first to indolence, but the affection must be weak which is so long overruled by that. Adieu.   TH: J.

1. Incorrectly dated 1790.

FROM MARTHA JEFFERSON RANDOLPH

Monticello January 16th 1791.

I very much regret not having answered yours My Dearest Papa sooner. But being misinformed with regard to the Charlottesville post which we heard was discontinued has till now prevented my writing and not as you supposed having nothing to say. It is unlucky that the matrasses cannot be sent now as we shall soon be in great distress. Aunt Fleming and probably one of her sons being expected here shortly I must accept of Mrs. Lewis's[1] kind offer who in returning one of the beds I sent home offered a second if necessary. I have reason to think my self far advanced in her good graces as she has really been friendly. Martin has left us and not relying much in the carefullness of the boys particularly when left to them selves I took an account of the plate china &c. and locked up all that was not in imediate use not recolecting that there was a set of queens ware here I sent to Richmond for some, by which means the china was preserved entire except our beautiful cups which being obliged to leave out are all broke but one. The spoons &c. that are in use are counted and locked up night and morning so that I hope to keep them all to gather till your return. It was very troublesome in the beginning tho now I have the boys in tolerable order. Every thing goes on pretty well. I have wrought an entire reformation on the rest of my household, nothing comes in or goes out without my knowledge and I believe there is as little wasted as possible. I visit the kitchen smoke house and fowls when the weather permits and according to your desire send the meat cut out. I can give but a poor account of my reading having had so little time to my self that tho I really have the greatest inclination I have not as yet been able to indulge it. Polly improves visibly in her spanish which she reads with much more facility than when you went away. She was surprised that I should think of making her look for *all* the words and the parts of the verb. Also when she made nonsense but finding me inexorable she is at last reconciled to her dictionary with whom she had for some time past been on very bad terms. She has been twice thru her grammar since your departure. As for the harpsichord tho I put in fine order, it has been to little purpose till very lately. I am in hopes she will continue to attend to that also. She is remarkably docile where she can surmount her Laziness of which she has an astonishing degree and which makes her neglect what ever she thinks will not be imediately discovered. I have entered

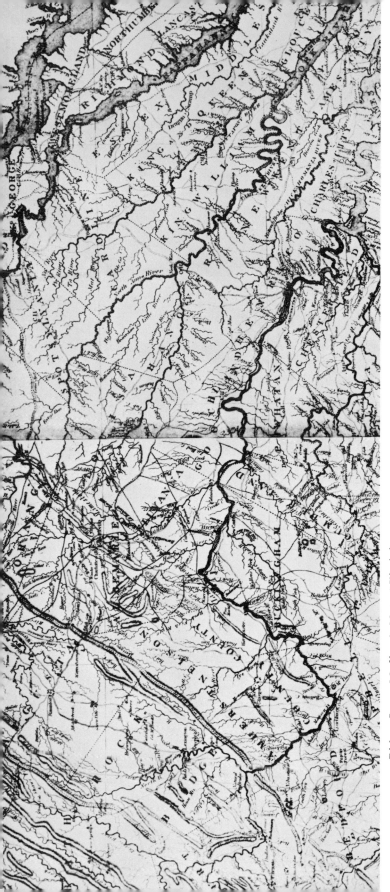

Bishop James Madison's *Map of Virginia*
(with corrections and additions to the year 1818)
Original in the University of Virginia Library

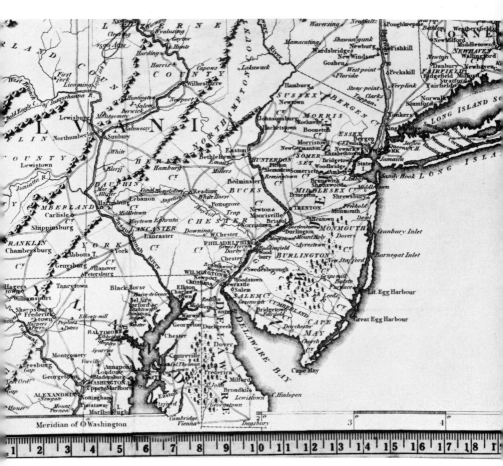

Map of the Northern Provinces of the United
States from La Rochefoucauld Liancourt's
*Travels Through the United States of
North America*, II (London, R. Phillips, 1799)
Copy in the University of Virginia Library

Thomas Jefferson. An engraving by St. Mémin after his life portrait done in 1804. This was a family favorite, especially with his daughters Martha and Mary. *Princeton University Library*

Martha Jefferson Carr. Wife of Dabney Carr and Jefferson's sister. In the family she was known as "Aunt Carr." *Thomas Jefferson Memorial Foundation*

Martha Jefferson Randolph. As a young lady of fifteen, when she was in France with her father. *Thomas Jefferson Memorial Foundation*

Francis Wayles Eppes. Grandson of Francis Eppes of Eppington and the only child of Mary Jefferson and John Wayles Eppes to survive infancy. Artist not known. *Thomas Jefferson Memorial Foundation*

Edgehill, the home of Martha Jefferson and Thomas Mann Randolph, Jr., from 1797 until 1809, when they removed to Monticello. The property in 1817 came into the possession of their son Thomas Jefferson Randolph, who resided on the estate until his death in 1875 but not in this house. *Mrs. Olivia Taylor*

Eppington, the home of Francis Wayles Eppes, located on the north side of the Appomattox River in Chesterfield County, Virginia. The porch was not a part of the original house.

into all these details because however trifling they would appear to others, to you my Dear Papa I think they will be interesting. I received a kind invitation from Aunt Eppes to spend the month of February at Eppinton but Mrs. Fleming's being here at that time will render it useless. The morning of the 13th. at 10 minutes past four we had an earth quake [2] which was severe enough to awaken us all in the house and several of the servants in the out houses. It was followed by a second shock very slight and an aurora borealis. I am extremely obliged to you for the cypress vine which with a bundle of seeds I found in rumaging up some drawer in the chamber, written on the back cupressus Patula and some others I intend to decorate my windows this spring. You promised me a colection of garden seeds for a young Lady in the west indies (*Bruni*)[3] for whom also I will send you a letter to be forwarded to her with them. Adieu My Dearest Father. Mr. Randolph and Polly join in love. Believe me ever your affectionate child, M RANDOLPH

1. Mrs. Nicholas Lewis was the wife of Nicholas Lewis of The Farm, Albemarle County, under whose care Monticello came while TJ was in France.
2. This was not the first recorded earthquake at Monticello. TJ had noted shocks on Februry 21 and 22, 1774. Account Book 1774.
3. Mme. Brunette de Châteaubrun, called "Bruni" or "Bruny," was a schoolmate and close friend of Martha's.

To MARTHA JEFFERSON RANDOLPH

Philadelphia Jan. 20. 1791.

MY DEAR DAUGHTER

Mr. Short in a late letter says that your acquaintances in Panthemont complain excessively of your inattention to them and desired him to mention it. Matters there are going on well. The sales of the church lands are successful beyond all calculation. There has been a riot in Paris in which M. de Castrie's[1] househould furniture was destroyed. I am opening my things from Paris as fast as the workmen will make room for me. In a box lately opened I find a copy of the octavo edition of the Encyclopedie, and a complete copy of Buffon's[2] works with Daubenton's part which I had written for to present to Mr. Randolph. But I do not know when I shall be able to send any thing forward, from the slowness of workmen in making houseroom for me to open my things and from the ice in the river. The cold of this place has made me wish for some stockings of cotton and hair's fur knit together. I do not recollect whether Bet[3] can knit. If she can do it well, it might be a good employment for her sometimes. If she cannot, I wish a good knitter could be found in the neighborhood to knit some for me. They should be very large. Present my cordial regards to Mr. Randolph, and kiss Polly for me, telling her I have received not a single letter from Monticello since I left it, except one from Mr. Randolph. Adieu my dear. Your's affectionately,   TH: JEFFERSON

P. S. The inclosed letter is for a neighbor of yours living somewhere on the waters of Buckisland. It is from her sister who is in Paris, the wife of one of the Duke of Orleans's grooms. He was of General Philips's army.

1. Marquis Charles de Castries was a one-time minister of the French navy. His town house, situated in the Rue de Varenne in the Faubourg Saint-Germain of Paris, was sacked by a mob on November 13, 1790, as a result of his duel with Charles de Lameth. The house still stands.

2. *Encyclopédie, ou Dictionnaire Raisonné des Sciences des Arts et des Métiers* . . . , edited by D'Alembert and Diderot [1750–1789]; TJ's was a thirty-nine-volume octavo edition. Louis-Jean-Marie Daubenton was one of the many contributors to Buffon's *Histoire Naturelle, générale et particulière* (1752–1788). Sowerby 1024, 4890.

3. Probably Betty Hemings.

FROM MARY JEFFERSON

Monticello, January 22d, 1791.

DEAR PAPA

I received your letter of December the 7th. about a fortnight ago, and would have answered it directly, but my sister had to answer hers last week and I this. We are all well at present. Jenny Randolph[1] and myself keep house, she one week, and I the other. I owe sister thirty-five pages in Don Quixote, and am now paying them as fast as I can. Last Christmas I gave sister the "Tales of the Castle," and she made me a present of the "Observer," a little ivory box, and one of her drawings; and to Jenny she gave "Paradise Lost," and some other things.[2] Adieu, dear Papa. I am your affectionate daughter,   MARIA JEFFERSON

1. Virginia Randolph was a younger sister of Thomas Mann Randolph, Jr., and was known as Jenny or Cousin Jenny.

2. This is one of the few references to an exchange of Christmas presents among members of the Monticello family. *Tales of the Castle* was a translation of *Les Veillées du château* by the Countess de Genlis, *The Observer*, a collection of philosophical essays by Richard Cumberland, Bishop of Peterborough.

TO MARTHA JEFFERSON RANDOLPH

Philadelphia Feb. 2. 1791.

MY DEAR MARTHA

I have this moment recieved your's of January 16. and answer it by the first post. It is indeed and interesting letter to me as it gives me the details which I am sure will contribute to your happiness, my first wish. Nothing is so engaging as the little domestic cares into which you appear to be entering, and as to reading it is useful for only filling up the chinks of more useful and healthy occupations. I am sincerely sorry that the mattresses cannot yet be forwarded. But the state of the river here forbids it, and while it is incertain whether it will be found open or shut no vessels come here from Virginia. They shall go by the first possible opportunity. Whenever your letter to Bruny comes I will reccompany it with the seeds: but you must inform me at the sametime what kind of seeds to send her. Congress will certainly rise the 1st. of March, when you will again have Colo. Munroe[1] and Mrs. Monroe in your neighborhood. I write to you out of turn, and believe I must adopt the rule of only writing when I am written to, in hopes that may provoke more frequent letters. Mr. Randolph's letter of Dec. 27. and yours now acknowledged are all I have recieved from Monticello since I left it. Give my best affections to him and Poll, and be assured my dear daughter of the sincere love of your's affectionately,   TH: JEFFERSON

1. James Monroe.

TO MARTHA JEFFERSON RANDOLPH

Philadelphia Feb. 9. 1791.

MY DEAR MARTHA

Your two last letters are those which have given me the greatest pleasure of any I ever recieved from you. The one announced that you were become a notable housewife, the other a mother.[1] This last is undoubtedly the key-stone of the arch of matrimonial happiness, as the first is it's daily ailment. Accept my sincere congratulations for yourself and Mr. Randolph. I hope you are getting well, towards which great care of yourself is necessary: for however adviseable it is for those in health to expose themselves freely, it is not so for the sick. You will be out in time to begin your garden, and that will tempt you to be out a great deal, than which nothing will tend more to give you health and strength. Remember me affectionately to Mr. Randolph and Polly, as well as to Miss Jenny. Your's sincerely,   TH: JEFFERSON

1. TJ is referring to the birth of Martha's first child, a daughter, who was born January 23, 1791.

FROM MARY JEFFERSON

February 13 [1791]

DEAR PAPA

I am very sorry that my not having wrote to you before made you doubt of my affection towards you and hope that after having read my last letter you were not so displeased as at first. In my last I said that my sister was very well but she was not. She had been very sick all day without my knowing any thing of it as I stayed up stairs the whole day. However she is very well now and the little one also. She is very pretty has beautiful deep blue eyes and is a very fine child. Adieu my Dear Papa. Beleive me to be your affectionate daughter,   MARY JEFFERSON

TO MARY JEFFERSON

Philadelphia Feb. 16. 1791.

MY DEAR POLL

At length I have recieved a letter from you. As the spell is now broke, I hope you will continue to write every three weeks. Observe I do not admit the excuse you make of not writing because your sister had not written the week before: let each write their own week without regard to what others do, or do not do. I congratulate you my dear aunt on your new title. I hope you pay a great deal of attention to your niece, and that you have begun to give her lessons on the harpsichord, in Spanish etc. Tell your sister I make her a present of Gregory's comparative view,[1] inclosed herewith, and that she will find in it a great deal of useful advice for a young mother. I hope herself and the child are well. Kiss them both for me. Present me affectionately to Mr. Randolph and Miss Jenny. Mind your Spanish and your Harpsichord well and think often and always of, Your's affectionately,

TH: JEFFERSON

P. S. Letters inclosed with the book for your sister.

1. John Gregory, *A Comparative View of the State and Faculties of Man with those of the Animal World* . . . , *seventh edition* . . . (London, 1777).

Martha's copy is in the Alderman Library at the University of Virginia. TJ owned a 1779 edition (Sowerby 1354). This was a popular and widely read work on child care.

To Martha Jefferson Randolph

Philadelphia Mar. 2. [1791]

MY DEAR DAUGHTER

The present will serve just to tell you that I am well, and to keep up my plan of writing once a week whether I have any thing to say or not. Congress rises tomorrow. They have passed no laws remarkeable except the excise law[1] and one establishing a bank.[2] Mrs. Trist and Mrs. Waters always enquire after you and desire me to remember them to you. I hope you are by this time able to be about again and in good health as well as the little one.[3] Kiss it and Maria for me. I have recieved her letter and will answer it next week. I inclose a letter for M. de Rieux.[4] Present my esteem to Mr. Randolph. Yours affectionately,

TH: JEFFERSON

1. This law provided for the assessment and collection of internal revenue duties on distilled liquors and also additional duties on imported spirits.
2. The first Bank of the United States was chartered in 1791 for twenty years, with the parent bank in Philadelphia. Branches were established in principal seaports.
3. The reference is to Martha's daughter. The parents wanted TJ to name her, but as of this date, if their request had reached him, his reply had not been received
4. The wife of Justin Pierre Plumard Derieux, a son-in-law of Philip Mazzei who resided at Colle, Mazzei's home in Albemarle County near Monticello.

From Mary Jefferson

march 6 [1791]

According to my dear Papa's request I now sit down to write. We were very uneasy for not having had a letter from you since six weeks till yesterday I received yours which I now answer. The marble Pedestal[1] and a dressing table are come. Jenny is gone down with Mrs. Fleming who came here to see sister while she was sick. I suppose you have not received the letter in which Mr. Randolph desires you to name the child. We hope you will come to see us this summer therefore you must not disapoint us and I expect you want to see my little neice as much as you do any of

us. We are all well and hope you are so too. Adieu dear Papa. I am your affectionate daughter, MARY JEFFERSON
P. s. My sister says I must tell you the child grows very fast.

1. Probably the large pedestal that Madame de Tessé presented to TJ in August of 1789. TJ brought it to Monticello, where it stood in the entrance hall, bearing the Ceracchi bust of Jefferson. It was sold to the United States Government and was later destroyed in a fire in the Library of Congress in 1851. For further information, consult Alfred Bush, *The Life Portraits of Thomas Jefferson* (Charlottesville, 1962), and *Papers*, XV, 363–64.

To Mary Jefferson

Philadelphia March 9. 1791.

MY DEAR MARIA

I am happy to have at length a letter of yours to answer, for that which you wrote to me Feb. 13. came to hand Feb. 28. I hope our correspondence will now be more regular, that you will be no more lazy, and I no more in the pouts on that account. On the 27th. of February I saw blackbirds and Robinred breasts, and on the 7th. of this month I heard frogs for the first time this year. Have you noted the first appearance of these things at Monticello? I hope you have, and will continue to note every appearance animal and vegetable which indicates the approach of spring, and will communicate them to me. By these means we shall be able to compare the climates of Philadelphia and Monticello. Tell me when you shall have peas &c up, when every thing comes to table, when you shall have the first chickens hatched, when every kind of tree blossoms, or puts forth leaves, when each kind of flower blooms. Kiss your sister and niece for me, and present me affectionately to Mr. Randolph and Miss Jenny. Yours tenderly, my dear Maria, TH: JEFFERSON

From Martha Jefferson Randolph

Monticello March 22 1791

MY DEAR PAPA

You gave me reason to hope in your last to Mr. Randolph that there was a probability of our seeing you this summer. Your little grand daughter thinks herself entitled to a visit. I hope you will not disapoint us. My house keeping and Pollys spanish have equally suffered from my confinement. She is beginning again to go on tolerably for so great a habit of idleness had she contracted in one month that it has taken [me almost] another to get the better of it. I have at last seriously [begun] writing to my European friends tho I fear it will be a difficult matter to forward my letters to you as the post has ceased to go. Doctor Gilmer's[1] eldest son is arrived from Scotland in a very deep consumption. His father and mother are gone down to Shirley[2] in all probability to take their last farewell of him if he is still alive which they almost dispaired of when they set off. A cousin of ours Randolph Lewis is lately married to Miss Lewis of the *bird* the bridegroom was 18 and she 15.[3] Young Mr. Monroe [and] a Miss Elizabeth Kerr daughter of old Jimmy Kerr have followed their example.[4] Polly and My self have planted the cypress vine in boxes in the window as also date seed and some other flowers. I hope you have not forgot the colection of garden seed you promised me for Bruni. I am under some obligation to her for several things which she has sent me and for which tho not yet come to hand I am not the less grateful. Flower seeds and fruit stones would no doubt be also very acceptable tho grain de jardinage was the expression she made use of. I will send you a letter to go with the seeds or be burnt if you can not get them. I should be extremely obliged to you My Dearest Papa for a green silk calash lined with green also, as a hat is by no means proper for such a climate as ours. The little girl grows astonishingly and has been uncommonly healthy. Adieu My dear Papa. I have read gregory and am happy to tell you it was precisely the plan who we had followed with her for her birth by Mrs. Lewis's advice.[5] We continue very great friends. She allways calls the child (who till you send her one will go by no other name) her grand daughter. Once more adieu My Dearest Papa. Your affectionate child,   M. RANDOLPH

1. Thomas Walker Gilmer, the eldest son of Dr. George Gilmer of Pen Park, Albemarle County, had been in Edinburgh studying medicine. He died in his twenty-second year; he is not to be confused with Governor Thomas Walker Gilmer.

2. Shirley, the Carter home in Charles City County.

3. Randolph Lewis was the son of Charles L. Lewis, Jr., and Lucy Jefferson, TJ's sister. Randolph Lewis was also a grandson of Charles L. Lewis, Sr., and Mary Randolph, a sister of Jane Randolph Jefferson, TJ's mother. His bride was Mary Lewis, a cousin, and daughter of Robert Lewis. See John Meriwether McAllister and Lura B. Tandy, editors, *Genealogies of the Lewis and Kindred Families* (Columbia, Missouri, 1906).

4. Joseph J. Monroe was the brother of James and Andrew Monroe.

5. Mrs. Nicholas Lewis.

To Martha Jefferson Randolph

Philadelphia Mar. 24. 1791.

MY DEAR DAUGHTER

The badness of the roads retards the post, so that I have recieved no letter from Monticello. I shall hope soon to have one from yourself, to know from that that you are perfectly reestablished, that the little Anne is becoming a big one, that you have received Dr. Gregory's book and are daily profiting from it. This will hardly reach you in time to put you on the watch for the annular eclipse of the sun which is to happen on Sunday sennight to begin about sun-rise. It will be such a one as is rarely to be seen twice in one life. I have lately recieved a letter from Fulwar Skipwith who is consul for us in Martinique and Guadaloupe. He fixed himself first in the former, but has removed to the latter. Are any of your acquaintances in either of those islands? If they are, I wish you would write to them and recommend him to their acquaintance. He will be a sure medium thro which you may exchange *souvenirs* with your friends, of a more useful kind than those of the convent. He sent me half a dozen pots of very fine sweetmeats. Apples and cyder are the greatest presents which can be sent to those islands. I can make those presents for you whenever you chuse to write a letter to accompany them, only observing the season for apples. They had better deliver their letters for you to F. Skipwith. Things are going on well in France, the revolution being past all danger. The national assembly being to separate soon.[1] That event will seal the whole with security. Their islands, but most particularly St. Dominque and Martinique are involved in a horrid civil war. Nothing can be more distressing than the situation of the inhabitants, as their slaves have been called into action, and are a terrible engine, absolutely ungovernable. It is worst in Martinique which was the reason Mr. Skipwith left it. An army and fleet from France are expected every hour to quell the disorders. I suppose you are busily engaged in your garden. I expect full details from you on that subject, as well as from Poll, that I may judge what sort of a gardener you make. Present me affectionately to all around you and be assured of the tender and unalterable love of Your's,   TH: JEFFERSON

1. The National Assembly at the beginning of the year indicated that instead of continuing its session, as the Long Parliament had done in England, it would enumerate a list of articles to be discussed previous to the establishment of a constitution. Following this, the Assembly declared its intention of dissolving itself and planned accordingly to resign its authority.

FROM MARY JEFFERSON

march the 26 [1791]

It is three weeks my Dear Papa, since I have had a letter from you however as it is now my turn I shall not be ceremonious. We are all waiting with great impatience to know the name of the child. Mrs. Lewis was so kind as to give me a Calico habit. Adieu my Dear Papa. I am your affectionate daughter,

MARY JEFFERSON

TO MARY JEFFERSON

Philadelphia, March 31st, 1791.

MY DEAR MARIA

I am happy to have a letter of yours to answer. That of March 6th came to my hands on the 24th. By-the-by, you never acknowledged the receipt of my letters, nor tell me on what day they came to hand. I presume that by this time you have received the two dressing-tables with marble tops. I give one of them to your sister, and the other to you: mine is here with the top broken in two. Mr. Randolph's letter, referring to me the name of your niece, was very long on the road. I answered it as soon as I received it, and hope the answer got duly to hand. Lest it should have been delayed, I repeated last week to your sister the name of Anne,[1] which I had recommended as belonging to both families. I wrote you in my last that the frogs had begun their songs on the 7th; since that the blue-birds saluted us on the 17th; the weeping-willow began to leaf on the 18th; the lilac and gooseberry on the 25th; and the golden-willow on the 26th. I inclose for your sister three kinds of flowering beans, very beautiful and very rare. She must plant and nourish them with her own hand this year, in order to save enough seeds for herself and me. Tell Mr. Randolph I have sold my tobacco for five dollars per c., and the rise between this and September. Warehouse and shipping expenses in Virginia, freight and storage here, come to 2s.9d. a hundred, so that it is as if I had sold it in Richmond for 27s.3d. credit till September, or half per cent. per month discount for the ready money. If he chooses it, his Bedford tobacco may be included in the sale. Kiss every body for me. Yours affectionately,

TH: JEFFERSON

1. Anne Cary Randolph.

To Martha Jefferson Randolph

Philadelphia April. 17. 1791.

My dear daughter

Since I wrote last to you; which was on the 24th. of March, I have received yours of March 22. I am indeed sorry to hear of the situation of Walker Gilmer and shall hope the letters from Monticello will continue to inform me how he does. I know how much his parents will suffer, and how much he merited all their affection. Mrs. Trist has been so kind as to have your calash made, but either by mistake of the maker, or of myself, it is not lined with green. I have therefore desired a green lining to be got, which you can put in yourself if you prefer it. Mrs. Trist has observed that there is a kind of veil lately introduced here, and much approved. It fastens over the brim of the hat and then draws round the neck as close or open as you please. I desire a couple to be made to go with the calash and other things. Mr. Lewis not liking to write letters I do not hear from him: but I hope you are readily furnished with all the supplies and conveniences the estate affords. I shall not be able to see you till September, by which time the young-grandaughter will begin to look bold, and knowing. I inclose you a letter to a woman, who lives, I believe, on Buck island.[1] It is from her sister in Paris, which I would wish you to send express. I hope your garden is flourishing. Present me affectionately to Mr. Randolph and Polly. Your's sincerely my dear,

TH: JEFFERSON

1. Buck Island Creek is located in southeastern Albemarle near Fluvanna County. In a letter to William Short in Paris on April 6, 1790, TJ enclosed a note from the sister at Buck Island in which he opined that her name was "Thompson, but am not sure." *Papers*, XVI, 319.

From Mary Jefferson

Monticello, April 18th, 1791.

Dear Papa

I received your letter of March 31st the 14th of this month; as for that of March 9, I received it some time last month, but I do not remember the day. I have finished Don Quixote, and as I have not Desoles yet, I shall read Lazarillo de Tormes.[1] The garden is backward, the inclosure having but lately been finished. I wish you would be so kind as to send me seven yards of cloth like

APRIL 24, 1791   79

the piece I send you. Adieu, my dear papa. I am your affectionate
daughter,   MARIA JEFFERSON

1. Probably *The Life and Adventures of Lazarillo de Tormes* and Antonio
de Solis, *Historia de la Conquista de Mexico* . . . (Madrid, 1783–84) 2 volumes.
Sowerby 4119.

To Mary Jefferson

Philadelphia Apr. 24. 1791.

I have received my dear Maria, your letter of Mar. 26. I find
I have counted too much on you as a Botanical and zoological
correspondent: for I undertook to affirm here that the fruit was
not killed in Virginia, because I had a young daughter there, who
was in that kind of correspondence with me, and who I was sure
would have mentioned it if it had been so. However I shall go on
communicating to you whatever may contribute to a comparative
estimate of the two climates, in hopes it will induce you to do the
same to me. Instead of waiting to send the two vails for your
sister and yourself round with the other things, I inclose them
with this letter. Observe that one of the strings is to be drawn
tight round the root of the crown of the hat; and the vail then
falling over the brim of the hat is drawn by the lower string as
tight or loose as you please round the neck. When the vail is not
chosen to be down, the lower string also is tied round the root of
the crown so as to give it the appearance of a puffed bandage for
the hat. I send also inclosed the green lining for the Calash. J.
Eppes[1] is arrived here. Present my affections to Mr. R. your sister
and niece.

    April 5. Apricots in blossom.
              cherry leafing.
        9.   Peach in blossom.
              Apple leafing.
        11.   Cherry in blossom
                  Your's with tender love,
                                        TH: JEFFERSON

1. John Wayles Eppes (or Jack, as TJ called him at this time) was the only
son of Elizabeth and Francis Eppes. He was in Philadelphia to further his
education, which was being done under TJ's supervision.

FROM MARY JEFFERSON

monticello may 1 [1791]

DEAR PAPA

As Bob[1] is going down the country tomorrow we shall all write to you by this opportunity. We expect jenny and nancy Randolph[2] here in July. Mr. Randolph has bought a horse called my heart and a saddle for me to ride out on, also a pretty whip. My niece is prettier and prettier. Every day this is beautiful now the peaches cherrys and strawberries are very big allready and there are a great number. Adieu my Dear Papa. I am your affectionate daughter,   MARY JEFFERSON

1. Robert Hemings. It was not unusual for certain of TJ's slaves to travel as he was doing.
2. Virginia and Anne Cary Randolph were daughters of Thomas Mann Randolph, Sr. Anne Cary was known in the family as Nancy.

TO MARTHA JEFFERSON RANDOLPH

Philadelphia May 8. 1791.

MY DEAR DAUGHTER

Your letter of April 13. tho' it came to hand on the 30th. is yet to be acknowleged. That of May 1. I received last night within seven days of it's date. The post from Richmond comes I believe in 4. days at this season of the year, so that our correspondence might be very prompt if you had a regular post from Charlottesville to Richmond. I thank you for all the small news of your letters, which it is very grateful to me to recieve. I am happy to find you are on good terms with your neighbors. It is almost the most important circumstance in life, since nothing is so corroding as frequently to meet persons with whom one has any difference. The ill-will of a single neighbor is an immense drawback on the happiness of life, and therefore their good will cannot be bought too dear. The loss of my vis-a-vis coming round by water from Richmond to this place taught me that it was best to trust nothing that way during the boisterous months of the winter and spring. I am afraid I have a second lesson of the same kind, as I had 4. hhds of tobo. on board a capt. Stratton, who was to sail from Richmond 3. weeks ago, but is not arrived here. On board him were J. Eppes's books and baggage. I fear he must be lost. I had been particularly waiting for him, as being a very careful man and going directly to Richmond, to send the Mattrasses &c. Tomorrow however I will have the packages finished, and send them by any other conveyance which occurs. They will contain as follows.

6. mattrasses.

A package of James's[1] bedding from Paris. To be kept for him.
   do.   Sally's   do.

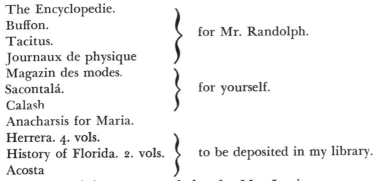

The Encyclopedie.
Buffon.
Tacitus.   } for Mr. Randolph.
Journaux de physique

Magazin des modes.
Sacontalá.   } for yourself.
Calash

Anacharsis for Maria.

Herrera. 4. vols.
History of Florida. 2. vols. } to be deposited in my library.
Acosta

A box containing 2. panes of glass for Mrs. Lewis.

Some Windsor chairs if the vessel can take them.

I am made happy by Petit's[2] determination to come to me. I had not been able to assume the name of a housekeeper for want of a real housekeeper. I did not look out for another, because I still hoped he would come. In fact he retired to Champaigne to live with his mother, and after a short time wrote to Mr. Short 'qu'il mouroit d'ennui.' and was willing to come. I shall acknowlege the receipt of Mr. Randolph's letter next week. Adieu, my dear, with affectionate esteem to you both. Your's,

TH: JEFFERSON

1. James Hemings, a slave, was taken to France for the express purpose of learning French cookery. Sally was his sister.

2. Adrien Petit was TJ's ablest and most trusted maître d'hôtel while in Paris. He came into TJ's service on May 22, 1785, and remained until after Jefferson's departure for America in 1789. He arrived in Philadelphia July 19, 1791, much to TJ's pleasure and remained until 1794, when he became homesick and returned to France. See Account Books 1785, 1791, and 1794.

To Mary Jefferson

Philadelphia May 8. 1791.

MY DEAR MARIA

Your letter of Apr. 18. came to hand on the 30th. That of May 1. I recieved last night. By the stage which carries this letter I send you 12. yards of striped nankeen of the pattern inclosed. It is addressed to the care of Mr. Brown mercht. in Richmond, and will arrive there with this letter. There are no stuffs here of the kind you sent.

April 30. the lilac blossomed.

May 4. the gelderrose, Dogwood, Redbud, and Azalea were in blossom. We have still pretty constant fires here. I shall answer Mr. Randolph's letter a week hence. It will be the last I shall write to Monticello for some weeks, because about this day sennight[1] I set out to join Mr. Madison[2] at New York, from whence we shall go up to Albany and Lake George, then cross over to Bennington and so through Vermont to the Connecticut river, down Connecticut river by Hartford to New-haven, then to New York and Philadelphia. Take a map and trace this rout. I expect to be back in Philadelphia about the middle of June. I am glad you are to learn to ride, but hope your horse is very gentle, and that you will never be venturesome. A lady should never ride a horse which she might not safely ride without a bridle. I long to be with you all. Kiss the little one every morning for me, and learn her to run about before I come. Adieu my dear. Your's affectionately,   TH: JEFFERSON

1. Seven days and nights.
2. James Madison.

FROM MARTHA JEFFERSON RANDOLPH

Monticello May 23, 1791

MY DEAR PAPA

As you have been so long without hearing from any of us Mr. Randolph begged me to write a few lines to you that you might not be uneasy he had began to do it him self but was prevented by a very bad cut in his thumb. It is almost 5 weeks since *I* have recieved a letter from you which I attribute to the iregularity of the post: that of Charlottesville they say is reestablished. Anthony has been to innoculate your trees. We had strawberies here the 2d of this month and cherries I think the 9th tho they had had both some time before that in Richmond. As I did not expect to have written this week it was so late before I began that I am obliged to be very concise for fear of missing the post which is expected in town early this morning and by which I am in hopes of receiving a letter from you. Adieu My Dear Papa. We have all been in perfect health here and are extremely obliged to you for

the veils you sent us. I am with the tenderest love your affectionate
child,   M. RANDOLPH

The largest of the beans you sent me is come up and very flourishing but none of the others have as yet made their appearance.

FROM MARY JEFFERSON

May 29 [1791]

MY DEAR PAPA

I am much obliged to you for the veil that you sent me and
shall allways were it. I have began to learn botany and arithmetic
with Mr. Randolph. The mare that he bought for me is come.
She is very pretty and is sister to brimmer.[1] She can only trot and
canter. The fruit was not killed as you thought. We have a great
abundance of it here. Adieu Dear Papa. I am your affectionate
daughter, MARY JEFFERSON. P.S. Little anna grows very fast an
is very pretty.

1. TJ's horse, which he sold February 1, 1793, to Samuel Clarkson for
$120. (Account Book 1793). This horse is not to be confused with Bremo, pur-
chased from Gen. John Hartwell Cocke on April 20, 1814 (Account Book 1814),
which Edmund Bacon, a long-time Monticello overseer, mistakenly identifies
as Brimmer. See *Farm Book*, 105.

TO MARY JEFFERSON

[draft]
Lake George May 30. 91.

MY DEAR MARIA

I did not expect to write to you again till my return to Philada.,
but as I think always of you, so I avail myself of every moment to
tell you so which a life of business will permit. Such a moment
is now offered while passing this lake, and it's border, on which
we have just landed, has furnished the means which the want of
paper would otherwise have denied me. I write to you on the
bark of the Paper birch, supposed to be the same used by the
antients to write on before the art of making paper was invented,
and which being called the Papyrus, gave the name of paper to
the new invented substitute. I write to you merely to tell you that
I am well, and to repeat what I have so often before repeated that
I love you dearly, am always thinking of you and place much of
the happiness of my life in seeing you improved in knowledge,
learned in all the domestic arts, useful to your friends and good

to all. To see you in short place your felicity in acquiring the love of those among whom you live, and without which no body can ever be happy. Go on then my dear Maria in your reading, in attention to your music, in learning to manage the kitchen, the dairy, the garden, and other appendages of the houshold, in suffering nothing to ruffle your temper or interrupt that good humor which it is so easy and so important to render habitual, and be assured that your progress in these things are objects of constant prayer with Your's affectionately,

To Martha Jefferson Randolph

Lake Champlain May 31. 1791.

My dear Martha

I wrote to Maria yesterday while sailing on L. George, and the same kind of leisure is afforded me to day to write to you. L. George is unquestionably the most beautiful water I ever saw; formed by the contour of mountains into a bason 35 miles long and from 2 to 4 miles broad, finely interspersed with islands, it's waters limpid as chrystal, and the mountain sides covered with rich groves of Thuya, silver fir, white pine, Aspen, and paper Birch down to the water edge, here and there precipies of rock to chequer the scene and saves it from monotony. An abundance of speckled trout, salmon trout, bass and other fish with which it is stored have added to our other amusements, the sport of taking them. Champlain, tho much larger is a far less pleasant water. It is muddy, turbulent and yields little game. After penetrating into it about 25 miles we have been obliged by a head wind and high sea to return having spent a day and a half in sailing on it. We shall take our rout again thro' L. George, pass thro' Vermont down Connecticut river, and thro' Long island to N. Y. and Phila. Our journey hither to has been prosperous and pleasant except as to the weather which has been as sultry hot thro' the whole as could be found I believe in Carolina or Georgia. I suspect indeed that the heats of Northern climates may be more powerful than those of Southern ones, in proportion as they are shorter. Perhaps vegetation requires this. There is as much fever and ague and other bilious complaints on L. Champlain as on the swamps of Carolina. Strawberries here are in the blossom, or just formed. With you I suppose the season is over. On the whole I find nothing anywhere else in point of climate which Virginia need envy to any part of the world. Here they are locked up in ice and snow for 6. months. Spring and autumn which make a paradise of our country are rigorous winter with them, and a tropical summer breaks on them all at once. When we consider how much climate contributes to the happiness of our condn, by the fine sensation it excites, and the productions it is the parent of, we have reason to value highly the accident of birth in such a one as that of Virginia. From this distance I can have little domestic to write to you about. I must always repeat how much I love you. Kiss the little Anne for me. I hope she grows lustily, enjoys good health, and will make us all and long happy as the center of our common love. Adieu my dear. Yours affectionately,

TH: JEFFERSON

TO MARTHA JEFFERSON RANDOLPH

Philadelphia June 23. 1791.

MY DEAR DAUGHTER

I wrote to each of you once during my journey, from which I returned four days ago, having enjoyed thro' the whole of it very perfect health. I am in hopes the relaxation it gave me from business has freed me from the almost constant headach with which I had been persecuted thro the whole winter and spring. Having been entirely clear of it while travelling proves it to have been occasioned by the drudgery of business. I found here on my return your letter of May 23. with the pleasing information that you were all in good health. I wish I could say when I shall be able to join you: but that will depend on the movements of the President who is not yet returned to this place. In a letter written me by young Mr. Franklin,[1] who is in London, is the following paragraph. 'I meet here with many who ask kindly after you. Among these the D. of Dorset, who is very particular in his enquiries. He has mentioned to me that his niece[2] had wrote once or twice to your daughter since her return to America; but not recieving an answer had supposed she meant to drop her acquaintance, which his neice much regretted. I ventured to assure him that that was not likely, and that possibly the letters might have miscarried. You will take what notice of this you may think proper.' Fulwar Skipwith is on his return to the United States. Mrs. Trist and Mrs. Waters often ask after you. Mr. Lewis being very averse to writing, I must trouble Mr. Randolph to enquire of him rela-

tive to my tobacco, and to inform me about it. I sold the whole
of what was good here. 17. hogsheads only are yet to come, and
by a letter of May 29. from Mr. Hylton[3] there were then but 2.
hogsheads more arrived at the warehouse. I am weary at the delay,
because it not only embarrasses me with guessing at excuses to
the purchaser, but is likely to make me fail in my payment to
Hanson,[4] which ought to be made in Richmond on the 19th. of
next month. I wish much to know when the rest may be expected.
In your last you observe you had not received a letter from me
in five weeks. My letters to you have been of Jan. 20. Feb. 9. Mar.
2. 24. Apr. 17. May 8. which you will observe to be pretty regularly once in three weeks. Matters in France are still going on
safely. Mirabeau is dead; also the Duke de Richlieu; so that the
Duke de Fronsac has now succeeded to the head of the family,
tho' not to the title, these being all abolished. Present me affectionately to Mr. Randolph and Polly, and kiss the little one for
me. Adieu my dear. Your's affectionately,   TH: JEFFERSON

1. William Temple Franklin was a grandson of Benjamin Franklin.
2. Lady Caroline Tufton.
3. Daniel L. Hylton was a Richmond resident and Comptroller of the Port
of the James River Upper District.
4. Richard Hanson was the attorney for William Jones of Farrel & Jones,
a Bristol, England, firm. TJ gave him seven bonds on March 6, 1790, which
would mature each July 19 until 1797. They were in the amount of £ 4444·5·8
(one third being interest) and were for his part of the Wayles debt to Farrel &
Jones. See Account Book 1790, Malone, *Jefferson the Virginian*, 441–45, and
Jefferson and the Ordeal of Liberty, [529]–30, and *Papers:* VII, 384, 423; IX,
395–96; and X, 483.

TO MARY JEFFERSON

Philadelphia June 26. 1791.

MY DEAR MARIA.

I hope you have recieved the letter I wrote you from lake
George, and that you have well fixed in your own mind the geography of that lake, and of the whole of my tour, so as to be able
to give me a good account of it when I shall see you. On my return
here, I found your letter of May 29. giving me the information
it is always so pleasing to me to recieve that you are all well. Would
to god I could be with you to partake of your felicities, and to tell
you in person how much I love you all, and how necessary it is
to my happiness to be with you. In my letter [to y]our sister written to her two or three days ago, I expressed my uneasiness at
hearing nothing more of my tobacco and asked some enquiries to

be made of Mr. Lewis on the subject. But I received yesterday a
letter from Mr. Lewis with full explanations, and another from
Mr. Hylton informing me the tobo. was on it's way to this place.
Therefore desire your sister to suppress that part of my letter and
say nothing about it. Tell her from me how much I love her, kiss
her and the little one for me and present my best affections to
Mr. Randolph, assured of them also yourself from yours,

TH: J.

FROM MARY JEFFERSON

Monticello, July 10th, 1791.

MY DEAR PAPA

I have received both your letters, that from Lake George and
of June the 26th. I am very much obliged to you for them, and
think the bark that you wrote on prettier than paper. Mrs.
Monroe[1] and Aunt Bolling are here. My aunt would have written
to you, but she was unwell. She intends to go to the North Garden.[2] Mr. Monroe is gone to Williamsburg to stay two or three
weeks, and has left his lady here. She is a charming woman. My
sweet Anne grows prettier every day. I thank you for the pictures
and nankeen that you sent me, which I think very pretty. Adieu,
dear papa. I am your affectionate daughter,

MARIA JEFFERSON

1. Mrs. James Monroe; Mary Jefferson Bolling (Mrs. John).
2. A small community about sixteen miles southwest of Charlottesville on
the road to Lynchburg.

TO MARTHA JEFFERSON RANDOLPH

Philadelphia July 10. 1791

MY DEAR DAUGHTER

I have no letter from Monticello later than Maria's of May 29.
which is now six weeks old. This is long, when but one week is
necessary for the conveyance. I cannot ascribe all the delay to the
Charlottesville post. However to put that out of the way I am
negotiating with the postmaster the establishment of a public post
from Richmond to Staunton. In this case all the private riders
will be prohibited from continuance, let their contracts be what
they will, and the whole being brought into one hand, the public
will be better served. I propose that the post shall pass by Tucka-

hoe, Goochld. court house, Columbia and Charlottesville in order that as many may be served by it as possible. The price on each newspaper will be to be settled between the printers and their customers. I have no information whether the things sent by Stratton have got safe to hand: tho' hope they have. I expect him here daily, and shall send by him some stores against my arrival at Monticello, the time of which however is not yet fixable. I rather expect it will be earlier than the last year, because my return here must be earlier. Tell Maria I shall expect to find her improved in all good things and particularly in her music, of which I hope you also are mindful. Kiss her for me and the little one, and present my best esteem to Mr. Randolph. Your's, my dear, affectionately,   TH: JEFFERSON

To Martha Jefferson Randolph

Philadelphia July 24. 1791.

MY DEAR DAUGHTER

Your last letter come to hand was of May 23. consequently it is now two months old.

Petit arrived here three or four days ago, and accosted me with an assurance that he was come pour rester toujours avec moi. The principal small news he brings is that Panthemont is one of the convents to be kept up for education, that the old Abbess is living, but Madame de Taubenheim dead, that some of the nuns have chosen to rejoin the world, others to stay, that there are no English pensioners there now, Botidorer [Botidoux] remains there, &c. &c. &c. Mr. Short lives in the Hotel d'Orleans where I lived when you first went to Panthemont.

The President is indisposed with a complaint similar to that he had in New York the year before last. It is commonly called a blind bile, and is in fact a tumour which will not come to a head. I do not yet know when I shall go to Virginia, and fear the visit will be short. It will probably be the beginning of September. I sent off yesterday by capt. Stratton 4. boxes and 14. kegs with stores to be delivered to Mr. Brown to be forwarded to Monticello. But I beg you not to await my coming for the opening and using of them, as they are for the common use. Kiss Maria and the little Anne for me and accept cordial love from yours affectionately,

TH: J.

To Mary Jefferson

Philadelphia July 31. 1791.

The last letter I have from you, my dear Maria, was of the 29th. of May which is 9 weeks ago. Those which you ought to have written the 19th. of June and 10th. of July would have reached me before this if they had been written. I mentioned in my letter of the last week to your sister that I had sent off some stores to Richmond which I should be glad to have carried to Monticello in the course of the ensuing month of August. They are addressed to the care of Mr. Brown. You mentioned formerly that the two Commodes were arrived at Monticello. Were my two sets of ivory chessmen in the drawers? They have not been found in any of the packages which came here, and Petit seems quite sure they were packed up. How goes on the music, both with your sister and yourself? Adieu, my dear Maria; kiss and bless all the family for me. Your's affectionately,   TH: JEFFERSON

To Martha Jefferson Randolph

Philadelphia Aug. 14. 1791.

MY DEAR DAUGHTER

Maria's letter of July 16. informs me you were all well then. However great my confidence is in the healthy air of Monticello, I am always happy to have my hopes confirmed by letter. The day of my departure is not yet fixed. I hope it will be earlier or later in the first week of September. I know not as yet how I am to get along, as one of my horses is in such a condition as to leave little hope of his life, and no possibility of his being in a condition to travel. I hope, before you recieve this, the articles sent by Capt. Stratton will be come to hand. The moment affording nothing new but what the gazettes will communicate, I have only to add my affections to Mr. Randolph and Maria, not forgetting the little one, and to yourself my dear Martha the warm love of your's affectionately,   TH: JEFFERSON

To Mary Jefferson

Philadelphia Aug. 21. 1791

MY DEAR MARIA

Your letter of July 10. is the last news I have from Monticello. The time of my setting out for that place is now fixed to some time in the first week of September, so that I hope to be there between the 10th. and 15th. My horse is still in such a condition as to give little hopes of his living: so that I expect to be under a necessity of buying one when I come to Virginia as I informed Mr. Randolph in my last letter to him. I am in hopes therefore he will have fixed his eye on some one for me, if I should be obliged to buy. In the mean time as Mr. Madison comes with me, he has a horse which will help us on to Virginia. Kiss little Anne for me and tell her to be putting on her best looks. My best affections to Mr. Randolph, your sister, and yourself. Adieu My dear Maria.

TH: JEFFERSON

TO MARY JEFFERSON

Tuesday morning Oct. 18. [1791]

MY DEAR MARIA

Mr. Giles[1] carries your trunk to Baltimore where he will see you tonight. Take out of it whatever you may want before you get to Philadelphia and leave the trunk with Mr. Grant[2] and I will call on him for it. The weather is so bad that perhaps I may not be able to overtake you in the morning as I had hoped: but I shall if possible. Adieu my dear Maria. Yours affectionately,

TH: JEFFERSON

1. Probably William Branch Giles.
2. A Baltimore innkeeper.

TO MARTHA JEFFERSON RANDOLPH

Philadelphia Nov. 13. 1791.

MY DEAR MARTHA

Maria and myself are waiting with impatience to hear that Mr. Randolph and yourself and dear little Anne are well. We now write alternately, once a week, so that the correspondence is become more equal. I now inclose to Mr. Randolph Freneau's paper instead of Bache's[1] on account of the bulk of the latter which, being a daily paper, was too much for the post. And Freneau's two papers contain more good matter than Bache's six. He will see that the affairs of the French West Indies are in a desperate state. A second set of deputies has arrived here to ask succours. Abundance of women and children come here to avoid danger. The men are not permitted to come. I should not wonder to see some of your friends among them. We expect hourly the arrival of capt. Stratton, by whom the clothes for the houseservants shall be sent. To forward them by any other vessel, is risking their miscarriage. Maria is fixed at Mrs. Pine's,[2] and perfectly at home. She has made young friends enough to keep herself in a bustle with them, and she has been honored with the visits of Mrs. Adams, Mrs. Randolph, Mrs. Rittenhouse, Sargeant, Waters, Davies &c. so that she is quite familiar with Philadelphia.[3] Present my sincere attachment to Mr. Randolph and kiss Anne for us. Adieu my dear, dear daughter. Your's affectionately,

TH: JEFFERSON

1. Benjamin Franklin Bache was a grandson of Benjamin Franklin and editor of the Philadelphia *Aurora*. Philip Freneau's paper was the *National Gazette*.

2. Maria resided with her and attended a school she operated; TJ maintained a residence in the city of Philadelphia.

3. Mesdames John Adams, Edmund Randolph, David Rittenhouse, Jonathan D. Sergeant, Nicholas Baker Waters, and Benjamin [?] Davies.

To MARTHA JEFFERSON RANDOLPH

Philadelphia Dec. 4. 1791.

MY DEAR DAUGHTER

We are well here, tho' still without news from Mr. Randolph or yourself, tho' we have been eight weeks from Monticello. Maria was to have written to you to-day, but she has been so closely engaged in pasting paper together in the form of a pocket book that she has not been able. She has been constantly getting colds since she came here. I have just put on board Capt. Stratton a box with the following articles for your three house-maids.

> 36. yds callimaneo
> 13½ yds calico of different patterns
> 25. yds linen
> 9. yds muslin
> 9. pr cotton stockings
> thread

I put into the same box for you la Cuisiniere Bourgeorsie[1] and the following books which Mr. Randolph wished to see. Ginanni del grano. Duhamel maniere de conserver le grain. Duhamel de l'insecte de l'Angoumois.[2] Mr. Randolph sees by the papers sent him what is the price of wheat here. Perhaps he might think it worth while to send his Varina wheat here. He could always have the money in Richmond within a fortnight from the arrival of the wheat. I shall be very ready to have it received and disposed of for him on the best terms, if he chuses. So as to corn or any thing else. My affectionate love attends you all. Adieu my dear dear daughter, TH: JEFFERSON

1. *La cuisinière bourgeoise,* a very popular 18th-century cookbook. There were seven Paris editions before TJ procured one for Martha, probably the 1789 edition. See Georges Vicaire, *Bibliographie Gastronomique* (London, 1954), 235–38 for comment.

2. Francesco Ginanni, *Della Malattie del Grano* . . . (Pesaro, 1759); Henri Louis Duhamel du Monceau, *Traité de la Conservation des Grains* (Paris, 1754), and Mathieu Tillet and Duhamel, *Histoire d'un Insecte qui devore les Grains de l'Angoumois* (Paris, 1762). Sowerby 740, 737, 738.

To Martha Jefferson Randolph

Philadelphia Dec. 25. 1791.

MY DEAR DAUGHTER

Your's of Nov. 29. and Mr. Randolph's of Nov. 28. came to hand five days ago. They brought us the first news we had received from Monticello since we left it. A day or two after, Mr. Millar[1] of Charlottesville arrived here and gave us information of a little later date, and particularly of Colo. Lewis[2] and Mrs. Gilmer's[3] illness. His account of Mrs. Gilmer was alarming, and I am anxious to hear it's issue. Our feelings on little Anne's danger as well as her escape were greatly excited on all your accounts. These alarms and losses are the price parents pay for the pleasure they recieve from their children. I hope her future good health will spare you any more of them. We are likely to get a post established through Columbia, Charlottesville and Staunton, on a permanent footing, and consequently a more regular one. This I hope will move all precariousness in the transportation of our letters. Tho I am afraid there is one kind of precariousness it will not remove; that in the writing of them, for you do not mention having written before the 29th. of Nov. tho' we had then left Monticello near seven weeks: I have written every week regularly. Present me affectionately to Mr. Randolph. Kiss dear Anne for me, and believe me to be your's with tender love. TH: JEFFERSON

1. Isaac Millar.
2. Probably Colonel Charles L. Lewis, Sr., of The Bird, Goochland County, an uncle of Nicholas Lewis.
3. Mrs. George Gilmer.

To Martha Jefferson Randolph

Philadelphia Jan. 15. 1792

MY DEAR MARTHA

Having no particular subject for a letter, I find none more soothing to my mind than to indulge itself in expressions of the love I bear you, and the delight with which I recall the various scenes thro which we have passed together, in our wanderings over the world. These reveries alleviate the toils and inquietudes of my present situation, and leave me always impressed with the desire of being at home once more, and of exchanging labour, envy, and malice for ease, domestic occupation, and domestic love and society, where I may once more be happy with you, with Mr. Randolph, and dear little Anne, with whom even Socrates might ride on a stick without being ridiculous. Indeed it is with difficulty that my resolution will bear me through what yet lies between the present day and that which, on mature consideration of all circumstances respecting myself and others, my mind has determined to be the proper one for relinquishing my office. Tho not very distant it is not near enough for my wishes. The ardor of these however would be abated if I thought that on coming home I should be left alone. On the contrary I hope that Mr. Randolph will find a convenience in making only leisurely preparations for a settlement, and that I shall be able to make you both happier than you have been at Monticello, and relieve you from *desagremens* to which I have been sensible you were exposed, without the power in myself to prevent it, but by my own presence. Remember me affectionately to Mr. Randolph and be assured of the tender love of Yours,   TH: JEFFERSON

To Martha Jefferson Randolph

Philadelphia Feb. 5. 92.

MY DEAR MARTHA

I was prevented writing to you last week by a bad cold attended with fever: and this week I have nothing to say but that I find myself nearly well, and to repeat the assurances of my love to you. Maria is well, and has come to a resolution to write to you no more. Whether this arises most from resentment or laziness I do not know. Mr. Randolph's last letter received was of Dec. 29. Yours of Nov. 29. In my last to him, knowing that Clarkson[1] could not write, I asked the favor of him to communicate to me from time to time the progress of my affairs. I wish much to know whether my wheat is getting to market, and the debts for which it was destined paying off? Negroes clothed etc. Adieu my dear. Your's affectionately, TH: JEFFERSON

1. Manoah Clarkson.

To Martha Jefferson Randolph

Phila. Feb. 11. 1792.

MY DEAR MARTHA

The hour of post is come and a throng of business allows me only to inform you we are well, and to acknolege the rec't of Mr. Randolph's letter of Jan. 24. with hopes that you are all so. Accept assurances of constant love to you all from your's my dear most affectionately, TH: J.

From Martha Jefferson Randolph

Montecello February 20 1792

MY DEAREST FATHER

Just arrived from a journey of 3 months in which I have not had it in my power to write to you. I am impatient to take the first opportunity of renewing a correspondence so very pleasing to me. I recieved your letters all together at Dick Randolph's[1] and should have answered them imediately but Mr. Randolph's writing rendered it unnecessary at that time. We have had a most disagreable journey travelling [the] greatest part of the way thro a deep snow and dismal weather generally raining or hailing. I never saw the end of any thing with more pleasure in my life. The anxiety you express to be at home makes me infinitely happy. I acknowledge I was under some aprehension that you would be prevailed upon to stay Longer than you intended and I feel more and more every day how necessary your company is to my happiness by the continual and ardent desire I have of seeing you. I suppose Mr. Randolph has told you that he is in possession of Edgehill. The old gentleman[2] has at Last made him a deed for it. He has also bought those negroes who had families here. We are so lately arrived that I have not heard any news as yet. Mrs. Gilmer has been in a state of insanity from which I *believe* she is recovered tho I am by no means certain. I have weaned Little Anne who begins to walk. She becomes every day more mischievious and more entertaining. I think she is also handsomer than she was and looks much better tho not as fat. Adieu my Dearest Papa. Tell me if we shall have the pleasure of seeing you this spring and believe me with tender and unchangeable love your affectionate child,   M RANDOLPH

My best love to Dear Maria. Tell her I will certainly write to her next week.

1. Richard Randolph of Bizarre, Cumberland County.
2. Thomas Mann Randolph, Sr. The deed was dated April 12, 1793. For additional insight on this transaction, see Thomas Mann Randolph, Jr., to Peter Carr, June 26, 1793: "I shall send to you the deed for Edgehill, which I must beg the favor of you to present to Colo. Randolph, and to witness his acknowledgement of the signature. It is probable there may be some of our neighbours below at present, if there are any within call of you, demand of them in my name the same neighbourly duty. The names below affixed were taken thro. necessity: You will see they are persons whose attendance I cannot expect." (ViU.) See footnote 4 of TJ to Martha Jefferson Randolph, April 26, 1790.

To Martha Jefferson Randolph

Philadelphia Feb. 26. 92.

MY DEAR MARTHA

We are in daily expectation of hearing of your safe return to Monticello, and all in good health. The season is now coming on when I shall envy your occupations in the feilds and garden while I am shut up drudging within four walls. Maria is well and lazy, therefore does not write. Your friends Mrs. Trist and Mrs. Waters are well also, and often enquire after you. We have nothing new or interesting from Europe for Mr. Randolph. He will preceive by the papers that the English are beaten off the ground by Tippoo Saib. The Leyden gazette assures that they were saved only by the unexpected arrival of the Mahrattas, who were suing to Tippoo Saib for peace for Ld. Cornwallis.[1] My best esteem to Mr. Randolph, I am my dear Martha your's affectionately,

TH: JEFFERSON

1. Reference is probably to conditions in the Indian province of Bengal. Tippoo Sahib was Sultan of Mysore and violently anti-British. The Mahrattas inhabited the district of Maharasthtra. Despite the report of the usually reliable Leyden *Gazette,* the British under Cornwallis won a victory near Seringapatam.

To Martha Jefferson Randolph

Philadelphia Mar. 22. 1792

My dear Martha

Your's of Feb. 20. came to me with that welcome which every thing brings from you. It is a relief to be withdrawn from the torment of the scenes amidst which we are. Spectators of the heats and tumults of conflicting parties, we can not help participating of their feelings. I should envy you the tranquil occupations of your situation were it not that I value your happiness more than my own. But I too shall have my turn. The ensuing year will be the longest of my life, and the last of such hateful labours. The next we will sow our cabbages together. Maria is well. Having changed my day of writing from Sunday to Thursday or Friday, she will oftener miss writing, as not being with me at the time. I believe you knew Otchakity,[1] the Indian who lived with the Marquis Lafayette. He came here lately with some deputies from his nation, and died here of a pleurisy. I was at his funeral yesterday. He was buried standing up according to their manner. I think it will still be a month before your neighbor Mrs. Monroe will leave us. She will probably do it with more pleasure than heretofore; as I think she begins to tire of the town and feel a relish for scenes of more tranquillity. Kiss dear Anne for her aunt, and twice for her grand-papa. Give my best affections to Mr. Randolph and accept yourself all my tenderness.

TH: JEFFERSON

1. TJ appears to have misspelled his name, which was Otsiguette; he was a young prince of the Oneida Nation then well known for its attachment to America. As an unlettered Indian he was taken to France by Lafayette, and under his patronage he became proficient in French and English. On his return to America in 1788 he became dissipated and more savage than ever.

To Martha Jefferson Randolph

Philadelphia Apr. 6. 1792.

My dear Martha

Mr. Randolph's letter of the 18th. has been received since my last. The one it covered for Great Britain is sent by the packet now about to sail from New York. His commission to Doctor Barton[1] shall be fulfilled to-day. Maria is with me keeping her Easter holidays. She is well. She allows herself to write but one letter a week, and having written to some acquaintance already she has nothing but her love for Monticello. I suppose you are busy in your garden. Shackleford[2] promised me *on his honor* to cover it well with manure. Has he done it? If not, tell him I have written to enquire. Two or three straggling numbers of Fenno's gazette being found in my office, we presume they belong to Mr. Randolph's set, and therefore I send them. Present my best affections to him, and be assured of the cordial love of Your's,

TH: JEFFERSON

1. Benjamin Smith Barton was a physician and botanist of Lancaster, Pennsylvania. Mr. Randolph was an able botanist in his own right.
2. Tom Shackleford was a TJ slave.

To Martha Jefferson Randolph

Philadelphia Apr. 27. 1792.

MY DEAR DAUGHTER

I received yesterday your's and Mr. Randolph's of the 9th. which shews that the post somehow or other slips a week. Congress have determined to rise on the 5th. of May. Colo. Monroe and Mrs. Monroe will set out on the 7th. and making a short stay at Fredericksburg pass on to Albemarle. I have reason to expect that my visit to Virginia this year, instead of September as heretofore, will be about the last of July, and be somewhat longer than usual, as it is hoped Congress will meet later. Tell Mr. Randolph that Mr. Hylton informs me 43. hhds. of my tobacco, meaning of my mark, are arrived at the warehouse, and that he shall send them on by the first opportunity. As this cannot possibly be all mine, it must contain Mr. Randolph's, and therefore it is necessary he should enable Mr. Hylton to distinguish his, or it will all come round here. I am to have 5. dollars for mine, payable in September, from which will be deducted about half a dollar expences. Maria is well and joins me in affections to Mr. Randolph and yourself. Adieu my dear. Your's,

TH: JEFFERSON

From Martha Jefferson Randolph

Monticello May 7, 1792

MY DEAREST PAPA

Mr. Randolph recieved your letter respecting the bonds 2 days before he set off for Richmond and carried them down with him. He has by Mr. Colquohoun's not appearing been cast in his suit with Rogers and fined 77 pounds which added to the other expences attending a suit amounts to upwards of a hundred. It is particularly unlucky at this time as he has met with many misfortunes which will render the payment of it rather distressing. I am rejoiced from my heart to hear that you are coming in july instead of september. You will see that I am a much better gardner than last year tho in truth old George[1] is so slow that [I] shall never shine in that way with out your assistance. Tom has been a man of honour with respect to the manure. We have had some very high winds here lately one of which blew down 5 large trees in and about the grove and did some other mischief. It was accompanied with very severe lightning. The noise of the wind kept us from hearing any thing of the thunder except when it was extreemely loud. We have discovered a very beautiful tree near the lower round about[2] a silver fir I believe, it differs from the common pine in having a smooth green bark and the bottom of the leave white and much finer than the other. Mr. Randolph is still in Richmond. We are all well. Doctor Gilmer is perfectly recovered. My little Anne tho not handsome on account of her being allmost entirely bald is a source of infinite happiness to her fond Parents. She begins to prattle and is remarkably lively. Tell My Dearest Maria that I will write to her next week. Her friend Nancy Randolph is coming up with Mr. Randolph and Judy[3] has a fine son. Adieu my Dearest Father. Believe me your ever affectionate child.   M. RANDOLPH

1. A slave gardener.
2. The Grove was located on the northern slope at Monticello between the First and Fourth roundabouts. It was the Monticello arboretum. TJ constructed on the slopes at Monticello at four different levels riding and/or walking paths or, as he called them, roundabouts. These were connected by oblique roads and formed the nuclei of the Monticello road system. *Garden Book*, Plate XXI.
3. Judy Randolph (Mrs. Richard), a sister of Thomas Mann Randolph, Jr.

TO MARTHA JEFFERSON RANDOLPH

Philadelphia May 11. 1792.

MY DEAR DAUGHTER

Excess of business prevented my writing to you the last week or even having time to inclose the papers to Mr. Randolph. Since my last I have received yours of Feb. 28. and Mr. Randolph's of Apr. 9. 16. and May 4. Congress rose three days ago. Colo. Monroe sets out three days hence, and by him I shall send your watch, and the 2d. part of Payne's Rights of man[1] for Mr. Randolph. Also, for yourself, my own copy of Lavater's aphorisms,[2] which I fancy are not to be got here, and which I think you will sicken of in a few pages. Mrs. Pine has determined to go to England, so that I shall be obliged to send Maria to Mrs. Brodeau's,[3] a better school, but much more distant from me. It will in fact cut off the daily visits which she is able to make me from Mrs. Pine's. I do not know whether I have before mentioned to you that the President will make his visit to Mount Vernon this year about the last of July: consequently mine to Monticello will be earlier than usual. Present my esteem to all my neighbors. My best affections to Mr. Randolph and yourself, not forgetting little Anne, who I suppose will be able to take a part in conversation by the time we see her. Adieu my dear daughter. Your's,

TH: JEFFERSON.

1. Thomas Paine, *Rights of Man. Part the second* . . . (London, 1792). Sowerby 2826.

2. Johann Kaspar Lavater, *Aphorisms on Man. Translated from the original manuscript of . . . 4th ed. . . .* (Boston, 1790). This is probably the edition mentioned, although there were others, a London and a Dublin edition, before 1791.

3. Mrs. Anne Brodeau, a Philadelphia schoolteacher, whose boarding school was located at 2 Lodge Alley. The Account Book lists no payments to a Mrs. Brodeau, and it is questionable if Mary ever attended her school.

TO MARTHA JEFFERSON RANDOLPH

Philadelphia May 27. 1792

MY DEAR DAUGHTER

I was too much occupied to write by Friday's post and fear it will occasion your recieving my letter a week later. Yours of the 7th. Inst. has come duly to hand. Colo. and Mrs. Monroe will probably be with you by the time you recieve this. Mr. Madison left us last Wednesday. I have promised, during his stay in Orange to inclose to him Fenno's paper for his perusal, to be forwarded on to Mr. Randolph, which will sometimes occasion his recieving it later than he would have done. We expect the President tomorrow on his return from Mount-Vernon. To the news in the public papers I may add the attempt to assassinate the K. of Sweden. He was dangerously wounded. French affairs are going on pretty well. Their assignats[1] begin to gain. The election in N. York will be interesting to Colo. Monroe. Tell him it is generally thought that Mr. Jay[2] has the most votes, but that one of the returns which contains 1000 in his favor is so deficient that it is imagined the judges of the election (who are all Clintonians) will not recieve them, and this is a greater number than it is thought he has to spare, consequently he will fail in his election. My tobacco arrived here yesterday. I have constantly forgotten to make enquiry about my bacon. If it is not come from Monticello, I would rather it should remain there till I go home, as it will suffice if it is here by the opening of the next Congress. My best esteem to Colo. and Mrs. Monroe, Mr. Randolph and your friends with you. To yourself my tenderest affections. Adieu my dear daughter. Your's,

TH: JEFFERSON

1. Paper currency issued during the French Revolution in order to redeem the huge public debt and to meet a growing governmental deficit.

2. John Jay was unsuccessfully opposed by De Witt Clinton for the governorship of New York State.

From Martha Jefferson Randolph

Monticello May 27, 1792

I intended writing to My Dearest Father by the last post but being prevented I have taken this opportunity rather than differ it an other week. Young Nicholas Lewis is just returned from Williamsburg with his Lady[1] whom I have not been to see as yet but I certainly intend it shortly altho I have some reason to complain of the airs that family has given them selves of late with me. They find it so difficult to divest themselves of the authority they once enjoyed here that they continue to this day to exert it over every part of the enclosure to my great vexation as I look upon that to be my domain and of course enfringing upon my rights to take any thing out of it with out my leave. I have however overlooked their impertinence with regard to that as I am determined not to fall out with them if I can possibly avoid it tho I acknowledge it hurts my pride not a little to be treated with so much contempt by those of whom I am conscious of not diserving it having allways been particularly attentive to the whole family as far as I had it in my power. I rejoice to think that this is the last year I have to put up with it. Bergere has six fine little puppies all of which I am in hopes of being able to raise. They have been peculiarly unlucky with those in the park.[2] I believe they have had no less than thirteen this spring of which six are dead, probably starved to death. Many of your sugar maples are alive and tolerably flourishing considering the drouth. Your acasias are not come up yet tho they were planted imediately. We

are burnt up for want of rain. The drouth has continued for upwards of 5 weeks and there is no appearance of its discontinuing
as yet. People are in great pain about their crops. Indeed they
have a wretched prospect before them and many of them are suffering for bread even at this time. Joseph Monroe has been
extreemely ill but he is perfectly recovered now. It is generally
supposed it was the gout. We are all in perfect health here myself
particularly. I do not recolect ever to have been so fat as I am at
present. Adieu my dearest father. Believe me ever yours most
affectionately,   M. RANDOLPH

1. The son of Nicholas Lewis of The Farm. His lady was Mildred Hornsby,
daughter of Joseph Hornsby of Williamsburg.

2. As early as 1769 TJ had cleared on the north side of Monticello mountain
a park of 1,850 yards' circumference in the vicinity of the North Spring near
the future location of the Fourth Roundabout. When the Marquis de Chastellux visited TJ in 1782 he reported a score of deer in the park. Howard C. Rice,
Jr., editor, *Travels in North America 1780, 1781 and 1782 by the Marquis de
Chastellux* (Chapel Hill, 1963), II, 394.

TO MARY JEFFERSON

Wednesday morn. [ca. June 1, 1792]

TH:J. TO HIS DEAR MARIA.

Ask, my dear, of Mrs. Pine, what would be the price of Mr.
Madison's picture,[1] and let me know when you come over to-day.

1. TJ is referring to the Robert Edge Pine portrait of James Madison, which
at one time hung in the Monticello parlor. It is now lost. The date of the
letter is probably May 30 because on that day he sent Mrs. Pine an order on
the Bank of the United States, and on June 2 he paid her "for Mr. Madison's
picture 39.33." (Account Book 1792.) It is also to be noted that TJ, in a letter
to Thomas Mann Randolph, Jr., of June 1, 1792, stated: "Maria's mistress
is just now on her departure for England. She came home yesterday." (ViU.)

TO MARTHA JEFFERSON RANDOLPH

Philadelphia June 8. 1792.

MY DEAR DAUGHTER

The last news we have from Monticello is by your letter of May
7. I am in hopes tomorrow's post will bring us something, for
some how or other your letters (if you write by post to Richmond)
miss a post and are sometimes a week longer coming than they
ought to be. The news from the French West India islands is
more and more discouraging. Swarms of the inhabitants are quit-
ting them and coming here daily. I wonder that none of your
acquaintances write to you. Perhaps they may be in Martinique

where the disturbance is not yet considerable. Perhaps they may be gone to France. Your friend Mrs. Waters is in a fair way of losing her husband, as he appears to be in a galloping consumption. The family are alarmed at his situation, tho he goes about his business still with activity. Maria's letter will inform you she is well. Present me affectionately to Mr. Randolph, kiss dear Anne for me, and be assured of my tender love. Your's,

TH: JEFFERSON

To Martha Jefferson Randolph

Philadelphia June 22. 1792.

MY DEAR MARTHA.

Yours of May 27. came to hand on the very day of my last to you, but after it was gone off. That of June 11. was received yesterday. Both made us happy in informing us you were all well. The rebuke to Maria produced the inclosed letter. The time of my departure for Monticello is not yet known. I shall within a week from this time send off my stores as usual that they may arrive before me. So that should any waggons be going down from the neighborhood it would be well to desire them to call on Mr. Brown in order to take up the stores should they be arrived. I suspect by the account you give me of your garden, that you mean a surprise. As good singers always preface their performance by complaints of cold, hoarseness &c. Maria is still with me. I am endeavoring to find a good lady to put her with if possible. If not, I shall send her to Mrs. Brodeaux, as the last shift. Old Mrs. Hopkinson is living in town but does not keep house. I am in hopes you have visited young Mrs. Lewis, and borne with the old one so as to keep on visiting terms. Sacrifices and suppressions of feeling in this way cost much less pain than open separation. The former are soon over: the latter haunt the peace of every day of one's life, be that ever so long. Adieu my dear, with my best affections to Mr. Randolph. Anne enjoys them without valuing them.

TH: JEFFERSON

From Martha Jefferson Randolph

Monticello July 2 1792

DEAR PAPA

I have just recieved yours of June 22. The sudden departure of the post who entered Charlottesville the morning and left it before dinner prevented my writing last week tho Mr. Randolph did and sent his letter after him as far as fluvana courthouse before they could overtake him. So his iregularity is owing that which you complain of in the receipt of my letters. I am very sorry you can not fix the time of your departure. As it aproches my anxiety augments. All other thoughts give way to that of shortly seeing two people so infinitely dear to me. What I told you of my garden is really true indeed if you see it at a distance it looks very green but it does not bear close examination, the weeds having taken possession of much the greater part of it. Old George is so slow that by the time he has got to the end of his labour he has it all to do over again. 2 of the acasia's are come up and are flourishing. I have visited the two Mrs. Lewis's. The young lady appears to be a good little woman tho most intolerable weak. However she will be a near neighbor and of course worth cultivating. Dear little Anne has been in very bad health her illness having been occasioned by worms. Dr. Gilmer advised the tincture of sacre the effects of which were allmost imediate. She still looks badly but I imagine that may be partly owing to her cutting teeth. I must now trouble you with some little commissions of mine. The glass of one of those handsome engravings I brought in with me has by some accident got broke and not being able to suply the place of it in Richmond I should be extremely obliged to you to bring me one according to the measure and also a small frame with a glass to it for a picture of the size of the enclosed oval paper. Adieu my dear papa. The heat is incredible here. The thermometer has been at 96 in Richmond and even at this place we have not been able to sleep comfortably with every door and window open. I dont recolect ever to have suffered as much from heat as we have done this summer. Adieu my Dearest Father. Believe me with tender affection yours,

M. RANDOLPH

To Martha Jefferson Randolph

Philadelphia July 3. 1792.

MY DEAR MARTHA

I now inclose you Petit's statement of the stores sent round to Richmond to the care of Mr. Brown. They sailed from hence yesterday morning, and the winds have been and are so favorable that I dare say they will be in Chesapeak bay tomorrow, ready for the first Southernly breeze to carry them up the river. So that they will probably be at Richmond some days before you receive this. I wrote to Mr. Randolph last week desiring he would speak to Mr. Claxton[1] to get the stores brought up immediately, which I hope he is doing, as I shall otherwise arrive before them. The President has fixed his departure on Thursday the 12th. inst. and I consequently fix mine to Saturday the 14th. According to the stages I have marked out I shall be at Mr. Madison's on Saturday the 21st. and if on that day you can send a pair of the plough or waggon horses to John Jones's, 17. miles from Monticello and about 12. miles from Mr. Madison's, I can be at Monticello the next morning by 10. or 11. oclock. I do not know whether Jones's is a tavern, but he surely will give them cover the Saturday night, if they carry their own provisions, and even a day or two longer, should any accident retard me in my departure or on the road. The road from Jones's to Monticello is so excessively hilly that it will injure my horses more than all the rest of the journey, as they will by that time be jaded with the heat. If I have rightly estimated the course of the post, you will recieve this on Saturday the 14th. the very day I leave Philadelphia. I shall write you again the day before I leave Philadelphia, which I presume you will receive on Saturday the 21st. in the morning of which day I expect to arrive at Mr. Madison's, unless any thing should arise to retard me, in which case that letter will probably give you notice of it. A Mr. Williams handed me yesterday a letter from Mr. Randolph. He was much gratified with the sight of my paintings. Mr. Randolph's desire shall be complied with. Petit's note will enable you to open any of the stores you may have occasion for, which I beg you not to hesitate to do, as they are intended more for you than myself. My best esteem to Mr. Randolph, and beleive me to be, my dear Martha, with the most tender affection Your's,

TH: JEFFERSON

1. Robert Claxton.

TO MARTHA JEFFERSON RANDOLPH

Philadelphia July 13. 1792.

MY DEAR MARTHA

Yours of the 2d. came yesterday. I wrote to Mr. Randolph two days ago, but by a bungle of the servt. it did not get to the post office in time, so I suppose that and this will get to hand together, and both probably only the evening before I shall reach Monticello. Still should my former one desiring horses, have missed, this will be in time for them to meet me on the road, and relieve mine in the last and worst part of it.

I set out this afternoon, and can pretty certainly be with you early on Sunday sennight. My affections to Mr. Randolph. Adieu my dear,   TH: JEFFERSON

TO MARTHA JEFFERSON RANDOLPH

Philadelphia Oct. 26. 1792.

MY DEAR DAUGHTER

Having not received a letter by yesterday's post, and that of the former week from Mr. Randolph having announced dear Anne's indisposition, I am under much anxiety. In my last letter to Mr. Randolph I barely mentioned your being recovered, when somewhat younger than she is, by recurrence to a good breast of milk. Perhaps this might be worthy of proposing to the Doctor. In a case where weakness of the digesting organs enters into the causes of illness, a food of the most easy digestion might give time for getting the better of the other causes, whatever they may be. I [trust] it should however be some other than your own, if a breast of milk is to be tried. I hope you are perfectly well and the little one also, as well as Mr. Randolph to whom present my sincere regards. Adieu my dear. Your's affectionately,   TH: JEFFERSON

TO MARTHA JEFFERSON RANDOLPH

Philadelphia Nov. 12. 1792

MY DEAR MARTHA

The last post day for Monticello, which was the 9th. slipt by me without my recollecting it. However as you are perhaps in Cumberland, a letter of this day may get to you only three days the later. I have nothing indeed to tell you but that I love you dearly, and your dear connections, that I am well, as is Maria. I hope your little one has felt no inconvenience from the journey, that Anne is quite recovered, and Mr. Randolph's health good. Yours is so firm, that I am less apt to apprehend for you: Still, however, take care of your good health, and of your affection to me, which is the solace of my life. Remember me cordially to Mr. Randolph. Yours,   TH: JEFFERSON

FROM MARTHA JEFFERSON RANDOLPH

Bizarre November 18 1792

I am afraid my dear Papa has by this time allmost dispaired of ever recieving an other line from me. I have no excuse for having neglected writing entirely, tho a very good one for not doing it often, my mind has been in such a continual state of anxiety on account of Ann as to render me unfit for any thing. The hopes I had concieved of her recovery are all blasted by a relapse and that too at the time she appeared out of all danger. Every moment of my life is embitered by the aprehensions of losing her. Indeed she has for many months been an untarissable [intarissable] source of pain to me and will I fear continue so for the weakness of her constitution is such that the smallest excess in her diet brings on her disorder. Your little namesake[1] is a remarkably fine boy. He bore the fatigue of the journey better than any of us. Adieu my dear Papa. You must excuse this scrawl. It is written by the bed side where my little angel lies with a high fever upon her and Mr. Randolph's absence at this time adds greatly to my distress. Once more adieu and believe me dearest father with unalterable love yours,   M RANDOLPH

Give my love to dear Maria. Tell her I have recieved her letter and will answer it as soon as I have it in my power.

1. Thomas Jefferson Randolph was Martha's eldest son and second child. He was born September 12, 1792.

TO MARTHA JEFFERSON RANDOLPH

Philadelphia Nov. 22. 1792.

MY DEAR MARTHA

The last letter received from Mr. Randolph or yourself is of Oct. 7. which is near seven weeks ago. I ascribe this to your supposed absence from Monticello, but it makes me uneasy when I recollect the frail state of your two little ones. I hope some letter is on the way to me. I have no news for you except the marriage of your friend Lady Elizabeth Tufton, to some very rich person, but whose name could not be recollected by Mr. Hammond,[1] my informer. Maria is well, but not yet become industrious in letter writing. Present my warmest esteem to Mr. Randolph. Adieu my dear. Your's affectionately and for ever,   TH: J.

1. George Hammond was the British Minister Plenipotentiary and the first British minister accredited to the United States.

To Martha Jefferson Randolph

Philadelphia Dec. 6. 92.

MY DEAR MARTHA

I have this day received yours of the 18th. Novembr. and sincerely sympathize with you on the state of dear Anne, if that can be called sympathy which proceeds from affection at first hand, for my affections had fastened on her for her own sake and not merely for yours. Still however experience (and that in your own case) has taught me that an infant is never desperate, let me beseech you not to destroy the powers of her stomach with medicine. Nature alone can re-establish infant-organs; only taking care that her efforts be not thwarted by any imprudencies of diet. I rejoice in the health of your other hope. Maria is well. Remember me affectionately to Mr. Randolph and be assured of my unceasing love for you both. Adieu my very dear Martha.   TH: JEFFERSON

To Martha Jefferson Randolph

Philadelphia Dec. 13. 1792.

MY DEAR MARTHA

By capt. Swaile, who sailed yesterday for Richmond I sent addressed to Mr. Randolph to the care of Mr. Brown a box containing the following articles for your three house maids.

2. peices of linen. 52. yards
9. pair cotton stockings (3 of them small)
13. yds. cotton in three patterns
36. yards Calimanco.
9. yards muslin.

Bob is to have a share of the linen. I had promised to send him a new suit of clothes. Instead of this I send a suit of superfine ratteen of my own, which I have scarcely ever worn. I forgot to get stockings for him: therefore must desire you to have him furnished with them from Colo. Bell's on my account. In the same box you will find 4. pair tongs and shovels which I observed the house to be in want of. I hope our dear Anne is got well and that all of you continue so. Maria is well. She begun a letter to you Sunday was sennight: but it is not finished. My affections to Mr. Randolph and your friends. Adieu, my dear, your's with all love,

TH: JEFFERSON

To Martha Jefferson Randolph

Philadelphia Dec. 31. 1792.

MY DEAR MARTHA

I received three days ago Mr. Randolph's letter of the 14th. from Richmond, and received it with great joy as it informed me of the re-establishment of dear Anne's health. I apprehend from an expression in his letter that some of mine may have miscarried. I have never failed to write every Thursday or Friday. Percieving by the Richmond paper that the Western post now leaves that place on Monday, I change my day of writing also to Sunday or Monday. One of the Indian chiefs now here, whom you may remember to have seen at Monticello a day or two before Tarlton drove us of[f], remembers you and enquired after you.[1] He is of the Pioria nation. Perhaps you may recollect that he gave our name to an infant son he then had with him and who, he now tells me, is a fine lad. Blanchard[2] is arrived here and is to ascend in his balloon within a few days. The affairs of France are going on well. Tell Mr. Randolph that I write him a letter by this post in answer to the application to rent Elkhill;[3] but under the possibility that the sale of it may be completed, I inclose his letter to Mr. Hylton with a desire that he will return it to me if the place is sold, otherwise to forward it to Mr. Randolph. My best esteem to him and our friends with you. Adieu, my dear. Your's affectionately,   TH: JEFFERSON

1. It was a detachment of Tarleton's troops, under Captain McLeod, that came to Monticello. Tarleton remained in Charlottesville.
2. Jean Pierre Blanchard the celebrated French balloonist. TJ was familiar with his flight across the English Channel and witnessed his Paris ascent in 1784. In Philadelphia on January 9, 1793, he paid five dollars for the privilege of seeing his ascent there (Account Book). For additional interest in aerial flights, see Account Books 1791–1803.
3. A plantation in Goochland County that TJ inherited from his wife and that was ravaged by Cornwallis during the Revolutionary War.

To Martha Jefferson Randolph

Philadelphia Jan. 14. 1793.

MY DEAR MARTHA

Mr. Randolph's letter of Dec. 20. from Richmond is the only one come to hand from him or you since your's from Bizarre of two months ago. Tho' his letter informed me of the re-establishment of Anne, yet I wish to learn that time confirms our hopes. We were entertained here lately with the ascent of Mr. Blanchard in a baloon. The security of the thing appeared so great that every body is wishing for a baloon to travel in. I wish for one sincerely, as instead of 10. days, I should be within 5 hours of home. Maria will probably give you the baloon details, as she writes to-day. Have you recieved the package with the servants clothes? My best attachments to Mr. Randolph. Adieu my dear. Your's affectionately,   TH: JEFFERSON

FROM MARTHA JEFFERSON RANDOLPH

Monticello January 16, 1793

With infinite pleasure I date once more from Monticello tho for the third time since my return. But from the negligence of the servant that carried the letters once and the great hurry of the post another time they never got farther than Charlottesville. Our dearest Anne has had an attack of a different nature from her former ones which the doctor imagines to proceed from her fatening too quickly. She is far from being well yet, tho considerably better. She is at present busily employed *yiting* to you, a thing she has never missed doing whenever her health has permitted her. Her memory is uncommonly good for a child of her age. She relates many circumstances that happened during her travels with great exactitude but in such broken language and with so many gestures as renders it highly diverting to hear her. Her spirits have as yet been proof against ill health so far as to recover them with the least intermission of it tho I much fear that will not long be the case if she does not mend speedily. The little boy continues well and is little inferior to his sister in point of size. He also begins to take a great deal of notice and bids fair to be as lively. I am afraid you will be quite tired of hearing so much about them but a fond Mother never knows where to stop when her children is the subject.

Mr. Randolph did not recieve the letter in which you mentioned the books and stalactite till after he had left Richmond with 4 or 5 other Letters of yours which had been detained by some accident. Peter [1] desires to be remembered to you and wishes to know if you have recieved one he wrote you from Richmond. Adieu dearest Papa. My Love to dear Maria. I will write to her by the next post. Believe me to [be] with tenderest affection Yours,

M RANDOLPH

1. Peter Carr, one of TJ's nephews and son of Martha and Dabney Carr.

To Martha Jefferson Randolph

Philadelphia Jan. 26. 93.

My dear Martha

I received two days ago your's of the 16th. You were never more mistaken than in supposing you were too long on the prattle &c. of little Anne. I read it with quite as much pleasure as you write it. I sincerely wish I could hear of her perfect reestablishment. I have for some time past been under an agitation of mind which I scarcely ever experienced before, produced by a check on my purpose of returning home at the close of this session of Congress. My operations at Monticello had been all made to bear upon that point of time, my mind was fixed on it with a fondness which was extreme, the purpose firmly declared to the President, when I became assailed from all quarters with a variety of objections. Among these it was urged that my retiring just when I had been attacked in the public papers, would injure me in the eyes of the public, who would suppose I either withdrew from investigation, or because I had not tone of mind sufficient to meet slander. The only reward I ever wished on my retirement was to carry with me nothing like a disapprobation of the public. These representations have for some weeks passed, shaken a determination which I had thought the whole world could not have shaken. I have not yet finally made up my mind on the subject, nor changed my declaration to the President. But having perfect reliance in the disinterested friendship of some of those who have counselled and urged it strongly, believing that they can see and judge better a question between the public and myself than I can, I feel a possibility that I may be detained here into the summer. A few days will decide. In the mean time I have permitted my house to be rented after the middle of March, have sold such of my furniture as would not suit Monticello, and am packing up the rest and storing it ready to be shipped off to Richmond as soon as the season of good sea-weather comes on. A circumstance which weighs on me next to the weightiest is the trouble I forsee I shall be constrained to ask Mr. Randolph to undertake. Having taken from other pursuits a number of hands to execute several purposes which I had in view for this year I cannot abandon those purposes and lose their labour altogether. I must therefore select the most important and least troublesome of them, the execution of my canal,[1] and (without embarrassing him with any details which Clarkson and George[2] are equal to) get him to tell them always what is to be done and how, and to attend to the levelling the bottom. But on this I shall write him particularly if I defer my departure. I have not received the letter which Mr. Carr wrote to me from Richmond nor any other from him since I left Monticello. My best affections to him, Mr. Randolph and your fireside and am with sincere love my dear Martha Yours,   Th: J.

1. A canal TJ was constructing on the south side of the Rivanna River. It was located about ¾ mile upstream from Milton and approximately six from Charlottesville. Its purpose was to carry water from the river to his Shadwell toll mill. See the *Farm Book,* 343–45 for additional details.

2. The individuals referred to were probably Manoah Clarkson, a Monticello overseer from 1792 to 1793, and "Big" George, a slave.

To Martha Jefferson Randolph

Philadelphia Feb 11. 1793

My Dear Martha

The hour of Post is come and a throng of business allows me only to inform you we are well, and to acknowledge the rect. of Mr. Randolph's letter of Jan. 24. with hopes that you are all so. Accept assurances [of] constant love to you all from Yours My Dear most affectionately,   Ths: Jefferson

To Martha Jefferson Randolph

Philadelphia Feb. 24. 1793.

My Dear Martha

We have no letter from Monticello since Mr. Randolph's of Jan. 30. to Maria. However we hope you are all well and that there are letters on the road which will tell us so. Maria writes to-day. Congress will rise on Saturday next, a term which is joyous to all as it affords some relaxation of business to all. We have had the mildest winter ever known, having had only two snows to cover the ground, and these remained but a short time. Heavy rains now falling will render the roads next to impassable for the members returning home. Colo. Monroe will stay some days after the rising of Congress. Bob was here lately, and as he proposed to return to Richmond and thence to Monticello I charged him with enquiring for the box with the servants clothes, should Mr. Randolph not yet have heard of it. It went from hence the 12th. of December by the Schooner Mary, Capt. Swaile, bound for Norfolk and

Richmd. The capt. undertook to deliver it to Mr. Brown in Richmond. From these circumstances it may certainly be found. Perhaps however an enquiry at Norfolk may be necessary. Present me affectionately to Mr. Randolph. Kiss dear Anne and ask her if she remembers me and will write to me. Health to the little one and happiness to you all. Your's affectionately my dear,

TH: JEFFERSON

FROM MARTHA JEFFERSON RANDOLPH

Monticello February 27, 1793

DEAR PAPA

I have just this moment recieved yours of Jan. 26, which by the negligence of the post has remained a fortnight longer than it ought to have done upon the road. We had already Learnt your resolution of continuing in Philadelphia by a letter of a later date to Mr. Randolph. I concieve your anxiety by what I feel myself. It was a cruel disapointment to me who had set my heart upon the pleasure of seeing you in March never to separate again farther than Edgehill.[1] Having never in my life been more intent upon any thing I never bore a disappointment with so little patience. My Little cherubs have both been very sick Latley. The Little boy has recovered but My Dear Anne continues extremely unwell. Poor Jenny Cary has Lost her husband and her sister Lucy is married to a Mr. Teril with whom she goes to Kentucke this spring so that Aunt Carr will have only one of her children with her it being the intention of Sam to settle imediately upon his own Land in this neighbourhood.[2] It is so Late that I shall not have time to write to Dear Maria this evening. Indeed I am affraid she thinks I never intend it again and that that is the reason she has left off writing to me however I hope to redeem my credit by the next post. In the mean time present my tenderest affections to her and be assured dear and much loved Father that no one breathing possesses them more entirely than your self. Yours,

M. RANDOLPH

I have unintentionally hurt Petit by neglecting to mention him in my Letters, therefore I should be much obliged to you to say *bien des choses* to him or any other message you think proper. I am affraid you will scarcely be able to read my Letter but it is one o'clock and the post goes off by day break. Once more adieu dear Father.

1. Martha's reference is to the breakdown in negotiations over the Edgehill property between Thomas Mann Randolph, Jr., and his father. Whatever this was, it may have accounted for the failure to have the deed recorded. It did not affect the Randolphs' ultimate possession and habitation at Edgehill. See notes for TJ to Martha Jefferson Randolph, April 26, 1790, and Martha to TJ of February 20, 1792.

2. Jane Barbara Carr Cary (Mrs. Wilson) and Lucy Carr Terrell (Mrs. Richard). Polly Carr was the daughter who remained with Aunt Carr.

To Martha Jefferson Randolph

Philadelphia Mar. 10. 1793.

MY DEAR DAUGHTER

Your letters of the 20th. and 27th. Feb. as well as Mr. Randolph's of the same dates, came to hand only yesterday. By this I percieve that your post must be under bad regulation indeed. I am sorry to learn that your garden is dismantled, and yourself thereby discoraged from attention to it. I beg that Mr. Randolph will employ the whole force, he has been so kind as to direct, in repairing the inclosure in preference to every other work I had proposed. Nothing can be placed in competition with the loss of the produce of the garden during the season, either for health or comfort, and my own are less dear and desirable to me than the health and comfort of yourself, Mr. Randolph and the little ones. I had hoped that from the same resources your supplies of wood in the winter would not have failed. I again repeat it that I wish every other object to be considered as secondary in my mind to your accomodation and insist that Mr. Randolph make the freest use of the people under his direction for his and your convenience in the first place. When I shall see you I cannot say: but my heart and thoughts are all with you till I do. I have given up my house here, and taken a small one[1] in the country on the banks of the Schuylkill to serve me while I stay. We are packing all our superfluous furniture and shall be sending it by water to Richmond when the season becomes favorable. My books too, except a very few, will be packed and go with the other things, so that I shall put it out of my own power to return to the city again to keep house, and it would be impossible to carry on business in the winter at a country residence. Tho' this points out an ultimate term of stay here, yet my mind is looking to a much shorter one if the circumstances will permit it which broke in on my first resolution. Indeed I have it much at heart to be at home in time to run up the part of the house the latter part of the summer and fall which I had proposed to do in the spring. Maria is well. Whether she writes or no to-day I know not. My best affections to Mr. Randolph; cherish your little ones for me, for I feel the same love for them as I did for yourself when of their age, and continue to me your own love which I feel to be the best solace remaining to me in this world. Adieu my dear. Your's affectionately,

TH: JEFFERSON

1. TJ moved on April 9 to a house located near Gray's Ferry on the Schuylkill River, then a few miles outside Philadelphia. See TJ to Moses Cox, March 7 and 12, 1793 (ViU), relative to renting this house. In the March 12 letter he mentions that he would move the beginning of April.

To Martha Jefferson Randolph

Philadelphia Mar. 24. 1793.

MY DEAR DAUGHTER

I have nothing interesting to tell you from hence but that we are well, and how much we love you. From Monticello you have every thing to write about which I have any care. How do my young chesnut trees? How comes on your garden? How fare the fruit blossoms &c. I sent to Mr. Randolph, I think, some seed of the Bent-grass which is much extolled. I now inclose you some seed which Mr. Hawkins[1] gave me, the name of which I have forgotten: but I dare say it is worth attention. I therefore turn it over to you, as I should hope not to reap what would be planted here. Within about a week I remove into the country. Tell Mr. Randolph that I send Fenno's papers thro' Mr. Madison, who left this place with Colo. and Mrs. Monroe on the 20th. Give my best attachments to Mr. Randolph and kiss the little ones for me. Your's affectionately my dear,   TH: JEFFERSON

1. Possibly John Hawkins, a Philadelphia merchant, or Benjamin Hawkins of Warren, North Carolina.

To Martha Jefferson Randolph

Philadelphia Apr. 8. 1793.

MY DEAR MARTHA

Since my letter of the last week Maria has recd. one from Mr. Randolph which lets us know you were all well. I wish I could say the same. Maria has for these three or four weeks been indisposed with little fevers, nausea, want of appetite, and is become weak. The Doctor thinks it proceeds from a weakness of the stomach, and that it will soon be removed. I learn from the head of Elk that a person of the name of Boulding set out from thence some days ago, to view my lands with an intention to become a tenant. He carried a letter from Mr. Hollingsworth,[1] whom I had desired to procure tenants for me; not addressed I beleive to any particular person. I am in hopes he will apply to Mr. Randolph. The lands I should first lease would be the upper tract joining Key: but if enough of them would join to take the whole lands on that side of the river, they might divide them as they pleased. I have never heard yet whether you got the servants' clothes which were sent by water. I have got all my superfluous furniture packed and on board a vessel bound to Richmond, to which place she will clear out to-day. I have written to Mr. Brown to hire a Warehouse or rather Ware-room for it, there being 1300. cubical feet of it, which would fill a moderate room. Some packages containing looking glass will have to remain there till next winter I presume, as they can only be trusted by water. Indeed I do not know how the rest will be got up. However, on this subject I will write to Mr. Randolph the next week. War is certainly declared between France, England and Holland. This we learn by a packet the dispatches of which came to hand yesterday. J. Eppes sets out for Virginia to-day, to go and finish his course of study at Wm. and Mary. Tell Mr. Carr his letter is just now received, and shall be answered the next week, as I am now in the throng of my removal into the country. Remember me affectionately to him, to Mr. Randolph and kiss the little ones for me. Adieu my dear. Your's most affectionately,   TH: JEFFERSON

1. Jacob Hollingsworth of Elkton, Maryland, who had found tenants for some of TJ's lands, among them Eli Alexander and Nicholas Biddle.

To Martha Jefferson Randolph

Philadelphia Apr. 28. 1793.

MY DEAR MARTHA

I am now very long without a letter from Monticello, which is always a circumstance of anxiety to me. I wish I could say that Maria was quite well. I think her better for this week past, having for that time been free from the little fevers which had harrassed her nightly. A paper which I some time ago saw in the Richmond gazette under the signature R. R. proved to me the existence of a rumor,[1] which I had otherwise heard of with less certainty. It has given me great uneasiness because I know it must have made so many others unhappy, and among these Mr. Randolph and yourself. Whatever the case may be, the world is become too rational to extend to one person the acts of another. Every one at present stands on the merit or demerit of their own conduct. I am in hopes therefore that neither of you feel any uneasiness but for the pitiable victim, whether it be of error or slander. In either case I see guilt but in one person, and not in her. For her it is the moment of trying the affection of her friends, when their commiseration and comfort become balm to her wounds. I hope you will deal them out to her in full measure, regardless of what the trifling or malignant may think or say. Never throw off the best affections of nature in the moment when they become most precious to their object; nor fear to extend your hand to save another, less you should sink yourself. You are on firm ground. Your kindnesses will help her and count in your own favor also. I shall be made very happy if you are the instruments not only of supporting the spirits of your afflicted friend under the weight bearing on them, but of preserving her in the peace, and love of her friends. I hope you have already taken this resolution if it were necessary; and I have no doubt you have: yet I wished it too much to omit mentioning it to you. I am with sincere love to Mr. Randolph and yourself, my dear Martha Your's affectionately,

TH: JEFFERSON

1. One of the most distressing scandals ever to take place in a prominent Virginia family. It is the alleged affair between Richard Randolph of Bizarre and a sister of his wife Judith, Anne Cary (Nancy) Randolph, also a sister of Thomas Mann Randolph, Jr. Richard was charged with infanticide. At his trial he was represented by Patrick Henry and John Marshall and acquitted. For an excellent but brief treatment of the affair, see Malone, *Jefferson and the Ordeal of Liberty*, 172–74; a longer account is in William Cabell Bruce, *John Randolph of Roanoke 1773–1833* (New York, 1922), I, 106–23. The novel by Jay and Audrey Walz, *The Bizarre Sisters* (New York, 1950), may also be of interest.

TO MARTHA JEFFERSON RANDOLPH

Philadelphia May. 12. 1793.

MY DEAR MARTHA

I have at length found time to copy Petit's list of the packages sent to Richmond. Tho' I have not heard of their arrival there, I take it for granted they must be arrived. I inclose you the list wherein I have marked with an * the boxes which must remain at Richmond till they can be carried up by water, as to put them into a waggon would be a certain sacrifice of them. They are the Nos. 2. 5. 10. 18. 19. 22. 23. 25. 26. 27. 28. Such of the others as contain any thing that you think would be convenient immediately, you may perhaps find means of having brought up. As to the rest they may lie till I can have waggons of my own or find some other oeconomical means of getting them up. In any way it will be expensive, many of the boxes being enormously large. I got a person to write to Scotland for a mason and house-joiner for me. I learn that they were engaged and only waited for a ship. They will be delivered at Richmond to the address of Mr. Brown. A person who is come here, and knows them personally, says they are fine characters, will be very useful to have on a farm; it is material therefore that they do not remain 24. hours in Richmond to be spoiled. I shall write to Mr. Brown to send them off instantly and shall be obliged to Mr. Randolph to have an eye to the same object. How to employ them will be the subject of consideration It will be puzzling till my return. It is one of the great inconveniences I experience by having been persuaded by my friends to defer carrying into execution my determination to retire. However when I see you, it will be never to part again. In the mean time my affairs must be a burthen to Mr. Randolph. You have never informed me whether the box containing the servant's clothes, which were sent in December last, have been received. I am anxious to hear, because if it has not, I will prosecute the captain. Maria's brain is hard at work to squeeze out a letter for Mr. Randolph. She has been scribbling and rubbing out these three hours, and this moment exclaimed 'I do not think I shall get a letter made out to-day.' We shall see how her labours will end. She wonders you do not write to her. So do I. Present me most affectionately to Mr. Randolph and be assured of my unceasing love to yourself. Kiss the dear little ones for me. Yours,

TH: JEFFERSON

FROM MARTHA JEFFERSON RANDOLPH

Monticello May 16 1793

DEAR PAPA

I recieved your kind letter of April the 28 a week ago and should have answered it imediately but that the house was full of company at the time. The subject of it has been one of infinite anx-

iety both to Mr. Randolph and my self for many months and tho
I am too sensible of the iliberality of extending to one person the
infamy of an other, to fear one moment that it can reflect any real
disgrace upon me in the eyes of people of sense yet the generality
of mankind are weak enough to think otherwise and it is painful
to an excess to be obliged to blush for so near a connection. I know
it by fatal experience. As for the poor deluded victim I believe
all feel much more for her than she does for her self. The villain
having been no less sucessful in corrupting her mind than he has
in destroying her reputation. Amidst the distress of her family she
alone is tranquil and seems proof against every other misfortune
on earth but that of a separation from her vile seducer. They have
been *tried* and acquited tho I am sorry to say his Lawers gained
more honour by it than they did as but a small part of the world
and those the most inconsiderable people in it were influenced
in there opinion by the dicision of the court. In following the
dictates of my own heart I was so happy as to stumble upon the
very conduct you advised me to, before I knew your opinion. I
have continued to behave with affection to her which her errors
have not been able to eradicate from my heart and could I suppose
her penitent I would redouble my attentions to her though I am
one of the few who have allways *doubted* the truth of the report.
As the opinion I had of R. R. was most exalted would to heaven
my hopes were equal to my fears but the latter often to often pre-
sides. The divisions of the family encrease daily. There is no knowing where they will end. The old gentleman has plunged into the
thickest of them governed by the most childish passions. He lends
the little weight his imprudence has left him to widen the breaches
it should be his duty to close. Mr. R—s conduct has been such as
to conciliate the affections of the whole family. He is the Link by
which so many discordant parts join. Having made up his difference with David Randolph there is not one individual but what
looks up to him as one, and the only one who has been uniform
in his affection to them. My Little cherubs are both in perfect
health. Anna was very much delighted with the *yather* and *fasty
old basselor* enclosed in it. She talks incessantly of you and Aunt
Polly. Your chestnuts are all alive but *one* and the acasia's all dead
but one. But that is very much grown and flourishing. Bergere has
added one to the number of genuine shepherds. The mungrels
increase upon us daily. My garden is in good order and would
really cut a figure but for the worms and catipillars which abound
so every where this year that they destroy the seed before it comes

up and even the Leaves of the trees. Adieu my dear Papa. We are
all impatient to see you. My love to Dear Maria and believe me
ever yours,   M. RANDOLPH

TO MARTHA JEFFERSON RANDOLPH

Philadelphia May 26. 1793.

MY DEAR MARTHA

Your and Mr. Randolph's welcome favors of the 16th. came to
hand yesterday, by which I perceive that your post-day for writing
is the Thursday. Maria is here and, tho not in flourishing health,
is well. I will endeavor to prevail on her to write, and perhaps may
succeed, as the day is too wet to admit her saunters on the banks
of the Schuylkill, where she passes every Sunday with me. We are
in sight of both Bartram's and Grey's gardens, but have the river
between them and us. We have two blind stories here. The one that
Dumourier[1] is gone over to the Austrians. The authority for this
is an English paper. No confidence in DuMourier's virtue opposes
it, for he has none: but the high reputation he has acquired is a
pledge to the world, which we do not see that these were any
motives on this occasion to induce him to forfeit. The other story
is that he has cut off 10,000 Prussians, and among them the K. of
Prussia and D. of Brunswick. The latter we know is out of command, and the former not in DuMourier's way. Therefore we concluded the story fabricated merely to set off against the other. It
has now come thro' another channel and in a more possible form
to wit that Custine has cut off 10,000 Prussians without naming
the King or Duke. Still we give little ear to it. You had at your
Convent so many —courts (as terminations of names) that I wish
the following paragraph of a newspaper may involve none of them.
'A few days ago several rich and respectable inhabitants were
butchered at Guadaloupe. The following are the names of the
unfortunate victims. Madame Vermont and Madame Meyercourt.
Monsr. Gondrecourt, three daughters just arrived from France
from 11. to 18. years of age. Messrs. Vaudrecourt &c.' Maria thinks
the Gondrecourts were at the convent.[2] The French minister Genet told me yesterday that matters appeared now to be tolerably
well settled in St. Domingo. That the Patriotic party had taken
possession of 600 aristocrats and monocrats, had sent 200 of them
to France, and were sending 400. here: and that a coalition had
taken place among the other inhabitants. I wish we could distribute our 400 among the Indians, who would teach them lessons

of liberty and equality. Give my best affections to Mr. Randolph and kiss the dear little ones for me. Adieu my very dear Martha. Your's constantly and affectionately,   TH: JEFFERSON

1. Charles-François Dumouriez, a French general who did in fact go over to the enemy.
2. Mary was correct. There were Gondrecourts at the convent.

TO MARTHA JEFFERSON RANDOLPH

Philadelphia June 10. 93.

MY DEAR MARTHA

I wrote you last on the 26th. of the last month. On the 3d. of the present I received Mr. Randolph's favor of May 22. I sincerely congratulate you on the arrival of the Mocking bird. Learn all the children to venerate it as a superior being in the form of a bird, or as a being which will haunt them if any harm is done to itself or it's eggs. I shall hope that the multiplication of the cedar in the neighborhood, and of trees and shrubs round the house, will attract more of them: for they like to be in the neighborhood of our habitations, if they furnish cover. I learn from Mr. Brown that all my furniture is safely arrived and stored at Rocket's.[1] Maria is here, but too lazy to write. She says in excuse that you do not write to her. Mrs. Shippen[2] lost her little son Bannister the last week. He died of a dysentery. Our letters from Mr. Bev. Randolph and the other commissioners[3] are that they were safely arrived at Niagara; and that their treaty was likely to be delayed a month longer than was expected. Consequently their return will be later. My sincere affections to Mr. Randolph and kiss dear Anne for me. Yours with constant love,

TH: JEFFERSON

1. A well-known landing site in Richmond, named for Robert Rockett, who established a ferry there. In 1787 it became a port of delivery.
2. Wife of Thomas Lee Shippen, the former Jane Wood of Albemarle County.
3. Beverley Randolph, Benjamin Lincoln, and Timothy Pickering were the commissioners sent to treat with Indians residing north of the Ohio River. They set out from Philadelphia on April 30, 1793, for Niagara.

FROM MARTHA JEFFERSON RANDOLPH

Monticello June 26, 1793

DEAR PAPA

We recieved your 3 Last letters yesterday which by the carelessness of the post master in Richmond have been detained many weeks, indeed Their negligence is intolerable. We have just heard of some of Mr. Randolph's Letters to you that have gone on to Lexington in kentucke. Those that we do get, come so irregularly with out any regard to Their dates that it is impossible to follow your directions with any degree of punctuality. Mr. Randolph thinks it would be adviseable to have all your furniture brought by water as it is not only much more oeconomical but also safer. I have a terible account to give you of your cyder. Of 140 bottles that were put away you will hardly find 12. It flew in such a manner as to render it dangerous going near them. Those that were carelessly corked forced their corks, the rest burst the bottles amongst which the havoc is incredible. The servants cloaths are not arrived nor have we been able to hear any thing about them. I am going on with such spirit in the garden that I think I shall conquer my *oponent* the *insect* yet, tho hither to they have been as indifatigable in cutting up as I have been in planting. I have added to your accasia which is at Least 2 feet high 2 lemmon trees and have the promise of an egg plant from Mr. Derieux. My dear little Anne [grows] daily more and more entertaining. She is very observing and very talkative and of course charming in the eyes of a mother. The dear Little boy tho not in perfect health is very well for one that is cutting teeth. *You* will easily concieve how great the satisfaction is I derive from the company of my sweet Little babes tho none but those who have experienced it can. I have allways forgot to mention Petit in any of my Letters. My negligence hurt his feelings I know, as it is not my Design to do so. You would oblige me infinitely by delivering some message to him *de ma part.* Adieu my Dear Papa. Believe me with tender affections yours,   M RANDOLPH

To Martha Jefferson Randolph

Philadelphia July 7. 1793.

MY DEAR DAUGHTER

My head has been so full of farming since I have found it necessary to prepare a plan for my manager, that I could not resist the addressing my last weekly letters to Mr. Randolph and boring him with my plans. Maria writes to you to-day. She is getting into tolerable health, tho' not good. She passes two or three days in the week with me, under the trees, for I never go into the house but at the hour of bed. I never before knew the full value of trees. My house is entirely embosomed in high plane trees, with good grass below, and under them I breakfast, dine, write, read and receive my company. What would I not give that the trees planted nearest round the house at Monticello were full grown. Can you make a provision of endive plants for the winter? Of celery I take for granted it may be done. But endive in great abundance would be a most valuable addition. I shall be in time for preparing covered places to transplant it to. Present me affectionately to Mr. Randolph and to the friends you have with you, and kiss the dear children for me. Adieu my dear. Yours with unceasing affection,

TH: JEFFERSON

To Martha Jefferson Randolph

TH: J. TO HIS DEAR DAUGHTER.

Philadelphia July 21. 1793.

We had peaches and Indian corn on the 12th. instant. When do they begin with you this year? Can you lay up a good stock of seed-peas for the ensuing summer? We will try this winter to cover our garden with a heavy coat of manure. When earth is rich it bids defiance to droughts, yeilds in abundance and of the best quality. I suspect that the insects which have harassed you have been encouraged by the feebleness of your plants, and that has been produced by the lean state of the soil. We will attack them another year with joint efforts. We learn that France has sent commissioners to England to treat of peace, and imagine it cannot be unacceptable to the latter, in the present state of general bankruptcy and demolition of their manufactures. Upon the whole the affairs of France, notwithstanding their difficulties external and internal, appear solid and safe. Present me to all my neighbors; kiss the little ones for me, and my warmest affections to yourself and Mr. Randolph.

To Martha Jefferson Randolph

Philadelphia Aug. 4. 1793.

MY DEAR MARTHA

I inclose you two of Petit's receipts.[1] The orthography will amuse you, while the matter of them may be useful. The last of the two is really valuable, as the beans preserved in that manner, are as firm, fresh, and green, as when gathered. Mr. D. Randolph is at Philadelphia and well. He delivered me your watch, which I will have ready to send by him. He proposes to set out for Monticello in 8. or 10. days. Present my best respects to Mrs. Randolph [2] and my regrets at my absence during the favor of her visit. I hope to be more fortunate another time. We have had a remarkeable death here which I will mention for example sake. Mrs. Lear,[3] wife of the gentleman who is secretary to the President, by eating green plumbs and apples brought on a mortification of the bowels which carried her off in six days. She was 23. years old, and of as fine healthy a constitution as I ever knew. Tell Anne this story, and kiss her for me, in presenting one of the inclosed caricatures. I put up several as Mrs. Randolph may have some of her family to whom they may give a moment's pleasure. My best affections are with Mr. Randolph and yourself. Adieu my dear.

1. For selected Monticello recipes that include certain of Petit's, consult Marie Kimball, *Thomas Jefferson's Cookbook* (Richmond, 1949).

2. Probably Mrs. Beverley Randolph. See TJ to Martha Jefferson Randolph, September 8, 1793.

3. Mrs. Tobias Lear. *The Pennsylvania Journal and Weekly Advertiser,* July 31, 1793, has her obituary notice.

TO MARTHA JEFFERSON RANDOLPH

Philadelphia Aug. 18. 93.

MY DEAR MARTHA

Maria and I are scoring off the weeks which separate us from you. They wear off slowly, but time is sure tho' slow. Mr. D. Randolph left us three days ago. He went by the way of Presquisle and consequently will not enrapture Mrs. Randolph till the latter end of the month. I wrote to Mr. Randolph sometime ago to desire he would send off Tom Shackleford or Jupiter[1] or any body else on the 1st. of September with the horse he has been so kind as to procure for me to meet at Georgetown (at Shuter's tavern). A servant whom I shall send from hence on the same day with Tarquin, to exchange them, Tarquin[2] to go to Monticello and the other come here to aid me in my journey. The messenger to ride a mule and lead the horse. I mention these things now, lest my letter should have miscarried. I received information yesterday of 500 bottles of wine arrived for me at Baltimore. I desired them to be sent to Richmond to Colo. Gamble[3] to be forwarded to Monticello. They will be followed the next week with some things from hence. Should any waggons of the neighborhood be going down they might enquire for them. With the things sent from hence will go clothes for the servants to replace those sent last winter, which I did not conclude to be irrecoverably lost till Mr. Randolph's last letter. My blessings to your little ones, love to you all, and friendly how d-ye's to my good neighbors. Adieu. Your's affectionately,   TH: JEFFERSON

1. A TJ slave.
2. Tarquin was one of TJ's riding horses.
3. Colonel Robert Gamble, a Richmond merchant and shipper.

To Martha Jefferson Randolph

Schuylkill Sep. 8. 93.

MY DEAR MARTHA

I received this day Mr. Randolph's letter of Aug. 31. with the horse, rather thin, having performed his journey in 7. days. However I shall hope to recruit him before I set out. The servant gives a very good account of him. The President sets out the day after tomorrow for Mount Vernon, and will be back about the last of the month. Within 4 or 5. days or a week after his return I can set out. The yellow fever, of which I wrote Mr. Randolph last week still increases. The last week about twice as many have died as did the week before. I imagine there are between 3. and 400. persons ill of it. I propose after the President's departure to remove my office into the country so as to have no further occasion to go into the town. I was just about ordering some few stores to be got and sent off to Richmond for Monticello: but I think it too unsafe now, and shall therefore write to Colo. Gamble to send up some from Richmond. Tell Mr. Randolph that the box for me in the Custom house at Bermuda[1] must be a small Orrery,[2] cost 2½ or 3 guineas. If Mrs. Beverley Randolph is still with you tell her that the Indians having refused to meet our Commissioners we expect Mr. Randolph her spouse here in the course of a week on his way back. Present my respects to her and your other friends with you. My best affections to Mr. Randolph, yourself and dear little ones. Adieu my dear dear Martha.   TH: J.

1. Bermuda Hundred was a small town and port on the James River at the mouth of the Appomattox River in Chesterfield County about eight miles south of Richmond.
2. An instrument for representing the various motions of the solar system. The small orrery referred to here is presumably the "portable orrery" (actually a pocket-sized one) that TJ purchased from the London firm of William and Samuel Jones. It is now in the possession of the Franklin Institute in Philadelphia. See *Princeton University Library Chronicle*, XV, No. 4 (Summer, 1954), 197, for an account of this instrument.

To Martha Jefferson Randolph

Germantown Nov. 10. 1793.

I wrote, my dear Martha, by last week's post to Mr. Randolph. Yesterday I received his of Oct. 31. The fever [1] in Philadelphia has almost entirely disappeared. The Physicians say they have no new infections since the great rains which have fallen. Some previous ones are still to die or recover, and so close this tragedy. I think however the Executive will remain here till the meeting of Congress, merely to furnish a rally point to them. The refugee inhabitants are very generally returning into the city. Mr. T. Shippen and his lady are here. He is very slowly getting better. Still confined to the house. She is well and very burly. I told her of her sister's pretensions to the fever and ague at Blenheim.[2] She complained of receiving no letter. Tell this to Mrs. Carter, making it the subject of a visit express, which will be an act of good neighborhood. The affairs of France are at present gloomy. Toulon has surrendered to England and Spain. So has Grand Anse and the country round about in St. Domingo. The English however have received a check before Dunkirk, probably a smart one, tho the particulars are not yet certainly known.[3] I send Freneau's papers. He has discontinued them, but promises to resume again. I fear this cannot be till he has collected his arrearages. My best regards to Mr. Randolph, accept my warmest love for yourself and Maria, compliments to miss Jane, kisses to the children, friendly affections to all. Adieu. Yours,   TH: J.

1. The yellow fever epidemic of 1793 began about the last of August, and by September hundreds had been stricken and nearly seventy had died. As mid-September approached, its intensity increased, causing a considerable number of the populace to flee the city. TJ remained at his desk until September 17, long after the other Cabinet members and the President had departed. He arrived at Monticello on September the 25. See Malone, *Jefferson and the Ordeal of Liberty*, 140–42, for an account of TJ and the epidemic; J. H. Powell, *Bring Out Your Dead: The Great Plague of Yellow Fever in Philadelphia in 1793* (Philadelphia, 1949), for broader aspects of it.

2. Jane Wood Shippen (Mrs. Thomas Lee) was a sister of Lucy Wood Carter (Mrs. Edward) of Blenheim, a Carter estate eight miles south of Monticello on the North Fork of the Hardware River.

3. The Duke of York was driven from there in September, 1793. By December Bonaparte had regained Toulon from the English, but TJ had no way of knowing this.

To Mary Jefferson

Germantown, Nov. 17. 1793

No letter yet from my dear Maria, who is so fond of writing, so punctual in her correspondence. I enjoin as a penalty that the next be written in French. Now for news. The fever is entirely vanished from Philadelphia. Not a single person has taken infection since the great rains about the 1st. of the month, and those who had it before are either dead or recovered. All the inhabitants who had fled are returning into the city, probably will all be returned in the course of the ensuing week. The President has been into the city, but will probably remain here till the meeting of congress to form a point of union for them before they will have time to gather knolege and courage. I have not yet been in, not because there is a shadow of Danger, but because I am afoot. Thomas[1] is returned into my service. His wife and child went into town the day we left them. They then had the infection of the Yellow fever, were taken two or three days after, and both dead. Had we staid those two or three days longer, they would have been taken at our house. I have heard nothing of Miss Fullarton. Her trunk remains at her house. Mrs. Fullarton[2] left Philadelphia. Mr. and Mrs. Rittenhouse remained there, but have escaped the fever. Follow closely your music, reading, sewing, housekeeping, and love me, as I do you, most affectionately.

TH: JEFFERSON

P. S. Tell Mr. Randolph that General Wayne has had a convoy of 22. wagons of provisions and 70. men cut off in his rear by the Indians.

1. Thomas was one of TJ's five servants at Philadelphia. He was paid eight dollars a month.
2. See note 1, TJ to Mary Jefferson, December 15, 1793.

To Martha Jefferson Randolph

Philadelphia Dec. 1. 1793.

MY DEAR MARTHA

This place being entirely clear of all infection, the members of Congress are coming into it without fear. The President moved in yesterday, as did I also. I have got comfortably lodged at the corner of 7th. and Market Street. Dr. Waters is returned; not well, but better. Still always Hectic. He and Mrs. Waters are just gone to housekeeping for the first time. Mrs. Trist is also returned to town and means to take a small house and 3. or 4. boarders. Mr. Randolph, the Atty Genl. having removed to German town during the fever, proposes not to return again to live in the city. Mrs. Washington is not yet returned. So much for small news. As to great, we can only perceive in general that the French are triumphing in every quarter. They suffered a check as is said by the D. of Brunswick, losing about 2000. men, but this is nothing to their numerous victories. The account of the recapture of Toulon comes so many ways that we think it may now be believed. St. Domingo has expelled all it's whites, has given freedom to all it's blacks, has established a regular government of the blacks and coloured people, and seems now to have taken it's ultimate form, and that to which all of the West India islands must come. The English have possession of two ports in the island, but acting professedly as the patrons of the whites, there is no danger of their gaining ground. Frencau's and Fenno's papers are both put down for ever. My best affection to Mr. Randolph, Maria and friends. Kisses to the little ones. Adieu affectionately,   Th: J.

To Mary Jefferson

Philadelphia, Dec. 15, 1793

My Dear Maria

I should have written to you the last Sunday in turn, but business required my allotting your turn to Mr. Randolph, and putting off writing to you till this day. I have now received your and your sister's letters of Nov. 27 and 28. I agree that Watson shall make the writing desk for you. I called the other day on Mrs. Fullarton,[1] and there saw your friend Sally Cropper. She went up to Trenton the morning after she left us and staid there till lately. The maid servant who waited on her and you at our house caught the fever on her return to town and died. In my letter of last week I desired Mr. Randolph to send horses for me to be at Fredericksburg on the 12th. of January. Lest that letter shoud miss carry I repeat it here and wish you to mention it to him. I also informed him that a person of the name of Eli Alexander[2] would set out this day from Elkton to take charge of the plantation under Byrd Rogers[3] and praying him to have his accommodations at the place got ready as far as should be necessary before my arrival. I hope to be with you all about the 15th. of January no more to leave you. My blessings to your Dear Sister and little ones: affections to Mr. Randolph and your friends with you. Adieu, My Dear, Yours tenderly,   Th: Jefferson

1. Mrs. Valeria Fullerton conducted a school on Mulberry Street in Philadelphia. Sarah Corbin Cropper was the daughter of General John and Margaret Pettitt Cropper of Bowman's Folly, Accomac County. Sally and Maria were close friends and were both students at Mrs. Fullerton's school. Jennings Cropper Wise, *Colonel John Wise of England and Virginia (1617–1695) His Ancestors and Descendants* (Richmond, 1918), 96–97.

2. Overseer at Shadwell from 1793 to 1795. He later leased the property and remained as a tenant until 1810.

3. Possibly the "Mr. Rogers" who resided at Elk Hill, TJ's property in Goochland County.

To Martha Jefferson Randolph

Philadelphia Dec. 22. 1793.

My dear Martha

In my letter of this day fortnight to Mr. Randolph, and that of this day week to Maria, I mentioned my wish that my horses might meet me at Fredericksburg on the 12th of January. I now repeat it, lest those letters should miscarry. The President made yesterday, what I hope will be the last set at me to continue; but in this I am now immoveable, by any considerations whatever. My books and remains of furniture embark tomorrow for Richmond. There will be as much in bulk as what went before. I think to address them to Colo. Gamble. As I retained longest here the things most necessary, they are of course those I shall want soonest when I get home. Therefore I would wish them, after their arrival to be carried up in preference to the packages formerly sent. The Nos. most wanting will begin at 67. I hope that by the next post I shall be able to send Mr. Randolph a printed copy of our correspondence with Mr. Genet and Mr. Hammond, as communicated to Congress. They are now in the press. Our affairs with England and Spain have a turbid appearance. The letting loose the Algerines on us, which has been contrived by England, has produced peculiar irritation. I think Congress will idemnify themselves by high duties on all articles of British importation. If this should produce war, tho not wished for, it seems not to be feared. My best affections to Mr. Randolph, Maria, and our friends with you. Kisses to the little ones. Adieu my dear Martha. Your's with all love,   Th: Jefferson

Virginia Planter

Varina Jan. 15 1795

We intended writing to my Dearest Father from Richmond, but that care devolving upon me on account of Mr. Randolph's business it was as is often the case with me put off till the hurry of packing obliged me to neglect it entirely. Col. Blackden[1] and W. C. Nicholas[2] had both left Richmond before we arrived there. The letter for the former was put in the post office imediately. That to Mr. Nicholas Mr. Randolph thought better to keep untill a direct opportunity offered, of sending it as the post does not pass near Warren. I have the paper you desired me to get, ready to send. It is not handsome but their was no choice their being only three pieces in Richmond that I could hear of except complete hangings for a room which they would not break in upon, borders were not to be had at any price.

I saw Bob[3] frequently while in Richmond. He expressed great uneasiness at having quitted you in the manner he did and repeatedly declared that he would never have left *you* to live with any person but his wife. He appeared to be so much affected at having deserved your anger that I could not refuse my intercession when so warmly solicited towards obtaining your forgiveness. The poor creature seems so deeply impressed with a sense of his ingratitude as to be rendered quite unhappy by it but he could not prevail upon himself to give up his wife and child. We found every thing here in such a ruinous condition that it is impossible to say what stay we shall be forced to make here. The monstrous crops of wheat which was represented to be 3000. bushels has dwindled away to 800 Most of the corn out still at the mercy of thieves hogs birds &c. and in short every thing in such disorder that Mr. Randolph has been obliged to discharge the overseer and take the management of the plantation in his own hands. We were quite happy at your having made use of the waggon as we were in no hurry at all for the horses indeed we did not leave Rock castle in several days after their arrival and then loitered away much of our time on the road. If you had any idea My dear Papa of the pleasure it gives us both for you to make use of any thing of ours you would never think of appologizing for it. Give my love to Maria and my two little angels and believe me My Dearest Father with constant tenderness your affectionate child,

M. RANDOLPH

Mr. Randolph will write to you from Dover[4] where the sale is to be. He desired me to tell you that he has executed all your commissions.

1. Probably Samuel Blagden, a Revolutionary War colonel, possibly from Connecticut.
2. Wilson Cary Nicholas was at one time governor of Virginia and was a friend of TJ's. He resided at Mount Warren, near the present site of Warren, near the mouth of Ballinger's Creek as it empties into the James River.
3. Robert Hemings.
4. A small settlement near Dover Creek in Goochland County. It lies between Sabot Island and Tuckahoe Creek, which flows into the James River.

TO MARTHA JEFFERSON RANDOLPH

Monticello Jan. 22. 95

TH. J. TO HIS DEAR M. J.

I received yesterday yours and Mr. Randolph's letters from Varina of the 15th. and 16th. inst. I had been in hopes that you would have come up from the Dover sale but am sorry to find that the affairs of Varina will claim Mr. Randolph's presence longer. In my last to him I asked the favor of him to remit the balance of Stras's money (after taking out Mr. Lyle's and Taylor's) to Mr. Mussi in Philadelphia.[1] Mr. Watson's[2] boats are bringing up the balance of my nailrod, and Snelson[3] has undertaken for the Drillplough. Gamble promises the clover seed and gongs shall come by the first conveyance: so that from all these Mr. Randolph is relieved. There remain on his hands Martin[4] and the Chariot. If the latter cannot be disposed of without better wheels I would be obliged to him to take the greater and larger diameters of the axle, and the length of the Nut of the wheel, as also the height of the fore and hind wheels, that I may have a set of good wheels made here, and sent down. Those now on the chariot will answer some purposes here. We have little new in the neighborhood. Mrs. Wood[5] and family are living at Milton. Derieux has begun to move, his family will go off this week. Mrs. Peter Marks[6] is dead after a very long illness. Dr. Gilmer declining rapidly. We have had about 12. days of very cold weather; the thermometer has been once as low as 10°. and only once in the whole time as high as the thawing point, 32°. So much the better for our wheat, and for the destruction of the weavil. But you are impatient to hear something of the children. They are both well, and have never had even a finger-ach since you left us. Jefferson is very robust. His hands are constantly like lumps of ice, yet he will not warm them. He has not worn his shoes an hour this winter. If put on him, he takes them off immediately and uses one to carry his nuts etc. in. Within these two days we have put both him and Anne into mockaseens, which being made of soft leather, fitting well and lacing up, they have never been able to take them off. So that I believe we may consider that as the only effectual shoe which can be made for them. They are inseparable in their sports. Anne's temper begins to develope itself advantageously. His tempests give her opportunities of shewing and exercising a placid disposition: and there is no doubt but that a little time will abate of his impatience as it has done hers. I called her in to ask what I should write for her to yourself and her papa. She says I must tell you that she loves you, and that you must come home. In both these sentiments we all join her. Maria gives all her love to you. We are alone at present; but are in hopes soon of a visit from my sister Anne. I shall address the next week's letter to Mr. Randolph. In the mean while present me to him affectionately, and continue to love me yourself as I do you most tenderly. Adieu; come home as soon as you can, and make us happy in seeing you here, and Mr. Randolph in better health.

1. This exchange reflects the freeing of Robert Hemings who was manumitted December 24, 1794. "Executed a deed of emancipation for Bob. by the name of Robert Hemmings. He has been valued at £ 60. which Stras [Dr. George Frederick Strauss, of Richmond] is to advance." (Account Book, December 24, 1794.) Hemings later worked for Dr. Strauss and married one

$$\frac{D}{51} - \frac{C}{67}$$

of his slaves. On January 8, 1795, TJ remitted ". . . 51 − 67 the balance of Stras's money to Mussie [Joseph Mussie] of Philadelphia." (Account Book.) He thus rid himself of an obligation to Mussie. The indenture freeing Hemings is at the MHi. See Malone, *Jefferson and the Ordeal of Liberty*, 208, and *Memoirs of a Monticello Slave* (1955), 10.

2. John Watson, a Milton resident.

3. Possibly William Snelson, Jr., a one-time resident of Hanover and Louisa counties. TJ had varied business dealings with a "Mr. Snelson." See Account Books 1795 and 1796, entries from June, 1795, to December, 1796.

4. TJ slave who often drove him in his light four-wheeled vehicle drawn by a pair of horses.

5. Probably Mrs. Lucy Wood, with whom TJ had business dealings. It is to be noted that there were nineteen Woods paying a property tax in Fredericksville Parish and six in Saint Anne's in 1795. Albemarle County Personal Property Book 1795, Virginia State Library, Richmond, Virginia.

6. Mother of Hastings Marks, TJ's brother-in-law.

To Martha Jefferson Randolph

Monticello Feb. 5. 95.

TH: J. TO HIS DEAR MARTHA

We are all well, and especially the children, who will forget you if you do not return soon. Jefferson is under daily discipline with our puppy. He mends a little of his fears, but very slowly. We have been all kept much within doors by a spell of very cold weather which has lasted now about 4. weeks. During this no ploughing done. The men Mr. Randolph hired for me arrived last Saturday with the 3. mares, all well. His having put Varina under Mr. Hughes, gives us hopes he will soon be relieved from his attendance there, and Jamey's[1] being ordered down with horses has quickened our expectations. I inclose Mr. Randolph a letter from Clarke.[2] I imagine it is as doleful as one I received from him, announcing a much shorter crop of tobo. than he had expected, as also the loss of horses. Our neighborhood offering nothing in the way of news, I have only to add my best affections to you both. Accept them tenderly and warmly. Adieu.

1. Jamey or Jame, Thomas Mann Randolph, Jr.'s slave who sometimes worked at Monticello. TJ also owned slaves by this name.
2. Bowling Clarke was overseer at Poplar Forest, a Jefferson farm in Bedford County, approximately seventy miles from Monticello.

To Martha Jefferson Randolph

Monticello July 31. 95.

DEAR MARTHA

We have no letter from you since your arrival at the Warmsprings, but are told you are gone on to the sweet springs.[1] Not knowing how to write to you by post, I take the opportunity of sending this by Dr. Currie.[2] He has mentioned to me the homeless situation of Nancy Randolph. She is now with Mrs. Carrington. I do not know whether she is on such a footing with Mr. Randolph and yourself as that her company would be desireable or otherwise to you. If the former, invite her here freely to stay with you. But if disagreeable, do not do it; my object in mentioning it being to place you both at your perfect ease on that subject.[3] Our own family is all well; the children remarkeably so. But the house has been a mere hospital of sick friends. Mrs. Bolling and Polly, and their servants sick. So also Mrs. Marks. Several others on their way to the springs; so that every corner of every room has been occupied. J. Eppes has been for some time gone to Champe Carter's[4] and that neighborhood with P. Carr. Mrs. Dunbar is just gone there also. Our weather has been very seasonable. But I hear an unfavorable account of a field of corn of Mr. Randolph's on the road, as being yellow and ill-looking, supposed to be too thick planted. We are very anxious to hear what effect the springs have on his health. My best esteem to him. Adieu. Yours affectionately,   TH: JEFFERSON

1. These watering places or spas were located in the western counties of Bath and Greenbrier. The latter is now in West Virginia.
2. Dr. James Currie of Richmond.
3. She did not come to Monticello.
4. William Champe Carter was a son of Edward Carter of Blenheim, Albemarle County. In 1790 he purchased Viewmont from Edmund Randolph and resided there until he sold it to his brother Edward Hill Carter on August 9, 1801. In December he purchased from Robert Beverley 1,904¼ acres in the northwest section of Culpeper County, near the present village of Brandy. See George S. Wallace, *The Carters of Blenheim* (Richmond, 1955), 64.

From Martha Jefferson Randolph

Dunginess[1] Jan 1st 1796

Mr. Randolph having determined to spend some months at Varina I am under the necessity of troubling you my dearest Father with a memorandum of the articles we shall want from Monticello. We have spent hollidays and indeed every day in such a perpetual round of visiting and recieving visits that I have not had a moment to my self since I came down and we shall leave this on our way to Richmond next sunday where I hope to recieve a letter from you. Give my love to Maria and the children and believe me dearest Father with unchangeable affection your's in great haste.   M RANDOLPH

The waggon will be at Monticello the 5th or 6th of the month.

1. Dungeness, the home of Isham Randolph in Goochland County, Virginia.

To Martha Jefferson Randolph

Jan. 25. 1796.

MY DEAR MARTHA

After the departure of my last letter to Mr. Randolph I found the details I had given him respecting the waggon were erroneous. The rise of the river had cut off our communications for several days. I presume it arrived at Varina as soon as my letter.

We are all well here. Jefferson particularly so. He is become the finest boy possible. Always in good humor, always amusing himself, and very orderly. It appears that his continued fretfulness before was owing to his being teazed by his companions. I hope Mr. Randolph received my letter covering the commission for taking the depositions of the Shockoe inspectors.[1] The notice given is for Saturday next, at noon at the warehouse. The notice has been duly served, so that if the business can be then done, we shall have no further trouble with it. We have had two or three days of extreme cold. The thermometer was down to 15°. I hear that P. Carr is at Philadelphia. He was to form the depositions of the Inspectors so as to leave nothing further to be done but to swear to them. But as I did not hear from him I presume he did nothing. Maria and Virginia[2] give their love to you. Jefferson is always talking of sending letters to you. Kiss Anne for me, and present my best esteem to Mr. Randolph. Adieu. Your's affectionately,   TH: JEFFERSON

1. Inspectors at the public warehouse along Shockoe Creek at Richmond. They checked and verified tobacco there for tax purposes.
2. Virginia Randolph.

To Martha Jefferson Randolph

Monticello Feb. 14. 96.

We are all well here, my dear daughter, and Jefferson particularly so. He often repeats that you told a story, 'that you did,' when you got into the carriage and said you would come back for him. His cheeks swell with emphasis as he asseverates this. We are just beginning our demolitions and find they will be very troublesome. It was high time to do it, from the rotten state in which we found some of our timbers.[1] The first time Mr. Randolph goes to Richmond, I will ask the favor of him to call on Swan, the cabinetmaker, who is agent for Mr. Lownes my iron merchant in Philadelphia.[2] Lownes is in arrears with me twenty three hundred weight of nailrod, and informed me that Swan had standing directions from him to furnish at all times any quantities I should call for. I wrote to Mr. Swan a month ago to know if he could furnish me this 23.₵ weight, but have no answer, and from his inattention to business, expect to get none, unless Mr. Randolph will be so good as to call on him, and write me his answer, and by no means trust to his doing it himself. Adieu affectionately my dear Martha; kisses to Anne, and my best salutations to Mr. Randolph.

1. Monticello is actually two houses, the present, or second, having evolved from the first. The earlier was begun about 1769 and had a central mass of two stories with octagonal projections. (See James A. Bear, Jr., *Old Pictures of Monticello, An Essay in Historical Iconography* [Charlottesville, 1957], 5–7.) This was the house that Mrs. Jefferson knew, the one that was nearing completion or had been completed when she died in September, 1782. This sad event caused the suspension of all future plans and construction, and the house stood in this condition until several years after TJ's return from France, where he undoubtedly began to contemplate remodeling. Such plans were formulated by 1793 and were mentioned in a letter of March 3, 1793 (DLC), to the carpenter, Stephen Willis. Active demolitions did not begin until February, 1796, and consisted chiefly of "taking down the upper story . . . and building it on the ground, so as to spread all my rooms on one floor." (To Benjamin Hawkins, March 22, 1796, DLC.) TJ envisaged a job of several years, but it was not completed (if indeed it ever was) until 1809. For a step-by-step account of the remodeling of the house, consult the "Construction File" at Monticello. This is a chronologically arranged file of extracts, chiefly from Jefferson, and family correspondence pertaining to all phases of construction and remodeling.

2. Samuel Swann and Caleb Lownes. Consult Account Books for numerous references to Lownes and the *Virginia Gazette and Richmond Chronicle*, May 20, 1794, p. 3, for a Swann advertisement.

To Martha Jefferson Randolph

Monticello Mar. 6. 96.

Our neighborhood my dear daughter furnishes us with not one word of news to you, and I am so fatigued with writing for this post that I can only inform you we are all well, Jefferson robust as a beef, and all our desires alive to see you. My kisses to dear Anne, and best affections to Mr. Randolph and yourself. Adieu my dear and love me as I do you.   TH: J.

To Martha Jefferson Randolph

Chester-town Maryland Feb. 28. 1797.

I have got so far, my dear Martha, on my way to Philadelphia which place I shall not reach till the day after tomorrow. I have lost one day at Georgetown by the failure of the stages, and three days by having suffered myself to be persuaded at Baltimore to cross the bay and come by this route as quicker and pleasanter. After being forced back on the bay by bad weather in a first attempt to cross it, the second brought me over after a very rough passage, too late for the stage. So far I am well, tho' much fatigued.

I hope Mr. Randolph and Maria joined you long ago, and that you are all well. Tell Mr. Randolph that eleven dollars have been given in Baltimore and Philadelphia for the best James river tobacco, and that it is believed it will still rise considerably. It will be worth his while to have the making of his crab cyder well attended to hereafter, as I learn here that good cyder of the qualities commonly at market sell for a quarter of a dollar the bottle, wholesale, including in that the price of the bottle. Crab-cyder would probably command more. Wheat is at 2. dollars at Baltimore, and no immediate apprehensions of a fall. Present him my affections. My best love to yourself, Maria and the little ones. Adieu.

Vice-President of the
United States of America

To Mary Jefferson

Philadelphia Mar. 11. 97.

MY DEAR MARIA

I recieved with great pleasure your letter from Varina, and though I never had a moment's doubt of your love for me, yet it gave me infinite delight to read the expressions of it. Indeed I had often and always read it in your affectionate and attentive conduct towards me. On my part, my love to your sister and yourself knows no bounds, and as I scarcely see any other object in life, so would I quit it with desire whenever my continuance in it shall become useless to you. I heard, as I passed thro' Wilmington, that your acquaintance Miss Geddis was well, and not yet married. I have here met with another who was at Mrs. Pine's with you, Miss McKain, who sings better than any body I have heard in America, and is otherwise well accomplished. I recieved a letter yesterday from Bruni,[1] praying a seat *in my carriage* to some place in Virginia where she could get a passage by water which would shorten that to Varina. I am sincerely sorry not only that I have not my own carriage to offer her a seat, but that I had engaged with a party to take the whole of the mail stage back, so that there was not a place left to offer her. I am obliged to apologize to her on this ground, but people under misfortune are suspicious, and I fear these little accidental checks may make her think them intentional. I leave this the day after tomorrow, and shall be at home on the 19th. or 20th. but my dear, do not let my return hasten yours. I would rather you should stay where you are till it becomes disagreeable to you, because I think it better for you to go more into society than the neighborhood of Monticello admits. My first letter from Monticello shall be to your sister. Present her my warmest love and be assured of it yourself. Adieu my dear daughter

1. Mme. Brunette de Châteaubrun.

141

To Martha Jefferson Randolph

Monticello Mar. 27. 97.

MY DEAR MARTHA

I wrote to Mr. Randolph two or three days ago, but I imagine he will recieve the letter at Richmond on his way up: for we expect he will of course come up this week. He has a more dangerous competitor in Billy Wood[1] than had arisen before. But I hear little about it. I arrived in good health at home this day sennight. The mountain had then been in bloom ten days. I find that the natural productions of the spring are about a fortnight earlier here than at Fredericksburg. But where art and attention can do any thing, some one in a large collection of inhabitants, as in a town, will be before ordinary individuals whether of town or country. I have heard of you but once since I left home, and am impatient to know that you are all well. I have however so much confidence in the dose of health with which Monticello charges you in summer and autumn that I count on it's carrying you well through the winter. The difference between the health enjoyed at Varina and Presquisle is merely the effect of this. Therefore do not ascribe it to Varina and stay there too long. The bloom of Monticello is chilled by my solitude. It makes me wish the more that yourself and sister were here to enjoy it. I value the enjoiments of this life only in proportion as you participate them with me. All other attachments are weakening, and I approach the state of mind when nothing will hold me here but my love for yourself and sister and the tender connections you have added to me. I hope you will write to me: as nothing is so pleasing during your absence as these proofs of your love. Be assured my dear daughter that you possess mine in it's utmost limits. Kiss the dear little ones for me. I wish we had one of them here. Adieu affectionately. I inclose you a letter I rec'd in Philadelphia from Mde. Salimber. As I came in a stage it was impossible to accomodate her. I wrote her the fact with such friendly expressions for us all as might tend to prevent her imputing it to unwillingness. Had it not been for the unroofing our house, I would have invited her to come here and spend the summer with you.

1. Thomas Mann Randolph, Jr., made a tentative decision to offer for the legislature from Albemarle County, but he failed to be present on election day, which cost him the contest and greatly embarrassed his friends and father-in-law. "Gaines," 77.

FROM MARTHA JEFFERSON RANDOLPH

Varina March 31st 1797

MY DEAREST FATHER

The first certain account we had of your arrival were conveyed by your letter to Mr. Randolph which would as you suposed have met on his way up had we not previously determined upon having the children innoculated. But every circumstance of season health &c. conspiring to make the present opportunity favorable Mr. Randolph thought no interest of his could excuse his letting it slip. I have often experienced that a mother's heart was of all things in nature the least subject to reason but never more fully than at present. The idea of exposing my children to such a disorder with out being able to accompany them alltho I have the certainty of their finding in their Father as tender and an infinitely more skillfull nurse than my self, makes me perfectly miserable. I never look at them but my eyes fill with tears to think how soon we shall part and *perhaps* for ever. The anxiety I feel on their account my Dear Father does not prevent my feeling most sensibly for the solitude and gloom of your present situation. I never take a view of your solitary fire side but my heart swells. However as nothing detains us now but the children I hope soon [to] be restored to your paternal embraces and dispel by the presence of your children the cloud which obscures the beauties of spring, no where so enchanting as at Monticello. My sister joins me in the tenderest love. As the boys are waiting I am obliged to conclude with Dearest Father yours most affectionate,

M. RANDOLPH

TO MARTHA JEFFERSON RANDOLPH

Monticello Apr. 9. 97.

I recieved yours, my dear Martha, of Mar. 31. four days ago. The inoculation at Richmond having stopped that post I send this by way of Fredsbg. I entirely approve of your resolution to have the children inoculated. I had before been so much convinced of the expediency of the measure that I had taken it for granted before your letter informed me of it. I am called to Philadelphia to a meeting of Congress the 15th. of May and shall leave Monticello on the 3d. or 4th. of that month, as Mr. Randolph informs me you would have quitted Varina and come up the beginning of this month but for the inoculations, would it not be best for you as soon as the children are quite recovered, from the disease, to come up, you, Maria and Ellen, and send the carriage back for Mr. Randolph and the children. In this way I shall have the pleasure of seeing you certainly and him and the children probably before my departure and can make better arrangements for your accomodation during my absence. Still however let all this depend on your convenience. My love to Maria. Tell her I have made a new law, which is only *to answer letters*. It would have been her turn to have recieved a letter had she not lost it by not writing. Adieu most affectionately both of you.

To Martha Jefferson Randolph

Philadelphia May 18. 1797.

My Dear Martha

I arrived here in good health on the 7th. day after my departure from home, without any intervening accident and am as well as when I left home. I recieved here the inclosed letter from Mr. Pintard[1] our Consul at Madeira who sais it was given him by one of your old convent acquaintances settled there. I suppose the letter will inform you of more particulars. We yesterday recieved the President's speech. Till the answer shall be given in we cannot judge what work the legislature will now take in hand, nor consequently how long we shall be here. Opinions vary from 4. to 6. weeks. My next letter will give a better idea of the time of my return which will be within a week after rising of Congress. Our affairs with France become more and more gloomy. Those of England every day more desperate. Nothing but their desperation prevents the stronger party in our government from making common cause with them. Prices of produce are at a stand. The current price of James river tobacco is 9. dollars. This information may be desirable to some of our mercantile neighbors. My love to my dear Maria. I write to Mr. Randolph on the presumption he is at Richmond. My affections are with yourself and Maria and my wishes be with you. Continue to love me. Adieu.

1. John M. Pintard.

To Mary Jefferson

Philadelphia, May 25th, 1797.

My dear Maria

I wrote to your sister the last week, since which I have been very slowly getting the better of my rheumatism, though very

slowly indeed; being only able to walk a little stronger.[1] I see by
the newspapers that Mr. and Mrs. Church and their family are
arrived at New York. I have not heard from them, and therefore
am unable to say any thing about your friend Kitty, or whether she
be still Miss Kitty.[2] The condition of England is so unsafe that
every prudent person who can quit it, is right in doing so. James[3]
is returned to this place, and is not given up to drink as I had
before been informed. He tells me his next trip will be to Spain. I
am afraid his journeys will end in the moon. I have endeavored
to persuade him to stay where he is, and lay up money. We are not
able yet to judge when Congress will rise. Opinions differ from two
to six weeks. A few days will probably enable us to judge. I am
anxious to hear that Mr. Randolph and the children have got
home in good health; I wish also to hear that your sister and yourself continue in health; it is a circumstance on which the happiness
of my life depends. I feel the desire of never separating from you
grow daily stronger, for nothing can compensate with me the want
of your society. My warmest affections to you both. Adieu, and
continue to love me as I do you. Yours affectionately,

TH: JEFFERSON

1. This attack does not appear to have been severe, since he failed to mention it in his letter of the 12th to Martha or in any following. These spells
on occasion were very painful and sometimes rendered him almost immobile.
Consult the "Medical Chronology" under appropriate dates.

2. Mrs. and Mrs. John Baker Church. He was an Englishman who married
Angelica Schuyler, daughter of General Philip Schuyler of New York. Cather-
ine (Kitty) Church was their daughter. She was a schoolmate of Martha and
Mary at Panthemont in Paris and a close friend of Mary.

3. James Hemings was taken to France by TJ in 1784 for the purpose of
learning the art of French cookery. He was freed by indenture February 5,
1796 (original at MHi), but not until he had instructed another member of
the Monticello household staff in French cuisine. On February 26 (Account
Book 1797) TJ gave him $30 for the trip to Philadelphia, where he presum-
ably was to take up residence. An examination, however, of Philadelphia direc-
tories fails to list him as a resident. His later whereabouts is unknown.

To MARTHA JEFFERSON RANDOLPH

Philadelphia June 8. 1797.

MY DEAR MARTHA

Yours of May 20 came to hand the 1st. inst. I imagine you recieved mine of May 18. about six days after the date of yours. It
was written the first post day after my arrival here. The commission you inclosed for Maria is executed, and the things are in
the care of Mr. Boyce of Richmond, who is returning from hence

with some goods of his own, and will deliver them to Mr. John-ston.[1] I recieve with inexpressible pleasure the information your letter contained.[2] After your own happy establishment, which has given me an inestimable friend to whom I can leave the care of every thing I love, the only anxiety I had remaining was to see Maria also so asociated as to ensure her happiness. She could not have been more so to my wishes, if I had had the whole earth free to have chosen a partner for her. I now see our fireside formed into a groupe, no one member of which has a fibre in their compo-sition which can ever produce any jarring or jealousies among us. No irregular passions, no dangerous bias, which may render prob-lematical the future fortunes and happiness of our descendants. We are quieted as to their condition for at least one generation more. In order to keep us all together, instead of a present provi-sion in Bedford, as in your case, I think to open and resettle the plantation of Pantops[3] for them. When I look to the ineffable pleasures of my family society, I become more and more disgusted with the jealousies, the hatred, and the rancorous and malignant passions of this scene, and lament my having ever again been drawn into public view. Tranquility is now my object. I have seen enough of political honors to know that they are but splendid torments: and however one might be disposed to render services on which any of their fellow citizens should set a value; yet when as many would deprecate them as a public calamity, one may well entertain a modest doubt of their real importance, and feel the impulse of duty to be very weak. The real difficulty is that being once delivered into the hands of others, whose feelings are friendly to the individual and warm to the public cause, how to withdraw from them without leaving a dissatisfaction in their mind, and an impression of pusillanimity with the public.

Congress, in all probability will rise on Saturday the 17th. inst. the day after you will recieve this. I shall leave Philadelphia Mon-day the 19th. pass a day at Georgetown and a day at Fredericks-burg, at which place I wish my *chair*[4] and horses to be Sunday evening the 25th. Of course they must set out Saturday morning the 24th. This gives me the chance of another post, as you will, the evening before that, recieve by the post a letter of a week later date than this, so that if any thing should happen within a week to delay the rising of Congress, I may still notify it and change the time of the departure of my horses. Jupiter must pursue the rout by Noel's to which he will come the first day, and by Chew's[5] to Fredericksburg the next. I fix his rout because were any acci-

dent to get me along earlier, or him later, we might meet on the
road. Not yet informed that Mr. Randolph is returned I have
thought it safest to commit this article to my letter to you. The
news of the day I shall write to him. My warmest love to yourself
and Maria. Adieu affectionately.   TH: JEFFERSON

1. Probably Charles Johnston of Charles Johnston & Co., a Richmond
mercantile house with which TJ often transacted business.
2. The engagement of Mary and John Wayles Eppes delighted TJ, for he was
very kindly disposed toward the Eppington household and especially toward
"Jack," as he had addressed him since childhood. After the wedding on October
13, 1797, he altered this form of address to a more dignified "Mr. Eppes."
3. For his daughter's dowry TJ, on October 12, 1797, deeded to "Mary
and her heirs" 819¼ acres of land "on the north east side of the Rivanna River
and adjacent thereto called Pantops." Included were slaves, cattle, and farm
equipment; unfortunately, there was no dwelling house, which certainly
influenced "Mr. Eppes's" decision not to settle near Monticello where his possessive father-in-law strongly desired them. Albemarle County Deed Book 12,
363–64.
For Mary's sole heir's inheritance, see footnote 1 to TJ to Francis Wayles
Eppes, May 6, 1824.
4. A light one-horse-drawn vehicle, that is, a chaise or gig.
5. Noel's, an Orange County inn. TJ often breakfasted here when traveling
north.

FROM MARY JEFFERSON

Monticello June 12th 1797

DEAR PAPA

Your letters to my sister and myself did not arrive here till the
9th. They were stopt in Fredericksburg by the sickness of the post
boy, and were at last sent round by Richmond. We learnt with
sorrow indeed that you had again been tormented by your rheumatism. The consolation of seeing you when you are ill is the only
one I know. I never feel the distress of separation as much as then.
I have at last written to Sally Cropper and inclose the letter to you
to direct to her in Acomac county, and if she will answer it [I] will
try for the future to keep up a more regular correspondence with
her. Mr. Randolph and the children arriv'd here last Tuesday all
in perfect health. Ann and Jefferson grown so much as to amaze
us, Ann seems to promise more every day of resembling her
mother. Her disposition is the same allready. She will no doubt
be worthy of her. We are alone at present. Mr. Hylton[1] and Mr.
Lawrence with whom he is travelling left us today after a visit of
ten days. We have seen no one else, I hope we shall not for some
time, solitude after such company as his is by no means unpleasant.
I am not able to tell you whether Mr. Richardson[2] is going on well.
They today, began to raise the walls of the hall, the other rooms

are done. The garden has supplied us better with vegetables and fine lettuce than it has ever yet done although we have been so much in want of rain. But I must finish my letter as they are waiting for it. The next we recieve from you I hope will let us know that you are recovered and when to expect you. We wait in hopes of that in no small anxiety. Adieu Dear Papa

I am your most affectionate daughter,   M. JEFFERSON

1. William Hylton was a brother of Daniel Hylton. See Daniel Hylton to TJ, May 24, 1793 (Carr-Cary Papers, ViU).

2. Richard Richardson was a Monticello workman/overseer who began work on April 10; his name last appears in the Account Book April 20, 1801.

To Mary Jefferson

[draft]
June 14. 97.

I learn, my d. M. with inexpressible pleasure that an union of sentiment is likely to bring on an union of destiny between yourself and a person for whom I have the highest esteem. A long acquaintance with him has made his virtues familiar to me and convinced me that he possesses every quality necessary to make you happy and to make us all happy. This event in compleating the circle of our family has composed for us such a group of good sense, good humor, liberality, and prudent care of our affairs, and that without a single member of a contrary character as families are rarely blessed with. It promises us long years of domestic concord and love, the best ingredient in human happiness, and I deem the composition of my family the most precious of all the kindnesses of fortune. I propose, as in the case of your sister, that we shall all live together as long as it is agreeable to you; but whenever inclination convenience or a curiosity to try new things shall give a wish to be separately established, it must be at Pantops, which in the mean time while under improvement will furnish to Mr. E. useful and profitable occupation as a farmer, and to you occasional rides to superintend the spinning house, dairy &c. You might even have a room there to be in comfort if business or variety should induce a short stay. From thence to Edgehill we can make a road on the dead level which shall make it as near as Monticello. But I should lose myself, my dear Maria, in these reveries as I always do when I think of yourself or your sister, did not the discordant noises, the oppressive heats and other disagremens of this place awaken me through the channel of every sense to very different scenes. I long the more to be with you and therefore see

with the utmost impatience day after day drawn out here in useless debate, and rhetorical declams. Take care of your health my
dear child for my happiness as well as your own and that of all
those who love you. And all the world will love you if you continue
good good humored, prudent and attentive to every body, as I
am sure you will do from temper as well as reflection. I embrace
you my dear in all the warmth of my love, and bid you affectionately adieu.

To Mary Jefferson Eppes

Monticello Dec. 2. 97.

My dear Maria

You will be surprised at recieving a letter from me dated here
at this time but a series of bad weather having suspended our
works many days, has caused my detention. I have for sometime
had my trunk packed and issued my last orders, and been only
waiting for it to cease raining. But it still rains. I have a bad
prospect of wars and work before me. Your sister moved to Belmont about three days ago. The weather ever since has kept us
entirely asunder. If tomorrow permits my departure I shall be in
Philadelphia in a week from this time. You shall hear from me
there, should it be only to provoke answers to my letters assuring
me of your health, of Mr. Eppes's and the good family of Eppington. I received his letter from Mrs. Payne's which gave us great
comfort; but we have apprehended much that you did not get to
Eppington before the bad weather set in. Tell Mr. Eppes that
I have orders for a sufficient force to begin and finish his house [1]
during the winter after the Christmas holidays; so that his people
may come safely after New year's day. The overseer at Shadwell
will furnish them provisions. Present my affections to him, and
the family, and continue to love me as you are tenderly beloved
by Your's affectionately,   Th: Jefferson

1. TJ was referring to the Pantops property. See Dumas Malone, "Polly Jefferson and Her Father," *The Virginia Quarterly Review*, VII, No. 1 (1931), 90.

From Mary Jefferson Eppes

Chestnut grove December the 8th 1797

Dear Papa

The fortnight that I spent at Eppington was so taken up in
recieving and returning visits, that it was out of my power while

there, to write to you. After a safe journey down, we arrived in perfect health all. My ankle so much mended that I had no further use for my stick, and except a great weakness which I still feel when I attempt to exert it, it is quite well. We left them yesterday, all well except Betsy Eppes, who came here with us on her way to Petersburg, where she is gone with her brother to have a tooth drawn which the doctors suppose occasion the swelling in her jaw. My Aunt suffering with hers, tho much easier than it has been, she is well otherwise. My Uncle Bolling[1] is much as usual, in a state of constant intemperance allmost, he is happy only with his glass in his hand, he behaves tho' much better to my Aunt than he did, and appears to desire a reconciliation with her and I think could she hide her resentment of his past behaviour to her, she might render her situation much more comfortable than it is. I shall return to Eppington in a day or two, where I shall spend the time that is not taken up in visiting Mr. Eppes relations; and where, as much happiness as I can feel, seperated from you and my dearest sister. I experience, in the kind attentions, and affectionate behaviour, of the whole family, and which to merit will be my endeavour through life. Adieu My Dear Papa. My Aunt has sent to me to join the company which is here. Adieu once more your most affectionate daughter,   M E

I have enclosed the size of chrystal of my watch and beg you to get one for I have not been able to find one large enough in Petersburg or Richmond.

1. John Bolling was TJ's brother-in-law.

To Martha Jefferson Randolph

Philadelphia Dec. 27. 97.

My dear Martha

I am at length got well of a terrible cold, which I think must have proceeded from the intense cold of the day I left Belmont. It became very bad by the time I got to Baltimore, and has been worse here. However it is now entirely passed off. We are here lounging our time away, doing nothing, and having nothing to do. It gives me great regret to be passing my time so uselessly when it could have been so importantly employed at home. I cannot but believe that we shall become ashamed of staying here, and go home in February or March at furthest. Nor are we relieved by the pleasures of society here. For partly from bankruptcies partly from party dissensions society is torn up by the roots. I envy those who stay at home, enjoying the society of their friendly neighbors, blessed with their firesides, and employed in doing something every day which looks useful to futurity. I expect you will of course charge me before my departure with procuring you such articles of convenience here as you can get best here. I shall be sending some things for my self in the spring. Tell Mr. Randolph I shall be glad from time to time to exchange meteorological diaries with him, that we may have a comparative view of the climates of this place and ours.[1] I received a letter from Maria last week. She had got quite well of her sprain and was then at the Chestnut grove. However I suppose you hear from one another more directly than through me. Let me also hear from you, as your welfare, Mr. Randolph's and the little ones are the things nearest my heart. Do not let them forget me. Adieu my dear Martha. Affectionately,

1. TJ made these observations from 1766 until 1820. They appear in three manuscript volumes: 1776–1820, 1785–1786, and 1802–1815 (MHi). He also made similar notations in certain of his account books. The exchange with Thomas Mann Randolph, Jr., was first made in New York City in 1790.

To Mary Jefferson Eppes

Philadelphia Jan. 7.98.

I acknowledge, my dear Maria, the reciept of yours in a letter I wrote to Mr. Eppes. It gave me the welcome news that your sprain was well. But you are not to suppose it entirely so. The joint will remain weak for a considerable time and give you occasional pains much longer. The state of things at Chestnut grove is truly distressing. Mr. B's habitual intoxication will destroy himself, his fortune and family. Of all calamities this is the greatest. I wish my sister could bear his misconduct with more patience. It might lessen his attachment to the bottle, and at any rate would make her own time more tolerable. When we see ourselves in a situation which must be endured and gone through, it is best to make up our minds to it. Meet it with firmness and accomodate every thing to it in the best way practicable. This lessens the evil, while fretting and fuming only serves to increase our own torment. The errors and misfortunes of others should be a school for our own instruction. Harmony in the marriage state is the very first object to be aimed at. Nothing can preserve affections uninterrupted but a firm resolution never to differ in will and a determination in each to consider the love of the other as of more value than any object whatever on which a wish has been fixed. How light in fact is the sacrifice of any other wish, when weighed against the affections of one with whom we are to pass our whole life and though opposition in a single instance will hardly of itself produce alienation; yet every one has their pouch into which all these little oppositions are put. While that is filling, the alienation is insensibly going on, and when filled, it is complete. It would puzzle either to say why; because no one difference of opinion has been marked enough to produce a serious effect by itself. But he finds his affections wearied out by a constant string of little checks and obstacles. Other sources of discontent, very common indeed, are the little cross purposes of husband and wife in common conversation, a disposition either to criticise and question whatever the other says, a desire always to demonstrate and make him feel himself in the wrong, and especially in company. Nothing is so goading. Much better therefore, if our companion views a thing in a light different from what we do to leave him in quiet possession of his view. What is the use of rectifying him if the thing be unimportant; and if important let it pass for the present, and wait a softer moment and more conciliatory occasion of revising the subject together. It is wonderful how many persons are rendered unhappy by inattention to these little rules of prudence. I have been insensibly led, by the particular case you mention, to sermonize to you on the subject generally. However if it is the means of saving you from a single heart-ache, it will have contributed a great deal to my happiness. But before I finish the sermon, I must add a word on economy. The unprofitable condition of Virginia estates in general, leaves it now next to impossible for the holder of one to avoid ruin. And this condition will continue until some change takes place in the mode of working them. In the mean time nothing can save us and our children from beggary but a determination to get a year beforehand, and restrain ourselves rigorously this year to the clear profits of the last. If a debt is once contracted by a farmer it is never paid but by a sale. The article of dress is perhaps that in which economy is the least to be recommended. It is so important to each to continue to please the other, that the happiness of both requires the most pointed attention to whatever may contribute to it, and the more as time makes greater inroads on our person. Yet generally we become slovenly in proportion as personal decay requires the contrary. I have great comfort in believing that your understanding and dispositions will engage your attention to these considerations; and that you are connected with a person and family who, of all within the circle of my acquaintance, are most in the dispositions which will make you happy. Cultivate their affections, my dear, with assiduity. Think every sacrifice a gain which shall tend to attach them to you. My only object in life is to see yourself and your sister, and those deservedly dear to you, not only happy, but in no danger of becoming unhappy.

I have lately recieved a letter from your friend Kitty Church. I inclose it to you. I think the affectionate expressions relative to yourself and the advance she has made will require a letter from you to her. It will be impossible to get a chrystal here to fit your watch without the watch itself. If you should know of any one coming to Philadelphia, send it to me, and I will get you a stock of chrystals. The river being frozen up, I shall not be able to send your things till it opens, which will probably be some time in February. I inclose to Mr. Eppes some pamphlets. Present me affectionately to all the family, and be assured of my tenderest love to yourself. Adieu,   TH: JEFFERSON

FROM MARTHA JEFFERSON RANDOLPH

Bellmont Jan. 22, 1798

Jupiter had given us so terrible an account of your sufferings from the ice on the potowmac that we began to be seriously alarmed about you before the arrival of your letters, which came both to gether; it was with infinite pleasure that we learned you had got the better of your cold and were at least comfortably if not agreably fixed for the winter. It is much more than we can boast of, for the extreme dampness of the situation and an absolute want of offices of every kind to shelter the servants whilst in the performance of their duties, have occasioned more sickness than I ever saw in a family in my life. Pleurisies, rhumatism and every disorder proceeding from cold have been so frequent that we have scarcely had at any one time *well* enough to tend the sick. Our intercourse with Monticello has been allmost *daily*. They have been generally well there except Tom and Goliah who are both *about* again and poor little Harriot[1] who died a few days after you left us. I shall joyfully accept the offer you made of executing my commissions in Philadelphia. Mr. Randolph has some money remaining in Barnes's hands[2] which I should be extremely obliged to you to lay out in plate, table spoons tea spoons, &c. as far as it will go. I imagine there is enough of it for that purpose and as much (considering the many other urgent calls for money building will occasion) as will be convenient to bestow upon that article and if such a thing is to be had a *game of the goose*.[3] It was a promise made to the children which Richmond does not furnish the means of paying. I look forward with great impatience to March. I am afraid to flatter my self with the hope of seeing you sooner and I feel every day more strongly the impossibility of becoming habituated to your absence. Sepparated in my infancy from every other friend, and accustomed to look up to you alone, every sentiment of tenderness my nature was susceptible of was for many years centered in you, and no connexion formed since that could weaken a sentiment interwoven with my very existence. I have heard from Maria thru Mr. Eppes. She deals much in promises but very little in deeds that are to be performed with a pen. She was in as good health and better spirits than usual. Adieu my dearest Father. The children unanimously join in love to you and believe me with every sentiment of tenderness gratitude and respect, your affectionate child,   M. RANDOLPH

1. Tom Shackleford and Goliah were slave laborers at Monticello. "Little Harriot" was the eldest daughter of Sally Hemings, the slave who accompanied Mary to Paris. She was born in 1795 and died October 5, 1797. Consult *Farm Book* for the slave rolls and also *Memoirs of a Monticello Slave* (1955), 55–57.

2. John Barnes, a Philadelphia factor with whom TJ had long and cordial business relations. These continued after Barnes's removal to Washington and TJ's retirement from public life.

3. A game played with counters on a board that has been divided into compartments. It is sometimes called "Fox and Geese."

FROM MARY JEFFERSON EPPES

Eppington February 1st 1798

May I thank you My Dear Papa for your last letter. The advice with which it is fill'd, I feel the importance of, and the solicitude it expresses for my happiness makes me sensible how gratefully I will endeavour to follow it. I hope I shall never do otherwise for I feel more and more every day how much the happiness of my life depends on deserving your approbation. You will have heard I suppose before you recieve this of my aunt Skipwiths[1] death an event which was render'd by her situation before it, a relief to her friends, who began to apprehend a long life of insanity. She had been for two months before she died, tho quite well otherwise and perfectly out of her senses, that she knew no one about her, and expir'd in that situation. The family here will go in a week to her funeral. We shall stay sometime there to comfort the poor children and most of all poor Betsy whose sufferings for her mothers situation have but too much allready affected her health. We left Richmond a few days ago and I should have written to you there, but I had not time. We saw Mr. W. Hylton there, who inform'd us that his son, with Mr. Lawrence, had rented Richneck[2] of him for 1000 pounds a year, in consequence of which he goes to live in Berkely[3] where he has bought land of a gentleman who is engaged to Mrs. Campbell his daughter and will be married to her this spring. This piece of news I thought would not be disagreable to you as he has given over all thoughts of settling in our neighbourhood. I will write to Kitty Church soon and enclose my letter in one to you. Adieu dear Papa. I am your affectionate daughter, M E

1. Anne Wayles Skipwith (Mrs. Henry).
2. Richneck was an estate of 4,000 acres in Warwick County owned by Wilson Miles Cary. Jane Carr Cary lived there after her husband's (Wilson Cary, son of Miles) death until financial conditions forced a sale. Daniel Hylton informed TJ on May 24, 1793 (Carr Cary Papers, ViU), "that in conjunction with Mr. Miles King Doctor Wm. Foushee and brother Mr. Wm. Hylton we have made a purchase of Mr. Wilson Miles Cary for his plantation call'd Richneck situated on the Warwick River to carry on the lumber business in its various branches."
An excellent map for locating Richneck, Ceeleys, Rock Castle, Eppington, and other Virginia and Maryland estates, and particularly churches, of the 17th and 18th centuries is Leonard Leland, *Map of the Chesapeake Bay Country . . . Featuring more Particularly Tidewater Virginia* (n.p., MCMXXXIX), original in the College of William and Mary Library. Photocopies at ViU and Monticello.
3. Probably Berkeley County (now West Virginia), which at this time was attracting a number of eastern Virginians.

TO MARTHA JEFFERSON RANDOLPH

Philadelphia Feb. 8. 98.

I ought oftener, my dear Martha, to recieve your letters, for the very great pleasure they give me, and especially when they express your affections for me. For though I cannot doubt them, yet they are among those truths which tho' not doubted we love to hear repeated. Here too they serve like gleams of light, to chear a dreary scene where envy, hatred, malice, revenge, and all the worse passions of men are marshalled to make one another as miserable as possible. I turn from this with pleasure to contrast it with your fire side, where the single evening I passed at it was worth more than ages here. Indeed I feel myself detaching very fast, perhaps too fast, from every thing but yourself, your sister, and those who are identified with you. These form the last hold the world will have on me, the cords which will be cut only when I am loosened from this state of being. I am looking forward to the spring with all the fondness of desire to meet you all once more, and with the change of season, to enjoy also a change of scene and of society. Yet the time of our leaving this is not yet talked of. I am much concerned to hear the state of health of Mr. Randolph and the family, mentioned in your letters of Jan. 22. and 28. Surely, my dear, it would be better for you to remove to Monticello. The south pavillion, the Parlour and Study will accomodate your family;[1] and I should think Mr. Randolph would find less inconvenience in the riding it would occasion him than in the loss of his own and his family's health. Let me beseech you then to go there, and to use every thing and every body as if I were there. If Mr. Randolph will take on himself to command the usual functions of the servants, carts, waggons, and other resources of the place, you may make yourselves comfortable there. I shall anxiously hope to hear that you adopt this plan. I wrote to Mr. Randolph on the subject of a rider for our Fredericksburg post who may be relied on. The proposition should be here, if any one will undertake it, by the 14th. inst. but the postmaster has promised to keep it open a little longer. £ 100. Virginia money will be given, if the person be approvedly trustworthy. All your commissions shall be executed, not forgetting the game of the goose, if we can find out what it is; for there is some difficulty in that. Kiss all the little ones for me: present me affectionately to Mr. Randolph, and my warmest love to yourself. Adieu.

1. This points out the very slow pace in the remodeling of Monticello. The house had been unroofed since about September, 1797, and five months later only two rooms had coverings, and these temporary.

To Mary Jefferson Eppes

Philadelphia Mar. 7. 98.

I have recieved yours, my dear Maria, of Feb. 1. and with that extreme gratification with which I recieve all the marks of your affection. My impatience to get from hence is urged by the double motives of escaping from irksome scenes here, and meeting yourself and others dear to us both. No time is yet spoken of for our adjournment; yet as there is likely to arise nothing which might keep Congress together, I cannot but hope we shall separate early in the next month. I still count on joining you at Eppington on my return. I recieve from home very discouraging accounts of Davenport's[1] doing nothing towards covering the house. I have written to him strongly on the subject, expressing my expectations to find the roof finished at my return. But I fear it will not pro-duce the effect desired. We are sure however of the Outchamber for you, and the Study for myself, and will not be long in getting a cover over some room for your sister. My last letter from Belmont was of Feb. 12. when they were all well. They have found the house there unhealthy, and their situation in general not pleasant. I pressed them to go to Monticello where they would be relieved from the inconvenience if just of a cellar full of water under them. I have not heard from them since. Mr. Trist is gone on to purchase Mr. Lewis's place.[2] They will not remove there till the fall. He is to be married to a Miss Brown of this place, an amiable girl, and who I hope will be of value to you as a neighbor. Having no news for Mr. Eppes but what he will find in a paper inclosed herewith, I do not write to him. My salutations to him, Mr. and Mrs. Eppes and the family at Eppington. To yourself my tenderest love,

TH: JEFFERSON

1. William Davenport was a sawyer and carpenter at Monticello.

2. Hore Browse Trist, son of Eliza House Trist (Mrs. Nicholas), purchased property in Albemarle County, Virginia, from James Lewis. The present estate of Birdwood was part of the original Trist purchase. Trist married Mary Brown of Philadelphia.

FROM MARY JEFFERSON EPPES

Eppington March 20th 1798

DEAR PAPA

We have been to Cumberland since I wrote to you last and saw while there the last melancholy rites paid to my Aunt Skipwith; I was never more affected, and never so sensible of the cruelty of requiring the presence of those who are most deeply afflicted at the ceremony. We came down immediately after it and brought poor Betsy for whom the scene had been too much with us, as her father fear'd her relapsing into her former state of melancholy if left alone so soon after it. We had a dreadful journey down and thought ourselves fortunate in escaping with one oversetting only, in which except the fright, none of us suffer'd, for the roads were as bad as they could possibly be. I am sorry to hear that my sisters situation at Belmont is not as agreeable as she expected, tho I shall rejoice if it occasions her return to Monticello. How much do I wish for that day which will reunite us all after so long an absence, but I am afraid it will be some time yet before it arrives. The family here would all be allmost as much dissapointed as myself were you not to return by this place, particularly my father, who can think he says of nothing but the improvements he saw at Monticello, and intends to get you to plan when you come, a cover'd way from the Maidens hall, to the house, with an alcove in it, and an octagon to the other wing. Aunt Carr is return'd from Celies[1] in good health and is at present with Aunt Bolling, who is in tolerable health, the former will be here soon, where she will stay I expect and go up with us. Adieu Dear Papa. That I may see you soon again and in good health is the earnest prayer of your affectionate daughter,   M E

1. Ceelys was a large plantation near Hampton in Elizabeth City County, about twenty miles below Williamsburg. It was owned by Wilson Cary, Aunt Carr's son-in-law.

To Mary Jefferson Eppes

Philadelphia Apr. 1. 98.

My dear Maria

Yours of Mar. 20. came to hand yesterday. You are not aware of consequences of writing me a letter in so fair a hand, and one as easily read. It puts you in great danger of the office of private secretary at Monticello, which would sometimes be a laborious one. Your letter was 11. days coming here, and Mr. Eppes's of Feb. 8. was 19. days on it's way. This shews that there is something wrong in the time they take to get into the mail; for from Richmond here is but about 5. or 6. days. I feared some of my letters may have miscarried. I hope Mr. Eppes recieved that of Feb. 18. covering an order to Quarrier to deliver my chariot to him, and asking his and your acceptance of it. Should that have miscarried, this serves to make the same tender. I have still hopes of being able to come by Eppington: but these become less firm in proportion as Congress lengthens their sessions; for that route would add a fortnight to the length of my journey. If I do not get home within a certain time, I shall not finish the hull of the house this year, and if I do not finish that this year, then I cannot build my mill the next. But whatever rout I am obliged to adopt, I will give you timely notice. They talk of not rising here till the last of this month. Should I not be able to come by the way of

Eppington, still, tell Mr. Eppes, I will make a visit from Monticello, rather than lose the colonnade and octagon.[1] So he will not get off from his purposes by that excuse. My last letter from Belmont was of the 19th. but Mr. Trist came from there since and reports that all were well. He is about sending off his furniture He has taken the house in Charlottesville that was George Nicholas's,[2] and will be living there before mid summer. My affectionate salutations to Mrs. Eppes, the gentlemen, and young ones, and kisses and everlasting love yourself. Adieu.

Mar. 16. The 1st. shad here.

28. The weeping willow begins to shew green leaves.

1. TJ did offer suggestions for the alteration of Eppington. A colonnade and octagonal projection were constructed. They are not visible today nor are they shown on a delineation of the front of the house that is included on a survey of the property made in 1865. This survey is now hanging in Eppington.

2. Wilson Cary Nicholas' brother. It was he who moved in the legislature for an investigation of TJ as war governor. He later removed to Kentucky.

To Martha Jefferson Randolph

Philadelphia. Apr. 5. 98.

Mr. Randolph's letter of Mar. 26. informs me you are all well at Belmont. My last news from Eppington was of Mar. 20. when all were well there. I have myself had remarkably good health through the winter, since the cold which I took on my way here. The advance of the season makes me long to get home. The first shad we had here was Mar. 16. and Mar. 28. was the first day we could observe a greenish hue on the weeping willow from it's young leaves. Not the smallest symptom of blossoming yet on any species of fruit tree. All this proves that we have near two months in the year of vegetable life, and of animal happiness so far as they are connected, more in our canton than here. The issue of a debate now before the H. of Representatives will enable us to judge of the time of adjournment. But it will be some days before the issue is known. In the mean time they talk of the last of this month. Letters by a late arrival from France give reason to believe they do not mean to declare war against us; but that they mean to destroy British commerce with all nations, neutral as well as belligerent. To this the Swedes and Danes submit, and so must we unless we prefer war. A letter from Mr. Short informs me of the death of the old Dutchess Danville. He talks of coming in this spring or summer. I have purchased an excellent harpsichord[1] for Maria, which I hope is by this time arrived at Monticello, with a box of trees to which I asked Mr. Randolph's attention by the last post. Among these were cranberries, raspberries and strawberries of great value. I am afflicted with the difficulty of procuring horses for the farm, or rather for the waggon in place of the mules to be turned over to the farm, which is a good idea. I am afflicted too with the fear that the roof of the house is not going on as my necessities require. I have engaged a fine housejoiner[2] here to go on with me. My most friendly salutations to Mr. Randolph and tenderest love to yourself and the little ones. Adieu affectionately,

1. TJ made the first payment on March 21: "Gave Harper ord. on Barnes for 40. D. in part for harpsichord." Account Book 1798.

2. James Dinsmore superintended the construction of Monticello and executed much of the woodwork, from 1798 until he went out of TJ's employ in 1809, the year the house is presumed to have been finished.

FROM MARTHA JEFFERSON RANDOLPH

Bellmont May 12 1798

DEAREST FATHER

Nothing makes me feel your absence so sensibly as the beauty of the season; when every object in nature invites one into the fields, the close monotonous streets of a city which offers no charms of society with in doors to compensate for the dreariness of the scene without, must be absolutely intolerable: particularly to you who have such interesting employment at home. Monticello shines with a transcendent luxury of vegetation above the rest of the neighbourhood. As yet, we have been entirely supplied with vegetables from there having no sort of a garden here nor any prospect of one this year. I am glad to have it in my power to give you a more favorable account of things than Mr. Randolph did in his last which was written immediately after a frost that blasted every appearance of vegetation, but John[1] informs me alltho the peaches cherries (except the kentish) and figs which had been uncovered were gone past recovery for *this* year, yet of strawberries, rasp berries, currants &c. &c. &c. there will be more than common. I dined at Monticello a fortnight ago and saw Maria's harpsichord which arrived safe except the lock and 1 or 2 pieces of the moulding which got torn off some way. It is a charming one I think tho certainly inferior to mine. You have probably not heard of the death of poor Aunt Fleming.[2] That of Mrs. Archer (Polly Bolling that was)[3] is still more recent. It took place at her

Father's house a few weeks since. We have been all well but
Jefferson who had declined rapidly for some time from a disorder which had baffled every attention and change of diet, the
only remedy we ventured to try, but Mr. Sneed[4] opening school
and Jeffy[5] being hurried out of bed every morning at sunrise and
obliged after a breakfast of bread and milk to walk 2 miles to
school: his spirits returned his complexion cleared up and I am in
hopes that his disorder has left him entirely. He is much mended
in appearance strength and spirits, which had been low to an
alarming degree. Anne just begins to read and little Ellen points
at grand Papa's picture[6] over the chimney when ever she is asked
where he is. Adieu my Dearest Father. Blest as I am in my family
you are still wanting to compleat my happiness. Monticello will
be interesting indeed when with the prospect of it the loved idea
of yourself and Dear Maria will be so intimately blended as they
will in a few weeks I hope. Once more adieu and believe me with
every sentiment of affection yours,   MRANDOLPH

1. A slave.
2. Mary Randolph Fleming (Mrs. Tarlton).
3. Martha Bolling Archer (Mrs. Field), a Jefferson niece.
4. Possibly Benjamin Snead.
5. Thomas Jefferson Randolph.
6. Probably the Mather Brown original of Jefferson, which was lost at
sea in 1823 while in transit from Monticello to Boston with other possessions
of Ellen Wayles Coolidge (Mrs. Joseph). See Alfred L. Bush, *The Life Portraits of Thomas Jefferson* (Charlottesville, 1962), [14]–16. This is the latest
and most authoritative study of Jefferson's iconography.

To Martha Jefferson Randolph

Philadelphia May 17. 98.

MY DEAR MARTHA

Having nothing of business to write on to Mr. Randolph this
week I with pleasure take up my pen to express all my love to
you, and my wishes once more to find myself in the only scene
where, for me, the sweeter affections of life have any exercise. But
when I shall be with you seems still uncertain. We have been so
long looking forward from 3. weeks to 3. weeks, and always with
disappointment, that I know not now what to expect. I shall immediately write to Maria and recommend to Mr. Eppes and her
to go up to Monticello as soon as my stores, which went from
here a week ago, shall be sent on from Richmond; because our
groceries &c. were pretty well exhausted when I left home. These
may well arrive at Richmond by about the 20th. instant, so that

if my recommendation is adopted they may be soon with you, and contribute some variety to your scene. For you to feel all the happiness of your quiet situation, you should know the rancorous passions which tear every breast here, even of the sex which should be a stranger to them. Politics and party hatreds destroy the happiness of every being here. They seem like salamanders, to consider fire as their element. I am in hopes you make free use of the garden and any other resources at Monticello. The children I am afraid will have forgotten me. However my memory may perhaps be hung on the game of the goose which I am to carry them. Kiss them for me, and present me affectionately to Mr. Randolph. To yourself my tenderest love and adieu.

TH: JEFFERSON

P. S. Since writing the above, Richardson has called on me. He has recieved a letter from Mr. Duke[1] expressing doubts whether he shall be able to go and do Mr. Randolph's work. He has therefore determined to leave this place in the first vessel, and you may expect him in 3. or 4. weeks to be with you ready for work, and much improved, from what he has seen and done here.

1. Probably Henry Duke, a brickmason at Monticello.

To Mary Jefferson Eppes

Philadelphia May 18. 98.

MY DEAR MARIA

It is very long since I have heard from Eppington. The last letter I [received] was from Mr. Eppes dated Apr. 4. So long without hearing from you, I cannot be without uneasiness for your health. I have been constantly in the hope that we were within 3. or 4. weeks of rising, but so often disappointed [and] I begin to lose my faith as to any period of adjournment; and some begin now openly to avow that it would not be proper for Congress to separate. Under this uncertainty I would wish you not to put off your return to Monticello, if Mr. Eppes and yourself would find it agreeable to be there and indeed I think his experience of ill health in the lower country, should urge him to quit it before the hot weather comes on. I sent from here on the 19th. instant the necessary groceries and stores for the use of the family. These will probably be arrived at Richmond by the time you recieve this, and I have desired Mr. Jefferson[1] to forward them up by water immediately, and to give Mr. Eppes notice; in order that you may time your journey so as to find them there. All other necessaries, either in the house or for me, have [administered] to you as if I were there. I have given notice to them at home that you will come and I shall have the pleasure of finding you there as soon as I can get from here, and in the mean time brood over the pain of being uselessly kept from among the society and scenes for which alone I would wish to prolong life one moment. For here it is worse than nothing. You will find your harpsichord arrived at Monticello, and without injury as Mr. Randolph informs me. I shall go of necessity by the shortest route to Monticello, and of course must deny myself the pleasure of taking Eppington in my way this time. Present my friendly salutations to Mr. and Mrs. Eppes; as also to our Mr. Eppes and the family. To yourself my tenderest love and Adieu.   TH: JEFFERSON

1. George Jefferson was a partner in the Richmond firm of Gibson and Jefferson and also TJ's cousin.

FROM MARY JEFFERSON EPPES

Eppington May 27th 98

DEAR PAPA

In hopes every day of recieving the long wish'd for and long expected summons to meet you at Monticello, I have delayed answering your last letter which you laughing and reproved me so justly for my negligence and inattention in writing. From your last to Mr. Eppes he does not expect that you will come in till near the 20th of next month, till which time unless your return should be sooner we shall stay down, as he is obliged to be here at that time. I have been to Petersburg lately with the girls, Bolling, and Tabby Walker,[1] one of her cousins, to take the small-pox which they have had most favourably; and from there we went to Shirley with my mother who is an old acquaintance and was recieved with much pleasure. We there met with Mr. John Walker and his lady, the latter seem'd pleas'd to see me and press'd me to visit her at her house, but I was not sorry that her husband did not think proper to invite me, for it would have been disagreeable to be forced to invent excuses where there was one so evident and so insurmountable.[2] I suppose you have not heard of Polly Archers death, render'd more afflicting to Aunt Bolling from her just suspicions that she hasten'd it by her intemperance in eating. She died of a bilious fever, a fort-night after her child was born, which is now alive and well and seems allready to afford much consolation to my aunt. She intends to go up this summer. I heard very lately from Mr. Randolph that my Sister and her children were well. Mr. Eppes met him in Richmond, but amongst the many enquiries he made he forgot to ask if my harpsichord had arrived safe at Monticello. Mr. Jefferson had before sent me word it was gone up. Adieu dear Papa. Aunt Carr is here and waits as impatiently as myself for the welcome letter that will inform us you are on your way home. Adieu once more and believe me your truly affectionate daughter.   MEPPES

1. The daughter of Colonel Henry Walker of Boydton, Mecklenburg County.

2. Mary and Mrs. Francis Eppes were paying a call on the Carters at Shirley. The Mr. John Walker and lady undoubtedly were those of the "Walker Affair" in which Jefferson as a youth made improper advances toward his Albemarle County friend's wife. See Malone, *Jefferson the Virginian*, Appendix III, 447–51, for a summation of the affair.

TO MARTHA JEFFERSON RANDOLPH

Philadelphia May 31. 98.

MY DEAR MARTHA

My letter by the last post was to Mr. Randolph, dated May 24. Yours of the 12th. inst did not get to hand till the 29th. so it must have laid by a post somewhere. The receipt of it, by kindling up all my recollections increases my impatience to leave this place and every thing which can be disgusting, for Monticello and my dear family, comprising every thing which is pleasurable to me in this world. It has been proposed in Congress to adjourn on the 14th. of June. I have little expectation of it myself: but whatever be their determination, I am determined myself; and my letter of next week will probably carry orders for my horses. Jupiter should therefore be in readiness to depart on a night's warning, with three horses, as a workman accompanies me from here. It will be necessary also to send for my letter to the post office the evening of it's arrival, or rather to order him to attend the arrival of the post at Milton, and carry the letters to Belmont to recieve his orders if any. Some think Congress will wait here till their envoys[1] return from France, for whom a vessel was sent the 1st. of April, so that they may be here the 2d week of July. Others think they will not adjourn at all, as they have past a bill for capturing French armed vessels found near our coast, which is pretty generally considered as a commencement of war without a declaration. So that we consider war as no longer doubtful.

Volney[2] and a ship load of others of his nation will sail from hence on Sunday. Another ship load will go in about 3. weeks. A bill is now brought in to suspend all communication with France and her dominions: and we expect another to declare our treaty with her void. Mr. Randolph will percieve that this certainty of war must decide the objects of our husbandry to be such as will keep to the end of it. I am sorry to hear of Jefferson's indisposition, but glad you do not physic him. This leaves nature free and unembarrassed in her own tendencies to repair what is wrong. I hope to hear or to find that he is recovered. Kiss them all for me. Remember me affectionately to Mr. Randolph and be assured yourself of my constant and tenderest love. Adieu,

TH: JEFFERSON

P.S. It would be well that Davenport should be immediately informed that I am coming home. Since writing this I have recieved a letter from Mr. Eppes, informing me that all are well there. He and Maria will set out for Monticello June 20th.

TH: JEFFERSON

1. Charles Cotesworth Pinckney, John Marshall, and Elbridge Gerry had been sent to France to secure a treaty of amity and commerce. Their contemptuous treatment by and the attitude of the French government thoroughly aroused public opinion in America. Congress, fearing war, attempted to consolidate the national defense by passing twenty acts between March 27 and July, 1798, aimed at improving our military posture. On June 13 a bill suspending commercial intercourse with France was enacted. Other bills of May and July authorized the seizure of armed French ships but not of merchantmen, and on July 7 Congress declared the treaty with France void.

2. Count Constantin François Volney was a French philosopher and a friend of TJ's then residing in Philadelphia.

To Mary Jefferson Eppes

Philadelphia [June. 6. 98.]

MY DEAR MARIA

I wrote you last on the 18th. of May since which [I have received Mr. Eppes's] letter of May 20. and yours of May 27. I have deter[mined to set out from this] place on the 20th. inst. and shall, in my letters of tomo[rrow, order] my horses to meet me at Fredericksburg on the 24th. and may therefore be at home on the 26th. or 27th. where I shall hope to have the happiness of meeting you. I can supply the information you want as to your harpsichord. Your sister writes me it is arrived in perfect safety except the lock and a bit of moulding broke off. She played on it and pronounces it a very fine one, though without some of the advantages of hers, as the Celestini for instance. If I did not mistake it's tone, it will be found sweeter for a moderate room, but not as good as hers for a large one.

I forward for Mr. Eppes some further dispatches from our envoys. To this it is said in addition that Mr. Pinckney is gone into the South of France for the health of his daughter, Mr. Marshall to Amsterdam, perhaps to come home for orders, and Mr. Gerry remains at Paris. They have no idea of war between the two countries, and much less that we have authorized the commencement of it.

I will convince you at Monticello whether I jested or was in earnest about your writing. And as, while it will relieve me, it may habituate you to an useful exercise, I shall perhaps be less scrupulous than you might wish. My friendly salutations to Mrs. Eppes, the two gentlemen and family. To yourself the most tender and constant affection and Adieu,　　　　Th: Jefferson

From Martha Jefferson Randolph

Bellmont Saturday Morning
recd July 1.98.

It is easier to concieve than express the sensations which the sight of the preparations for your return inspires us. I look forward to Thursday with raptures and palpitations not to be described; that day which will once more reunite me to those most dear to me in the world. Adieu Dearest and adored Father. The heart swellings with which I address you when absent and look forward to your return convince me of the folly or want of feeling of those who dare to think that any *new* ties can weaken the first and best of nature. The first sensations of my life were affection and respect for you and none others in the course of it have weakened or surpassed that. The children all send their love to grand Papa and count the days with infinite anxiety. Yours with the tenderest love and reverence,　　　　MRandolph

To Mary Jefferson Eppes

Monticello July 13. 98.

My dear Maria

I arrived here on the 3d. inst. expecting to have found you here and we have been ever since imagining that every sound we heard was that of the carriage which was once more to bring us together. It was not till yesterday I learnt by the reciept of Mr. Eppes's letter of June 30th. that you had been sick, and were only on the recovery at that date. A preceding letter of his, referred to in that of the 30th. must have miscarried. We are now infinitely more anxious, not so much for your arrival here as your firm establishment in health, and that you may not be thrown back by your journey. Much therefore, my dear, as I wish to see you, I beg you not to attempt the journey till you are quite strong enough, and then only by short day's journies. A relapse will only keep us the longer asunder and is much more formidable than a first attack. Your sister and family are with me. I would have gone to you instantly on the reciept of Mr. Eppes's letter, had that not assured me you were well enough to take the bark. It would also have stopped my workmen here, who cannot proceed an hour without me, and I am anxious to provide a cover which may enable me to have my family and friends about me. Nurse yourself therefore with all possible care for your own sake, for mine, and that of all those who love you, and do not attempt to move sooner or quicker than your health admits. Present me affectionately to Mr. Eppes father and son, to Mrs. Eppes and all the family, and be assured that my impatience to see you can only be moderated by the stronger desire that your health may be safely and firmly re-established. Adieu affectionately,   TH: J.

To Mary Jefferson Eppes

Monticello July 14. 1798

I arrived here, my dear Maria, on the 3d. inst. and was in the daily hope of recieving you, when Mr. Eppes's letter of June 30. by the post of day before yesterday, gave us the first notice of your being sick.[1] Some preceding letter we infer had explained the nature of your indisposition, but it has never come to hand. We are therefore still uninformed of it. Your sister and myself wrote yesterday to you by post, but I have concluded to-day to send express that we may learn your situation of a certainty, and in a shorter time. I hope the bearer will find you so advanced in recovery as to be able ere long to set out for this place. Yet anxiously as we wish to see you, I must insist on your not undertaking the journey till you are quite strong enough, and then only by very short stages. To attempt it too soon will endanger a relapse which will keep us longer apart, and is always more tedious than the origi[nal] attack. I have been confined some days by very sore eyes.[2] This is the first day they seem to have mended. I should otherwise probably have set out to see you immediately [on] reciept of Mr. Eppes's letter. My workmen too are unable to proceed one day without me [and] I am anxious to have a cover for my family and friends. I sh[all conti]nue in great uneasiness till the return of the bearer by whom I shall hope to know the truth of your situation, [and] in every event to learn that you maintain good spirits and do every thing necessary [to] restore yourself to health and to those who love you with the tenderest sensibility. Adieu my dear, and ever dear Maria. Let me know that you are well, [and bravely] determined [to be so speedily], (for these things depend much on our own will). Write to shorten our longing expectations of seeing you. Again adieu. Your's affectionately,

TH: JEFFERSON

1. Mary's ailment is not known.
2. The cause of TJ's sore eyes is not established; it is to be noted that this is the first mention of them. On May 21 he purchased spectacles from William Richardson of Philadelphia. Account Book 1798.

TO MARTHA JEFFERSON RANDOLPH

Wednesday. Aug. 15. 98.

TH: J. TO HIS DEAR MARTHA

Ellen appeared to be feverish the evening you went away: but visiting her a little before I went to bed, I found her quite clear of fever, and was convinced the quickness of pulse which had alarmed me had proceeded from her having been in uncommon spirits and been constantly running about the house through the day and especially in the afternoon. Since that she has had no symptom of fever, and is otherwise better than when you left her. The girls indeed suppose she had a little fever last night, but I am sure she had not, as she was well at 8. oclock in the evening and very well in the morning, and they say she slept soundly through the night. They judged only from her breathing. Every body else is well: and only wishing to see you. I am persecuted with questions 'when I think you will come?' My respects to Mr. and Mrs. Carter[1] and affectionate salutations to our more particular friends. If you set out home after dinner be sure to get off between four and five. Adieu my dear.

1. Mr. and Mrs. William Champe Carter were then residing in the southern part of Albemarle County, in Saint Anne's Parish.

To Mary Jefferson Eppes

Monticello Dec. 8. 98.

MY DEAR MARIA

I wrote to Mr. Eppes three weeks ago. Immediately after the date of that letter Lucy increased her family. She is doing well except as to her breasts. The one so much out of order when you went away, still continues in the same state, and the other threatens to rise also, which would entirely prevent her giving suck. She could not be moved in their present condition. I expect to set out for Philadelphia within ten days, within which time I hope to see the two Mr. Eppes's here. Mr. Randolph is not yet returned from Richmond, tho' now expected in a day or two. His family is here and all well. Ellen continues as much so as a weak digestion will permit. Our house I hope will all be covered in in the course of three or four weeks more so as to be out of the way of suffering, but Buck's[1] leaving us, without laying any more floors has prevented our getting the use of any other room. We shall hear from you I hope by Mr. Eppes and learn that you are well, and all the good family at Eppington. Present me to them affectionately and tell [remainder torn away]

1. John H. Buck, a Monticello workman.

To Martha Jefferson Randolph

Philadelphia Dec. 27. 98.

MY DEAR MARTHA

I reached Fredericksburg the day after I left you, and this place on Christmas day, having (thanks to my pelisse[1]) felt no more sensation of cold on the road than if I had been in a warm bed. Nevertheless I got a small cold which brought on an inflammation in the eyes, head ach &c., so that I kept within doors yesterday and only took my seat in Senate to-day. I have as yet had little opportunity of hearing news; I only observe in general that the republican gentlemen whom I have seen consider the state of the public mind to be fast advancing in their favor. Whether their opponents will push for war or not is not yet developed. No business is as yet brought into the Senate, and very little into the other house: so that I was here in good time. I shall be at a loss how to direct to you hereafter, uncertain as I am whether you will leave home and where you will be. On this subject you must inform me. Present me affectionately to Mr. Randolph, and kiss all the little ones for me, not forgetting Elleanoroon. Be assured yourself of my constant and tender love. Adieu my ever dear Martha,

1. A long outer garment or cloak generally made of fur or lined with it.

To Mary Jefferson Eppes

Philadelphia Jan. 1. 99.

My dear Maria

I left Monticello on the 18th. of Dec. and arrived here to breakfast on the 25th. having experienced no accident of inconvenience except a slight cold, which brought back the inflammation of my eyes and still continues it, though so far mended as to give hopes of it's going off soon. I took my place in Senate before a single bill was brought in or other act of business done, except the Address which is exactly what I ought to have nothing to do with. And indeed I might have staid at home a week longer without missing any business, for of the last 11. days the Senate have met only on 5. and then little or nothing to do. However when I am to write on politics I shall address my letter to Mr. Eppes. To you I had rather indulge the effusions of a heart which tenderly loves you, which builds it's happiness on your's, and feels in every other object but little interest. Without an object here which is not alien to me, and barren of every delight, I turn to your situation with pleasure in the midst of a good family which loves you, and merits all your love. Go on, my dear, in cultivating the invaluable possession of their affections. The circle of our nearest connections is the only one in which a faithful and lasting affection can be found, one which will adhere to us under all changes and chances. It is therefore the only soil on which it is worth while to bestow much culture. Of this truth you will become more convinced every day you advance into life. I imagine you are by this time about removing to Mont-blanco.¹ The novelty of setting up house-keeping will, with all it's difficulties, make you very happy for a while. It's delights however pass away in time, and I am in hopes that by the spring of the year they will be no obstacle to your joining us at Monticello. I hope I shall on my return find such preparations made as will enable me rapidly to get one room after another prepared for the accommodation of our friends, and particularly of any who may be willing to accompany or visit you there. Present me affectionately to Mrs. and Mr. Eppes, father and son, and all the family. Remember how pleasing your letters will be to me, and be assured of my constant and tender love. Adieu, my ever dear Maria. Your's affectionately,

TH: JEFFERSON

1. John Wayles Eppes and Mary removed from Eppington and resided here, a few miles from Petersburg, during the first months of their marriage.

FROM MARY JEFFERSON EPPES

Eppington January 21st 99

I was writing to you My Dear Papa and apologizing for my silence which has for sometime past had been occasion'd by a slight indisposition when I recieved your last letter. How much does your kindness affect me my dear Papa? A kindness which I so little merit and surely, if the most grateful sense of it, if the tenderest love could in any degree entitle me to it, I should not be undeserving of it. Suffer me dear Papa to tell you, how much above all others you are dear to me. That I feel more if possible every day how necessary your presence is to my happiness, and while blest with that and your affection I can never be otherwise. But the time is not far-distant I hope that will again reunite us all. With what pleasure do I look forward to it, to see you once more settled at home and to be after so long an absence allways within a mile or two of you and my dear sister. An if you are indeed with us whose happiness can be compared with our! Mr. Eppes is now at the Hundred. He had turn'd off his overseer and finds his presence there indispensable. I shall join him as soon as it is in my power which will be in a week or two at the farthest. We shall remain there till he gets another. We shall then remove to Mont Blanco, and there I hope it will not be long before we shall see you. Let me remind you of your promise my dear Papa if not too inconvenient for you to perform, and tell you what delight I feel at the hope of seeing you there. Adieu my dear Papa, excuse this hasty scrawl for it is very late. Believe me your affectionate daughter,   M E
P S Mr. Eppes desired me to tell you that his father expects to recieve the next Cumberland court 30 pound more for you and wishes to know into whose hands he must commit it. The family here all join in love to you.

To Martha Jefferson Randolph

Philadelphia Jan. 23. 99.

The object of this letter, my very dear Martha, is merely to inform you I am well and to convey to you the expressions of my love. It will not be new to tell you that your letters do not come as often as I could wish. I have not heard from Albemarle or Chesterfield since I left home, now 5. weeks. This deprives me of the gleams of pleasure wanting to relieve the dreariness of this scene, where not one single occurrence is calculated to produce pleasing sensations. Tho' I hear not from you, I hope you are all well, and that the little ones, even Ellen talk of me sometimes. If your visit to Goochland has been relinquished as I expect, I shall hope to find you on my return still at Monticello. Within a post or two I shall announce to you the day for my cavalry to be sent off. In the mean time I feed my self with the pleasure which the approach of that day always gives me. I hope you will aid John in his preparations in the garden. I have heard nothing from Mr. Richardson about the hiring of labourers and consequently am anxious about my summer operations. Dr. Bache[1] will set out for our neighborhood next month. I have persuaded Mrs. Bache to let him go first and prepare a *gite*.[2] In the mean time they are packing their furniture. Let George[3] know that the nail rod sent from here in December has, with the vessel in which it was, been cast away at sea: and that another supply was shipped here two or three days ago, and will probably be at Richmond about the 10th. of February. Present me affectionately to Mr. Randolph to whom I inclose Gerry's correspondence and Pickering's[4] report. Kiss all the little ones, and recieve the tender and unmingled effusions of my love to yourself. Adieu, TH: JEFFERSON

1. Dr. William Bache was a son of Benjamin Franklin's daughter.
2. *Gite.* A resting or lodging place; a place of shelter.
3. "Great" or "Big" George, a slave who directed the operations of the Monticello Nailery from 1796 to 1799. He was Ursula's husband and father of Isaac. For the latter's memoirs, see *Memoirs of a Monticello Slave* (1955).
4. Timothy Pickering, Secretary of State.

To Martha Jefferson Randolph

Philadelphia Feb. 5. 99.

MY DEAR MARTHA

I wrote to Mr. Randolph on the 30th. of Jan. having just then recieved his of the 19th. It was not till yesterday that I learned from the Post office that our post now departs on Wednesday morning from this place. My letters hitherto have been written for Thursday morning, so that you will have recieved them a week later. Tell Mr. Randolph that the day on which I wrote to him, but after I had sealed my letter, a bill was brought in to raise 30. regiments of infantry, cavalry and artillery, on the event of an invasion or in case of imminent danger of invasion in the opinion of the President. Regiments are now proposed to be about 1000. Our land army will then be the *existing* army 5000. The additional army *9000*, this *eventual* army 30,000. (instead of the Provisional one of 10,000 the act for which is expired) and the *volunteer* army, which is now to be formed into brigades and divisions and to be exercised. We have no particular information as to the price of tobo. but generally that that as well as all other produce is higher in England than ever known. The immense quantities of paper which their circumstances have forced them to create are now sensibly felt in the enlivening effect which always takes place in the first moment in the delusive shape of prosperity. They are accordingly now singing Hosannas for the unparalleled rise of their finances, and manufactures. We shall catch a little of the benefit in the beginning as their paper money price for tobo. will be hard money to us. But it will soon be fetched up as their paper money price for manufactures will be a hard money price to us. We ought to prepare against being involved in their embarassments by setting in by times to domestic manufacture. Jupiter with my horse must be at Fredericksburg on Tuesday evening the 5th. of March. I shall leave this place on the 1st. or 2d. You will recieve this the 14th. inst. I am already lighthearted at the approach of my departure. Kiss my dear children for me. Inexpressible love to yourself and the sincerest affection to Mr. Randolph. Adieu.

To Mary Jefferson Eppes

Philadelphia Feb. 7. 99.

Your letter, my dear Maria, of Jan. 21. was recieved two days ago. It was, as Ossian[1] says, or would say, like the bright beams of the moon on the desolate heath. Environed here in scenes of constant torment, malice and obloquy, worn down in a station where no effort to render service can aver any thing, I feel not that existence is a blessing but when something recalls my mind to my family or farm. This was the effect of your letter, and it's affectionate expressions kindled up all those feelings of love for you and our dear connections which now constitute the only real happiness of my life. I am now feeding on the idea of my departure for Monticello which is but three weeks distant. The roads will then be so dreadful, that, as to visit you even by the direct route of Fredsg. and Richmond, would add 100. miles to the length of my journey, I must defer it in the hope that about the last of March or first of April, I may be able to take a trip express to see you. The roads will then be fine. Perhaps your sister may join in a flying trip, as it can only be for a few days. In the mean time let me hear from you. Letters which leave Richmond after the 21st. inst. should be directed to me at Monticello. I suppose you to be now at Mountblanco and therefore do not charge you with the delivery of those sentiments of esteem which I always feel for the family at Eppington. I write to Mr. Eppes. Continue always to love me, and to be assured that there is no object on earth so dear to my heart as your health and happiness, and that my tenderest affections always hang on you. Adieu my dear Maria.

TH: JEFFERSON

1. TJ is referring to the *Poems of Ossian* by James Macpherson. He was very fond of reading them even after he learned that Macpherson had composed rather than translated them from Gaelic. Sowerby 4377.

FROM MARTHA JEFFERSON RANDOLPH

Bellmont February 8, 1799

I am ashamed indeed my Dearest Father to have so *justly* incurred the reproach contained in your last. Allthough the trip down the country was soon relinquished, yet my time has been more varied than is usual with me. After your departure we spent ten days with Mrs. Divers,[1] Carr, Trist, &c. &c. &c. during which time I went to a ball in Charlottesville, *danced* at it and returned home fatigued and unwell to prepare for our return to Bellmont; where for the consideration of 20 £ Allen[2] consented to let us remain till the fifteenth of March. This will give Mr. Randolph time, at least to empty a barn for the reception of our furniture. The visit from Mrs. Jefferson[3] with preparations for a second ball where I accompanied her and the girls, added to the cares of the house hold some what increased by so long an absence from them, will account in some measure for the neglect of so sacred and agreable a duty. John has been once only to recieve orders about the garden; his excuse was the negligence of Phil in furnishing but one load of manure, the want of which he seemed to think rendered his attentions useless. Mr. Randolph will give you the details of the farm which he has visited twice during your absence, and the newspapers have informed you of the loss the friends of Liberty have sustained in the death of young Thomson[4] of Petersburg; which is the only event of any consequence that has taken place since you left us. For the rest, every thing stands as you left it, even your house. Davenport has I am afraid sold the plank he engaged to furnish for it, at least McGehee[5] told Mr. Randolph so, and he has certainly agreed to furnish some one in Milton with plank immediately. Mr. Randolph has some thoughts of employing a young man who has engaged to work for him (an acquaintance and recommended by McGehee) to do it if Davenport delays any longer. The children all join in tender love to you, from Virginia to *Annin Zoon*[6] who speaks much of you, and as a constant resource against *ill treatment* from her Papa and my self, whom she frequently threatens with going to *Phildelphy*. She sends her love to you and begs you will bring her a *cake*. I must beg the favor of you to bring for Jefferson the *newest* edition of Sandford and Merton.[7] The old edition consisting of two volumes are to be had in Richmond but as we have heard there is a third and perhaps fourth volume come out which are not to be met with there, I must apply to you to acquit my word with him. Since I began to write we have been informed that Davenport has this very day set about your work. Mr. Randolph finds it impossible to write by this post but bids me tell you the tobacco is just prized (13 hogsheads in all) and by the next post he will give you the details of the other operations of the farm. Adieu Dearest Father. I write in the midst of the noise of the children and particularly your little *seet heart*[8] who has interrupted me so often that I have scarcely been able to connect one sentence with another. Believe me with tenderest reverence and affection yours unchangeably,

M. RANDOLPH

1. Martha Walker Divers (Mrs. George), who resided at Farmington.
2. Probably Richard H. Allen, who in 1799 paid taxes on 328 acres in Fredericksville Parish, where Belmont was located. There were no Allens residing in Saint Anne's Parish. Albemarle County Land Book 1799, Albemarle County Courthouse.
3. Possibly Mrs. George Jefferson of Richmond or Mrs. Randolph Jefferson, TJ's sister-in-law.
4. John Lewis Thomson was author of *The Letters of Curtius*.
5. William McGehee.
6. Virginia (Jenny) Randolph was then living at Monticello and probably Anne Cary, a TJ granddaughter.
7. Thomas Day, *The History of Sandford and Merton* (London, 1783–1789), 3 volumes. A work intended for the use of children. Martha was referring probably to the 7th edition, of 1795. There was also a French edition [1798] and others.
8. Ellen Wayles Randolph.

FROM MARTHA JEFFERSON RANDOLPH

Bellmont February 22, 1799

Uncertain whether this will still find you at Philadelphia or no, I shall write but a few lines happy in the thoughts of it's being the last time I shall have it in my power to do so, before we embrace you. I have heard from Maria since the letter I recieved from you containing an account of her indisposition and recovery, and Mr. Eppes mentioned that she had been again unwell, too much so to go to Mont Blanc the appointed day. I have not heard from her since by which I hope she has not proved serious. Your tobacco is not gone down yet, George (smith) continues *ill* confined in Milton and some of the others are unwell, I do not recollect who but Mr. Randolph has been over several times lately so I suppose they have not suffered. Adieu Dearest Father. Your return is the favorite theme of us all, even little Ellen talks incessantly of you and I am certain she will know you, for she speaks with great tenderness of you, more, than she would of a person she did not remember, and love. Her constant message is to come home and bring her a cake. Adieu once more. Believe me with tenderness unspeakable your affectionate child,

M. RANDOLPH

TO MARY JEFFERSON EPPES

Monticello Mar. 8. 99.

MY DEAR MARIA

I am this moment arrived here, and the post being about to depart, I set down to inform you of it. Your sister came over with me from Belmont where we left all well. The family will move over the day after tomorrow. They give up the house there about a week hence. We want nothing now to fill up our happiness but to have you and Mr. Eppes here. Scarcely a stroke has been done towards covering the house since I went away, so that it has remained open at the North end another winter. It seems as if I should never get it inhabitable. I have proposed to your sister a flying trip when the roads get fine to see you. She comes into it with pleasure; but whether I shall be able to leave this for a few days is a question which I have not yet seen enough of the state of things to determine. I think it very doubtful. It is to your return therefore that I look with impatience and shall expect as soon as

Mr. Eppes's affairs will permit. We are not without hopes he will take a trip up soon to see about his affairs here, of which I yet know nothing. I hope you are enjoying good health, and that it will not be long before we shall be again united in some way or other. Continue to love me, my dear, as I do you most tenderly. Present me affectionately to Mr. Eppes and be assured of my constant and warmest love. Adieu my ever dear Maria.

TH: JEFFERSON

To Mary Jefferson Eppes

Monticello Apr. 13. 99.

Your letter, my dear Maria, of Mar. 13. came safely to hand and gave us the information, always subject of anxiety, and therefore always welcome, that yourself and Mr. Eppes were well. It would yet have been better that we could all have been well together, as the health we enjoy separately would be more enjoyed together. Whether we can visit you is still uncertain, my presence here is so constantly called for when all our works are going on. However I have not altogether abandoned the idea. Still let it not retard your movements towards us. Let us all pray the fish to get into motion soon that Mr. Eppes may be done with them. His affairs here are going on well. Page [1] has made a noble clearing of about 80. thousand of the richest tobo. land and is in good forwardness with it. I have provided the place with corn till harvest. Our spring has been remarkeably backward. I presume we shall have asparagus tomorrow for the first time. The Peach trees blossomed about a week ago, the cherries are just now (this day) blossoming. I suppose you have heard before that Peter Carr had a son and Sam a daughter. Sam and his wife are daily expected from Maryland.[2] Dr. Bache is now with us at Monticello. His furniture is arrived at Richmond. He goes back to Philadelphia to bring on Mrs. Bache.[3] I expect he will buy James Key's land;[4] but what he will do for a house this summer is uncertain. Champe Carter is endeavoring to move into our neighborhood, and we expect Dupont de Nemours (my old friend) every day to settle here also. Baynham[5] is not quite decided. Ellen gives her love to you. She always counts you as the object of affection after her mama and uckin Juba.[6] All else join in love to you and Mr. Eppes. Add mine to the family at Eppington, and continue me your most tender affections so necessary to my happiness, and be assured of mine for ever. Adieu my ever dear Maria. TH: J.

1. William Page, a Monticello workman, who at one time leased the Shadwell Farm. It is presumed the land cleared was at Pantops, where TJ still hoped to entice the Eppeses to make their home.

2. It appears that TJ may have confused Peter and Sam in reporting the births of their children. Peter had married Hetty (Smith) Stevenson, a sister of General Samuel Smith of Baltimore; Sam had married Eleanor (Nelly) Carr, daughter of his uncle John Overton Carr. The children TJ was referring to were Nelly, Peter's daughter, and John Addison, Sam's son. See Edison I. Carr, *The Carr Family Records* (Rockton, Illinois, 1894), 181–82.

3. Dr. William Bache moved to Albemarle and lived there for a time on a 600-acre farm, Franklin, lying on the eastern side of the Rivanna River near Charlottesville. For additional information of Dr. Bache's residence in this county, see Edgar Woods, *Albemarle County in Virginia* (Bridgewater, n.d.), a reprint of the 1900 edition. The Richmond *Enquirer*, July 28, 1804, carries an advertisement offering it for sale; Richard Sampson purchased it that same year.

4. Key's land was in the southern part of the county.

5. Son of Dr. John Baynham of Caroline County. After sixteen years of study in England he returned and settled in Essex County.

6. Jupiter was one of TJ's trusted slave servants.

FROM MARY JEFFERSON EPPES

Eppington June 26th 99.

I am sorry indeed my dear Papa that my silence has continued so long as to have given you displeasure. Could you know my heart you would least of all suspect me of any thing like forgetfulness, and tho' I must acknowledge that indolence has been in great measure the cause, yet from Mont Blanco to Petersburg, opportunitys are so rare that it is seldom in our power to write. You can have but a slight idea of my affection my dear Papa. Could you suppose it possible for me a moment to forget you? Could my letters be agreeable to any one it might induce me oftener to write; but as you excuse them such as they are, it shall not be the case again. They will prove to you whatever they are that tender love which I can never express which is interwoven with my existence. I should have gone up last month could Mr. Eppes who has long wish'd it have staid but it would have been very inconvenient to him as his affairs would have requir'd his presence down here till now. I am in hopes however that it will not be long before his interest will induce him to build up there and we shall then allways be one of the first to welcome your arrival. He will find it easy to sell the Hundred should your friend

not take it, as he has had several applications from gentlemen
well able to purchase it. I anticipate the time with real pleasure,
had I no other reasons, regard for my health would make it desirable for the sallow complexions of my neighbours and their own
complaints even at this season are sufficient proofs of the unhealthiness of the country. But I have been desir'd by Mr. Eppes's
father to assure you that would you try the air of this place you
would find it as healthy as any situation below the mountains. It
is indeed uncommon for any one to be sick here. Adieu dear Papa.
This is the last letter I hope that I shall write to you this year.
The 15th or 16th I shall again behold dear Monticello and with
it all that is most dear to me in the world and in that idea I allready feel a degree of happiness which makes me more sensible
of that which I shall experience when that moment arrives, that
heartfelt happiness which I only feel with you and my dear Sister.
Adieu once more my dear Papa. Believe me your affectionate
daughter,   M E

To Mary Jefferson Eppes

Philadelphia Jan. 17. 1800

My dear Maria

I recieved at Monticello two letters from you, and meant to
have answered them a little before my departure for this place;
but business so crowded on me at that moment that it was not
in my power. I left home on the 21st. and arrived here on the
28th. of Dec. after a pleasant journey of fine weather and good
roads, and without having experienced any inconvenience. The
Senate had not yet entered into business, and I may say they have
not yet entered into it: for we have not occupation for half an
hour a day. Indeed it is so apparent that we have nothing to do
but to raise money to fill the deficit of 5. millions of Dollars, that
it is proposed we shall rise about the middle of March; and as the
proposition comes from the Eastern members who have always
been for setting permanently, while the Southern are constantly
for early adjournment, I presume we shall rise then. In the mean
while they are about to renew the bill suspending intercourse with
France, which is in fact a bill to prohibit the exportation of tobacco and to reduce the tobacco states to passive obedience by
poverty. J. Randolph has entered into debate with great splendor
and approbation. He used an unguarded word in his first speech,

applying the word raggamuffin to the common souldiery. He took it back of his own accord and very handsomely the next day, when he had occasion to reply. Still in the evening of the 2d. day he was jostled and his coat pulled at the theatre by two officers of the Navy who repeated the word raggamuffin. His friends present supported him spiritedly so that nothing further followed. Concieving, and, as I think justly, that the H. of Representatives (not having passed a law on the subject) could not punish the offenders, he wrote a letter to the President, who laid it before the house, where it is still depending. He has conducted himself with great propriety, and I have no doubt will come out with increase of reputation; being determined himself to oppose the interposition of the house when they have no law for it.[1] M. du Pont, his wife and family are arrived at New York, after a voyage of 3 months and 5 days. I suppose after he is a little recruited from his voyage, we shall see him here. His son is with him, as is also his son in law Bureau-Pusy the companion and fellow sufferer of La fayette. I have a letter from La fayette of April. He then expected to sail for America in July; but I suspect he awaits the effect of the mission of our ministers. I presume Made. de la fayette is to come with him, and that they mean to settle in America. The prospect of returning early to Monticello is to me a most chearing one. I hope the fishery will not prevent your joining us early in the spring. However on this subject we can speak together, as I will endeavor if possible to take Mont Blanco and Eppington in my way. A letter from Dr. Carr,[2] of Dec. 27. informed me he had just left you well. I become daily more anxious to hear from you, and to know that you continue well, your present state being one which is most interesting to a parent; and it's issue I hope will be such as to give you experience what a parent's anxiety may be. I employ my leisure moments in repassing often in my mind our happy domestic society when together at Monticello, and looking forward to the renewal of it. No other society gives me now any satisfaction, as no other is founded in sincere affection. Take care of yourself, my dear Maria, for my sake, and cherish your affections for me, as my happiness rests solely on yours and that of your sister and your dear connections. Present me affectionately to Mr. Eppes, to whom I inclosed some pamphlets some time ago, without any letter; as I shall write no letters the ensuing year for political reasons which I explained to him. Present my affections also to Mrs. and Mr. Eppes, Senr. and all the family for whom I feel every interest that I do for my own. Be assured yourself, my dear, of my most tender and constant love. Adieu. Your's affectionately and forever,   TH: JEFFERSON

1. Randolph was speaking to a resolution offered by John Nicholas of Virginia leading to a reduction of the regular army. Captain James McKnight and Lieutenant Michael Reynolds, Marine Corps officers, were the individuals who jostled him. The matter of Randolph's intemperate language finally came to President Adams' attention and hence to a congressional debate. The sum of the affair appears only to have enhanced Randolph's public reputation. See William Cabell Bruce, *John Randolph of Roanoke 1773–1833* (New York, 1922), I, 156–65 for a full account.
2. Dr. Frank Carr was a son of Garland Carr and nephew of Martha Jefferson and Dabney Carr.

TO MARTHA JEFFERSON RANDOLPH

Philadelphia Jan. 21, 1800.

MY DEAR MARTHA

I wrote on the 13th. inst. to Mr. Randolph. I now inclose you a letter from your friend Mde. Salimben. It came under cover to me. And without looking at the second cover, or suspecting it not for me, I broke the seal. A few words in the beginning shewed me it was not, and on looking at the back I found it was addressed to you. M. Bureau Pusy, the companion of la Fayette, with his family and Mde. Dupont arrived at N. York some time ago. Dupont, with his son (late consul) and family arrived there a few days ago. I have a letter from La Fayette in which he says he should sail for America in July, but as he also expressed a wish to see the event of our negociation I suppose he will not come till reconciliation is established by that. J. Randolph's affair is not over. A rancorous report was made to the H. of R. yesterday by a committee. It would seem as if the army themselves were to hew down whoever shall propose to reduce them. The non-intercourse law is to be renewed, but whether only for the tobacco states; or for all, is a question. Were it not for the prospect of it's expiring by the effect of a treaty, our state would do better to drop the culture of tobo. altogether. I am made happy by a letter from Mr. Eppes, recd two or three days ago and informing me that Maria was become a mother and was well.[1] It was written the day after the event. These circumstances are balm to the painful sensations of this place. I look forward with hope to the moment when we are all to be reunited again. It is proposed that we shall adjourn about the middle of March; and as the proposition comes from the Eastern members it will probably prevail. There is really nothing to do but to authorise them to make up their deficit of 5. millions by borrowing at 8. or 10. per cent. My friend Govr. Rutledge[2] of S. Carolina is dead. News is this moment recieved here of the death of Govr. Mifflin[3] at Lancaster; and there is a rumor of the death of George the 3d.[4] The great and antient house of Cuningham & Nesbitt of this place has stopped paiment. It is but the beginning of a great crush. No commerce was more deeply interested than our's in the deposits at Hamburgh. Indeed our commerce and navigation generally are in a state of prostration. I am anxious as you may suppose to hear from you, having heard nothing since I left home. I hope you all continue well, yet should be happier to know it. I inclose a little tale for Anne. To Ellen you must make big promises, which I know a bit of gingerbread will pay off. Kiss them all for me. My affectionate salutations to Mr. Randolph and tender and unceasing love to yourself. Adieu my ever dear Martha. Affectionately.   TH: JEFFERSON

1. The name or sex of this first Eppes grandchild is not established. Since it lived less than two weeks, it is doubted if a name had been given.
2. John Rutledge.
3. Thomas Mifflin.
4. George III died in 1820.

FROM MARTHA JEFFERSON RANDOLPH

Edgehill January 30 1800

I have this moment recieved your 2 letters to Mr. Randolph and my self (together) and by the same post one from Mr. Eppes informing me of the loss of his child. My heart is torn by an event which carries death to hopes so long and fondly cherished by my poor sister. I would give the world to fly to her comfort at this moment but having been dissappointed before in doing what perhaps my *anxiety only* termed a moral duty (visiting her during her lying in) I am afraid to indulge any more hopes upon that subject. To your enquiries relative to poor Jupiter he too has paid the debt to nature, finding him self no better at his return home, he unfortunately conceived him self poisoned and went to consult the negro doctor who attended the Georges. He went in the house to see uncle Randolph[1] who gave him a dram which he drank and seemed to be as well as he had been for some time past, after which he took a dose from this black doctor who pronounced that it would *kill or cure*. 2½ hours after taking the medecine he fell down in a strong convulsion fit which lasted from ten to eleven hours, during which time it took 3 stout men to hold him, he languished nine days but was never heard to speak from the first of his being seized to the moment of his death. Ursula[2] is I fear going in the same manner with her husband and son, a constant puking, shortness of breath and swelling first in the legs but now extending it self. The doctor I understand had also given her means as they term it and upon Jupiter's death has absconded. I should think his murders sufficiently manifest to come under the cognizance of the law. Mr. Trist had left Charlottesville before I recieved your letters but should Mr. Randolph be able to procure any other conveyance he will send them. As he is not at home at present I have of course answered those parts of his letter which required an immediate one. Adieu my dearest Father. I have written this with the messenger who is to carry it at my elbow impatiently waiting. I will write by the next post more deliberately. We are all well. Ellen sends her love to dear *seet* grand papa. Believe me with tenderest affection yours,   M RANDOLPH

1. Randolph Jefferson.
2. The Georges, "Little" and "Great," were slaves; Ursula was their mother and wife, respectively. "Little" George died in June of 1799 and his father on November 2 of this same year. See *Memoirs of a Monticello Slave* (1955), 66, and the *Farm Book*.

TO MARTHA JEFFERSON RANDOLPH

Philadelphia Feb. 11. 1800.

MY DEAR MARTHA

I wrote to Mr. Randolph on the 2d. inst. acknoleging the receipt of his letter of the 18th. Jan. I had one also at the same time from Mr. Richardson giving me the details from Monticello. The death of Jupiter obliges me to ask of Mr. Randolph or yourself to give orders at the proper time in March for the bottling my cyder. I forgot to bring with me a morsel cut from one of our sheets, as a sample to guide Mr. Barnes in providing some sheeting for me. Being entirely ignorant of it myself I must ask the favor of you to inclose me a bit in a letter by the return of post. I suppose our French sheets to be of the proper fineness and quality. A person here has invented the prettiest improvement in the Forte piano I have ever seen. It has tempted me to engage one for Monticello, partly for it's excellence and convenience, partly to assist a very ingenious, modest and poor young man, who ought to make a fortune by his invention. His strings are perpendicular, so that the instrument is only 3.f. 4.I. wide, 15.I. deep, and 3.f. 6.I. high.

It resembles when closed the underhalf of a book case, and may be moved by it's handles, to the fire side. He contrives within that height to give his strings the same length as in the grand forte-piano, and fixes his 3. unisons to the same screw, which screw is in the direction of the strings and therefore never yields. It scarcely gets out of tune at all, and then for the most part the 3. unisons are tuned at once. The price of one with 5. octaves is 200. D. with 5½ octaves 250.D.[1]

I recieved a letter of Jan. 17. from Mr. Eppes announcing the death of his child, and that poor Maria was suffering dreadfully, both her breasts having risen and broke. She was still ill from that cause. I have not heard from her since. There is abundant cause of deep concern in this, and especially for the peculiar affliction it will be to them, as I think they would have been made very peculiarly happy by the possession of a child. I am extremely uneasy to hear further from her. The H. of Representatives have sent a resolution to the Senate to adjourn on the 1st. Monday of April. The Eastern men being for the first time eager to get away for political reasons, I think it probable we shall adjourn about that time. There is really no business which ought to keep us one fortnight. I am therefore looking forward with anticipation of the joy of seeing you again ere long, and tasting true happiness in the midst of my family. My absence from you teaches me how essential your society is to my happiness. Politics are such a torment that I would advise every one I love not to mix with them. I have changed my circle here according to my wish; abandoning the rich, and declining their dinners and parties, and associating entirely with the class of science, of whom there is a valuable society here. Still my wish is to be in the midst of our own families at home. Present me affectionately to Mr. Randolph. Kiss all the dear little ones for me. Do not let Ellen forget me; and continue to me your love in return for the constant and tenderest attachment of Your's affectionately,   TH: JEFFERSON

1. The instrument TJ saw was John Hawkins' "portable grand." As interesting as this instrument was, says Arthur Loesser, in *Men, Women and Pianos,* 461, "it may not have had a satisfactory tone quality and may have seemed too queer-looking a domestic object for fashionable people to take up. In any event, it made no headway. We do not know what became of Hawkins." The Account Book fails to record any such purchase at this time.

TJ's attraction for the new instrument was typical of his approach toward music, for more often than not he appears more interested in the how than the what of it.

To Mary Jefferson Eppes

Philadelphia February 12. 1800.

My dear Maria

Mr. Eppes's letter of Jan. 17. had filled me with anxiety for
your little one, and that of the 25th. announced what I had feared.
How deeply I feel it in all it's bearings, I shall not say, nor attempt
consolation where I know that time and silence are the only mede-
cines. I shall only observe as a source of hope to us all that you
are young and will not fail to possess enough of these dear pledges
which bind us to one another and to life itself. I am almost hope-
less in writing to you, from observing that at the date of Mr.
Eppes's letter of Jan. 25. three which I had written to him and
one to you had not been recieved. That to you was Jan. 17. and
to him Dec. 21. Jan. 22. and one which only covered some pamphlets. That of Dec. 21. was on the subject of Powell and would
of course give occasion for an answer. I have always directed to
Petersburg. Perhaps Mr. Eppes does not have enquiries made at
the post office there. His of Jan. 1. 12. 17. and 25. have come safely
tho' tardily. One from the Hundred never came. I will inclose this
to the care of Mr. Jefferson.

The Representatives have proposed to the Senate to adjourn
on the 7th. of April, and as the motion comes from the Eastern
quarter and the members from thence are anxious, for political
reasons, to separate, I expect we shall adjourn about that time.
I fully propose, if nothing intervenes to prevent it, to take Chesterfield in my way home. I [am] not without hopes you will be
ready to go on with me; but at any rate that you will soon follow.
I know no happiness but when we are all together. You have perhaps heard of the loss of Jupiter. With all his defects, he leaves
a void in my domestic arrangements which cannot be filled.

Mr. Eppes's last letter informed me how much you had suffered
from your breasts: but that they had then suppurated, and the
inflammation and consequent fever abated. I am anxious to hear
again from you, and hope the next letter will announce your re-
establishment. It is necessary for my tranquility that I should hear
from you often: for I feel inexpressibly whatever affects either
your health or happiness. My attachments to the world and whatever it can offer are daily wearing off, but you are one of the links
which hold to my existence, and can only break off with that. You
have never by a word or a deed given me one moment's uneasiness;
on the contrary I have felt perpetual gratitude to heaven for
having given me, in you, a source of so much pure and unmixed

happiness. Go on then, my dear, as you have done in deserving the love of every body: you will reap the rich reward of their esteem, and will find that we are working for ourselves while we do good to others. I had a letter from your sister yesterday. They were all well. One from Mr. Randolph had before informed me they had got to Edgehill, and were in the midst of mud, smoak, and the uncomfortableness of a cold house. Mr. Trist is here alone, and will return soon. Present me affectionately to Mr. Eppes, and tell him when you cannot write, he must. As also to the good family at Eppington to whom I wish every earthly good. To yourself my Dear Maria I cannot find expressions for my love. You must measure it by the feelings of a warm heart. Adieu.

TH: J

TO MARY JEFFERSON EPPES

Philadelphia April 6. 1800.

I have at length, my ever dear Maria, recieved by Mr. Eppes's letter of Mar. 24. the welcome news of your recovery. Welcome indeed to me, who have past a long season of inexpressible anxiety for you: and the more so as written accounts can hardly give one an exact idea of the situation of a sick person. I wish I were able now to leave this place and join you. But we do not count on rising till the 1st. or 2d. week of May. I shall certainly see you as soon after that as possible at Mont Blanco or Eppington, at whichever you may be; and shall expect you to go up with me according to the promise in Mr. Eppes's letter. I shall send orders for my horses to be with you, and wait for me if they arrive before me. I must ask Mr. Eppes to write me a line immediately by post to inform me at which place you will be during the 1st. and 2d. weeks of May, and what is the nearest point on the road from Richmond where I can quit the stage and borrow a horse to go on to you. If written immediately I may recieve it here before my departure. Mr. Eppes's letter informs me your sister was with you at that date; but from Mr. Randolph I learn she was to go up this month. The uncertainty where she was has prevented my writing to her for a long time. If she is still with you, express to her all my love and tenderness for her. Your tables have been ready some time, and will go in a vessel which sails for Richmond this week. They are packed in a box, marked I. W. E. and will be delivered to Mr. Jefferson, probably about the latter part of this month. I write no news for Mr. Eppes, because my letters are so

slow in getting to you that he will see every thing first in the newspapers. Assure him of my sincere affections, and present the same
to the family of Eppington if you are together. Cherish your own
health for the sake of so many to whom you are dear, and especially for one who loves you with unspeakable tenderness. Adieu
my dearest Maria.

To Martha Jefferson Randolph

Philadelphia Apr. 22. 1800.

My dear Martha

It is very long since I wrote to you, because I have been uncertain whether you would not have left Eppington before the arrival
of my letters there and the rather as I found them very long getting
there. Mr. Randolph's letter of the 12th. informs me you had then
returned to Edgehill. In a letter of Mar. 24. which is the last I
have recieved from Eppington, Mr. Eppes informed me Maria
was so near well that they expected in a few days to go to Mont-
blanco. Your departure gives me a hope her case was at length
established. A long and a painful case it has been, and not the
most so to herself or those about her. My anxieties have been
excessive. I shall go by Mont-blanco to take her home with me,
which Mr. Eppes expressed to be their desire. I wrote last week
to Mr. Richardson to send off my horses to Mont Blanco on the
9th. of May. But both houses having agreed to rise on the 2d
Monday (12th. of May) I shall write to him by this post, not to
send them off till Friday the 16th. of May; as I shall be 7. or 8
days from the 12th. getting to Mont Blanco, and near a week afterwards getting home. I long once more to get all together again:
and still hope, notwithstanding your present establishment, you
will pass a great deal of the summer with us. I would wish to urge
it just so far as not to break in on your and Mr. Randolph's desires and convenience. Our scenes here can never be pleasant. But
they have been less stormy, less painful than during the XYZ.
paroxysms. Our opponents perceive the decay of their power. Still
they are pressing it, and trying to pass laws to keep themselves in
power. Mr. Cooper[1] was found guilty two days ago, under the
Sedition law, and will be fined and imprisoned. Duane[2] has 16.
or 17 suits and indictments against him. The sheriff and justices
who got the letters of Mr. Liston[3] which Sweeny the horse thief
abandoned, are indicted. This is all the news I have for Mr. Randolph. Of foreign news we know nothing but what he will see in

the papers. I inclose a little story for Anne, and many kisses for Ellenaroon. Present my affections to Mr. Randolph. To yourself constant and unbounded love. Adieu my dear Martha.

1. Thomas Cooper.
2. William Duane was editor of the Philadelphia *Aurora*. His charges under the Sedition Act were dismissed when TJ became President.
3. Sir Robert Liston the British Ambassador Extraordinary and Minister Plenipotentiary. He remained in the United States until the Peace of Amiens.

From Martha Jefferson Randolph

Edgehill May 15 1800

Being prevented by the unexpected arrival of company today, I have it in my power to write but a few lines to my Dearest Father while the rest of the family sleep. To repeat what he so well knows allready how tenderly loved how anxiously expected he is by every member of the family. They are all unwell at present with colds so bad as to create suspicions of the hooping cough particularly the two youngest. Ellen has been very ill. We were much disturbed and allarmed for three nights successively being in constant apprehension of her going in to convulsion *fits* with which she was seriously threatened. She is however better tho extremely weak and languid and Anne is quite well. For the upper two they have constitutions proof against every thing. Alltho the little one [1] is at the crisis of the disorder what ever it is and has really a horrid cough she has never been feverish. Adieu Dear and respected Father. Hasten I entreat you, the blest moment which will reunite me to all my heart holds dear in the world. Give my tenderest affections to Maria. Tell her I would have written to her but for the reason above mentioned not forgetting the dear and amiable family with whom this will find you. I remain with an affection truly inexpressible your most tenderly,   M. RANDOLPH

1. Cornelia Jefferson, born July 26, 1799, at Edgehill, was the third child of Martha and Thomas Mann Randolph, Jr.

To Mary Jefferson Eppes

Monticello July 4. 1800.

My dear Maria

We have heard not a word of you since the moment you left us. I hope you had a safe and pleasant journey. The rains which began to fall here the next day gave me uneasiness lest they should have overtaken you also. Dr. and Mrs. Bache have been with us till the day before yesterday. Mrs. Monroe is now in our neighborhood to continue during the sickly months. Our Forte-piano arrived a day or two after you left us. It had been exposed to a great deal of rain, but being well covered was only much untuned. I have given it a poor tuning. It is the delight of the family, and all pronounce what your choice will be. Your sister does not hesitate to prefer it to any harpsichord she ever saw *except her own.* And it is easy to see it is only the celestini which retains that preference. It is as easily tuned as a spinette, and will not need it half as often. Our harvest has been a very fine one. I finish to day. It is the heaviest crop of wheat I ever had. A murder in our neighborhood is the theme of it's present conversation. George Carter shot Birch[1] of Charlottesville, in his own door, and on very slight provocation. He died in a very few minutes. The examining court meets tomorrow. As your harvest must be over as soon as ours, we hope soon to see Mr. Eppes and himself. I say nothing of his affairs lest he should be less impatient to come to see them. All are well here except Ellen, who is rather drooping than sick; and all are impatient to see you. No one so much as him whose happiness is wrapped up in yours. My affections to Mr. Eppes and tenderest love to yourself. Hasten to us. Adieu.

TH: JEFFERSON

1. Samuel Birch. Peter Carr gives an account of this affair in a letter to Mary Carr of July 24, 1800. Carr-Cary Papers, ViU.

From Mary Jefferson Eppes

Bermuda Hundred Dec. 28. 1800.

I feel very anxious to hear from you My Dear Papa. It is a long time since you left us, and it appears still longer from not having heard from you, opportunitys from Eppington to Petersburg so seldom occur that I could not write to you while there, here I hope we shall recieve your letters more regularly. By directing them to City Point[1] which Mr. Eppes thinks will be the best, we can get them the same day they arrive there and in the expectation of hearing from you a little oftener I shall feel much happier. We have had the finest spell of weather ever known allmost for the season here, fires were uncomfortable till within a day or two past, and it still continues very mild and pleasant. It happen'd fortunately for us, as the house was not in a very comfortable state and every thing was to be moved from Mount Blanco here. We have not finish'd yet moving and the carpenters are still at work in the house but we have two rooms that are comfortable and I prefer it infinitely to living in a rented place. We are still in anxious suspence about the election. If the event should be as it is expected I shall endeavor to be satisfied in the happiness I know it will give to so many tho I must confess mine would have been greater Could I be forever with you and see you happy. I could enjoy no greater felicity but it is very late and I must bid you adieu My dear Papa. May every blessing attend you. Your affectionate daughter.

M EPPES

1. A small port and post village in Prince George County on the right bank of the James River at its confluence with the Appomattox River and twelve miles below Petersburg.

TO MARY JEFFERSON EPPES

Washington Jan. 4. [1801].

Your letter, my dear Maria, of Dec. 28. is just now recieved, and shall be instantly answered, as shall all others recieved from yourself or Mr. Eppes. This will keep our accounts even, and shew by the comparative promptness of reply which is most anxious to hear from the other. I wrote to Mr. Eppes Dec. 23. but directed it to Petersburg. Hereafter it shall be to City point. I went yesterday to Mount Vernon, where Mrs. Washington and Mrs. Lewis[1] enquired very kindly after you. Mrs. Lewis looks thin, and thinks herself not healthy; but it seems to be more in opinion than any thing else. She has a child of very uncertain health. The election is understood to stand 73.73.65.64. The Federalists were confident at first they could debauch Colo. B.[2] from his good faith by offering him their vote to be President, and have seriously proposed it to him. His conduct has been honorable and decisive, and greatly embarrasses them. Time seems to familiarise them more and more to acquiescence, and to render it daily more probable they will yield to the known will of the people, and that some one state will join the eight already decided as to their vote. The victory of the republicans in N. Jersey, lately obtained, by carrying their whole congressional members on an election by general ticket, has had weight on their spirits. Should I be destined to remain here, I shall count on meeting you and Mr. Eppes at Monticello the first week in April, where I shall not have above three weeks to stay. We shall there be able to consider how far it will be practicable to prevent this new destination from shortening the time of our being together. For be assured that no considerations in this world would compensate to me a separation from yourself and your sister. But the distance is so moderate that I should hope a journey to this place would be scarcely more inconvenient than one to Monticello. But of this we will talk when we meet there, which will be to me a joyful moment. Remember me affectionately to Mr. Eppes: and accept yourself the effusions of my tenderest love. Adieu my dearest Maria.

1. Betty Washington Lewis (Mrs. Fielding), sister of George Washington.
2. Aaron Burr.

To Martha Jefferson Randolph

Washington Jan. 16, 1801.

MY DEAR MARTHA

I wrote to Mr. Randolph on the 9th. and 10th. inst. and yesterday recieved his letter of the 10th. It gave me great joy to learn that Lilly[1] had got a recruit of hands from Mr. Allen,[2] tho' still I would not have that prevent the taking all from the nailery[3] who are able to cut, as I desired in mine of the 9th. as I wish Craven's ground[4] to be got ready for him without any delay. Mr. Randolph writes me you are about to wean Cornelia. This must be right and proper. I long to be in the midst of the children, and have more pleasure in their little follies than in the wisdom of the wise. Here too there is such a mixture of the bad passions of the heart that one feels themselves in an enemy's country. It is an unpleasant circumstance, if I am destined to stay here, that the great proportion of those of the place who figure are federalists, and most of them of the violent kind. Some have been so personally bitter that they can never forgive me, tho' I do them with sincerity. Perhaps in time they will get tamed. Our prospect as to the election has been alarming: as a strong disposition exists to prevent an election, and that case not being provided for by the constitution, a dissolution of the government seemed possible. At present there is a prospect that some tho' federalists, will prefer yielding to the wishes of the people rather than have no government. If I am fixed here, it will be but three easy days journey from you: so that I should hope you and the family could pay an annual visit here at least; which with mine to Monticello of the spring and fall, might enable us to be together 4. or 5. months of the year. On this subject however we may hereafter converse, lest we should be counting chickens before they are hatched. I inclose for Anne a story, too long to be got by heart, but worth reading. Kiss them all for me: and keep

them in mind of me. Tell Ellen I am afraid she has forgotten me. I shall probably be with you the first week in April, as I shall endeavor to be at our court for that month. Continue to love me my dear Martha and be assured of my unalterable and tenderest love to you. Adieu. TH: JEFFERSON
P. S. Hamilton is using his uttermost influence to procure my election rather than Colo. Burr's.

1. Gabriel Lilly was a Monticello overseer.
2. Probably Hancock Allen, an Albemarle County resident and sometime sawyer at Monticello.
3. In 1794 TJ established a nailery at Monticello along the Mulberry Row section of the First Roundabout on the southern side of the mountain. It was primarily for the commercial manufacture of nails and for a time was very successful. It remained in operation (but not always returning a profit) until 1823. In it was one of the first nail-cutting machines in Virginia. See TJ's "Nailery Account Book," the original at the University of California at Berkeley, and James A. Bear, Jr., "Mr. Jefferson's Nails," *The Magazine of Albemarle County History*, XVI (1957–1958), 47–52 for additional information on the operation of the Nailery.
4. John H. Craven came to Albemarle County from Loudon County about 1800. The lands he leased were a part of the Tufton farm, across the Rivanna River and southeast of Monticello.

FROM MARTHA JEFFERSON RANDOLPH

January 31 1801

I should not have waited for your letter my Dearest Father had it been in my power to have written sooner but incredible as it may appear, that in period of 2 months not one day could have been found to discharge so sacred and pleasing a duty. It is litterally true that the first fortnight of your absence excepted and 3 or 4 days of the last week, I have not been one day capable of attending even to my common domestic affairs. I am again getting into the old way with regard to my stomach, totally unable to digest any thing but a few particular vegetables; harrassed to death by little fevers, for 6 week I scarcely ever missed a night having one untill by recurring to my accustomed remedy in such cases, giving up meat milk coffee and a large proportion of the vegetable tribe that have allways been innimical to my constitution I have at last found some relief. It requires some self denial but I find my self so much recruited both in health and spirits, and every transgression so severely punished, that I shall rigorously adhere to it as long as my health requires it. Cornelia shows the necessity there was for weaning her by her surprising change for the better since that time. The children are all well except Jefferson who caught (that filthiest of all disorders) the itch from a little aprentice boy in the family. He was 6 or seven weeks in constant and familiar intercourse with us before we suspected what was the matter with him, the moment it was discovered that the other little boy had it, we were no longer at a loss to account for Jefferson's irruption which had been attributed all along to his covering too warm at night. I am delighted that your return will happen at a season when we shall be able to enjoy your company with out interuption. I was at Monticello last spring 1 day before the arrival of any one, and one day more of interval between the departure of one family and the arrival of another, after which time I never had the pleasure of passing one sociable moment with you. Allways in a crowd, taken from every useful and pleasing duty to be worried with a multiplicity of disagreable ones which the entertaining of such crowds of company subjects one to in the country. I suffered more in seeing you allways at a distance than if you had still been in Philadelphia, for then at least I should have enjoyed in anticipation those pleasures which we were deprived of by the concourse of strangers which continually crowded the house when you were with us. I find my self every day becoming more averse to company. I have lost my relish for what is usually deemed pleasures and duties incompatible with it have surplanted all other enjoyments in my breast. The education of my children to which I have long devoted every moment that I could command, but which is attended with more anxiety now as they increase in age without making those acquirements which other children do. My 2 eldest are uncommonly backward in every thing much more so than many others, who have not had half the pains taken with them. Ellen is wonderfully apt. I shall have no trouble with her, but the two others excite serious anxiety with regard to their intellect. Of Jefferson my hopes were so little sanguine that I discovered with some surprise and pleasure that he was quicker than I had ever thought it possible for him to be, but he has lost so much time and will necessarily lose so much more before he can be placed at a good school that I am very unhappy about him. Anne does not want memory but she does not improve. She appears to me to learn absolutely without profit. Adieu my Dear Father. We all are painfully anxious to see you. Ellen counts the weeks and continues storing up complaints against Cornelia whom she is perpetually threatning with *your* displeasure. Long is the list of misdemeanors which is to be communicated to you, amongst which the stealing of 2 potatoes carefully preserved 2 whole days for you but at last stolen by Cornelia forms a weighty article.

Adieu again dearest best beloved Father. 2 long months still before we shall see you. In the mean time rest assured of the first Place in the heart of your affectionate child,   M. RANDOLPH

FROM MARY JEFFERSON EPPES

Bermuda hundred Febry 2nd [1801]

DEAR PAPA

Your letter to Mr. Eppes arrived yesterday from City Point where I imagine from the date it had been some time. The river had been and is often so rough that a canoe could not venture over, tho' it is the most certain way of hearing from you. I am afraid it will not be a very regular one which I lament as in your absence it is the greatest pleasure I recieve, nor have I any thing so valuable as your letters. Sensible of the distance which Nature has placed between my sister and myself, the tender affection I feel for her, makes me judge what yours must be, and I rejoice that you have in her so great a source of comfort and one who is in every way so worthy of you, satisfied if my dear papa is only assured that in the most tender love to him I yeild to no one. You mention'd in your letter that your intention of being at Monticello in april and I shall then enjoy the heartfelt happiness of being with you and my dear Sister tho' only for a short time after which I suppose you will not be there again till the fall. Nothing can be more retired than the life we lead here, it has its pleasures tho', as it leaves us perfect Masters of our own time, and the different occupations we have I hope will prevent our ever feeling ennui. Will you be so good as to keep the little sum which the tobacco Mr. Eppes gave me will amount to and lay it out for me. I will let you know in what way when you recieve it. If you have not engaged the harpsichord to Aunt Bolling or any one else I will if you please put off chusing between them till April as I fear the Piano will not hold in tune long and I shall be able to judge by that time. Adieu My dear Papa. Mr. Eppes will write to you a few days hence. Beleive me with the tenderest affection yours,   M EPPES

TO MARTHA JEFFERSON RANDOLPH

Washington Feb. 5. 1801.

MY DEAR MARTHA

Yours of Jan. 31. is this moment put into my hands, and the departure of the post obliges an answer on the same day. I am

much afflicted to learn that your health is not good, and the particular derangement of your stomach. This last is the parent of
many ills, and if any degree of abstinence will relieve you from
them it ought to be practiced. Perhaps in time it may be brought
to by beginning with a single one of the hostile articles, taking a
very little of it at first, and more and more as the stomach habitu-
ates itself to it. In this way the catalogue may perhaps be enlarged
by article after article. I have formed a different judgment of both
Anne and Jefferson from what you do; of Anne positively, of Jefferson possibly. I think her apt, intelligent, good humored and of
soft and affectionate dispositions and that she will make a pleasant,
amiable and respectable woman. Of Jefferson's disposition I [have]
formed a good opinion, and have not suffered myself to form any
other good or bad of his genius. It is not every heavy-seeming boy
which makes a man of judgment, but I never yet saw a man of
judgment who had not been a heavy seeming boy, nor knew a boy
of what are called sprightly parts become a man of judgment. But
I set much less store by talents than good dispositions: and shall
be perfectly happy to see Jefferson a good man, industrious farmer,
and kind and beloved among all his neighbors. By cultivating those dispositions in him, and they may be immensely
strengthened by culture, we may ensure his and our happiness:
and genius itself can propose no other object. Nobody can ever
have felt so severely as myself the prostration of family society from
the circumstance you mention. Worn down here with pursuits in
which I take no delight, surrounded by enemies and spies, catching
and perverting every word which falls from my lips or flows from
my pen, and inventing where facts fail them, I pant for that society where all is peace and harmony, where we love and are
loved by every object we see. And to have that intercourse of soft
affections hushed and supported by the eternal presence of
strangers goes very hard indeed, and the harder as we see that the
candle of life burning out, so that the pleasures we lose are lost
forever. But there is no remedy. The present manners and usages
of our country are laws we cannot repeal. They are altering by
degrees, and you will live to see the hospitality of the country
reduced to the visiting hours of the day, and the family left to
tranquility in the evening. It is wise therefore under the necessity
of our present situation to view the pleasing side of the medal
and to consider that these visits are evidences of the general esteem
which we have been able all our lives trying to merit. The character
of those we recieve is very different from the loungers who infest

the houses of the wealthy in general: nor can it be relieved in our case but by a revolting conduct which would undo the whole labor of our lives. It is a valuable circumstance that it is only thro' a particular portion of the year that these inconveniences arise. The election by the H. of R. being on Wednesday next, and the next our post day, I shall be able to tell you something certain of it by my next letter. I believe it will be as the people have wished, but this depends upon the will of a few moderate men; and they may be controlled by their party. I long to see the time approach when I can be returning to you, tho' it may be for a short time only. These are the only times that existence is of any value to me. Continue then to love me my ever dear Martha, and to be assured that to yourself, your sister and those dear to you, every thing in my life is devoted. Ambition has no hold on me but thro' you. My personal affections would fix me for ever with you. Present me affectionately to Mr. Randolph, kiss the dear little objects of our natural love, and be assured of the constancy and tenderness of mine to you. Adieu.   TH: JEFFERSON

To Mary Jefferson Eppes

Washington Feb. 15. 1801.

Your letter, my dear Maria, of the 2d. inst. came to hand on the 8th. I should have answered it instantly according to our arrangement, but that I thought, by waiting till the 11th. I might possibly be able to communicate something on the subject of the election. However, after 4. days of balloting,[1] they are exactly where they were on the first. There is a strong expectation in some that they will coalesce tomorrow: but I know no foundation for it. Whatever event happens, I think I shall be at Monticello earlier than I formerly mentioned to you. I think it more likely I may be able to leave this place by the middle of March. I hope I shall find you at Monticello. The scene passing here makes me pant to be away from it: to fly from the circle of cabal, intrigue and hatred, to one where all is love and peace. Tho' I never doubted of your affections, my dear, yet the expressions of them in your letter give me ineffable pleasure. No, never imagine that there can be a difference with me between yourself and your sister. You have both such dispositions as engross my whole love, and each so entirely that there can be no greater degree of it than each possesses. Whatever absences I may be led into for a while, I look for happiness to the moment when we can all be settled together, no more to separate. I feel no impulse from personal ambition to the office now proposed to me, but on account of yourself and your sister, and those dear to you. I feel a sincere wish indeed to see our government brought back to it's republican principles, to see that kind of government firmly fixed, to which my whole life has been devoted. I hope we shall now see it so established, as that when I retire, it may be under full security that we are to continue free and happy. As soon as the fate of the election is over, I will drop a line to Mr. Eppes. I hope one of you will always write the moment you recieve a letter from me. Continue to love me my dear as you ever have done, and ever have been and will be your's affectionately,   TH: JEFFERSON

1. The balloting in the Electoral College ended in a tie between TJ and Burr; each received 73 votes. This threw the election into the House of Representatives, where another deadlock occurred. The Federalists in caucus decided to support Burr; Alexander Hamilton, however, backed TJ as the lesser of two evils, and on the 36th ballot on February 17 TJ was named President.

President of the
United States of America

To Mary Jefferson Eppes

Monticello Apr. 11. 1801.

MY DEAR MARIA

I wrote to Mr. Eppes on the 8th. instant by post, to inform him I should on the 12th. send off a messenger to the Hundred for the horses he may have bought for me. Davy Bowles[1] will accordingly set out tomorrow, and will be the bearer of this. He leaves us all well, and wanting nothing but your's and Mr. Eppes's company to make us compleatly happy. Let me know by his return when you expect to be here, that I may accomodate to that my orders as to executing the interior work of the different parts of the house. John[2] being at work under Lilly, Goliah is our gardener, and with his veteran aids, will be directed to make what preparation he can for you. It is probable I shall come home myself about the last week of July or first of August to stay two months, and then be absent again at least six months. In fact I expect only to ma[ke a sh]ort visit to this place of a fortnight or three weeks in April and two months during the sickly season in autumn every year. These terms I shall hope to pass with you here, and that either in spring or fall you will be able to pass some time with me in Washington. Had it been possible, I would have made a tour now on my return to see you, but I am tied to a day for my return to Washington to assemble our new administration, and begin our work systematically. I hope, when you come up, you will make very short stages, drive slow and safely, which may well be done if you do not permit yourselves to be hurried. Surely the sooner you come the better. The servants will be here under your commands and such supplies as the house affords. Before that time our bacon will be here from Bedford. Continue to love me, my dear Maria, as affectionately as I do you. I have no object so near my heart as your's and your sister's happiness. Present me affectionately to Mr. Eppes and be assured yourself of my unchangeable and tenderest attachment to you.   TH: JEFFERSON

1. A trusted slave.
2. John Hemings.

FROM MARY JEFFERSON EPPES

Eppington April 18th [1801]

I recieved your letter only yesterday My Dear Papa nor did I know 'till a few days before that you were at Monticello, as we have been here for some time past which has prevented our hearing from you. The prospect of seeing you so much sooner than I expected has in some degree consoled me for not being able to join you at this time, tho' I am afraid I shall lament more than ever the distance which separates me from Monticello as I fear it will be an obstacle not allways to be surmounted and that I shall not have the satisfaction even of allways spending with you the short time that you will now remain there. It will not be in our power to go up before the 20th of july Mr. Eppes says, and from that time My dear Papa till you return it will not be necessary to make any difference in your arrangements for us. The servants we shall carry up will be more than sufficient for ourselves and you would perhaps prefer yours being employed in some way or other. I send you the lettuce seed which Mr. Bolling promis'd you last year. Adieu My dear Papa. I shall be much obliged to you if you will take the trouble of keeping that small sum which is at present in Mr. Jeffersons hands for the tobacco, for me as I should prefer laying it out in Washington. Adieu once more my dear Papa. Pardon this scrawl for I have had scarcely time to write it and believe me with tenderest affection yours,   MEPPES

TO MARTHA JEFFERSON RANDOLPH

Washington May. 28. 1801.

MY VERY DEAR MARTHA

I recieved yesterday Mr. Randolph's letter of the 23d. giving me the always welcome news of your health. I have not heard from Maria since I have been here. It is a terrible thing that people will not write unless they have materials to make a long letter: when three words would be so acceptable. Mrs. Madison left us two days ago, to commence housekeeping, so that Capt. Lewis[1] and myself are like two mice in a church. It would be the greatest comfort imaginable to have you or Maria here. But this wish must be subordinate to your family affairs. Mrs. Madison's stay here enabled me to begin an acquaintance with the ladies of the place, so as to have established the precedent of having them at our dinners. Still their future visits will be awkward to themselves in the present construction of our family. I inclose for Anne some trifles cut out of the newspapers.[2] Tell Ellen I will send her a pretty story as soon as she can read it. Kiss them all for me; my affectionate esteem to Mr. Randolph and warmest love to yourself.

TH: JEFFERSON

1. Meriwether Lewis.
2. This was a TJ practice that he carried on with the older Randolph grandchildren, particularly Ellen. Unfortunately, none of these scrapbooks have survived; however, TJ's own volume "The Jefferson Scrapbook" is in the Alderman Library at the University of Virginia. This contains a great variety of material, including several poetical works sent to his grandchildren for their scrapbooks. For a discussion of the contents of Jefferson's, consult John W. Wayland, "The Poetical Tastes of Thomas Jefferson," *Sewanee Review*, XVIII, 283–99, and William H. Peden, "Thomas Jefferson: Book Collector," an unpublished dissertation at the University of Virginia (1942), 61–63.

To Mary Jefferson Eppes

Washington May 28. 1801.

An immense accumulation of business, my dear Maria, has prevented my writing to you since my arrival at this place. But it has [not] prevented my having you in my mind daily and hourly, and feeling much anxiety to hear from you, and to know that Mr. Eppes and yourself are in good health. I am in hopes you will not stay longer than harvest where you are, as the unhealthy season advances rapidly after that. Mr. and Mrs. Madison staid with me about three weeks till they could get ready a house to recieve them. This has given me an opportunity of making some acquaintance with the ladies here. We shall certainly have a very agreeable and worthy society. It would make them as well as myself very happy could I always have yourself or your sister here but this desire, however deeply felt by me, must give way to the private concerns of Mr. Eppes. I count that in autumn both yourself and sister, with Mr. Eppes and Mr. Randolph will pass some time with me but this shall be arranged at Monticello where I shall be about the end of July or beginning of August. Ask the favor of Mr. Eppes, to inform me as soon as he can learn himself the age, and blood of the several horses he was so kind as to purchase for me. Present him my affectionate attachment, as also to the family at Eppington when you have an opportunity. Remember that our letters are to be answered immediately on their reciept, by which means we shall mutually hear from each other about every three weeks. Accept assurances of my constant and tender love.

TH: JEFFERSON

FROM MARY JEFFERSON EPPES

Bermuda Hundred June 18th [1801]

DEAR PAPA

Mr. Eppes is at present busily engaged in his harvest, it has been somewhat retarded by rain which will make us rather later in our journey up than we intended. I am however very busily employed preparing to leave this for Eppington where I shall remain 'till Mr. Eppes can join me and I hope in three or four weeks at the farthest to be at Monticello, and that you will be there allmost as soon [as] we shall.

How happy I feel dearest Papa at the idea of spending a month or two with you again. I was afraid as the time approached that you would not have found it convenient to leave Washington for that time tho not long. My sister will I hope be with us during your short stay. Her friends will not surely be so inconsiderate as to visit her during the only time it will be in her power to be with you. It will compensate somewhat for the long separations which I fear I shall now experience if when we do meet we can be alltogether. But I must bid you adieu My Dear Papa it is so dark I can scarcely distinguish what I write. If Mr. Eppes remembers the ages and blood of the horses he will put it down in this letter. He goes to Petersburg before we leave this and can easily learn there if he does not. Adieu once more dear Papa. Your affectionate daughter,   M EPPES

FROM MARTHA JEFFERSON RANDOLPH

Edgehill June 19 1801

In an absence of 3 months I blush to think that this is the first time I have written to My Dear Father. It does not arise however as you suppose from want of materials, and still less of inclination, but from a spirit of procrastination which by inducing me to defer allways to the last moment, finally ocasions the total loss of opportunity. My affections my thoughts are however perpetually with you, incessantly hovering over you, there is no one scene in your solitary establishment in which they have not visited you. And never with out deeply regretting the unavoidable necessity of your spending so much of your time cut off from that society which alone gives a charm to life, and which you of all others in the world estimate most highly. However the time is at hand when every thing will be forgotten in a blest reunion of every individual of those we most love once more at Monticello and as the time approaches the spirits of the family proportionably increase. You have suffered a little from the last tremendous hail storm, from the [circumstance?] of 2 of the sky lights being uncovered. *They* were totally demolished and I believe it is owing to the accident of the storm's raging with so much more fury in the valley than on the mountains that you escaped so much better than your neighbours. The damage was immense in Charlottesville and Milton, allmost every window broken in some houses; we also suffered considerably and the more so as we have not been able to replace in either of the above mentioned places the glasses which has occasioned us to the violence of every succeeding rain in a degree that renders the house scarcely tenantable.

Your stockings are at last disposed of, but not to my satisfaction because I am sure they will not be so to yours. Aunt Carr after many ineffectual efforts to put them *out* acceded at last to the united and importunate entreaties of Mrs. Randolph[1] and Mrs. Lilburn Lewis[2] to let them knit them for you; and Aunt Lewis dining with me a few days after and hearing of the failure of the means upon which I had counted in accomplishing my part of the under taking, insisted in a manner [baffled?] resistance upon my letting her and her Daughters take them home and do them. It is a disagreable piece of business, but one not to have been fore seen in the first instance and not to be avoided afterwards with out hurting the feelings and perhaps giving offence to those without hurting the feelings and perhaps giving offence to those ladies. Inclosed are samples Fontrice[3] was to have carried, of the cotton one is too fine, the other too coarse. A size between the two would answer better than either. The sheeting is also I think rather coarse but not much so. Adieu dearest Father. The children are all confusing me with messages of various descriptions but the post hour is past and I am afraid my letter will scarcely be in time. Believe me with ardent affection yours,   M. RANDOLPH

1. Possibly Jane Cary Randolph Randolph (Mrs. Thomas Eston).
2. Lucy Jefferson Lewis (Mrs. Charles Lilburn, Jr.) was TJ's sister; she had five daughters.
3. Valentine Fontress was an Albemarle County resident who hauled for the Monticello family.

To Mary Jefferson Eppes

Washington June 24. 1801.

My dear Maria

According to contract, immediately on the reciept of Mr. Eppes's letter of the 12th. I wrote him mine of the 17th and having this moment recieved yours of June 18th. I hasten to reply to that also. I am very anxious you should hasten your departure for Monticello, but go a snail's pace when you set out. I shall certainly be with you the last week of July or first week of August. I have a letter from your sister this morning. All are well. They have had all their windows almost broken by a hailstorm, and are unable to procure glass, so that they are living almost out of doors. The whole neighborhood suffered equally. Two skylights at Monticello which had been left uncovered, were entirely broken up. No other windows, there were broke. I give reason to expect that both yourself and your sister will come here in the fall. I hope it myself: and our society here is anxious for it. I promise them that one of you will hereafter pass the spring here, and the other the fall; saving your consent to it. All this must be arranged when we meet. I am here interrupted so with my affectionate regards to the family at Eppington and Mr. Eppes and tenderest love to yourself I must bid you adieu.   Th: Jefferson

To Martha Jefferson Randolph

Washington June. 25. 1801.

My dear Martha

Your's of the 19. came to hand yesterday. As it says nothing of your health I presume all are well. I recieved yesterday also a letter from Maria of the 18th. She was then well and preparing to go to Eppington, and in about 4. weeks expected to set out for Albemarle. Mr. Eppes was engaged in his harvest much obstructed by rain, and regretting he had not before deposited Maria at Monticello. I hope she will get there safe. Tho' it is yet more than a month before I can set out for the same destination, yet I begin with pleasure to make memorandums, lay by what is to be carried there &c. &c. for the pleasure of thinking of it, of looking forward to the moment when we shall be all there together. Amidst the havoc made by the hailstorm in Albemarle I think myself well off to have had only two windows demolished. I should have ex-

pected my large panes of glass would have broken easily. I inclose
a little story for Anne as I have sometimes done before. Tell Ellen
as soon as she can read them, I will select some beautiful ones for
her. They shall be black, red, yellow, green and of all sorts of
colours. I suppose you have had cucumbers and raspberries long
ago. Neither are yet at market here, tho some private gardens have
furnished them. Present me affectionately to Mr. Randolph who
I suppose is now busy in his harvest. I rejoice at the prospect of
price for wheat, and hope he will be able to take the benefit of
the early market. If his own threshing machine is not ready, he
is free to send for mine, which is in order and may expedite his
getting out. Kiss the little ones for me and be assured of my constant and tenderest love.   TH: JEFFERSON

To Martha Jefferson Randolph

Washington July 16. 1801.

MY DEAR MARTHA

I recieved yesterday Mr. Randolph's letter of the 11th. and at
the same time one from Mr. Eppes. He had just carried Maria to
Eppington with the loss of a horse on the road. They are to
leave Eppington tomorrow at farthest for Monticello, so that by
the time you recieve this they will be with you. From what Mr.
Randolph writes I should think you had better go over at once
with your sister to Monticello and take up your quarters there. I
shall join you in the first seven days of August. In the mean time
the inclosed letter to Mr. Craven (which I pray you to send him)
will secure you all the resources for the house which he can supply.
Liquors have been sent on and I learn are arrived, tho' with some
loss. Lilly has before recieved orders to furnish what he can as if
I were there. I wish you would notify him to be collecting geese
and ducks and to provide new flour. Of lambs I presume he has
plenty. I have had groceries waiting here some time for a conveyance. Would it not be well for you to send at once for Mrs. Marks? [1]
Remus [2] and my chair are at Monticello, and Phill [3] as usual can
go for her. I this day inclose to Dr. Wardlaw [4] some publications
on the kine pox, with a request to make himself acquainted with
them. I shall probably be able to carry on some infectious matter
with a view of trying whether we cannot introduce it there. The
first essay here has proved unsuccessful but some matter recieved
6. days ago and immediately used, will prove this day whether it

takes or not; and I am promised by Dr. Waterhouse[5] of Boston successive weekly supplies till it takes. If the matter be genuine there is no doubt it prevents the Small pox. I send you a piece of music sent to me. If the music be no better than the words it will not shine. Also some small things for Anne. Kiss them all for me. Present me affectionately to Mr. Randolph, and be assured yourself of my warmest love. TH: JEFFERSON

1. Anna Scott Marks (Mrs. Hastings). TJ supplied the transportation for his sister to visit Monticello.
2. A horse.
3. A slave.
4. Dr. William Wardlaw was an Albemarle County physician.
5. Dr. Benjamin Waterhouse.

TO MARY JEFFERSON EPPES

Washington July 16. 1801.

MY DEAR MARIA

I recieved yesterday Mr. Eppes's letter of the 12th. informing me you had got safely to Eppington, and would set out tomorrow at furthest for Monticello. This letter therefore will, I hope, find you there. I now write to Mr. Craven to furnish you all the supplies of the table which his firm affords. Mr. Lilly had before recieved orders to do the same. Liquors have been forwarded and have arrived with some loss. I insist that you command and use everything as if I were with you, and shall be very uneasy if you do not. A supply of groceries has been lying here some time waiting for a conveyance. It will probably be three weeks from this time before they can be at Monticello. In the mean time take what is wanting from any of the stores with which I deal on my account. I have recommended to your sister to send at once for Mrs. Marks. Remus and my chair with Phill as usual can go for her. I shall join you between the 2d. and 7th. more probably not till the 7th. Mr. and Mrs. Madison leave this about a week hence. I am looking forward with great impatience to the moment when we can all be joined at Monticello, and hope we shall never again know so long a separation. I recommend to your sister to go over at once to Monticello, which I hope she will do. It will be safer for her, and more comfortable for both. Present me affectionately to Mr. Eppes, and be assured of my constant and tenderest love.

TH: JEFFERSON

From Martha Jefferson Randolph

Edgehill July 25 1801

Your letters found us all *together* at Edgehill. Maria does not look well but considering all things she seems to be in as good health as can be expected. My own has been uncommonly so, since my return from Monticello. With your request of going over immediately it is utterally impossible to comply; Mrs. Bache's family being with us at present, and to remain untill, the Doctor's return. Maria stays with *us* untill you join us and from what she says will not I hope require *my* attentions until I am *able* to bestow them entirely upon her. We have not sent for Aunt Marks because of the present size of our family which would render it, (with the expected addition) impossible to accomodate her. She might feel hurt at the idea of being at Monticello. Your other commissions shall be faithfully executed with regard to Lilly and altho it will not be in my power to be with you as soon as I could wish yet the idea of being so near you and the pleasure of seeing you sometimes will enliven a time otherwise dreary and monotonous. Adieu ever dear Father. Believe me with unchangeable affections yours,

M. RANDOLPH

To Martha Jefferson Randolph

Washington Oct. 19. 1801.

I am in hopes, my dear Martha, that I shall hear by the arrival of tomorrow morning's post that you are all well. In the mean while the arrangement is such that my letter must go hence this evening. My last letter was from Mr. Eppes of Oct. 3. when all were well. I inclose a Crazy Jane[1] for Anne, and a sweetheart[2] for Ellen. The latter instead of the many coloured stories which she cannot yet read. From the resolution you had taken I imagine you are now at Edgehill surrounded by the cares and the comforts of your family. I wish they may be less interrupted than at Monticello. I set down this as a year of life lost to myself, having been crowded out of the enjoiment of the family during the only recess I can take in the year. I believe I must hereafter not let it be known when I intend to be at home, and make my visits by stealth. There is real disappointment felt here at neither of you coming with me. I promise them on your faith for the ensuing spring. I wish however that may be found as convenient a season of absence for Mr. Randolph. Mr. Madison and family are with us for a few days, their house having been freshly plaistered and not yet dry enough to go into. Such is the drought here that nobody can remember when it rained last. My sincere affections to Mr. Randolph and Mr. Eppes, kisses to the young ones and my tenderest love to Maria and yourself.   TH: JEFFERSON

1. Crazy Jane, a game.
2. Probably a small sugar cake in the form of a heart.

TO MARY JEFFERSON EPPES

Washington Oct. 26. 1801.

MY EVER DEAR MARIA

I have heard nothing of you since Mr. Eppes's letter dated the day sennight after I left home. The Milton mail will be here tomorrow morning when I shall hope to recieve something. In the mean time this letter must go hence this evening. I trust it will still find you at Monticello, and that possibly Mr. Eppes may have concluded to take a journey to Bedford and still farther prolonged your stay. I am anxious to hear from you, lest you should have suffered in the same way now as on a former similar occasion. Should any thing of that kind take place and the remedy which succeeded before fail now. I know nobody to whom I would so soon apply as Mrs. Suddarth.[1] A little experience is worth a great deal of reading, and she has had great experience and a sound judgment to observe on it. I shall be glad to hear at the same time that the little boy is well. If Mr. Eppes undertakes what I have proposed to him at Pantops and Poplar Forest the next year, I should think it indispensable that he should make Monticello his headquarters. You can be furnished with all plantation articles for the family from Mr. Craven who will be glad to pay his rent in that way. It would be a great satisfaction to me to find you fixed there in April. Perhaps it might induce me to take flying trips by stealth, to have the enjoiment of family society for a few days undisturbed. Nothing can repay me the loss of that society, the only one founded in affection and bosom confidence. I have here company enough, part of which is very friendly, part well enough disposed, part secretly hostile and a constant succession of strangers. But this only serves to get rid of life, not to enjoy it. It is in the love of one's family only that heartfelt happiness is known. I feel it when we are all together and alone beyond what can be imagined. Present

me affectionately to Mr. Eppes, Mr. Randolph and my dear
Martha, and be assured yourself of my tenderest love.

TH: JEFFERSON

1. Possibly Mrs. James Suddarth, a midwife. TJ was suggesting that she
assist Mary in recovering from any aftereffects of the birth of her son Francis
Wayles Eppes, who was born September 20 at Monticello.

FROM MARY JEFFERSON EPPES

Monticello November the 6th [1801]

I did not write to you last week My dear Papa, I had discover'd
my little Francis had the hooping cough and my apprehensions
about him were so great that I could not at that time write. He
has now struggled with it eleven days and tho he coughs most
violently so as to become perfectly black with it in the face he is
so little affected by it otherwise that my hopes are great that he
will go through with it. He has as yet lost no flesh and has had
only one fever. We shall endeavour to travel with him the last
of next week if he is not worse. I have borrow'd Crita [1] as a nurse
for this winter. Betsy's ill health was such that I could not depend
on her as one and we shall return with Crita in the spring to meet
you. The children at Edgehill stand the disorder very well,
Cornelia suffers most with it but she still looks very well (Mr.
Eppes says who saw her yesterday). Ellen next to her is most unwell, the other three are better, Virginia [2] particularly. I have not
seen my sister since her return to Edgehill. She remain'd here four
weeks after you left us during which time except a few days we
were entirely alone. How much we did wish for you then, My
dear Papa, but I am afraid that except in the spring we shall never
enjoy the happiness of being alone with you. Nothing would give
me greater pleasure could Mr. Eppes so arrange it as to spend the
next summer here. The hope of a flying visit sometimes from you,
would alone make it most desirable independent of every thing
else. Adieu dear Papa. Believe me most tenderly yours,

M EPPES

1. Crita was a slave daughter of Betty Hemings.
2. Virginia Jefferson Randolph was born August 22, 1801, at Monticello.

FROM ELLEN WAYLES RANDOLPH

recd Nov. 10. [1801]

How do you do my dear Grand papa. I thank you for the picture you sent me. All my sisters have got the hooping cough. Vir-

ginia has got a very bad cold. I hope you will bring me some books my dear grand papa. I thank you. When I was writing the children made such a noise I could not write well. Your affectionate Grand daughter,   ELLENANORA. W. RANDOLPH

Make hast to come home to see us and all our books in the press.

FROM MARTHA JEFFERSON RANDOLPH

recd. Nov. 10. 1801

I am doomed to write to you in a hurry allways My Dearest Father. Abraham [1] who will be the bearer of this has arrived. I began my letter, and it will not be proper to make him wait [longer] than I can possibly help it. My children are doing generally well except Ellen and Cornelia the latter has had fever for three days and with triffling intermissions morning and evening tho very short. We have reason to fear they have worms in which case the worst consequences [are] to be apprehended unless they can be destroyed before the disorder weakens them too much to resist. That we are told has generally been the fate of those who have died of it. Francis is doing well. His cough is extremely violent but he continues to thrive in which case I apprehend the danger not to be great. Virginia is in the same state, coughing most violently so as to endanger strangling but evidently gaining strength to contend with it. I have been very unwell my self from cold taken by frequent getting up in the night and want of sleep but am infinitely better today however I have no reason to expect to be well again untill the fatigue of nursing is over. Adieu Dearest Father. Believe me with tender affection yours,

M RANDOLPH

1. Abraham Goulding, one of TJ's Washington servants. He was not a slave.

FROM MARTHA JEFFERSON RANDOLPH

Edgehill November 18 1801

DEAREST FATHER

Mr. Trist who will deliver this can also give a better account of the children than (limited as I am for time) I possibly can however I must write a few lines to you if it is only to wonder at your long silence. Each successive post has been anxiously expected and desired, only to bring along with it fresh dissapointment. My sister left us on Monday with her little boy better than would be expected, but in a very precarious state of being. He is (altho healthy except for the whooping cough) the most delicate creature I ever beheld. Mine are doing well, all but poor Ellen, who looks wretchedly is much reduced and weakened by the cough which still continues upon her with extreme violence. Little Virginia is recovering, still distressing us at times but the crisis seems to be over with all of them. It was a terrible moment. Ellen and Cornelia were particularly ill both delirious one singing and laughing the other (Ellen) gloomy and terrified equally unconscious of the objects around them. My God what moment for a Parent. The agonies of Mr. Randolph's mind seemed to call forth every energy of mine. I had to act in the double capacity of nurse to my children and comforter to their Father. It is of service perhaps to be obliged to exert one self upon those occasions. Certainly the mind acquires strength by it to bear up against evils that in other circumstances would totally overcome it. I am recovering from the fatigue which attended the illness of my children and I am at this moment in more perfect health than I have been for years. Adieu beloved Father. You would write oftener if you knew how much pleasure your letters give. There is not a child in the house that does not run at the return of the messenger to know if there is a letter from Grand Papa. Stewart[1] your white smith is returned. The plaistering at Monticello goes on, not as well as the first room which was elegantly done but better than the 3d and fourth, the two I think you would have been most anxious about, being below stairs. Moran[2] goes on slowly. Every one the children with the whoping cough excepted is well and they are none of them bad but every thing upon the land (at Monticello) has it. Once more Adieu. Believe me with ardent affection yours. To tell you that it is past one o'clock will appologize for a great deal of incorectness in this scrawl and the hurried way in [which] I generally work will account for the rest.   M. RANDOLPH

1. William Stewart the very able Monticello blacksmith fashioned much of the ironwork used in Monticello.
2. Joseph Moran was a Monticello workman, a stonemason.

TO ELLEN WAYLES RANDOLPH

Washington Nov. 27. 1801.

MY DEAR ELLEN

I have recieved your letter and am very happy to find you have made such rapid progress in learning. When I left Monticello you could not read, and now I find you can not only read, but write also. I inclose you two little books as a mark of my satisfaction, and if you continue to learn as fast, you will become a learned lady and publish books yourself. I hope you will at the same time continue to be a very good girl, never getting angry with your playmates nor the servants, but always trying to be more good humored and more generous than they. If ever you find that one of them has been better tempered to you than you to them, you must blush, and be very much ashamed, and resolve not to let them excel you again. In this way you will make us all too fond of you, and I shall particularly think of nothing but what I can send you or carry you to shew you how much I love you. I hope you are getting the better of your whooping cough. You will learn to bear it patiently when you consider you can never have it again. I have given this letter 20. kisses which it will deliver to you: half for yourself, and the other half you must give to Anne. Adieu my dear Ellen.   TH: JEFFERSON

TO MARTHA JEFFERSON RANDOLPH

Washington Nov. 27. 1801.

MY DEAR MARTHA

Your's of Nov. 18. by Mr. Trist has been duly recieved. My business is become so intense that, when post day comes, it is often out of my power to spare a moment. The post too, being now on the winter establishment is three days longer in carrying our letters. I am sincerely concerned at the situation of our dear little ones with the whooping cough, but much rejoiced that they have past the crisis of the disease safely. There is no disease whatever which I so much dread with children. I have not heard from Maria since she left you: but generally sucking children bear that disease better than those a little past that stage. I hope therefore her little Francis will do well. I am afraid from what I hear that Moran and Perry[1] have gone on badly with my works at Monticello. I am anxious to see the hull of the buildings once done with. We are all overjoyed with the news of peace. I consider it as the most fortunate thing which could have happened to place the present administration on advantageous ground. The only rock we feared was war; and it did not depend on ourselves but others whether we should keep out of it. We hope Great Britain will have so much to do at home that she will not have time to intrigue and plot against this country. We are now within 10. days of Congress when our campaign will begin and will probably continue to April. I hope I shall continue to hear from you often, and always that the children are doing well. My affections and contemplations are all with you, where indeed all my happiness centers. My cordial esteem to Mr. Randolph, kisses to the little ones, and tenderest love to yourself.   TH: JEFFERSON

1. John Perry, a Monticello carpenter.

TO MARY JEFFERSON EPPES

Washington Dec. 14. 1801.

MY DEAR MARIA

I recieved in due time yours and Mr. Eppes's letters of Nov. 6. and his of Nov. 26. This last informed me you would stay in Eppington 2. or 3. weeks. Having had occasion to write during that time to Mr. F. Eppes without knowing at the moment that you were there, you would of course know I was well. This with the unceasing press of business has prevented my writing to you. Presuming this will still find you at Eppington, I direct it to Colesville.[1] Mr. Eppes's letter having informed me that little Francis was still in the height of his whooping cough, and that you had had a sore breast, I am very anxious to hear from you. The family at Edgehill have got out of all danger. Ellen and Cornelia have been in the most imminent danger. I hear of no death at Monticello except old Tom Shackelford. My stonemasons have done scarcely anything there. Congress is just setting in on business. We have a very commanding majority in the house of Representatives and a safe majority in the Senate. I believe therefore all things will go on smoothly, except a little ill-temper to be expected from the minority, who are bitterly mortified. I hope there is a letter on the road informing how you all are. I percieve that it will be merely accidental when I can steal a moment to write to you, however that is of no consequence; my health being always so firm as to leave you without doubt on that subject. But it is not so with yourself and little one. I shall not be easy therefore if either yourself or Mr. Eppes do not once a week or fortnight write the three words 'all are well.' That you may be so now and so continue is the subject of my perpetual anxiety, as my affections are constantly brooding over you. Heaven bless you my dear daughter. Present me affectionately to Mr. Eppes and my friends at Eppington if you are there.   TH: JEFFERSON

P. S. After signing my name, I was called to receive Doctr. Walker[2]

who delivers me a letter from Mr. Eppes informing me of your
state on the 7th. inst. which is not calculated to remove anxiety.

1. A small community in Chesterfield County, about thirty-six miles southwest of Richmond.
2. Dr. Thomas Walker.

To Martha Jefferson Randolph

Washington Jan. 17. 1802.

This is merely, my dear Martha, to say that all is well. It is very
long since I have heard from you. My last letter from Edgehill
being of the 6th. of Dec. A letter of Jan. 6. from Mr. Eppes at
Richmond informed me that Maria was entirely reestablished in
her health, and her breast quite well. The little boy too was well
and healthy. Dr. Gantt[1] has inoculated six of his Cow-pox patients
with the small pox, not one of which took it. Many have been tried
in Philadelphia, and with the same issue. As the matter here came
from Monticello, and that at Philadelphia from this place, they
establish the genuineness of our inoculations and may place our
families and neighbors in perfect security. Congress have as yet
passed but one bill. The repeal of the Judiciary law[2] is rather
doubtful in the Senate, by the absence of two republican Senators.
Great opposition is made to the reduction of the army, the navy,
and the taxes. They will be reduced; but some republican votes
will fly the way on the occasion. Mr. Dawson[3] arrived here three
or four days ago. Present me affectionately to Mr. Randolph, and
the young ones, and be assured yourself of my constant and
tenderest love.   TH: JEFFERSON
P. S. In my last week's letter to Mr. Randolph I inclosed one for
Mr. Lilly with 940.D. in it, which I shall be glad to hear got safe
to hand.

1. Dr. Edward Gantt was a Washington physician who shared his investi-
gations of smallpox and vaccine with TJ.
2. The Judiciary Act of 1801; it was repealed March 8.
3. Martin Dawson was an Albemarle County resident and friend of TJ's.

From Mary Jefferson Eppes

Eppington jan 24th [1802]

It makes me blush to think of the length of time which has
elaps'd since I wrote to you last My Dear Papa. Deprived for 6
weeks of the use of my hands, I was after recovering them so

closely[1] employ'd with work which during that time had greatly accumulated that without intending it it has been postponed 'till now. I have only thought the more of you My Dear Papa, of that I hope you need never be assured, that you are of all most dear to my heart and most constantly in my thoughts. With how much regret have I look'd back on the last two months that I was with you, more as I fear it will allways be the case now in your summer visits to have a crowd, and in the spring I am afraid it not be in my power to go up. It would make me most happy to go to Washington to see you but I have been so little accustom'd to be in as much company as I should be in there to recieve the civilitys and attentions which as your daughter I should meet with and return, that I am sensible it is best for me to remain where I am. I have not heard from Edgehill since I left it. Mr. Eppes wrote once to my sister when I was unable to do it. But I must bid you adieu My dear Papa. Could I be as certain of the continuance of your good health as you may now be of mine I should endeavour to be satisfied in not hearing from you oftener, but while you are devoting your days and nights to the business of your country I must feel anxious and fearful that your health will suffer by it. Adieu once more my dear Papa. I shall write to you once more from here. My little son is getting much better tho' he still engrosses so much of my time that it is scarcely in my power to do any thing else. He is cutting teeth now which makes him more fretful than usual. Adieu. Yours with the most tender affection,   M EPPES

1. The nature of Maria's ailment is not known.

FROM ANNE CARY RANDOLPH

Edgehill Feb. 26. 1802

DEAR GRAND PAPA

I am very glad that I can write to you. I hope you are well. We are all perfectly recovered from our whooping cough. I thank you for the book you sent me. I am translating Justin's ancient history.[1] I want to see you very much believe me. Cornelia sends her love to you and has been trying to write to you. Adieu my Dear Grand Papa. Believe me your affectionate Grand Daughter.

ANNE CARY RANDOLPH

1. Marcus Junianus Justinus [*De historiis Philippicis et totius Mundi originibus* . . .]. TJ owned the London 1701 edition, and it may be presumed this is what the eleven-year-old Anne Cary was translating. Sowerby 36.

To ANNE CARY, THOMAS JEFFERSON, AND ELLEN WAYLES RANDOLPH

Washington Mar. 2. 1802.

MY DEAR CHILDREN

I am very happy to find that two of you can write. I shall now expect that whenever it is inconvenient for your papa and mama to write, one of you will write on a piece of paper these words 'all is well' and send it for me to the post office. I am happy too that Miss Ellen can now read so readily. If she will make haste and read through all the books I have given her, and will let me know when she is through them, I will go and carry her some more. I shall now see whether she wishes to see me as much as she says. I wish to see you all: and the more I perceive that you are all advancing in your learning and improving in good dispositions the more I shall love you, and the more every body will love you. It is a charming thing to be loved by every body: and the way to obtain it is, never to quarrel or be angry with any body and to tell a story. Do all the kind things you can to your companions, give them every thing rather than to yourself. Pity and help any thing you see in distress and learn your books and improve your minds. This will make every body fond of you, and desirous of doing it to you. Go on then my dear children, and, when we meet at Monticello, let me see who has improved most. I kiss this paper for each of you: it will therefore deliver the kisses to yourselves, and two over, which one of you must deliver to your Mama for me; and present my affectionate attachment to your papa. Yourselves love and Adieux.   TH: JEFFERSON

To MARY JEFFERSON EPPES

Washington, Mar. 3. 1802.

MY VERY DEAR MARIA

I observed to you some time ago that during the session of Congress I should be able to write to you but seldom; and so it has turned out. Yours of Jan. 24. I recieved in due time, after which Mr. Eppes's letters of Feb. 1. and 2. confirmed to me the news, always welcome, of your's and Francis's health. Since this I have no news of you. I see with great concern that I am not to have the pleasure of meeting you in Albemarle in the spring. I had entertained the hope Mr. Eppes and yourself would have past the summer there. And being there, that the two families

could have come together on a visit here. I observe your reluctance at the idea of that visit, but for your own happiness must
advise you to get the better of it. I think I discover in you a willingness to withdraw from society more than is prudent. I am convinced our own happiness requires that we should continue to
mix with the world, and to keep pace with it as it goes; and that
every person who retires from free communication with it is
severely punished afterwards by the state of mind into which they
get, and which can only be prevented by feeding our sociable principles. I can speak from experience on this subject. From 1793.
to 1797. I remained closely at home, saw none but those who came
there, and at length became very sensible of the ill effect it had
upon my own mind, and of it's direct and irresistible tendency to
render me unfit for society, and uneasy when necessarily engaged
in it. I felt enough of the effect of withdrawing from the world
then, to see that it led to an antisocial and misanthropic state of
mind, which severely punishes him who gives in to it: and it will
be a lesson I never shall forget as to myself. I am certain you would
be pleased with the state of society here, and that after the first
moments you would feel happy in having made the experiment. I
take for granted your sister will come immediately after my spring
visit to Monticello, and I should have thought it agreeable to both
that your first visit should be made together. In that case your best
way would be to come direct from the Hundred by Newcastle, and
Todd's bridge to Portroyal where I could send a light Coach to
meet you, and crossing Patomac at Boyd's hole you would come
up by Sam Carr's to this place. I suppose it 60. miles from Portroyal to this place by that route, whereas it would be 86. to come
from Portroyal up the other side of the river by Fredericksburg
and Alexandria. However if the spring visit cannot be effected then
I shall not relinquish your promise to come in the fall: of course,
at our meeting at Monticello in that season we can arrange it.
In the mean time should the settlement take place which I expect
between Mr. Wayles's and Mr. Skelton's executors, and Eppington
be the place, I shall rely on passing some time with you there.
But in what month I know not. Probably towards mid summer.
I hardly think Congress will rise till late in April. My trip to
Monticello will be about a fortnight. I am anxious to hear from
you, as during the period of your being a nurse, I am always afraid
of your continuing in health. I hope Mr. Eppes and yourself will
soon make your calculations as to leave the Hundred by the beginning of July at least. You should never trust yourselves in

the lower country later than that. I shall pass the months of August and September at Monticello where I hope we shall all be reunited. Continue to love me, my dear, as I do you and be assured that my happiness depends on your affections and happiness. I embrace you with all my love.   TH: JEFFERSON

FROM THOMAS JEFFERSON RANDOLPH

recd Mar. 3 1802.

MY DEAR GRAND PAPA

I hope you are well. It gives me great pleasure to be able to write to you. I have been through my latin grammar twice and mamma thinks that I improved in my reading. I am not going to school now but cousin Beverly[1] and my self are going to a latin school in the spring. Adieu my dear Grand Papa. I want to see you very much indeed. Believe me your affectionate Grandson,

THOMAS J R

1. Thomas Beverley Randolph was the son of William and Lucy Bolling Randolph; his father was a younger brother of Thomas Mann Randolph, Jr.

TO MARY JEFFERSON EPPES

Washington Mar. 29. 1802.

I wrote, my ever dear Maria, to Mr. Eppes and yourself on the 3d. inst. since which I have recieved Mr. Eppes's letter of the 11th. informing me all were well. I hope you continue so. A letter of the 20th. from Mr. Randolph informed me all were well at Edgehill. Mr. Randolph, allured by the immensely profitable culture of cotton, had come to a resolution to go to the Missisipi territory and there purchase lands and establish all his negroes in that culture.[1] The distance 1500. miles of which 600. are through an uninhabited country, the weakness of that settlement, not more than 800 men, with a population of blacks equal to their own, and surrounded by 8000. Choctaw warriors, and the soil and commercial position moreover not equal to Georgia for the same culture, has at length balanced his determination in favor of Georgia, distant only about 470. or 480. miles from Edgehill. The plan is now arranged as follows. Congress will rise from the 15th. to the 20th. of April. I shall be at Monticello within a week or 10. days after they rise. Mr. Randolph then goes to Georgia to make a purchase of lands, and Martha and the family come back with me and stay till his return, which probably will not be till the latter part of July when I shall be going on to Monticello for the months of Aug. and Sep. I cannot help hoping that while your sister is here you will take a run, if it be but for a short time to come and see us. I have enquired further into the best rout for you, and it is certainly by Portroyal,[2] and to cross over from Boyd's hole,[3] or somewhere near it to Nangemy. You by this means save 30. miles, and have the whole of the way the finest road imaginable, whereas that from Fredericksburg by Dumfries and Alexandria is the worst in the world. Will Mr. Eppes not have the curiosity to go up to his plantation in Albemarle the 1st. or 2d. week of May? There we could settle every thing, and he will hear more of the Georgia expedition. I inclose you two medals,[4] one for yourself, the other with my best affections for Mrs. Eppes. They are taken from Houdon's bust. Present me affectionately to Mr. Eppes and be assured of my tenderest love. TH: JEFFERSON

1. Thomas Mann Randolph, Jr., never went to the Mississippi Territory or to the state of Georgia.

2. A small Caroline County landing on the south side of the Rappahannock River, about 23 miles below Fredericksburg.

3. Boyd's Hole is in King William County, on the western side of the Potomac River.

4. These were by John Reich, and the delineation is found on the 1801 Indian Peace Medal.

TO MARTHA JEFFERSON RANDOLPH

Washington Apr. 3. 1802.

MY DEAR MARTHA

I recieved Anne's letter by the last post, in which she forgot to mention the health of the family, but I presume it good. I inclose you a medal executed by an artist lately from Europe and who appears to be equal to any in the world. It is taken from Houdon's bust, for he never saw me. It sells the more readily as the prints which have been offered the public are such miserable caracatures.[1] Congress will probably rise within three weeks and I shall be on in a week or ten days afterwards. My last to Mr. Randolph explained my expectations as to your motions during his journey. I wrote lately to Maria, encouraging her to pay us a flying visit at least while you are here, and proposing to Mr. Eppes so to time his next plantation visit in Albemarle as to meet me there in the beginning of May. My last information from the Hundred stated them all well, little Francis particularly healthy. Anne writes me that Ellen will be through all her books before I come. She may count therefore on my bringing her a new supply. I have desired Lilly to make the usual provision of necessaries for me at Monticello, and if he should be at a loss for the particulars to consult with you. My orders as to the garden were to sow and plant as usual, and to furnish you with the proceeds. Order them therefore freely: you know they will do nothing if you leave it to their delicacy. I am looking forward with impatience to the moment when I can embrace you in all my affection and the dear children. It already occupies much of my thoughts as the time approaches. Present me affectionately to Mr. Randolph, and be assured yourself of my tenderest love.   TH: JEFFERSON

1. The Reich medal. Consult Stanislaus V. Henkels, *The Hampton L. Carson Collection of Engraved Portraits of Thomas Jefferson* (Philadelphia, n.d.), for a listing of the engravings of TJ.

FROM MARTHA JEFFERSON RANDOLPH

Edgehill April 16 1802

I recieved with gratitude and pleasure unexpressible, my dearest Father, the elegant medal you sent me. It arrived safely with out a scratch even, and is I think a good likeness; but as I found fault with Houdon for making you too old I shall have the same quarrel with the medal also. You have many years to live before the likeness can be a perfect one. Mr.R. desired me to tell you that as his trip to Georgia was but to take a view of the country, a few weeks sooner or later would make no material difference with him and his anxiety to conduct such a family of little children thro the difficulties of the journey would naturally induce him to pospone his as it will be attended by no inconvenience to himself. Ellen and Cornelia have had an erruption attended with fever which has been prevalent in the neighbourhood; certainly not the chicken pox but what else we cannot determine. Ellen is well and Cornelia much better. Virginia is certainly for size and health the finest child I ever had. Cutting her teeth with out fever, disordered bowels or other indication of her situation but the champing of her gums and the appearance of the teeth them selves. The others go on better than they did last winter. Jefferson is reading latin with his Papa but I am seriously uneasy at his not going to school. Mr. Murray[1] with whom we proposed putting him has his number complete and will not I fear take another. Anne translates with tolerable facility, and Ellen reads, not very correctly it is true, but in a way speedily to do so I hope for which I really think we are indebted to your letter expressing your surprise at her having in so short a time learned to read and write; she began with it her self, and by continually spelling out lines and putting them together and then reading them to who ever would listen to her, she convinced me of the practicability of carrying on reading and spelling together before in the regular course of the business she had got into two syllables. The writing she attempted also but the trouble was so much greater than any end to be answered by teaching her at so early a period that very reluctantly I prevailed upon her to defer that part of her education to a more distant one. So much for my hopes and fears with regard to those objects in which they center. The former preponderate upon the whole, yet my anxiety about them frequently makes me unreasonably apprehensive. Unreasonably I think for surely if they turn out well with regard to morals I *ought* to be satisfied, tho I *feel* that I never can sit down quietly under the idea of their being blockheads. Adieu Dear adored Father. We look forward with transport to the time at which we shall all meet at Monticello tho not on my side unmixed with pain when I think it will be the precursor of a return to the world from which I have been so long been secluded and for which my habits render me every way unfit, tho the pleasure of seeing you every day is a good that will render every other evil light. Once more adieu. The children are clamorous to be remembered to you and believe your self *first* and unrivaled in the heart of your devoted child.   M. RANDOLPH

1. Possibly the Reverend Mr. Matthew Maury, son of the Reverend James, who succeeded his father in his classical school as well as in the Rectory of Fredericksville Parish.

To Anne Cary Randolph

Apr. 18. 1802.

TH: JEFFERSON TO HIS VERY DEAR GRANDAUGHTER
ANNE C. RANDOLPH

I send you, my dear Anne, more poems for our 1st. volume.[1] Congress will rise about the last day of the month, and it will not be many days after that before I shall be in the midst of you. In the mean time all is well here, and I have not time to say more, except that you must kiss all the little ones for me and deliver my affections to your papa and mama. Health and tender love to you all.

1. A scrapbook.

FROM MARY JEFFERSON EPPES

Eppington April 21st [1802]

I have written to you twice My Dear Papa by Dr. Walker who was prevented the first time from setting out by the death of one of his sisters. After having seen the last sad duties paid to her he return'd to the Hundred and gave me my letter. I then wrote again but it was forgot by Mr. Eppes who was the only one up when the Doctor went off in the morning. I recieved your last with the medals which I think very much like you. Mine will be very precious to me dear Papa during the long separations from you to which I am doomed and which I feel more cruelly at this time than ever. My father kindly offer'd the only pair of horses he had, to enable us to go up, but more were wanting and Mr. Eppes could not spare his own from the plough at this time. It gives me pleasure to know that you will have my dear Sisters society this summer. If I could how gladly would I join you during part of it but 'till the last of july the horses will be constantly in the plough. My little son grows daily and is daily becoming more dear and interesting to us. He indeed supplies the place of all company to us when at home for there we have no neighbours. He has no teeth yet tho' I think it cannot be long before he has as his gums have appear'd to be very painful to him at times for a long time. I have not said any thing to you about the money in Mr. Jeffersons hands as Mr. Eppes used it while in Richmond. Adieu My dear Papa I shall write again by Crity when she goes up. I hope you had no objection to her spending this winter with me. She was willing to leave home for a time after the fracas which happen'd there and is now anxious to return. Adieu once more my dear Papa. Believe me ever yours with warmest affection,

M EPPES

P. S. Mama desires me to send her best affections to you and thanks for the medal. I have been also desired to remind you of the spectacles you promised to procure for her.

TO MARTHA JEFFERSON RANDOLPH

Washington Apr. 24. 1802.

MY DEAR MARTHA

Your letter of the 16th. and Mr. Randolph's of the 9th. both came to hand by the last post. Since that too I have seen S. Carr who tells me you do not mean to include Virginia and Anne in your visit to this place. Against this I must remonstrate. Every principle respecting them, and every consideration interesting to yourself, Mr. Randolph or myself, is in favor of their coming here. If Virginia owes a visit to Dungeoness (as S. Carr says) the winter season will be more safe and convenient for that. Knowing that Mr. Randolph's resources must all be put to the stretch on his visit to Georgia, I insist that they not be touched by any wants which the visit of the family to this place might produce; but that all that shall be mine. As to the article of dress particularly, it can be better furnished here, and I shall intreat that it be so without limitation, as it will not be felt by me. Let there be no preparation of that kind therefore but merely to come here. Congress will rise in a few days. I think I can now fix the 5th. or 6th. of May for my departure and the 8th. or 9th. for my being with you. Mr. and Mrs. Madison go about the same time: that of their return is unknown to me, but cannot be much later than mine. I think it will be for your ease and convenience to arrive after Mrs. Madison's return, and consequently that this will give time for me after I get back here to send a carriage to meet you on a day to be fixed between us. Some groceries, intended for use while we are at Monticello, were sent from here a week or 10. days ago. I hope they will arrive in time, and with their arrival at Milton to be attended to. Mr. Milledge will dine with me to-day, and be able perhaps to tell me on what day he will be with you. A Mr. Clarke,[1] son of Genl. Clarke of Georgia, and a very sensible young man goes with him. I think they will be at Edgehill a day or two after you recieve this. Present me affectionately to Mr. Randolph and the family, and be assured of my tenderest love.

TH: JEFFERSON

P.S. On further enquiry I doubt if Congress will rise before the last day of the month. This will retard Mr. Milledge's[2] departure, but not mine.

1. John Clarke was the son of General Elijah Clarke of Georgia.
2. John Milledge was a congressman from the same state.

TO MARY JEFFERSON EPPES

Washington May 1. 1802.

MY DEAR MARIA

I recieved yesterday your's of April 21. bringing me the welcome news that you are all well. I wrote 2. or 3. days ago to Mr. Eppes to inform him that Congress would rise the day after tomorrow, that on the 6th. I should set out for Monticello where I should stay a fortnight, and had some hopes of meeting him there. It is even possible that Congress may rise to-day, which makes me so full of business that I have barely time to repeat to you the above information. I deem this necessary because I directed the other letter to City point, whereas I find you are at Eppington. I send by Dr. Logan[1] to the care of Mr. Jefferson Richmond some books for you, which I imagine you will find means of getting from thence. Mrs. Eppes's spectacles I will carry with me to Monticello. Doctr. Walker was here, but did not call on me or I should have sent them to her by him. The want of horses shall not prevent your paying us a visit, long or short, while your sister is here, as I can hire a good coacher here to go for you to the Hundred, on any day that shall be agreed on. Your sister will come in the same way. Present my affections to Mr. Eppes father and son, Mrs. Eppes and family, and accept my constant and tenderest love.

TH: JEFFERSON

1. Dr. George Logan was a physician and United States senator from Philadelphia.

TO MARTHA JEFFERSON RANDOLPH

Washington June 3. 1802.

MY DEAR MARTHA

I arrived here on Sunday morning (May 30.) to breakfast without having experienced any accident on the road, other than being twice taken in soaking rains: but my waterproof coat was a perfect protection. Mr. and Mrs. Madison arrived the day after. I find they have not yet got clear of the measles here, so that either at home or here your family will hardly escape it. It is now time for you to fix a day for my having you met at Mr. Strode's,[1] and it would be well if you could do it so that a postday should intervene, and give me an opportunity of acknoleging the reciept of your letter so that you may be sure it has not miscarried. Observe that the post which leaves Milton on Monday cannot carry back an answer till the Sunday following, and that which leaves Milton on Friday, returns with an answer on the Thursday following, taking a compleat week each. I will state on the 2d. leaf of this letter the stages and distances of the road and some notes. You must let me know whether you would rather that I should send horses and a carriage, or horses alone, as it will be perfectly equal to the person who furnishes me. I shall send John[2] with them as the driver will not be acquainted with the road, and it is a difficult one to find. It is generally a good and a safe one except the last day's journey which is very hilly, and will require you to get out of the carriage in several places on the Alexandria road between Fairfax court house and Colo. Wren's which is 8. miles, and once after you pass Wren's. I am not without fear that the measles may have got into your family, and delay the pleasure of seeing you here: but I expect to hear from you by the post which arrives tomorrow morning. My affectionate attachment to Mr. Randolph, kisses to the children, and tenderest love to yourself.

TH: JEFFERSON

1. An inn and stopping place eleven miles north of Stevensburg, Culpeper County, on a route often used by TJ traveling to and from Washington. It was eighty-three miles southwest of Washington.

2. John (Jack) Shorter was a Washington servant.

From Edgehill

To Gordon's 18. miles.	A good tavern, but cold victuals on the road will be better than any thing which any of the country taverns will give you.
Lodge at Gordon's go to	Orange courthouse 10. miles to breakfast. A good tavern. On leaving Orange courthouse be very attentive to the roads, as they begin to be difficult to find.
Adam's mill 7. miles.	Here you enter the flat country which continues 46. miles on your road.
Downey's ford 2.	Here you ford the Rapidan. The road leads along the bank 4 miles further, but in one place, a little below Downey's, it turns off at a right angle from the river to go round a cut. At this turn, if not very attentive, you will go strait forward, as there is a strait forward road still along the bank, which soon descends it and enters the river. If you get into this, the space on the bank is so narrow you cannot turn. You will know the turn I speak of, by the left hand road (the one you are to take) leading up directly towards some

huts, 100 yards off, on a blue clayey rising; but before getting to the huts, your road leads off to the right again to the river. No tavern from Orange courthouse till you get to

Stevensburg 11. miles   You will have to stop here at Zimmerman's tavern (brother in law of Catlett) to feed your horses, and to feed yourselves, unless you should have brought something to eat on the road side, before arriving at Stevensburg. Zimmerman's is an indifferent house. You will there probably see Mr. Ogilvie: He will certainly wish to be sent for to see Mr. Randolph.

Mr. Strode's 5. miles.   It will be better to arrive here in the evening. On stopping at his gate you will see Herring's house about 2 or 300 yards further on on the road. You had better order your servants (except your nurse) horses and carriages and baggage (not absolutely wanting at night) to go straight there, where those sent from here will be waiting for you.

Bronaugh's tavn. at Elk-run church. 13. miles.   The only tavern you will pass this day sleeping people.

Slate run church. 14½ miles.   Here you leave the flat country and engage in a very hilly one.

Brown's tavern 5½ miles.   Here you will have to dine and lodge being the first tavern from Bronaugh's. A poor house but obliging people.

Fairfax courthouse. 18. miles.   You can either breakfast here, or go on to Colo. Wren's tavern. 8. miles, a very decent house and respectable people. Georgetown ferry. 6. miles.

To Martha Jefferson Randolph

Washington June 18. 1802.

I recieved, my dear daughter, your's of the 13th. by post. I regret extremely the situation of your family, not only for my disappointment here, but for what they are to suffer. I acknolege that, know-

Thomas Jefferson Randolph. The eldest son of Martha Jefferson and Thomas Mann Randolph, Jr. The silhouette was probably made at Monticello and shows him in his sixteenth year. *Thomas Jefferson Memorial Foundation*

Elizabeth Wayles Eppes. "Aunt Eppes" was the wife of Francis Eppes of Eppington and a half sister of Mrs. Thomas Jefferson. *Thomas Jefferson Memorial Foundation*

Anne Cary Randolph. The eldest of the twelve Jefferson grandchildren. She was the wife of Charles Lewis Bankhead and the first grandchild to leave Monticello. *Thomas Jefferson Memorial Foundation*

Francis Eppes. Father of John Wayles Eppes, called "Uncle" and "Father" Eppes. *Thomas Jefferson Memorial Foundation*

Virginia Jefferson Randolph. The wife of Nicholas Philip Trist. They were the last of the family to live at Monticello, leaving there in 1829. *Laurence G. Hoes*

John Wayles Eppes. Mary Jefferson's husband, whom Jefferson addressed as "Jack" until his marriage; he then became the more dignified "Mr. Eppes." *Thomas Jefferson Memorial Foundation*

Ellen Wayles Randolph. She became the wife of Joseph Coolidge in 1825 and moved to Boston, where she lived until her death in 1876. The portrait is by an unidentified artist. *Charles Baker Eddy*

Thomas Mann Randolph, Jr. Husband of Martha Jefferson, whom Jefferson invariably referred to as "Mr. Randolph." *The Commonwealth of Virginia*

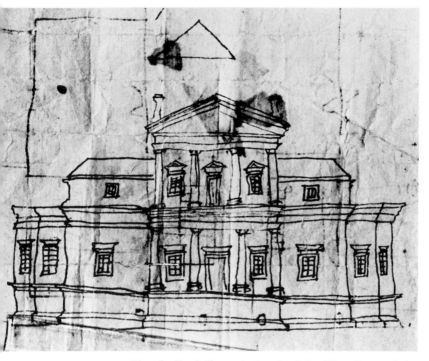

Monticello. Jefferson's sketch of the West Front of the house as it appeared in 1782. This is the house that Martha Wayles Jefferson lived in. *Thomas Jefferson Memorial Foundation*

West Front of Monticello. The remodeling that commenced about 1793 was not completed until 1809.
Thomas Jefferson Memorial Foundation

ing when I came away the measles were in the neighborhood.
I saw it was but too possible your visit here would be delayed. As
it is, we must agree to the fall visit; and as Maria will be at Monticello, I trust she will come on with you. I believe we shall conclude
here to leave this place the last week of July; probably I shall be
with you by the 24th. say 5. weeks from this time, and I shall endeavor that Mr. Eppes and Maria be there also by that time. I hope
Peter Hemings [1] will get the better of his complaint, or I know not
what we should do, as it is next to impossible to send Ursula [2] and
her child home and bring them back again. The servants here have
felt great disappointment at your not coming. The coachman is
particularly chagrined. I suppose he wishes to have an opportunity
of shewing himself on his box; which with me he has never had.
Mr. and Mrs. Trist are to set out in a few days for Albemarle, and
I believe the two young ladies go with them. He, I fancy will proceed immediately to the Missisipi. Present my best esteem to Mr.
Randolph, abundance of soft things to the children, and warmest
affections yourself.   TH: JEFFERSON

1. Peter Hemings was the ninth son of Betty Hemings.
2. A slave, but not to be confused with Ursula, the wife of "Great" George
who died in 1799. Her child was born in March, 1802. It is interesting to note
that as a servant in the President's House she received a salary of $2 a month.
Consult *Memoirs of a Monticello Slave* (1955), 66, the *Farm Book*, and Account Book 1802.

FROM MARY JEFFERSON EPPES

Eppington June 21st [1802]

My little son and Myself have both been very sick since I wrote
to you last My Dear Papa. We are now however getting better tho'
he is still very far from being well. His indisposition proceeded
from mine I believe and cutting teeth together, which occasion'd
constant fevers and have reduced him extremely, and perhaps
nursing him in my weak state of health made me worse for I had
only slight tho constant fevers on me and my stomach at last so
weak that nothing that I took remained on it. Change of air and
bark tho' have been allready of great service to me, for my dear
mother hearing of my sickness went down, and continued with
us tho to her extremely inconvenient at that time till I was able
to bear the journey up with her. I have kept Crity with me in consequence of it my Dear Papa. She should have gone up otherwise in
may but I was not well enough to undertake changeing his nurse.
I am very much in hopes now that he will mend daily as we have

procured a healthy nurse for him till I am stronger. I recieved a letter from my sister the other day mentioning they were all well and that she expected to go on to you in this month. I am afraid tho' she will put it off 'till the visit be hardly worth making. I have been very uneasy about the measles as it is said to be in that neighbourhood and am very anxious to hear from there. I should dread it infinitely more than the whooping-cough for Francis and the dear children. Through you My dear Papa I hope to hear something of it for my sister writes so seldom that I should hardly hear from her again if she was to remain there 'till I saw her. Mr. Eppes will finish his harvest tomorrow and after that is over there will be nothing to prevent our going up, should it be necessary sooner than we intended. Adieu My Dear Papa. I recieved the books and am very much obliged to you for them. Believe me with the tenderest affection yours ever,   M EPPES.

TO MARY JEFFERSON EPPES

Washington July 1. 1802.

MY DEAR MARIA

Mr. Eppes's letter of May 11. is the last news I have heard of you. I wrote to him on June 13. Your sister has been disappointed in her visit here by the measles breaking out in her family. It is therefore put off to October. I propose to leave this on the 21st. inst. and shall be at Monticello on the 24th. or 27th. according to the route I take; where I shall hope to find you on my arrival. I should very much apprehend that were you to continue at the Hundred till then, yourself, Mr. Eppes or the little one might be prevented by the diseases incident to the advancing season, from going up at all. It will therefore give me great pleasure to hear of your leaving the Hundred as soon as Mr. Eppes's affairs will permit. Mr. Trist and Doctr. Bache will both set out within a few days for the Missisipi with a view to remove their families thither in the fall: so we shall lose those two late accessions to our neighborhood. However in the Summer season our complaint is not the want of society; and in the winter there can be little even among neighbors. Dabney Carr was married on Monday (28th.) and set out yesterday (30th.) with his new wife for Albemarle where he will join his mother now keeping house at Dunlora, till he can fix himself in Charlottesville which will be soon. Sam Carr returns decidedly to live at Dunlora. The marriage of the other sister to

Dabney seems to have effected this. Peter and his wife are expected here daily on their way to Baltimore.[1] From this sketch you may judge of the state of our neighborhood when we shall meet there it will be infinitely joyful to me to be with you there, after the l[ong se]paration we have had for years. I count from one meeting to another as we do between port and port at sea: and I long for the moment with the same earnestness. Present me affectionately to Mr. Eppes and let me hear from you immediately. Be assured yourself of my tender and unchangeable affections.

TH: JEFFERSON

1. Another son of Martha Jefferson Carr (Mrs. Dabney), who married Elizabeth (Betsy) Overton Carr, daughter of his uncle Overton Carr. Samuel Carr had previously married another of Overton Carr's daughters, Eleanor (Nelly) Carr. Dunlora was a Carr farm a few miles north of Charlottesville. Peter was another nephew of TJ.

To Martha Jefferson Randolph

Washington July 2. 1802.

My dear Martha

I yesterday recieved letters from Mr. Eppes and Maria. She has been for a considerable time very unwell, with low but constant fevers, and the child very unwell also. Mrs. Eppes had gone there and staid with her till she was well enough to be removed to Eppington, where the air and the bark had already produced a favorable effect. She wishes to proceed to Monticello as soon as she is strong enough, but is in dreadful apprehensions from the measles. Not having heard from you she was uninformed whether it was in your family. I have this day informed her it is there, and advised her when she goes, to pass directly on to Monticello; and that I would ask the favor of Mr. Randolph and yourself to take measures for having the mountain clear of it by the 15th. of this month, by which time she may possibly arrive there, or by the 20th. at farthest. After that date should any one on the mountain have it they must remove. Squire's house[1] would be a good place for the nail boys, should they have it, and Betty Hemings's for Bet's or Sally's children. There are no other children on the mountain. I shall be at home from the 25th. to the 28th. My affectionate esteem to Mr. Randolph and tenderest love to yourself.

TH: JEFFERSON

1. Squire, a slave; the location of his house is not known. Betty Hemings' house was on the Third Roundabout Road several hundred yards southeast of the east portico of Monticello. Bett and Sally were her children.

To Mary Jefferson Eppes

Washington July 2. 1802.

My dear Maria

My letter of yesterday had hardly got out of my hand, when yours of June 21st. and Mr. Eppes's of the 25th. were delivered. I learn with extreme concern the state of your health and that of the child, and am happy to hear you have got from the Hundred, to Eppington, the air of which will aid your convalescence, and will enable you to delay your journey to Monticello till you have recovered strength to make the journey safe. With respect to the measles they began in Mr. Randolph's family about the middle of June; and will probably be a month getting through the family; so that you had better, when you go, pass on direct to Monticello, not calling at Edgehill. I will immediately write to your sister, and inform her I have advised you to this. I have not heard yet of the disease having got to Monticello, but the intercourse with Edgehill being hourly, it cannot have failed to have gone there immediately; and as there are no young children there but Bet's and Sally's, and the disease is communicable before a person knows they have it, I have no doubt those children have past through it. The children of the plantation being a mile and a half off, can easily be guarded against. I will write to Monticello and direct that should the nail boys or any others have it, they be removed to the plantation instantly on your arrival. Indeed none of them but Bet's sons stay on the mountain; and they will be doubtless through it. I think therefore you may be there in perfect security. It had gone through the neighborhood chiefly when I was there in May; so that it has probably disappeared. You should make enquiry on the road before you go into any house, as the disease is now universal through the state and all the states. Present my most friendly attachments to Mr. and Mrs. Eppes. Tell the latter I have had her spectacles these 6. months waiting for a direct conveyance. My best affections to Mr. Eppes if with you and the family, and tender and constant love to yourself.   Th: Jefferson

P. S. I have always forgotten to answer your apologies about Critta, which were very unnecessary. I am happy she has been with you and useful to you. At Monticello there could be nothing for her to do; so that her being with you is exactly as desireable to me as she can be useful to you.

FROM MARTHA JEFFERSON RANDOLPH

Edgehill July 10th 1802

My children have escaped the measles most wonderfully and unaccountably for so strongly were we all prepossessed with the idea of it's being impossible that from the moment of it's appearing upon the plantation I rather courted than avoided the infection and the children have been on a regimen for 4 or 5 weeks in the constant expectation of breaking out. Anne has been twice declared full of it by Doctor Bache and another time by the whole family but it went in as sudenly as it came out and has left much uneasiness upon my mind for fear of her being subject to something like Mrs. Kingkade's. I think the smoothness of her skin is affected by it and it shews, upon her heating herself immediately. Cornelia has been very low. The sickness which I mentioned to you in my last was but the beginning of a very long and teasing complaint of which however she is getting the better. She is still very pale and much emaciated but has recovered her appetite and spirits and I hope will be perfectly well before you return. We are entirely free from the measles here now. Those of our people who had it have recovered and Mr. Watson's family[1] living on the same plantation every individual of which had it are all recovered. The intercourse between them and us thro the servants was daily yet it has stopped and there is not at this moment one instance of it here. At Monticello the last time I heard from there 3 of the nail boys had it and others were complaining but whether with the measles or not I could not learn. I will send over to Lilly immediately to let him know your orders upon the subject. I regret extremely my children have missed it. The season was so favorable and it was so mild generally that no time or circumstance for the future can ever be as favorable again, besides having had the anxiety for nothing. I delayed writing to Maria untill I could give her a favorable account, for I know she has had great apprehensions on that score for a long time. Adieu my dear Papa. I do not know if I gave you a list of the things most wanting in the house. I do not exactly recollect what they were but sheets towels counterpanes and tea china were I think foremost on the list. Your linen has not arrived or it would have been made up before your return. The children all join in love and anxious prayer that nothing may retard your wished for return and believe me with tenderest affection yours.   MRANDOLPH.

Peter Hemmings is entirely well.

1. Possibly either David or John Watson

To Mary Jefferson Eppes

Washington July 16. 1802.

MY DEAR MARIA

Your sister informs me she has lately given you information of the health of the family. It seems her children have escaped the measles tho' some of the negroes have had it. The following is an extract from her letter dated July 10. 'We are entirely free from the measles here now. Those of our people who had it have recovered. At Monticello the last time I heard from there three of the nail boys had it and others were complaining, but whether with the measles or not I could not learn. I will send over to Lilly immediately to let him know your orders on the subject.' These orders were to remove every person from the mountain who had or should have the measles. I have no doubt you may proceed with the utmost security. I shall be there before you, to wit on Saturday the 24th. and will take care to have a clear stage, if any body should still have it: but there can be no doubt it will have gone through all who were to have it before that date. I am satisfied Francis will have more to hope from the change of air, than to fear from the measles. And as to yourself it is of great importance to get up into the country as soon as you are able, the liability to bilious diseases being exactly in proportion to the distance from the sea. I leave this on the 24th. and shall be in great hopes of recieving yourself and Mr. Eppes there immediately. I recieved two days ago his letter of the 8th. in which he gives me a poor account of your health, tho' he says you are recruiting. Make very short stages, be off always by daylight and have your day's journey over by ten. In this way it is probable you may find the moderate exercise of the journey of service to yourself and Francis. Nothing is more frequent than to see a child reestablish by a journey. Present my sincerest affections to the family at Eppington, and to Mr. Eppes. Tell him the tory newspapers are all attacking his publication, and urging it as a proof that Virginia has for object to change the constitution of the US. and to make it too impotent to curb the larger states. Accept yourself assurances of my constant and tenderest love.

TH: JEFFERSON

FROM MARY JEFFERSON EPPES

Eppington July 17th [1802]

Mr. Eppes thinks we had best remain here My Dear Papa till we hear further from you about the measles, I must therefore beg you will write as soon as you can conveniently after arriving at Monticello. You know not how anxious I am to see you, after having so long look'd forward to this period with so much pleasure. To be disappointed at the very moment which was to reunite us after so long an absence requires a greater degree of fortitude then I have to bear it, and your stay at home will be so short that it makes me doubly anxious to be with you. If my little sons health was not in the precarious state it is I should not fear the disorder so much on his account but he suffers so much and is so ill with every tooth that comes out that I should dread any additional complaint.

We had proposed going by the green springs[1] as we went up but the danger of finding the measles there has made us give up that journey. Your last letter to Mr. Eppes my dear Papa must be deferr'd answering till the happy moment which brings us together, yet suffer me to tell you how much I feel it. Your kindness knows no bounds nor is it the first time that it has gone so far as to pain the heart entirely yours. You have allready disfurnish'd yourself too much for us Dearest Papa. Suffer me to remind you of it and do not take it amiss if with grateful hearts we should not accept this present offer. It will I hope have this good effect on Mr. Eppes as to make him exert himself to begin a building of some sort at Pantops. He knows I should be satisfied with any for a while and would chearfully agree to any rules of economy when there that would enable him to continue independent and clear of debt. It must before long take place certainly. He is himself becoming very sensible of the many inconveniences attending the life we lead and which are increasing on us the longer we continue it. Adieu My dear Papa. This day week I expected to have met you and to have forgotten in the delight of meeting you the pain I have felt in being so long separated from you for I experience more at each separation. How little the heart can ever become accustom'd to them. Adieu. Believe me yours with tenderest love,

M EPPES

1. Possibly a Carr dwelling in Louisa County and located in the Green Springs area several miles east of Gordonsville. See Joseph Martin, *Comprehensive Gazetteer of Virginia and District of Columbia* (Charlottesville, 1835), 217.

To Ellen Wayles Randolph

Washington. Tuesday. July 20. 1802.

MY VERY DEAR ELLEN

I will catch you in bed on Sunday or Monday morning.
Your's affectionately,   TH: JEFFERSON

To Martha Jefferson Randolph

Washington Oct. 7. 1802.

MY DEAR MARTHA

I arrived here on the fourth day of our journey without accident. Travelling early one or two mornings through fog brought on some degree of indisposition, which I felt strongly on the day and day after my arrival, but it is wearing off slowly. It has been chiefly an excessive soreness all over and a deafness and ringing in the head. I have desired Mr. Jefferson to procure you whatever you may call for on my account, and I pray you to do it freely. It never was my intention that a journey made for my gratification should bring any expence on you. I must press on you to let me send horses to meet you, as I am convinced that no horses after the three first days journey, can encounter the 4th. which is hilly beyond any thing you have ever seen below the mountains. I shall expect soon to hear from you. Present me affectionately to Mr. Randolph and kiss the children for me. To yourself my tenderest love.   TH: JEFFERSON

To Mary Jefferson Eppes

Washington Oct. 7. 1802.

MY DEAR MARIA

I arrived here on the fourth day of my journey without accident. On the day and day after my arrival I was much indisposed with a general soreness all over, a ringing in the head and deafness. It is wearing off slowly, and was probably produced by travelling very early two mornings in fog. I have desired Mr. Jefferson to furnish you with whatever you may call for, on my account; and I insist on your calling freely. It never was my intention that a visit for my gratification should be at your expence. It will be absolutely necessary for me to send fresh horses to meet you, as no horses, after the three first days journey, can encounter the 4th. which is hilly beyond any thing you have ever seen. I shall expect to learn from you soon, the day of your departure, that I may take proper arrangements. Present me affectionately to Mr. Eppes, and accept yourself my tenderest love. TH: JEFFERSON

P. S. Mr. Eppes's bridle is delivered to Davy Bowles.

To Martha Jefferson Randolph

Washington Oct. 18. 1802.

MY DEAR MARTHA

I have been expecting by every post to learn from you when I might send on to meet you. I will expect it daily. In the mean time I enclose you 100 Dol for the expences of yourself, Maria and all your party. Mr. Randolph would do well to exchange the bills for gold and silver which will be more readily used on the road. The indisposition I mentioned in my letter by Bowles[1] turned out to be rheumatic. It confined me to the house some days, but is now nearly gone off so that I ride out daily. The hour of the post obliges me to conclude here with my affectionate attachment to Mr. Randolph and tender love to yourself and the children.

TH: JEFFERSON

1. Davy Bowles.

To Mary Jefferson Eppes

Washington Oct. 18. 1802.

MY DEAR MARIA

I have been expecting by every post to learn from yourself or your sister when I might send to meet you. I still expect it daily. In the mean time I have sent to Mr. Randolph, who I understand is to be your conductor money for the expences of the road, so that that may occasion no delay. The indisposition mentd in my letter by Davy Bowles turned out to be rheumatic. It confined me to the house some days, but is now nearly gone off. I have been able to ride out daily for a week past. The hour of the post leaves me time to add only assurances of my constant and tender love to you; and to pray you to tender my best affections to Mr. Eppes when he returns. TH: JEFFERSON

FROM MARTHA JEFFERSON RANDOLPH

October 29. [1802]

DEAR PAPA

We recieved your letter and are preparing with all speed to obey its summons; by next friday we hope we shall be able to fix a day, and probably the shortest time in which the horses can be sent after recieving our letter will determine it. Tho as yet it is not entirely certain that we can get off so soon. Will you be so good as to send orders to the milliner Mde. Pick I believe her name is, thro Mrs. Madison who very obligingly offered to execute any little commission for us, to send to Philadelphia for 2 wigs the colour of the hair enclosed and of the most fashionable shapes, that they may be at Washington when we arrive. They are universally worn and will relieve us as to the necessity of dressing our own hair a business in which neither of us are adepts. I believe Mde. Pick is in the habit of doing those things when desired and they can be procured in a short time from Philadelphia where she corresponds much handsomer and cheaper than elsewhere. Adieu Dearest Father. Maria is with [us] in good health and Spirits. Believe me with tender affection Yours,   M. RANDOLPH.

TO MARTHA JEFFERSON RANDOLPH

Washington Nov. 2. 1802.

MY DEAR MARTHA

Your letter of the 29th. has relieved me from the great anxiety I had felt on your previous entire silence about your journey. There was no hair inclosed in your letter: but I sent the letter to Mrs. Madison who has had the order given as you desired, for colours from her own judgment, perhaps those of your own hair. If this should not please, send her hair in your Friday's letter and within a fortnight from that time others suitable can be here from Philadelphia. Remember to tell me in your next whether I am to send a carriage, or whether you prefer coming on in your own. It makes no odds here whether horses are sent with or without a carriage. I spoke to you soon after the arrival of my sister Marks about getting necessaries for her from Higginbotham's.[1] It escaped me to repeat it when I came away. I hope however it has been done, or that she may be still with you and it can yet be done. Pray enable yourself to direct us here how to make muffins in Peter's method. My cook here cannot succeed at all in them, and they are a great luxury to me. Deliver to my dear Maria my love, and my rebukes that she should not once have written to me. Kiss the little ones, and be assured yourself of my unceasing affections.

TH: JEFFERSON

1. David Higginbotham was a Milton merchant.

FROM MARY JEFFERSON EPPES

November 5th [1802]

Mr. Randolph has been summon'd to Richmond My Dear Papa about the time we were to set off, which will prevent his going with us and obliges us to request Mr. Lewis to meet us at Strodes on Tuesday week. Mr. Eppes will go that far with us but says he cannot possibly go farther. I lament sincerely that it has not been possible for us to go sooner, as the visit will be scarcely worth making for so short a time and should prefer waiting till the spring and returning there with you as we could then remain with you some time but my sister will not agree to put it off any longer. On Tuesday week then if Mr. Lewis can meet us at Strodes we shall be there. Adieu dearest Papa. I am afraid the post will be gone and must conclude this scrawl, excuse it and believe me with the tenderest love yours,   M EPPES

P. S. I send the lock of hair which is to be the colour of the wig.

FROM MARTHA JEFFERSON RANDOLPH

November 9th [1802]

DEAR PAPA

It will be more convenient to us to leave this on wednesday than monday. It will occasion a delay of 2 days only, as this is a flying visit only to shew that we are in earnest with regard to Washington. I have determined to leave the children all but Jefferson considering the lateness of the season and the bad weather we may reasonably expect in december. The short time [I] shall have to spend with you it is better to part with them for a time than risk such a journey with a carriage full of small children. Next spring I hope I shall have it in my power to return with you and carry them all: Maria thinks it would be better to send a carriage with the horses as Mr. Eppes['s] in which we shall go is much out of repair and ours absolutely not in travelling condition. Adieu Dearest Father. Yours most truly affections,   M R

FROM MARY JEFFERSON EPPES

Edgehill january 11th [1803]

DEAR PAPA

We arrived here safe yesterday after a most disastrous journey sufficiently distressing in itself but more so at the time from the depression of spirits felt on leaving you. The pain of seeing you turn back alone after having experienc'd so many happy hours with you My dear Papa in the little room to us endear'd by your sitting in it allways, and the recollection of the heavy expense this journey has been to you for indeed it must be in all immense, made my heart ache I must confess in no slight degree. Suffer me to dwell upon it a moment My dear Papa to mention partly in excuse for myself that inexperience in some respects was greatly the cause on my own part of the great abuse of your indulgence towards us.

The horses have been so much fatigued as to render it necessary for them to rest a day. They will set off tomorrow with John, whom I hear you have miss'd very much in the dining room. I found Martin[1] here waiting for me, but as there is a possibility of the childs having taken the measles I shall remain here 'till the time is past in which it would appear if taken, and shall not leave this if he escapes it 'till the first of next week. Mrs. Trist is here and desires to be particularly remember'd to you, she has at last re- cieved a letter from her son dated from the Natches. They are themselves living at Pen Park[2] and will remain there I believe while here.

You will hear soon I imagine from Aunt Marks. It is said here that H. Marks[3] is dead or dying and the report is supposed to be true. Adieu dear Papa. My Sister is well and desires me to give her love to you. Virginia would not recognise her till she changed her dress for one that she remember'd from its being a calico. Adieu once more. How much do I think of you at the hours which we have been accustom'd to be with you alone My dear Papa and how much pain it gives me to think of the unsafe and solitary manner in which you sleep upstairs. Adieu dearest and Most beloved of fathers. I feel my inability to express how much I love and revere you. But you are the first and dearest to my heart. Yours with sincere affection,   M E

1. John Shorter, a Washington servant; Martin was a slave.
2. The Gilmer home in Albemarle County.
3. Hastings Marks died circa 1813.

To Mary Jefferson Eppes

Washington, Jan. 18. 1803.

My dear Maria

Your's by John came safely to hand, and informed me of your ultimate arrival at Edgehill. Mr. Randolph's letter from Gordon's,[1] recieved the night before gave me the first certain intelligence I had recieved since your departure. A rumor had come here of your having been stopped two or three days at Ball run,[2] and in a miserable hovel; so that I had passed ten days in anxious uncertainty about you. Your apologies my dear Maria on the article of expense, are quite without necessity. You did not here indulge yourselves as much as I wished, and nothing prevented my supplying your backwardness but my total ignorance in articles which might suit you. Mr. Eppes's election[3] will I am in hopes secure me your company next winter and perhaps you may find it convenient to accompany your sister in the spring. Mr. Giles's[4] aid indeed in Congress, in support of our administration, considering his long knoledge of the affairs of the Union, his talents, and the high ground on which he stands through the United States had rendered his continuance here an object of anxious desire to those who compose the administration: but every information we recieve states that prospect to be desperate from his ill health, and will relieve me from the imputation of being willing to lose to the public so strong a supporter, for the personal gratification of having yourself and Mr. Eppes with me. I inclose you Lemaire's reciepts.[5] The orthography will be puzzling and amusing: but the reciepts are valuable. Present my tender love to your sister, kisses to the young ones, and my affections to Mr. Randolph and Mr. Eppes whom I suppose you will see soon. Be assured of my unceasing and anxious love for yourself.   Th: Jefferson

1. N. Gordon operated an Orange County inn about fifteen miles from Monticello, on the road to Orange Court House.
2. A small tributary of the Appomattox River in Powhatan County.
3. He was elected to Congress in 1802 while residing at Eppington and served until March 3, 1811, when defeated by John Randolph of Roanoke; re-elected from Buckingham County in 1812 and again defeated by Randolph in 1814. Chosen a senator in 1816, John W. Eppes served until ill health caused his resignation in 1819.
4. William Branch Giles, a Virginia congressman.
5. Etienne Lemaire, TJ's maître d'hôtel while in the President's House.

To Martha Jefferson Randolph

Washington Jan. 27. 1803.

MY DEAR MARTHA

The last post-days have slipt away from me without adverting to them till too late. I learnt by a letter from Maria that you all got home safe after a very disagreeable journey. Indeed I suffer for you in imagination beyond any thing I had long felt. I found the road, in the short distance I went with you, so much worse than I expected, that I augured a dreadful journey, and sincerely lamented you did not await a better time. I felt my solitude too after your departure very severly. Your acquaintances here are well, except Mrs. Brent and Mrs. Burrowes.[1] I find Mr. Lilly was to begin filling his icehouse the 21st. We have had no thaw here since that till yesterday, and the river is still entirely blocked up; so that if the weather has corresponded there, I am in hopes he will have got his house full. I must pray you to press on the making my shirts, so that I may have them on my arrival, which will probably be the 9th. of March. Edy[2] has a son, and is doing well. I inclose poetry for Anne's book. I must pray her to become my correspondent. It will be useful to her, and very satisfactory to me. Jefferson promised to write to me from Orange court house but was not as good as his word. I presume you were amused with the reciepts for making panne-quaiques[3] and other good things. Present my affectionate respects to Mr. Randolph, kisses to the young ones, and be assured of my tenderest love to yourself.

TH: JEFFERSON

1. The wives of Robert Brent, the first mayor of Washington, and of Lieutenant-Colonel William W. Burrows, first Commandant of the United States Marine Corps.
2. A slave servant in the President's House.
3. A form of pancake. See Marie Kimball, *Thomas Jefferson's Cook Book* (Richmond, 1949), 103, for a Monticello recipe.

To Thomas Jefferson Randolph

Washington, Feb. 21st, 1803.

I have to acknowledge the receipt of your letter of the 3d, my dear Jefferson, and to congratulate you on your writing so good a hand. By the last post I sent you a French Grammar, and within three weeks I shall be able to ask you, 'Parlez vous Français, monsieur?' I expect to leave this about the 9th, if unexpected business should not detain me, and then it will depend on the weather and the roads how long I shall be going — probably five days. The roads will be so deep that I can not flatter myself with catching Ellen in bed. Tell her that Mrs. Harrison Smith desires her compliments to her. Your mamma has probably heard of the death of Mrs. Burrows. Mrs. Brent is not far from it. Present my affections to your papa, mamma, and the young ones, and be assured of them yourself.   TH: JEFFERSON

FROM THOMAS JEFFERSON RANDOLPH

[Edgehill] Recd. Feb. 24. 1803.
DEAR GRAND PAPA

We have been expecting the measles but have escaped it as yet. Virginia has learnt to speak very well. Ellen is learning french. Cornelia sends her love to you. I would be very much obliged to you if you would bring me a book of geography. Adieu Dear Grand Papa. Your affectionate Grand son,   THOMAS JEFFERSON R

TO ANNE CARY RANDOLPH

Washington Feb. 26. 1803.
MY DEAR ANNE

Davy Bowles is to call on me this morning, and if he can carry your dictionary I will deliver it to him, having recieved it yesterday from Mr. Duane. If he cannot, I will endeavour to carry it when I go. In the last case you will recieve it about the 9th or 10th of March, or as soon after health, the weather and roads will permit. Tell Jefferson that there is not a book of geography to be had here, but I will give him one I have at Monticello. Tell Ellen, Cornelia and Virginia how d'ye. [. . .]¹ Give my affectionate esteem to your Papa and to your Mama. My constant love for yourself. I deliver numberless kisses on this letter which you are to take from it. I hope in a few days we shall all be happy together at Monticello.   TH: JEFFERSON

1. Word following *d'ye* is illegible in original.

TO MARTHA JEFFERSON RANDOLPH

Washington Apr. 23.1803.
MY DEAR MARTHA

A promise made to a friend some years ago, but executed only lately, has placed my religious creed on paper. I have thought it just that my family, by possessing this, should be enabled to estimate the libels published against me on this, as on every other possible subject. I have written to Philadelphia for Doctr Priestly's history of the corruptions of Christianity, which I will send you, and recommend to an attentive perusal, because it establishes the groundwork of my view of this subject.[1]

I have not had a line from Monticello or Edgehill since I parted with you. P. Carr, and Mrs. Carr, who staid with me 5. or 6. days, told me Cornelia had got happily through her measles, and that Ellen had not taken them. But what has become of Anne? I thought I had her promise to write once a week, at least the words 'all's well.' It is now time for you to let me know when you expect to be able to set out for Washington, and whether your own carriage can bring you half way. I think my Chickasaws, if drove moderately, will bring you well that far. Mr. Lilly knows you will want them, and can add a fourth. I think that by changing horses half way, you will come with more comfort. I have no gentleman to send for your escort. Finding here a beautiful blue Casimer, waterproof, and thinking it will be particularly à propos for Mr. Randolph as a travelling coat for his journey, I have taken enough for that purpose, and will send it to Mr. Brown, postmaster at Fredericksbg to be forwarded by Abraham, and hope it will be recieved in time. Mr. and Mrs. Madison will set out for Orange about the last day of the month. They will stay there but a week. I write to Maria to-day, but supposing her at the Hundred, according to what she told me of her movements, I send my letter there. I wish you to come as early as possible: because tho' the members of the government remain here to the last week in July, yet the sickly season commences in fact by the middle of that month: and it would not be safe for you to keep the children here longer than that, lest any one of them being taken sick early, might detain the whole here till the season of general danger, and perhaps through it. Kiss the children for me. Present me affectionately to Mr. Randolph, and accept yourself assurance of my constant and tenderest love.   TH: JEFFERSON

1. TJ was recounting a conversation with Dr. Benjamin Rush in 1798/99 (see TJ to Rush, April 21, 1803, DLC). Included in this letter was his "Syllabus of an Estimate of the Merit of the Doctrines of Jesus, compared with those of others." Priestley's work, *An History of the Corruptions of Christianity* (Birmingham, 1793), 2 volumes, presented by TJ to his family, has not been located. See Malone, *Jefferson and the Ordeal of Liberty*, 482–83, and Julian P. Boyd, "Mr. Jefferson to Dr. Rush with Affection," *Library of Congress Quarterly Journal of Current Acquisitions*, Vol. I, No. 1 (October–December, 1943), 3–8.

To Mary Jefferson Eppes

Washington Apr. 25. 1803.

MY DEAR MARIA

A promise made to a friend some years ago, but executed only lately, has placed my religious creed on paper. I have thought it just that my family, by possessing this, should be enabled to estimate the libels published against me on this, as on every other possible subject. I have written to Philadelphia for Dr. Priestley's history of the corruptions of Christianity, which I will send to you, and recommend to an attentive perusal, because it establishes the ground work of my view of this subject.

In a letter from Mr. Eppes dated at the Hundred Apr. 14. he informed me Francis had got well through his measles; but he does not say what your movements are to be. My chief anxiety is that you should be back to Monticello by the end of June. I shall advise Martha to get back from here by the middle of July, because the sickly season really commences here by that time, altho' the members of the government venture to remain til the last week of that month. Mr. and Mrs. P. Carr staid with me 5. or 6. days on their way to Baltimore. I think they propose to return in June. Nelly Carr continues in ill health. I believe they expect about the same time to get back to Dunlora.[1] I wrote Mr. Eppes yesterday. Be assured of my most affectionate and tender love to yourself, and kiss Francis for me. My cordial salutations to the family of Eppington when you see them. Adieu.   TH: JEFFERSON

1. Samuel Carr's home on the South Fork of the Rivanna River and a few miles north of Charlottesville. Eleanor Carr Carr (Mrs. Samuel).

To Anne Cary Randolph

Washington May 20. 1803.

It is very long, my dear Anne, since I have recieved a letter from you. When was it? In the mean time mine have been accumulating till I find it necessary to get them off my hands without further waiting. With them I send an A.B.C.[1] for Miss Cornelia, and she must pay you a kiss for it on my account. The little recipe about charcoal is worth your Mama's notice. We had peas here on Tuesday the 17th. and every day since. We had then also fullgrown cucumbers: but I suppose they had been forced. What sort of weather had you from the 6th. to the 10th. Here we had frost, ice and snow, and great damage in the garden and orchards. How stands the fruit with you in the neighborhood and at Monticello and particularly the peas, as they are what will be in season when I come home. The figs also, have they been hurt? You must mount Midas and ride over to Monticello to inform yourself or collect the information from good authority and let me have it by next post. Tell your papa that I delivered waterproof blue Casimer for a coat for him to Mr. Madison a fortnight ago. He has been expecting to set out any day. He will forward it by the rider from Orange court house whenever he does go. Present my tenderest affections to your Mama, and accept my kisses for yourself and the little ones. To your papa [. . .]² and attachment.   TH: JEFFERSON

1. Any of several primers containing the alphabet and teaching the elements of reading.
2. Word following *papa* in last line is illegible in original.

FROM MARTHA JEFFERSON RANDOLPH

Edgehill July 12 1803

I have suffered so much from fatigue and anxiety since my return home that I have not had spirits to write to My Dearest Father. The day Mr. Randolph left me I discovered My Dear Ellen to be in a very advanced stage of a most horrible dissentery which had run on many days unnoticed except by a little restriction in her diet, from the idea of it's being a slight bowel complaint occasioned by strawberries, which had affected all the children (as I supposed at the time) in the same way and all of whom had recovered without medecine. The speed with which Mr. R. moves and accomplishes his business prevented my sending for him as he could only have been brought back 2 days sooner than he intended to return. His business was urgent and the heat of the weather, his anxiety, and fatigue, would have endangered his health so much I determined to depend upon my own strength and the advice of the physician. The complaint from the beginning seemed to be of the most inveterate kind with so much fever that she became thro the day delirious but employing every lucid interval in reading. Judge of my feelings My Dearest Father at seeing her escaping from me so rapidly and often when hanging over her in agonies indescribable to have some question of natural history which she was reading at the time addressed to me by the little sufferer the activity of whose mind even the most acute bodily pain was never capable of subduing. She sank at last in a state of stupor however which seldom ever left her. She was as certainly saved by bleeding[1] My Dear Father as others have been killed by it. The evacuations instantly fell from 60 to 70 in the 24 hours down to 6. The complaint being thus sudenly and as it were by magic arrested in it's progress. The fever gradually subsided untill it left her entirely but so debilitated that some little indiscretion of diet brought it on her again and we have been very much distressed by the danger which threatened her of it's terminating in a slow fever the event of which we had too much reason to apprehend might be fatal to one allready exhausted by the dissentery. Thank god it has intermitted yesterday for the first time and again this morning. At the time Ann wrote you the crisis had taken place in consequence of the bleeding and my self exhausted with watching, want of food which my stomach rejected and anxiety I had taken to my bed under a sever attack of the same complaint but thanks to the very judicious and friendly attention of Doctors Everet and Gilmer[2] who by sitting up with Ellen relieved me from the fatigue and anxiety and also a fortunate management of the complaint in it's beggining it was speedily terminated in me. I was not confined more than 5 days with it. The fever and derangement of the stomach lasted perhaps 10. Indeed to the false strength which that gave was I indebted for the incessant attention night and day which it enabled me to pay My Darling and by which perhaps she was saved. The others were all of them sick at the same time. They required also unwearied attention to their diet that they might not be suffered to get too low. Jane[3] from home and not a female friend to assist me, I reflect with horror upon that week that no language can paint. The children are all getting better and my self well allthough greatly debilitated. Adieu My Dear Father I must conclude for fear of losing the post. When you send the groceries on will you remember glasses, tumblers and wine glasses both are much want[ing here][4] and again believe me with unchangeable love yours,   MR.

1. TJ did not believe in bleeding as an effective treatment for any ailment. There is no record that he was ever bled, and this is the only recorded instance in which any of the Monticello grandchildren were subjected to it.

2. Doctor Charles Everett, later secretary to James Monroe, and Doctor John Gilmer, son of Doctor George Gilmer.

3. Jane Barbara Carr Cary (Mrs. Wilson) or Jane Cary Randolph Randolph (Mrs. Thomas Eston).

4. Original letter torn.

FROM THOMAS JEFFERSON RANDOLPH

Edgehill Oct. 30 1803

DEAR GRAND PAPA

I was at Monticello yesterday and Mr. Dinsmore had almost finished the cornice in the hall and was to set of for Philadelphia to day. They have almost done the canal and the mill house also.[1] I have read Goldsmith's grecian history Thucidides and I am now reading Goldsmith's Roman history.[2] Give my love to Papa and uncle Epes. Adieu Grand Papa. Your most affectionate Grand son,

THOMAS JEFFERSON RANDOLPH.

1. TJ's several mills occupied a site on the Rivanna River about ¾ miles from Milton and nearly six from Charlottesville. The mill herein mentioned was a small one, probably used chiefly by TJ and Mr. Randolph. It is not to be confused with the larger Toll Mill, not completed until 1806. See *Farm Book* for that section treating his Rivanna River operations.

2. Oliver Goldsmith, *The Grecian History, from the earliest state to . . . Alexander the Great* (Philadelphia, 1800), 2 volumes (not in Sowerby), and *The Roman History, from the Foundation of the City of Rome, to the Destruction of the Western Empire* (London, 1770), 2 volumes, Sowerby 100. Thucydides, *The History of the Peleponnesian War . . .* (London, [1753]), Sowerby 17.

TO MARTHA JEFFERSON RANDOLPH

Washington Nov. 7. 03.

So constant, my dear daughter, have been my occupations here since Congress met, that it has never been in my power to write any thing which could admit of delay at all: and our post now passing but once a week, lessens the opportunities, tho the rapidity is increased to 24. hours between this place and Charlottesville. I recieved by Mr. Randolph the frills and a pair of stockings. It will be impossible to judge as to the proportion of fur until the season comes for wearing them. I think that with the stock I now have, a supply of 2. pair every winter will keep me furnished. I judge from your letter that you are approaching an interesting term,[1] and consequently we shall be anxious to hear from you or of you by every post. I hope you have Mrs. Suddarth[2] with you, and that on the first alarm you will require the attendance of a physician, because being on the spot, a word of advice often saves a case from being serious which a little delay would render so. Never fail therefore to use this precaution. We are all well here, but immersed in the usual bickerings of a political campaign. The feds[3] are few, with little talent on their side, but as much gall at least as those who are wicked and impotent usually have. How much happier you in the midst of your family, with nobody approaching you but in love and good will. It is a most desireable situation, and in exchanging it for the scenes of this place we certainly do not calculate well for our happiness. Jerome Bonaparte[4] is to be married tomorrow to a Miss Patterson of Baltimore. Give my warm affections to my Maria and tell her my next letter shall be to her. Kiss all the fireside, and be assured yourself of my never-ceasing love.

TH: JEFFERSON

1. She was pregnant for the seventh time.
2. A midwife.
3. Federalists.
4. Napoleon's youngest brother. In 1803 he married Elizabeth Patterson, daughter of William Patterson, president of the Bank of the United States. The marriage was later dissolved by Napoleon, and Jerome returned to Europe without his bride. For additional information on the reaction of the bride's family and the international aspects of this marriage, see TJ to Robert Livingston, November 4, 1803, Lipscomb and Bergh, *Writings of Thomas Jefferson*, 10, 424–25.

To Mary Jefferson Eppes

Washington Nov. 27. 03.

It is rare, my ever dear Maria, during a session of Congress, that I can get time to write any thing but letters of business: and this, tho' a day of rest to others, is not at all so to me. We are all well here, and hope the post of this evening will bring us information of the health of all at Edgehill and particularly that Martha and the new bantling[1] are both well: and that her example gives you good spirits. When Congress will rise no mortal can tell: not from the quantity but dilatoriness of business. Mr. Lillie having finished the mill, is now I suppose engaged in the road[2] which we have been so long wanting, and that done, the next job will be the levelling of Pantops. I anxiously long to see under way the works necessary to fix you there, that we may one day be all together. Mr. Stewart is now here on his way back to his family, whom he will probably join Thursday or Friday. Will you tell your sister that the pair of stockings she sent me by Mr. Randolph are quite large enough and also have fur enough in them. I inclose some papers for Anne; and must continue in debt to Jefferson a letter for a while longer. Take care of yourself my dearest Maria, have good spirits and know that courage is as essential to triumph in your case as in that of the souldier. Keep us all therefore in heart by being so yourself: give my tender affections to your sister, and recieve them for yourself also, with assurances that I live in your love only and that of your Sister. Adieu my dear daughter.

TH: JEFFERSON

1. Mary Jefferson Randolph, Martha's sixth child, was born November 2, 1803, at Edgehill.
2. Probably the East (North) Road that led from the east front of the house to the ford at Shadwell. This was not completed until about 1806. See Frederick D. Nichols, *Thomas Jefferson's Architectural Drawings* (Boston, 1961), Drawing Number 17, for the relation of this road to the Monticello house.

To Mary Jefferson Eppes

Washington Dec. 26. 03.

I now return you, my dearest Maria, the paper which you lent me for Mr. Page, and which he has returned some days since. I have prevailed on Doctr. Priestly to undertake the work of which this is only the syllabus or plan. He says he can accomplish it in the course of a year. But in truth his health is so much impaired, and his body become so feeble, that there is reason to fear he will not live out even the short term he has asked for it. You may inform Mr. Eppes and Mr. Randolph that no mail arrived the last night from Natchez. I presume the great rains which have fallen have rendered some of the watercourses impassable. On New year's day however we shall hear of the delivery of New Orleans to us. Till then the legislature seem disposed to do nothing but meet and adjourn.[1] Mrs. Livingston, formerly the younger Miss Allen, made kind inquiries after you the other day. She said she was at school with you at Mrs. Pine's. Not knowing the time destined for your expected indisposition,[2] I am anxious on your account. You are prepared to meet it with courage I hope. Some female friend of your Mama's (I forget whom) used to say it was no more than a knock of the elbow. The material thing is to have scientific aid in readiness, that if any thing uncommon takes place, it may be redressed on the spot, and not be made serious by delay. It is a case which least of all will wait for Doctors *to be sent for*. Therefore, with this single precaution, nothing is ever to be feared. I was in hopes to have heard from Edgehill last night, but I suppose your post has failed. I shall expect to see the gentlemen here next Sunday night, to take part in the Gala of Monday. Give my tenderest love to your sister of whom I have not heard for a fortnight; and my affectionate salutations to the Gentlemen and young ones.

Continue to love me yourself and be assured of my warmest affections.

1. TJ was referring to the Louisiana Purchase. The United States took formal possession of the Territory on December 20, 1803.
2. They were expecting the birth of Mary's child.

To Anne Cary Randolph

Washington Jan. 9. 1804.

My dear Anne

I recieved last night your letter of the 7th. with your Mama's postscript. As your's was the principal the answer is due to you. I am glad to find you are pursuing so good a course of reading. French, History, Morals, and some poetry and writings of eloquence to improve the stile form a good course for you. How does Jefferson get on with his French? Will he let Ellen catch him? The American muse has been so dull for some time past as to have furnished nothing for our volume. I have here a pair of beautiful fowls of enormous size of the East India breed: and can get in the city a pair of Bantams. I should prefer sending you the latter, if an opportunity occurs, provided you will undertake to raise them, and furnish me a pair for Monticello. Tell your Mama I shall be extremely glad to have my chair brought by Davy Bowles, as it would be impossible for me to go home in my Phaeton in the spring, and I should have to perform the journey on horseback. I shall hope therefore to recieve the chair by Davy. I am glad to hear your Aunt Jane[1] is so near you. It will add exercise, and chearfulness to your enjoiments. Give my tenderest love to your Mama and Aunt Maria, and kiss all the little ones for me. I deliver kisses for yourself to this letter.   TH: JEFFERSON

1. Jane Cary Randolph Randolph (Mrs. Thomas Eston).

From Martha Jefferson Randolph

Edgehill Jan. 14, 1804

My Dearest Father

It was so late the other day before I could write that I had only time to add a postscript to Anne's letter to inform you of Davy Bowle's intention of going to Washington, and the offer he made of carrying your chair if you wished it; he is still here and will be on thursday, so that your intentions with regard to it may be complied with if known, on that day. He leaves this sometime next week altho I do not know when. Lilly has been here to advise with me about Kit.[1] He is now in Charlottesville jail where he passed himself for a negro of Mr. Randolph's, Lilly is afraid to take him out for fear of his going off again. He thinks you wished him sold and the money laid out in another, but he says his head was so confused during, and for some time after his illness that he cannot recollect whether you gave him any orders to that effect or not; the result of the conversation however was that if he could get 120 or 25£ before he could hear from you he should sell him rather than miss the sail but that he would be much obliged to you to let him know by the next post what you wish done with him in case of his not having been able to dispose of him. Higginbotham begged me to tell you that Stewarts goods having been attached during the time of his supposed flight the sale was to take place in a few days. That with regard to himself a word from you would satisfy *him,* and no doubt the other creditors would be as well pleased to have the debt in your hands, of those however he said nothing nor do I exactly understand the use of saying what he did for Mrs. Stuart being dead,[2] and Mrs. Lewis having taken charge of the girls, it appears to me of very little importance to prevent the sale of the furniture. Humanity cannot be interested in the fate of a man so well able to provide for himself. And his sons are old enough to be put to any trade he chuses. Nor do I believe the desire of supporting them selves to be wanting on their side, but how far they can do any thing without his concurrence or whether they can obtain that I am unable to say. I have fulfilled my commission in delivering Higginbothams message. You are the best judge of what remains to be done. So much for business. Suffer me now to touch upon subjects more interesting and certainly more important than any business to be transacted by or through me. We are *all* of us "as well as can be expected." Maria's spirits are bad, partly occasioned by her situation which precludes every thing like comfort or chearfulness, and partly from the prospect of congress not rising till April which Mr. Randolph writes us is the general opinion. I hope we shall do as well as if Mr. Eppes was here but certainly her mind would be more at ease could he be with her. Little Francis is doing well but it is in the best health allways that he has been attacked with those dreadful fits; I cannot help fearing them to be epileptic. The noise in the throat the foaming at the mouth and drawing back of the head certainly bear a much greater resemblance to that than convulsions which My aunt's children have been subject to. My sister Jane[3] who held him during the last one he had two days only before Mary's birth mentioned it to me but the distress it might occasion his parents for such an idea to get abroad determined us to confine our suspicion within our own breast's. He may and I hope will outgrow them. Time only can shew what the event will be. My own children are remarkably healthy and freer from colds than common. Ann informed you of the acquisition we have made in Jane as a neighbour. We have walked back and fro repeatedly. She spends much of her time with us and her husband has been as attentive as an own brother could have been. He is a man of the purest heart and most amiable temper in the world. Adieu My Dearest Father. I must beg you to recollect that I write amidst the noises and confusion of six children interrupted every moment by their questions, and so much disturbed by [their][4] pratling around me that I catch my self repeatedly writing [their words] instead of my own thoughts. That will account for, and I hope [apologize] for any inconsistencies or repetitions in my letters. Perhaps it will be deemed some excuse for not writing oftener certain as I am that it is impossible for you to doubt for one moment of the warmth of my affection. I remain with unchangeable and tender love yours,   M RANDOLPH

Your letter to Anne has this moment come to hand having gone thro a mistake to Charlottesville. I wish it may not have come too late for enquiry. They tell me Davy Bowles contrary to his promise to me is gone to Richmond intending from thence to Washington. I shall hear more certainly presently and act accordingly. If St. Memin[5] comes to Washington will you remember your promise to Maria and Myself.

1. A slave. He was sold to John Perry a sometime Monticello carpenter for £ 125 on April 20, 1804. See Account Book for this date.

2. Mary Stewart, the wife of William Stewart, the very able Monticello blacksmith. She is buried in the Monticello graveyard. See *The Annual Report of the Monticello Association* ([Charlottesville], 1940), 29.

3. Jane Cary Randolph Randolph (Mrs. Thomas Eston).

4. Bracketed words in this and the following sentence have been supplied, as originals are illegible.

5. Charles-Balthazar-Julien Févret de Saint-Mémin was the French *émigré* artist. He did not delineate TJ until 1804, for which service TJ noted in his Account Book on November 27: "Gave St. Mémin order on bk US. for 29.50." For this payment he received the original crayon drawing, a small copper plate engraved from the drawing, and forty-eight small engravings struck from this plate. For further information, consult these excellent publications: Fillmore Norfleet, *Saint-Mémin in Virginia: Portraits and Biographies* (Richmond, 1942); Howard C. Rice, Jr., "Saint-Mémin's Portrait of Jefferson," *The Princeton University Library Chronicle*, XX, No. 4 (Summer, 1959), 182–92, and Alfred L. Bush, *The Life Portraits of Thomas Jefferson* (Charlottesville, 1962), 65–67.

From Anne Cary Randolph

Edgehill Jan. 21 1804

I received my Dear Grand Papa's letter but it was too late to answer it. Jefferson will not let Ellen catch him for he is now translating the history of Cyrus by Xenophon. I will very gladly undertake to raise a pair of Bantams for Monticello if you will send them to me. I am very sorry to inform you that the plank house is burnt down.[1] John Hemming's was here last night and he told us that the floor of the hall and the Music gallery was burnt up and that it was as full of plank as it could of which not one inch was saved. Your ice house will be full by ten oclock today. I suppose you have heard of Aunt Bolling's death.[2] Aunt Virginia is engaged to Cousin Wilson Cary and Aunt Hariet to a Mr. Hackley of New York.[3] Adieu My Dear Grand Papa. Your affectionate grand daughter,   A C R

1. The exact location and the date of the burning of this structure is not established; however, it burned prior to January 21; Mary mentioned it in her letter of that date to John Wayles Eppes (ViU). It was probably located at the site of the "kiln" shown at the northeast arc of the First Roundabout on the 1809 Survey, No. 17, of Nichols, *Jefferson's Architectural Drawings*.

2. Mary Jefferson Bolling (Mrs. John).

3. Virginia (Jenny) and Harriet Randolph were Thomas Mann Randolph, Jr.'s sisters. Virginia was engaged to Wilson Jefferson Cary, a son of Jane Barbara Carr Cary (Mrs. Wilson); Harriet's fiancé was Richard S. Hackley of New York City.

To Martha Jefferson Randolph

Washington Jan. 23. 04.

My dear Martha

Our Milton post not having come in last night, we are without news from you. I suppose he has been delayed by the weather, a severe snow storm having begun yesterday morning and still continuing. The snow is supposed to be now a foot deep, and is still falling with unabated fury. As it is the first, so I hope it will be the last of our severe winter weather. It is so tempestuous that I presume Congress will hardly meet to-day, and the rather as they have nothing pressing. The little before them will permit them to proceed at leisure, and finish when they please, which I conjecture will be about the 2d. week of March. I expect that Mr. Eppes will leave it before it rises in order to be with Maria at the knock of an elbow in February. I hope she will keep up her spirits. Should she be later than she has calculated, perhaps we may all be with her. Altho' the recurrence of those violent attacks to which Francis is liable, cannot but give uneasiness as to their character, yet be that what it will, there is little doubt but he will out-grow them; as I have scarcely ever known an instance to the contrary, at his age. On Friday Congress give a dinner on the acquisition of Louisana. They determine to invite no foreign ministers, to avoid questions of etiquette, in which we are enveloped by Merry's and Yrujo's families. As much as I wished to have had yourself and sister with me, I rejoice you were not here. The brunt of the battle now falls on the Secretary's ladies, who are dragged in the dirt of every federal paper. You would have been the victims had you been here, and butchered the more bloodily as they would hope it would be more felt by myself. It is likely to end in those two families putting themselves into Coventry until they recieve orders from their courts to acquiesce in our principles of the equality of all persons meeting together in society, and not to expect to force us into their principles of allotment into ranks and orders.[1] Pour into the bosom of my dear Maria all the comfort and courage which the affections of my heart can give her, and tell her to rise superior to all fear for all our sakes. Kiss all the little ones for me, with whom I should be so much happier than here; and be assured yourself of my tender and constant love.   TH: JEFFERSON

1. Following his precepts, TJ allowed his guests to enter the dining room pellmell or first come first served. This almost precipitated an international incident in the case of Anthony Merry, the British Minister, whose wife was overlooked in one of these scrambles. The Marquis de Casa-Yrujo also had a similar grievance and joined Merry in a strong protest. It was to no avail; republican simplicity prevailed. For TJ's reaction to the Merry protest, see his letter to James Monroe of January 8, 1804 (DLC). Irving Brant, in his *James Madison, Secretary of State 1800–1809* (Indianapolis, 1953), 163–69, gives an excellent account of this "etiquette quarrel."

TO MARY JEFFERSON EPPES

Washington Jan. 29. 04.

MY DEAREST MARIA

This evening ought to have brought in the Western mail, but it is not arrived. Consequently we hear nothing from our neighborhood. I rejoice that this is the last time our Milton mail will be embarrassed with that from New Orleans; the rapidity of which occasioned our letters often to be left in the post-offices. It now returns to it's former establishment of twice a week, so that we may hear oftener from you: and in communicating to us frequently of the state of things I hope you will not be sparing, if it be only by saying that "all is well." I think Congress will rise the 2d. week in March, when we shall join you. Perhaps Mr. Eppes may sooner. On this I presume he writes you. It would have been the most desireable of all things could we have got away by this time. However I hope you will let us all see that you have within yourself the resources of a courage, not requiring the presence of any body. Since proposing to Anne the undertaking to raise Bantams I have recieved from Algiers two pair of beautiful fowls, something larger than our common fowls, with fine aigreetes. They are not so large nor valuable as the East India fowl, but both kinds, as well as the Bantams are well worthy of being raised. We must therefore distribute them among us; and raise them clear of mixture of any kind. All this we will settle together in March, and soon after I hope we shall begin the levilling, and establishing of your hen-house at Pantops. Give my tenderest love to your sister; to all the young ones kisses, to yourself every thing affectionate.

TH: JEFFERSON

FROM MARY JEFFERSON EPPES

Edgehill february 10th [1804]

Your letters My dear Papa have been long unanswerd but while low in spirits and health I could not prevail on myself to do it, the hope however of soon seeing you and Mr. Eppes for the time is now approaching makes me feel all of happiness that anticipation can give in my present situation. It is indeed only by looking forward to that much wish'd for moment that I acquire spirits to support me in the tedious interval, but to be with you both again would compensate for any suffering.

In the mean time I have a favor to beg of you that I hope will not be refused. It is one which my sister as well as myself is deeply interested in. We had both thought you had promised us your picture if ever St. Mimin went to Washington. If you did but know what a source of pleasure it would be to us while so much separated from you to have so excellent a likeness of you you would not I think refuse us. It is what we have allways most wanted all our lives and the certainty with which he takes his likenesses makes this one request I think not unreasonable. He will be in Washington the middle of this month and I can not help hoping you will grant us this one favor. I am very much afraid you will be disappointed in getting your faeton. Davy Bowles went to Richmond intending to return here before he went on, but it is so long since he left us that as his wife is now staying in Richmond it is most probable he has hired himself there. Your acacias are very beautiful My dear Papa, there are eight of them very flourishing that have changed their foliage entirely. They have remain'd in my room to the warmth of which I believe they are indebted for their present flourishing state as they appear to be more delicate the smaller they are. I wish you could bring us a small piece of your Geranium in the spring if it is large enough to admit of it. Perhaps Mr. Eppes could more conveniently take charge of it than yourself. Adieu dearest Papa. We are all well here and all most anxious for the happy moment that will reunite us again after this long separation. Believe me with the tenderest love yours ever,   M EPPES

FROM ANNE CARY RANDOLPH

Edgehill Feb. 14 1804

MY DEAR GRAND PAPA

I received your letter on the 13th of Feb: and am much obliged to you for it and the poetry also. I will very gladly undertake to write to you every post. Jefferson is going to a very good latin school in the neighbourhood.[1] Mama is now in very good health and her apetite is quite restored. She has never been out yet for fear of catching cold. All the children send their love to you and Francis and we are all delighted to hear that we shall have the pleasure of seeing you soon. Adieu my Dear Grand Papa. Your most affectionate Granddaughter,   A C RANDOLPH

Aunt Virginia sends her love to you also.

1. Probably John Robertson's, which was located near the eastern slope of the Southwest Mountains.

FROM ANNE CARY RANDOLPH

Edgehill Feb 22 1804

I wrote to my Dear Grand Papa last post but I suppose he did not receive my letter or he certainly would have answered it. In my last letter I mentioned the changing my name to Anastasia but you did not say whether you approved it. I am afraid my letters must be very tiresome to you as I have nothing to say but I intend to write to you every post. Adieu my Dear Grand Papa. Your most affectionate Grand daughter,   A C R

To Mary Jefferson Eppes

Washington Feb. 26. 04.

A thousand joys to you, My dear Maria, on the happy accession to your family.[1] A letter from our dear Martha by last post gave me the happy news that your crisis was happily over and all well. I had supposed that if you were a little later than your calculation, and the rising of Congress as early as we expected, that we might have been with you at the moment when it would have been so encouraging to have had your friends around you. I rejoice indeed that all is so well. Congress talk of rising the 12th. of March but they will probably be some days later. You will doubtless see Mr. Eppes and Mr. Randolph immediately on the rising of Congress. I shall hardly be able to get away till some days after them. By that time I hope you will be able to go with us to Monticello and that we shall all be there together for a month and the interval between that and the autumnal visit will not be long. Will you desire your sister to send for Mr. Lilly and to advise him what orders to give Goliah for providing those vegetables which may come into use for the months of April, August and September. Deliver her also my affectionate love. I will write to her the next week. Kiss all the little ones, and be assured yourself of my tender and unchangeable affection.   TH: JEFFERSON

1. Maria Jefferson Eppes, who was born February 15, 1804, at Edgehill.

To Mary Jefferson Eppes

Washington Mar. 3. 04.

The account of your illness my dearest Maria was known to me only this morning. Nothing but impossibilities prevent my instant departure to join you. But the impossibility of Congress proceeding a single step in my absence presents an insuperable bar. Mr. Eppes goes off and I hope will find you in a convalescent state. Next to the desire that it may be so, is that of being speedily informed of it and of being relieved from the terrible anxiety in which I shall be till I hear from you. God bless you my ever dear daughter and preserve you safe to be the blessing of us all.

TH: JEFFERSON

To Martha Jefferson Randolph

Washington Mar. 8. 04.

Your letter of the 2d. my dear Martha, which was not recieved till the last night has raised me to life again. For four days past I had gone through inexpressible anxiety. The mail which left you on the 5th. will probably be here tonight, and will I hope strengthen our hopes of Maria's continuing to recover, and Mr. Eppes's arrival which I presume was on the 6th. will render her spirits triumphant over her Physical debility. Congress have determined to rise on Monday sennight (the 19th). Mr. Randolph will probably be with you on the 22d. and myself within 3. or 4. days after. Maria must in the mean time resolve to get strong to make us all happy.[1] Your apologies my dear for using any thing at Monticello for her, yourself, family or friends, are more than unnecessary. What is there is as much for the use of you all as for myself, and you cannot do me greater pleasure than by using every thing with the same freedom I should do myself. Tell my dear Maria to be of good chear, and to be ready to mount on horseback with us and continue to let us hear of her by every post. If Mrs. Lewis be still with you deliver her my affectionate respects and assurances of my great sensibility for her kind attentions to Maria. Kiss the little ones for me, and be assured of my tenderest love to Maria and yourself.   Th: Jefferson

1. TJ recorded these vital statistics about Mary in his family Bible: "Mary
                              H M
Jefferson born. Aug. 1, 1778. 1 30 A.M. died Apr. 17. 1804. between 8. and 9.
A.M." The child survived.

To Martha Jefferson Randolph

Washington May 14. [1804]

My dear Martha

I arrived here last night after the most fatiguing journey I have experienced for a great many years. I got well enough to Orange C. H. the first day. The 2d. there was a constant heavy drizzle through the whole day sufficient to soak my outer great coat twice, and the roads very dirty and in places deep. The third the roads became as deep as at any season, and as laborious to the horse. Castor got into ill temper and refused to draw, and we had a vast deal of trouble and fatigue with him and obliged to give him up at last. I was from day light to sunset getting from Fauquier C. H.

to Colo. Wren's where I left John with the carriage, mounted my horse and arrived here at 9. oclock in the night more sore and fatigued than I ever remember to have been with a journey. With the circuitous route I was obliged to take it made about 55. miles, of as deep and laborious road as could be travelled. A night's sleep has little rested me, but I am yet extremely the worse for my labour. I hope a day or two will entirely relieve me, certainly I shall never again so far forget my age as to undertake such another day of fatigue. I have written you this long chapter about myself, because I have really nothing else to write about, having as yet not seen any body but of the house. I picked up by the way some ice-lettuce seed, which I inclose you to enable you to raise seed for yourself this year. My affections to Mr. Randolph and kisses to the young ones. To yourself my tenderest love,   TH: JEFFERSON

FROM MARTHA JEFFERSON RANDOLPH

Edgehill May 31, 1804

Pardon me Dearest Father for having so long delayed answering your letter. Great was the anxiety I suffered untill it arrived, nor was that any way, relieved by hearing what a terrible journey you had had, allthough it may ultimately prove fortunate if it serves as a warning against future exposure to cold and fatigue which every day of your life you will be less able to bear. No appology can be necessary for writing lengthily to me about your self. I hope you are not yet to learn that no subject on earth *is* or *ever can be* so dear and interesting to me. I speak so entirely without an exception that I do not hesitate to declare if my other duties could possibly interfere with my devotion to you I should not feel a scruple in sacrifising them, to a sentiment which has litterally "grown with my growth and strengthened with my strength,["] and which no subsequent attachment has in the smallest degree weakened. It is truly the happiness of my life to think that I can dedicate the remainder of it to promote yours. It is a subject however upon which I ought never to write for no pen on earth can do justice to the feelings of my heart. Ann is gone down with Aunt Eppes and I am shortly to join her if they send the carriage for me which my Aunt pressed so warmly that I could not refuse her. A letter from Ann informs me of their being all well on the 26th but the baby who continues mending, but slowly. We are as usual well here. I have my self had an attack of something like the cramp

in the stomach. The spasms were violent and came on with a desire
to puke which however produced nothing more than an insuperable distension of the breast at the moment and a difficulty of
breathing amounting allmost to suffocation. I was much allarmed
my self. Mr. Randolph has since affirmed it to have been hysterics
but I certainly know him to be wrong there. It was occasioned by
eating radishes and milk at the same meal both of which are unfriendly to my stomach and the affection of the speech of which
I was very sensible at the time proves it to have been some thing
more serious than mere hysterics. I was relieved by pepper mint
repeating the dose till my stomach was brought to act again, but
it was several hours before I was sufficiently easy to sit or lye down.
I have been perfectly well since. I shall however allways stand in
dread of another attack of the same nature and which may not
be as easily checked the second time. Adieu Dearly beloved Father.
Believe me with a tenderness not to be expressed yours most
affectionately,   M. RANDOLPH

To MARTHA JEFFERSON RANDOLPH

Washington July 17. 04.

It is a considerable time, my very dear Martha, since I have
written because I have been in expectation you were all at Eppington; and tho' I have not heard of your return to Edgehill, I presume it has taken place. I have some hope of being able to leave
this on the 23d. and to be with you on the 26th. but it is possible
I may not be able to get thro' my business. Mr. Gallatin and Smith
are gone. General Dearborne[1] and Mr. Madison will go in three
or four days. M. and Made. Pichon,[2] who have lately lost their
child are inconsoleable; and will pass the remainder of the season
in travelling about. They will pass some time with Mr. Madison
and us. I have written to my sister Marks to press a visit from her
and that I would send for her on my arrival. I hope the little ones
are all well and that you have left the family at Eppington, and
particularly our dear portion of it well, and in the intention of
visiting us. The necessaries for our comfort at Monticello have
been sent off long ago at two or three different times. Kiss the dear
children for me, and present me affectionately to Mr. Randolph.
My impatience to be with you all increases more as I approach
the moment of that happiness. God bless you my ever dear child,

and permit me to find you in good health. A tender adieu till I
see you.   TH: JEFFERSON
P. S. I presume Mr. Randolph's newspapers will inform him of
the death of Colo. Hamilton, which took place on the 12th.

1. Albert Gallatin, Secretary of the Treasury, Robert Smith, Secretary of
the Navy, and General Henry Dearborne, Secretary of War in TJ's Cabinet.
2. Louis André Pichon was the Chargé d'Affaires for the French Empire.
There is no known account of their visit to Monticello.

To Martha Jefferson Randolph

Washington Oct. 7. 04.

MY DEAR MARTHA

I arrived here this day week, having travelled through the rain
of that day rather than stay in disagreeable quarters. I experienced
no inconvenience from it. The Marquis Yrujo arrived two days
after me, and Mr. Madison and Genl. Dearborne got here last
night. The latter has left his family in Maine for the winter. Yrujo
is said to be very ill, taken two days ago. I inclose a magazine for
Jefferson, merely for the sake of the plate which may add to the
collection for his room. You will see in the magazine an account
of a new work by Mrs. Robinson, Mrs. Cosway and Mrs. Watson [1]
which must be curious. A great deal of sickness has been and still
exists in this place: I trust however that the hard frosts we had a
week ago has destroyed the germ of new cases. The sickliness of
the summer has been so general that we may consider the exemp-
tion of our canton from it as very remarkeable. Four weeks tomorrow our winter campaign opens. I dread it on account of the
fatigues of the table in such a round of company, which I consider
as the most serious trials I undergo. I wish much to turn it over
to younger hands and to be myself but a guest at the table, and
free to leave it as others are; but whether this would be tolerated
is uncertain. I hope Mr. Randolph, yourself, and the dear children
continue well. I miss you all at all times, but especially at breakfast, dinner and the evening when I have been used to unbend
from the labours of the day. Present me affectionately to Mr.
Randolph, and my kisses to the young ones.

1. Mary Robinson, an English authoress, who was sometimes known as Mrs.
Perdita Robinson. The magazine account may have referred to the work,
Progress of Female Virtue and Female Dissipation, a set of aquatint engrav-
ings designed by Maria Cosway (Mrs. Richard), an artist of note and friend of
TJ, and executed by Mrs. Caroline Watson, an English engraver.

To Martha Jefferson Randolph

Washington. Nov. 6. 1804.

MY DEAREST MARTHA

I send you the inclosed magazine supposing it may furnish you a few moments amusement, as well as to the reading members of your family. Mr. Randolph arrived here Sunday evening in good health and brought me the welcome news, that you were all well. Congress has as yet formed but one of it's houses, there being no Senate. My heart fails me at the opening such a campaign of bustle and fatigue: the unlimited calumnies of the federalists have obliged me to put myself on the trial of my country by standing another election. I have no fear as to their verdict; and that being secured for posterity, no considerations will induce me to continue beyond the term to which it will extend. My passion strengthens daily to quit political turmoil, and retire into the bosom of my family, the only scene of sincere and pure happiness. One hour with you and your dear children is to me worth an age past here. Mr. Eppes is here, with Francis in the highest health. He tells me he left our dear little Maria very well at Eppington, and all the family there. Tell Anne it is time for her to take up her pen. She shall have letter for letter. For Ellen I have a beautiful pair of little Bantams; but how to get them to her is the difficulty. In the spring I shall be able to send them. Kiss all the young ones for me, and be assured yourself of my tenderest unchangeable love.

TH: JEFFERSON.

From Martha Jefferson Randolph

Edgehill Nov 30, 1804

MY DEAREST FATHER

Lilly was here a fortnight ago to beg I would write to you immediately about some business of his, but a change in the post day disappointed me in sending the letters written to have gone by it. He says you desired him to part with 100 barrils of corn as more than you required, but he says he has got it on very good terms 16 and 16, 6 a barril and that there is not one bushell too much, on account of the heavy hauling he has to do. He says if the horses are not highly fed they will not be able to do the work and he thinks Anderson[1] from whom some of it was purchased will wait till the first of february for his money. After recieving your letter he went to see Moran[2] about the double payment that had been made, he pretended he knew nothing about it but that he would see Irving and it should be rectified, and that Lilly should hear from him in a fortnight. The time has past without hearing from him and he fears he is gone to Kentucky. He is obliged to give up K. Smiths negro's[3] tomorrow as he wished to get all the work possible out of them before they went. He defered going after Irving till their time was out, when he will immediately see him. The man that run away the first of August has never been recovered. He begged me also to speak particularly about John.[4] He is utterly averse to the idea of having any thing to say to him another year. His conduct is such that there can be nothing like honesty or subordination where he is. His wish is that he should be sent off the plantation and indeed the instances of depravity that he mentioned in him, his art in throwing every thing into confusion, encouraging the hands to rebellion and idleness and then telling upon them so as to put Lilly out of his senses allmost, are beyond conception. He says that John has frequently created such confusion by his art as to render it impossible to punish the very hands of whom he complained most, and pieces of ill will and mischief to himself inumerable, such as cutting up his garden destroying his things and once he suspects him of having attempted to poison him. He thinks it necessary for him to be allways upon his guard against his malice. He says giving up his labour is giving up nothing for he loses ten times more labour by his presence than ten such would do. Thus far I believe I have mentioned every thing necessary, for the [story][5] of John conduct would extend beyond [the limit] of any letter. I really believe him to be a most determined villain equal to any crime on earth. We recieved the most flattering accounts from Jeffersons Master as a boy of uncommon industry and application. The others are all going on pretty well and are all remarkably healthy. Adieu My Dearest Father. Lilly's business has taken up so much of my time and paper that I have only room to subscribe my self with inexpressible tenderness. Your affectionate Daughter,   M R.

1. Probably David Anderson, an Albemarle County farmer.

2. Joseph Moran was a sometime Monticello workman. Martha is referring to the payments her father noted in his Account Book on December 7, 1802, when Moran was paid $200, and on January 11, 1803, when another $200 was paid him, and finally, February 8, when $98 was given. Following this there is no further mention of Moran in the Account Book.

3. Christopher and Charles Smith were Louisa County residents. Jefferson had been leasing slaves from C. Smith since 1801. On March 12, 1804 (MHi), he wrote Smith that he was able to pay only one half of the fee for that year (the lease apparently ran from January to January) and on the same day enclosed a note to George Jefferson in Richmond for $433.50 "due to

him and Charles Smith for negro hire." (Account Book.) See Account Book
for entries of January 7, 1802, February 8, 1803, and March 12, 1804. There
are no other specific notations of payments to the Smiths.

4. This John obviously was a slave, and unfortunately nothing is known
of how TJ finally acted in the matter.

5. Words supplied in brackets are unclear in original.

To Martha Jefferson Randolph

Washington Dec. 3 04.

My dearest Martha

Taking for granted that Mr. Randolph writes to you regularly
and much engaged by business and company myself, I have been
more remiss. We are all well here, and our accounts from Eppington are favorable, and particularly that our dear little one there
has two teeth. Francis is in remarkeable health: and I hope the
objects of our affections with you are equally so. I send you some
magazines which may amuse you and them. I have some poetry
for Anne, but I reserve it for my answer to her first letter. Congress has scarcely any thing to employ them, and complain that
the place is remarkably dull. Very few ladies have come on this
winter, and we have lost Madmes. Yrujo, Pichon, Merry, and Law.[1]
The theatre fails too for want of actors. You are happy to need
none of these aids to get rid of your time and certainly they are
poor substitutes for the sublime enjoiment of the affections of our
children and of our cares for them. Mr. Burwell[2] being a member
of the Virginia legislature has left us to attend it; and Mr. Isaac
Coles[3] remains with me during his absence being this moment
called off, I must here conclude with my kisses to all the dear
children, and my tenderest and unalterable love to you.

Th: Jefferson

1. Mrs. Thomas Law was the wife of a Washington land speculator.

2. William Armistead Burwell, at one time TJ's secretary.

3. Isaac Coles was a son of John Coles of Enniscorthy and TJ's private
secretary. The Coles family were neighbors and close friends of the Monticello
family.

To Martha Jefferson Randolph

Washington Jan. 7. 05.

My dearest Martha

A letter from Mr. Randolph to Mr. Coles informs him he shall
bring you here but does not say if with or without the family. I
shall rejoice my dear to recieve you here, and them, or as many
of them as you can bring. I feel much for what you will suffer on

the road: for such a spell of severe weather we have not known for years. The thermometer has been down of mornings at 14. 12. 10. and once as low as 4°. The rivers are all solid. It will be absolutely necessary to provide yourselves with the most abundant covering for the road. I am sorry Mr. Randolph did not take my pelisse: as nothing can be more dangerous for you than to be exposed to a great degree of long continued cold. On this subject let me beseech you to make ample provision of covering.

I send you a book of gardening which I believe has merit.[1] It has at least that of being accomodated to our seasons.

We have but few strangers in town. Fewer ladies than I have ever known. The gentlemen complain that the place is very dull but it is the more comfortable. We shall expect you at the beginning of the next week. My affections to Mr. Randolph, kisses to the children and tenderest love to yourself.

TH: JEFFERSON

1. Probably Bernard McMahon, *The American Gardener's Calendar* (Philadelphia, 1806). Sowerby 810.

To Martha Jefferson Randolph

Washington Jan. 21. 05

MY DEAREST MARTHA

Your letter of the 11th. was recieved and gave me the first intimation of your illness. It has filled me with anxiety respecting you, and this is increased by your not having communicated it to me. Because in endeavoring to spare my feelings on your real situation it gives me the pain of fearing every thing imaginable; even that the statement of your recovery may not be exact. Let me pray you always to give me the rigorous state of things that I may be sure I know the worst. Had not Congress been sitting, I would have seen you as soon as my horses could have carried me. This dreadful spell of weather makes me fear lest you should suffer from it. If in such a season one day can be selected as worse than another yesterday and to-day have the preeminence. I have seen nothing like this since the last winter we were in Paris. A letter of last week from Mr. Randolph to Mr. Coles gives us reason to expect him here to-day. Yet I hope he has not set out in such weather. Consider my dear Martha to what degree, and how many persons have the happiness of their lives depending on you, and consider it as a duty to take every care of yourself that you would think of for the dearest of those about you. I hope by the post of tomorrow morning to hear you are perfectly reestablished. In the mean time this letter must go off by the post of this evening. Our last news from Eppington assured us of Maria's health, but Mrs. Eppes has been very ill. Francis enjoys as high health and spirits as possible. He wants only a society which could rub off what he contracts from the gross companions with whom he of necessity associates. He is a charming boy. Kiss all my dear little ones for me, and be assured yourself of my tenderest and unalterable love.

TH: JEFFERSON

To MARTHA JEFFERSON RANDOLPH

Washington Jan. 28. 05.

MY EVER DEAR MARTHA

Your letter of the 11th. recieved here on the 15th. is the last news I have of you. Mr. Randolph having written to Mr. Coles that he should be here on the 15th. and not having come, and no letter from you by that post, I was thrown into inexpressible anxiety lest a relapse into your complaint should have called him to Edgehill. From this I was not relieved till three days ago when a letter from Mr. Burwell (in Richmond) to Mr. Coles mentioned incidentally that Mr. Randolph had been detained there longer than he expected. The continuance too of this dreadful weather is an additional cause of fear for you. The ground had just got uncovered with a snow which had covered it 24. days, when yesterday another fell of 6. or 8. I. deep, and the weather, tho' now fair, is very severe. I hope you will not expose yourself to a renewal of the inflammatory complaint. That of the stomach must be opposed by a strict attention to what you find it digests most easily, and to a course of exercise for strengthening the system generally and invigorating the stomach with that. I hope by the post of tomorrow morning to hear your recovery is confirmed, but at any rate to know your exact situation. Kiss our dear little children for me, among whom I wish so anxiously to be and be assured of my tenderest affections.   TH: JEFFERSON

FROM ELLEN WAYLES RANDOLPH

Feb 22 1805

MY DEAR GRAND PAPA

I recieved your letter and am very much obliged to you for it, as it is very seldom that I get one. You cannot think how glad I was at it. I am very much obliged to you for the Bantams you promised me and will take great care of them. I go on very slowly with my French for I have got through but one book of Telemachus[1] but I hope that I shall now go on better since Mamas healt is so much better that she is able to hear us our lessons regularly. Give my love to Papa and Mrs. H Smith.[2] Adieu my Dear grand Papa. Believe me to be your affectionate grand Daughter,

ELLEN WAYLES RANDOLPH.

1. François de Salignac de la Motte Fénélon's *Télémaque* was a standard French reader of the time. Sowerby 4305–7.

2. Mrs. Samuel Harrison (Margaret Bayard) Smith was the wife of General Smith of Baltimore and a close friend of Jefferson's. Ellen became very attached to her during a visit to Washington, as subsequent letters will point out. Mrs. Smith is referred to variously as Mrs. S. H. S., Mrs. Smith, and Mrs. S. H. Smith.

FROM MARTHA JEFFERSON RANDOLPH

Feb. 28, 1805

I have been again greatly indisposed My Dearest Father but am now so much better that I should have left my room today if the weather had been good. I was for one night and a part of the next very ill, and having what I never in my life had before (an hysteric fit) thought my self dying whilst in it. Doctor Everett[1] says it is not uncommon in the complaint I had, which was brought on by *cold* in the first instance. My stomach is still extremely weak but I am in hopes as soon as the weather will admit of My taking exercise on horseback which he has strongly recommended I shall speedily recover. I am upon the whole much mended in health and appearance since Mr.R. left me. Adieu My Dearest Father. I will write you on saturday again but Jerry's[2] notice was so short that I had but one moment to write in. Believe me with tenderest love yours,   MR.

1. Dr. Everett, a Charlottesville physician.

2. A TJ slave who traveled a great deal between Monticello, Washington, and Poplar Forest.

TO ELLEN WAYLES RANDOLPH

Washington Mar. 4. 05.

MY DEAREST ELLEN

I owe a letter to you and one to your sister Anne. But the pressure of the day on which this is written, and your Papa's departure permits me to write only to you, to inclose you a poem about another namesake of yours, and some other pieces worth preserving. As I expect Anne's volume is now large enough, I will begin to furnish you with materials for one. I know you have been collecting some yourself; but as 1 expect there is some tag, rag, and bobtail verse among it you must begin a new volume for my materials. I am called off by company therefore god bless you, my dear child, kiss your Mama and sisters for me, and tell them I shall be with them in about a week from this time. Once more Adieu.

TH: JEFFERSON

FROM ANNE CARY RANDOLPH

Edgehill March 22 1805

This is the fourth letter I have written to My Dear Grand Papa without receiving an answer. I suppose you have not received them or else your business prevented your answering them. Mama has been very sick and two of the children but they are now quite well. We heard that you were to set of from Washington the 8 of March. I wish in your next letter you will let me know whether it is true. Adieu My Dear Grandpapa. Your most affectionate Grand daughter,   A C R

FROM MARTHA JEFFERSON RANDOLPH

Monticello April 19 1805

MY DEAREST FATHER

Mr. Randolph's election is almost certain. The polls stand, Alb. TM.R 503 W.L. 140. Amh. TM.R. 390. WL. 474 which leaves Mr. Randolph a majority of 279, so that independent of his influence in Fluvanna which is great, he is safe.[1] We are all well, but I am moored here till Thursday as he merely stopped a day with us on his way to Fluvanna where he now is, of course I am obliged to stay till his return. The weather is very favorable to your new plantations but many of the thorns[2] I am told are certainly dead. Adieu My Dear Father. It is so late 1 am in danger of losing the post. Yours most tenderly,   MR.

1. Mr. Randolph was contesting with Walter Leake for a delegate's seat in the Virginia legislature from the counties of Albemarle, Amherst, and Fluvanna. He won, as Martha had predicted.

2. These were introduced in 1805 to surround the Monticello orchards. TJ's reason for not attempting live fencing sooner was the lack of a hardy plant of suitable size and strength and in sufficient quantity. Thomas Main,

an Alexandria nurseryman, convinced him the Washington thorn (*Crataegus phaenopyrum* Med.), which grew wild in the environs of Washington, would suffice, and TJ procured about 4,000 plants in March, 1805. These were set out in the South Thorn Hedge, which encompassed the South Orchard and Vegetable Garden except the segment along Mulberry Row. His interest in this type of fence continued, for later he procured a copy of Main's pamphlet, *Directions for the Transplantation and Management of young Thorn or other Hedge Plants* (District of Columbia, 1807). Sowerby 723. For additional information, consult the *Garden Book*, 298ff., and Account Book, October 21, 1805, and June 28, 1806.

To Martha Jefferson Randolph

Washington May 6. 1805.

My dearest Martha

Your letter of Apr. 19. and Mr. Randolph's of Apr. 27. have given me the agreeable information of Mr. Randolph's success, and the more agreeable and important information that you are getting well. For the restoration of your stomach my chief dependance is on your own resolution to observe rigorously whatever regimen you find from experience to agree with you: and it will take a long course of this rigorous regimen to place you beyond the danger of relapse. To guard against cold will be more difficult. I negotiate with your friends here who enquire whether you will come the next winter, and find them readily acquiesce in the necessity of agreeing that you shall never be out of an evening. I am in hopes therefore you will come and bring the whole family. Arrangements made up stairs since you were here, and additional furniture now providing will accomodate them all, and the necessity of lessening the fatigues of the table, which have borne too heavily on me, will oblige me to dine company less frequently, and to live more in a family way. A good deal of sickness is shewing itself here exactly among those individuals who were sick the last year. The same is said to be the case in the part of the country afflicted the last year. This will probably induce us to break up here a little earlier than usual: I suppose about the middle of July. As this is within little more than 2 months, I am now preparing to send off our groceries for Monticello, that they may get up the river before it falls. Present me affectionately to Mr. Randolph and in kisses to all the dear children. To yourself tenderness without bounds.   Th: Jefferson

To Ellen Wayles Randolph

May 21. 05.

MISS ELEANOR W. RANDOLPH TO TH: JEFFERSON   DR.
1805. May 21. To a letter which ought to be written once in
every 3. weeks, while I am here, to wit
from Jan. 1. 1805. to this day 15. weeks   5.
CR.
Feb. 23. By one single letter of this day's date   1
Balance due from E. W. Randolph to Th: J Letters   4

                                                           ──

                                                            5

So stands the account for this year, my dear Ellen, between you
and me. Unless it be soon paid off, I shall send the sheriff after
you. I inclose you an abundant supply of poetry, among which
you will find Goody Blake,[1] which I think you wanted. I will thank
you if you will put on your boots and spurs and ride to Monticello
and inform me how my thorns live. This part of the country is
beautifying with them so fast that every ride I take makes me
anxious for those at Monticello. Your Papa in his last letter informs me that mumps have got into the family. Let me know who
have it and how all do. Kiss your dear Mama for me and shake
hands with all the little ones. Present me affectionately to your
Papa and accept mes baise-mains yourself.

TH: JEFFERSON

1. Unidentified. For other information on TJ's grandchildren's reading,
see James A. Bear, Jr., "Childrens' Books at Monticello," in press and to be
published in 1966 by the McGregor Library of the Alderman Library at the
University of Virginia.

To Martha Jefferson Randolph

Washington June 10. 05

MY DEAREST MARTHA

I have been a month now without hearing from Edgehill, Mr.
Randolph's letter of May 11, being the last I have recieved. Anne
then had the mumps which of course were expected to go thro'
the family, and heightens my anxiety to hear from you. Our post
is now I believe prcmanently established at three times a week.
The spring here continues sickly and cold, and poor prospects of
crops. We had yesterday cauliflowers and artichokes at table. The
40. days corn I mentioned to Mr. Randolph to have recieved and

had planted here has failed: but I learn that a few of the same seeds have succeeded with a gardener at Baltimore. He had however but 4. grains, and of course there is still much risk. I count about this day five weeks (July 15.) to set out for Monticello, and after a few days rest to proceed to Bedford. I hope in the mean time to hear from you frequently and to know how your own health is particularly and how the dear children get on with the mumps. Kiss them all for me, accept yourself my tenderest love, and affectionate salutations to Mr. Randolph.

TH: JEFFERSON

P.S. I send you some magazines[1] for your amusement.

1. It is difficult to ascertain the titles of these magazines. According to the Account Books 1791–1803, TJ subscribed to only four: *The Connecticut Republican* in 1802; *The Columbian Magazine,* 1793; *The National Magazine,* 1799, and *The Weekly Magazine of Original Essays.* For others not subscribed to but available, see Frank L. Mott, *A History of American Magazines 1741–1850* (New York, 1930), and Winifred Gregory, editor, *Union List of Serials in Libraries of the United States and Canada* (New York, 1943).

TO MARTHA JEFFERSON RANDOLPH

Washington June 12. 05

MY DEAREST MARTHA

I have barely time to tell you that Mrs. Madison has executed your desires and I dare say to your mind. The commission to me has given me the greatest pleasure, as it always would that you would say to me freely at all times what want you have which I could gratify. My wishes are always to do what would be pleasing to you; but knowing nothing of what would be proper or acceptable, I do nothing. I see nothing as yet to hinder my departure on Monday and my being with you to breakfast on Thursday. Mrs. Madison is very anxiously confined by surgical care which disables her from walking, and which it is feared may disable her from visiting Orange this season.[1] The danger to Mr. Madison of staying here, may induce them to undertake the journey by short stages. My tenderest love my dear to yourself and all about you.

TH: JEFFERSON

1. She developed an ulcerated tumor on her leg near the knee and went to Philadelphia for treatments by Dr. Philip Physick. It was October before it had healed sufficiently for her to be about, but still too tender for travel. She remained in Philadelphia while Mr. Madison returned to Washington. See Brant, *James Madison, Secretary of State,* 280, 288.

To Martha Jefferson Randolph

Washington June 24. 05.

MY DEAREST MARTHA

I last night recieved a letter from Mr. Taylor of Baltimore informing me he had sent by the stage to this place the trunk of articles ordered by Mr. Kelly. I sent this morning to the Stage office; the trunk was arrived, and goes on this evening to Fredericksburg, where I shall desire Mr. Benson[1] to forward it by the first stage to Milton. I had paiment made here for transportation as far as Fredericksbg that no delay might happen on that account. Further could not be paid here, on account of it's being a different concern with which the stage-company here is unconnected. I hope you will get the trunk by the first stage. I have had here a considerable time ½ doz. pr. of shoes for Virginia and ½ doz. pr. for Anne, but am afraid to trust so small a parcel by the stage without a guardian. Perhaps it will not come on till I go myself which will be this day three weeks. I take for granted that Virginia's marriage[2] is to take place at Monticello, as we have so much more room there for our friends, and conveniencies of other kinds also. I will accomodate my trip to Bedford to the matrimonial arrangements. We have just heard from Capt. Lewis, who wintered 1600. miles up the Missouri; all well. 45. chiefs of 6. different nations from that quarter are forwarded by him to St. Louis on their way to this place. Our agent at St. Louis will endeavor to prevail on them to stay there till autumn and then come on. Should they insist on coming immediately they will arrive in July, and may derange my departure. I am glad to find the family has got so easily thro' the mumps, and hope you will discover that you have had them, as I think you had when very young. My love to every body; to yourself unceasing affection. Greet Mr. Randolph also affectionately for me.   TH: JEFFERSON

1. Benjamin Taylor was a Baltimore merchant, John Kelly a Milton merchant, and Benson a Fredericksburg innkeeper with whom TJ often lodged while traveling to and from Washington.
2. Virginia (Jenny) Randolph.

From Ellen Wayles Randolph

recd. June 27. 05

DEAR GRAND PAPA

I now set down to write to you and hope you will answer my letter. I have often tried to do it before but never could succeed, but now I am determined to do it. I suppose you have heard that Cousin Eliza Pleasants is gone away. Uncle William[1] and Mr. Hackley have been here and left us yesterday. Excuse the faults and bad writing of this letter since nothing but my anxiety to write to you and to show you I had not forgotten you could have made me do it. Your affectionate Grand Daughter,

ELLEONORA W RANDOLPH

1. Elizabeth Randolph Pleasants (Mrs. Robert, Jr.) and William Randolph, an elder sister and brother of Thomas Mann Randolph, Jr.

To ELLEN WAYLES RANDOLPH

Washington June 28. 05

MY DEAREST ELLEN

I recieved your letter (without date) with great pleasure, for it always gives me pleasure to hear from Edgehill. In return for your news from thence, I have none to give you from this place which would interest you, except that Mrs. Harrison Smith is well, dined with me the other day, and desired me to present her love in the first letter to you. She is now in the country at a neat little box they have a few miles from the city. You do not inform me whether you have all read all the books I have given you; because till that is done you know I am not to give any more. I send you some pieces for your volume of poetry some of which have merit, and intend to catch you in bed in the morning of the 18th. of July; against which I know not how you are to guard yourself but by not going to bed at all the over night. Kiss your Mama for me, and tell her I write to her through you. Salute our dear Anne for me also, and all the little ones: and present my affections to your papa. Tender salutations to yourself, to Virginia's meditations no interruption will be welcome. Salute her for me however the moment of respite she has from reveries.   TH: JEFFERSON

FROM ELLEN WAYLES RANDOLPH

July 4 1805

I have just recieved my Dear Grand Papa's letter, and am very much obliged to him for it, since I cannot have a greater pleasure than to recieve letters from him. I have a question to ask you that

I did not put in my last letter, it is what is [the] seventh fine art?
I know six of them, Painting, Sculpture, architecture, Music,
Poetry, Oratory, but mama nor my self either cannot recollect the
seventh. All the children have had the mumps except Mary who
is the sweetest little creature in the world, always laughing talking
and singing. She has a great many ideas and is a very forward child
for her age. Cornelia begins to read very well; we have none of us
deserved new books. We have not got half through those you gave
us the last time you were at Monticello, but as far as I have got
I am very much interested and we are going on with great spirit.
Aunt Virginia Sister Ann and all the other children give their love
to you. Give mine to Mrs. H Smith. Mama's health is daily improving. She has ridden out a good deal since you left us. Adieu my
dear Grandpapa, believe me to be your affectionate Grand Daughter,   ELEOANORA WAYLES RANDOLPH

To Anne Cary Randolph

Washington July 6. 05.

MY DEAREST ANNE

I do not know whether it is owing to your laziness or mine that
our letters have been so long intermitted. I assure you it is not to
my want of love to you, and to all of those about you, whose welfare I am always so anxious to learn. But it is useless to discuss old
bankrupt scores. We will therefore burn our old accounts, and
begin a new one on the 1st. day of October next. I have expected to
be able to set out for Monticello on Monday the 15th. but as I have
not yet recieved Capt. Lewis's letters and the Western mail will not
come in till Tuesday morning the 16th. very possibly I may not be
able to set out till that or even the next day Wednesday. In the
last case Ellen will not be able to go to bed for three nights, lest I
should catch her there. It is possible the letters may come sooner in
which case I see nothing to hinder my setting out on the Monday.
You will be able to give me an account of your stewardship of the
fowls. I expect but a short one from Ellen. I inclose a letter from
Dr. Mitchell[1] in answer to one which accompanied a packet from
your Papa. Deliver my endearments to all the family, and above
all to your Mama: and accept kisses and salutations for yourself.

TH: JEFFERSON

1. Dr. Samuel Latham Mitchell was a Quaker who resided on Long Island,
New York. He was also a chemist and botanist.

To Ellen Wayles Randolph

Washington July 10. 05.

MY DEAREST ELLEN

To answer the question in your letter of the 4th. I must observe that neither the *number* of the fine arts, nor the particular arts entitled to that appellation have been fixed by general consent. Many reckon but five Painting, sculpture, architecture, music and poetry. To these some have added Oratory, including within that Rhetoric which is the art of style and composition. Others again, add Gardening as a 7th. fine art. Not horticulture, but the art of embellishing grounds by fancy. I think Ld. Kaims¹ has justly proved this to be entitled to the appellation of a fine art. It is nearly allied to landscape painting, and accordingly we generally find the landscape painter the best designer of a garden. No perfect *definition* of what is a fine art has ever yet been given. Some say that as those are *mechanical* arts which consist in manual operation unconnected with the understanding, those are *fine* arts which to manual operation join the exercise of the imagination or genius. This would comprehend sculpture, painting, architecture and gardening, but neither music, poetry, nor oratory. Others say that the sciences are objects of the understanding, the fine arts of the senses. This would add gardening, but neither poetry nor oratory. A definition which should include Poetry and Oratory and no more would be very difficult to form. I have delivered your love to Mrs. Smith. I will bring mine to you all on Thursday, Friday or Saturday next. The thermometer was yesterday at 97½° here, and at 96.° the two preceding days. I think it will be at 96.° today. Should it be as hot when I am ready to depart, I shall certainly delay my departure. God bless you all.   TH: JEFFERSON

1. The reference is to Henry Home, Lord Kames, *Elements of Criticism,* and probably to the third edition, published in Edinburgh in 1765. Sowerby 4699.

FROM ANNE CARY RANDOLPH

Edgehill July 11 1805

I received my Dear Grand Papas letter on the 11 of July and am the more obliged to him for it as I did not deserve it. Your thorns were growing very well when I was at Monticello where we dined one day last month. I am afraid the ice will give out this summer. The house is very much improved by being painted. They showed me a cane[1] which they said Buonaparte sent you. It is a very handsome one but I hope you never will have ocassion for it. It is made of fish bone I believe as it is too long to have been the horn of any animal, although it has that appearance. It is capped and pointed with gold very handsomely embost. You will certainly catch Ellen in bed for she is the laziest girl I ever saw and takes the longest to dress of any one I know. Adieu my Dear Grand Papa. Permit me to subscribe myself your most affectionate Grand Daughter,   A C R

1. TJ owned several canes or walking sticks, but this description does not seem to fit any of them.

FROM MARTHA JEFFERSON RANDOLPH

Edgehill July 11, 1805

MY DEAREST FATHER

The trunk you were so good as to forward from Washington, arrived safe by the same post which brought your letter. It contained the wedding cloaths, which rendered it of so much importance to some of the family that I shall make no apology for the trouble it put you to. The marriage will take place at Monticello early in August entirely private except the old Gentleman and Lady and Aunt Carr.[1] There is however a possiblity of it's being delayed by the illness of Mrs. Cary's[2] youngest daughter whose situation is extremely critical and will be lingering, which ever way it terminates. I am afraid however the phisicians will *expedite* the business; a feeble constitution reduced as low as she is, is not apt to linger in their hands. I have this moment recieved a letter from Mr. Eppes informing me of the health of the children and a promise to see Francis early in August. The little Girl[3] not quite so soon, as My Aunt's attentions to her daughter Baker[4] will retard her motions. It will be the latter end of the month before we can expect to see her. I must beg your pardon for having omitted till this moment to inform you of the dismantled state of our tea equipage being reduced to *4 tea* cups. Of every thing else there is enough. The tea pots are too small consequently a large black one with 2 cream pots to match would add both to the comfort and appearance of the board, the plated ones being so much worn as to shew the copper. Coffee cups etc. we have in abundance. I am afraid having delayed so long will occasion you some trouble for which I am truly sorry but it slipt my memory till this moment and had like to have done it all together. Will you be so good as to bring Cornelia *Mrs. Barbauld's first lessons.*[5] She is so young at reading that the print of the books common to children of her age puzzles her extremely whereas Mrs. Barbauld is allways printed in large type in 4 small volumes. Adieu My Dearest Father. It is with great pleasure I write to you for the *last* time this summer. Believe me with every sentiment of respect and tenderness yours most affectionately.   M R.

We have this moment heard of the death of S. Carr's eldest daughter, the little girl my Aunt had with her at Monticello.[6]

1. Possibly the Wilson Miles Carys, maternal grandparents of the groom. His father Wilson Cary died in 1793. Aunt Carr was Martha Jefferson Carr.

2. Jane Blair Cary. Her death is reported in the July 24 issue of the Virginia *Gazette.*

3. Maria Jefferson Eppes.

4. Martha Bolling Eppes Baker (Mrs. Jerman), John Wayles Eppes's elder sister.

5. Anna Letitia Barbauld, *Lessons for Children from Four to Five Years Old.* TJ may have bought the Philadelphia editions of 1780 or 1798 or the Wilmington of 1801.

6. The Carr genealogy previously cited fails to mention Sam Carr as having a daughter by his first marriage; there was one by his second, but she would not have been born at this time. A search of the Dunlora graveyard failed to reveal a grave marker for this child.

FROM ELLEN WAYLES RANDOLPH

recd. July 20. 05.

How was I disappointed at not recieving a letter from my Dear Grand Papa, this Post in answer to one I wrote him: you said in your letter to Sister Ann, that you expected but a short one from me, however I am determined to keep up a regular correspondence if possible. You said also, that you would catch me in bed the morning of the 18 19 or 20 of this month; I hope you will not, for I shall rise betimes all three mornings I expect you. Aunt has had the mumps, and is not quite recovered. I am very much obliged to you for the Poetry you sent me and think it all very Pretty, particularly Little John and the Ode to Modesty.[1] Sister Ann's fowls are increased greatly. My hen has laid a great many eggs, not fit for hatching. Adieu my Dear Grand Papa. Believe me to be your affectionate Grand daughter,   E W. RANDOLPH

1. In "The Jefferson Scrapbook" (ViU), p. [139], there is a clipping of this poem, which was probably clipped from an August, 1805, issue of the Virginia *Argus.* The poem was published in *The Monthly Anthology and Boston Review* (May, 1805), II, 196–97 over the pseudonym, Dominus Providebit. Unfortunately, the poem "Little John" has defied identification.

To Martha Jefferson Randolph

Washington Oct. 13. 05

MY DEAREST MARTHA

I performed my journey to this place without any accident or disagreeable circumstance except travelling half a day in a pretty steady rain, which I thought preferable to staying at Brown's.[1] I experienced no inconvenience from it. This place, which had been healthy thro' the summer is now rather sickly. Some cold mornings and frost after my arrival, it was hoped would remove all disease, but the present warm spell if it continues will probably produce a good deal of sickness. Two of our family are down with bilious fevers, one of them ill. As you did not propose to come till November, the frosts before that time will render every thing safe. As soon as you inform me of the time for your journey, every thing necessary shall be done on my part, and I insist you shall bring the whole family. Mrs. Madison is still at Gray's ferry.[2] Altho' the part affected is healed, it is thought as yet too tender to venture on the journey. But we hope to see her in a few days. I omitted to mention to you that I had agreed to lend Mr. Freeman[3] a mattras and straw bed till he could supply himself. From Mr. Strode's[4] character of him I am in hopes the disagreeable circumstances from him proceeded partly from his sickness, and had part of their colouring from the medium through which they passed. I inclose a paper for Ellen. My friendly salutations to Mr. Randolph and love to yourself and the children.   TH: JEFFERSON

1. Probably the Centreville, Fairfax County, inn where TJ on other occasions had lodged.
2. A ferry site north of Philadelphia.
3. John Holmes Freeman was a Monticello overseer who proved unsatisfactory and was replaced by Edmund Bacon.
4. Possibly Mr. Strode, the Culpeper innkeeper.

To Martha Jefferson Randolph

Washington Oct. 22. 05

MY DEAREST MARTHA

I have been from home now three weeks without having heard from you or of you through any channel. This being our stage postday I had hoped for a line from some of the family. Knowing the uncertain state of your health this long silence makes me uneasy. I hope I shall soon be relieved by a letter. Your rooms will be in readiness for you here by the beginning of the month. Mrs.

Madison still continues in the neighborhood of Philadelphia. The affected part healed, but too tender for her to quit her surgeon for some time yet. Indeed I consider it as a case of indefinite length. We have had a good deal of sickness and death in this place since I came, very little before. I presume the hard frost of yesterday will correct our atmosphere. The almost certainty of a continental war in Europe gives us time to bring Spain to reason peaceably, and considerably relieves our prospects. Kiss all the young ones for me. My affections to Mr. Randolph and warmest love to you.   TH: JEFFERSON

FROM MARTHA JEFFERSON RANDOLPH

Edgehill Oct. 26, 1805

It is become so probable that I am to spend the winter with you My Dearest Father that I must impose upon your goodness the procuring of some articles not be had in Washington or with certainty even in Richmond. A fashionable wig of the colour of the hair inclosed, a set of combs for dressing the hair, a bonnet shawl and white lace veil, for paying morning visits. Mrs. Madison can chuse them as she passes through Baltimore and deposit them with you where only they will be wanted and that before I could with any certainty furnish my self. Will you be so good as to add to the above mentioned articles, 2 lace half handerchiefs. Nothing but my present situation could justify my leaving home at a time when it is so little convenient to Mr. Randolph as he induce me to saddle you with any part of the expense which my going will occasion but my courage shrinks from the horrors of a trial so severe under the most favorable circumstances but rendered infinitely more so in this instance from the uncertainty of my accustomed medical aid and the want of a female friend, Jane being a fellow sufferer. Adieu My Dearest Father yours most tenderly,
M R.

TO MARTHA JEFFERSON RANDOLPH

Washington Nov. 7. 05.

MY DEAREST DAUGHTER

Immediately on the reciept of your last letter, as Mrs. Madison was and is still in Philadelphia, I wrote to her for the articles you desired, and they may be expected by the stage probably in a few days. I now inclose you an hundred dollars for your expences on the road, and you must consider every thing which yourself or the family will want here as to be furnished by me so that the visit may not at all affect Mr. Randolph's pecuniary arrangements. You have not told me in your letter whether I am to send a carriage for you half way or the whole way. Tho' there will be some reluctance in the carriage owners to undertake the whole way, yet we can effect it with two or three days notice. The stages and distances are as follows:

From Edgehill to Gordon's 16. miles to Orange C. H. 10. = 26. miles

to Stevensburg 20. Herring's 5. Norman's ford 4. Elkrun church 9. = 38

To Slate run church 14½. Brown's 5½ Centerville 9½ Fairfax C. H. 8. = 37½

Wren's 7. Georgetown ferry 6. President's house 2 = 15 to dinner.

I think the sooner you come the better, as fine weather will be the more probable. You will not find Mrs. Madison here I expect, for tho' her recovery is pronounced to be compleated, yet the tender state of the part will induce her to continue there some time. Mr. Madison has been here near a fortnight. Let me hear from you immediately as to a carriage, and when you may be expected. Kiss all the young ones for me, and give Ellen the inclosed poetry. My best affections to Mr. Randolph and yourself.

Th: Jefferson

FROM ELLEN WAYLES RANDOLPH

Edgehill November 10 1805

DEAR GRAND PAPA

I expect you think I have forgotten the Promise I made you of writing to you every Post but I have not for I have tried several times but could not effect it for want of implements to do it. You must answer my letters for it would give me great Pleasure to keep up a regular Correspondence with you. I have no news to tell you except the report that prevails of Mrs. Trists marriage with Governor Claiborne.[1] I suppose you have heard it. It is time to finish my letter. I have written enough for this time. Sister Ann gives her love to you and says she will write to you shortly. Mama gives hers to you also as do all the children. Give mine to Mrs. Smith and tell her I hope I shall see her soon. Adieu Dear Grand Papa. Believe me to be your affectionate Grand Daughter,

ELLEN WAYLES RANDOLPH

1. William Charles Coles Claiborne was governor of the Territory of New Orleans. Although married three times, he was never married to Mrs. Trist.

FROM MARTHA JEFFERSON RANDOLPH

Nov. 23, 1805

The hurry of preparation My Dearest Father must apologise for this note. We shall be at Centreville the last day of the month where Mr. Randolph thinks the horses he can procure will easily take us, and sunday evening or Monday morning we shall be with you. We are all in health and spirits preparing to join you as soon as possible. Adieu. Believe me with inexpressible tenderness yours,   M R

TO ELLEN WAYLES RANDOLPH

Washington Nov. 24. 05.

MY DEAREST ELLEN

Your letter of the 10th. did not get here till the 19th. and this is the first post day since that [for answering it.] I am afraid that sending your letters a few minutes too late they arrive at Milton after the departure of the post and lie there a week. I am very doubtful that something like this must have happened with the letters of the 16th. If any were written, as they ought to have been recieved on the 19th. but now cannot be till tomorrow morning when the post will come in. In the meantime ours goes out this evening. I am the more fearful of such an accident, because your Mama may possibly have given me notice to send off a carriage which notice is not recieved although it was expected. It is expected that Mrs. Madison will leave Philadelphia tomorrow and be here with Mrs. Cutts[1] in the course of the week. She will of course be here before you. I believe I formerly inclosed the poem now sent. But not being certain and it's merit considerable I now forward it. In hopes of soon seeing you I shall only add kisses for

your Mama and sisters and yourself, and my affectionate salutations to your Papa.   TH: JEFFERSON

1. Mrs. Richard Cutts was wife of the Maine congressman and sister of
Dolley Madison.

TO MARTHA JEFFERSON RANDOLPH

Washington Nov. 25. 05

MY DEAREST MARTHA

I was uneasy at not hearing from you by the last post, that is to
say, by the one which arrived Tuesday morning last, the 19th.
I thought it certain I should recieve information as to sending a
carriage. I take for granted I shall have a letter tomorrow morning; but in the mean time this goes out this evening. We find more
difficulty than I had expected in getting a carriage. It seems that
all Congress being to come on this week all the carriages are
engaged for bringing them on. Joseph[1] was out on this business
yesterday and will be to-day. If we fail here he will go to Alexandria where doubtless we shall succeed: so that you may count on
the exactitude of our movements to your wishes, if we get them in
time. You must come short stages, as it will be better to lodge
badly than endanger being in the night in your situation,[2] and
with so many in the carriage with you. Mrs. Madison sets off this
day from Philadelphia but will probably not be here till the latter
end of the week. My cordial respects to Mr. Randolph, kisses to
yourself and the children.   TH: JEFFERSON
P.S. I hope you recieve my letter of the 7th with the remittance.

1. Joseph Daugherty was a Washington hostler and sometime servant to TJ
while in the President's House.
2. She was expecting the birth of her eighth child, James Madison Randolph, who was to be the first child born in the President's House.

TO MARTHA JEFFERSON RANDOLPH

Washington Nov. 29. 05.

MY DEAREST MARTHA

The carriage goes off in the morning for Centerville, in time, if
you should arrive there early and be so disposed, to bring you on
to Fairfax court house in the evening. That will make your ride
the next morning easy. But should you not leave Centerville till
Sunday morning, you may with ease get here to dinner which we
shall accordingly keep back for you till 4. oclock. If you could

start by sunrise or soon after, and breakfast either at Fairfax C. H. or Wren's as may suit, you may get here[1] in time. The driver is an extremely careful, sober, excellent hand. He finds himself every thing by agreement. My kisses to the children and best affections to Mr. Randolph and yourself.   TH: JEFFERSON

1. Despite the oft-quoted and popular legend that Martha acted as hostess for her father in the President's House, she was there only twice, the first time with Mary from mid-November, 1802, to some time in January, 1803; the second was from about December 2 until May, 1806. These would be the only times she could have been TJ's "official" hostess in Washington.

FROM ELLEN WAYLES RANDOLPH

recd June 10. 06.

I cannot let slip so good an opportunity of writing to My Dear Grandpapa as now offers it self. Although I cannot write a very long letter yet at least I will a few lines to let him see how much I love and respect him and that I intend to correspond with him. We are going over to Edgehill to morrow there to wait impatiently untill we can see you again. I do not intend to let you catch me in bed that day as I will get up with the sun that you may not for I should be very sorry if you found me as averse to getting up early as I was when you left us. Sister Ann and the children give their love to you. Give mine to Mrs. S. H. Smith. Adieu Dear Grandpapa. Believe me to be your most affectionate Grand daughter,
                    ELEONORA W. RANDOLPH

TO MARTHA JEFFERSON RANDOLPH

Washington June 16. 06.

I arrived here, my dear Martha, to breakfast, on the Saturday morning before the last, without accident, and without wetting from the various showers which fell. Mr. Eppes proceeded to Annapolis the next day (Sunday) and was back on Tuesday, all that matter being entirely broken off. I understand it was from the disagreement of the mother, solely, who has some other match for her daughter in her eye, more to her mind.[1] I have not seen Mrs. Dearborne since I came; so know not whether she visits us this summer; but presume she will. Mrs. Gallatin will certainly, and probably Mrs. R. Smith. At least Mr. Smith wishes it and will endeavor to prevail on her. Mr. Short[2] will pass the month of September with us; so that we shall have a thronged season. I find by a letter from Chisolm that I shall have to proceed to Bedford

almost without stopping in Albemarle. I shall probably be kept
there a week or 10. days, laying the foundation of the house,
which he is not equal to himself.[3] So that it will be near the middle
of August before I shall be fixed at Monticello. Do you know anything of my Antenor's Travels?[4] I do not find them here. Perhaps
they are lent out. I write this just at the commencement of an
eclipse of the sun, total at Boston and 50 miles North and South
of that, of 11¾ digits at Philadelphia, and I suppose at 11½ here
and perhaps 11. with you.[5] Tell Ellen I shall acknolege her letter
by the next post. Mr. and Mrs. Madison are still a little lamish.
They will probably visit us also in September. Kiss all the young
ones for me. Present my affections to Mr. Randolph and be assured yourself of my constant and tenderest love.

TH: JEFFERSON

1. John Wayles Eppes was courting an Annapolis lady who unfortunately
remains unidentified. He was more successful in another quest, for in 1809
he married Martha Burke Jones of Halifax, N. C., and became the father of
a family of four children — two sons and two daughters, who resided at Millbrook, in Buckingham County.

TJ remained on good terms with them and gave as a wedding present
the epergne or "glass tree" presently standing on the dining table at Monticello. For additional information on Eppes, consult James H. Bailey, "John
Wayles Eppes, Planter and Politician," unpublished Master's thesis at the
University of Virginia.

2. William Short.

3. One of TJ's able carpenters. They were going to Bedford County to
begin construction of the house on the Poplar Forest tract.

4. Antenor was a pseudonym. There are several editions of this work: Les
Voyages d'A. en Grece et Asie traduit par E. F. Lantier, which could have
been in the Monticello library. It is not included in Sowerby.

5. For an account of the eclipse as seen at Washington, see the Richmond
Enquirer, July 1, 1806.

TO ELLEN WAYLES RANDOLPH

Washington June 24. 06.

I learn with deep concern, my dearest Ellen, that the family
has been unwell generally, that you have been ill and your Mama
indisposed. Anne informs me you are getting better but does
not say whether your Mama is so also. Yet, in the absence of your
Papa, her health is doubly important because her care is necessary
for you all. I hope this will find you all recovered. Your friends
here are generally well. Mrs. S. H. Smith remains constantly in
the country; and this place is duller than I ever saw it. I certainly
have never been so tired of it; yet I do not at present expect to
leave it till the 21st. of July, and on the 24th. shall expect to catch

you in bed, and to be happy in the midst of you. In the meantime God bless you all, and have you and your precious Mama in his holy keeping. Give her my tenderest kisses, and to all of the little ones; to your Papa, if returned my sincere affections.

TH: JEFFERSON

TO ANNE CARY RANDOLPH

Washington June 29. 06.

MY DEAREST ANNE

I have now to acknolege your letter of the 20th. from which I learnt with real affliction that sickness in the family had prevailed generally, that Ellen was still ill, and your dear Mama not well. I hope this will find all re-established, and that tomorrow's letters will tell me so. I shall count with long scores the three weeks to come, after which I hope to be with you. An unfortunate accident happened in Genl. Mason's island yesterday.[1] About sun-rise his house was discovered to be afire, and in spite of all the aid carried to him, one wing was burnt down and the middle part nearly so. They saved their furniture. Suspicions arising that it was done by one of his house servants who wished the family to go back to Georgetown, he was arrested and on his way to prison with the constable, he jumped out of the boat and drowned himself. I understand the family will continue through the summer in the remaining wing. Genl. Dearborne continues ill of a fever. Mrs. S. H. Smith is always at her country house, tho' she came in and dined with us two days ago. We have had the thermometer one day (the 25th.) at 96°. Kiss your beloved Mama for me, and all the little ones. Present my warm affections to your Papa, and accept yourself assurances of my tender love.

TH: JEFFERSON

1. A small island, also known as Analostan Island, of seventy acres, in the Potomac River opposite Georgetown. It was the seat of General John Mason. See Joseph Martin, *A New and Comprehensive Gazeteer of Virginia and the District of Columbia . . .* (Charlottesville, 1835), 494, and James F. Duhamel, "Analostan Island," *Records of the Columbia Historical Society*, XXXV, 133-45.

FROM ANNE CARY RANDOLPH

Edgehill July 4, 1806

I recieved my Dear Grandpapas letter and am much obliged to him for it. All the family are quite well except Mary who is still unwell and very much reduced. There was a great Barbacue at Charlottsville to day at which Mr. Jones delivered an oration.[1] Aunt Jane has returned home and Aunt Lucy and Harriet with her. I got a letter from Miss Nicholson[2] and she told me that she was afraid that Mr. [and] Mrs. Gallatin would not come to Monticello this summer. Do you know whether they will or not? Aunt Carr has been to see us. She is a good deal better but still complains of a pain in her neck. All the children and Mama send their love to you. Adieu my Dear Dear Grand Papa. I cannot tell you how much I love and respect you. Believe me your most affectionate Grand daughter,   A C R

1. The Richmond *Enquirer* for July 26 reported the celebration by stating it began at 3:00 P.M., with Elijah Garth providing a handsome barbecue. The speakers were not identified. Mr. Jones may have been John R. Jones, a county resident.
2. Probably the daughter of Joseph H. Nicholson, a congressman from Maryland whose wife was Maria Gallatin, sister of Albert Gallatin.

From Ellen Wayles Randolph

Edgehill Friday July 4 1806

I recieved My Dear Grandpapas letter with great pleasure and should have answered it last post but by some neglect it remained untill tuesday in the office and therefore I could not answer it as the post went out Saturday. We are all recovered now except Mary who is still unwell but she is now much better than she was a few days ago and I hope she will soon be entirely well. Aunt Jane has returned and with her Aunt Lucy and Aunt Harriot[1] who design to stay no longer than a month up the country. You must write to me very soon for I am allways exceedingly happy to get a letter from you. All the children give their love to you. Excuse this short letter My Dear Grand Papa. Adieu. Believe me to be your affectionate Grand Daughter.   E. W. RANDOLPH

1. Jane Cary Randolph (Mrs. Thomas Eston), Lucy Eppes Thweatt, and Harriet Randolph Hackley.

To Martha Jefferson Randolph

Washington July 6. 06.

MY DEAREST MARTHA

The last letter I have had from Edgehill was Anne's of June 20 that informed me that the family had been generally unwell, that Ellen was still ill, and yourself too sick to write. I am very anxious to hear from you and hope that this day's post will inform me you are all well. This day fortnight I propose to leave this place and to be with you Thursday morning the 24th. Absence from you becomes every day more and more insupportable and my confinement here more disgusting. I have certainly great reasons for gratitude to my constituents. They have supported me as cordially as I could ever have expected; and if their affairs can preserve as steady a course for two years to come, and I can then carry into retirement the good will they have hitherto bestowed on me, the day of retirement will be the happiest I have now to come. It will relieve me from a load of care too burthensome for my time of life, and it will restore me to those domestic scenes where alone I can be happy. We have nothing new to communicate. All public matters are in a state of tranquility, and seem as if they will continue so: and I recollect nothing among your acquaintances here, except that Miss Clifton was near losing her life by a small piece of biscuit lodging in her throat which could not be removed till she was near expiring. She is still ill of the effects of it. Present me affectionately to Mr. Randolph, kiss the young ones for me, and be assured of my tenderest and unalterable love.

TH: JEFFERSON

FROM MARTHA JEFFERSON RANDOLPH

Mont. Oct 14. 1806

DEAREST FATHER

Some trifling repairs to our house which were to have been finished in three days after you left us, but which the slothfulness of the workmen have spun out to 14 have kept us here till now; and as it is we are returning to rooms newly plaistered and the house not yet clear of the workmen. But so much is to be done before winter to make us comfortable that we think it best to go immediately either to hurry them in their work or arrest the business in it least inconvenient stay if it cant be finished in time. John was anxious to have set off 3 days after the fever left him but he was evidently so weak that we thought it better to detain him a few days longer to prevent the danger of a relapse on the road. Adieu My Dearest Father. We are all in all moving and the pen is so bad I can scarcely form a letter with it. Yours most tenderly,

MR.

To Martha Jefferson Randolph

Washington Oct. 20. 06.

MY DEAREST MARTHA

John delivered safely your letter of the 14th. I am sorry you did not continue at Monticello until your house was in compleat readiness for you. You will run the double risk of green plaister, and less perfect preparation of it for your winter's residence. I do not know what stores remained for your consumption, but it is always my wish you should take whatever does remain. Many of them will not keep, such as crackers, cheese, fish &c. Porter is so peculiarly salutary for your stomach, that I took a larger supply than usual that there might be some for you and in laying in the stores for the ensuing year, I never count on the fragments of the last. I beseech you therefore to consider every thing of that kind as intended for you, and to use any of the wines, and at all times, which you prefer to your own. Having been so long in the midst of a family, the loansomeness of this place is more intolerable than I ever found it. My daily rides too are sickening for want of some interest in the scenes I pass over: and indeed I look over the two ensuing years as the most tedious of my life. You will have with you in a few days a Mr. Brodie, an elderly English gentleman, who is seeking an asylum in this quiet country to bring his family to. He is a very worthy, inoffensive polite man. He turns his eyes to our neighborhood, and I have given him a letter to Mr. Randolph merely to prevent his being imposed on in any bargain. He has his eye on Henderson's and Overton's lands,[1] but of preference on the latter. I send in a separate package to Mr. Randolph 25. advertisements from Mr. Shoemaker[2] which we ask the favor of him to have set up in the most public places for 20. miles round, and without delay. By the return of Davy I shall send a piece of linen to be made up for me against March. Present me affectionately to Mr. Randolph and the young ones, and be assured of my constant and tenderest love.

TH: JEFFERSON

1. Mr. Brodie did not remove to Albemarle.
2. Johnathan Shoemaker was the miller at the Shadwell Toll Mill.

From Ellen Wayles Randolph

Edgehill November 14 1806.

I am now preparing my self to write a short letter to my Dear Grandpapa and hope he will let me hear from him as soon as he recieves it. Aunt Jane has gone down the country and it is probable will not return this winter. I shall be very sorry if she does not for we shall be very lonesome by ourselves here. I have no news to tell you but I do not suppose you would expect any from me who am in the country. Mama and all the children are well and send their love to you. Give my love to Mrs. H. Smith. Adieu my Dear Grandpapa. Believe me to be your most affectionate Grand Daughter,   E. W. R.

To Martha Jefferson Randolph

Washington Nov. 21. 06.

My dearest Martha

Davy arrived last night and will set out tomorrow on his return. By him I send the flower-pot and plant in it which you left here, and a box No. 5. containing a bonnet for yourself. He carries also a cage with a pair of Bantams for Ellen. I must ask the favor of you to have the box No. 4. opened, to take out a piece of linen, and then let the box go on to Monticello. The linen I must ask you to have made into shirts for me so as to be ready for me when I come home in March. Rigden[1] is not yet returned from Europe, of course your watch not here. It is thought that Rigden proposes to establish himself in Alexandria. I expected ere this to have recieved a watch for my brother from Philadelphia and to have sent it by Davy. But it is not yet come. I mention this, as it is possible my brother may send or come to Edgehill in expectation of finding it there. I am afraid it may be long before another opportunity occurs of sending it from here by a safe hand. I was happy to learn by the letters of last week that you were all well. Present my affections to Mr. Randolph and the young ones and be assured of my constant and tenderest love.   Th: Jefferson

P. S. Mrs. Nourse[2] has just sent a bundle of Wall flowers for you. With these are some tussocks of Peruvian grass she sent me, and which I will ask Anne to take care of till March, when I will carry them to Monticello.

1. John E. Rigden was a Washington watchmaker.
2. Probably Mrs. Joseph Nourse, wife of the Register of the Treasury.

From Ellen Wayles Randolph

recd Nov. 24. [1806]

DEAR GRAND PAPA

The post is going directly and I only have time to write a few lines to let you know that we are all well and I hope you are so. I wrote to you last saturday and shall wait impatiently to hear from you soon. I have not time to write any more to you now but I will very shortly make amends for this short letter. Mama and all the children send their love to you. Give mine to Mrs. H. Smith. Adieu my Dear Grandpapa. Believe me to be your affectionate Grandaughter,   E. W. R.

To Ellen Wayles Randolph

Washington Nov. 30. 06.

MY DEAREST ELLEN

I have recieved two letters from you since I left Monticello. By Davy I sent you a pair of Bantam fowls; quite young: so that I am in hopes you will now be enabled to raise some. I propose on their subject a question of natural history for your enquiry: that is whether this is the Gallina Adrianica, or Adria, the Adsatick cock of Aristotle? For this you must examine Buffon etc. Mr. Burwell asks in the name of your Mama, for a Nautical almanac.[1] She will find those of many years in the library at Monticello, in the press on the right hand of the Eastern outward door of the cabinet.[2] I send you inclosed much newspaper poetry. Adieu my dear Ellen: kiss your mama for me and all the young ones. For yourself recieve the kiss I give this paper.

TH: JEFFERSON

1. *The Nautical Almanac and Astronomical Ephemeris* was published in London. TJ purchased his first while in Paris in 1786.
2. The Cabinet is that room at Monticello opposite TJ's bedroom. It was one of the rooms of the library suite and where his chaise longue writing apparatus was situated.

To Anne Cary Randolph

Washington Dec.8.06.

MY DEAREST ANNE

I owe you the acknolegement of your letter of Nov. 15. and I shall hope this evening to recieve one from some one of the family informing us all are well. Here we are suffering under a very severe spell of cold weather. The thermometer was at 25. this morning and we have had two inches of snow. I hope Davy got safely home with his plants, fowls, and other charges. I consigned to you some roots of Peruvian grass to be taken care of for me till I come home. Davy must have made a bad hand of his journey, as he left this on a Saturday and from your papa's account could not have reached Edgehill till the Sunday sennight following, making it a journey of 9. days instead of 5. All are well here, except my crippled hand from which I had the whole nail of the middle finger torn off by accident. It is now nearly healed up. Kiss your mama for me and all the little ones, and accept for yourself my affectionate Adieux.   TH: JEFFERSON

FROM ANNE CARY RANDOLPH

Edgehill December 12 *1806*

I recieved my Dear Grand Papa's letter and am much obliged to him for it. The grass fowls and flowers arrived safe on monday afternoon. I planted the former in a box of rich earth and covered it for a few nights untill I thought it had taken root and then by degrees for fear of rendering it too delicate exposed it again. It looks extremely well indeed. If you think it will not stand the winter out it is not too late to take it in. The weather here is very cold. Our first snow was between 8 and 10 inches deep. Before it had melted one fell of 2 and it is still snowing quite fast. It is the general opinion that we shall have a hard winter. Mr. Shoemaker has been unwell but is now better. Mr. Peyton[1] has returned well. Mama and the children are well also and send their love to you. Adieu my Dear Grandpapa. Believe me to be your sincerely affectionate Grand daughter,

ANN C RANDOLPH

1. Craven Peyton was a Milton merchant who married Jane Jefferson Lewis, daughter of Lucy Jefferson Lewis, TJ's sister.

FROM ELLEN WAYLES RANDOLPH

Edgehill Decemember 12th 1806

DEAR GRANDPAPA

I recieved the Bantams for which I am very much obliged to you. They seem to be larger, and younger, than the first and I think them handsomer. I have no news to tell you for being in the country I seldom have any thing worth relating and that being the case I can never write long letters unless you suffer me to speak of myself. I have begun the Grecian History in which I am very much interested and have got to multiplication in arithmetic. I am going on with Dufief[1] and am reading Plutarque de la Jeuness in French[2] of which I read ten pages for my lesson sometimes more but not often less. I copyd the historical part of Lord Chesterfield's letters for a lesson in writing, all which is generally concluded by dinner time after which I play and at night sew while Sister Ann reads aloud to us. Adieu my Dear Grandpapa. Mama and the children join in love to you. Believe me to be your affectionate Grand Daughter, E. W. R.

Mama says Buffon[3] cannot answer the question you propose to me.

1. Nicolas Gouin Dufief, *Nature Displayed, in her Mode of Teaching Language to Man* (Philadelphia, 1804), 2 volumes (Sowerby 4819), a popular French grammar of that day. Dufief presented Jefferson with the set; Volume I is now at Monticello. Dufief was also a book dealer and a correspondent of Jefferson's. For more on him, see Edith Phillips, *Louis Hue Girardin and Nicholas Gouin Dufief and Their Relations with Thomas Jefferson; An Unknown Episode of the French Emigration in America* (Baltimore, 1926).

2. Plutarque de la Terinesse. It is difficult to establish the specific title of Ellen's book. It might have been any of several abridgements, as: *Abrégé des Hommes, illustres de Plutarque, à l'usage de la jeunesse* . . . Beauvais, impr. de Des Jardins *an IV; —— an V–IX, Beauvais l'auteur;* or *Abrégé des Vies de Plutarque, par M. Archer . . . Nouvelle Edition . . .*

3. Martha was correct; the solution was not in Buffon.

To Ellen Wayles Randolph

Washington Dec. 15. 06

My dearest Ellen

This is our postday, and I have been so engaged that the hour of dinner and company are arriving before I could begin a letter to you. I shall therefore merely say we are all well, and I hope we shall hear to-night that all are well at Edgehill. Tell your Mama, while you kiss her for me, that Rigden has returned and delivered me her watch neatly done which will be sent by your papa. I send you something for your collection. Kiss and bless all the young people for me, and be assured of my affectionate love.

Th: Jefferson

FROM ELLEN WAYLES RANDOLPH

Edgehill December 19 1806

Your letter my Dear Grand Papa found us well and conveyed the gratefull intelligence of your being so indeed. Mama and the children have enjoyed better health this winter than common. There has not been even a cold amongst them except James and Mary who were a little unwell for two or three days. As for the rest they have been in perfect health ever since our return home. Fine weather has at length returned and the grass and wallflowers look remarkably well. Adieu my Dear Grandpapa. Believe me to be your affectionate Grand Daughter,   E. W. RANDOLPH.

Sister Ann desires me to tell you that she will write next post. She joins the children in love to you.

FROM ELLEN WAYLES RANDOLPH

Edgehill December 27th 1806

I could not miss so good an opportunity of writing to you my Dear Grand Papa as now offers itself to tell you I do not regard your not punctually answering my letters as I know how many you have to write. Your grass still continues to look very well and will I hope all the winter. I rely upon your indulgence to excuse this short letter as I have not any thing to say to you. Mama, Sister Ann, and the children send their love to you. Give mine to Mrs. S. H. Smith. Adieu my Dear Grandpapa. Believe me to be your affectionate Grand Daughter,   E. W. RANDOLPH.

FROM ELLEN WAYLES RANDOLPH

Edgehill January 30th 1807

It has been a long time since I have heard from my Dear Grandpapa although he is two letters in my debt one of which I expected last post but not recieving it I concluded it would be better to set down and write to [put] you in mind of your promise of writing to me sometimes. Jefferson has returned and so has Mr. Ogilvie[1] who is going to be married to a Mrs. Bankhead[2] of Port Royal[3] who is the widow of a gentleman who had been his pupil. She is (I am informed) a fine woman and very rich. Besides she is rather handsome than otherwise. Mr. O. intends to settle with

her in Milton. It will [be] a great addition to our neighbourhood. James[4] is very much grown and I think now is a very handsome and sprigtly child. Mama Sister Ann and the children are well and send their love to you. Give mine to Mrs. S. H. S. Adieu my dear Grandpapa. Believe me to be your affectionate Grand Daughter,   E. W. RANDOLPH
    Your Grass looks very well.

1. James Ogilvie had been operating a school at Milton since January, 1806. See Richmond *Enquirer,* November 26, 1805, for his advertisement announcing its curriculum and opening date.

2. Mrs. Stewart Bankhead of Port Royal. She did not marry Ogilvie. Following her husband's death this much married lady took as her third husband Robert Gilchrist Robb of Gaymont, Caroline County.

3. A small tobacco port on the Potomac River in Caroline County.

4. James Madison Randolph, the second son of Martha and Thomas Mann Randolph, Jr., was born January 17, 1806, the first child to be born in the President's House. He was born during Martha's second visit to Washington.

To ELLEN WAYLES RANDOLPH

Washington Feb. 8. 07.

MY DEAREST ELLEN

    I believe it is true that you have written me 2. letters to my one to you. Whether this proceeds from your having more industry or less to do than myself I will not say. One thing however I will say that I most sincerely wish to be with you all and settle the point vivâ voce (if you do not understand these two Latin words you must lay Jefferson's Latin under contribution that you may know because they are often used in English writing). To return to our correspondence, you have a great advantage as to matter for communication. You have a thousand little things to tell me which I am fond to hear; for instance of the health of every body, and particularly of your dear Mama, every thing relating to her being of the first concern to me: then what you are reading, what are your other occupations, how many dozen Bantams you have raised, how often you and Anne have rode to Monticello to see if the Tulips are safe &c. &c. &c. However I shall be with you about the 11th or 12th proxima (more Latin, madam) and then we will examine the tulips together. Kiss your dear Mama a thousand times for me, and all the sisters, q.s.[1] (more Latin) and be assured yourself of my tender affections.   TH: JEFFERSON

1. An abbreviation for *quantum sufficit,* "as much as suffices." See Adriano Cappelli, *Dizionario di Abbreviature* (Milano, 1929), 314.

From Ellen Wayles Randolph

recd. Feb. 17. 07.

DEAR GRAND PAPA

I suspect that it would be more reasonable to think that your owing me 3 letters proceeds from my having more time than industry although a very little part of this winter has been spent by me in Idleness still however I think that you must have a great deal more to do than I have. Mama has been unwell for several days but I hope she will soon recover. All the children are in good health. As for the Bantam she laid one egg in the cold weather and eat it up. I am very much afraid she will do all the others so. If she does she will be as worthless as the others but in spite of that I am very fond of them and think them very handsome. The old ones are quite tame but the new much to the contrary. I have not finished the Grecian history[1] but I shall very soon. I have read in French the first volume of Plutarque de La Terinesse[2] which contains almost entirely Grecian Lives. I do not intend to read the lives of the modern great Men yet. I have advanced but slowly in my arithmetic but the reason was that Mama wished me to be perfect in one rule before I went into another. Your grass looks very well but I am afraid your Wallflower is Dead. I, Mama Sister Ann and the children send their love to you. Give mine to Mrs S. H. Smith. Adieu My Dear Grandpapa. Believe me to be your most affectionate Grand Daughter,

E. W. RANDOLPH

1. Probably Temple Stanyan, *The Grecian History*, the two-volume edition printed in London in 1739. Sowerby 39.
2. Consult footnote 2 for letter December 12, 1806, Ellen Wayles Randolph to TJ, for several editions Ellen was reading.

To Ellen Wayles Randolph

Washington Mar. 1. 07.

MY DEAREST ELLEN

I am afraid I shall be bankrupt in my epistolary account with Anne and yourself. However the tide of business, like that of the ocean, will wait for nobody. I send for Cornelia a little poem, the grasshopper's ball,[1] to begin her collection. The Yankee story is for yourself. Thank Mary for her letter, but tell her it is written in a cypher of which I have not the key. She must therefore tell it all to me when I come home. I shall write to Anne by the cart, because it will carry a box of flower roots which I shall consign to her care, but not to be opened till we get to Monticello, and have every thing ready for planting them as soon as they are opened. I shall write by this post to your Mama, so I conclude with my kisses to you all.   TH: JEFFERSON

1. TJ had undoubtedly confused the title, which was *The Butterfly's Ball and Grasshopper's Feast,* a poem by William Roscoe. See George Chandler, *William Roscoe of Liverpool* (London, 1953), 118–19 and 410–11, for the words and early publication media. It is also worth noting that in the "Jefferson Scrapbook" (ViU), p. [69], there is a newspaper clipping of this poem.

To Martha Jefferson Randolph

Washington Mar. 2. 07.
MY DEAREST MARTHA

Tomorrow Congress will close; but I hardly expect to get away under a week. It will take that time at least to get all the laws put into a course of execution and some other matters settled. On Monday last Mr. Randolph and myself took a ride to Maine's to engage our thorns. The day was raw, he was without a great coat, and was before indisposed, as I had mentioned to you. That evening he [1] was taken with a chill and fever, which went off on Wednesday, but returned in the same evening. The last night he has had another intermission, and the return this morning is so moderate that we hope it will quit him finally this evening. He is considerably reduced and weakened and I shall endeavor to prevail on him not to attempt his return till I go; because I could keep him down to short journies, whereas, if alone, he might push so as to produce a relapse. He will return in my chair and, if with me, I should be with him and stay with him should he have any fever on the road. Mr. Burwell will leave this on Wednesday or Thursday and will call on you. Our obligations to him for his attentions to Mr. Randolph are infinite; and so also to Dr. Jones [2] who scarcely ever leaves him. He has decided absolutely not to offer again for Congress. In saying that I expect to get away in a week, I merely guess. It may be some days longer: so that I cannot fix the day when we shall call to take you on to Monticello. Adieu my beloved Martha, take care of yourself for my sake and every one's sake.   TH: JEFFERSON

1. Before Randolph had been in Washington two weeks he was so ill of a fever that it was feared he would not recover. "Jefferson evidenced great con-

cern and tried unsuccessfully to move him to the Presidential Mansion where he could obtain better care and treatment, but the sick man chose to remain at the boarding house. . . . Randolph passed the crisis and proceeded to make slow and painful recovery, but he was not well again until the end of March. As soon as he was able to travel, he returned to Albemarle and resumed the life of a gentleman farmer." "Gaines," 120.

2. Not further identified, but obviously Thomas Mann Randolph, Jr.'s Washington physician.

From Ellen Wayles Randolph

Edgehill March 6th 1807

Dear Grandpapa

Your fear of being a bankrupt is not badly founded for I think if we were to count our letters you would owe me a great many. I do not however desire that you should pay me all as you have already too many to write. I only wish that you should keep up the correspondence by writing sometimes to me. Cornelia is very much pleased with the piece of poetry you sent her. Mary says she would tell you what was in her letter gladly if she knew herself. Your grass looks very well and when you come you will see that it is quite green and handsome. Sister Ann and the children send their loves to you. Give mine to Mrs S. H. Smith when next you see her. Adieu my Dear Grandpapa. Believe me to be your most affectionate Grand Daughter,   E. W. Randolph

To Martha Jefferson Randolph

Washington Friday Mar. 6. 07.

My dearest Martha

I wrote you on Monday evening, and then expected that a morning or two more would have produced a compleat intermission of Mr. Randolph's fever. But it did not. Yesterday morning the remission was such as to leave the fever scarcely sensible, and at 3. P.M. the usual hour of it's access it was more moderate than it has ever been. I left him at 4. P M with not much fever, entirely at ease and in good spirits. I write this too early in the morning to have heard from him this morning, because Mr. Burwell sets out early and is expected to call for it every moment. He will be able to give you particulars as he has attended him very assiduously. Dr. Jones and Capt. Lewis[1] never quit him. Mr. Coles[2] is much with him also, and Joseph constantly[3] to whose attentions he is particularly attached. I have had a very bad cold, which laid me up with a fever one day. This indisposition will occasion me to be here some days longer than I expected, and indeed with the mass which is before me, I cannot fix a day at all for my departure. I think that it will take Mr. Randolph, as long, after his fever leaves him, to recover strength for the journey, as it will me to get thro' my business: so that you will see us both together, as certainly I shall not go till he is strong enough to accompany me. I shall write you by your stage mail which arrives on Thursday, and a horse post will now arrive at Milton every Monday morning. God bless you my beloved Martha, and all the young ones.

TH: JEFFERSON

1. Meriwether Lewis.
2. Isaac Coles.
3. Thomas Mann's body servant.

To Martha Jefferson Randolph

Monday Mar. 9. 07.

MY DEAREST MARTHA

I have the happiness to inform you that Mr. Randolph is entirely well. His fever had left him at the date of my last but I did not then know it. He moved here on Saturday and Dr. Jones with him. He has now nothing but weakness to contend with. He was able to walk two or three times across the room to-day,[1] he eats with some appetite and sleeps tolerably. The Doctor will leave us tomorrow, as nothing is now wanting but care of our patient. But it will be many days before he will be able to set out on his journey. I would willingly compound for ten days. However he must not set out too soon. We shall detain the carts some days yet. As we have now two posts a week you shall hear from me every 3. or 4. days. God bless you my ever dear daughter and all our young ones.   TH: JEFFERSON

1. Mr. Randolph had finally yielded to TJ's entreaties and removed from his boardinghouse to the President's House.

To Martha Jefferson Randolph

Washington Mar. 11. 07. (Tuesday)

MY DEAREST MARTHA

Altho' I wrote to you by post yesterday, yet as an opportunity offers by Capt. Clarke at noon to-day, and I know you will still be anxious, I write again to assure you that Mr. Randolph continues perfectly well. He slept finely last night, eats with appetite to-day, is in fine spirits, and has nothing amiss but weakness. The first sun-shiney day he will begin to take air and exercise in the carriage, in a few days he will do it on horseback and as soon as he is able to ride half a dozen miles on horseback without fatigue, we will set out with him in my chair. Doctr. Jones thinks it will be 10. days first; but his recovery proceeds so rapidly that I expect it will be sooner. The Doctor has just left us. I have recieved your's of the 7th. and thank you for the profile of Mr. Wythe.[1] My next letter to you will be by the horsepost which will arrive at Milton on Monday morning. Adieu my beloved Martha, and continue to love me as I do you.   Th: Jefferson

1. George Wythe was TJ's close friend and former law teacher. TJ wrote to Charles Willson Peale on June 27, 1806, about this likeness: "I have a shade profile of a very dear friend [Judge Wythe] whose portrait was never taken. It is a complete whole length of about 6 or 8. inches." (DLC.)

To Martha Jefferson Randolph

Washington. Thursday Mar. 12. 07.

My dearest Martha

Altho' this letter which goes by the carts, will not reach you till Monday evening, and that which I shall write you by the post of tomorrow evening will reach you on Monday morning, yet I cannot omit to drop you a line lest any accident should delay that by mail. Mr. Randolph continues well. Eats with appetite sleeps tolerably, reads: and has not had the smallest return of fever since it left him which is 6. days ago. The day before yesterday he walked in the Circular room upstairs[1] about 5. or 600. steps, yesterday he walked 1200. and to-day he will come downstairs and take a ride in the chariot. His convalescence will now be rapid. He thinks he shall not be strong enough to set out on his journey till Monday the 23d. which is the day he sets for it. I think he will be able sooner. However on this subject you will have further opportunities of being informed by your Monday's and Thursday's posts. Your letter of the 7th. shews you had supposed him worse than I stated him to be. This was not so. I know that unless a statement is faithful enough to command credit, it leaves the mind in the most distressing uncertainty. Mr. R's fever was of 12. days. The first 2 days it was slight; it then continued extremely violent for a week with but small abatements. Yet he had so much strength as never to be in immediate danger, altho had it continued so some days longer danger would have supervened. On the 10th. day it abated evidently still more on the 11th. and went off on the 12th. which was the day I wrote you by Mr. Burwell. We are now at the 18th. day since he was taken. Adieu my dearest Martha. Kiss all the little ones for me. Should I by any post omit to write, do not be alarmed; for as he is quite well it is very possible my business may sometimes prevent my recollecting a post day.

TH: JEFFERSON

1. The Oval Room was on the second floor of the President's House and was used as a drawing room or study, William V. Elder, Curator of the White House, to James A. Bear, Jr., December 28, 1962.

TO MARTHA JEFFERSON RANDOLPH

Washington. Friday afternoon. Mar. 13. 07.

MY DEAREST MARTHA

I wrote to you by the carts yesterday morning; but as you will not get that letter till Monday evening, and may recieve this written a day later on Monday morning, I again inform you that Mr. Randolph continues well. He rode yesterday 5. miles, without fatigue, was much exhilarated by it, and had a fine night's sleep. An Easterly storm having set in this morning will interrupt this salutary recruit to his spirits and health. He still looks to Monday sennight (the 23d) as the date by which he will be strong enough to set out on his journey: I think we may set out sooner. He is now so well, that I may possibly forget the post day sometimes, tho' I will not willingly. We both think it will be better for you to move over to Monticello a little before we get there; because as we shall probably not set out from Gordon's till 9. oclock in the morning, any stoppage at Edgehill might keep him out to an improper hour of the evening. But on this subject I shall have other occasions of writing to you. Accept my tenderest love for yourself and the children.   TH: JEFFERSON

FROM MARTHA JEFFERSON RANDOLPH

March 14. 1807

MY DEAREST FATHER

I have but a moment to return you a thousand thanks for your goodness in writing so regularly to me during Mr. R illness. I have been in a state of great anxiety upon his account. Thank heavens it is past. We are all well and after saturday shall look for you hourly. God bless you My Dear Father. Believe me to be yours unalterably,

Mr. Burwell arrived on thursday only and is still with us.

To Martha Jefferson Randolph

Washington Mar. 16. 07.

My dearest Martha

Mr. Randolph continues well. Nothing has happened to throw him back. He rides out now on good days in the carriage. He came down to breakfast with us to-day. But the quantity of blood taken from him occasions him to recover strength slowly. It is now certain that his calculation for departure will be truer than mine. Judging by the advance of his strength for the last week, it will take another week fully to get enough for his journey. Above all things we must take care that too early an attempt does not expose him to a relapse. My letter of next Friday will inform you more certainly. I am poorly myself,[1] not at all fit for a journey at this time. The remains of a bad cold hang on me, and for a day or two past some symptoms of periodical head-ache. Mr. Coles and Capt. Lewis are also indisposed, so that we are but a collection of invalids. I hope yourself and the family are in good health, and that we shall find you so on our arrival. I have been late in forwarding my stores for Richmond. They only leave this to-day. God bless you and all our dear young ones.

Th: Jefferson

1. TJ was sick for the greater part of a month, beginning with a cold on March 6. His periodical headache began about the 14th and by the 20th he was "shut up in a dark room from early in the forenoon til night." (TJ to Albert Gallatin, March 20, 1807. DLC.) It was not until April that he completely recovered.

From Martha Jefferson Randolph

Edgehill March 20. 1807

My Dearest Father

I am very uneasy at the account you give of your own health. You would not set out of course whilst in any danger of the *head ach* but if otherwise indisposed from cold or the fatigues of the session it would be better to defer your journey, as the roads are in a state not to be concieved. The carts have not arrived yet; Davy broke down near orange court house[1] and past by on horseback to get the waggon to go down for his load. They could not have proceeded but for the circumstance of being able to double their team by being together. At the bad places some days they only came 6 miles. To give you a still better idea of the *labours* which await you, Mr. Carr[2] told me of their putting 9 horses to one waggon; finally they had to take out the load and prize out 2 of the horses who *mired*. If you determine to venture your self my dear Father which I think will be imprudent untill you feel quite recovered yet would it be very improper for Mr. Randolph whose fear of detaining you may make him venture upon it sooner than prudence would authorise. If you come shortly pray advise him to stay untill thoroughly recruited. I know it will put him more at his ease and your servants are so attentive that he will be as well attended to as if you were with him. I mention this merely to put you both entirely at your ease. I know he would rather be left than detain you one moment, or set off himself sooner than entirely prudent. Pray take care of your self. Your constitution is not adequate to the labours of your place. I look forward to the 2 remaining years with more anxiety than I can express. Those past with what joy shall I hail that return which will be followed by no sepparation. I make no exception when I say the *first* and most important object with me will be the dear and sacred duty of nursing and chearing your old age, by every endearment of filial tenderness. My fancy dwells with rapture upon your image seated by your *own* fire side surrounded by your grand children contending for the pleasure of waiting upon you. Every age has its pleasures, with health I do not know whether youth is to be regretted. I have been very much delighted with a tract of Cicero's upon that subject; he has certainly seen it in its true light, as a harbour from the cares and storms of life to which the turbulence of the passions expose us in youth. Adieu My Dearest Father. Once more pray take care of your precious health and believe me with unalterable tenderness yours,   M. R.

Isaac has just arrived. I think it will be better for us to go to Monticello before you come. As soon as that is determined upon I shall regulate my motions accordingly.   M. RANDOLPH

1. Orange Court House, the county seat of Orange County, was a stopping point in traveling between Monticello and Washington. It was 25 miles north of Charlottesville.
2. Probably Samuel Carr.

To Martha Jefferson Randolph

Washington Mar. 20. 07.

MY DEAREST MARTHA

Mr. Randolph continues well without the least retrograde circumstance. He sleeps well, walks a good deal about the house, rides out in the carriage every day this cruel weather will permit and breakfasts and dines with us. But his strength returns so slowly that he certainly will not be able to undertake his journey on Monday as we had hoped. Indeed I do not think a time can be fixed when he shall be able to get on horseback and ride half a dozen miles without fatigue. I think he may venture to set out in a chair. You shall hear twice a week of his advance towards this. I am now in the 7th day of a periodical head-ache, and I write this in the morning before the fit has come on. The fits are by no means as severe as I have felt in former times, but they hold me very long, from 9. or 10. in the morning till dark. Neither Calomel nor bark have as yet made the least impression on them. Indeed we have quite a hospital, one half below and above stairs being sick. Lemaire is seriously ill. John Freeman [1] just getting about after a 6. weeks confinement with a broken jaw. I hope you are all well, and send you my tenderest affections,   TH: JEFFERSON

1. The Monticello overseer or a servant.

To Martha Jefferson Randolph

Washington Mar. 23. 07.

MY DEAREST MARTHA

Mr. Randolph's convalescence proceeds steadily, not a single circumstance having arisen to throw him back. Yet his strength increases slowly. As yet he only rides out in the carriage every day. It will not be till he can get on horseback that we can judge when he will be able to travel. My fits of head-ach have shortened from 9 hours to 5. but they have stuck some days at 5. hours, and when they will give further way cannot be divined. In our present situation it is impossible to fix a day of departure. It has always seemed to be about a week off; but, like our shadows, it walks before us, and still keeps at the same distance. I do believe however that Mr. Randolph will be able to travel within one week from the time of his getting on horseback. I write while a fit is coming on and therefore must conclude with my kisses to you all.

TH: JEFFERSON

To Martha Jefferson Randolph

Washington Mar. 27. 07

MY DEAREST MARTHA

I presume Mr. Randolph writes to you and informs you he continues well. He has rode twice on horseback; and yesterday about 4. miles without feeling it. My fit of yesterday was so mild that I have some hope of missing it to-day. I write this in the morning, but will keep it open till the evening to add the result of the day. We both think we may very safely fix on Monday sennight for our departure, to wit, the 6th. of April, and that you had better move over to Monticello the first fair day after that, as we shall be there on the Friday to dinner. Should any thing derange our plan, we have still two other posts to write to you, to wit, those which will arrive at Milton on the 2d. and 6th. of April. Before this reaches you you will have heard of the arrival of Burr at Richmond for trial.[1] There may be a possibility of something connected with this circumstance arising which might detain me a little, but I do not foresee that that can be. Accept kisses for yourself and our dear children.   TH: JEFFERSON

P. S. Afternoon. I have scarcely had any sensation of a fit to-day: so that I consider it as missed.

1. Aaron Burr's trial for conspiracy to separate the western states from the United States. He was brought before Chief Justice John Marshall, who presided over the United States Circuit Court in Richmond beginning March 30, 1807.

To Martha Jefferson Randolph

Mar. 30. 07.

MY DEAREST MARTHA

I presume Mr. Randolph informs you himself that he is quite well. Indeed I have no doubt he could now very safely undertake the journey; but we continue to fix on Monday next for departure. As to myself altho' I have no actual head-ach, yet about 9. oclock every morning I have a very quickened pulse come on, a disturbed head and tender eyes, not amounting to absolute pain. It goes off about noon, and is doubtless an obstinate remnant of the head-ach, keeping up a possibility of return. I am not very confident of it's passing off. I shall write to you again on Friday, and should nothing have changed our purpose by that time, we shall hope you will be removed to Monticello so as that we shall find you there on the 10th. I send Ellen a little piece of poetry; yet I am not certain if I had not sent it before. Recieve my kisses for yourself and our dear children, and be assured of my tenderest love.

TH: JEFFERSON

TO MARTHA JEFFERSON RANDOLPH

Washington Apr. 2. 07.

MY DEAREST MARTHA

Being apprehensive we have mistaken, by one day, the departure of the horse post from hence, I write this on Thursday instead of Friday. Mr. Randolph is quite strong enough to begin his journey even now. I think that to-day for the first time I have had no sensation of any remains of my head-ach. We continue our purpose of setting out on Monday, but I forsee a particular circumstance which may put it off to Tuesday. After that you must allow for the accidents of bad weather, which continue to prevail wonderfully; as we shall not move on the road on either wet or very cold days. I thank you, my dear, for your attention to the cyder, and hope you have had it bottled. Our stores will probably arrive at Richmond about the 7th. and I hope may be at Monticello about the 13th. or 14th. We shall count on your moving there on Tuesday, or the first good day after. Kisses to all our dear children and tenderest love to you. TH: JEFFERSON

TO MARTHA JEFFERSON RANDOLPH

Washington April 5. 07

We are all well here, My ever dear Martha, but I shall not be able probably to set out tomorrow, but shall on Tuesday. We shall be five days on the road. In the mean time the roads will be getting better, and the weather perhaps milder, but indeed it looks as if this winter would run through the summer. Not a bud is swelled here yet, except of the red Maple. Kiss our dear children for me, and be assured of my tenderest love. TH: JEFFERSON

TO MARTHA JEFFERSON RANDOLPH

Washington June 1. 07.

MY DEAREST MARTHA

I am in hopes this evening's mail will bring me information that you are all well, tho in the mean time this letter will have gone on. My health has been constant since my return here. I inclose a newspaper for Mr. Randolph, a magazine for yourself, and a piece of poetry for Ellen. Tell her she is to consider this as a substitute for a letter and that I debit her account accordingly. I shall have a letter for Anne next week, by which time I am in hopes to recieve a report from her of the state of our affairs at Monticello. We had cucumbers here on the 20th. of May, strawberries the 24th. and peas the 26th. I am in hopes she has noted when you first had cherries and strawberries. Of small news in this place we have not much. Doctr. Bullas[1] and his family have left it for the Mediterranean. S. H. Smith proposes to give up his press. Whether he will remain here afterwards will probably depend on his obtaining office. It is thought he will offer as successor to Beckley.[2] Altho' we had fires on the 19th. 20th. and 21st. the summer seems now to have set in seriously. On the 30th. the thermometer was at 84°. Will you tell Mr. Randolph that I have found here the pure breed of Guinea hogs, and shall endeavor to send on a litter of the pigs when my cart comes in autumn. Is there any thing here I can get or do for you? It would much add to my happiness if I oftener could know how to add to your convenience or gratification. Remember me affectionately to Mr. Randolph and the young ones, and be assured yourself of my tenderest love.

TH: JEFFERSON

1. Dr. John Bullus was later appointed as customs agent for the port of New York City.
2. Possibly John Beckley, author of *Address to the People of the United States; with an Epitome and Vindication of* . . . *TJ* (1800) and Clerk of the House of Representatives until 1797, when defeated for re-election; he was named Librarian of Congress in 1802.

To Anne Cary Randolph

Washington June 7. 07.

MY DEAR ANNE

I recieved last week from your papa information that you were all well except your Mama, who had still some remains of the pain in the face. I hope I shall hear this week that she also is restored to her health. From yourself I may soon expect a report of your first visit to Monticello, and of the state of our joint concerns there. I find that the limited number of our flower beds will too much restrain the variety of flowers in which we might wish to indulge, and therefore I have resumed an idea, which I had formerly entertained, but had laid by, of a winding walk surrounding the lawn before the house, with a narrow border of flowers on each side. This would give us abundant room for a great variety. I inclose you a sketch of my idea,[1] where the dotted lines on each side of the black line shew the border on each side of the walk. The hollows of the walk would give room for oval beds of flowering shrubs. Will you tell your papa that Joseph has put into my hands Marmontel's memoirs,[2] and 7. Dollars being the surplus of money left after paying Duane's account. The 7. Dollars are included in a remittance I now make to Mr. Bacon,[3] who is instructed to deliver them to Mr. Randolph. The books, making too large a packet for the post, I shall reserve them to bring with me, unless some earlier conveyance offers. Kiss your dear Mama and the young ones for me. Present me affectionately to your Papa, and accept the assurances of my love for yourself.

Th: Jefferson

1. The spring visit to Monticello is of special interest because during it TJ laid out and planted the oval and round flower beds around the house. The winding or serpentine flower borders around it and mentioned in this letter were not laid out until 1808. The drawing that accompanied this letter has been omitted. See *Garden Book*, 330 and 331; also Edwin M. Betts and Hazelhurst B. Perkins, *Thomas Jefferson's Flower Garden at Monticello* (Richmond, 1941).

2. *Oeuvres posthumes de Marmontel* . . . (Paris, 1804, 1807), Sowerby 234. written originally by Jean François Marmontel for his children.

3. Edmund Bacon was TJ's best and longest-employed overseer.

To Martha Jefferson Randolph

Washington June 14. 07.

My dearest Martha

I have just recieved information from Mr. Jefferson that my shipwrecked goods are gone on from Richmond to Monticello (3. casks excepted which he supposes plundered) and that they appear to be in good condition. As a knolege of what gets safe and in good condition will dispense with my sending on a duplicate provision, I have directed Mr. Bacon to open all the packages and report to me their condition by return of post; also to inform you of their condition and take your advice as to what had best be done with any of them which may have been wet, which advice I hope you will give. Tell Anne I have recieved no report from her yet as to our affairs at Monticello. I subjoin for your informa-

tion a list of these shipwrecked packages. My tender love to you
all, and to yourself above all.   TH: JEFFERSON

No. 1. a barrel. white Musco-
vado sugar.
2. cask. cheese and sun-
dries.
3. do. raisins, rice, loaf
sugar.
4. do. crackers.
5. do. brandy. double
cased
6.7.8.9. four boxes. 200 bottles cyder
10.11.12. barrels of potatoes.
13. box. 36. beef's tongues

14.15. barrels of cyder for vinegar.
16. box. containg 12. boxes
prunes, 4. do. figs
17. do. 18 bottles oil. 4. do. an-
chovies
18.19. boxes. 1. doz. Hungary
wine in each.
20.21. boxes. 59 bottles syrup of
punch.
22. box. horns, books, paper,
prints
23. box. chimney facings.
24.25. boxes. ornaments in led.

To ELLEN WAYLES RANDOLPH

Washington June 29. 07.

MY DEAR ELLEN

I believe I have recieved no letter from you since I came from
Monticello, but perhaps there is one on the road for me. Hope is
so much pleasanter than despair, that I always prefer looking into
futurity through her glass. I send you some poetical gleanings.
Our newspapers have been rather barren in that ware for some
time past. Whether the muses have been taking a nap, or our news
writers have been prevented from making their weekly visits to
mount Parnassus,[1] by their occupations with Burr and the Chesapeake I cannot decide. But we will leave these idle ladies to their
dreams in the Castalian valley, and descend to the more useful
region and occupations of the good housewife, one of whom is
worth more than the whole family of the muses. How go on the
Bantams? I rely on you for their care, as I do on Anne for the
Algerine fowls, and on our arrangements at Monticello for the
East Indians. These varieties are pleasant for the table and furnish
an agreeable diversification in our domestic occupations. I am
now possessed of individuals of four of the most remarkeable
varieties of the race of the sheep.[2] If you turn to your books of
natural history, you will find among these 1. the Spanish sheep

or Marino. 2. the Iceland sheep, or Ovis Polycerata. 3. the Barbary sheep, or Ovis laticauda and 4. the Senegal sheep, or that of Bengal which is the same. I have lately recieved a ram of the 2d. kind, who has 4. horns, a round and beautiful animal, rather small. The 3d. or broad tailed is remarkable for it's flavor. I lately had a quarter sent me which I found the highest flavored lamb I had ever tasted. The 4th. or Senegal is supposed to be the original stock of the sheep. It's flavor is said to be equal to that of Venison. Tho' I possess individuals of one sex only of the 2d. 3d. and 4th. kinds, yet 4. crossings are understood by naturalists to produce the true breed. I mean to pay great attention to them, pro bono publico (call on Jefferson to translate your Latin). Tell your Papa the only true account of the affair of the Chesapeake is that in Smith's paper, the others are full of falsehoods.[3] Present my warm affections to your Papa, Mama, and the young ones, and be assured of a full share of them yr. sf.,   TH: JEFFERSON

1. Mount Parnassus was near the site of the Delphic oracle, and the Castalian Valley was the location of a spring sacred to Apollo.
2. TJ raised sheep to supply food and also for the wool with which to make coarse woolens for his slaves. See the *Farm Book*, 111–13.
3. On June 22, 1807, the British frigate *Leopard* fired on the U.S.S. *Chesapeake*, killing three and wounding eighteen Americans; four British deserters were removed.

FROM MARTHA JEFFERSON RANDOLPH

July 11 1807

MY DEAREST FATHER

I send you a shoe that fits perfectly. The only objection to it is, the heel which is too high. I must beg the favor of you to add a comb for tucking up the hair, to the shoes. Will this affair of the Chesapeake affect your return? We have had thro' the medium of the newspapers, news of a later date than your letter contained which announce an actual commencement of hostilities on the side of the british which I am afraid will retard your return to us. Bacon applied to for information with regard to the fresh meat necessary for the summer but being totally ignorant of the time you would spend with us I could not direct him. He said he had several beeves and I advised him to engage some lambs. Perhaps you had better write a line to him. Adieu My Dearest Father the post is going. I have only time to subscribe my Self with tenderest affection yours unchangeably,   MRANDOLPH

I should wish my shoes made a little higher in the hind quarter because they keep up better at the heel and lower heels but otherwise exactly like the pattern.

To Martha Jefferson Randolph

Washington July 27. 07.

My dearest daughter

As it seems now tolerably probable that the British squadron in our bay[1] have not in contemplation to commit any hostile act, other than the remaining there in defiance, and bringing to the vessels which pass in and out, we are making all the arrangements preparatory to the possible state of war, that they may be going on while we take our usual recess. In the course of three or four days a proclamation will be issued for calling Congress on some day in October. These matters settled, I can leave this for Monticello some day I think from Friday to Monday inclusive, unless something unforeseen happens. I am endeavoring to persuade Genl. Dearborne to go and stay with me at Monticello; but I do not see much likelihood of prevailing on him. In expectation of being with you somewhere from Monday to Thursday I tender my best affections to Mr. Randolph and the family and my warmest love to yourself.   Th: Jefferson

1. They were anchored in the Norfolk Roads.

To Martha Jefferson Randolph

Washington Oct. 12. 07.

My dearest Martha

My journey to this place was not as free from accident as usual. I was near losing Castor[1] in the Rapidan, by his lying down in the river, where waste deep, and being so embarrassed by the shafts of the carriage and harness that he was nearly drowned before the servants, jumping into the water, could lift his head out and cut him loose from the carriage. This was followed by the loss of my travelling money, I imagine as happened on the Sopha in the morning I left Monticello, when it was given me again by one of the children. Two days after my arrival here I was taken with the Influenza, but it was very slight, without either fever or pain and is now nearly passed off. I send you a letter and pamphlet from your old acquaintance Dashwood, now Mrs. Lee,[2] who you will percieve not to have advanced in prudence or sound judgment.

Return me the letter if you please, as I may perhaps answer it, if from a perusal of the pamphlet I find it worth while. I have not yet read it. She sent me a dozen copies. I inclose a letter for Mr. Randolph to whom present me affectionately and to all the young ones. Be assured yourself of my warmest love.

TH: JEFFERSON

1. A horse that TJ regarded very highly.
2. Mrs. Rachel Fanny Antonina Lee, a daughter of Sir Francis Dashwood, was an English authoress and friend of Martha's in Paris.

To ELLEN WAYLES RANDOLPH

Washington Oct. 19. 07.

MY DEAR ELLEN

I have nothing better to send you than an old song. But indeed I could send you nothing better. It was much in vogue when I was of your age, and has lost nothing of it's pathos by time. It shews the wonderful sources of comfort which open themselves to every condition of man. I have not heard from the family since I left them at Monticello, but I always hope the next post will bring me a letter. Your friends here are all well. As Congress will meet this day week, we begin now to be in the bustle of preparation. I am this week getting through the dining all my friends of this place, to be ready for the Congressional campaign. When that begins, between the occupations of business and of entertainment, I shall become an unpunctual correspondent. This letter is written Stylographically,[1] not Polygraphically. The latter mode you know; the former is new and may be explained to you hereafter. Kiss your dear Mama for me not forgetting your sisters: remember me affectionately to your Papa, to whom I send newspapers and accept for yourself my tender love,   TH: JEFFERSON

1. William Lyman informed TJ in a letter of July 11, 1807 (DLC), that he had forwarded him one of "R Wedgwoods improved Stylographic Manifold Writer[s]." It arrived some time prior to this letter. TJ acknowledged its arrival April 30, 1808 (DLC). Unfortunately, this copying machine has been lost.

To ANNE CARY RANDOLPH

Washington Nov. 1. 07.

MY DEAR ANNE

I wish to learn from you how the tuberoses &c. do, and particularly to have a list from you of the roots and seeds you have saved that I may know what supplies to ask from Mc.Mahon[1] for the next spring. When Davy comes I shall send some Alpine strawberry roots, and some tussocks of a grass of a perfume equal to Vanilla, called the Sweet-scented Vernal grass, or Anthoxanthum odoratium. These I must consign to your care till the spring. I expect a pair of wildgeese of a family which have been natives for several generations, but they will hardly be here in time for Davy.[2] They are entirely domesticated, beautiful have a very musical note, and are much superior to the tame for the table. I have recieved from Capt. Pike[3] a pair of grisly bears brought from the head of the Arkansa. These are too dangerous and troublesome for me to keep. I shall therefore send them to Peale's Museum.[4] We have nothing new here except a new importation of Influenza by the Western and Southern members who take it on the road and bring it on. I am anxious to hear that you are all recovered from it. Convey my warm affections to your papa, mama and the family and be assured of them yourself.   TH: JEFFERSON

1. Bernard McMahon, the Philadelphia nurseryman and author of *The American Gardener's Calendar.*
2. A trusted slave who carted a great deal of TJ's supplies between Monticello and Washington.
3. Zebulon Pike.
4. An exhibition hall and museum in Philadelphia operated by Rembrandt and Charles Willson Peale.

FROM ELLEN WAYLES RANDOLPH

Edgehill November 6th 1807

I hope my dear grandpapa, will excuse my long silence, when he knows the reason of it which was that I had no paper, but now that papa has come from Richmond and brought some with him, I will gladly answer your letter. The song, which you sent me, I have always admired as a very beautiful and pathetic piece and am very glad that you sent it as it has always, been one of my favorites. Mama and all the children are well; James has grown a great deal, and begins to talk. He is a sweet child; Mama and Sister Ann send their love to you, give mine to Mrs. S. H. S. Adieu my dear Grandpapa. Believe me to be your very affectionate Grand Daughter.   E. W. RANDOLPH

From Anne Cary Randolph

Edgehill November 9 1807

My Dear Grand Papa

The tuberoses and Amaryllises are taken up. We shall have a plenty of them for the next year. The tulips and Hyacinths I had planted before I left Monticello. They had increased so much as to fill the beds quite full. The Anemonies and Ranunculuses are also doing well. Fourteen of Governor Lewis's Pea ripened which I have saved.[1] The Pinks Carnations Sweet Williams Yellow horned Poppy Ixia Jeffersonia everlasting Pea Lavetera Columbian Lilly Lobelia Lychnis double blossomed Poppy and Physalis failed, indeed none of the seeds which you got from Mr. McMahon came up. Ellen and myself have a fine parcel of little Orange trees for the green house[2] against your return. Mrs. Lewis[3] has promised me some seed of the Cypress vine. Mama Aunt Virginia and all the children are well and send their love to you. Good night my Dear Grand Papa. Believe me to be your sincerely affectionate Grand daughter.   A C R

I will be very much obliged to you if you will send me [last line wanting].

1. A flowering pea sent from Arkansas by Meriwether Lewis.
2. The glass-enclosed southern piazza, just off the library suite at Monticello. This area also housed TJ's workshop and greenhouse and probably served other utilitarian purposes.
3. Mrs. Nicholas Lewis.

From Ellen Wayles Randolph

Edgehill November 11th 1807

This is the second letter I have written to My dear grandpapa without recieving an answer but as I know the reason I will continue to write untill you have leisure to answer my letters. One of my poor little Bantams is dead and the one which I liked best although it was the old one. He had got so tame that he would fly up in my lap and eat out of my hand. All the children were sorry at his death. Cousin Polly Harrison was in the neighbourhood lately and has left Jane to stay with me untill the exhibition which is to commence Wednesday the 11th and will finish saturday when there will be a ball to which we are all going. I have only two dances to go to before the school will be broken up for which I will be sorry. Aunt Virginia has not quitted us yet but

expects to go down soon. Mama Aunt Virginia Sister Ann and all
the children send their love to you. Give mine to Mrs S H Smith.
Pray write to me when you have time. Adieu my dear Grandpapa.
Believe me to be your affectionate Grand Daughter,

ELEONORA WAYLES RANDOLPH

To Martha Jefferson Randolph

Washington Nov. 23. 07.

MY DEAR MARTHA

Here we are all well; and my last letters from Edgehill informed
me that all were so there except some remains of Influenza hanging on yourself. I shall be happy to hear you are entirely clear of
it's remains. It seems to have gained strength and malignancy in
it's progress over the country. It has been a formidable disease in
the Carolinas; but worst of all in Kentucky; fatal however only
to old persons. Davy will set out on his return tomorrow. He will
carry an earthen box of Monthly strawberries which I must put
under Anne's care till Spring, when we will plant them at Monticello. I have stuck several sprigs of Geranium in a pot which contained a plant supposed to be Orange, but not known to be so.
We have little company of strangers in town this winter. The only
ladies are the wives of Messrs. Newton, Thruston, W. Alston,
Marion, Mumford, Blount, Adams, Cutts, and Mrs. Mc.Creary
expected.[1] Congress are all expectation and anxiety for the news
expected by the Revenge,[2] or by Colo. Monro,[3] whose immediate
return however may be doubted. The War-fever is past, and the
probability against it's return is rather prevalent. A Caucus of
malcontent members has been held, and an organized opposition
to the government arranged, J. R. and J. C.[4] at it's head. About
20. members composed it. Their object is to embarras, avoiding
votes of opposition beyond what they think the nation will bear.
Their chief mischief will be done by letters of misrepresentations
to their constituents; for in neither house, even with the assured
aid of the federalists can they shake the good sense and honest
intentions of the mass of real republicans. But I am tired of a life
of contention, and of being the personal object for the hatred of
every man, who hates the present state of things. I long to be
among you where I know nothing but love and delight, and where
instead of being chained to a writing table I would be indulged
as others are with the blessings of domestic society, and pursuits

of my own choice. Adieu my ever dear Martha. Present me affectionately to Mr. Randolph and the family.

TH: JEFFERSON

1. Wives of members of Congress: Thomas Newton, Jr., Virginia; Buckner Thruston, Kentucky; Willis Alston, South Carolina; Robert Marion, South Carolina; Gurdon S. Mumford, New York; Thomas Blount, North Carolina; John Q. Adams, Senator from Massachusetts; Richard Cutts, Massachusetts; and William McCreery, Maryland.
2. The *Revenge* was a ship.
3. James Monroe.
4. John Randolph of Roanoke and John C. Calhoun of South Carolina.

To ANNE CARY RANDOLPH

Washington Nov. 24. 1807.

MY DEAR ANNE

I wrote yesterday to your Mama and mentioned what I should send to your charge by Davy, for fear I might be prevented from writing to you by him. I have just time to say that I have sent the following articles.

1. A small pot containing several sprigs of Geranium, stuck round a plant supposed to be Orange.
2. A long earthen box of Monthly strawberries, which I pray you to take care of till spring when we will plant them at Monticello. The gardener says they need never be watered during winter. Yet I should think a little stale water, in warm weather, from time to time would be safest.
3. A bag of paccan nuts (about 100.) for your papa for planting. I am this moment called off, therefore Adieu my dear Anne.

TH: JEFFERSON

To ELLEN WAYLES RANDOLPH

Washington Dec. 8. 07.

MY DEAREST ELLEN.

I owe you a letter, and very fortunately have one to inclose from an acquaintance which you must consider as a paiment in full of my debt. For having nothing to write about I should otherwise have been puzzled to make paiment, had it not been for this godsend. I could tell you we are all well. But that is a thing of course. I could tell you it is now very cold: but the air of the morning has already told you that, especially if you have been to your hen-

house. I could say much about politics, our only entertainment
here, but you would not care a fig about that. Now I recollect one
thing which you will care about. Colo. Munroe left London Oct.
14. and probably sailed about the 20th. We may expect him therefore every hour and as it is probable he will come here first, he
will not be with you till you will have heard of his arrival. Another
recollection, new arrangement of the Western mail begins this
day which will enable you to recieve to your letters written Saturday morning, the answers the Thursday following instead of the
Thursday sennight. For fear of more recollections which might
incroach on other pressing business I will here close with the addition only of my affectionate remembrance to your Papa Mama,
and the others of the family, not forgetting yourself.

TH: JEFFERSON

To Martha Jefferson Randolph

Washington Dec. 29. 07

MY DEAREST MARTHA

I was taken with a tooth-ache[1] about 5. days ago, which brought
on a very large and hard swelling of the face, and that produced
a fever which left me last night. The swelling has subsided sensibly, but whether it will terminate without suppuration is still
uncertain. My hope is that I shall be well enough to recieve my
company on New Year's day. Indeed I have never been confined
by it to my bed-room. This would not have been worth mentioning to you, but that rumour might magnify it to you as something
serious. Present my warm affections to Mr. Randolph and the
family and be assured of my unceasing love.

TH: JEFFERSON

1. One of the few instances of TJ's having trouble with his teeth or
gums. The ailment began about Christmas Eve; the jawbone exfoliated, and
a piece was extracted about January 5. For fear of complications he remained
indoors for nearly a month. As late as February 23 there still was a small
knot on his jawbone. Consult the "Medical Chronology."

From Martha Jefferson Randolph

Edgehill Jan. 2, 1808

I am very much obliged to you My Dearest Father for your
kindness in saving me from the anxiety which an exaggerated report
would have occasioned me. I am in hopes the swelling will go off

with out suppuration. Mr. Eppes found me with exactly such a one as you describe when he returned from Washington in the spring 1804 except that the pain had brought on an affection of the stomach and head which kept me with an incessant puking for 3 or four days. The swelling remained many weeks. Mr. Randolph has been a fortnight in Richmond setling David Randolph's affairs.[1] He has not property to pay his debts. Sister Randolph's house servants have been saved by a prior mortgage to an old Lady of the name of Stith[2] in Williamsburg who means to leave the debt to *him* at her death, in the mean time the interest must be paid and from what funds it is not easy to say. Sister Randolph has opened a boarding house in Richmond, but she has not a single boarder yet. Her husband has gone to England upon some mercantile scheme with barely money to defray his expenses. The ruin of the family is still extending it self daily. William is ruined. His negroes during his absence remained three days in the dwelling house to save them selves from the sherif. Archy is without a shelter for his family but her Father's, and Will. Fleming goes constantly armed to keep the sherif off.[3] I ought rather to say *went* for in consequence of the pistol's going off in his pocket he is rendered a cripple for life. He has never moved but as he has been lifted and probably will not for many months. Mr. Randolph's trials have been great but thank heaven he has resisted their solicitations and has had the prudence not to hamper himself by security ships. His contributing to his Sister's necessities as far as he is able is a sacred duty. But a recent occurence under which he is still smarting, with my *urgent entreaties* have kept him clear of all *new* engagements. The desolation which surrounds us has kept us both in a state of great anxiety which the present appearance of affairs is not likely to dissipate. Adieu My Dear Father. Believe me with every sentiment of tenderness and veneration your affectionate Daughter,

MRANDOLPH

1. David Meade Randolph was appointed a marshal by Washington. A die-hard Federalist who neither died nor resigned after TJ's election as President, he was perforce removed from office. Following this, his finances fell into disarray, and he was forced to sell his Richmond home. Thomas Mann Randolph, Jr., was in Richmond presumably looking after the interests of Mary (Molly) Randolph (or Sister Randolph), his sister and the wife of David Meade.

2. Mary Stith was a granddaughter of Thomas Mann Randolph, Sr., of Tuckahoe. She never married, and she died in 1816.

3. Archibald Carry and William Fleming Randolph were cousins of Thomas Mann Randolph, Jr.

To Martha Jefferson Randolph

Washington Jan. 5. 08.

MY DEAREST MARTHA

I recieved yesterday yours of the 2d. My fever left me the day I wrote to you, and the swelling abated through the whole face, but still remains in a knot as big as a pigeon's egg, over the diseased tooth, which has now been suppurating so long that the Doctr. thinks he shall have to extract the tooth (altho' perfectly sound) to prevent a caries of the bone. A day or two will decide. In the mean time I am confined to the house, though without pain, and indeed in good health. I always apprehended that Mr. Randolph would be in great embarrasment between the imprudencies of some members of his father's family, and the necessity of taking care of a large one of his own, and knowing his liberal dispositions I thought it possible that present pressure might sometimes prevail over a prudent foresight of the future. If he keeps himself clear of engagements on their behalf, and only assists them with money when he has it, this will prevent any serious injury to himself. I never in my life have been so disappointed as in my expectations that the office I am in would have enabled me from time to time to assist him in his difficulties. So far otherwise has it turned out that I have now the gloomy prospect of retiring from office loaded with serious debts, which will materially affect the tranquility of my retirement. However, not being apt to deject myself with evils before they happen, I nourish the hope of getting along. It has always been my wish and expectation, that when I return to live at Monticello, Mr. Randolph, yourself and family would live there with me, and that his estate being employed entirely for meeting his own difficulties, would place him at ease. Our lands, if we preserve them, are sufficient to place all the children in independance. But I know nothing more important to inculcate into the minds of young people than the wisdom, the honor, and the blessed comfort of living within their income, to calculate in good time how much less pain will cost them the plainest stile of living which keeps them out of debt, than after a few years of splendor above their income, to have their property taken away for debt when they have a family growing up to maintain and provide for. Lessons enough are before their eyes, among their nearest acquaintances if they will but contemplate and bring the examples home to themselves. Still there is another evil against which we cannot guard, unthrifty marriages; because characters are not known until they are tried. But even here, a wife imbued with principles of prudence, may go far towards arresting or lessening the evils of an improvident management. In your moralising conversations with your children, I have no doubt you endeavor to warn them against the rocks on which they see so many shipwrecked. Altho we cannot expect that none of our posterity are to become the victims of imprudence or misfortune, yet we cannot but be particularly anxious to ward off the evil from those in present being, who having been brought up in our bosoms, cannot suffer without our own suffering equally.

Colo. Monroe left us the day before yesterday. He talks of settling in Richmond. I have ventured to advise him against being hasty in that determination. Present me affectionately to Mr. Randolph and the children, and be assured of my constant and tenderest love.   TH: JEFFERSON

FROM ELLEN WAYLES RANDOLPH

Edgehill January 8 1808

DEAR GRANDPAPA

I should have written to you post before last but I was not at home and newyears day I did write but I did not send the letter because it was not well written as I had bad pens and it was late before I sat down to write. I went sometime ago to a ball given by Mr. Ogilvie and his sholars. Several of the boys recited pieces some of which were done very well particularly a piece by Peter Pindar[1] which was spoken by Henry Taylor.[2] An Elephant passed through Milton lately. Jefferson went to see him but we did not. He was only 7 foot high. Aunt Virginia has quitted us. Sister Ann spent her Christmas in the North Garden with Cousin Evelina.[3] Papa has returned from Richmond. The Orange trees do not look well. Davy let the box that had the Geraniums fall out of the cart and break by which means we have lost them. Mama and Sister Ann send their love to you. Give mine to Mrs. H. Smith the next time you see her. Adieu my Dear Grandpapa. Believe me to be your most affectionate Grand Daughter,

ELEONORA WAYLES RANDOLPH

1. Pen name of Dr. John Wolcot, author of *Susan and the Spider*. He was a cousin of St. George Tucker, whose pen name was Jonathan Pindar. See Copybook of Martha Jefferson Trist Burke in the Monticello Archive and

also the "Jefferson Scrapbook" (ViU) for evidences of the poetry of Peter Pindar in the Monticello family.

2. Henry Taylor was possibly one of James Ogilvie's students.

3. Evelina Bolling was the daughter of John Bolling and Mary Kennon and the granddaughter of Mary Jefferson Bolling (Mrs. John).

TO ELLEN WAYLES RANDOLPH

Washington Jan. 12. 08.

MY DEAR ELLEN

I send you some poetry, but am not sure whither I may not have sent you the same pieces before. My letters to your Mama will have informed you of my having been indisposed with a swelled face. It rose, suppurated, and has left me with a hard swelling still on the jawbone, which however I am in hopes will go down. It still confines me to the house for fear cold should affect it. Otherwise I am well. Your particular friends here are all well as far as I can recollect. Mr. Eppes has been confined a month by an Erysipelas. He went out yesterday for the first time. Francis is in good health and goes to school every day. He just reads. Mr. Rose's[1] delay on board his ship is still unexplained to us; but as you are no politician I shall add nothing further in that line. Kiss your dear Mama for me, and sisters. Present me affectionately to your papa, and be assured of my tender love for yourself. Adieu.

TH: JEFFERSON

1. George Rose was the special British envoy sent to adjudicate the *Chesapeake-Leopard* affair of June 22, 1807. See footnote 3 for TJ to Ellen Wayles Randolph, June 29, 1807.

FROM ELLEN WAYLES RANDOLPH

Edgehill. January 15th 1808

DEAR GRANDPAPA

I recieved your letter of the 12 yesterday and am very much obliged to you for the Poetry you sent me. I wrote to you the last post but I did not know when Jefferson went to the post office and he went without it. I inclose it to you now. I am sincerely sorry that you have that swelling on your face however I hope it will go down. How I long for the time that you are to come home to live and then we shall all go to Monticello to live with you. All is well here. James is well and begins to speak very plain. He is the sweetest little fellow you ever saw. Mama and Sister Ann send their love to you. Cornelia begins to write and I hope will soon be able to write to you. Virginia reads a little in fables of one sallable and Mary can spell. My Bantams are well but I am afraid I shall never raise any. Adieu my dear Grandpapa. Believe me to be your affectionate Grand daughter,

ELENORA WAYLES RANDOLPH

FROM MARTHA JEFFERSON RANDOLPH

Edgehill Jan. 16 1808

MY DEAREST FATHER

The subject of your last letter has cast a gloom over my spirits that I can not shake off. The impossibility of paying serious debts by crops, and living at the same time, has been so often proved, that I am afraid you should trust to it. If by any sacrifice of the Bedford Lands[1] you can relieve your self from the pressure of debt I conjure you not to think of the children, your own happiness is alone to be considered. Let not the tranquility of your old age be disturbed and we shall do well. I never could enjoy happiness to see you deprived of those comforts you have allways been accustomed to and which habit has rendered necessary to your health and ease. The children are all young *their* habits are yet to form and upon those only will depend their happiness that, moderate desires, youth, and health can not fail to insure as far as they will be capable of enjoying it and wealth it self could do no more. I can never forgive my self for having so wantonly so cruelly added to your embarrassments by the expense my last visit to Washington put you to. It cuts me to the heart to think how much it will cost you in retirement to raise what I so wantonly squandered in going to live with you My Dear Father. It was never our intention to burthen you with the maintenance of our large family. The same supplies which they consume here, ought to be sent there. Mr. R. has entered into no *new* engagements the consequences of the old are yet at issue and upon the event will rest the situation of our children. Let it come to the worst my land will insure them food and raiment. If the addition of Sister R–s family comes upon us we must still ensure that. It is some comfort to reflect that what ever may happen his children and myself have never contributed. Our expenses have been regulated by the most rigid economy. God send I had been as moderate with you my

Dear Father but I never can forgive my self for that unfortunate trip to Washington. I conjure you once more not to consider the children but secure your own tranquility and ours will follow of course.

Mr. Hackley has written to Mr. Randolph to know with certainty what he can count upon. He understood the promise of the consulship of Cadiz implied by an expression of yours "that if he was already there (in Spain) some thing might be done for him" where as Mr. Mead[2] tells him *he* expects it and has found powerfull friends to support his claim. Mr. Randolph begged me also to reccomend to your kindness a cousin of his (Tarlton Webb)[3] a grandson of Aunt Fleming's and one of a large family of beggared orphans. A midshipmans place is what they wish for the youth. Pardon me if I tease you. It is my misfortune to be so circumstanced as not to be able to avoid it allways as much averse to it as I am. Adieu My Dear Father. Remember that our happiness is so involved in yours as to depend upon it for never can I know peace if yours is disturbed. Yours devotedly,

MRANDOLPH

1. TJ at this time owned 4,164½ acres in the Poplar Forest tract in Bedford County.
2. A lieutenant in the United States Navy who hoped to obtain Don Joseph Yznardi's consular post at Cadiz. It later went to Richard S. Hackley.
3. A grandson of Tarlton Fleming and Mary Randolph, the latter an aunt of Thomas Mann Randolph, Jr.

FROM ANNE CARY RANDOLPH

Edgehill January 22 1808

I have intended to write to My Dear Grand Papa for several post's but we are so much engaged in our lesson's that I had not time. Ellen and myself are learning geography with which I am very much pleased indeed.

I read Coocks voyages in French and Livy in english besides a lesson in Dufief and my Arethmetic and writing every day.[1] I have not been to Monticello since we came from there but Jefferson was there the other day and says that the green house is not done. Both your ice house and ours are filled. I was at Mrs. Lewis's on my way from the North Garden. She told me she had saved some of the seed of the Cypress vine for you and some prickly ash trees. The Alpine Strawberries are doing very well. We were so unfortunate as to lose the Mignonett entirely although Mama devided it between Mrs. Lewis Aunt Jane[2] and herself but none of it seeded. Mrs. Lewis supposes that the climate is too cold for it for she has had it repeatedly before and it never would seed. We have a plenty of the two kinds of Marigold that you gave us. I suppose you have heard that Aunt Lewis is gone to Kentucky with her sons. I went to see her before she set off. She appeared to be very much pleased with the thoughts of Living with her children. All the children send their love to you. Virginia desires me to tell you that she can read and Mary that *she* can read "go up". Adieu My Dear Grand Papa. It wont be long now thank God before you come home to live with us. Believe me to be My Dear Dear Grand Papa your sincerely affectionate Grand Daughter,

A C RANDOLPH

1. In the Albemarle County Courthouse, Will Book 2, 346–49, is "An Apraisement of the Books of Thos. M. Randolph decd." This does not include any of James Cook's travel volumes; however, it does list a Titus Livius. The Dufief is his *Nature Displayed*.

2. Mrs. Charles Lilburn Lewis was TJ's sister and Anne Cary's great-aunt. Aunt Jane was Jane Cary Randolph Randolph (Mrs. Thomas Eston).

FROM ELLEN WAYLES RANDOLPH

Edgehill. January. 29 1808

I hardly think it worthwhile to write to you for I have no news nor any thing agreable to tell you but as I know you are always glad to hear from Edgehill I will take up my pen to inform you that all are well here. I am reading Millot[1] in French and Homers Illiad in English. I have begun to study Geography and I am very much pleased with it. James grows sweeter and better every day. He can speak some words very plain. He cannot pronounce my name yet but calls me Ann. Cornelia goes on very well with her writing. Virginia and Mary also go on well. We have heard lately from Aunt Virginia. She says that the embargo has thrown the dissipated inhabitants of Williamsburg in great confusion. The Ladies say they cannot give up tea and coffee and the gentlemen wine. Mama and Sister Ann send their love to you. Adieu my dear Grandpapa. Believe me to be your affectionate Grand Daughter,   ELEONORA WAYLES RANDOLPH

1. Undoubtedly Claude François Xavier Millot, *Élémens de l'Histoire de France* . . . (Paris, 1787). Sowerby 189. This title was usually included on TJ's recommended reading lists.

FROM MARTHA JEFFERSON RANDOLPH

Jan. 30 1808

I must beg the favor of you My Dearest Father to forward the inclosed, it is from Jane to her Sister and there is no mode of comunication at present unless through you.[1] I suppose you have heard of the loss of your dam.[2] Mr. Randolph begs particularly that you will transmit your orders about the repairs to *him*. He has nothing to do having two overseers to overlook his business and will do the dam with your own hands without it's costing you any thing; he thinks Bacon has not under standing and Shoemaker[3] wants honesty to do it properly. I know it will give him real pleasure to recieve any little commission from you and it can not possibly put him to the least inconvenience. Adieu My Dearest Father. We have no post yet I suppose from hight of the water courses. Yours sincerely,   M RANDOLPH

1. Jane Randolph (Mrs. Thomas Eston) to her sister, Harriet Hackley (Mrs. Richard S.), in Cadiz, Spain.
2. A flood during the late summer of 1807 caused the loss of half of TJ's mill dam. See *Farm Book,* 367.
3. Isaac Shoemaker and his father Jonathan were the mill tenants at the Shadwell Mill. TJ had very unsatisfactory relations with both, and the mill instead of being an income-producer became a source of great trouble. *Farm Book,* 341ff.

FROM CORNELIA JEFFERSON RANDOLPH

recd Feb. 1. 08.

DEAR GRANDPAPA

I do not know how to write myself but as I am very anxious to write to you I must get Sister Ellen to do it for me. I hope that I shall soon be able to do it myself and not to depend upon others. I am reading Sandford and Merton. Every day I get a peice of poetry by heart and write a copy. I have not begun arithmetic yet but I hope I soon shall. Virginia and Mary send their love to you. Adieu my dear Grand Papa. Believe me to be your affectionate Grand daughter,   CORNELIA RANDOLPH

TO MARTHA JEFFERSON RANDOLPH

Washington Feb. 2. 08.

MY DEAREST MARTHA

The letter to Mr. Hackley shall go by a government vessel which sails for Cadiz the 10th. of this month: such a one will sail monthly for Falmouth, Brest, Lisbon and Cadiz during the embargo. This will furnish his friends a regular means of writing to him. Mr. Hackley has nothing to apprehend from Mr. Meade as the successor to Mr. Yznardi. Meade's intrigues against Yznardi, and his indecent attempt to engage the body of the merchants and even Congress itself to force the Executive to remove Yznardi, have shut the door of that appointment for ever to him. Yznardi is a very old and faithful servant of the US. A vacancy by his resignation or death cannot be very distant. Indeed it is believed he would resign in favor of a person whom he should like to prevent Meade who is his greatest enemy. I wish Mr. Hackley would cultivate the old gentleman's good will. He might perhaps make way for him. However a vacancy may happen. Mr. Hackley will be very safe, if it is in my time, and equally so if Mr. Madison should be my successor. I have had Tarleton Webb put on the list of competitors for a Midshipman's place. The number is fixed and full, and many applicants stand before him and must have their turn. Mr. Smith[1] will enable me to give you a more definite idea of his prospects. But it is a poor business. We shall not have any large vessels during the prevalence of present opinions, and the command of a gun boat is a poor prospect.

I shall avail myself with great pleasure of Mr. Randolph's kind offer to direct the repairs of the dam. Bacon's incompetence had made me consider the misfortune as nearly irreparable. I will direct Bacon to follow Mr. Randolph's directions; but the hour of the post being at hand, and other business pressing I can not do it till next post. This will be the less important as a permanent repair cannot be attempted till warm weather. In the meantime should the water fail it may be raised by throwing loose rocks into the gap. My intention is during the ensuing summer to double the breadth of the dam, by extending it 15. feet below the present one, and to reduce it's height one foot, if, as I believe the present height gives more water than is wanting. Recurring to Mr. Hackley's case, you will be sensible that the communication to him must be made with caution so as not to commit my name, of which Meade would make great use. Mr. Hackley may be told he is in no danger from Meade, that the dispositions of the Executive are extremely favorable to him, that Yznardi as an antient and faithful servant possesses their esteem and it should be recommended to him to cultivate the old man's friendship as he might be induced by that to make an opening for him. So much may be said to him. Such is likely to be the posture of public affairs this year that I fear I shall be able to absent myself but little from this place. My spring visit will [I] apprehend be very short. Present me affectionately to Mr. Randolph, and kiss all the young ones for me. To yourself is devoted my unalterable love.

TH: JEFFERSON

1. Robert Smith was Secretary of the Navy in TJ's Cabinet.

To Martha Jefferson Randolph

Washington Feb. 6. 08.

MY DEAREST MARTHA

I wrote to you the last week, but a pressure of business at the time prevented my answering a part of your letter of the 16th. Jan. The regret which you there expressed at the supposed effect of your visit to this place on my ordinary expences, gives me real uneasiness, and has little foundation. Your being here with your family scarcely added any thing sensible to the ordinary expences of the house, and was richly compensated by the happiness I have when with you compared with the comfortless solitude of my general situation. I mean a solitude as to the objects dear to me, for of others I have more than enough. I mentioned my embarrasments merely as a reason for my having been unable to assist Mr. Randolph. The economies which I may practice this year with my crops of the last and present year, if the embargo does not deprive me of the proceeds, will not leave serious difficulties on my hands. That in going into private life I should return to a private stile of living is a thing of course: and this I shall be able to meet without interfering as you mention with the productions of Mr. Randolph's farms, which I wish he should be able to apply entirely to the easement of his own affairs. Indeed I know no difference between his affairs and my own. My only reason for anxiety to keep my property unimpaired is to leave it as a provision for yourselves and your family. This I trust I shall be able to do, and that we shall be able to live in the mean time in love and comfort. In proportion as the time of my rejoining you permanently approaches, every day seems longer, and the load of business appears heavier. But still every day shortens it. Kiss all the children for me, and be assured of my tenderest love.   TH: JEFFERSON

To Anne Cary Randolph

Washington Feb. 16. 08.

My dearest Anne

The time at which Congress will adjourn is very uncertain, but certainly not till April, and whether I shall be free to come home even then is doubtful. Under these prospects I shall not attempt to get any more flower roots and seeds from Philadelphia this season, and must rely entirely on you to preserve those we have by having them planted in proper time. This you will see from McMahon's book, and Mr. Bacon will make Wormley prepare the beds whenever you let him know, so that they may be ready when you go over to set out the roots. The first time I come home I will lay out the projected flower borders round the level so that they shall be ready for the next fall; and in the spring of the next year I will bring home a full collection of roots and plants. We shall then have room enough for every thing.

Tell your papa that the Algerine war is at an end. Present him my affections, and to your Mama and family the same keeping them for yourself also.   Th: Jefferson

From Anne Cary Randolph

Febuary 19 1808

My Dear Grand Papa

I recieved your letter and we are all very sorry to hear that you are not certain of coming home in April. I shall plant Governor Lewis's Peas as soon as the danger of frost is over. The bed they were in last summer was so much shaded that all of them did not ripen and as there are a good many empty one's, I think it will be better to change it. The shady one will suit violets or any other flower's that like shade. The Tube rose and Amaryllis's are the only roots which I have not put in the ground and you will be at home I expect before it is time to plant them. I believe I can get some everlasting Pea's in this neighbourhood. If so I shall sow them in the bed in which they were last year, but did not come up. It is reported that Evelina Bolling is going to be married to Mr. Garett of Charlottesville. All the children are well and send their love to you. Adieu My Dear Grand Papa. Your truly affectionate Grand daughter,   A C R

FROM MARTHA JEFFERSON RANDOLPH

Edgehill Feb. 20, 1808

This will be Delivered to you My Dear Father by Beverly Randolph[1] whom you may recollect to have seen at your house in the Spring 1806. Mrs. Madison has been so kind as to procure for him young Nourse's[2] place during his absence or untill some thing better offers. Enclosed is a little seal of My Mothers that I Must beg the favor of you to have mended and My watch key if it is possible to make it strong but as it is, it never will stand; the pin or the steel pipe continually breaking where it is bored. Adieu My Dear Father. I did not know of Beverly's intention to leave us to Morrow untill a few minutes ago or I should have written in the day, as it is I must leave you it being late bed time. Yours most affectionately,   MR.

1. Thomas Beverley Randolph was a son of William and Lucy Bolling Randolph of Chilower, Cumberland County. He was also a nephew of Thomas Mann, Jr.'s. TJ obtained for him an appointment to the military academy at West Point.
2. Charles Nourse was a son of Joseph Nourse, the registrar of the United States Treasury.

TO ELLEN WAYLES RANDOLPH

Washington Feb. 23. 08.

MY DEAREST ELLEN

I am several letters in your debt, but I am in hopes that age and occupation will privilege me against your counting letter for letter rigorously with me. The loss of your geraniums shall be replaced. I have this day planted a sprig in a small and very portable pot of earth. You give a bad account of the patriotism of the ladies of Williamsburg who are not disposed to submit to the small privations to which the embargo will subject them. I hope this will not be general and that principle and prudence will induce us all to return to the good old plan of manufacturing within our own families most of the articles we need. I can assure you from experience that we never lived so comfortably as while we were reduced to this system formerly; because we soon learnt to supply all our real wants at home, and we could not run in debt, as not an hour's credit was given for any thing. It was then we were obliged to act on the salutary maxim of 'never spending our money before we had it.' I expect it will not be long before you will spin me a dimity waistcoat. It is believed Congress will rise early in

April: but quite uncertain whether I shall get away then. My swelled face is not yet entirely well. A small knot remains on the bone, which enlarged considerably on my riding out on a raw day lately. By keeping house a few days it is again reduced to a small size. Give my tenderest love to your mama and accept it for yourself and sisters.   TH: JEFFERSON

FROM ELLEN WAYLES RANDOLPH

Edgehill Feb 26th 1808

My Dearest Grand Papa must have a bad opinion of my affection for him if he can suppose that I would stand upon ceremony with him and wait for answers to my letters without considering how much he has got to do and how little in comparison I have. It was not any thing (I am almost ashamed to confess it) but laziness which I am determined to conquer and pursuant with my Inclination write a long letter every other post (that I am not prevented) to you and will be perfectly satisfied at recieving one every month from you. If you will make the agreement I will keep up to it and often go beyond it by writing sometimes four or five posts hand running and this I will do as often as I can which will be very frequently as I have but two correspondents besides you and they never write regularly owing perhaps to my not answering their letters till many weeks after I recieve them though they are as bad in that as I am. I fear that I shall never be able to spin you a dimity waistcoat for I cannot now even spin candle wick although I could do it once. It has been 3 years since I have spun any. I have heard lately from Aunt Virginia. Her little boy[1] and herself are both quite well. Cousin Polly Carr is here at present. Cousin Dabneys little daughter[2] had a narrow escape the other day. She was in the yard and she fell down. She cried as she had hurt herself. A mule was tied near her. He broke loose and going to the place where she was stamped on her untill he had broken a silver hook and eye off of her frock. When she was carried in the house she was horribly bruised but none of her bones broken.

Cousin Evelina is to be married to Sandy Garrett of Charlottesville. Mama and Sister Ann send their love to you. You must excuse the bad writing of this letter as my pen is shocking. Adieu my dear Grandpapa. Believe me to be your most affectionate Grand Daughter.   E. W. R.

1. Wilson Miles Cary, the son of Wilson Jefferson and Virginia Randolph Cary, was born in 1806.
2. Jane Carr.

FROM ANNE CARY RANDOLPH

Edgehill March 4 *1808*

MY DEAR GRAND PAPA

As I do not know when the ship goes to Spain I have written and inclose my letter to Aunt Harriet to you. Mr. Ogilvie has broken up his school in Milton and does not mean to keep one any where this year but to devote himself to public speaking. Papa has not determined where he is to send Jefferson yet. Mama intends to make him employ the time he stays at home in learning french Arethmetic Geography and reading history. Mrs. Barber the daughter of Mr. Strode has been trying to get a female boarding school in Charlottesville. I have not heard whether it is likely she will succeed or not. Evelina is certainly to be married after March court. Cousin Polly Carr left us to day. She spent a week with Aunt Jane and Mama. Poor Aunt Lewis I believe had a dreadful journey. Mr. Peyton[1] recieved a letter from them after they had been gone ten weeks and they were 4 hundred miles from the place to which they were going. All the children are well and send their love to you. Virginia and Mary are going on very well with their lessons and will be able to read before you come. Adieu my Dear Grand Papa. Your truly affectionate Grand daughter,   A C RANDOLPH

Jefferson has just returned from Milton and says that Mr. Ogilvie has made a fresh determination to continue his school. I wish it may be a firm one.

1. Craven Peyton was a son-in-law of Lucy Jefferson Lewis (Mrs. Charles), TJ's sister.

TO ANNE CARY RANDOLPH

Washington Mar. 8. 08.

MY DEAR ANNE

I recieved yesterday your letter of the 4th. and as it said nothing of the health of the family, I presume all are well. Your letter to your aunt Harriet shall be taken care of. I wish Mrs. Barber may succeed in getting her school. She is a woman of extraordinary good sense, information and merit. Should Mr. Ogilvie discontinue his school, Jefferson cannot be better employed from morning till night than in reading French, and reading much to your mama in order to get the pronunciation. If he is not perfect master of French when he goes to Philadelphia he will not reap half the advantage of his situation. In fact there is not a science (medicine excepted) in which the best books are not in French. If he employs himself diligently in that, under your mama's help, as to pronunciation, he will lose nothing by the discontinuance of the school. I am in hopes I shall be with you in about a month. Present me to your papa and Mama and the family with tender affections,   TH: JEFFERSON

FROM ELLEN WAYLES RANDOLPH

Edgehill March 11th 1808

In compliance with my promise I take up my pen to write to my Dear Grandpapa. I was disappointed at not recieving a letter from him last post but as I was in hopes I shall get one the next I shall (this being the second week since I have written to you) perform my promise of writing every other post to inform you how we all are. I am in a fair way to raise some Bantams as the hen is now setting. She has taken up her residence in the cellar. Has laid 13 eggs and I hope will hatch some chickens. Mr. Ogilvie has broken up keeping school and Jefferson is going to the Green Springs to a Mr. Maury who they say is a very good teacher. He knows French and means to teach it. I heard yesterday from Aunt Virginia. There has been a terrible riot at *Williamsburg*.[1] 15 boys were expelled and 5. thrown in Jail and fined 20. dollars a piece. Aunt V's child is sick. Sister Ann says she would have written but as I write this post you will hear from her the next. Mama is a little unwell to day. Sister Ann has had an imposthisma on her neck. It is well now. Aunt Jane's health is still delicate although much better than it has been. How is Mrs. H. Smith? Tell me when you answer this. Are all the birds and flowers well? I soon will have a garden of my own in which I shall plant the seeds you gave me. The orange trees look very well but one of the finest is dead. We had a visit yesterday from colonel Munroe. Cornelia will soon be in joining hand. Virginia reads a little and Mary can spell words of 3 letters. She imagines that she is far before Cornelia although she often expresses apprehensions lest Cornelia should catch her and learn to read before she does. James is a sweet little fellow speaks quite well and has really grown handsome. He thinks of nothing but guns horses and dogs. Mama and sister Ann send their love to you. Give mine to Mrs. S H S. Cousin Polly Carr has quitted us. Mary desires me to tell you that she is spelling c a t cat, f a t fat, p a t pat and reading Go-to-Ann-she-is-ill. Jane-has-made-a-nice-plum-tart and will-you-have-some-of-it. Cornelia says

will you soon answer her letter. She hopes the next you get from
her will be in her own hand writing. Virginia sends her love to
Francis, and yourself. We have not had such a thing as a ball for a
long time in Milton and my dancing school is over so that I have
not been to a dance for a long time however I never regreted the
want of such kinds of amusement although I am fond of dancing I
can always find employments infinitely more amusing and instructing. I am sorry there is so little poetry in the newspapers as my
book is not full. If I can fill it sister Ann and myself will have together an excellent collection. We each have books in which we
copy such poetry as we cannot get in newspapers. My dear Grandpapa will excuse this long catalogue but I have no news to tell him
and rather than not write I will relate to him what passes among us
which though dull and uninteresting to another will serve to show
him that rather than not write at all I will this. All of us are
in health. Mama since I have been writing has got up off the bed
and feels a great deal better. My pen is shocking so that you must
excuse the bad writing of this letter. Adieu my Dear Grand Papa.
Believe me to be your most affectionate Grand Daughter,

E. W. R.

1. There was a riot at this time, but unfortunately there are no faculty
or Board of Visitors minutes for the period. It was reported in the Virginia
Argus, March 15, 1808, that the following students were expelled: "John Evins
[Evans] . . . for disorderly conduct" and also "Andrew Holmes, John Goodall,
John Ragland, William Taylor, William Buchanan, Joseph John Hill, William
Tomlin and Thomas Hayes . . . for riotous conduct." See Thomas Todd to
Charles S. Todd, June 4, 1808, and Albert Allmond (Allmand) to Andrew
Reid, Jr., April 15, 1808, in *William and Mary College Quarterly Historical
Magazine,* 1st Series, Vol. VIII (April, 1900), 222–23, and XXII, No. 1 (July,
1913), 22–23.

To Ellen Wayles Randolph

Washington Mar. 14. 08.

My dearest Ellen

Your letter of the 11th is recieved and is the best letter you have
ever written me because it is the longest and fullest of that small
news which I have most pleasure in recieving. With great news I
am more than surfieted from other quarters, and in order that your
letters may not be shortened by a bad pen of which you complain,
I have got a pen for you which will be always good, never wearing
or needing to be mended. Among my books which are gone to
Monticello, is a copy of Madame de Sevigne's letters,[1] which being
the finest models of easy letter writing you must read. If Anne

and yourself will take it by turns to write by every post, I shall
always know of the health of the family; the first object of my
concern. I am glad to learn you are at length likely to succeed with
your Bantams. They are worthy of your attention. Our birds and
flowers are well and send their love to yours. Mrs. S. H. Smith is
also well; as I learn, for I have not seen her for a long time. She
promises to visit us at Monticello this summer. I hope to be with
you about the middle or latter part of April. The trumpet of war
seems to have frightened the muses from our land or from some
other cause they do not get admission into the newspapers of late.
I hope this will find your Mama entirely recovered. Kiss her
warmly for me, not forgetting the rest of the family. I salute you
with love.   TH: JEFFERSON

1. Marie de Rabutin-Chantal, Marquise de Sévigné, *Lettres de Madame de
Sévigné à sa fille et à ses amis* . . . (Paris, 1806). Sowerby 4637.

FROM ANNE CARY RANDOLPH

Edgehill March 18 *1808*

MY DEAR GRAND PAPA

Ellen and my self have agreed that we will write to you every
post that Mama and Papa do not so that you may never be more
than a week without hearing from us. I am very anxious to go to
Monticello to see how the flowers come on but Papa has not a
horse that can be riden by a lady with safety. I hear however from
them once or twice a week by Burwell[1] for I never fail to enquire
after their health. The last news was that they were all coming up
very well particularly the tulips of which he counted at least
forty flourishing one's. You will be at home time enough to see
them all bloom. The Straw berries I am sorry to say I cannot give,
so good an account of. I put them when they came in a sheltered
place but the cold weather killed them, I have put out fresh
leaves this spring and I hope some more of them will. The earth
in which they were put was very bad and I have been afraid to
transplant them. It is very poor clay and gets baked as hard as a
brick by the sun. The winter has been so wet that they have not
required watering, but I have done it occasionally this spring
with water that had been standing in the sun, and used a watering
pot with such small holes, that it was exactly like a shower. The
embargo has set every body to making homespun, Mama has made
157 yards since October, you will see all the children clothed in it.
There has been the greatest number of wild pigeons this spring

that I ever saw, Mr. Craven they say by means of his net has cought nearly three thousand. He kills some days 700 and seldom less than three or four hundred. He salts and barrels them like fish for his people. All the children send their love to you and are well but Mary who is a little indisposed. I am afraid the cider you got of Mrs. Clarke this year is bad ours is, and I hear great complaints of it in general. It is said that the summer was so wet that all the apples were watery and the cider also. Adieu my Dear Grand Papa. Your truly affectionate Grand daughter,

A C. R

I enclose you some white violets but fear they will lose their smell before they reach you.

1. Burwell was a trusted slave of TJ's.

From Ellen Wayles Randolph

Edgehill March 18th 1808

I am glad my Dear Grandpapa expresses approbation at my writing about little things as I always shall have enough to say to you in my letters. I shall be much obliged to you for the pen. It will be very convenient and usefull to me as I have a great deal of writing to do. Pray in your next inform me what it is made of. I guess it is glass. I shall certainly read Madame de Sevigne's letters. I have heard they were the most elegantly written letters in the world. Cornelia has got in joining hand at last. She has begun arithmetic. Virginia goes on tolerably poor. Mary is sick. Mama is entirely recovered. I have not yet heard of cousin Evelinas marriage although I suppose it was yesterday as report says that the 17th was the day fixed on. Uncle William is with us now. Mr. Ogilvie has gone to Staunton. He is very much ashamed of the indecission he has shown concerning the breaking up of his school. He first said he would not then that he would then he was uncertain but at last he has gone away. Jefferson has changed his plan. He is to remain at home and carry on his arithmetic his geography History Latin and French. James has given the paper a kiss to be sent to you. The orange trees still look well. I am glad to hear that all your birds and flowers are well. We have had one or two violets in bloom and several persian Iris's. We all look forward with great impatience to the time when you are to come back to Monticello. How slow time passes away and how heavy it hangs on our hands when we expect to see any one whom we all love so tenderly as we do you. Papa has been to Monticello. He says the hall is very beautifull now that it is done.[1] A fire broke out here some time ago. It burnt a mile of fencing and two empty tobacco houses. This news is very trifling but as you have assured me you like it I shall not hesitate to fill up my letter with it. My bantam will hatch in 10 days and I hope I shall raise some of her chickens but they are so delicate. She hatched some last year. We took great care of them but they died. I am still reading Millot to mama and Justin to myself.[2] Aunt Jane is very well. You are the only correspondent I have and therefore I can write to you very often. You desire me to write every other post but I shall sometimes break through that rule and trespass on your patience by writing every post as I have no body else to correspond with and when I get the pen you have given me I shall write a great deal indeed. Harriet Aunt Janes second daughter has been very ill and poor little Mary is sick. She sends her love to you as do mama Sister Ann and all the rest of the children. They are very much pleased at the thoughts of seeing Francis next summer. I think James is a little like him in person. Does he nurse as much as he used to do formerly? All the little ones send their love to him. Give mine to Mrs. S. H. Smith. I am very glad to hear she is coming to Monticello. I wish to see her again. She is a most excellent woman. I shall always be gratefull to her for her kindness to me when I was in Washington. I suppose by your saying you have not seen her lately she is in the country. I am very sorry that Mars has driven the muses away from the united States as I fear my book will never get full. Mama intends to clothe us in homespun this year. I shall like it very well. We have had fine weather for a long time which has done a great deal of good to our plants. The violets are green and budding. One bloomed on the 17th. The honeysuckle has several green leaves. The orange trees look as fresh and as well as can be. I shall say nothing of Sister Anns charges as she intends herself to give you an account of your tulips tuberoses strawberries &c. &c. &c. I do not know how to make an et cetera and therefore you must think there is one after strawberries and not take that awkward mark for one. I think my dear Grand Papa you can have no reason to complain of the shortness of this letter as I have spun it out to a great length. [So, I] therefore bid you adieu and will only subscribe myself as my [dear] Grandpapa your affectionate grand Daughter,   E. W. RANDOLPH

1. Progress was slow at Monticello when it is recalled that the remodeling had begun fifteen years before the hall was completed.

2. Possibly *Justin's History of the World* (London, 1606). See footnote, TJ to ACR, February 26, 1802.

To Anne Cary Randolph

Washington Mar. 22. 08.

My dear Anne

My reason for desiring Ellen and yourself to write alternately was not that I did not wish to hear from you both oftener, but that I could not probably find time to answer more than one letter a week. I am sorry our strawberries are unpromising; however I trust they will put out soon. If some sand and stable manure were put on the earth, the waterings would carry both down into the clay and loosen and enrich it. But we had better not transplant them till we get them to Monticello, where we will take out the whole sod unbroken, and set it in the ground without having disturbed the roots. I ate strawberries from these plants last October after my return to this place. I inclose you some seed of the Beny, or Oriental Sesamum.[1] This is among the most valuable acquisitions our country has ever made. It yields an oil equal to the finest olive oil. I recieved a bottle of it, and tried it with a great deal of company for many days, having a dish of sallad dressed with that and another with olive oil, and nobody could distinguish them. An acre yields 10. bushels of seed, each bushel giving three gallons of oil. An acre therefore, besides our sallad oil, would furnish all kitchen and family uses, most of them better than with lard or butter. You had better direct Wormly to plant these seeds in some open place in the nursery, by dropping two or three seeds every 10. or 12. I. along a row, and his rows 2. feet apart. The plant grows somewhat like hemp. It was brought to S. Carolina from Africa by the negroes, who alone have hitherto cultivated it in the Carolinas and Georgia. They bake it in their bread, boil it with greens, enrich their broth etc. It is not doubted it will grow well as far North as Jersey, tho' McMahon places it among greenhouse plants. Adieu my dear Anne. Present my tender affections to the family.   TH: JEFFERSON

1. Oriental Sesamum (*Sesamum indicum* or *orientale*): used in salad dressings; was first cultivated in Africa and Asia. TJ usually referred to it as benne seed.

From Ellen Wayles Randolph

Edgehill March 25th. 1808.

I shall write a few lines to inform my dear Grandpapa that all are well here except James and he is not very sick. All the plants are well. We have a great many flowers in bloom Narcissus's Daffadils Hyacinths Periwinkle and a great number of white violets. My bantam will hatch next week. That is all the news I have got to tell you except that Jefferson is going on very well with his studies. I am reading Diodorus Sicubus.[1] Cornelia goes on tolerably with her writing and Virginia and Mary still continue fond of their books. Give my love to Mrs. S. H. S. when you see her next. Write to me next post. My pen is not very good you can perceive by the writing of this letter. Mama Sister Ann and all the children send their love to you. Adieu my dearest grand Papa and beleive me to be your most affectionate Grand Daughter,

ELLENORA W. RANDOLPH

1. Diodorus Siculus wrote a world history in forty books c. 21 B.C. Sowerby 37 and 38.

TO ELLEN WAYLES RANDOLPH

Washington Mar. 29. 08.

MY DEAR ELLEN

I recieved yesterday yours of the 25th. and have also to acknolege that of the 18th. You asked whether the pen which is not to wear out is made of glass? No. Guess again. I am glad to hear you expect a family of Bantams. Take good care of them. Is it not best to put the hen into a tobacco stick coop in and round which the chickens will always stay. The properest way to make an et-caetera is thus &c. Can you guess why? If you cannot, call Jefferson to your aid. Our newspapers are so barren that I have been obliged to go to Paris for a piece of poetry for you, or at least to a Paris paper. I must here close, being under an attack of periodical head-ach.[1] It began on Friday last. Sunday it was severe. Yesterday more moderate so that I hope it is on the wane. About an hour in the morning is all the time I have to write in the day. I have given you a part of that. I have kissed this paper, which James must take off with his lips. There is one also for your Mama, yourself and sisters. I bless you all. Adieu.   TH: JEFFERSON

1. This was a relatively mild attack lasting only about two weeks.

FROM ELLEN WAYLES RANDOLPH

Edgehill April 1st 1808.

My dear Grand papa's letter of the 29th arrived safe yesterday and brought the disagreeable news of his being unwell but we all

sincerely wish and hope that he will soon recover and come on to
see us all again. I will give another guess about the pen. It is
steel is it not? My bantam has hatched 8. pretty little chickens and
I shall follow your advice about her treatment. The orange trees
are well. Sister Ann is gone to Monticello to see about the flowers
and plant the Beny. 3 of your Alpine strawberries are flourishing.
Mr. Burwell has just sent me some of the seed of the Ice plant.
I am told it is a very beautifull flower. I cannot guess why an
et-caetera should be made in the manner you wrote the word.
If it is not that the figure represents the E. T. and the C. caetera.
Mama Sister Ann and all the children are quite well and send
their love to you. Adieu my dearest grandpapa. Believe me to be
(with the sincerest wishes for your health) your most affectionate
grand daughter,   E. W. RANDOLPH

TO CORNELIA JEFFERSON RANDOLPH

Washington Apr. 3. 08.

MY DEAR CORNELIA

I have owed you a letter two months, but have had nothing to
write about, till last night I found in a newspaper the four lines
which I now inclose you: and as you are learning to write, they will
be a good lesson to convince you of the importance of minding
your stops in writing. I allow you a day to find out yourself how to
read these lincs so as to make them true. If you cannot do it in
that time you may call in assistance. At the same time I will give
you four other lines which I learnt when I was but a little older
than you, and I still remember.

        I've seen the sea all in a blaze of fire
        I've seen a house high as the moon and higher
        I've seen the sun at twelve oclock at night
        I've seen the man who saw this wondrous sight.[1]

All this is true, whatever you may think of it at first reading
I mentioned in my letter of last week to Ellen that I was under
an attack of periodical head-ach. This is the 10th. day. It has
been very moderate and yesterday did not last more than 3. hours.
Tell your Mama that I fear I shall not get away as soon as I
expected. Congress has spent the last 5. days without employing
a single hour on the business necessary to be finished. Kiss her
for me, and all the sisterhood. To Jefferson I give my hand, to
your papa my affectionate salutations. You have always my love,

                                             TH: JEFFERSON

1. See F. J. Harvey Dalton, *Children's Books in England* (Cambridge, 1958), 59–61. There were twelve lines to this little poem, which came from Thomas White, *A Little Book for Little Children*, which appeared in the latter half of the 17th century in England. TJ's version varies slightly from the original, but is without any doubt from White's six rhyming couplets.

On the verso in Cornelia's hand:
The boundaries
The mountains
The capes
The isthmuses
The peninsulas
The islands
The oceans
The inland season gulphs
The straits
The lakes
The rivers

To Ellen Wayles Randolph

Washington Apr. 12. 08.

My dearest Ellen

Your letter of Apr. 1. came to hand only yesterday. I presume you sent it a little too late for the post and that it has lain a week at Milton. You have guessed rightly both as to the pen and the &c. I am entirely recovered of my head-ach. Congress have come to a resolution to adjourn on the 25th. of this month. I suppose I shall get away some time in the first week in May. What particular morning I shall catch you abed I cannot say. We had our first shad[1] here on the 19th. of March, and the first Asparagus on the 6th. of this month. When had you these things? Your letters of the 16th. 23d. and 30th. will still find me here. My affectionate love to everybody.   Th: Jefferson

1. According to the *Farm Book,* TJ used fish to vary the diet of pork and beef not only for his own table but also for his slaves'. The fish diet included herring, carp, and shad when the run occurred during the spring; shad was served chiefly on TJ's own table. See *Farm Book.*

From Ellen Wayles Randolph

Edgehill April 14. *1808*

I have at length guessed right my dear Grandpapa, about the pen, and am very glad to find it is made of steel. The change in the post was the cause of your not recieving my letter of the first of the month. It goes out now much earlier than it formerly did. I am delighted to hear that your head-ach is over and that you are to come home so soon. Mr. Mrs. and the two Miss Lindseys[1] spent a few days with us; the young ladies, Sister Ann, and myself, went over to Monticello; I think the hall, with its gravel coloured border is the most beautifull room I ever was in, without excepting the drawing rooms at Washington. The dining room is also greatly improved. The pillars of the portico are rough cast and look very well. All the railing on the top of the house finished and painted. I wont say any thing of the flower beds. That is sister Anns part. The level is spoilt nearly. Mr. Bacon has made a mistake (I presume) and covered it with charcoal instead of manure; it looks rather dismal where ever the grass has not grown. It is quite black and is excessively dirty to walk on. It is not near as bad as it was but it is still disagreable and ugly. They are finishing your terrace now. The sheep eat up 4 orange trees and bit half of the finest besides, when we put them out; however I have 3 tolerably good though they are only 2 inches high. They are all mean little things except that which the sheep bit, but they are very young. The third of April snow drops bloomed. You have none I believe. They are very beautiful and I will give you mine if you want them, and have them set in your garden when we go to Monticello. We have had shad the latter end of march; we have got no asparagus beds here and I was so much taken up with looking at the house that I did not inquire about the vegetables at Monticello, besides we stayed but a short time. Aunt Virginia is well. All our family except James are well also. Cornelia was very much delighted with your letter, she easily found out the verse as she had seen many before of the same kind. Virginia and Mary send their love to you. I am reading Diodorus Siculus. I began to learn Spanish, but I have not said a lesson for a long time. I must take it up again for I wish to know it. I cannot read french entirely without a dictionary yet. Adieu my dearest Grandpapa, I am your most affectionate Grand Daughter,   E. W. RANDOLPH.

P S. I beg you to send the inclosed to Miss Forrest.

1. Colonel and Mrs. Reuben Lindsay were Albemarle friends and neighbors of the Monticello family. Reference here is to two of their three daughters, Sarah, Elizabeth, and Maria.

FROM ANNE CARY RANDOLPH

Edgehill April 15 *1808*

I should certainly have answered My Dear Grand Papas letter by the last post, but I was very busy preparing to go to Evelinas wedding which I declined afterwards, on hearing that it was not to be untill the 16. of this month. I have been twice to Monticello to see the sesamum and governor Lewis's pea planted. The hyacinth's were in bloom, they are superb ones. The Tulips are all budding. Neither the hyacinths nor Tulips grow as regularly this spring as they did the Last. Wormley in taking them up left some small roots in the ground which have come up about in the bed and not in the rows with the others. The Strawberries Artichokes Salsafie Asparagus and Golden willow all look very well. Of the Alpine Straw berries that Davy brought, 3 are flourishing. But I am afraid the others are entirely dead. All the children are well and send their Love to you. Adieu My Dear, Dear Grand Papa. Your most affectionate Grand Daughter,   A C R

TO MARTHA JEFFERSON RANDOLPH

Washington Apr. 17. 08.

MY DEAREST MARTHA

My latest news from Edgehill was Ellen's letter of the 1st. inst. which seems to have closed her weekly engagements, as otherwise the 8th. and 15th. would have been here. I think Congress will certainly rise on the 25th. The only question of length is the giving the Executive a power to suspend the embargo in the events of peace or of the orders and decrees being withdrawn. The members seem determined to set it out and take the question to-night, and for that purpose have ordered refreshments to be carried to the capitol for them. If this question is closed to-night, there will be nothing to prevent their rising on the day fixed: in that case I think I shall leave this within 10. days after; probably on the 5th. and breakfast with you on the 8th. Mr. Burwell and Mr. Coles will be with me. I am in hopes that Mr. Bacon, under your direction, will have laid in those provisions which the market of the day does not offer, and that the groceries which left this on the 12th. of March will have been safely stored at Monticello. If not, I will ask the favor of Mr. Randolph to be on the look-out for their arrival at Milton, and notify Bacon of it immediately. I tender to him, yourself and all the fireside my warmest affections.

TH: JEFFERSON

From Ellen Wayles Randolph

Edgehill April 21st 1808.

My dearest Grandpapa must not imagine because he received no letter last post that I did not write for the post now goes out Friday and my letter was too late for it but I send it to him now. We have had blue and white lilacs blue and white flags and Jonquils. I found also in the woods a great many mountain cowslips and wild Ranunculus besides other wild flowers. I have got the seed of the Jerusalem cherry which I am told is very beautifull. Aunt Jane had asparagus the same time that you had. Will you fetch me a sprig of geranium when you come in. Your 3 strawberries look very well. All our family are in good health. How delighted we shall be when we see you drive up to the door. Uncle Randolph Jefferson[1] is with us and Cousin Nancy Neville[2] in the neighbourhood. You must excuse this short letter and the badness of the writing for my pen is horrible and I can scarcely see to subscribe myself. My dearest Grandfather your affectionate Grand Daughter.   E. W. R.

1. Randolph Jefferson was TJ's younger brother and a twin of Anna Scott Jefferson Marks (Mrs. Hastings). He resided at Snowden, a Buckingham County farm located across the James River from the present-day Scottsville in Albemarle County. Little is known of him, the best source being *Thomas Jefferson and His Unknown Brother Randolph* (Charlottesville, 1942), edited by Bernard Mayo. This contains a brief biographical sketch and a number of letters between TJ and Randolph.
2. Anna Scott Jefferson, a daughter of Randolph Jefferson, who married Colonel Zachariah Nevil of Nelson County, a one-time United States congressman.

To Martha Jefferson Randolph

Washington Apr. 25. 08.

My dear daughter

Davy arrived last night with your letter of the 23d. and as he will stay some days and then return slowly with a lame horse I take advantage of this day's post to answer it. The recommendations for military appointment came too late. As it was impracticable for the Executive to select the best characters for command through all the states, we apportioned the men to be raised and the officers to command them among the states in proportion to their militia, then gave to each delegation in Congress all the recommendations we had recieved, and left to them to make the selection out of these or such better subjects as they knew. They in general distributed the appointments among their districts, and each selected for his district. In Virginia there were about 3. officers for every two districts and the members joined in clubs as suited them. Congress having risen last night, it was of course too late to add your list to that before given to the members and already acted on. But it was probably of little consequence for Virginia had only 33 officers to furnish and there were between one and two hundred candidates. I have not yet seen the names of those selected, which I presume have been given in to the Secretary at War. I hope to leave this on the 5th. of May and to breakfast with you on the 8th. The fatigue of the session and my long absence from you render me extremely impatient to be with you and the dear family once more. Present me affectionately to Mr. Randolph and the young ones and believe me tout à vous,

TH: JEFFERSON

To ELLEN WAYLES RANDOLPH

Washington May 3. 08.

MY DEAR ELLEN

As you insist I shall write you one more letter before my departure. This is to inform you that altho' I have not entirely abandoned the hope of setting out on the 5th. yet I think it more probable I shall be detained to the 6th. so that if I do not catch you in bed on Sunday, expect it on Monday. Your's affectionately,

TH: JEFFERSON

To MARTHA JEFFERSON RANDOLPH

Washington June 21.08.

MY DEAR MARTHA

We got in good time to dinner at Montpelier[1] the day I left you, and the next two days being cool, we reached this place a little in the night, having come a little over 100. miles in the two days without inconvenience to ourselves or horses. Mr. Madison arrived here the next day. Mr. Gallatin and Rodney[2] are still absent. Mr. Ogilvie has been here sometime lecturing, to very unequal audiences of from 15. to 50. but with universal applause. He had proposed to set out for Baltimore to-day but I believe he has agreed to stay a week longer. He expressed surprise and chagrin at the deficiency in the return of my books. He seems strongly persuaded that he did not take out the Baskerville Milton or Smith's wealth of nations,[3] because he had a Milton and Smith of his own, but was confident they would be found among his books. I sent off a few days ago a supply of groceries for Monticello. I did not send either coffee or tea, under an idea, I do not know whether recieved from you or not, that there is enough of those articles remaining to serve during the next visit. I must pray you to inform me immediately if this is not so, as there is yet time enough to forward a supply. The good health and calm of this place leaves us without news, except as to Mrs. Harrison, who is in an irrecoverable state of health. All doubt of the election of Mr. Madison has vanished, altho' some of the New York papers still keep up an useless fire. Present me affectionately to Mr. Randolph and to all our dear children, and be assured of my tenderest and unchangeable love for yourself.   TH: JEFFERSON

1. The home of James and Dolley Madison in Orange County.
2. Caesar A. Rodney was United States Attorney General from 1807 until 1809.
3. *Paradise Regain'd. A Poem, in Four Books . . . Printed by John Baskerville . . .* (London [1759]), or *Paradise Lost. A Poem in Twelve Books . . . Printed by John Baskerville . . .* (London [1758]). See Sowerby 4287, 4288, and 4289. Adam Smith, *An Inquiry into the Nature and Causes of the Wealth of Nations . . .* (London . . . [1784]). Sowerby 3546.

FROM MARTHA JEFFERSON RANDOLPH

Edgehill June 23 [1808]

Your conjecture with regard to the tea and Coffee was correct as we just began upon the last stock with out making any sensible impression upon them. I have no doubt therefore but there will be enough of both of those articles as well as of chocolate. Cooking wine will be wanting and the Madeira gave out before you left us. There was no white wine therefore but what was in the octagon cellars. I must beg the favor of you My Dear Father to pay a debt of Ann's very unintentionally contracted. She sent a pearl clasp to Mrs. Madison to exchange in some of the jewellers shop's for a gold chain. The price of the clasp was more than sufficient to pay for the chain, but Mrs. Madison informed me in sending the chain that she had been obliged to make a considerable sacrifice. From what she said I conjecture the chain to have cost perhaps 6 or 7 dollars more than she got for the clasp. Will you be so good as to ask her and discharge the debt. We have not heard of Colonel

Monroe's arrival yet although we presume he must be at home by this time as Higginbotham passed him on the road some days since. Eliza[1] is to be married as soon as they come up. As soon as we hear of their arrival Mr. Randolph and Ann will wait upon them. Adieu My Dearest Father. We are all well and look forward with great pleasure to the last of July. Yours with unchangeable affection,   MRANDOLPH

I forgot to mention coffee cups amongst the difficiencies of the house. We have tea cups enough but a dozen coffee cups will be requisite to meet the summer visitations and also 2 or 3 doz shallow plates.

1. The elder daughter of James Monroe, who married Judge George Hay of Virginia.

FROM ELLEN WAYLES RANDOLPH

July the 1st 1808.

It has been three weeks since my Dear Grandpapa has been away and I have not written once but I am determined now to let him see I have not forgotten my promise. We have all resumed our lessons and go on very well. Virginia is now reading and Mary spells very well. Mama has been sick but she has now quite recovered. Poor little James has a very bad breaking out. He is still a sweet fellow and begins to talk plain and so as to be understood. My bantams have grown prodigiously and are beautifull. We have had artichokes for some time and roasting ears yesterday. There is to be a great Barbacue on the 4th of July in Charlottesville to which Sister Ann is going.[1] Mama begs you will send the key of the trunk that had the curtains in it as it was not with the keys of the eight large trunks. I have no news to tell you and therefore you must excuse the shortness of this letter but next post I may be able to write a very long one to you. Adieu my dearest Grandpapa. Beleive me to be with gratitude for your kindness to us all your most affectionate grand Daughter,   E. W. R.

Sister Ann desires me to tell you she will write next post to you. Please to send the inclosed to Miss Forrest.

1. The big holiday of the year for Charlottesville and Albemarle County was the Fourth of July. The celebration included a picnic, with barbecue, fireworks, and speeches. See the Richmond *Enquirer*, July 26, 1808.

TO ELLEN WAYLES RANDOLPH

Washington July 5. 08.

MY DEAR ELLEN

Your letter was safely delivered to Miss Forrest who was here yesterday well. I thank heaven that the 4th. of July is over. It is always a day of great fatigue to me, and of some embarrasments from improper intrusions and some from unintended exclusions. We have had such a week of hot weather as has never probably been known before in this country. My thermometer has been as follows:

Monday June 27. 93.
             28. 98 (95)
             29. 96
             30. 95
      July   1. 98½ (98½)
              2. 98   (98)
              3. 95½

Yesterday I took no observation. To-day it is quite moderate. I hope this severe spell will be an acquittal for us, at least till I get home, for which I shall leave this place about the 22d. inst. You have been before hand with us in roston ears. We had cimlings[1] yesterday. Kiss your dear Mama for me and all the young ones, and assure your papa of my constant affection. Be assured yourself of my tender love.   TH: JEFFERSON
P. S. 2. men died here on the 1st. instant drinking cold water. We shall probably hear of many more in other places.

1. A simlin was a white scalloped summer squash.

TO MARTHA JEFFERSON RANDOLPH

Washington July 11. 08.

MY DEAREST MARTHA

My last letters from Edgehill mentioned that you had been indisposed but had got the better of it. Having no letter from Edgehill by this mail I can only hope you continue well. In a conversation with you on the subject of Jefferson's going to Philadelphia[1] you mentioned that Mr. Randolph thought of declining it, and I do not know whether I inferred rightly from what you said that a supposed inconvenience to me might make a part of his reason. If a disapprobation of the measure or any other reasons prevail with him against his going there, the measure certainly rests with him altogether. I only wish that so far as any supposed inconvenience to me might be a motive for declining, that that may cease to have any weight. What I mentioned in a former letter, that I would furnish his expences during my stay here, and attend to whatever concerned him, I wish to do, and can do without inconvenience. His fixed expences there will not exceed 40. or 50. D. a month, which I shall not feel while I am here. Should therefore this be the only ground of Mr. Randolph's hesitation, I intreat that it may be done away, without however any opposition to his own judgment on any other grounds which may excite any doubt with him as to the advantage of the measure. Ann's matter with Mrs. Madison has been attended to. I think it possible I may be able to leave this three or four days earlier than I mentioned in my letter to Ellen: perhaps on the 19th. 20th. or 21st. Several matters still to be done render the moment uncertain when I can clear out. But I think you will see me from Friday to Sunday or Monday. Present me affectionately to Mr. Randolph and the children and be assured of my tenderest love.   TH: JEFFERSON

1. Although merely grandfather to Thomas Jefferson Randolph, TJ was vitally interested in his education and sought to channel it into what he considered the proper direction, but never over the objections of the boy's father. He used the same method of suggesting schooling for Francis Wayles Eppes, but John Wayles Eppes gave his father-in-law a freer hand here than he did in other phases of their relationship.

FROM MARTHA JEFFERSON RANDOLPH

Edgehill July 15 1808

MY DEAREST FATHER

My health is what it allways is in the same circumstances, so precarious that for fear of accident, I shall go to Monticello on sunday 17th. where you will find us all unless any unforeseen event should happen to detain us. Mrs. Trist and Miss Brown have been with us a week and will be in the neighbourhood if not at Monticello when you arrive. With regard to Jefferson our objections were incurring so great an expense with out any certain benefit. His education is too back ward I am afraid to enable him to profit by any instructions conveyed by *lectures* and his indolence so great as to render it doubtfull whether he can be trusted to himself as much as he would be in the situation in vue. I believe that a good *common* school is the only one that would answer for him as yet. Of course My Dear Father it would *be wrong* to incur a certain evil for a very uncertain benefit and perhaps the danger of giving expense for one who certainly has very little prospect at present of any thing more than bare competency. Ann is very much obliged to you for having discharged her debt to Mrs. Madison. I must beg the favor of you if such things are to be met with in Washington to bring me a little ivory memorandum book[1] such as you used to have. I find my chicken accounts troublesome without some assistance of the kind. Adieu My Dearest Father. I write in such haste that I am afraid you will scarcely be able to read My letter. Believe me with unchangeable tenderness yours,   MR

1. TJ had been able to procure such a memorandum book while in Paris, as attested by his Account Book entry for April 2, 1786: "Pd . . . a doz ivory leaves 12/." MHi.

To Martha Jefferson Randolph

Washington July 19. 08

My dearest Martha

I drop this line merely to inform you that it is still doubtful whether I shall be ready to set off tomorrow or not till the next day. But indeed should the weather be as warm as it has been for some days I doubt whether I should venture on the road as I believe it impossible the horses should stand it or even ourselves. This day however is moderate, and if it continues so I shall have the pleasure of breakfasting with you on Saturday or Sunday at Monticello. I am glad to hear of Mrs. Trist's arrival. Present my affectionate salutations to her and tell her I shall hope to find her at Monticello and that she will make it her head quarters. All Georgetown and Washington have been searched and no such thing as an ivory book to be found. Salute Mr. Randolph and the family for me, and be assured yourself of all my love.

Th: Jefferson

To Martha Jefferson Randolph

Montpelier Sep. 30. 08.

My dearest Martha

I forgot to bring with me the gravy spoons to be converted into Dessert spoons.[1] I must therefore pray you to send them to me. I think you mentioned a spare ladle. Two ladles I think are necessary. If there be more it may come. If any body should be coming from your neighborhood to Washington, *by the stage,* they might be packed in a great mass of waste paper and a light box. Shoemaker[2] or J. Peyton could know when such a passenger offers. If none offers, Bacon may bring them in his saddle bags well done up in paper. We were delayed here by the rain yesterday, but start this morning. Mr. Madison sets out also. My new horse[3] is perfectly gentle, but so fractious and ill-tempered in difficult roads that I fear he will not answer. I salute you with tenderest affection. Mr. Randolph and the family also,

Th: Jefferson

1. TJ occasionally did this with odd and large pieces of silverware. See TJ to John Letelier, March 27, 1810, in which he directs the melting down of two silver cans given him by George Wythe (MHi).

2. Either Jonathan or Isaac, who lived in Milton, through which the stage passed; likewise, John Peyton, the unmarried brother of Craven Peyton.

3. Diomede, bought for TJ by John Wayles Eppes on about September 5, 1808, in Richmond, from Eppes's brother-in-law Richard Thweatt for $250. See Account Book December 6, 1808, and *Farm Book,* 104.

MEMORANDUM THOMAS JEFFERSON TO
THOMAS JEFFERSON RANDOLPH

Oct. 13. 08

Baltimore.   Call on Mr. P. Williamson Market street No. 72. and pay him for a dozen steel pen points sent me.

Call on Mr. Rigden, watchmaker and pay him for repairing my repeating watch, and pray him to send it by some person coming here who will undertake to bring it in his pocket.

Philadelphia.   Deliver my alarm watch to Mr. Voigt and pay him what the repair will amount to. Perhaps I may owe him for some former service of the same kind. Pay it also. Enquire for Mr. James Ronaldson, and deliver him the letter and fleece of wool. Get my Mamaluke bridle plated.

Should you be able at any time to find in the shops of Philadelphia a handsome Alabaster lamp, inform me of it, and it's price, and describe it's form, that I may judge whether to buy it or not.

I have lodged, and shall from time to time remit to Mr. Peale, money for your board, washing, fire, candles, and tickets for the lectures. You should buy a copy of John and Charles Bell's Anatomy as soon as you arrive that you may *use it* while attending the lectures in Anatomy. It is in 4. vols 8vo. and Mr. Peale will pay for it. Enter yourself for the lectures in Anatomy Natural history and Surgery all of which begin in November, and end in March. Mr. Peale will pay for the tickets amounting to 42. Dollars.

The Botanical course does not begin till April. Then you must buy a Copy of Dr. Barton's botany, new edition.

To Martha Jefferson Randolph

Washington Oct. 18. 08.

My dear Martha

I inclose you a letter for T. B. Randolph containing his appointment as a Cadet. But the lodgings at the Military school at Westpoint being entirely full, he cannot be recieved there till the 1st. of March. Indeed he could do nothing there sooner, as their vacation begins with November and ends with February. Genl. Dearborne proposed to me yesterday a new regulation respecting the Cadets. There is to be one to each company. And he proposes that those for whom there is as yet no room at the military school shall be attached at once to the company to which they are to belong and shall proceed immediately to do duty. In this case their pay and rations would commence immediately. Otherwise not till there is room for them at the school. Should we finally determine on this T. B. R.[1] will recieve instructions to repair to some particular company. If we knew in the mean time what particular captain he would prefer, perhaps we might be able to indulge his choice.

Jefferson left this on Friday. He would Stay Saturday and Sunday at Baltimore, and reach Philadelphia this day. While here he visited Maine's[2] thorn hedges, the hanging bridge,[3] Navy yard,[4] and Alexandria. When going to the latter I proposed to him to take a horse, but as he had never been in a sailing boat he preferred the packet. On his way down the river he took the masts of the vessels at Alexandria, which were in view, for Lombardy poplars, and at length asked the master of the packet if they were so. He will have a fortnight to sate himself with Philadelphia, before the lectures begin, which will be the 1st. of November. I am glad to hear that Benjamin's[5] eye is hoped not to be serious. Tell Anne that my old friend Thouin[6] of the National garden at Paris has sent me 700. species of seeds. I suppose they will contain all the fine flowers of

France, and fill all the space we have for them. My affectionate love
to all and most of all to yourself,   TH: JEFFERSON

1. Thomas Beverley Randolph.
2. Thomas Maine, nurseryman at Alexandria.
3. The bridge reached from the low promontory on the southwest shore in
Alexandria across the river to an area near the present foot of Maryland
Avenue. It was completed about 1809.
4. Located on the eastern branch of the Potomac; it was the main manufacturing establishment in Washington.
5. Benjamin Franklin Randolph, Martha's third son, was born July 16,
1808, at Edgehill.
6. André Thouin was a famous French botanist and the head gardener at
the Jardin du Roi, Paris.

FROM ELLEN WAYLES RANDOLPH

Edgehill October 20th 1808.

DEAR GRANDPAPA

Altho I have only a torn sheet of paper to write upon yet rather
than to neglect writing at all I will make use of it; as I have no
paper. It will not be in my power to write again shortly to you or
any body. Little Benjamins eye is almost well and I hope the next
letter you receive from me will inform you that there is no more
of that troublesome rising which incommoded him and alarmed us
for so long a time. Papa Mama and all the rest of the family are
well and send their love to you. Cornelia and Myself have been
going to dancing school 2 dances. Remember me to Mrs. Harrison Smith when you see her next; excuse the shortness of this
letter my dear Grandpapa for I have no news to tell you and beleive me to be your most affectionate Grand daughter, E W R.
Sister Ann sends her love to you.   EWR

Mama is afraid she will not have time to write to you this post
and bids me mention to you that Aunt Marks and myself returned
to Monticello to have the wine bottled. Two pipes of Termo[1]
which were in a crazy condition were bottled. One cask Oeras[2]
wine had leaked in the summer. The remainder was drawn off in
203 bottles. Another cask of the same wine which was tumbling
to pieces was drawn off in two smaller casks. I beleive we left all
of the wine in perfect safety if the two smaller casks which were
the best we could get are to be depended on. Burwell thinks they
will do. They had been used for water casks. Mama has sent over
twice since we came away to look at them. They were perfectlly
sound and she intends to send every week or ten days to have

them examined untill you return. Your affectionate Grand Daughter,   ELEONORA WAYLES RANDOLPH

1. Actually Terme, a Bordeaux wine from the Château Marquis de Terme. According to the Account Book purchases, this was not one of TJ's favorite wines.
2. Possibly Oiry, a champagne from the Oiry district in the Marne Valley.

TO THOMAS JEFFERSON RANDOLPH

Washington, Oct. 24th, 1808.

DEAR JEFFERSON

I inclose you a letter from Ellen, which, I presume, will inform you that all are well at Edgehill. I received yours without date of either time or place, but written, I presume, on your arrival at Philadelphia. As the commencement of your lectures is now approaching, and you will hear two lectures a day, I would recommend to you to set out from the beginning with the rule to commit to writing every evening the substance of the lectures of the day. It will be attended with many advantages. It will oblige you to attend closely to what is delivered to recall it to your memory, to understand, and to digest it in the evening; it will fix it in your memory, and enable you to refresh it at any future time. It will be much better to you than even a better digest by another hand, because it will better recall to your mind the ideas which you originally entertained and meant to abridge. Then, if once a week you will, in a letter to me, state a synopsis or summary view of the heads of the lectures of the preceding week, it will give me great satisfaction to attend to your progress, and it will further aid you by obliging you still more to generalize and to see analytically the fields of science over which you are travelling. I wish to hear of the commissions I gave you for Rigden, Voight,[1] and Ronaldson,[2] of the delivery of the letters I gave you to my friends there, and how you like your situation. This will give you matter for a long letter, which will give you as useful an exercise in writing as a pleasing one to me in reading.

God bless you, and prosper your pursuits.

TH: JEFFERSON

1. John E. Rigden; Henry Voight, a one-time Philadelphia watchmaker and a coiner at the United States Mint in Philadelphia.
2. James Ronaldson, a member of the firm of Binney & Ronaldson of Philadelphia, the first successful type-founding company in America.

To Ellen Wayles Randolph

Washington Oct. 25. 08.

My dear Ellen

Your's and your Mama's letters of the 20th. are recieved. Tell her I will take care of her accounts with Mrs. Madison. I thank you for your care of my wines. I will endeavor to send bottles for the two doubtful casks into which you have drawn a part. I put a letter from Jefferson to your Mama into your Papa's newspaper packet which went by the stage yesterday. Yours to him shall be immediately forwarded. Our races[1] begin to-day but I am kept from them by an attack of rheumatism[2] which came upon me in my sleep the night before last. It is precisely the same as that which I had at Monticello and which I then ascribed to a wrench from my horse, but now consider as a real rheumatism. When that disease is coming on us, some jostle great or small marks the moment of attack, but is falsely tho' often considered as the cause. I keep up, but can scarcely walk, and that with great pain. I suppose it will take the same course as it did at Monticello, and that I shall be well at the meeting of Congress. Give my warm affections to your Papa and Mama. Tell the latter not to forget to send the silver spoons which are to be altered by Mr. Bacon who sets off for this place on Sunday next, the 30th. Salute all the young ones, and recieve the kisses I imprint for you on this paper.

Th: Jefferson

1. TJ often attended the races while President. His Account Book entry for November 9, 1803, "Small expences at the races 1. D.–10. do. 1.D.–11. do. 1. D.," is typical of the expenses incurred. The races mentioned in this letter were presumably those of the Washington Jockey Club that were held at their track just north of the city. They staged both flat and trotting races.

2. As may be noted in a subsequent letter, to Martha on November 1, this was a mild attack.

From Martha Jefferson Randolph

Edgehill Oct. 27, 1808

My Dear Father

I have sent the 4 spoons and a large french ladle there being 2 others left, one french and one english belonging to the B S M spoons. Bacon will also give you a bundle for Jefferson which I must beg the favor of you to forward to him. In packing up the books which was left to himself to do, we have discovered them. He has left nearly one half of the Buffon. I presume the best way will be to pack them and send them to Mr. Jefferson as he will have occasion I suppose for all of them. It was *corks* and not bottles that were wanting to bottle the rest of the wine. My orders were that they should continue untill their corks gave out, which they did not do for Ellen told me there were still some corks left but as there were not enough for the whole cask they would not make a begginning but prefered using 2 water casks that may or may not answer. I shall send often to inspect them having been greatly decieved in 2 of the same description once before. I am truly concerned to hear that your rheumatism has fixed in so dreadful a part as the back. You will be obliged to try flannel next the skin in which I have very great confidence, particularly as you have never *abused* the use of it. Should the pain continue I am sure you would find relief from it. Adieu My Dear Father. I am with tenderest affection your,   M RANDOLPH

To Martha Jefferson Randolph

Washington Nov. 1. 08.

MY DEAREST MARTHA

Mr. Bacon delivered your letter and every thing else safely. I had ordered a gross of bottles to be bought: but I will now countermand them. I send on corks by the stage, for I think that water casks should be trusted no longer than necessary. The letter and bundle for Jefferson shall be forwarded. Certainly the residue of Buffon ought to be sent on to him to the care of Mr. Jefferson. When he went to Philadelphia I gave him letters to some of my friends, apprising them at the same time that I did not wish it to be the means of drawing him into society so as to interfere with the pursuits which carried him there and for which all his time would be little enough. I have since recieved the inclosed from Dr. Rush[1] which I send for your perusal and that of Mr. Randolph and to be returned to me. I had advised Jefferson every evening to commit to writing the substance of the two lectures he will have heard in the day. If to that he adds the Doctor's advice, he will be fully employed. As soon as my attak of rheumatism came on, I applied flannel to the part, and toasted a great deal before the fire. It carried it off compleatly in four days, and I am persuaded the attack at Monticello might have been shortened in the same way had it been suspected to be rheumatism. Mr. Burwell[2] passed through town a day or two ago, in such a hurry to his wedding that he did not call on us. Our campaign opens on Monday, for which we are all preparing. Present me affectionately to Mr. Randolph and the family. Ever tenderly yours,

TH: JEFFERSON

1. Dr. Benjamin Rush of Philadelphia.
2. William Armistead Burwell was hurrying to Baltimore for his marriage to Miss Letitia McCreery.

TO THOMAS JEFFERSON RANDOLPH

Washington Nov. 3. 08.

DEAR JEFFERSON

I inclose you a letter which came to me under cover of one from your mama. It was accompanied by a bundle too large for the post, and too small to be trusted by itself to the stage. I will send it under the care of the first person who shall be going on to Philadelphia, within my knolege. Your box of books and that of the model of the mammoths head, did not leave Milton till a fortnight ago. They will be a month on their passage to you. Your mama says you left out near half the volumes of Buffon. They will be packed in a box and sent after the others. Can my Marmaluke bridle bit be plated in Philadelphia? I have a letter from Dr. Rush in which he speaks favorably of you. He mentions his recommendations to you to journalize all the observations worthy of note which you hear in conversation every day. If you can do this in addition to the committing your lectures to writing, it will certainly be well to do it. It will exercise your attention to conversation, your recollection, and habituate you to composition. I salute you with constant affection.   TH: JEFFERSON

FROM THOMAS JEFFERSON RANDOLPH

Museum Nov. 5 08

DEAR GRAND FATHER

I am very sorry your watch was not ready to send by Drs. Porter or Michell as Voight had not finished it and I am afraid he has slighted it if he did it as he did mine. I purchased the lamp and sent your bridle bit to be plated which will be done in a few days. There is no such thing as a pure crystal seal in this place but I will send to N. York for one by the first of my acquaintance who goes there.

The lectures begin on the seventh and I have not been able to get Bells Anatomy nor is there a prospect of getting it shortly. I was therefore obliged to get Fifer for the present.[1] I am pleased with my situation and feel (contrary to my expectations) as happy here as I ever was, when I hear often from home. Yours affectionately,   THOMAS J RANDOLPH

1. John and Sir Charles Bell, *The Anatomy of The Human Body* (London, 1802–1804), and Andrew Fyfe, *A Compendium of the Anatomy of the Human Body* (Edinburgh, 1800), 2 volumes.

TO ANNE RANDOLPH BANKHEAD

Washington Nov. 8. 08.

MY DEAR ANNE

Not having heard of your departure [1] from Albemarle I address this letter to you expecting it will find you at that place. It covers one from Jefferson to Mr. Bankhead. In a letter I recieved yesterday from Jefferson he says 'I am pleased with my situation and feel (contrary to my expectation) as happy here as I ever was, when I hear often from home.' I hope this will stimulate yourself and Ellen particularly to write to him often, and as I shall be a safe channel of conveyance I may come in for a letter also occasionally. It will give me great pleasure to hear from yourself and Mr. Bankhead while at Port royal. I will make you returns in the same way whenever my business will permit. I trust it is Mr. Bankhead's intention to join us at Monticello in March and to take his station among my law books in the South pavilion.[2] Whatever field of practice he may propose, I do not think he can take a more advantageous stand for study. I hope therefore that he will consent to it, and that you will both ever consider yourselves as a part of our family until you shall feel the desire of separate establishment insuperable. Salute him and your Papa in my name. My love and kisses to your Mama, yourself, Ellen and the others,

TH: JEFFERSON

1. Anne Cary was married to Charles Lewis Bankhead at Monticello on September 19, 1808, by the Reverend Mr. William Crawford. Consult Albemarle County Marriage Record 1806–1808 in the county courthouse in Charlottesville, Virginia.

2. That small structure on the south side of the west lawn at the termination of the south terrace walk. His law books, as well as others, were stored here awaiting the completion of the library suite in the main house.

FROM ELLEN WAYLES RANDOLPH

November 11th 1808

DEAR GRANDPAPA

I expect every moment that They will come to carry my letters to the post office but still I have begun to write in hopes that I shall conclude my letter before the others are sent away. The sweet scented grass[1] I shall take all possible care of. The pot was broken on the way. It was tied together but I shall have to remove the grass soon in another box. Your Orange trees come on very well as to their looks but I never saw such little short things in my life. They are near eighteen months old and they are not as high (any of them) as my hand is long. Sister Ann and Mr. Bankhead left us some days before your letter arrived. Benjamins eye is entirely well except the redness which the rising has left. All the family are well and send their love to you. I beg you will forward the inclosed to My brother. Adieu my dear Grandpapa. Beleive me to be your most affectionate Grand Daughter,

E. W. R.

1. Sweet scented grass, *Anthoxanthum odoratum* L.

FROM THOMAS JEFFERSON RANDOLPH

Nov 11 Museum [1808]

DEAR GRANDFATHER

The Introductory Lectures have began this week, before I could attend any lecture at the University I was obliged to Matriculate, that is, to become a student of Medicine, which cost 4$ and Dr. Phisick raised his ticket to 15$. Dr. Wistar would not recieve any thing for his and he says I must attend Dr. Woodhouse untill he hears from you. I have purchased Bells Anatonny at 22$ being the only one for sale in the united states. Your bridle is plated tolerable well and will go in the packet with the lamps. Dr. Say[1] has your watch. I wish to join the desecting class if you have no objections, the expense will be 15 or 20$. Yours sincerely,

1. Dr. Philip Syng Physick, Dr. Caspar Wistar, Dr. James Waterhouse, and Dr. Benjamin Say.

To Ellen Wayles Randolph

Washington Nov. 15. 08.

MY DEAR ELLEN

I recieved yesterday yours of the 11th. and rejoice to hear that all are well with you. I inclose a letter from Dr. Wistar the perusal of which will be agreeable to your Papa and Mama as it respects Jefferson, and to your Papa what relates to the Mammoth.[1] Return it to me. I am glad to hear that the sweet scented grass got safe, altho' the pot did not. The sooner you put it into a larger box the better. Perhaps your papa will take the trouble to separate the roots so as to spread without endangering them. It is the anthoxanthum odoratum of the botanists, and you must now become the botanist in addition to your charge over the basse-cour. This last department will be recruited when I come home by 6. wild geese born of tamed parents, 2. summer ducks, a pair of wild turkies, 6 grey geese, much larger and handsomer than the common race of which the ganders are white. For the former department I have 700. species of seeds sent me by Mr. Thouin from the National garden of France. What will you do under all this charge? And more especially as the geese ducks &c. will be very clamorous from daylight till visited. It is lucky for you that the milk pen and sheep-cote from their distance, cannot be ascribed to your care undercolour of their belonging to the field of Natural history. I sent by Mr. Bacon some corks to compleat the bottling our wines. Was my letter forwarded to Anne? Those to Jefferson will go on to-day. Affectionate Adieux to every body.

TH: JEFFERSON

1. TJ and Dr. Caspar Wistar, Curator of the American Philosophical Society, collaborated in classifying the fossil remains sent by William Clarke to Washington from the dig at Big Bone Lick, Kentucky. This was an archeological expedition directed by William Clarke and underwritten by TJ. For one of the best articles on TJ and fossils, see Howard C. Rice, Jr., "Jefferson's Gift of Fossils To The Museum of Natural History in Paris," *Proceedings of the American Philosophical Society*, Vol. 95, No. 6 (December, 1951), 597–627.

From Martha Jefferson Randolph

Edgehill Nov. 18, 1808

I gave the keys of the wine cellar in to Dinsmore's hands who promiscd to superintend the bottling of the wine. If the bottles and corks hold out would you wish them to begin upon any other cask? And which should have the prefference? Your letter to Ann was forwarded by the same post. She left us the monday before only, in a state of such extreme dejection at the sepparation from her family that it rendered the scene a very distressing one. I have not heard from her since her arrival but I depend much upon the natural chearfulness of her disposition and the kindness of the family to restore her spirits in a short time. I have been made very happy by the accounts your correspondants give you of Jefferson. His understanding I have for many years thought favorably of. His judgement when not under the influence of passion is as good as can be expected at his age but he is indolent impatient of reproof and *at times* irritable. He is however anxious to learn rigidly correct in his morals and affectionate in his temper. I see enough of the Randolph character in him to give me some uneasiness as to the future but I hope the society into which he is thrown and the habits he may acquire at this period will counteract any propensities inimical to his future happiness. Nothing I should suppose so effectual to eradicate Jealousy and *suspicion* from a mind not absolutely confirmed in those vices as good company. I mean virtuous and well bred where he will learn that it is not customary for genteel society to indulge mean and little passions. Good manners are I believe more important in forming the character than good sense and reflection because called in to action before our habits are formed and before that period at which the understanding is sufficiently matured to be of much importance in preventing bad one's. I never was fully aware of the influence of good manner upon the morals untill I read a very sensible little book upon that subject called Le bon de la bonne compagnie[1] in which the author proves that the various little rules of etiquette which though scrupulously observed have been thought lightly of as *ceremonies* are really derived from the most amiable and virtuous feelings of the heart. The post is waiting and I must bid you adieu for fear of losing it. Ellen is at Dancing school but your grass shall be attended to with the little orange and lemon trees which being Grand Papa's are respected and remembered in all changes of the weather by every child in the house. Adieu My Very Dear Father. Believe me with no common degree of filial love yours devotedly,   MR.

Chisholm[2] took a letter out of the post office directed in your hand to Mr. Steptoe[3] but which having no other direction but the name had stopped in Milton. He begged me to break the seal insisting that there must be a letter in it for him. I did so gave him the letter and having explained the circumstance to Mr. Steptoe in the cover of the letter sealed, directed and sent it to the office.

1. Louis Dubroca, *Le ton de la bonne compagnie, ou régles de la civilité, à l'usage des personnes des deux sexes* (Paris, 1802). Martha's copy of this work is in the Alderman Library at the University of Virginia. It bears her signature, "M. Randolph Monticello." This is followed by "G W Randolph" in his handwriting.

2. Hugh Chisholm, a trusted employee of TJ's and literally a man of many trades. He worked for TJ from 1796 until 1824.

3. James Steptoe was clerk of Bedford County, a close friend of TJ's, and he resided near Poplar Forest.

FROM MARTHA JEFFERSON RANDOLPH

Edgehill Nov. 24, 1808

MY DEAREST FATHER

The small pox has broke out in Staunton and spread a general alarm, least through the medium of the stages it should be communicated. If it is easy to obtain the vaccine we should be greatly obliged to you to send us some as our three youngest children and many of our negroes have not been innoculated at all.

Looking over some of the literary magazines the other day we met with the beginning of a tale by Miss Edgeworth[1] which interested us so much that we are all anxious to see the end of it. Perhaps Mrs. H. Smith who is such a general reader may be able to tell you from what work of Miss Edgeworth's it is taken, and if not exceeding one volume in size I should be very much obliged to you to get it and send it to me. "The Modern Griselda" is the name of the tale, or novel, I do not know which, having read only as much as one number of a magazine contained and not possessing the following numbers. Old Col. Lewis[2] is confined to his bed and has lost the use of his hands entirely. Mr. Randolph went to see him last sunday and thinks from his general appearance that he can hold out but very little longer. Virginia leaves us to morrow.[3] They have obtained the old gentleman's consent to go to house keeping at Cary's brook next summer; Mr. Randolph proposed to Doctor Bankhead to purchase for his son *her* portion of the Bedford Lands, which will be laid off adjoining Ann's.[4] He has consented and by that means they will have near 1000 acres of the best land where they mean finally to settle, and Virginia's portion being converted in to *money* will enable Wilson to buy Miles's part of the Cary's brook estate.[5] So that nothing but a sad experience of the uncertainty of the fairest prospects of happiness, would prevent my being perfectly satisfied with the situation of our two eldest Daughters but such is the instability of human affairs that no man can be pronounced a "happy one before his death" so said Solon, and so too many of us have experienced. Adieu My Very Dear Father. To contribute to the utmost of my abilities to the happiness of your life shall constitute the supreme felicity of mine. Yours tenderly,   MR.

1. Maria Edgeworth, *The Modern Griselda*. For a complete bibliography of Miss Edgeworth's writing, see Bertha Coolidge Slade, *Maria Edgeworth, 1767–1849; A Bibliographical Tribute* (London, [1937]).

2. Colonel Nicholas Lewis of The Farm, or Charles Lewis of North Garden.

3. Virginia Randolph and Wilson Jefferson Cary were married at Monticello on August 5, 1805.

4. This plan was not acted upon. See Albemarle County Deed Book, Number 23, 96–97, for the property settlement between Dr. John L. Bankhead and Thomas Mann Randolph, Jr., for Anne Cary Randolph and Charles L. Bankhead.

5. The Carysbrook estate belonged to Wilson Miles Cary, the Miles mentioned by Martha; he was Wilson Jefferson Cary's grandfather. On October 9, 1809, "in consideration of the natural love and affection," he deeded 100 acres of this estate to his grandson, the remainder after his death in 1817. See Fiduciary Account Book, Number 3, page 2a, in Fluvanna County Clerk's office, Palmyra, Virginia.

To Thomas Jefferson Randolph

Washington Nov. 24th. o8

MY DEAR JEFFERSON

I have just recieved the inclosed letter under cover from Mr. Bankhead which I presume is from Anne and will inform you she is well. Mr. Bankhead has consented to go and pursue his studies at Monticello, and live with us till his pursuits or circumstances may require a separate establishment. Your situation, thrown at such a distance from us and alone, cannot but give us all, great anxieties for you. As much has been secured for you, by your particular position and the acquaintance to which you have been recommended, as could be done towards shielding you from the dangers which surround you. But thrown on a wide world, among entire strangers without a friend or guardian to advise so young too and with so little experience of mankind, your dangers are great, and still your safety must rest on yourself. A determination never to do what is wrong, prudence, and good humor, will go far towards securing to you the estimation of the world. When I recollect that at 14. years of age, the whole care and direction of my self was thrown on my self entirely, without a relation or friend qualified to advise or guide me, and recollect the various sorts of bad company with which I associated from time to time, I am astonished I did not turn off with some of them, and become as worthless to society as they were. I had the good fortune to become acquainted very early with some characters of very high standing, and to feel the incessant wish that I could even become what they were. Under temptations and difficulties, I could ask myself what would Dr. Small, Mr. Wythe, Peyton Randolph do in this situation? What course in it will ensure me their approbation? I am certain that this mode of deciding on my conduct tended more to it's correctness than any reasoning powers I possessed. Knowing the even and dignified line they pursued, I could never doubt for a moment which of two courses would be in character for them. Whereas seeking the same object through a process of moral reasoning, and with the jaundiced eye of youth, I should often have erred. From the circumstances of my position I was often thrown into the society of horseracers, cardplayers, Foxhunters, scientific and professional men, and of dignified men; and many a time have I asked myself, in the enthusiastic moment of the death of a fox, the victory of a favorite horse, the issue of a question eloquently argued at the bar or in the great Council of the nation, well, which of these kinds of reputation should I prefer? That of a horse jockey? A foxhunter? An Orator? Or the honest advocate of my country's rights? Be assured my dear Jefferson, that these little returns into ourselves, this self-cathechising habit, is not trifling, nor useless, but leads to the prudent selection and steady pursuits of what is right? I have mentioned good humor as one of the preservatives of our peace and tranquillity. It is among the most effectual, and it's effect is so well imitated and aided artificially by politeness, that this also becomes an acquisition of first rate value. In truth, politeness is artificial good humor, it covers the natural want of it, and ends by rendering habitual a substitute nearly equivalent to the real virtue. It is the practice of sacrificing to those whom we meet in society all the little conveniences and preferences which will gratify them, and deprive us of nothing worth a moment's consideration; it is the giving a pleasing and flattering turn to our expressions which will conciliate others, and make them pleased with us as well as themselves. How cheap a price for the good will of another! When this is in return for a rude thing said by another, it brings him to his senses, it mortifies and corrects him in the most salutary way, and places him at the feet of your good nature in the eyes of the company. But in stating prudential rules for our government in society I must not omit the important one of never entering into dispute or argument with another. I never yet saw an instance of one of two disputants convincing the other by argument. I have seen many of their getting warm, becoming rude, and shooting one another. Conviction is the effect of our own dispassionate reasoning, either in solitude, or weighing within ourselves dispassionately what we hear from others standing uncommitted in argument ourselves. It was one of the rules which above all others made Doctr. Franklin the most amiable of men in society, 'never to contradict any body.' If he was urged to anounce an opinion, he did it rather by asking questions, as if for information, or by suggesting doubts. When I hear another express an opinion, which is not mine, I say to myself, He has a right to his opinion, as I to mine; why should I question it. His error does me no injury, and shall I become a Don Quixot to bring all men by force of argument, to one opinion? If a fact be misstated, it is probable he is gratified by a belief of it, and I have no right to deprive him of the gratification. If he wants information he will ask it, and then I will give it in measured terms; but if he still believes his own story, and shows a desire to dispute the fact with me, I hear him and say nothing. It is his affair, not mine, if he prefers error. There are two classes of disputants most frequently to be met with among us. The first is of young students just entered the threshold of science, with a first view of it's outlines, not yet filled up with the details and modifications which a further progress would bring to their knoledge. The other consists of the ill-tempered and rude men in society who have taken up a passion for politics. (Good humor and politeness never introduce into mixed society a question on which they foresee there will be a difference of opinion.) From both of these classes of disputants, my dear Jefferson, keep aloof, as you would from the infected subjects of yellow fever or pestilence. Consider yourself, when with them, as among the patients of Bedlam needing medical more than moral counsel. Be a listener only, keep within yourself, and endeavor to establish with yourself the habit of silence, especially in politics. In the fevered state of our country, no good can ever result from any attempt to set one of these fiery zealots to rights either in fact or principle. They are determined as to the facts they will believe, and the opinions on which they will act. Get by them, therefore as you would by an angry bull: it is not for a man of sense to dispute the road with such an animal. You will be more exposed than

others to have these animals shaking their horns at you, because
of the relation in which you stand with me and to hate me as a
chief in the antagonist party your presence will be to them what
the vomit-grass is to the sick dog a nostrum for producing an
ejaculation. Look upon them exactly with that eye, and pity
them as objects to whom you can administer only occasional ease.
My character is not within their power. It is in the hands of my
fellow citizens at large, and will be consigned to honor or infamy
by the verdict of the republican mass of our country, according
to what themselves will have seen, not what their enemies and
mine shall have said. Never therefore consider these puppies in
politics as requiring any notice from you, and always shew that
you are not afraid to leave my character to the umpirage of public
opinion. Look steadily to the pursuits which have carried you to
Philadelphia, be very select in the society you attach yourself to;
avoid taverns, drinkers, smoakers, and idlers and dissipated persons generally; for it is with such that broils and contentions arise,
and you will find your path more easy and tranquil. The limits
of my paper warn me that it is time for me to close with my affectionate Adieux.   TH: JEFFERSON
P. S. Present me affectionately to Mr. Ogilvie, and in doing the
same to Mr. Peale tell him I am writing with his polygraph[1] and
shall send him mine the first moment I have leisure enough to
pack it.

1. Literally a machine for making several copies of writing at once. TJ
owned several of the kind mentioned in this letter, which was the invention
of a Mr. Hawkins, an Englishman, who at one time resided near Frankfort,
Pennsylvania. This was the two-pen type and is the one TJ suggested improvements on to Charles Willson Peale. See correspondence between TJ
and Peale in the Library of Congress and Historical Society of Pennsylvania.

FROM ANNE RANDOLPH BANKHEAD

Port Royal November 26 *1808*

I should have answered My Dear Grand Papas letter by the Last
post but Mr. Bankhead wrote and as I have seldom time we agreed
never to write to gether that you might hear from us often. On
coming from Edgehill I left all the flowers in Ellens care, however
I shall be with you early enough in march to assist about the
border, which the old French Gentlemans[1] present if you mean
to plant them there, with the wild and bulbous rooted ones we
have already, will compleatly fill. Although no longer under

Mama's eye I do not altogether neglect my lessons, but make it a point to spend every morning in my room reading French, History and in doing sums. That at least I may not Lose what has cost her so much pains and anxiety to teach me. The former I read with more ease than ever. Arethmetic I have so little occasion for, that without *that* precaution I should entirely forget it. The Histories that I brought with me are, an abridgment of the Roman history (merely to refresh my memory) Middletons Cicero Thomsons Caesars and Tacitus. I shall be as industrious as the dissipation of the place will permit, our evenings are spent in sewing while one of the family reads a play to us. They are all very kind and Friendly to me, indeed I am as happy as I can be seperated from all my relations. Adieu My Dear Grand Papa. I long for the time to come when we shall meet again. Untill then believe me to be your most affectionate Grand Daughter,

A C B

I inclose you some Acasia flowers which Mr. Lomax[2] sent me from the tree that you gave him I think he says in 76.

1. André Thouin.
2. Thomas Lomax was a friend and fellow horticulturalist of TJ's who was born at Portotabago (Port Tobacco, Port Tobaco), Caroline County, in 1746.

To Martha Jefferson Randolph

Washington Nov. 29. 08.

My dearest Martha

Yours of the 18th. has been recieved. I recieved a letter lately from Mr. Bankhead informing me he and Anne were well and agreeing to come and live with us until the population of the hive shall force a swarm or the concourse of clients call for and afford a separate establishment. I am happy that they think of settling ultimately at Poplar forest. It is a fine establishment and good neighborhood. I rejoice also that Virginia's accomodation has been increased by it. I inclose you Mrs. Harrison Smith's answer on the subject of the Novel. By the post-rider I send your watch, key, and ring. In the same paper you will find a scab of vaccine which I have this moment recieved from Dr. Worthington.[1] He sais the surface of the scab is to be paired with the point of a lancet to near the middle of it's thickness. Then putting on it a drop of tepid water, work it up with the point of the lancet till that is well impregnated, and then insert the launcet horizontally between the scarf skin and skin without making any wound.

This scab is old, and therefore the Doctr. has not entire confidence in it. He will write to Baltimore this evening for fresh matter which you shall have by the next post. I have been delayed to the very moment of making up the mail, and must therefore close with my best affections to Mr. Randolph and the children, and my constant and tenderest love to yourself.

TH: JEFFERSON

1. Dr. Charles Worthington.

FROM THOMAS JEFFERSON RANDOLPH

Philadelphia Museum Dec 3 [1808]

DEAR GRANDFATHER

I recieved yours of the 24th and it gives me great pleasure to hear that sister Ann and her husband will live with us. I am aware of the dangers of my situation and of my own inexperience; I have heard much, and seen little of the vices and follies of the world and distrusting my own knowlegde of human nature, I have shuned all unnecessary intercourse with persons not previously recommended to my acquaintance, by some friend more experienced than myself; I go no where and I live in retirement amongst thousands; without your advice, Politics would have been, the rock upon which I should have split ere long; Although I never speak on the subject myself, yet when I hear these vile pensioners and Miscreants expressing Tory sentiments and abusing you, it is with difficulty I can restrain myself. You have no doubt expected a performance of my promise, I attempted it once, but it took me all day sunday and I could not finish in twelve what the professors expressed in fourteen. I however do it every night on Anatomy and chemistry, but on surgery I do not understand it sufficiently to do it regularly; when he (Dr. physick) lectures on the fresh subject I hope I shall understand it better. Yours affectionately,   THOS. J. RANDOLPH

P S The cover of the letter you inclosed from Mother bore evident marks of having been broken open as likewise several others.

TO MARTHA JEFFERSON RANDOLPH

Washington Dec. 6. 08.

MY DEAREST MARTHA

I inclose you a letter from Jefferson which I presume will inform you he is well, and I send you one from Dr. Wistar which will give you satisfaction. Be so good as to return it. I had one from Anne 2. or 3. days ago, when all were well. She says they will be with us early in March. I sent you the last week by the post rider your watch, watch key and ring, which I hope got safe to hand. I forgot to mention that the chrystal side of the watch opens with perfect ease, if while you insert your left thumb nail at the place of opening, you at the same time press with the other thumb, the stem of the watch, as you would to make a watch repeat. I have been confined to the house these 3. weeks with a swelled face. For 4. or 5. days I suffered much, but was relieved by a suppuration and have since been able to extract the tooth. There is too much swelling still to go out, but I hope to be able to take my usual rides in 3. or 4. days more.[1] Present me affectionately to Mr. Randolph and the family, and be assured yourself of my warmest love.   TH: JEFFERSON

1. Probably an abscessed tooth that was successfully extracted. He was actually confined to the house for about six weeks. See "Medical Chronology."

To THOMAS JEFFERSON RANDOLPH

Washington Dec. 7. 08

DEAR JEFFERSON

I have recieved a letter from Anne which informs me she is well. I had letters from home two days ago, when all were well there; I must get you to call on Mr. Mc.Alister,[1] optician in Chestnut street and pay him 2. Dollars for me; and on old Mr. Pemberton[2] with the inclosed letter, and pay him the price a book sent me, which I believe is 4. Dollars. My remittance to Mr. Peale yesterday was meant to cover these little paiments. The letter to Mr. Pemberton is also one of introduction for you, as the worth of his character, and his being at the head of the society of friends makes him worthy your respects. I have not yet heard of the lamp and bridle. Have they left Philadelphia? I shall send on a box with a Polygraph to Mr. Peale by the stage, as soon as I can find a passenger to take care of it, and in the box is a small bundle recieved from home for you some time since.

The difficulty you experience in abridging the lectures is not unexpected. I remember when I began a regular course of study I determined to abridge in a common place book,[3] every thing of value which I read. At first I could shorten it very little: but after a while I was able to put a page of a book into 2. or 3. sentences, without omitting any portion of the substance. Go on therefore with courage and you will find it grows easier and easier. Besides obliging you to understand the subject, and fixing it in your memory, it will learn you the most valuable art of condensing your thoughts and expressing them in the fewest words possible. No stile of writing is so delightful as that which is all pith, which never omits a necessary word, nor uses an unecessary one. The finest models of this existing are Sallust[4] and Tacitus, which on that account are worthy of constant study. And that you may have every just encouragement I will add that from what I observe of the natural stile of your letters I think you will readily attain this kind of perfection. I am glad you are so determined to be on the reserve on political subjects. The more you feel yourself piqued to express a sentiment on what is perhaps said at you, the more the occasion is to be seized for preserving in silence, and for acquiring the habit of mastering the temptations to reply, and of establishing an absolute power of silence over yourself. The tendency of this habit too to produce equanimity and tranquility of mind is very great. On this subject perhaps I may say a word in some future letter. I must now close with my affectionate attachment.   TH: JEFFERSON

1. John McAlister.
2. James Pemberton, a Quaker merchant of Philadelphia who succeeded Benjamin Franklin as president of the Society for Promoting the Abolition of Slavery.
3. *The Commonplace Book of Thomas Jefferson*, Gilbert Chinard, editor (Baltimore, 1926). (Original DLC.) This includes only legal abstracts, etc., and is not as complete as the manuscript volume.
4. TJ was perhaps interested in this Roman historian because he was the first to use the monograph form.

To ANNE RANDOLPH BANKHEAD

Washington Dec. 8. 08.

MY DEAR ANNE

Your letter of Nov. 26. came safely to hand, and in it the delicious flower of the Acacia, or rather the Mimosa Nilotica from Mr. Lomax. The mother tree of full growth which I had when I gave him the small one, perished from neglect the first winter I was from home. Does his produce seed? If it does I will thank him for some, and you to take care of them: altho' he will think it a vain thing at my time of life to be planting a tree of as slow a growth. In fact the Mimosa Nilotica and Orange are the only things I have ever proposed to have in my Green house. I like much your choice of books for your winter's reading. Middleton's life of Cicero is among the most valuable accounts we have of the period of which he writes; and Tacitus I consider as the first writer in the world without a single exception. His book is a compound of history and morality of which we have no other example. In your arithmetic, if you keep yourself familiar with the 4. elementary operations of addition, subtraction, multiplication and division or rather of addition and division, because this last includes subtraction and multiplication, it is as much as you will need. The rule of three, of universal utility, is a thing of meer common sense: for if one yard of cloth costs 3. Dollars, common sense will tell you that 20. yards will cost 20. multiplied by 3. I inclose you a letter from Jefferson which I presume will inform you he is well. Present my respects to Mr. Bankhead, and the good family you are with: also to my antient and intimate friend Mr. Lomas[1] when you have the opportunity. To yourself my affectionate love.   TH: JEFFERSON

1. Thomas Lomax.

To Anne Randolph Bankhead

Washington Dec. 10. 08.

MY DEAR ANNE

Jefferson writes to enquire of me whether he ever had the smallpox, and cannot attend the anatomical dissections till he gets an answer for fear of catching that disease. I am almost certain that he and yourself were carried by your Papa to Richmond when very young and inoculated there under his eye. You were probably old enough to remember it. Write me an answer by return of post that I may communicate it to Jefferson without further loss of time. Affectionate love to you.

TH: JEFFERSON

From Ellen Wayles Randolph

Edgehill December 15th 1808

MY DEAR GRANDPAPA

With this letter I send you a book which is in a miserable and tattered condition which if you will have bound for me I will be very much obliged to you. It is old and rotten but being valuable to me on account of the person who gave it. If it can be stuck together any way so as to prevent it from tumbling to pieces it will do. Many of the leaves are lost for it has seen hard service though not since I have had it. Col. Lewis died last Thursday night. The sweet scented grass looks very well. It was transplanted carefully in a larger box. My Bantams are very mischievous. They have pecked all the leaves off of some fine orange trees. They have increased very much. There are at least a peck of tuberose and 12 or 14 Amaryllys roots all packed in bran. The Geese and ducks shall be attended to when we go to Monticello. The seed I hope will succeed better than those which Sister Ann and yourself planted in the oval beds. The OERAS Wine which was in the little crazy casks is bottled off, there are not bottles enough to draw any other kind but it is no matter for All the rest is perfectly safe. When the book is bound I will thank you to return it for Cornelia to read. All the children send their love to you. Adieu dear Grandpapa. Believe me to be your most affectionate Grand daughter,   ELEONORA W. RANDOLPH

Mama says she will write next post. The watch, key and ring came safe but as the Vaccine was old Papa prefered waiting untill you got better.

FROM ANNE RANDOLPH BANKHEAD

Port Royal Dec. 19 *1808*

I recievd My Dear Grand Papas letters and in one of them he desires to know whether Jefferson ever had the small pox, he had it in Richmond at the same time that Aunt Virginia and myself did and was inoculated three times for fear of taking it in the natural way. I have not seen Mr. Lomax yet but make no doubt of geting the seed as I heard that he had some. He is very anxious to get one of your Likenesses by St. Memin and I promised to ask you for him, if you have another. I would be much obliged to you if you will send me in a letter some of the ice plant seed. A Lady here has Lost it and is to give me a few roots of the Lilly of the valley and a beautiful pink for it. I know it is to be had in Washington. Mr. Burwell got some there for Ellen. Adieu my Dear Grand Papa, your most affectionate Grand Daughter, A C B. It is so dark that I cannot see to write any longer. Nothing but the weather being too cold to travel in an open carriage has prevented our paying you a visit. Mr. Bankhead wished to hear the Debates in Congress.

I send you a watch paper. Miss Judy Lomax[1] gave it to me, but my watch will not admit one.

1. Miss Judy Lomax was a daughter of Thomas Lomax. This is the only notice that TJ may have collected watch papers.

FROM CORNELIA JEFFERSON RANDOLPH

recd. Dec. 19. 08.

DEAR GRANDPAPA

I hope you will excuse my bad writing, for it is the first letter I ever wrote, there are a number of faults, in it I know, but those you will excuse; I am reading a very pretty little book called dramatic dialogues,[1] that Mrs. Smith gave sister Elen when she was a little girl; I am very much pleased with it. All the children send their love to you. We all want to see you very much. Adieu my dear Grandpapa. Beleive me to be your most affectionate Granddaughter. C. R.

1. Mrs. Pinchard, *Dramatic Dialogues for the Use of Young Persons* (Boston, 1798).

TO THOMAS JEFFERSON RANDOLPH

Washington Dec. 19. 08.

DEAR JEFFERSON

I inclose you two letters from home, which I presume will inform you all are well there. I have no answer yet respecting your inoculation, but perhaps your father's letter may contain it. But will not the scar on your arm shew it? Will you ask Dr. Wistar to send me some vaccine matter to forward to Edgehill where they wish to vaccinate, being under apprehensions of the small pox. Will there be such an intermission of your lectures about Christmas as that you can come and pass a few days here? If there is, we shall be happy to see you here. If your funds with Mr. Peale will not meet the expences of the journey, let me know it and I will replenish them immediately. We mean to exhibit ourselves here on New Year's day in homespun. To compleat my provision, I want something for a pair of small cloths, which cannot be got here. I must get you to examine the manufactures of Philadelphia and send me something. I think it probable they make there some of those thick, ribbed, or corded cottons which are now so much used for pantaloons &c. That or any other thick cotton will do, or even black cloth if homespun. Nobody can better advise you where you may find what is good than Mr. Ronaldson to whom you carried the fleece of wool for me. I am your's affectionately,

TH: JEFFERSON

P. S. Do it up very close and hard in paper and send it by post.

To ELLEN WAYLES RANDOLPH

Washington Dec. 20. 08.

MY DEAR ELLEN

I recieved yesterday yours of the 15th. and I shall take care to have your book bound. The letter to Jefferson went on direct. I have not heard from him for sometime, but Doctr. Rush in a letter just recieved says 'your grandson has not called upon me as often as I expected, but I hear with great pleasure that he is absorbed and delighted with his Anatomical and other studies.' I have been expecting Vaccine matter from Dr. Worthington here: but he has been disappointed, and I yesterday wrote to Jefferson to get Dr. Wistar to send me some. I have been confined to the house since 18th. of Nov. by a diseased jaw. An exfoliation of the bone is taking place, and will in time relieve me. I feel no pain from it, and the only inconvenience is the confinement to the house, from the fear that a cold air might make the case worse. Altho' you have been long silent, the muses have been uncommonly loquacious. They have enabled me to send you three of their effusions which do not want merit. I have written to Jefferson if there is sufficient intermission in his lectures at Christmas, to come and pass his free interval with us. Tell Cornelia I give her credit for her letter, and shall repay the debt before long. Kiss your dear Mama and the little ones for me and remember me affectionately to your papa. To yourself I am all love.

TH: JEFFERSON

To CORNELIA JEFFERSON RANDOLPH

Washington Dec. 26. 08.

I congratulate you, my dear Cornelia, on having acquired the invaluable art of writing. How delightful to be enabled by it to converse with an absent friend, as if present. To this we are indebted for all our reading; because it must be written before we can read it. To this we are indebted for the Iliad, the Aeneid, the Columbiad, Henriade, Dunciad, and now for the most glorious poem of all, the tarrapiniad, which I now inclose you.[1] This sublime poem consigns to everlasting fame the greatest atchievement in war ever known to antient or modern times. In the battle of David and Goliath the disparity between the combatants was nothing in comparison of our case. I rejoice that you have learnt to write for another reason; for as that is done with a goose quill, you now know the value of a goose, and of course you will assist Ellen in taking care of the half dozen very fine grey geese which I shall send by Davy. But as to this I must refer to your Mama to decide whether they will be safest at Edgehill or at Monticello till I return home, and to give orders accordingly. I recieved letters a few days ago from Mr. Bankhead and Anne. They are well. I had expected a visit from Jefferson at Christmas had there been a sufficient intermission in his lectures but I suppose there was not, as he is not come. Remember me affectionately to your Papa and Mama, and kiss Ellen and all the children for me.

TH: JEFFERSON

P S. Since writing the above I have a letter from Mr. Peale informing me that Jefferson is well, and saying the best things of him.

1. Joel Barlow, *The Columbiad a Poem* (Philadelphia, 1807); *La Henriade,* an epic poem on Henry IV of France by Voltaire, and "The Dunciad," a satirical heroic poem by Alexander Pope. W. H. Peden, in "Thomas Jefferson: Book Collector," states on page 64, "Cornelia, having just learned to write, had sent Jefferson a bit of doggerel verse, 'The Terrapiniad.'" Cornelia's letter to TJ, received January 16, 1809, suggests it might have been a clipping, perhaps verses on the fable of the race between the tortoise and the hare.

FROM THOMAS JEFFERSON RANDOLPH

Museum Dec 28 [1808]

DEAR GRANDFATHER

I heard to day from a Virginia student who had recieved letters from home stating an Insurrection in Amherst. If you have heard any of the circumstances attending it, pray inform me, as it is too near to every thing which is dear to me, to fail being very interesting.[1] I have paid, Mr. McAllister and Mr. [Purkes?] for clarksons history, which you had forgot to mention.[2] I went to see Mr. J. Pemberton, he mentioned he had made you present of the book and I thought after what he said that I had better not offer him the Money. You were informed no doubt by Mr. Peales letter that your remittances were larger than necessary. Yours affectionately,

T J R

NB. When I had more time, I wrote more intelligible and more lengthy.

1. Thomas Jefferson Randolph was particularly interested in this insurrection in Amherst County because he was courting Jane Hollins Nicholas, who lived at Warren, not far removed from the site of the trouble.

2. Thomas Clarkson, *History of the Rise, Progress & Accomplishment of the Abolition of the African Slave-Trade* (Philadelphia, 1808).

FROM ELLEN WAYLES RANDOLPH

[1809]

I have sent a letter to be inclosed to Uncle Hackley which I beg you will forward by the first ship that sails to Spain.

E. W. R.

FROM MARTHA JEFFERSON RANDOLPH

recd. Jan. 1. 09

I enclose you another letter My Dearest Father, irksome as it is for me to add to your vexations of the kind Mr. R. thinks he can not refuse without danger of giving offense [to] friends who think they have a claim upon him. Mr. Hackley also wrote to beg him to mention his name to you. We recieved the vaccine safe and will innoculate our children immediately as well as our neighbours. Jefferson was innoculated with the small pox in Richmond With Virginia and Anne. Mr. Randolph recieved your letter in Milton and not having time by that mail to write to both wrote on to Jefferson to prevent his losing a lecture. Adieu My Dearest Father. You must excuse this hurried scrawl but I have been so closely at work for these 10 days past that I have never been able to take up My pen till the moment of the departure of the mail. Yours with unchangeable affection,   M RANDOLPH

Will you return Moultrie's letter[1] it has not been answered?

1. Relating to his appointment to West Point and that he would not be called until the spring.

TO THOMAS JEFFERSON RANDOLPH

Washington Jan. 3. [1809]

DEAR JEFFERSON

I had letters from home of last Thursday informing that all there were well. The disturbance among the negroes of which you heard took place in Nelson county (part of Amherst) under the blue ridge, and so remote from Charlottesville that it had no other effect there than to produce some vigilence. It was prevented entirely by a previous arrest of the small band concerned in it. I have never yet heard of the vessel with my Alabaster vase and bridle bit, which in yours of Dec. 7. you mentioned to be bound for Alexandria. Can you furnish me with the name of the vessel and master and time of sailing? Have the boxes containing your books, and the model of the Mammoth head ever arrived at Philadelphia? Will you enquire of Mr. Peale whether he has or has not the skin, horns &c. of the fleecy goat from Govr. Lewis? And of him, and Dr. Wistar what they make of it? I call it the Potiotragos.

I formerly advised you to pay but a general attention to Surgery. I have since reflected on this more maturely. I do not know whether your father intends you for a profession, or to be a farmer. This last is the most honourable and happy of all. But farmers as well as professional men are apt to live beyond their income and thus to be reduced to bankruptcy. You know too many examples of this in Virginia not to see that it is possible as to yourself, and probable unless you have that resolution to live within your income, the want of which has swallowed up the patrimonial estates of so many of your friends. Under this possibility it is provident and comfortable to possess some resource within ourselves some means by which we can get a living if reduced by misfortune or imprudence to poverty. I know of none which you might look to with more expectation than Surgery. We have no good surgeons in the country; so that emploiment would be certain. It is a comfortable art because in operating we find from those doubts which must forever haunt the mind of a conscientious practitioner of the equivocal art of medicine, and in the mean time, while you do not follow it as a profession it will be a most valuable acquisition for family use. What therefore you should now be most attentive to are the manual operations, and treatments which you have so excellent a model in Doctr. Physic. Your great attention therefore should be to this part of the business; because you can read and study the books at home, but the benefit of practice in the hospitals you can never have again, and therefore you should attend most particularly to them, and be careful never to fail seeing all the important operations performed, whenever an occasion offers. These are built on an accurate knowledge of the anatomy of the human body, and therefore the two things go on intimately together. I fear you are at present engaged in almost too much. However wonders may be done by incessant occupation, and refusing to lose time by amusements during the few months you have to pass in Philadelphia. You will be encouraged in this by the reflection that every moment you lose there, is irrecoverably lost. If you are obliged to neglect any thing, let it be your chemistry. It is the least useful and the least amusing to a country gentleman of all the ordinary branches of science. In the exercises of the country and progress over our farms, every step presents some object of botany natural history, comparative anatomy &c. But for chemistry you must shut yourself up in your laboratory and neglect the care of your affairs and of your health which calls you out of doors. Chemistry is of value to the amateur inhabiting a city. He has not room there for out of door amusements. I am your's with all possible affection.

TH: JEFFERSON

To Martha Jefferson Randolph

Washington Jan. 10. 09.

MY DEAR DAUGHTER

I recieved yesterday your letter of the 5th. and Mr. Randolph's of the 6th. and I have this morning sent an extract of the latter to Mr. Nicholas.[1] I sincerely wish it success, but I am afraid Mr. Carr[2] has been misinformed of Mr. Patterson's[3] views, or, which is as likely, that Mr. Patterson has changed them. He has certainly concluded to settle on a tract of 5. or 600. acres which he gets from Mr. Nicholas about 2. miles from Warren. However we shall soon know the result of this offer. Joseph is now gone out in quest of the Imperial spelling book. If he gets it, and in time it shall go by this post. After being confined to the house about 6. weeks, I am now quite well. The diseased jaw bone having exfoliated, the piece was extracted about a week ago, the place is healed, the swelling nearly subsided, and I wait only for moderate weather to resume my rides. As the term of my relief from this place approaches, it's drudgery becomes more nauseating and intolerable, and my impatience to be with you at Monticello increases daily. Yet I expect to be detained here a week or 10. days after the 4th. of March. This will be unfavorable to our forwardest garden provisions. Can you have a sowing or two of the forwardest peas, lettuces, radishes etc. made at Edgehill to fill up the chasm till the first Monticello sowings, which cannot be till the middle of March. I have not heard lately from Jefferson or Anne. Present me affectionately to Mr. Randolph and kiss the young ones for me. Ever yours most tenderly,

TH: JEFFERSON

1. Wilson Cary Nicholas.
2. Peter or Samuel Carr.
3. John Patterson was the husband of Mary Nicholas, daughter of Wilson Cary Nicholas.

FROM CORNELIA JEFFERSON RANDOLPH

recd. Jan. 16. 09.

DEAR GRANDPAPA

I am very much obliged to you for the Tarripiniad. I have pasted it in a little book mama Made me to put all the piece's that you send me in. Pray answer this letter next post. Virginia sends her love to you. She can read tolerable well.

I am dear Grandpapa your most affectionate Granddaughter,

CORNELIA RANDOLPH

TO CORNELIA JEFFERSON RANDOLPH

Washington Jan. 23. 09

MY DEAR CORNELIA

I recieved by the last post your letter which you desire me to answer by the succeeding one. I have accordingly set down to do it, and to find out the points in your letter to which you wish an answer. They are rather blunt and difficult to ascertain. They seem however to be these. 1. You thank me for the Terrapiniad. To this I answer, you are welcome. 2. You have pasted it in a book. I answer, that is very well. 3. Virginia reads well and sends her love to me. I answer that that is best of all. That she is a very good girl, and I return her my love. Your letter being now fully answered, I have only to add that I inclose you two pieces for your book, and desire you to kiss your Mama and all the young ones for me with assurances of my tenderest love,

TH: JEFFERSON

From Ellen Wayles Randolph

Recd. Jan. 23. 09

DEAR GRANDPAPA

I have not time this post but will certainly write the next. I am dear Grandpapa your affectionate grand Daughter.

E. W. R.

From Ellen Wayles Randolph

Edghill January 26th 1809

DEAR GRANDPAPA

I would have written to you last post, if I had had time, but I am determined to do it this, although, I have not much to say, unless I talk about the plants; those in the large box were killed to the roots, but they are coming up all over the box; those in the small pot were killed also, but are putting out small fresh buds; the evergreens have lost all their leaves but one branch on each, which look lively enough; in the large pot, there is not the least appearance of life, but Mama preserved a little pod full of seed from it. Poor James has been inoculated with the Vaccine and is very unwell. Benjamin has had it but he did not have a fever. You must pardon this letter so full of mistakes, for it is written by candle light. I have been writing almost all day; give my love to Mrs. S. H. Smith, the children and mama send theirs to you. I am dear Grand Papa your most affectionate Grand Daughter,   ELLENORE WAYLES RANDOLPH

The sweet scented grass looks very badly although Mama seperated the roots and planted them with great care in a box of fine rich mould and the season in which it was done was warm and rainy. Yours affectionately,   E W R.

From Thomas Jefferson Randolph

Museum February 4 [1809]

DEAR GRANDFATHER

I have obtained permission to have a fire in the hall of the Philosophical Society[1] where I can study in solitude; Dr. Wistar and Mr. Peale have as yet made nothing of the Fleecy goat owing to the imperfection of the sample. All the lectures will end this Month and I wish very much to go to washington the 1st of

March to see you, as I will not have it in my power to see any of the family before July. If I may, pray inform me soon and furnish me with money to defray the expences of the journey. Your affectionate grandson, T J RANDOLPH

1. The American Philosophical Society's building was located on the southeast side of State House Square in Philadelphia.

To ELLEN WAYLES RANDOLPH

Washington Feb. 6. 09.

MY DEAR ELLEN

I have recieved your letter on the subject of my plants and will now explain to you what they were, tho' I cannot say what was in each box or pot particularly.

Savory. A dead plant. It's leaves very aromatic. A little resembling thyme. My dependance is that it's seeds are shed on the earth in the box and will come up.

Arbor vitae. A small evergreen tree, in a small pot.

Ice-plant. Not entirely dead, but I suppose it's seed shed on the earth and will come up.

Tarragon. A plant of some size. The leaves mostly dead. I expect the seed is scattered and will come up.

Geranium. I think there was a plant of this but am not certain.

Besides the above there was a box containing many sods of sweet-scented grass, packed one on another, and in the same box a bunch of monthly raspberry plants, which box Davy was directed to carry to Monticello. I much fear he did not, as Bacon writes me he recieved no raspberry plants, saying nothing of the grass. Kiss every body affectionately for me,

TH: JEFFERSON

To MARTHA JEFFERSON RANDOLPH

Washington Feb. 14. 09

MY DEAREST MARTHA

In the instant of the departure of the post Genl. Dearborn calls on me to know the name of a person for whom I applied to be made a Cadet; and I have forgotten the name, and cannot find it on a review of your letters, altho' I know it was through you that the application came. Pray let me know it by return of post, and I will keep the place open a few days. Genl. Dearborne leaves us in a few days; I have only time to add that Jefferson is well, and as his lectures will finish this month he will come on here to see me the 1st. of March, and return to commence the botanical lectures. My affections to Mr. Randolph and the young ones and tenderest love to yourself.   TH: JEFFERSON

FROM MARTHA JEFFERSON RANDOLPH

Edgehill Feb. 17, 1809

MY DEAREST FATHER

The name of the young gentleman for whom the application was made is Moultrie. The Christian name I do not remember but it is probably mentioned in his Father's letter to Mr. Randolph which you told me had been filed with the papers of the Office. If it is not to be found there, Mr. Randolph thinks it probable that David R. Williams[1] may know it. He is the eldest son of Doctor James Moultrie of Charlston S. Carolina. The inclosed I must beg the favor of you to send by the first vessel that sails. This letter will be delivered to you by My Brother William's son Beverley who will spend a day in Washington on his way to west point. If you are not engaged when he arrives I would be much obliged to you if you would ask him to dine with you any little attention from you being particularly grateful to the family. He will spend some days in Philadelphia where Jefferson will spend as much of his time with him as is consistent with his studies. The first of March he is obliged to be at west point. The two little boys were *vaccinated* and had the disease finely. Benjamin's arm was very sore but he had no fever nor a moment's indisposition of any kind that we were sensible of with it. James on the contrary had a very small place on the arm but was seriously indisposed for several days. The Geraniums in the little pot have come up from the root and are flourishing. The Arbre vitae is budding out also and a box which I take to be the savory is very flourishing. One more pot with a dead plant we have but of the other boxes and plants you mentioned I have heard nothing. The sweet scented grass that was sent on in the fall scarcely exhibits the least sign of life. I some times think there is a little green about the roots but am not allways certain even of that. I must beg the favor of you to send Mary "the road to learning made pleasant" and "Select rhymes for the nursery".[2] Adieu My Dearest Father. As the *period* of your labours draws near My heart beats with inexpressible anxiety and impatience. Adieu again My ever Dear and honoured Parent. That the evening of your life may pass in serene and unclouded tranquility is the daily prayer, and as far as my powers will cont[inue you] will be the dearest and most sacred duty of your devoted child,   MR.

Mrs. Trist wrote to beg I would ask you if some hammocks that William Brown had sent her directed to you had arrived. There were three of them, one for yourself one for Mr. Randolph and a third for *her*. There was also a barrel of Peccans. The hammocks[3] were from Campeachy and were sent on in the month of October so William Brown wrote to Mrs. Trist, directed to you, but she has never heard of their arrival. If I have time to write by Isaac Coles to Botidoux will you be so good as to let me know? This is written in the midst of the children with never less than three talking to me at once which is a sufficient apology for the many inacuracies in it for they really distract me with their noise and incessant questions.

1. Colonel David R. Williams was superintendent of the United States Military Academy at West Point, New York.

2. "The road to Learning, Made Pleasant, with Lessons and Pictures" (Philadelphia, n.d.). Title from *J. Johnson's Juvenile Catalogue of Useful and Entertaining Books for Children* [Philadelphia, n.d.], affixed to a copy of *Johnson's Virginia Almanack, 1807*. A copy is at MWA.

Jane Rogers, *Rhymes for the Nursery*. The first edition was published in London in 1806; later published under the title, *Select Rhymes for the Nursery*. There was a Philadelphia edition of 1810 using this same title.

3. These were comfortable leather-covered reclining chairs made of a particular type of mahogany that grows in the State of Campeche, Mexico. Their profile resembles a modern deck chair except that they do not fold and cannot be adjusted. TJ asked William Brown in a letter of August 18, 1808 (MHi), to procure three for him. This Brown did, but they were lost at sea while in transit. A number of years later (1819) TJ requested Thomas Bolling Robertson in New Orleans to procure them, which Robertson did. One of these is now at Monticello.

To Thomas Jefferson Randolph

Washington Feb. 17. 09

DEAR JEFFERSON

Will you be so good as to call at the office of Hope's Philadelphia price-current, enter me as a subscriber, and pay 3. dollars, the year's subscription. The paper must be addressed to 'Thomas Jefferson, Monticello, near Milton.'   TH: JEFFERSON

FROM VIRGINIA JEFFERSON RANDOLPH

Feb. 17. 1809

DEAR GRANDPAPA

I want to see you very much. I am reading a little book called Rosamond.[1] I have read seven books since december. The little geranium has grown a great deal. I had a good deal to say to you the other morning but I have forgotten it. Ben sends you a kiss. Cornelia is learning french. Sister Ellen sends her love to you and says she will write next post. I am spelling [words of] two syllables and [soon hope] to be in four. Adieu dear Grandpapa. Believe me to be your most affectionate Grand Daughter,

VIRGINIA RANDOLPH[2]

1. A child's book by Maria Edgeworth.
2. Letter written by Ellen W. Randolph.

TO ELLEN WAYLES RANDOLPH

Washington Feb. 20. 09.

MY DEAR ELLEN

My last letter to you stated the plants which had been sent, and I was in hopes, after you had been enabled to distinguish them, you would have informed me of their respective conditions. But no post has arrived for this week from Milton and consequently no letter from you. In about three weeks I hope to be with you, and then we shall properly be devoted to the garden. What has become of Mrs. Trist? I have not heard a word about her since I left Monticello. I inclose you a budget of poetry to be distributed according to their address. Tell your Papa that the ultimate decision of Congress is as uncertain at this moment as it ever was. I rather believe the embargo will be removed on the 4th. of March, and a nonintercourse[1] with France and England and their dependencies be substituted. But it is by no means certain. My affections to him, and kisses to your dear Mama and sisters. All love to yourself.   TH: JEFFERSON

1. The Non-Intercourse Act of March 1, 1809, repealed the Embargo, effective March 15, 1809; it reopened trade with all nations except France and Great Britain. The President was authorized by this act to resume trade with these nations if they should cease violating our neutrality rights.

FROM MARTHA JEFFERSON RANDOLPH

Edgehill February 24, 1809

MY DEAREST FATHER

Mr. Randolph has been applied to by the people of the County generally to know if you would have any objection to their meeting you on the road and escorting you to Charlottesville. Not only the militia companies but the body of the people. They wish it as the last opportunity they can have of giving you a public testimony of their respect and affection.[1] If you will write to him by the return of the post the 6th being court day he will have an opportunity of seeing them and giving them the answer required. I wrote to you by the last mail but from Ellens letter it appear'd that you had not recieved mine and although I suppose you must have recieved it ere this yet for fear of accident will again mention the name of young Moultrie. His Father's letter to which I must refer you for his christian name you informed me at the time, was filed with the papers of the office, if it should not be found Mr. Randolph thinks David R Williams may probably know the name. He is the eldest son of Doctor James Moultrie of Charlston S. C. To divide the confusion of your arrival and my moving and thereby lessen it I think I shall go to Monticello the 9 or 10th.[2] It will give me time to fix my self before the arrival of your waggons and servants which will naturally occasion some bustle in the family. Adieu My Very Dear Father your Devoted child,

MR.

Mr. Randolph begs the favor of you to send the inclosed by some of the members of congress who are probably acquainted with Mr. Barker. I have taken avantade of Your power of franking letters My Dear Papa to convey a parcel to Ann almost too bulky for the post. Will you be so kind as to inclose it to her immediately.

1. The local citizenry had proposed that they meet and escort TJ to Monticello with a great deal of ceremony. He declined, saying that his date of arrival was too indefinite. This proposed public ovation gave way to a welcome-home address, which he answered. TJ did not arrive at Monticello until March 15.

2. Martha invariably moved her family to Monticello whenever her father was there from Washington. This time she did not return to Edgehill. It is assumed that Mr. Randolph followed her to Monticello but probably with little enthusiasm.

TO MARTHA JEFFERSON RANDOLPH

Washington Feb. 27. 09

MY DEAR DAUGHTER

Your letters of the 17th. and 24th. are both recieved. Beverly T. Randolph[1] called at the hour at which I had rode out, and left your letter of the 17th. Taking for granted he was to stay a day as you mentioned, I wrote an invitation to him the next morning to come and dine with me. But he had already gone on. He called in like manner on his namesake Beverley here,[2] who being out did not see him. I had written a letter of introduction and recommendation to Colo. Williams, the superior of the whole institution, to be delivered by him in person: but as I did not see him, I sent it on by post. We have found the paper which gave Moultrie's Christian name, and his warrant was forwarded to him at Charleston 4. days ago: so Mr. Randolph can answer his friend on that ground. The schooner Sampson, Capt. Smith with the Campeachy hamocks &c. owned in this place, left N. Orleans for this destination about the 6th. of October, as the Captain's reciept, forwarded to me, shews: and has never been heard of since. No doubt remains here of her being lost with every person and thing on board her. Mr. Coles will leave this about the 9th. of March. Consequently if you will write to Botedour by the return of post, it will find him here, as it will myself. I send the two books you desired for Mary.

I am glad you have taken the resolution of going over to Monticello before my return, because of the impossibility of fixing the day of my return. I shall be able, I expect, to dispatch the waggon with the servants from hence, about the 9th. of March, and they will reach home about the 14th. But how many days after their departure I shall be detained in winding up here, I cannot determine. I look with infinite joy to the moment when I shall be ultimately moored in the midst of my affections, and free to follow the pursuits of my choice. In retiring to the condition of a private citizen and reducing our establishment to the style of living of a mere private family, I have but a single uneasiness. I am afraid that the enforcing the observance of the necessary economies in the internal administration of the house will give you more trouble than I wish you to have to encounter and I presume it is impossible to propose to my sister Marks to come and live with us. Perhaps, with a set of good and capable servants, as ours certainly are, the trouble will become less after their once understanding the regulations which are to govern them. Ignorant too, as I am, in the management of a farm, I shall be obliged to ask the aid of Mr. Randolph's skill and attention, especially for that of Tufton, when it comes to me. It will be my main dependance, and to make it adequate, with my other Albemarle resources, to support all expences, will require good management. If I can sell the detached tracts of land I own, so as to pay the debts I have contracted here (about ten thousand Dollars) and they are fully adequate to it, my wish would be to live within the income of my Albemarle possessions. They will yield 2000. D. rent, besides the profits of the lands and negroes of Monticello and Tufton,[3] the toll mill, and nailery. My Bedford income, about 2000. to 2500. D. would then be free to assist the children as they grow up and want to establish themselves. In all this I look to nothing but the happiness of yourself, Mr. Randolph, and the dear children. My own personal wants will be almost nothing beyond those of a chum of the family. On these subjects however we can confer more in detail when I shall have the happiness of being with you. I write to Mr. Randolph on the subject of my friends of the county. My love to the children and most of all to yourself.   TH: JEFFERSON

1. Thomas Beverley Randolph was the son of Lucy Bolling and William Randolph, a younger brother of Thomas Mann Randolph, Jr.

2. TJ doubtless meant Robert Beverley of Acrolophos, now Dumbarton Oaks, in Georgetown.

3. One of TJ's plantations, east of and adjacent to Monticello.

FROM MARTHA JEFFERSON RANDOLPH

March 2 1809

MY DEAREST FATHER

I shall go to Monticello a day or two before you arrive as it is probable by the return of the waggon you will be able to fix a day. The arrangements necessary for retrenching all possible expense no one can be more thoroughly convinced of the necessity than my self. *Your* comfort My Dearest Father must however be the only criterion. Any encroachment upon that were it productive of millions to the children would be distracting to me. I can bear any thing but the idea of seeing you harrassed in your old age by debts or deprived of those comforts which long habit has rendered necessary to you. Our children are young and healthy and their habits may be formed to what we please therefore I conjure you by the Dear the sacred tie that unites us to make your

arrangements so as to relieve your self, and we shall all be happy
if you are so. I assure you again and again that the possession of
millions would not compensate for one year's sadness and discomfort to you. The trouble you speak of so far as it regards my
self is nothing. You know "nothing is troublesome that we do
willingly." Your difficulties will be a stimulus that would render
rest the most intolerable of all cares to me. My health is good and
exercise will still confirm it but I am afraid you will be very much
disappointed in your expectations from Shoemaker. It is the
opinion of the neighbourhood that it would be better for you to
get the mill back upon any terms than to let him keep it. In the
first place he is not a man of business his bargains are ruinous to
himself and more over he has not one spark of honesty. His credit
is so low that nothing but necessity induced any one to trust him
with their grain; and the general complaint is that it can not be
got out of his hands. He told Higginbotham that if *perfectly con-
veninient* he might perhaps pay the 500 $ on your order but not
one cent more would he pay untill there had been a settlement
between you. And it is the general opinion that he means to keep
the mill and set you at defiance. From some circumstances I am
afraid you have been decieved in the character of his Father.
There are strong doubts of his honesty in the minds of many here.
In short My Dear Father disagreeable as it is to tease you with
tales of the kind I think it my duty to tell you the opinion of the
whole neighbourhood of the man and your prospects from him.
If the bargain was made with the Father perhaps you may secure
your self though even that is *doubted.* As for the son your chance
is I fear desperate for certainly a greater rascal or a more bitter personal enemy to you does not exist. They say farther that he will
contrive to destroy the geer of the mill so as to make it scarcely
hold out his time. You may depend upon it that I have not exaggerated the reports and I have reason to believe them too well
founded. People allow your mill to be invaluable from its situation and if it was in the hands of a tolerably honest or indrustious
man it would be a public benefit. As it is by the time his lease is
out it will be totally destroyed as far as it will be possible to do
it and you get nothing from him in the mean time. I should not
have mentioned these things now, but that perhaps it may enable
you to do something with the old man if your bargain is with him.
As for the sons they have no character to maintain and never
intended to comply with their contract. Excuse me again for intruding so disgusting a subject upon you. Nothing as I have al-

ready said but a strong sense of the necessity of your being informed of your situation while there is a possibility of bettering it would have made me meddle in so disagreeable a business. The rest of our difficulties we will talk over to gether. As to Aunt Marks it would not be desirable to have her if it was proper.[1] I had full proof of her being totally incompetent to the business the last summer. The servants have no sort of respect for her and take just what they please before her face. She is an excellent creature and a neat manager in a little way, but she has neither head nor a sufficient weight of character to manage so large an establishment as yours will be. I shall devote my self to it and with feelings which I never could have in my own affairs. And with what tenderness of affection we will wait upon and cherish you My Dearest Father [and] will experience but I cannot tell. If you can be tranquil we shall not suffer. The arrangements you propose for clearing your estate answer so much the better if they do not which will be soon ascertained, you must releave your self in some other way, certain than we can only be happy by seeing you so. God bless you and restore you speedily to your truly affectionate child.

M R.

I believe I shall send these letters by the post for fear of the waggons being detained by some accident on the road and my letter to Botidour missing Mr. Coles. If you have one of your profiles by St. Memin I wish you would enclose it with My letter. I know her respect and affection for you will make it most grateful to her. I have sent by the waggon a box for Mrs. Madison which I must beg the favor of you to send to her. Ellen has not been at home for 3 weeks which will account for her not having written to you. Adieu.

1. Aunt Marks's becoming TJ's housekeeper would perhaps have aroused Martha's violent objections even if she had been a capable manager.

First Citizen of Virginia

To Thomas Jefferson Randolph

Monticello May 6. 09.

DEAR JEFFERSON

Your's of the 28th. ult. came to hand by our last post. I have consulted your father on the subject of your attending Mr. Godon's lectures in mineralogy, and we consent to it so long as the Botanical lectures continue. We neither of us consider that branch of science as sufficiently useful to protract your stay in Philadelphia beyond the termination of the Botanical lectures. In what you say respecting the preservation of plants, I suppose you allude to Mr. Crownenshield's specimens which I shewed you. But I could not have promised to give you his method because I did not know it myself. All I know was from Genl. Dearborne, who told me that Mr. Crownenshield's method was, by extreme pressure (with a screw or weight) on the substance of the plants but that he could never make it adhere to the paper until he used garlick juice either alone or in composition with something else. I communicated to Mr. Randolph your wish respecting the specimens of antimony. But how shall we convey them. By an unintended omission in the act of Congress allowing my letters to be free, they omitted those *from* me, mentioning those *to me* only. It will be corrected at their ensuing session as the letters of my predecessors were privileged both *to* and *from*. And in truth the office of president commits the incumbent, even after he quits office, to a correspondence of such extent as to be extremely burthensome. To avoid the expence of postage to Mr. Peale, I inclose his letter in yours, that it may be paid out of your funds. I send you one also for Mr. Hamilton[1] open for your perusal. When read, stick a wafer in it before delivery. Attend particularly to the assurances of using his indulgence with discretion and to the study of his pleasure grounds as the finest model of pleasure gardening you will ever see. I wrote to Lemaire to send me some Vanilla and vinegar syrop, and that you would pay him for it on presenting my letter. I must desire you to send me 9. feet of brass chain to hang the Alabaster lamp[2] you got for me. I inclose you 4. links as a specimen of the kind and size. This was furnished me by Messrs. Caldcleugh & Thomas, stationers No. 66. and 68. Chesnut street at 67. cents per yard, who probably can furnish the same now. I must also pray you to get for me a gross of vial-corks of different sizes, and 4. dozen phials of 1. 2. 3. and 4. ounces, one dozen of each size. The largest mouthed would be the best as they are for holding garden seeds. I have not yet seen Dr. Watson. The family here are all well, and I recollect no small news of the neighborhood worth mentioning. We wish to hear from you oftener. God bless you,   TH: JEFFERSON

P. S. The above articles to be packed in a box addressed to Gibson & Jefferson and sent by water. It would be well if Lemaire's articles were packed in the same box, as they would all come safer in one than two boxes. But for this purpose you must see him immediately, or he will have sent away his alone. I must pray you to put half a dozen pounds of scented hair powder into the same box. None is to be had here, and it is almost a necessary of life with me. To spare your funds I shall have the postage of this package paid here.

1. William Hamilton was a Philadelphia horticulturist, and he owned The Woodlands, a botanical garden from which he sent TJ many species of plants.

2. This lamp now hangs in the Book Room of the library suite at Monticello.

FROM THOMAS JEFFERSON RANDOLPH

May 29 1809 Museum Philadelphia

DEAR GRANDFATHER

I recieved your letter of the 5th about the 20th. Mr. Lemaire had sent the Articles which you wrought [wrote] for before. I have got phials and hair powder; [the] chain I have sent to New york for, there being none her; corks, I have not been able to get, as yet of that size. I have paid Mr. Lemaire, as you will see by his receipts which, however, he sent before I could find him out.

You desire to hear from me oftener; I have written three times, this making the fourth, and have received one letter 50 days after I left you. My mother Father and yourself who are so much occupied, I could hardly expect to hear from; Mr. Bankhead[1] I suppose is so *studious*; he can think of nothing else but *Blackstone*; Sister Ann, and Ellen, particularly are so fond [of] darning stockings, that I could not expect to hear from them. Yours affectionately,   THOS J. RANDOLPH

PS I shall leave this place in four weeks.

NB Dr. Barton[2] has informed me the Lectures end the 12th of June.

1. Charles L. Bankhead was reading law at Monticello under TJ's direction.
2. Dr. Benjamin Barton was a Philadelphia botanist who taught at the College of Philadelphia.

TO THOMAS JEFFERSON RANDOLPH

Monticello June 20. 09

DEAR JEFFERSON

In the even current of a country life few occurrences arise of sufficient note to become the subject of a letter to a person at a distance. It would be little interesting to such an one to be told of the distressing drought of the months of April and May, that wheat and corn scarcely vegetated and no seeds in the garden came up; that since that we have had good rains but very cold weather, so that prospects are disheartening for the farmer and little better to the gardener &c. &c. Yet these circumstances excite a lively interest on the spot, and in their variations from bad to good, and the reverse fill up our lives with those sensations which attach us to existence, altho' they could not be the subject of a letter to a distant friend. Hence we write to you seldom, and now after telling you we are all well, I have given you all our news which would be interesting to you. But tho' we do not write we think of you, and have been for some time counting the days before you will be with us. The death of Dr. Woodhouse and loss of his lectures leave no inducement to protract your stay after the Botanical lectures are ended, for I do not think the mineralogical course important enough for that. We shall expect you therefore when the botanical course is finished. In the mean time it is necessary I should know the state of your funds. Before I left Washington I remitted to Mr. Peale what I supposed would suffice during your stay: but having made some draughts on you, and the one for Lemaire more considerable than I had expected there will probably be a deficiency. Your Mama desires you will get for Mary a little book she has seen advertised called the Adventures of Mary and her cat. Anticipating the pleasure of your return, and assuring you of the happiness it will give us to have you again among us, to the salutations of the family I add only my own affectionate Adieu.   TH: JEFFERSON

To Anne Randolph Bankhead

Monticello Dec. 29. 09.

MY DEAR ANNE

Your

Mama has given me a letter to inclose to you, but whether it contains any thing contraband; I know not. Of that the responsibility must be on her. I therefore inclose it. I suppose she gives you all the small news of the place such as the race in writing between Virginia and Francis, that the wildgeese are well after a flight of a mile and a half into the river, that the plants in the greenhouse prosper &c. A 'propos of plants, make a thousand acknolegements in my name and with my respects to Mrs. Bankhead for the favor proposed of the Cape Jessamine. It will be cherished with all the possible attentions: and in return proffer her Calycanthuses, Paccans, Silk trees, Canada martagons or any thing else we have. Mr. Bankhead I suppose is seeking a Merry Christmas in all the wit and merriments of Coke Littleton. God send him a good deliverance. Such is the usual prayer for those standing at the bar. Deliver to Mary[1] my kisses, and tell her I have a present from one of her acquaintances, Miss Thomas for her, the minutest gourd ever seen, of which I send her a draught in the margin. What is to become of our flowers? I left them so entirely to yourself, that I never knew any thing about them, what they are, where they grow, what is to be done for them. You must really make out a book of instructions for Ellen, who has fewer cares in her head than I have. Every thing shall be furnished on my part at her call. Present my friendly respects to Doctr. and Mrs. Bankhead. My affectionate attachment to Mr. Bankhead and yourself, not forgetting Mary.   TH: JEFFERSON

1. Mary Jefferson Randolph was Martha's sixth child to survive infancy; she was born at Edgehill November 2, 1803. She was the Randolphs' fourth daughter.

To Thomas Jefferson Randolph

Monticello Dec. 30.09.

DEAR JEFFERSON

It may seem odd that while I was involved in so much business at Washington, I could yet find time to write to you sometimes, and that I have not been able to do it in my present situation; but the fact is that letter writing was there my trade. From sunrise to near dinner was to be of course devoted to it, and a letter more

or less made little odds, but in our country economy, letter writing
is a hors d'oeuvre. It is no part of the regular routine of the day.
From sunrise till breakfast only I allot for all my pen and ink
work. From breakfast till dinner I am in my garden, shops, or on
horse back in the farms, and after dinner I devote entirely to relaxation or light reading. Hence I have not written to you. Still I
have wished to know what you have entered on, what progress you
have made, and how your hours are distributed. For it is only by
a methodical distribution of our hours, and a rigorous, inflexible
observance of it that any steady progress can be made. From what
I learn through the letter to your mother, I would advise you to
make the Mathematics your principal and almost sole object.
Consider Natural philosophy as quite secondary, because the
books will teach you that as well as any master can. Whereas
Mathematics require absolutely the assistance of a teacher. You
should therefore avail yourself to the utmost of your present situation, because of the uncertainty how long it may continue, and
the certainty that you will have no chance for another when this
fails. As you are entered with the class of Nat. philosophy, give to it
the hours of lecture, but devote all your other time to Mathematics, avoiding company as the bane of all progress. Mr. Jefferson is desired to furnish you all necessaries and to pay your tui-
tion and board. Of the two last articles give him punctual notice
at the end of every quarter that they may never be a day in arrear.

The family are all well, and late letters from Anne inform us
that she and Mary are so. But I presume you have lately seen
them as it was understood you meant to pass your Christmas with
them. Can you always, by the return of your father's boatmen
send us some oysters prepared as those you lately sent us. Robert
Hemings would I think prepare them for us, and call on Mr. Jefferson by your directions for the cost. I shall be glad to hear from
you from time to time, and be assured of my constant and affectionate attachment.   TH: JEFFERSON

To Thomas Jefferson Randolph

Monticello Mar. 14. 10.

DEAR JEFFERSON

I recieved by the last post your letter of 9th. expressing your
desire to study half the day in your own room rather than in the
school, if Mr. Gerardin's[1] consent should be obtained; and I
have consulted your father on the subject. We both find ourselves

too much uninformed of the regulations of the school to form a proper judgement on the proposition. If it would break through any rule which Mr. Gerardin thinks necessary for the government of his school, and would set a precedent which he could not extend to others under equal circumstances, we should be entirely unwilling to infringe the regular course by which he wishes to conduct the institution. Again, supposing it perfectly agreeable to Mr. Gerardin, we must still leave to your own discretion whether you can pursue your studies one half of the day more usefully in your chamber, than in the presence, and with the aid, of your instructor. You know that our views in giving you opportunities of acquiring sciences are directed to your own good alone; to enable you, by the possession of knolege, to be happier and more useful to yourself, to be beloved by your friends, and respected and honored by your country. We believe that you feel these considerations, and that you will study with equal assiduity in your room as in the school. Our confidence in your discretions therefore induces us to leave the matter to yourself rather than hazard a decision on our imperfect information. Perhaps the half day you propose for your room may be while the school and preceptors are occupied in branches of science which we have thought less useful to be pursued by you at present than the Mathematics. This would weigh with us in favor of the inclination you have expressed. I would wish you to shew this letter to Mr. Gerardin that he may see that while we suppose there may be circumstances which might render retirement to your chamber more advantageous to the particular studies we wish you to pursue, we yet would not, in any case desire an indulgence either to you or ourselves which would prove inconvenient to him as a precedent. Assure Mr. Wood, on my part, that I will with care and pleasure send his letters for France by a public vessel under cover to our minister there for delivery according to their address. Your's with all affection,   TH: JEFFERSON

1. Louis Hue Girardin. At this time he was conducting a school in Richmond. Later, he conducted them in Milton and Staunton. Volume 4 of Burk's *History of Virginia* (Sowerby 464) was completed by Girardin.

To Thomas Jefferson Randolph

Monticello Apr. 16. 10.

DEAR JEFFERSON

We are out of sallad-oil, and you know it is a necessary of life here. Can any be had in Richmond? I must get you to inquire, and

to be particular as to it's quality. If fine I would be glad to have
half a dozen quarts. If midling 2. or 3. bottles will do. If absolutely not good get a single bottle only to serve till I can get some
from Philadelphia. Mr. Jefferson will be so good as to have it
paid for, and I must get you to have it well packed, *in much
straw,* and sent up by in a boat. Mr. T. Eston Randolph's[1] boat
left Milton yesterday for Richmond, by the return of which you
can send it. Your father's boats do not now come up this river.
That the oil should be packed in *much straw* is to protect it from
the heat of the sun.

We are all full of complaints against you for not writing to us.
Independant of the wish to hear from you, I would advise you,
as an exercise, to write a letter to somebody every morning, the
first thing after you get up. As most of the business of life, and
all our friendly communications are by way of letter, nothing is
more important than to acquire a facility of developing our ideas
on paper; and practice alone will give this. Take pains at the same
time to write a neat round, plain hand, and you will find it a
great convenience through life to write a small and compact hand
as well as a fair and legible one. I shall probably see you in Richmond in May. The family is all well except Benjamin whose
health is not good. Affectionately yours,   TH: JEFFERSON

1. Thomas Mann Randolph, Jr.'s brother-in-law and the husband of Jane
Cary Randolph. He resided at Ashton, near Milton, where he was a merchant and, at one time, postmaster.

To Thomas Jefferson Randolph

Monticello May 14. 10.

DEAR JEFFERSON

I have safely recieved the 4. bottles of oil you sent me and find it
very good insomuch that I wish to get more of the same batch.
For this purpose I inclose you 10.D. and pray you to get as much
more as that will pay for, letting me know at the same time the
price, and how much more of the same oil the person has: because
if it be cheap, I may still lay in a larger stock of it. Send it up
by some boat to Mr. Higginbotham. I cannot but press on you my
advice to write a letter every day. It is necessary to begin the exercise of developing your ideas on paper. This is best done at first
by way of letter. When further advanced in your education it
will be by themes and regular discourses. Practice in this as in all
other cases, will render that very easy which now appears to you

of insuperable difficulty. Your father and family are all well, and will return here in 2. or 3 days, having gone to Edgehill during my absence in Bedford and remained there since from some pressure of the business of the farm. Their return is hastened by the situation of Mrs. Hackley who will increase her family probably in a very few days, and therefore must move hither in time, probably about Thursday or Friday. Altho' I have written to you more rarely, yet I am not the less anxious to be informed of your progress in Mathematics. In your letters to me therefore state always in what particular part you are engaged: and never forget that on the closeness of your application at this time depends the future respectability and happiness of your life. Ever most affectionately yours,   TH: JEFFERSON

FROM THOMAS JEFFERSON RANDOLPH

Richmond June 4 1810

DEAR GRANDFATHER

I recieved your letter of the 14, not untill the 28 when I immediately bought the oils but there has not been a boat from Milton since, by which I could send it; by the bottle it cost a Dollar; by the dozen 10 Dollars. There is to be a short vacation in the school on the first of July; If I continue here the fall Months I would wish to go home then, if not I should prefer staying here untill the 13 of August when my quarter will expire and then return home. That however will depend entirely on your wishes and papas. Will you write me soon after you recieve this, (because your letters seldom reach me under ten days) whether [I] remain here or not. Yours affectionately,

THOS J RANDOLPH

N B I have been confined three weeks from a cut of the Tendo Achilles, I shall be able to walk however in two or three days at farthest.

TO MARTHA JEFFERSON RANDOLPH

Poplar Forest Feb. 17. 11

MY EVER DEAR MARTHA

Our post to Milton is but once a week, and I missed the opportunity of sending my letter to Lynchburg the last week. I performed my journey to this place with as little fatigue and by the same stages as in my chair. And by losing myself the first day I made it 40. miles to Mr. Scott's.[1] I have sold my tobo. here for 7. Dollars: but my wheat is in an embarrassing situation. The dam of the mill in which it is has now broke a second time, and the Miller refuses to deliver my wheat back, altho he had promised in that event to redeliver it. It will take another month to mend his dam, by which time the price and the river both may fail us. I propose to make another formal demand of it, and if he refuses, I may have parted with my crop for a lawsuit instead of money. Besides that he is not able to pay all who are in my situation with him. I expect to obtain his final decision within a few days, and whatever it be to set out then on my return if the weather will permit. We have had 4. snows since my arrival here, one of 4. Inches, the others slight. They have put the roads into a horrible situation. I was two days ago at Belleplaine, Beaulieu, Bellavista, Mount Dougherty &c.[2] All well except a man (William) who is habitually otherwise. Slaughter[3] is much surprised that the two men expected are not yet arrived, and the more on my telling him they were to set out from Monticello the day after I left it now three weeks past. Kiss and bless all the fireside for me, and be assured yourself of my unceasing and tenderest love.

TH: JEFFERSON

1. C. A. Scott operated a ferry in Cumberland County on the James River. TJ lodged there on the night of January 28.

2. These several names have doggedly resisted complete identification. TJ departed Poplar Forest February 8 for Lynchburg, returned on the 9th or 10th and, according to his itinerary set down in his account book, remained at Poplar Forest until he left for Monticello on the 28th. The checklist of his correspondence at the University of Virginia lists letters dated the 13th and the above of the 17th, both written at Poplar Forest. This, coupled with his limited mobility, would have put him on February 15 no more than 30 to 40 miles, at the most, from his Bedford County seat. These places then were probably farm sites, possibly TJ's, in the vicinity of Poplar Forest.

3. Possibly Joseph Slaughter, a Bedford County farmer.

To Martha Jefferson Randolph

Poplar Forest Feb. 24. 11.

MY DEAR MARTHA

When I wrote you this day week, I thought I should have been with you as soon as my letter, so I think with respect to the present one. My whole crop of wheat had been put completely out of my power, and the miller who had recieved it has, by twice losing his dam, become insolvent and has delivered over his mill to a person more able to carry it on, but who will need time to repair it. I have a hope of getting possession of 1100 bushels of my wheat, out of 1400. I have promises of it. I think that within two or three days I can ascertain whether they will be performed, and shall set out the moment it is secured. I have wished for Anne but once since I came here, and that has been from the moment of my arrival to the present one. The weather has been such that I have seen the face of no human being for days but the servants. I am like a state prisoner. My keepers set before me at fixed hours something to eat and withdraw. We have had seven snows since I came making all together about 10½ Inches. The ground has been now covered a fortnight. I had begun to prepare an Asparagus bed, and to plant some raspberry bushes, gooseberry bushes &c. for Anne. But it has been impossible to go on with it, the earth is so deep frozen, and I expect to leave it so: I trust that Bacon does not let the family suffer for any thing in his department, and your note in my name will command groceries or whatever else may be wanting from Higginbotham's. My best affections attend you all and constant love to yourself.

TH: JEFFERSON

To Anne Randolph Bankhead

Monticello May 26. 11.

My dear Anne

I have just recieved a copy of the Modern Griselda[1] which Ellen tells me will not be unacceptable to you. I therefore inclose it. The heroine presents herself certainly as a perfect model of ingenious perverseness, and of the art of making herself and others unhappy. If it can be made of use in inculcating the virtues and felicities of life, it must be by the rules of contraries. Nothing new has happened in our neighborhood since you left us. The houses and trees stand where they did. The flowers come forth like the belles of the day, have their short reign of beauty and spendor, and retire like them to the more interesting office of reproducing their like. The hyacinths and tulips are off the stage, the Irises are giving place to the Belladonnas, as this will to the Tuberoses &c. As your Mama has done to you, my dear Anne, as you will do to the sisters of little John,[2] and as I shall soon and chearfully do to you all in wishing you a long, long, goodnight. Present me respectfully to Doctr. and Mrs. Bankhead and accept for Mr. Bankhead and yourself the assurances of my cordial affection, not forgetting that Cornelia shares them.

TH: JEFFERSON

1. Probably the 1810 Philadelphia edition published by Joseph Milligan.

2. Anne Cary and Charles L. Bankhead had four children: John Warner, Thomas Mann Randolph, Ellen Wayles, and William Stuart Bankhead. For additional biographical information on these and other of TJ's children, grandchildren, and great grandchildren, consult "Collection of Papers to Commemorate Fifty Years of the Monticello Association of the Descendants of Thomas Jefferson," edited by Dr. George Green Shackelford and to be published in 1966.

To CORNELIA JEFFERSON RANDOLPH

Monticello June 3. 11.

MY DEAR CORNELIA

I have lately recieved a copy of Mrs. Edgeworth's Moral tales,[1] which seeming better suited to your years than to mine, I inclose you the first volume. The other two shall follow as soon as your Mama has read them. They are to make a part of your library. I have not looked into them, preferring to recieve their character from you after you shall have read them. Your family of silk-worms is reduced to a single individual, that is now spinning his broach. To encourage Virginia and Mary to take care of it, I tell them that as soon as they can get III wedding gowns from this spinner they shall be married. I propose the same to you that, in order to hasten it's work, you may hasten home; for we all wish much to see you, and to express in person, rather than by letter. the assurances of our affectionate love.   TH: JEFFERSON

P. S. The girls desire me to add a postscript to inform you that Mrs. Higginbotham has just given them new Dolls.

1. *Moral Tales for Young People;* possibly the three-volume London edition of 1804.

FROM FRANCIS WAYLES EPPES

Millbrook Sep 2 1811

DEAR GRANDPAPA

I wish to see you very much. I am very sorry that you did not answer my letter. Give my love to aunt Randolph and all of the children. Believe me to be your most affectionate Grandson,

FRANCIS EPPES

To Francis Wayles Eppes

Monticello Sep. 6.11.

Dear Francis

Your letter of Aug. 19. came to hand only 4. or 5. days ago. I should have answered it by post had not Martin[1] arrived with your second. I am glad to learn you are becoming a Roman, which a familiarity with their history will certainly make you. The putting you into qui, quae, quod, was only to strengthen your memory, which you may do quite as well by getting pieces of poetry by heart. Jefferson and myself intend you a visit in November, and it will then be a question for the consideration of your papa and yourself whether you shall not return with us and visit your cousins. This will be acceptable to us all, and only deprecated by the partridges and snow birds against which you may commence hostilities. Adieu my dear Francis, be industrious in advancing yourself in knolege, which with your good dispositions, will ensure the love of others, and your own happiness, and the love and happiness of none more than of Yours affectionately,

Th: Jefferson

1. A slave of John Wayles Eppes.

From Francis Wayles Eppes

Lynchburg April 11 day 1813

Dear Grand Papa

I wish to see you very much. I am Sorry that you wont Write to me. This leter will make twice I have wrote to you and if you dont answer this leter I Shant write to you any more. I have got trough my latin Gramer and I am going trough again. I enclose a leter in this from My Cousin Wale Baker.[1] Give my love to all of the family.

Believe me to remain with the filial love your most affectionate Grand Son,   Francis Eppes

1. Wayles Baker was his first cousin and the son of Martha Bolling Eppes and Jerman Baker.

To Martha Jefferson Randolph

Poplar Forest. May 6. 13.

We arrived here, my dear Martha, well and without accident, favored on the road by the weather. The caravan also came well, except overpassing their stage the 2d day, sleeping in the woods all night, without cover, and overwhelmed by a rain, in the center of which they were, while it did not extend 5 miles in any direction from them. The spinning Jenny is at work, well while with washed cotton, but very ill when with unwashed. At least this is Maria's[1] way of accounting for the occasional difference of it's work. The flying shuttle began a little yesterday, but owing to a variety of fixings which the loom required it exhibited very poorly. We hope to see it do better to-day. I am afraid I shall be detained here in getting Perry[2] off before I go away. If I leave him here I shall have no confidence in his following me. Still I shall not fail to be at home within a week or ten days from this date. Present me affectionately to Mr. Randolph and our beloved children, if Ellen will permit herself to be included under that appellation, and be assured yourself of all my love and tenderness.

TH: JEFFERSON

1. A Jefferson servant who was particularly adept at spinning and weaving.
2. Reuben Perry was a Poplar Forest workman.

To Francis Wayles Eppes

Poplar Forest. Aug. 28. 13

MY DEAR FRANCIS

After my return from this place to Monticello in May last I recieved the letters which yourself and your cousin Baker wrote me. That was the first information I recieved of your being at school at Lynchburg, or I should certainly have sent for you to come and see me while I was here. I now send 2. horses for yourself and your cousin and hope your tutor will permit you both to come and stay with me till Monday morning then I will send you back again. I left your aunt and all your cousins well in Albemarle. In hopes of seeing you here immediately I remain affectionately yours,

TH: JEFFERSON

To Francis Wayles Eppes

Poplar Forest Nov. 26.13.

DEAR FRANCIS

I have written to ask the favor of Mr. Halcomb to permit your cousin Baker and yourself to come and pass tomorrow and next day with me here. I send horses for you both, and will send you

back on Monday morning. I left your aunt and cousins well at
Monticello, and in the hope of seeing you here this evening, I
remain affectionately Your's,   TH: JEFFERSON

TO ELLEN WAYLES RANDOLPH

Poplar Forest Nov. 26. 13.

MY DEAREST ELLEN

The situation in which I left your dear Mama makes me very
anxious to hear of her during my stay here. Uncertain whether
this may not find her in bed, I address it to you to pray you to
write me a line letting me know how she is. If it is done on the
reciept of this letter and put immediately into the post office of
Charlottesville, it will still find me here. Direct to me at Poplar
Forest near Lynchburg. If you have heard any thing from your
Papa since I left you, let me know it. Indeed, as I shall see no
newspaper till I get back, if it be known with you whether a stroke
is struck either against Kingston or Montreal the news will be
acceptable. I had a terrible journey up, thro two days of rain,
which tho' light, was nearly constant, but the roads dirtier and
heavier than I have ever found them on this rout. The 2d. day I
was able to get but 25. miles, and on the 3d. which brought me
here I was from day-light to dark getting 34. miles. I was so well
guarded that I was not at all wet, and my rheumatism is sensibly
abated. According to my present prospect I shall be with you after
an absence of three weeks. Kiss your dear Mama for me, and deliver my affections to all the fireside assuring yourself of my
tender love.   TH: JEFFERSON

FROM THOMAS JEFFERSON RANDOLPH

Carys-brook. March 25 1814

MY DEAR GRANDFATHER

Mr. Cary[1] is unfortunately from home. I have ordered Phil[2]
to wait and have left a message for him with his wife. I am afraid
there is little prospect of getting him. Your sincerely affectionate
grandson,   TH: J. RANDOLPH

1. Wilson Jefferson Cary.
2. A trusted slave of TJ.

TO MARTHA JEFFERSON RANDOLPH

Poplar Forest June 6. 14.

MY DEAR MARTHA

I have for some time been sensible I should be detained here longer than I had expected, but could not till now judge how long. Chisolm will finish his work in about 10. days, and it is very essential that I should see the walls covered with their plates, that they may be in a state of preservation. This will keep me 3. or 4. days longer, so that I expect to be here still about a fortnight longer. There have not been more than 2. or 3. days without rain since I came here, and the last night the most tremendous storm of rain, wind and lightening I have ever witnessed. For about an hour the heavens were in an unceasing blaze of light, during which you might at any moment have seen to thread a needle. They had been deluged with rain before I came; and the continuance of it threatens injury to our wheat, which is indifferent at best. I have not seen a pea since I left Albemarle, and have no vegetable but spinach and scrubby lettuce. Francis and Wayles Baker are with me. My journey was performed without an accident. The horses and postilions performed well. James will be an excellent driver, and Israel will do better with more strength and practice. You will always be perfectly safe with their driving. If Wormly and Ned should get through the ha! ha![1] and cleaning all the grounds within the upper roundabout, they should next widen the Carlton road,[2] digging it level and extending it upwards from the corner of the graveyard up, as the path runs into the upper Roundabout, so as to make the approach to the house from that quarter on the Northside instead of the South. Present me affectionately to all the family, and be assured of my warmest love. TH: JEFFERSON

1. The idea for a ha-ha (a ditch or sunken fence) is found in TJ's "General ideas for the improvement of Monticello," circa 1804 (MHi). It was to run behind the Mulberry Row, being the boundary of the northern side of the vegetable garden terrace. There is no evidence this was ever constructed; in 1808–1809, however, a paling fence was erected along the same route as proposed for the ha-ha.

2. A Monticello road. See *Farm Book*, 70, for additional information on this road.

FROM THOMAS JEFFERSON RANDOLPH

Richmond Aug 31st 1814

MY DEAR GRANDFATHER

You are no doubt anxious to hear what we are doing and what are our expectations as it respects defence, and the arrival of the enemy.[1] Our governor[2] as pompous, perhaps, as patriotic, has taken the field and is encamped at fairfeild, two miles from town with H. Lee[3] Mercer, H. Nelson, aids, and about 2500. men under the immediate command of Gen. Cocke.[4] There are 2,000 at Camp Holly 10 miles below this under Gen. Porterfield[5] and about 5 or 600 in town, local militia and volunteer corps; making an aggregate of about 5,000. Volunteers, are hourly arriving. They are to be organized, both horse and foot under command of my father as a legion to meet the enemy where he lands, and fight him incessantly until he reaches the town.[6] At the same time impeding his march by breaking up bridges and felling trees in the road. There is no confusion here, because the enemy is not at their doors, and not from a confidence in them or activity in their preparation. They rest satisfied as the enemy did not destroy private property at Washington, that they will not here. The federalists allways the least active in their preparation are as usual the more violent and abusive upon every miscarriage. I have made yet no disposition of myself. I find all my young friends and acquaintances here and will be able to fix myself agreably. God forbid, that I should have been last to come forward in defence of my country, for which I shall always be proud to sacrifice my life. Your most devoted and affectionate grandson,

TH: J. RANDOLPH

1. The British were expected to seize Richmond by an attack up the peninsula from Norfolk.

2. Wilson Cary Nicholas, who was soon to be Randolph's father-in-law.

3. Henry Lee, a son of Henry "Lighthorse Harry" Lee, was a major in the 36th Virginia Infantry Regiment.

4. General John Hartwell Cocke was the commanding officer of the Virginia militia guarding Richmond.

5. General Robert Porterfield was a general officer in the Virginia militia in 1812, commanding troops stationed at Camp Holley on the Chickahominy River.

6. Probably Richmond, Virginia.

To Francis Wayles Eppes

Monticello Sep. 9. 14.

My first wish, my dear Francis, is ever to hear that you are in good health, because that is the first of blessings. The second is to become an honest and useful man to those among whom we live. You are now in the high road of instruction for this object, and I have great confidence you will pursue it with steadiness and attain the end which will make all your friends happy. I shall carry with me to Poplar Forest the proper books for instructing you in French. Whether you can pass your time with me while there, and be employed in learning French must depend on the will of your father and of your tutor. I expect to go there within about three weeks, and to make a longer stay that usual. If that should be employed wholly on French, and you can afterwards pass your Christmas at Monticello where your aunt and cousins can assist me in helping you on, you will afterwards be able to proceed of yourself. In this you will be obliged to separate from your cousin who is too young for an undertaking to be pursued afterwards alone. In the hope of seeing you soon, and conveying to you the wishes of your aunt and cousins to be remembered to you, be assured of my affectionate love,

TH: JEFFERSON

From Thomas Jefferson Randolph

Timberlake,[1] Sep 9th 1814

My Dear Grandfather

By accident I have obtained in this wretched country paper enough to write a letter upon. We arrived at camp (on the sixth) about two miles from West Point, in want of every thing necessary for the support of the army, both man and horse; we get some beef but never, enough, and that such as we find in the old field, not good, without salt and often without bread, the supply of which is allways precarious; our horses go often twenty four hours without food. We have nothing in abundance, but ticks and musketoes, not as many of the latter as we expected to find. If we remain here many days longer, we must depend entirely upon supplies brought from Richmond as the country between this and that place was found too poor to support us on our march. We very often see large establishments apparently the abode of wealthy persons. Upon approaching them we find them occupied by squalid indigent, wretches, who can not give a meal of any kind to two persons.

Our sick list is rapidly encreasing; the water drank by part of the corps is such as our horses in Albemarle would not drink.

Your kind offer of a draught upon Gibson[2] would be very acceptable. Your affectionate Grandson,   TH J RANDOLPH

1. Timberlake is in King and Queen County, at the confluence of the Pamunkey and Mattaponi rivers that forms the York River.
2. Patrick Gibson was a partner in the Richmond firm of Gibson and Jefferson.

To Francis Wayles Eppes

Poplar Forest Nov. 11. 14.

MY DEAR FRANCIS

I arrived here a few days ago, and sent for you immediately and did not learn till the return of the messenger that your school had separated, and would not reassemble until after Christmas. As your father will probably be from home all that time, would it not be better that you should pass it at Monticello. In two months we can advance you so much in French that you would be able to pursue it by yourself afterwards, and especially when aided by our occasional meetings at this place. On this subject consult with your Mama who will decide for you what is best, and to whom present my friendly respects. In the hope she will conclude in favor of your visit to Monticello I give you here the assurances of my love.   TH: JEFFERSON

From Francis Wayles Eppes

Millbrook Nov 23 1814

DEAR GRANDPAPA

I wish to see you very much. I have not been able to go to School this Session. I cannot Come to Monticello Christmas for I expect my Father Home. Give my love to Aunt Randolph and all of my Cousins. Believe me to be your most Affectionate Grandson, FRANCIS EPPES

To Thomas Jefferson Randolph

Monticello Mar. 31. 15.

DEAR JEFFERSON

Ellen's visit to Warren[1] has been delayed by an unlucky accident. On Monday we heard that my brother was very sick.[2] Mrs. Marks wishing to go and see him I sent her the next morning in the gig with a pair of my horses, counting on their return the next day so that Ellen and Cornelia might have gone on Thursday according to arrangement. After Mrs. Marks had got about 7. miles on her road, one of the horses (Bedford) was taken so ill that she thought it best to return. He died that night, and no pair of the remaining three could be trusted to draw a carriage. Mrs. Marks going off again to-day to Snowden, I make Wormley take Seclah, and direct him to return by Warren and exchange him with you for the mare Hyatilda. She is an excellent draught animal, and with a match I have for her at Tufton will carry the girls very well; only that as it is sometime since she was in geer, it will be advisable to drive her in the waggon two or three days. In the mean time as your business will probably bring you to court the girls will have the benefit of your escort to Warren. This is the best arrangement it is in my power to make. Ellen is still unwell, and her face is tied up, which however she would not have permitted to disappoint her visit. The family here wish to be presented with respect to Mrs. Nicholas and the family of Warren. To our new friend[3] whom you have brought into so near a relation with us, give assurances that we recieve her as a member of our family with very great pleasure and cordiality and shall endeavor and hope to make this an acceptable home to you both. Ever affectionately yours,   TH: JEFFERSON

1. A small village in southern Albemarle County, on the James River.
2. Randolph Jefferson died on August 7, 1815, at the age of sixty.
3. Thomas Jefferson Randolph was married at Mount Warren, the Nicholas home in Albemarle County, on March 6, 1815, to Jane Hollins, a daughter of Wilson Cary Nicholas and Margaret Smith of the distinguished Baltimore family.

From Martha Jefferson Randolph

Monticello Aug. 13, 1815.

MY DEAR FATHER

The emergency of the occasion must apologise for the liberty I took in opening the enclosed. But as to morrow is Buckingham court and not knowing the danger that might accrue from a disappointment I ascertained by opening the letter Whether it was your self or the Witnesses only that were wanting. In which latter case they could have been summoned with out applying to you, but as some thing more seems requisite perhaps you can by writing do the business. Adieu. We are all as you left us the sick mending and no new cases. Yours,   MR.

To Martha Jefferson Randolph

Montpelier Aug. 13. 15.

The letter you forwarded, my dear Martha, desiring me to attend the Buckingham court of this month, requires an impossibility because that is tomorrow. I know also that the trial of the question cannot be at the same court at which the two wills are presented. Time must be given to summon witnesses, and I suppose I shall be served with a summons notifying the day I must appear. We have had a safe journey, shall return to Mr. Lindsay's[1] tomorrow night and shall be at home to dinner on Tuesday. Yours with unalterable and tender affection,   TH: JEFFERSON

1. Reuben Lindsay was a close friend of TJ and resided in Albemarle County.

To Martha Jefferson Randolph

Poplar Forest Aug. 31. 15.

My dear Martha

We all arrived here without accident, myself the day after I left home, having performed the journey in two days, reaching Noah Flood's[1] the 1st. day. The story of the neighborhood immediately was that I had brought a crowd of workmen to get ready my house in a hurry for Bonaparte. Were there such people only as the believers in this, patriotism would be a ridiculous passion. We are suffering from drought terribly at this place. Half a crop of wheat, and tobacco, and two thirds a crop of corn are the most we can expect. Cate,[2] with good aid, is busy drying peaches for you. We abound in the luxury of the peach, these being as fine here now as we used to have in Albemarle 30. years ago, and indeed as fine as I ever saw any where. I find the distance from hence to the Natural bridge,[3] by Petit's gap is only 29. miles. I shall therefore go there on horseback; but not until I return from

Buckingham court, where I presume I shall meet Jefferson, and hear something from home. Indeed it would be a great comfort to me if some one of the family would write to me once a week, were it only to say all is well. I see no reason to believe we shall finish our work here sooner than the term I had fixed for my return. It is rather evident we must have such another expedition the next year. Remember me affectionately to the family and be assured yourself of my warmest and tenderest love my dearest Marth.

TH: JEFFERSON

1. A Buckingham County inn; TJ arrived there on August 20.
2. A Jefferson slave.
3. TJ referred to this natural formation in present-day Rockbridge County as "the most sublime of nature's works." He patented 157 acres of land lying along Cedar Creek, then in Botetourt County, in 1774, for 20 shillings under a grant from George III. The original deed is recorded in the courthouse in Fincastle, Virginia. For Jefferson's description, see William Peden, editor, *Notes on the State of Virginia by Thomas Jefferson* (Chapel Hill, 1955), 24–25.

To MARTHA JEFFERSON RANDOLPH

Poplar Forest Nov. 4. 15.

MY DEAREST MARTHA

We arrived here on the third day of our journey, without any accident; but I suffered very much both mornings by cold. I must therefore pray you to send my wolf-skin pelisse and fur-boots by Moses's Billy, when he comes to bring the two mules to move the Carpenters back. He is to be here on the 27th. by my directions to Mr. Bacon. In the closet [1] over my bed you will find a bag tied up, and labelled 'Wolf-skin pelisse,' and another labelled 'fur-boots,' wherein those articles will be found. The pelisse had better be sowed up in a striped blanket to keep it clean and uninjured; the boots in any coarse wrapper.

Mr. Baker called on me yesterday, and tells me Francis is gone to Monticello. I am in hopes Ellen will give him close employment. Mr. Baker is come to look for land in this quarter, and will return here this evening and start with me tomorrow morning to Mr. Clark's,[2] to examine his land which is for sale. It will place his family exactly under the sharp peak of Otter,[3] 20. miles only from hence, and along a good road. Lands of 2d quality are selling here now for 25. Dollars. I am this moment interrupted by a crowd of curious people come to see the house. Adieu my Dear Martha, kiss all the young ones for me; present me affectionately to Mr. Randolph, and be assured of my tenderest love.

TH: JEFFERSON

P. S. I was most agreeably surprised to find that the party whom I thought to be merely curious visitants were General Jackson and his suite, who passing to Lynchburg did me the favor to call.

1. The only reference to the use of the small room above TJ's bed. The three oval openings, which tradition says were used as look-outs for his body-guards, were there only for letting light into the closet. The closet was reached via a stairway at the head of TJ's bed.

2. Probably John Clarke, a Bedford County resident.

3. The Peaks of Otter are located on the boundary line between Bedford and Botetourt counties, about thirty miles southwest of Lynchburg. The tall-est peak is 4,260 feet above sea level.

To Ellen Wayles Randolph

Monticello Mar.14.16.

I have been, my dear Ellen, without subject for a letter to you until one has been furnished by the sale of my tobacco. In this you also will feel somewhat of interest, inasmuch as it enables me to replenish your moyens de jouissance, by remitting to Mr. Barnes 100.D. for you. I do this by the present mail, and have chosen his cover because I thought it would go safer in that way, and because also it has given me an opportunity of requesting that he would furnish your wants beyond that to any extent you may call for, with an assurance of immediate replacement. You have only there-fore to draw on him for the present and any further sums, as you may want them; and I assure you, my dear Ellen, you cannot give me so great a proof of your affection and confidence as by a free use of the opportunity now furnished me of doing what may be acceptable to you. Your Mama and the girls, I expect, anticipate me in all the small news of the neighborhood; perhaps even in that we have heard but this morning, the death of an aunt, and birth of a niece. We had scarcely wished Jefferson joy of his daugh-ter[1] when we recieved the news of the death of Mrs. Judy Ran-dolph.[2] Have they told you that our neighbor Mr. Sthreshly has sold out to Capt. Meriwether this giving us a double subject of regret?[3] I thought you were to have given me occasional if not regular reports of Congressional incidents and fracasseries, not omitting entirely the babble of the coteries of the place. Do not write me studied letters but ramble as you please. Whatever books you want, desire Milligan[4] to furnish them and to put them into my account. By the bye do you know anything of him? By the im-possibility of my getting answers from him I begin to suspect some-thing is the matter. When are you coming home? I shall be in

Bedford all April. The void you have left at our fire side is sensibly felt by us all, and by none more than your's with most affectionate love,   TH: JEFFERSON

P. S. My friendly respects to the President, and homage to Mrs. Madison and Mrs. Cutts.[5]

1. Margaret Smith Randolph was born at the Governor's Mansion in Richmond on March 7, 1816.

2. Mrs. Richard Randolph of Bizarre, Cumberland County.

3. Robert B. Streshley sold William D. Meriwether a tract of 312 acres lying along Moore's Creek and opposite the house of Charles L. Bankhead and approximately one mile down the mountain from the Thoroughfare Gap gate to Monticello. See Albemarle County Deed Book No. 20, page 122, Albemarle County Courthouse, Charlottesville.

4. Joseph Milligan was a Washington bookseller and friend of TJ's.

5. Mrs. Richard Cutts was the sister of Dolley Madison.

FROM ELLEN WAYLES RANDOLPH

Washington March 19th 1816

MY DEAR GRANDPAPA

Your letter of the 14th reached me yesterday and I hasten to return you thanks for this new proof of your affection. The remittance made to Mr. Barnes will indeed add considerably to my moyens de jouissance, and I need not tell you how gratefull I am for your kindness. I have no idea that my wants will exceed the 100. D. but if they should I will apply as you have directed. If I have not written to you hitherto it has been because I found myself unable to perform my promise of giving you the little news of Congress. I do not hear subjects of the kind much spoken of either at home or abroad. I have very little acquaintance with the members, who are not in the habit of visiting familiarly in the family; some of them attend the drawing rooms regularly, but these parties are always crowded, and the conversation consists of compliments, and common place observations made in passant. I did not know untill I came here, how much more amusement may sometimes be found in the solitude of one's own chamber, than in a gay circle. The election of the next President is a subject so interesting to every body, that even the most idle and indifferent think and talk a good deal about it. The merits of the candidates are discussed, and even the ladies of their families come in for their full share of praise or blame. Mrs. Monroe has made herself very unpopular by taking no pains to conceal her aversion to society, and her unwillingness to be intruded on by visitors. The English Minister and his lady and Mrs. Bagot[1] arrived in town last evening. She is niece to the Duke of Wellington and said to be a great dasher, if the word is well applied; she will not make a good model for our city ladies, who are generally willing to fashion themselves after any thing foreign, and particularly English.

There was a report in circulation some short time ago that Milligan had broken, but I believe it was without foundation, for Mr. Barnes tells me he is doing very well. I heard of the death of my aunt and the birth of Jefferson's daughter immediately after they took place.

I have so little interesting to write about my dearest Grandpapa, that I cannot flatter myself, my letters will give you pleasure, except as they are proofs of my affection. With congressional incidents and fracasseries I am unacquainted, because those with whom I associate, either take no interest or forbear to speak of them; and the babble of the coteries of the place I can never remember an hour. I wish very much to visit Baltimore this Spring. I have a curiosity to see the place, and shall probably never again have so good opportunity; this wish gratified, I shall have no others but to return to the bosom of my family, where alone I can expect to find real happiness.

Adieu my dearest Grandpapa, I remain most affectionately yours,   E. W. RANDOLPH
P. S. Mrs. Madison and Mr. Todd[2] desire to be particularly remembered to you. Mrs. Cutts I have not seen since I received your letter.

1. Sir Charles Bagot, British Minister to the United States.
2. Payne Todd, Dolley Madison's son by her first marriage.

To FRANCIS WAYLES EPPES

Monticello May 21.16.

I send you, my dear Francis, a Greek grammar, the best I know for the use of schools.[1] It is the one now most generally used in the United States. I expect you will begin it soon after your arrival at the New London academy.[2] You might, while at home, amuse yourself with learning the letters, and spelling and reading the Greek words, so that you may not be stopped by that when Mr. Mitchell puts you into the grammar. I think you will like him, and old Mr. and Mrs. Dehavens, from the character I have of them. I am sure Mr. Mitchell will do every thing for you he can and I have no fear that you will not do full justice to his institution.

But, while you endeavor, by a good store of learning, to prepare yourself to become an useful and distinguished member of your country you must remember that this can never be, without uniting merit with your learning. Honesty, disinterestedness, and good nature are indispensible to procure the esteem and confidence of those with whom we live, and on whose esteem our happiness depends. Never suffer a thought to be harbored in your mind which you would not avow openly. When tempted to do any thing in secret, ask yourself if you would do it in public. If you would not be sure it is wrong: in little disputes with your companions, give way, rather than insist on trifles. For their love and the approbation of others will be worth more to you than the trifle in dispute. Above all things, and at all times, practice yourself in good humor. This, of all human qualities, is the most amiable and endearing to society. Whenever you feel a warmth of temper rising, check it at once, and suppress it, recollecting it will make you unhappy within yourself, and disliked by others. Nothing gives one person so great advantage over another, as to remain always cool and unruffled under all circumstances. Think of these things, practice them and you will be rewarded by the love and confidence of the world. I have some expectation of being at Poplar Forest the 3d. week of June, when I hope I shall see you going on cleverly, and already beloved by your tutor, curators, and companions, as you are by your's affectionately,

TH: JEFFERSON

1. Sowerby, in *The Library of Thomas Jefferson*, V, No. 4756, does not indicate which of the several listed titles TJ favored as a school text. She does state that a translation of *Elementa Linguae Graecae* . . . (Glasguae, [1795]) was one of the first books ordered by TJ after the sale of his library to Congress in 1815.

2. This is one of the oldest secondary schools in the United States that has continuously operated on a single site. It was chartered in 1795 and today is part of the Bedford County school system.

To Martha Jefferson Randolph

Poplar Forest Nov. 10. 16.

We are all well here, my dear Martha, and thinking of our return home which will be about the 30th. or perhaps a day or two sooner. It is necessary therefore that the boys, Johnny and Randall with the mules should set off from Monticello on the 19th. or 20th. to take the cart and baggage. I must pray you to desire Mr. Bacon to let them have a good mule and geer in addition to Tilman and his. Tell Wormley also to send some Calycanthus plants well done up in moss and straw, and about a bushel of Orchard grass seed out of the large box in the Green house.[1] Would it be possible for you so to make up some of the hardy bulbous roots of flowers as to come safely on the mule? Daffodils, jonquils, Narcisouses, flags and lillies of different kinds, refuse hyacinths &c. with some of the small bulbs of the hanging onion. I think if wrapped and sowed up tight in two balls, one to come in each end of a wallet with nothing else in it to bruise them, they would come safe. Present me affectionately to Mr. Randolph, kiss all the young ones for me and be assured of my most tender affection.

TH: JEFFERSON

P.S. Ellen writes to you more fully and I write to Jefferson.

The boys must come to Gibson's the 1st. night, Hunter's the 2d. and here the 3d.[2]

1. The glass-enclosed southern piazza. It was the southernmost room at Monticello and was entered through the library suite. Here was also TJ's workbench and shop.

2. Mrs. Gibson's was a Buckingham County inn. Hunter's was just across the line in Campbell County, south of Noah Flood's. On various occasions TJ utilized each of these inns. Consult Account Book.

FROM MARTHA JEFFERSON RANDOLPH

Monticello Nov. 20, 1816

MY DEAREST FATHER

We recieved your letters last night only, and the necessary preparations for the boy's Journey would take up so much of the day that we determined not to send them till to morrow morning 21st. Wormley will see to every thing but the bulbous roots. The kinds you mention are all growing at present and could not be moved with out destroying them but I have sent you a number of off sets of tulips and hyacinths some blooming roots and some that will not bloom till the ensuing year but I believe all of the finest kinds. They were intended to have been planted in the borders last fall but were kept out waiting for a bed to be prepared for them. The others can be dug up at the proper season and planted next summer or fall. You will have seen by the papers the death of Gouverneur Morris. His loss will be irreparable to his wife by lessening the *little* consequence that I am afraid she had, and exposing her unprotected to the persecution of his heirs who have been dissapointed by the birth of her child of his large possessions. I wrote to her upon the occasion although we had not previously corresponded, but poor creature she is surrounded by ennemies and never in more need of the support of her family than at present. Adieu My Dearest Father we are All well but poor Ann. Mr. Bankhead[1] has returned and recommenced his habits of drunkeness. Mr. Randolph[2] has taken in to his own hands the mannagement of his affairs and if his family are much disturbed or endangered will take at once the steps necessary for their protection, as circumstances may require. Sending him to the mad house is but a temporary remedy, for after a few weeks he would be returned with renewed health to torment his family the longer. I really think the best way would be to hire a keeper for him to prevent his doing mischief, and let him finish him self at once. His Father is utterly in dispair, and told Aunt Marks that but for Ann and the children he never wished to see his face again. He so entirely threw off all respect for the old gentleman as to tell him he would be master in his own house and called for a decanter of whiskey and drank of two draughts to his face the more to brave him. Adieu My Dearest Father. With tender and unchangeable love Your affectionate Daughter,

MRANDOLPH

The large crown imperial root is for Mrs. Eppes, if you go that way. The smaller ones are not blooming roots yet, but will be in a year or 2. The tulips and hyacinths are mixed but Cornelia knows them all. I have sent you besides the first letter, 3 I believe of which I altered the direction. 3 packets enclosing many letters each the second via Richmond and the 3 went of[f] yesterday 19th before I recieved your letter, for they close the mail on Monday which will account for one packet going by Richmond. The mail being closed before my letters were sent to Charlottesville. I have also sent all the weekly registers as I recieved them.

1. Charles Lewis Bankhead, Anne Cary Randolph's husband. He had been visiting his family in Caroline County.
2. Thomas Mann Randolph, Jr.

TO MARTHA JEFFERSON RANDOLPH

Poplar Forest. Tuesday Dec. 3. 16.

We have been, my ever dearest Martha, now weather bound at this place since Sunday was sennight. We were then to have set off on our return home, but it began to rain that day, and we have had three regular N. E. rains successively, with intermissions of a single day between each. During the first intermission, Mr.

Flower left us for Monticello, but by the way of the Natural bridge. By him I wrote to Mr. Randolph that we should set out in 2. or 3. days; but the 2d. storm set in the next day, and the 3d. cleared up last night, leaving us a snow of 4. inches on the ground. We shall wait 2. or 3. days for that to go off, the roads to harden, and the waters to fall, and we shall be 6. days on the road, that is to say, 2 days to Millbrook, 2. there and 2. home; so that I suppose we shall be at Monticello about this day or tomorrow sennight, allowing in addition for any further bad weather. Johnny Hemings & co. will set off on Thursday and be at home on Sunday. It is well that during our delay we have been in comfortable quarters. Our only discomfort is the not being with you. The girls have borne it wonderfully. They have been very close students, and I am never without enough to do to protect me from ennui. God bless you all.   TH: JEFFERSON

To Martha Jefferson Randolph

Poplar Forest Aug. 18. 17.

I inclose the within, to you, my dearest daughter and friend, because it is of great consequence, to be put into the post office at Charlottesville from which place it will go safer to Staunton than from hence. Ellen writes to you and of course will give the news of this place if she can muster up any. The history of our expedition to the Natural bridge she will write you of course. The sun, moon and stars move here so much like what they do at Monticello, and every thing else so much in the same order, not omitting even the floods of rain, that they afford nothing new for observation. It will not be new that we give all our love to young and old, male and female of the family, and our kisses to Septimia [1] particularly, with gingerbread which she will prefer to them.

TH: JEFFERSON

1. Septimia Anne Randolph, Martha's youngest daughter, was born January 3, 1814, at Monticello. Here the Randolphs' first child had been born twenty-three years earlier.

To Martha Jefferson Randolph

Poplar Forest Aug. 31. 17.

MY EVER DEAR MARTHA

Ellen tells me that a request is communicated thro' Mr. Randolph and yourself from the Freemason societies of Charlottesville to be permitted to lay the first brick of the Central college. I do not know that I have authority to say either yea or nay to this proposition; but as far as I may be authorised, I consent to it freely. The inhabitants of Charlottesville deserve too well of that institution to meet with any difficulty in that request, and I see no possible objection on the part of the other visitors which exposes me to risk in consenting to it.[1]

Ellen and Cornelia are the severest students I have ever met with. They never leave their room but to come to meals. About twilight of the evening, we sally out with the owls and bats, and take our evening exercise on the terras. An alteration in that part of the house, not yet finished, has deprived them of the use of their room longer than I had expected; but two or three days more will now restore it to them. Present me affectionately to Mr. Randolph, the girls and family. I trust to Ellen and Cornelia to communicate our love to Septimia in the form of a cake. My tenderest love attends yourself.   TH: JEFFERSON

1. The Central College was the planned institution's name until a charter by the legislature altered it to the University of Virginia. The cornerstone of the first pavilion, the present-day Colonnade Club, was laid October 6, 1817, by the Widow's Son Masonic Lodge No. 60 and Charlottesville Lodge No. 90. Present were James Madison, James Monroe, and TJ, members of the institution's Board of Visitors. See Philip Alexander Bruce, *University of Virginia,* I, 183–90.

To MARTHA JEFFERSON RANDOLPH

Poplar Forest Nov. 22. 17.

I arrived here, my dear daughter after a disagreeable journey, one day shut up at Warren by steady rain, the next travelling thro a good deal of drizzle and rain, and the last excessive cold, the road being full of ice. But all well in the end. Johnny Hemings had made great progress in his work. His calculation is that he may possibly finish by this day fortnight but possibly and almost probably not till this day three weeks. It is necessary therefore that Cretia's Johnny should be here this day fortnight with the cart for which purpose he must leave Monticello Thursday morning the 3d. of December. I shall be glad if you will send by him my old Rocquelo which will be found on the couch in the chamber. Mr. Burwell, and Mrs. Trist have staid a day with me and are now starting off after an early breakfast. I have time therefore only to add my affections to all and my most especiall love to yourself, inclosing a letter for Mr. Bacon on the mission of Johnny.

TH: JEFFERSON

To Martha Jefferson Randolph

Poplar Forest Nov. 29. 17.

My dear Martha

The calculation in my former letter of the time when Johnny Hemings would be done, was made on a guess of his own. By what he has since done I can estimate the time it will take him more exactly, and I find the cart need not leave Monticello till Thursday the 11th. of December, on which day therefore I wish it to be dispatched.

I have been two days engaged from sunrise to sunset with a surveyor in running round my lines, which have never before been run round. I find that one neighbor (Cobbs) has cleared one half of his field on my land, and been cultivating it for 20. years chiefly in corn, having cut down the line trees so as to leave it nearly impossible to find out the lines. They are by no means unravelled as yet.

News from this place you will not expect. My health continues good except my sprained shoulder; and every body here well. My affectionate love attends always on yourself and the family.

TH: JEFFERSON

From Francis Wayles Eppes

Washington Dec. 28 1817

Dear Grandpapa

I am now though not permanently fixed at school I expect to quit this place the ensueing Spring and if the central College is not ready my Father intends to place me in some school in Virginia untill it goes into operation. Their are a great many objections to this Georgetown College. In the first place they are bigoted Catholics extremely rigid and they require the boys to observe all the regulations of their Church which makes a great interuption in the course of our studies. We rise at Six o Clock and go into the chapell to Mass. We study about two hours and three quarters in the whole of the day the rest of the time being taken up with reciteing lessons and church, an hour and a half excepted for recreation but it would be tedious and unnecessary to inumerate all the particulars. Suffice it is to Say that they are very strict and punish for the most trivial offence. Pappa and Mama unite with me in presenting love to yourself and family. I believe they are very tired of a city life and indeed I think that there is a vast diference between the uproar and bustle of this place and our peaceful home in virginia, I feel the effects of confinement very much, Shut up within the walls of the college scarcely ever permitted to go out except when I am sent for by My Father. Greatly diferent from my past life and it is what I dislike very much. Thire is a gentleman here a Spaniard whom My Father intends to employ to carry on My Spanish but their is a great dificulty in procuring books. Believe me to remain with great respect your affectionate Grandson, FRANCIS EPPES

TO FRANCIS WAYLES EPPES

Monticello Feb. 6. 18.

DEAR FRANCIS

I have deferred acknoleging the reciept of your letter of Dec. 28 in the daily hope of being able to speak with more certainty of the time when our Central college will be opened, but that is still undecided and depending on an uncertainty which I have explained to your father. I do not wonder that you find the place where you are disagreeable, it's character, while I lived in Washington was that of being a seminary of mere sectarism. The only question is how to dispose of yourself until the Central college opens. There is now at the N. London academy an excellent teacher, and that place is on a better footing than it ever has been. Indeed I think it now the best school I know. Dr. Carr[1] has also a school in our neighborhood, but I doubt whether you would find it as good, or as comfortable as the other. James[2] goes to that. If your father should conclude on N. London, you had better come here before the 15th. of April when I shall go to Bedford, and could carry you with me. If Dr. Carr should be preferred, come as soon as you please and I will endeavor to get a place for you with him. But this is not certain as he is very full. In all events I shall hope to see you here whenever your situation will permit, and that you will be assured of my constant love.

TH: JEFFERSON

1. Dr. George Carr operated a school at the east end of Main Street in Charlottesville.
2. James Madison Randolph, Martha's second son and seventh living child. He was born January 17, 1806.

FROM FRANCIS WAYLES EPPES

Washington City Feb, 14th 1818

DEAR GRANDPAPA

I have just recieved your letter of the sixth inst. and I am extremely sorry to learn, that the central college will not be opened next spring. My Father justly estimateing the advantages of a situation in which I could enjoy the benifit of your care and attention had looked forward to this establishment as a place where without the inconvenience of future change and loss of time I might prepare myself for Some university at which my education might be finished. It appears however from your letter that neither his hopes or your own will be realized, as a considerable period may yet intervene before a single professorship will be in operation. Papa intends as I informed you in my last to remove me from the George Town College after the adjournment of congress. Before that period arrives, we shall know with more certainty prospects of the central College. In the mean time I understand from him, that it is his intention to carry me back to Virginia and place me in some situation where I can remain untill the central college goes into operation. Papa and Mama are well and unite with me in wishes for your health and happiness. Believe me to remain with Sincere affection your Grandson,   FRANCIS EPPES

FROM ANNE RANDOLPH BANKHEAD

Recd. Mar. 25. 18.

MY DEAR GRAND PAPA

Mr. Bankhead feels a delicacy in mentioning to you the subject on which Mr. Lightfoot has written to us and I am very sorry to be obliged to give you the trouble of reading his letter. But he has always been so kind and attentive to me that I should like to perform his requests as far as it is in my power and conclude that the best way that I can serve him is by sending his letter to speak for itself. I hope you will excuse my interfering in this affair as I do not know how to avoid it without giving offence. And believe me to be My Dear Grand Papa your truly affectionate grand daughter,   A C BANKHEAD

FROM FRANCIS WAYLES EPPES

New London Academy August 2d 1818

DEAR GRANDPAPA

I found on my arrival here the day that we parted that the Trustees were assembling for the trial of Watts, after Spending most of the day in warm debate he was Suspended untill he should beg Mr. Dashiels pardon, and promise good behaviour in future, and this in the presence of the whole school. To my great surprise he agreed to these humiliating conditions and was admitted. All goes on now as before and a sullen calm has succeeded to the storm that was once threatening in its aspect. Mr. Dashiel is not as much respected I think by the Students as formerly.

By this time you have decided on the place for the University and I hope that the Central College is adopted, as the situation is an healthy one and the most cligible indeed in the state, and because it would afford me the greatest pleasure imaginable to finish my education there it being under your direction. I have commenced Xenophon, and Horace also, though I am afraid that I cannot get through the Arithmetic this Session. I have heard nothing from the Forest Since I saw you. Give my love to Aunt Randolph and the family. Believe me to remain your Affection-ate Grandson, FRANCIS EPPES

TO MARTHA JEFFERSON RANDOLPH

Rockfish gap Aug. 4. 18.

MY DEAR DAUGHTER

All our members, except 3 who came not at all arrived on Saturday morning so that we got to work by 10. oclock, and finished yesterday evening.[1] We are detained till this morning for fair copies of our report. Staunton has 2. votes, Lexington 3. the Central college 16. I have never seen business done with so much order, and harmony, nor in abler nor pleasanter society. We have been well served too. Excellent rooms, every one his bed, a table altho' not elegant, yet plentiful and satisfactory. I proceed today with judge Stuart to Staunton.[2] Every body tells me the time I allot to the Springs is too short. That 2. or 3. weeks bathing will be essential. I shall know better when I get there. But I forsee the possibility and even probability that my stay there must be longer than I expected. I am most afraid of losing Mr. Correa's visit.[3] I shall write to him from the springs. Cooper[4] has failed in his election, Dr. Patterson having obtained the Chemical chair. I imagine he has written to me, but I must inform him from the springs of the cause of delay in answering him. Kiss all the family for me, and be assured of my warmest love.

TH: JEFFERSON

P. S. Send bill immediately for my bed &c.

1. This committee met at a tavern at Rockfish Gap in the Blue Ridge Mountains on August 1. Their first duty was to report a site for the location of a university, to be called the University of Virginia. This they did by choosing a site near Charlottesville. See Roy J. Honeywell, *The Educational Work of Thomas Jefferson* (Cambridge, Mass., 1931), 67–87. Appendix J, page 248 gives the "Report of the Commissioners Appointed to Fix the Site of the University of Virginia . . ." See also Bruce, *University of Virginia*, I, 209–35 for a narrative of this commission.

2. Judge Archibald Stuart of Staunton.

3. José F. Correa da Serra was the Portuguese botanist and a friend of TJ's. He did not come to Monticello at this time.

4. Dr. Thomas Cooper was hoping to gain the chair of chemistry at the University of Pennsylvania, a position that paid a higher salary than the University of Virginia could offer. TJ was relieved when Dr. Robert M. Patterson was named to the post in Pennsylvania.

To Martha Jefferson Randolph

Warm springs Aug. 7. 18.

MY DEAREST DAUGHTER

I have heard that Dr. Cooper has come on to Richmond, which however I doubt. If so he may possibly have come to Monticello. Under this uncertainty where a letter may find him, I inclose one to you for him, with a request to forward it to him by mail wherever he is. I have left it open as it may enable you to judge what to do with it in every case.

I left Judge Stuart's yesterday after breakfast, and breakfasted here this morning between 9. and 10. I have performed the journey entirely on horseback and without fatigue.[1] An attack of rheumatism in the knee yesterday, without retarding my journey, affects my walking. I have tried once to-day the delicious bath and shall do it twice a day hereafter. The company here is about 45. The table is very well kept by Mr. Fry, and every thing else well. Venison is plenty, and vegetables not wanting. I found the houses on the road from Staunton more detestable than any thing I have ever met with: but little *gay* company here at this time, and I rather expect to pass a dull time. Express all my affections to our dear family and most of all be assured of them yourself.

TH: JEFFERSON

1. TJ was seventy-five years of age. The ride from Staunton to the Warm

Springs was approximately sixty miles. For an itinerary from Richmond to the Warm Springs, see *Johnson's Virginia Almanack . . . 1807* (Richmond, 1806). A copy is in the almanac collection at the American Antiquarian Society, Worcester, Massachusetts.

To Martha Jefferson Randolph

Warm springs Aug. 14. 18.

My dear Daughter

I wrote to you by our last mail of the 8th. having been now here a week and continued to bathe 3 times a day, a quarter of an hour at a time. I continue well, as I was when I came. Having no symptom to judge by at that time I may presume the seeds of my rheumatism eradicated, and desirous to prevent the necessity of ever coming here a 2d time, I believe I shall yeild to the general advice of a three weeks course. But so dull a place, and so distressing an ennui I never before knew. I have visited the rock on the high mountain, the hotsprings, and yesterday the falling spring, 15. miles from here; so that there remains no other excursion to enliven the two remaining weeks.[1] We are at present about 30, and at the Hotsprings 20. Yesterday we were reduced to a single lady (Miss Allstone) but there came in 4. more in the evening. Mrs. Egglestone (Matilda Maury that was) left us yesterday for the Hotsprings, obliged to be carried to the bath in a chair, being unable to walk. The 2. Colo. Coles[2] came in last night, and John Harris the night before. Yesterday too Genl. Brackenridge[3] left us, who had accompanied me from the Rockfish gap, and who has been my guide and guardian and fellow lodger in the same cabin. We were constantly together, and I feel his loss most sensibly. He tells me you were at his house (in the neighborhood of Fincastle)[4] on your tramontane excursion. I have contracted more intimacy with Colo. Allstone than any other now remaining. He is father of the Mr. Allstone[5] who married Burr's daughter. The whole of the line of springs seems deserted now for the white Sulphur,[6] where they have 150. persons and all latter-comers are obliged to go into the neighborhood for lodging. I believe in fact that the spring with the Hot and Warm, are those of the first merit. The sweet springs retain esteem, but in limited cases. Affectionate remembrance to all the family and to yourself devoted love.

Th: Jefferson

1. The high mountain was probably the Warm Springs or Jackson's Mountain; others in the vicinity are not of great height. Hot Springs is in Bath County, as is Warm Springs, and about five miles southwest of it. TJ may

have meant the Flowing Springs, sixteen miles northeast of the Warm, rather than the Falling or Healing Springs, and only three miles southwest of the Hot Springs.

2. John A. and Tucker Coles.

3. James Breckenridge of Botetourt County.

4. The county seat of Botetourt County.

5. Joseph Allston was at one time governor of South Carolina.

6. In Greenbrier County, now West Virginia, and about forty miles south and west from Warm Springs.

To Martha Jefferson Randolph

Warmsprings Aug. 21. 18.

My dearest daughter

I wrote to you this day week and this day fortnight. We have been here in a continued state of fluctuation between the numbers of 40. and 60. A greater proportion of ladies than formerly: but all invalids, and perfectly recluse in their cabins. Mr. Glendy joined us to-day and will stay til Sunday. We had been many days without venison till the day before yesterday, in the course of which 8. deer were brought in. Their price 3d. a lb. nett. I do not know what may be the effect of this course of bathing on my constitution; but I am under great threats that it will work it's effect thro' a system of boils. A large swelling on my seat, increasing for several days past in size and hardness disables me from sitting but on the corner of a chair. Another swelling begins to manifest itself to-day on the other seat. It happens fortunately that Capt. Harris is here in a carriage alone, and proposes to set out on the same day I had intended. He offers me a seat which I shall gladly accept. We propose to set out on Friday or Saturday next, to be 2 days on the road to Staunton, stay there one day, and 2 days more to get home. He will deposit me 4. miles below Rockfish gap, from whence I shall make my way home in the gig. Perhaps these swellings may yet disappear, but I have little hope of that. Adieu my dear daughter. Receive my affectionate love for yourself and express it to all the dear family.   TH: JEFFERSON

To Francis Wayles Eppes

Monticello Sep. 11. 18.

Dear Francis

I am lately returned from the warm springs with my health entirely prostrated by the use of the waters. They produced an imposthume and eruptions which with the torment of the journey back reduced me to the last stage of weakness and exhaustion.[1] I am getting better, but still obliged to lie night and day in the same reclined posture which renders writing painful. I cannot be at Poplar Forest till the middle of October, if strong enough then. If you should have to go to another school, if you will push your Greek Latin and Arithmetic, there will be no time lost, as that prepares you for reception at the University on the ground of a student of the sciences. Altho' I now consider that as fixed at the Central College yet it will retard the opening of that till the spring, as the conveyance of all our property to the Literary fund[2] subjects us now to await the movements of the legislature. Be assured, My dear Francis of my affectionate and devoted attachment to you. TH: JEFFERSON

1. TJ was at Warm Springs from August 8 to 27. While there he contracted an "erruptive complaint," undoubtedly boils or carbuncles, which he stated were treated with "unctions of mercury and sulphur." This would indicate only local medication, but in a letter to Henry Dearborn of July 5, 1819 (DLC), he infers that this treatment may have been internal as well: "The cause of the eruption was mistaken and it was treated with severe unctions of mercury and sulphur. These reduced me to death's door and on ceasing to use them I recovered immediately and consider my health as perfectly reestablished except some small effects on the bowels produced by these remedies." Whatever the causes of his indisposition, he was ill for about three months. See TJ to Lafayette, November 23, 1818 (DLC).

2. Established by the Virginia legislature in 1810, it formed the nucleus for the popular support of free education in the state. For a brief explanation of its history and activities, see Cornelius J. Heatwole, *A History of Education in Virginia* (New York, 1916), 104–9; also, Bruce, *University of Virginia,* I, 85–91.

FROM FRANCIS WAYLES EPPES

Millbrook Nov: 26th. 1818

DEAR SIR

You will no doubt be surprised at seeing the date of this letter, thinking that I have been at school for some time past. I have however been detained at home much longer than I myself expected by the indisposition of our family. A bilious Fever has been prevalent in our neighbourhood this fall and carried off many. It is now much abated. I set out this week at Furtherest for Mr. Bakers and will let you hear from me as soon as I arrive there. It is very uncertain whether Mr. Barbour will continue his school after Christmas, if he does not I shall pursue the course you recommended to me untill the Central College goes into operation.

I have taken a list of My Fathers Books as you desired and find that but few classical ones are among them and as I suppose that you merely wished to see those I only Send you a list of them. In looking over them I found a quarto edition of Hedericks Lexicon[1] and a superb copy of Homer but the latter is too large to be of Much use.

By this time I hope you enjoy the blessings of Health without which happiness cannot be enjoyed on this earth. Papa has written to us from Washington and I believe is heartily tired of public life. Present me affectionately to the family. I remain your affectionate Grandson,   FRANS: EPPES

1. Benjamin Hederich, *Graecum Lexicon Manuale.* There were several editions of this work, the first in 1727. Sowerby 4762.

To Francis Wayles Eppes

Monticello Jan.1.19.

DEAR FRANCIS

Leschot[1] has repaired Mrs. Eppes's watch and changed the pipe of the key, but the watch was so short a time in his hands that she could not be well regulated. She will therefore probably need further regulation to make her keep good time. I am sorry you are disappointed in your teacher, but it depends on yourself whether this is of any consequence. A master is necessary only to those who require compulsion to get their lessons. As to instruction a translation supplies the place of a teacher. Get the lesson first by dictionary; and then, instead of saying it to a master go over it with the translation, and that will tell you whether you have got it truly. Dacier's Horace is admirable for this. As to parsing you can do that by yourself both as to parts of speech and syntax. You can perfect yourself too in your Greek grammar as well alone as with a teacher. Your Spanish too should be kept up. All depends on your own resolution to stick as closely to your book as if a master was looking over you. If Dr. Cooper comes to us, he will open our grammar school the 1st. of April. We shall be decided in a few days and I will let you know. You complain of my not writing to you, writing has become so irksome to me that I have withdrawn from all correspondence and and scarcely answer any body's letter. You are young and it is one of the best exercises for you. I shall hope therefore to hear from you often; but can write to you myself only when I have something to communicate or advise. Present my respects to Mrs. Eppes and be assured of my constant affection.   TH: JEFFERSON

1. Louis Leschot, a Charlottesville merchant and watch repairman. Tradition has it that TJ brought him to America, but there is no evidence to support this. Leschot and his wife Sophie were buried in the Monticello graveyard.

To Martha Jefferson Randolph

Pop. For. July 28. [1819]

MY DEAREST MARTHA

I have just learned from the Enquirer the death of my old and valuable friend Cathalan[1] of Marseilles, an important loss to me, and at this time particularly requiring attention, as my orders are now on the way to him for the supplies of the year, and the money to pay for them. But I can do nothing without his papers which I request you to send me. In my Cabinet, and in the window on the right of my writing table you will see 4. or 5. cartoons of papers. The 2d. and 3d. of these contain a compleat set of alphabeted papers, and in the 2d where the alphabet begins you will find Cathalan's papers in one or more bundles, for I believe they are in more than one. The latest of these in point of date is the one I want. If it includes the present and last year or two it will be sufficient.[2] Be so good as to send it by the 1st. mail of which the girls apprise you. We should have felt great uneasiness at your sickness had not the same letter informed us of your convalescence. We have been near losing Burwell[3] by a stricture of the upper bowels; but he has got about again and is now only very weak. Bless all the young ones for me, and be blessed yourself.

TH: JEFFERSON

1. Stephen Cathalan, a Marseilles merchant with whom TJ had been doing business since his stay in Paris.
2. For TJ's filing method, see "Description of his presses and their contents," an undated manuscript (circa 1827) in a hand not identified (MHi).

From Martha Jefferson Randolph

Monticello Aug. 7. 19

MY DEAREST FATHER

I found very readily the two bundles of papers which I enclose. Capt. Peyton[1] who has been with us lately says that he has your cement, and books, but that the river is so low that not a boat can float. The smith's shop took fire a few days since and but for the circumstance of his being here with Mr. Randolph and T. Gilmer it would certainly have burnt down. There was no man upon the mountain but Joe and old John, and whilst Joe was disengaging the bellows the 3 gentlemen passed on their way to visit the president when they percieved the fire. Capt. Peyton tore the planks off of the roof by main force. The rafters were so much burnt that they fell in immediately. Both Mr. Randolph and himself were smartly burnt particularly Mr. R whose cloaths caught. Nothing was lost but the roof which they are repairing with all speed. Captain Peyton will probably be with you, as he had some intention of returning that way and of calling upon you. He will give you a better account of the president than I can.[2] But he appears so entirely exhausted that I should think him in danger. He sits almost double from weakness, and his voice is so low that you can hardly hear what he says: the gentlemen all agreed in their account of his being worn to a shadow and looking so ill and so old as to shock them. I recieved a letter from Ann the other day in which she tells me that they have jointly with Capt. Miller rented a small farm 3 miles from Doctor Bankhead's. The Capt. will live with them at which I am delighted for they will always require a protector. Mr. Bankhead has begun to drink again. Capt. Peyton said something of his intention to return in to this neighbourhood, some one came in at the moment and I had not an opportunity of asking any particulars upon the subject but I suppose if he does that he is still liable to be brought to trial.[3] We are still suffering with the drought here. Jefferson thinks that not much of his corn is so far gone but what it might still recover if we have rain soon. The thermometer in your window was many days at 94 the other one at 95½. Adieu My Dearest Father. Believe me with feelings which I have not language yours most devotedly,

MRANDOLPH

We got the letters from New London Post mark 29. July, the 3d day of August, the day on which we sent to the post office. Poor old Robert Hemming is dead. Since writing the above a report has reached us that Col. Nicholas has been *protested* for a large sum. Jefferson believes it and Mr. Randolph says talks of sending an express to you.[4]

1. Bernard Peyton was a Richmond factor and friend of TJ's.
2. James Madison.
3. Martha was referring to the outcome of a fight on the Courthouse Square in Charlottesville between Thomas Jefferson Randolph and Bankhead in

which Randolph was seriously wounded. Bankhead was arrested and then released after posting bond. He left the county, thus forfeiting his bond, and for some unexplainable reason was never brought to trial. Several years later he returned but was not called to account for his wounding of Randolph. See Joseph C. Vance, "Thomas Jefferson Randolph," 61–75, for an excellent account of the affair.

4. In 1817 TJ had applied to the Richmond branch of the Bank of the United States for a loan. An audit of his accounts revealed him in debt to the United States government as a result of his stay in France. The loan was granted, but an endorser was needed; Wilson Cary Nicholas, a member of the board of the bank, obliged TJ in this matter. Very shortly thereafter, TJ acted as an endorser for two of Nicholas' notes totaling $20,000. The following year (1819), one of these was protested, but Nicholas assured TJ that he would not suffer as a result. However, Nicholas was not able to meet the demand, and TJ informed the bank he would cover his own endorsement. This he was able to do by mortgaging his property. For additional details of this matter, consult the Jefferson-Wilson Cary Nicholas correspondence, March 26, 1818, through August 17, 1819, in the Jefferson Papers in the Library of Congress.

To Martha Jefferson Randolph

P. F. Aug. 24. 19.

My dear daughter

It is our purpose to set out from this place for Monticello on Monday the 13th. or perhaps on Sunday the 12th. of next month. As Henry, his mule and little cart will be necessary to carry our baggage, I would wish him to leave Monticello on Sunday morning the 5th. making stages at Tooler's on this side the river at Warren, at Noah Flood's, Hunter's and this place.

I am much recovered from my rheumatism,[1] altho' the swellings are not entirely abated, nor the pains quite ceased. It has been the most serious attack of that disease I ever had. While too weak to sit up the whole day, and afraid to increase the weakness by lying down, I long for a Siesta chair which would have admitted the medium position. I must therefore pray you to send by Henry the one made by Johnny Hemings. If it is the one Mrs. Trist would chuse, it will be so far on it's way, if not, the waggon may bring hers when it comes at Christmas. John or Wormly should wrap it well with a straw rope, and then bowed up in a blanket. Besides this, ticklenburg should be got from Mr. Lietch's[2] and a cover made for the cart. Wormly will see to it's being safely placed in.

We have nothing new here but comfortable rains which it is thought will make us half a crop of corn, sufficient for bread and perhaps for fattening some hogs. Present me affectionately to Mr.

Randolph and the young ones and be assured yourself of all my love.   TH: JEFFERSON

1. TJ for a long time suffered from rheumatism, and the older he became the worse the ailment seemed to plague him. This particular attack began early in August and affected both shoulders and his wrists and knees and did not terminate until late September or early October.

2. James Leitch was a Charlottesville merchant.

FROM FRANCIS WAYLES EPPES

Millbrook Decmbr: 28th. 19.

DEAR GRANDPAPA

I found on my return all our family well except my Father. He is still mending but I fear will never entirely recover. The precarious state of his health for some years past has caused me much uneasiness, but his late violent attack which was much more alarming in its nature than any of the Former, makes me tremble at the prospect of the greatest misfortune which could now befal me. If bereft of him I have only yourself to turn to. It has pleased Providence to take away all of my other Friends, and though I feel little need of a Protector, I still have the greatest, For an adviser, a sincere Friend who would point out my Faults, hitherto I have found this friend in the person of my Father. I hope the Almighty in his infinite goodness, will prolong his days perhaps with due care and attention he may yet recover. In a great measure, his situation I think is owing to the many physicians whom he has employed. They with their different remedies and advice have danger of its being dislodged. As Barnaby is on Foot I think it danger of its being dislodged. As Barnaby is on Foot I think it better to defer sending the Thorn bushes, I will bring them on my return. We have a Harpsichord here which formerly belonged to my mother. I believe that with new strings it will be as good as ever, as none of our Family play, and you have no instrument at Poplar Forest, papa told me to offer it to you, thinking it might afford some amusement to the young Ladies. As your cart passes, you might send for it without much inconvenience. Present me affectionately to Aunt Randolph and family. Your affectionate Grandson,   FRANCIS EPPES

To Francis Wayles Eppes

Poplar Forest Sep. 21. 20

DEAR FRANCIS

I leave at Flood's with this letter a packet containing 3. small volumes of my petit format library[1] containing several tragedies of Euripedes, some of Sophocles and one of Aeschylus. The 1st. you will find easy, the 2d. tolerable so; the last incomprehensible in his flights among the clouds. His text has come to us so mutilated and defective and has been so much plaistered with amendments by his commentators that it can scarcely be called his.

I inclose you our measured distances expressed in miles and cents. We leave this tomorrow morning and shall be at Monticello the next night. From thence you shall hear from me about the end of the 1st. week of October. By that time I shall either see Doctr. Cooper, or know that I shall not see him. I was decieved in the weather the day we left Milbrook. We passed thro' 2. hours of very heavy rain, and got to Flood's at 11. oclock where we staid the day. We did not suffer ourselves but the servants got very wet. Present our cordial love to the family. Ever and affectionately yours,   TH: JEFFERSON

1. TJ maintained at Poplar Forest a small library of about seventy titles, chiefly for pleasurable reading. The Petit Format Library was a part of this. See *Catalogue of a Private Library . . . the Messrs. Leavitt, Auctioneers . . .* (New York, 1873), (NNP), the only record known of this library. The Petit Format Library is Item No. 647, and typical of the authors were Virgil, Tacitus, Ovid, Sophocles, Pindar, etc. There were 98 volumes in 12- and 32-mo. sizes, and they were principally from the Wetstein, Elzevir, and Jansonii presses.

To Francis Wayles Eppes

Monticello Oct.6. 20.

DEAR FRANCIS

Your letter of the 28th. came to hand yesterday, and, as I suppose you are now about leaving Richmond for Columbia,[1] this letter will be addressed to the latter place. I consider you as having made such proficiency in Latin and Greek that on your arrival at Columbia you may at once commence the study of the sciences: and as you may well attend two professors at once, I advise you to enter immediately with those of Mathematics and Chemistry. After these go on to Astronomy, Natl. philosophy, Natl. history and Botany. I say nothing of Mineralogy or Geology, because I presume they will be comprehended in the Chemical course. Nor shall I say any thing of other branches of science, but that you should lose no time on them until the accomplishment of those above named, before which time we shall have opportunities of further advising together. I hope you will be permitted to enter at once into a *course of Mathematics,* which will itself take up all that is useful in Euclid, and that you will not be required to go formally thro' the usual books of that Geometer. That would be a waste of time which you have not to spare, and if you cannot enter the Mathematical school without it, do not enter it at all, but engage in the other sciences above mentioned. Your Latin and Greek should be kept up assiduously by reading at spare hours: and, discontinuing the desultory reading of the schools. I would advise you to undertake a regular course of history and poetry in both languages. In Greek, go first thro' the Cyropaedia, and then read Herodotus, Thucydides, Xenophon's Hellenus and Anabasis, Arrian's Alexander, and Plutarch's lives, for prose reading: Homer's Iliad and Odyssey, Euripides, Sophocles in poetry, and Demosthenes in Oratory; alternating prose and verse as most agreeable to yourself. In Latin read Livy, Caesar, Sallust Tacitus, Cicero's Philosophies, and some of his Orations, in prose; and Virgil, Ovid's Metamorphoses, Horace, Terence and Juvenal for poetry. After all these, you will find still many of secondary grade to employ future years, and especially those of old age and retirement. Let me hear from you as soon as you shall have taken your stand in College, and give me a general view of the courses pursued there, and from time to time afterwards advise me of your progress. I will certainly write to you occasionally, but you will not expect it very frequently, as you know how slowly and painfully my stiffened wrist now permits me to write, and how much I am oppressed by a general and revolting correspondence, wearing me down with incessant labor, instead of leaving me to the tranquil happiness with which reading and lighter occupations would fill pleasantly what remains to me of life. I had written to Dr. Cooper that I should leave Monticello for Poplar Forest about the 11th. of this month. He informs me he cannot be here so soon as that but will call on me at Poplar Forest in the 3d. week of the month. Adieu, my dear Francis. Consider how little time is left you, and how much you have to attain in it, and that every moment you lose of it is lost for ever. Be assured that no one living is more anxious than myself to see you become a virtuous and useful citizen, worthy of the trusts of your country and wise enough to

conduct them advantageously, nor any one more affectionately
yours.   TH: JEFFERSON

1. He was attending the South Carolina College, later the University of
South Carolina, at Columbia.

FROM FRANCIS WAYLES EPPES

Columbia Octbr. 31st. 20

DR GRANDPAPA

I waited untill this time (before writing) that I might be able to
give a more satisfactory, and circumstantial account, of the course
and regulations of this institution, which are pretty nearly the
same as those of the northern colleges, differing only in two points.
In the first place the course here is neither as full nor as comprehensive a one as that of Cambridge, secondly the discipline is more
lax and consequently better adapted, to the feelings and habits of
the southern students. This latter circumstance too is somewhat
surprising as the Faculty themselves (with the exception of Dr.
Cooper) are Clergymen. The objection too to their course is ob-
viated by the consideration of a college library the free use of
which is permitted to the students. They have four classes and
to the studies of each one year is allotted, so that the lowest
1. takes four years to graduate; in it Graeca Minora, Virgils AEneid,
2. and Arithmetic are the studies, those of the next in grade are, the
1st part of the 1st vol: of Graeca Majora, Horace, Algebra as far as
3d cubick equations, Geography. &c. Those of the junior are Blairs
Lectures, Watts's Logick, Kames's elements of Criticism, Paleys
Moral Philosophy, cubick equations, Geometry, Trigonometry &c.
Hutton alone is used, his demonstrations are much shorter than
4 Simpsons. The senior year Logarithms, conick sections and Flux-
ions, Cavallo's Natural Philosophy Butlers Analogy of Religion,
Chemistry. No one is allowed the privilege of entering as student,
without pursuing this course, unless he does under the Title of
Honorary, which besides being an unusual is moreover a disad-
vantageous standing. I have therefore entered as a regular student,
and am a candidate for the junior class, whose examination comes
on in two weeks. After it is over I will write again and perhaps may
be enabled then, to give you more satisfactory information concerning the elections of a President and Professor of Mathematics.
The only objection to Elliot who is talked of as President is his
not being a minister of the Gospel, this too is urged as a very

weighty one. Wallace whose merits you are better informed of than I, and who was formerly a Professor in the Georgetown College, is a candidate for the Mathematical chair. It is said however that Judge De Saussure, one of the Trustees and a man of great influence is opposed to him.[1] What the result of these conjectures may be, it is impossible for me to say. I can only add that I hope they will terminate in the election of those whose abilities may confer a lasting advantage and prosperity on this institution. Dr. Cooper is very much beloved by the students here and is in fact one of the most popular Professors that they have ever had. I find that this place is very healthy, a young man from the neighbourhood of Poplar-Forest, (who is the only Virginian in college except myself) stayed here the whole summer without experiencing the slightest inconvenience. Wayles has not arrived though I expect him daily. Present me affectionately to Aunt Randolph and Family. I often think of the happy moments spent in your society, the happiest perhaps of my life. I remain your affectionate Grandson,

FR: EPPES.

1. Stephen Elliott was president of the South Carolina College in 1820. Judge Henry William DeSaussure was a member of the South Carolina legislature and had been instrumental in helping to found the South Carolina College. James Wallace was professor of mathematics at the college. See Daniel W. Hollis, *University of South Carolina, South Carolina College* (Columbia, 1951), I, 22, 74, and M. Laborde, *History of the South Carolina College* (Columbia, 1859), 187.

To Francis Wayles Eppes

Poplar Forest Dec. 13. 20.

DEAR FRANCIS

Yours of Oct. 31. came to me here Nov. 28. having first gone to Monticello. I observe the course of reading at Columbia which you note. It either is, or ought to be the rule of every collegiate institution to teach to every particular student the branches of science which those who direct him think will be useful in the pursuits proposed for him, and to waste his time on nothing which they think will not be useful to him. This will certainly be the fundamental law of our University to leave every one free to attend whatever branches of instruction he wants, and to decline what he does not want. If this be not generally allowed at Columbia, I hope they may be induced to indulgence in your case, in consideration of the little time you have left, and which you cannot afford to waste on what will be useless to you, or can be acquired by reading hereafter without the aid of a teacher. As I do not know any professor at Columbia but Doctr. Cooper, request, in my name, his interest and influence to be permitted to adapt your studies to your wants.

Reviewing what you say are the courses of the 4. classes, I pass over the 1st. and 2d. which you are done with, and should select for you from the 3d. Algebra, Geometry, trigonometry and Natural philosophy, and from the 4. Logarrithms and chemistry to which I should add astronomy, Botany and natural history, which you do not mention in any of the classes. I omit Blair's Rhetoric, Watt's logic, Kaims, Paley, Butler &c. which you can read in your closet after leaving College as well as at it. And in Mathematics I do not think you have time to undertake either Conic sections or fluscions. Unless you can be indulged in this selection I shall lament very much indeed the having advised your going to Columbia because time is now the most pressing and precious thing in the world to you; and the greatest injury which can possibly be done you is to waste what remains on what you can acquire hereafter yourself, and prevent your learning those useful branches which cannot will be acquired without the aids of the College.

Whether our University will open this time, 12 month or be shut up 7. years, will depend on the present legislature's liberating our funds by appropriating 100,000 D. more from the Literary fund. If you watch the newspapers you will see what they do, and be able to judge what may be expected.

Ellen and Virginia are here with me. We leave this the day after tomorrow for Monticello, where we hope to meet your aunt, who will be returning at the same time from Richmond. We learn by your letter to Virginia that Wayles is with you. To him and to yourself I tender my affectionate attachments. To Dr. Cooper also give my friendly souvenirs. The difficulty with which I write puts that much out of my power.   TH: JEFFERSON

To Francis Wayles Eppes

Monticello Jan. 19. 21.

DEAR FRANCIS

Your letter of the 1st came safely to hand. I am sorry you have lost Mr. Elliot, however the kindness of Dr. Cooper will be able to keep you in the tract of what is worthy of your time.

You ask my opinion of Ld. Bolingbroke and Thomas Paine.

They were alike in making bitter enemies of the priests and Pharisees of their day. Both were honest men; both advocates for human liberty. Paine wrote for a country which permitted him to push his reasoning to whatever length it would go: Ld. Bolingbroke in one restrained by a constitution, and by public opinion. He was called indeed a tory: but his writings prove him a stronger advocate for liberty than any of his countrymen, the whigs of the present day. Irritated by his exile, he committed one act unworthy of him, in connecting himself momentarily with a prince rejected by his country. But he redeemed that single act by his establishment of the principles which proved it to be wrong. These two persons differed remarkably in the style of their writing, each leaving a model of what is most perfect in both extremes of the simple and the sublime. No writer has exceeded Paine in ease and familiarity of style; in perspicuity of expression, happiness of elucidation, and in simple and unassuming language. In this he may be compared with Dr. Franklin: and indeed his Common sense was, for awhile, believed to have been written by Dr. Franklin, and published under the borrowed name of Paine, who had come over with him from England. Ld. Bolingbroke's, on the other hand, is a style of the highest order: the lofty, rythmical, full-flowing eloquence of Cicero. Periods of just measure, their members proportioned, their close full and round. His conceptions too are bold and strong, his diction copious, polished and commanding as his subject. His writings are certainly the finest samples in the English language of the eloquence proper for the senate. His political tracts are safe reading for the most timid religinist, his philosophical, for those who are not afraid to trust their reason with discussions of right and wrong.

You have asked my opinion of these persons, and, *to you,* I have given it freely. But, remember, that I am old, that I wish not to make new enemies, nor to give offence to those who would consider a difference of opinion as sufficient ground for unfriendly dispositions. God bless you, and make you what I wish you to be.

TH: JEFFERSON

To Francis Wayles Eppes

Monticello. Apr. 8. 21.

DEAR FRANCIS

Yours of Mar. 27. has been duly recieved. The effect of what our legislature did for us at their last session is not exactly what you suppose. They authorized us to borrow another 60,000. D. pledging however our own funds for repayment. This loan enables us to finish all our buildings of accomodation this year, and to begin The Library, which will take 3. years to be compleated. Without waiting for that, it is believed that when the buildings of accomodation are finished, the legislature will cancel the debt of 120,000. D. and leave our funds free to open the institution. We shall then require a year to get our Professors into place. Whether the legislature will relingquish the debt the next session, or at some future one is not certain. In the mean time you cannot do better than to stay where you are until the end of 1822 confining your studies to Mathematics, Natl. Philosophy, Natl. History and Rhetoric. All other branches you can pursue by yourself, should we not open here by that date.

I note what you say of the late disturbances in your College. These dissensions are a great affliction on the American schools, and a principal impediment to education in this country. The source of discontent arising from dieting the students, we shall avoid here, by having nothing to do with it, and by leaving every one to board where he pleases. Nor do I see why this remedy might not have been resorted to in your late case, rather than that of making it a ground of difference with the Professors. There may have been reasons however of which I am uninformed.

The family here is all well, always remember you with affection, and recieve your letters with gratification. To theirs I add the assurance of very affectionate love.   TH: JEFFERSON

To Francis Wayles Eppes

Monticello June 27. 21.

DEAR FRANCIS

Your letter of May 7. was recieved in due time, and in it you ask my opinion as to the utility of pursuing metaphysical studies. No well educated person should be entirely ignorant of the operations of the human mind, to which the name of metaphysics has been given. There are three books on this subject, Locke's essay on the human understanding, Tracy's elements of Idiology, and Stewart's Philosophy of the human mind,[1] any one of which will communicate as much on the subject as is worth attention. I consider Tracy as the most correct Metaphysician living; and I inclose you a small tract of his worth reading because it is short, profound, and treats an interesting question, to wit that on the certainty of human knolege. He prostrates the visions of Malebranche[2] and Barclay and other sceptics, by resting the question on the single basis of 'we feel.' With him who denies this basis, there can be no ground of reasoning at all. To pursue the science further is following a Will of the wisp, and a very useless waste of time much better given to sciences more palpable, and more useful in the business of life.

Tracy's Review or Commentaries on Montesquieu is the best elementary book on government which has ever been published. Being afraid to publish it in France, he sent his manuscript to me in 1809, and I got it translated and published in Philadelphia in 1811. It will be the text-book of the Political lectures of the University. The buildings of the University (except the library) will all be finished the ensuing winter. Towards this object the Legislature permitted an advance of 120.M.D. from the literary fund, but under the name of a loan, taking in pledge our annuity of 15,000 D. If it is to be really redeemed by this, many years will be necessary to clear that fund but it is hoped they will consider it as an appropriation and discharge the annuity within one year. After that discharge we may open the institution, as it will require that time to bring our professors into place. Mr. Watts when here asked me for a copy of the Report containing the plan of that institution. I did not know then that I had a spare copy. I have since found one, which I inclose for his acceptance with the tender of my great respect.

Our family is all well; remember you always with affection and join me in hoping you will be able to visit us during your next vacation, as they do in assuring you of our constant attachment.

TH: JEFFERSON

1. Antoine Louis Claude Destutt de Tracy, *Project d'Élémens* . . . and Dugald Stewart, *Elements of the Philosophy of the Human Mind,* Sowerby 1239, 1244.

2. Nicolas de Malebranche was a French philosopher whose *De la Recherche de la vérité* (Amsterdam, 1688) was in TJ's great library. Robert Barclay was a Scottish Quaker apologist. TJ owned his *An Apology for the True Christian Divinity . . . an explanation of the Principles and Doctrines of the People called Quakers* (Birmingham, 1765). Sowerby 1243, 1537.

To Francis Wayles Eppes

Poplar Forest Nov. 17. 21.

DEAR FRANCIS

On my return to this place on the 5th. inst. I found here your letter of Oct. 22. I learnt from that with real affliction that it was doubtful whether you would be permitted at Columbia to pursue those studies only which will be analogous to the views and purposes of your future life. It is a deplorable considn that altho neither your father nor myself have spared any effort in our power to press on your education, yet so miscrable are the means of educn in our state that it has been retarded and baffled to a most unfortunate degree. And now that you have only a single year left, you cannot be permitted to employ that solely in what will be useful to you. Every instn however has a right to lay down it's own laws, and we are bound to acquiescence. There seems from your ltr. to be still a possibility that you may be permitted to remain as an irregular student. That is the most desirable event. If not, then to obtain from Dr. Cooper and Mr. Wallace the favor of attending them as a private student unconnected with the College. From them you can recieve every instruction necessary for you, to wit in Mathematics, Astronomy, Nat. Philosophy and Chemistry. If that cannot be permitted, there will remain nothing but the disastrous alternative of again shifting your situation. I know nothing of the plan or degree of instruction at Chapel-hill.[1] Perhaps you might be excluded there also by similar rules. If so, William & Mary is your last resource. There students are permitted to attend the schools of their choice, and those branches of science only which will be useful to them in the line of life they propose. The objection to that place is it's autumnal unhealthiness.

The thankfulness you express for my cares of you bespeaks a feeling and good heart: but the tender recollections which bind my affections to you, are such as will for ever call for every thing I can do for you. And the comfort of my life is in the belief that you will deserve it. To my prayers that your life may be distinguished by it's worth I add the assurance of my constant and affectionate love.   TH: J.

1. Why TJ had such strong feelings against the college at Chapel Hill, North Carolina, are not clear. That he had them is evident in a letter from John Wayles Eppes to Francis Wayles Eppes: "I could not reconcile to my feelings going against your Grand Father and his prejudices against Chappell hill appear invincible." November 18, 1818 (MHi).

To THOMAS JEFFERSON RANDOLPH

                                                         Mar. 15. 22.
TH: J to TH: J. R.

Do not give up the bonds to Morrison. Your right to them is sound. Colo. Nicholas covenated to assign certain bonds to Mor rison. Until actual assignment the legal property remained in Colo. N. and on his death that legal property vested in his execurs and in yourself as one. He was indebted to you and the law allows an excr. to pay himself. Morrison can get no hold of those bonds at law. He must go into a court of chancery, and it is a sacred principle with the Chancellor never to take a legal advantage from one creditor to give it to another.

The record of the Covenant is only additional evidence of there being such a covenant, but adds nothing to it's force, or to it's lien on the bonds. It is only an equitable lien which the Chancellor will not enforce against another creditor who has possession and legal right.

FROM FRANCIS WAYLES EPPES

Columbia March 22. 1822

DR. GRANDPAPA

I had determined to write to you sometime ago, but was prevented partly by the expectation of an answer to my last letter, and partly by business, which has occupied nearly the whole of my time for several weeks past. I regret this circumstance the more as necessity compels me to take a step which I should wish in the first place to recieve the sanction of your approbation. I am about to return home, and tho' it is unpleasant to communicate the reasons which prompt me, yet in the present instance delicacy must give way to duty and gratitude. You are not ignorant that my Father has during my stay in college allowed me a certain sum to defray my expences: this he informed me was as *much* as he could afford and I must therefore take care not to excede it; and this he enjoined more particularly last October. I accordingly on my arrival calculated my expences for the winter in college and found that my allowance would hold out until the first of May, which would have carried me through the Lectures on Chemistry, and a part of those on Mineralogy, and I was very well content as I thought the latter would prove of little use to me in life, and I was certain that in Mathematics, I should then be far enough advanced to go on without the aid of a Professor. In a letter of my Father's a few weeks ago he informed me that he was pressed for money and could not possibly forward any more until the sale of his crops, and as I foresaw that this would place me not only in a disagreable but distressing situation, I determined to make the best use of that in my possession and return as soon as it was expended. This has brought me nearly through the Lectures on chemistry and so far in Nat. Philosophy that Mr. Wallace tells me I shall find no more difficulty, and may pursue the study to as much advantage at home. As to Astronomy the course taught here is scarcely better than that contained in every petty treatise on the use of the Globes, as it is an abridgement of the outline in Cavallo's Nat. Philosophy, by Brosius, and hardly worth perusal; so that I should not have gained much by staying for this. Had it so happened, I would have prefered staying until the Lectures on chemistry were quite over, but I have in a measure remedied this deficiency by studying the few remaining subjects in our text Book, which is an excellent one. Dr C's lectures will I expect certainly be over next week, and then Mr. Vanuxum begins with *Geological Mineralogy,* as the chair is entitled. Tomorrow I set off and in 10 days expect to reach Millbrook, when I hope to find your answer as I shall feel disatisfied until I know that you are not displeased with me for acting in the way that I have done. If you approve my intention I will turn in immediately to the Study of Law and divide my time between it and other studies.

Remember me to Aunt Randolph and family and accept this as testimony of my sincere love. Your affectionate Grandson,

FRS. EPPES

TO FRANCIS WAYLES EPPES

Monticello Apr. 9.22.

DEAR FRANCIS

Your letter of Mar. 22. did not reach me till a few days ago. That of Feb. 6. had been recieved in that month. Being chiefly a statement of facts, it did not seem to require an answer, and my burthen of letter-writing is so excessive as to restrain me to answers absolutely necessary. I think, with you, that you had now better turn in to the study of the law, as no one can read a whole day closely on any one subject to advantage, you will have time enough in the other portions of the day to go on with those essential studies which you have not as yet compleated. If you read Law from breakfast 4. or 5. hours, enough will remain before dinner for exercise. The morning may be given to Natural philosophy and Astronomy, the afternoon to Rhetoric and Belles lettres, and the night to history and ethics. The first object will be to procure the necessary law books for reading. They will come 25. per cent cheaper from England than bought here; and some indeed can only be had there. I will subjoin a catalogue of what should be obtained as soon as practicable and their cost there. About as much the next year will be a sufficient library for reference in practice. The course of reading I should advise would be Coke Littleton and his other Institutes, Bacon's abridgment, Blackston's Commentaries, Woodeson's lectures and Reeves, in common law, and in chancery the Abridgment of cases in equity, Bridgman's digested Index, and Fonblanque, interspersing some select cases from the Reporters both in law and equity. The course will employ 2. years to be superficial, and 3. to be profound. This may be done at Mill-brook or Monticello as well as in a lawyer's office. You know of course that you are as much at home at Monticello as at Millbrook, so that you can chuse freely, or divide your time between them to your own wish. You would have perhaps less interruption by company at Millbrook, but access here to books which may not be there. I have fortunately just recieved from England Thomas's Coke Littleton, a most valuable work. He has arranged Coke's matter in the method of Blackstone, adding the notes of Lords Hale and Nottingham, and Hairgraves, adding also his own which are excellent. It is now, beyond question the first elementary book to be read, as agreeable as Blackstone, and more profound. This will employ you fully till the other books can be recieved from England. They will cost there about 200. D. to which is to be added duties of about 30. D. freight and charges. If I can be useful in procuring them I shall do so with pleasure. The sum I have to pay your father is about sufficient to accomplish it, and shall be so app[roved] if it is his pleasure. I shall be in Bedford during the last week of this month and the first of the next. You will of course visit us there or here, when we can make more particular arrangements. I have here the two best works on Nat. Philos. and Astronomy, Haüy and Biot,[1] which I have imported for you from Paris, knowing they were not to be had here. Present me affectionately to Mr. and Mrs. Eppes, and be assured of my warmest attachments to yourself.   TH: JEFFERSON

Bracton English
Brooke's abridgment. 4to. edn.
Thomas's Coke Littleton 3.v. 8vo.
Coke's 2d.3d. and 4th. institutes. 3.v. 8vo
Bacon's abridgment by Gwyllim. 7.v. 8vo the last edition.
Comyns's Digest by Manning, a new edition
Blackstone's Commentaries by Christian. 15th. edn. 4.v. 8vo
Woodeson's lectures. 3.v. 8vo.

Reeves's history of the English law. 4.v. 8vo.
Jacob's Law dictionary by Russhead. fol.
Abridgment of Cases in Equity
Bridgman's digested Index of cases in Chancery. 3.v. 8vo.
Fonblanque's a treatise of equity. 5th. edition. 1819. 2.v. 8vo.

1. René Just Haüy, the well-known French mineralogist and author of
Traité de Minéralogie (Sowerby 1089), and Biot, *Traité élémentaire d'Astron-
omie Physique.*

FROM FRANCIS WAYLES EPPES

Millbrook May 13. 1822

DR. GRANDPAPA

I merely write a few lines to inform you of the success of my
negociation. Papa can only spare at present money for the purchase of two books, Bacons Abridgment, and Thomas's Coke Littleton, which I beg you will send for with yours. The money you
have in your hands it will therefore be no trouble to retain a
sum sufficient to purchase the books and pay their freight, and
this my Father authorises me to say. I have a copy of Blackstone
and a very good Law Dictionary and by the time that the others
arrive will perhaps be enabled to send for more. Bad crops and
bad prices, added to my Fathers ill health and the loss of 9000.
wt. of tobacco by fire last winter have rendered it impossible to
incur any other expences than those which are absolutely necessary. Knowing these circumstances and moreover in conversation
having discovered that he had otherwise appropriated the greater
part of the money we had calculated on, I forebore to ask any
thing more than what I conceived essentially requisite. I am
pursuing the plan you advised and have already made some
progress in my Lord Coke: I do not find him any thing like as
difficult as I had anticipated, and presume from this circumstance
that the almost insuperable obstacles encountered by others were
owing entirely to the want of arrangement in the old editions. I
have as yet met with nothing that a little more, than ordinary
attention could not master. My Father is still in very delicate
health and at present almost a cripple in consequence of a wound
in the arm by an unskilful bleeder; he desires to be affectionately
remembered to you and requests that you and Aunt Randolph
will take Millbrook in your way on your return in which request
I most sincerely join. Accept the assurance of my constant affection,   FR: EPPES

To Francis Wayles Eppes

Monticello June 12. 22.

DEAR FRANCIS

I recieved while at Poplar Forest your's of May 13. and am glad to learn that you find Coke Lit. not as difficult as you expected. The methodical arrangement of his work and the new notes and cases have certainly been a great improvement. According to your information I have retained in my hands enough to import for you this edition of Coke Lit. and Bacon's abridgement. The present high exchange, our enormous duties and other charges bring them very high. Still I observe the Bacon will come at 45.89 D. which is 4. D. less than the American price. The Coke Littleton being a new publication comes to 10. D. a vol. of which more than 1. D. a volume is our own duty. At the close of your reading of the 1st. vol. we shall hope to see you. I suppose you have heard that the Trists have lost their mother. Ever and affectionately your's,

TH: JEFFERSON

From Francis Wayles Eppes

Millbrook Octbr. 31. 22.

MY DR GRAND FATHER

I have been waiting several weeks to hear of your leaving monticello for Bedford intending to meet you there, but as the trip seems protracted and I know not the reason, or how long it may continue, I have determined to write, not to redeem my credit as a regular correspondent (for that I fear is past redemption!) but to assure you of my constant and lively affection. I would have written sooner but the interruptions to which I have been almost continually exposed straitened my time exceedingly and caused me to hope, that in consideration of this circumstance, and that of my writing occasionally to my cousins, you would be disposed to indulgence. To the plan which you advised me to pursue, there is an obstacle of which I myself am just apprised. On coming to an explanation with my Father I find that he does not intend (and indeed he says it is out of his power) to afford me any pecuniary aid in settling my plantation.[1] I shall therefore be compelled to go in debt for Horses, farming utensils, corn, meat, and every necessary expence immediately. These at a moderate calculation will take 12, perhaps $1400; and as the expence of House keeping will add only a hundred more, or at most something trifling in comparison to this, will it not be better as my interest must be promoted by personal attention, to incur that likewise. With good security which I can give, the money may perhaps be obtained in Richmond on condition of its being returned in two years, one half the principal with interest the first, the remainder the next. Besides this, there is one other shift. My Father proposes that I shall join hands and work a plantation of his in Cumberland sharing the profits in proportion to the force of each. This would free me it is true from present expence, but reckoning on good prices, will yield only $800 which will not come to hand till april twelvemonth, besides the loss of labour in clearing anothers land while my own is lying idle, or yielding little profit. These are the circumstances to which I am reduced; and the different considerations which attend on either step appearing equally advantageous have brought me nearly to a stand. In this dilemma I apply to your better judgment and experience, and am determined to be guided by your advice. My Father had a severe attack on his journey, but in consequence of not being bled as the Physicians say, recovered speedily. He returned in much better health than when he left us and with his memory considerably improved. He is at present in Amelia, but expected back tomorrow. I obtained from Col. Burton[2] the address of several gentlemen who make the Carolina wine. He was much opposed to giving the information being willing and indeed anxious to procure it for you, but upon my insisting told me that Thomas Cox & co. Commission Merchants Plymouth, would be more likely to please than any others. The makers of the wine are persons in easy circumstances, who do not care to oblige, generally keeping the best for themselves. It was from Cox that your last and (I believe) my Fathers which you admired, were obtained. In case however, that you might still prefer the wine makers themselves, he informed me that Ebinezer Pettigrew P. O. Edenton, and George E. Spruel P. O. Plymouth make it best. The former will not always sell being very wealthy, the latter is not in as good circumstances, and owns the famous vine covering an acre of ground. Col. B. informed us that the vine does not grow from the slip, which accounts for the failure of yours.

If you can conveniently, I wish you would answer this as soon as it comes to hand. I am compelled to go down to Richmond on the 17th of novbr. at farthest, which will leave me two mails, the 14th and 16th. My *time* since I saw you, which I know you care most about, has been as well employed as circumstances would allow. I am just making up my mind to attack my Lord Cokes master peice, the chapter on Warranty which from all accounts will be a good winters campaign. My warmest love to yourself, Aunt Randolph, and family. Affectionately yours,

FRANS. EPPES

1. This explanation probably is in reference to his proposed marriage with Mary Elizabeth Cleland Randolph, which took place November 28, 1822, at Ashton in Albemarle County, the home of Thomas Eston Randolph, the father of the bride.

2. Colonel G. Hutchins Burton of Halifax, N. C. The wine in question was scuppernong. On May 1, 1817, TJ recorded in his account book that he had sent an order to J. W. Eppes to pay for "a barrel of Scuppernon wine bot for me by Mr. Burton."

TO FRANCIS WAYLES EPPES

Mo. Apr. 21.23.

DEAR FRANCIS

I am necessarily detained here by a negocia'n for the Univy. With the Literary board not yet closed, and our next Ct. which I must attend is now so near as not to allow me time for my visit to you and to get back to court. I must then defer it until our court is over. I mentd. to yourself and to Jefferson that you must make use of our dairy, our flock of sheep &c. for your table until your own should become sufficient, and lest Mr. Gough should not have been apprised of this I write him the inclosed letter, which I pray you to deliver him. I think I shall be with you about the 10th. or 12th. of May. My crippled wrist and hand are still in an useless situation and not likely soon to be otherwise.[1] Joe having got his axle-tree broken yesterday, is detained here to-day while we make a new one. Present me affectionately to Elizabeth and be assured yourself of my constant attachment.

TH: JEFFERSON

1. TJ injured his arm some time between October 29 and November 9, 1822, when he fell from one of the terraces at Monticello, fracturing one of the smaller bones in his left forearm and small ones in the same wrist. See TJ to John Barnes, November 30, 1822 (MHi), and William Branch Giles, June 9, 1823 (DLC). Also consult the "Medical Chronology" at Monticello.

FROM FRANCIS WAYLES EPPES

Poplar Forest April 23. 24.

I should have written sooner My Dr. Grandfather, but being very busy, and like most busy-bodies very thoughtless, I found it extremely easy to rest contented with the continued assurances of your health recieved thro' the letters of my cousins. I now write in apprehension of some difficulties with the representatives of my late Father[1] both to obtain your advice, and to learn whether you may have in possession any letter of his expressive of his designs as to my settlement in life. Any written corroboration of intentions which I have affirmed and acted upon would be grateful to my feelings, as the executors seem disposed to wring from my grasp all that the law will allow. They now demand a copy of the conveyance made in August last of six negroes, with the intention of disputing the title, or of compelling me to take them in part of the reversionary interest. The deed is worded in consideration "of natural affection and of promises heretofore made;" without specifying what promise: you consulted Col. Barbour on this head but mentioned the former condition only. I thought it probable, that as the subject has on several occasions been in agitation between you (as to cite one, when the exchange of Pantops for land here was proposed) there might be some letter containing full and explicit views on the subject: some one at least that may serve to convince My Mother that the reversion of Pantops is not an ephemeral claim; an idea which seems to hang upon her mind. This month has been extremely cold and disagreable with us. We have had frequent storms of wind, often accompanied by rain, and several smart frosts. The fruit however is as yet safe. Crops of wheat are promising. Yours uncommonly fine; better than that of Mrs. Mosely, which is a great point in reputation and profit. Some recent sales of tobacco in Lynchburg as high as 10 and 11 dollars: one crop of eight hogsheads very fine averaged 8.50. The neighbours are all well, and make frequent enquiries about you. They hope that your visit will not be much longer protracted, and that you will give us a larger share of your time. I need not add how much it would gratify me. With my love to you all in which Elizabeth joins I must now conclude. Believe me ever and affectionately yrs., FRANS. EPPES.

P. S. If it will not be too troublesome I wish you to bring me a little bit of Pyracantha with the root to it. The method of propagation by rows is so tedious and uncertain that I am inclined to rely more on this tho' the season maybe unfavourable.

1. John Wayles Eppes resigned from Congress in April, 1819, because of failing health. He was only fifty when he died at Millbrook on September 5, 1823; he was buried in the family cemetery there. TJ's opinion of his will may be found under the date 1823 in the Ambler Papers (ViU).

To Francis Wayles Eppes

Monto. May 6. 24.

DEAR FRANCIS

Your favor of the 23d ult. has been recieved. I have diligently gone over your father's correspondence with me, which is very voluminous, and I send you the only letters which seem to answer the purposes you have in view. There are 4. in number, to wit June 12. July 11. and Oct. 14. 1812. and June 12. 1820. The 3. first of these will shew he was aware that he was tenant for life only by courtesy in Pantops, the fee simple having descended on you, and further that he meant to hold it only till you should come of age and then surrender to you his life estate in it. And when we contemplated an exchange of that for equivalent lands in Bedford [1] he still meant you should recieve the equivalent lands there when of age. The last letter of June 12. 20 shews that the negroes [2] purchased from me with the 4000. D. your money, were purchased for you and were to be delivd. to you on coming of age, with 'such others as he could add to them.' The deed for the 6 negroes in Aug. 1823. was therefore but fulfillment of the intention expressed in this letter, and meant as an additional prov'n for you as a father, and not as in paiment of a debt and as a debtor. The consid'n too of 'natural affection and of promises heretofore made' by expressing what the consid'n was proves what it was not, to wit that it was a free gift and not meant as a paiment of a debt. That debt was not payable till his death. Was it then impossible he should be able to make you a free gift, in the mean time by any words if possible by [illegible] by what words could do it better than those saying it was a free gift. When he declares it to be a free gift, are his own words to be rejected, his expressed intention set aside, and a construction forced on him to make it the payment of a debt instead of a parental prov'n and advancemt. to you as desired it be. A voluntary gift of negroes, if they are delivered, is good either with or without a deed, and if not delivered, it is still good agt claimants equally voluntary, and all persons whatever except creditors or bona fide purchasers. To be good agt them, if the negroes were not delivered, the deed must have been recorded. I consider therefore the expression of the consid'n as a declaration of the intention of the donor and excluding all others, and the latter of June 12. 20. as a corroboration of what was expressed in the deed, and so I think it must be decided in a court of justice. I am engaged in a piece of work here which will probably detain me till the next month, when I hope I may be able to pay you a short visit. Give my love to Elizabeth and be assured of my best affections to yourself,   TH: J.

1. Specific boundaries for the acreage and house in the Poplar Forest plantation left Francis W. Eppes is recorded in TJ's will dated March 16–17, 1826. A copy is reproduced in Randall, III, 665–67; the original is in the Albemarle County Courthouse. See also Albemarle County Deed Book, 23, 253–54. The remainder of the Poplar Forest tract was reserved for the payment of TJ's debts.

2. This transaction is reflected in the account book notation for October 18, 1820.

To Francis Wayles Eppes

Monto. Feb. 17. 25.

DEAR FRANCIS

We heard some time ago indirectly and indistinctly thro' your friends at Ashton of the injury sustained by your house at P. F. and I have waited in hopes you would inform me of the particulars that I might know how far I could help you. I will spare J. Hem. to you and his two aids and he can repair every thing of wood as well or perhaps better than any body there. I understand that the roofs of the 2. NW rooms and Ding. room are burnt. Are the Portico and stairway burnt? The joists of the 3. rooms? The cornice of the Ding. room? The doors and windows destroyed? Let me know this and every particular. If the joists are burnt you will have to get others sawed at Capt. Martin's while his mill has water to spare. I used to cut and haul him stocks, and he sawed one half for the other. Those for the Dg. Room had better not be sawed till J. H comes up which will be as soon as I hear from you and he has finished a necessary job here.

Our last Professors from England are arrived in Hampton and we have announced the opening of the Univty. on the 1st. Monday of March.[1] All well here and at Ashton. Affectly yours,

TH: J.

1. These three professors were Robley Dunglison, Thomas Hewitt Key, and Charles Bonnycastle. They arrived at Norfolk on February 10.

From Francis Wayles Eppes

Poplar Forest Feb. 25.25.

I should have written to you sooner, My Dr. Grandfather, and given all the particulars of our late accidint, had I not supposed them already detailed by Elizabeth, who writes every mail to some one of your family. It occurred during the last snow, which by its depth induced me to burn the chimnies become very foul from long neglect. The wind it seems, had blown the snow off in several places, and in two of these the fire caught: one under the ballustrade and the other at the bottom of the platform, which supports the top railing. The first notice given us of the fire was the house's filling with smoke. I ran up to the top immediately and thought all over, for the fire was burning rapidly under the ballustrade and platform, and except the hosler my hands a mile off shut up in a tobacco house. It was nearly an hour before we had any help, and in that time we had scarcely got the railing down and floor off to come at the fire. But it was soon extinguished on the arrival of sufficient force. And now to the damages which I am glad to say are not as serious as you apprehend. 2000 shingles with some of the sheeting were burnt and torn off the N. W. Corner. The ballustrade in the same quarter burnt and cut down. The entire railing at top nearly destroyed. The platform and shinglels under it in the same quarter burnt and pulled off. The cornice of the Dining room was saved by the thickness of the plaistering tho' a large hole over the fireplace is burnt in the ceiling. This I believe is the total damage sustained at present, but such an accident in the night, or in windy weather, would be fatal to the house and perhaps its inhabitants; and from the tinder like state of the shingles which are extremely old and decayed I think the recurrence not at all improbable. Thinking your carpenters engaged, I had the roof repaired in a temporary manner with slabs, and had intended to make my carpenter tho' a rough hand, reshingle the whole if you think it advisable but the ballustrade and railing are I am afraid beyond his art. The terrace too is entirely gone. The joists and floor are rotted completely, and nothing but an entire renewal can render the offices again habitable. If you can furnish it I should be much obliged to you for a plat of the land upon which I live. A difficulty has occured on the line between Cobbs and you, where I have cleared out to the Waterlick road, not being able to find any but corner trees; and I wish very much to have the tract surveyed for the purpose of laying off the fields equally.

Have Cummings & Hilliard arrived?[1] And if they have are you still willing to take my Coke and give me the value in other books? My love to you all. Believe me ever and affectionately yrs.,

FRANS. EPPES.

P. S. If your catalogue for the university library is published I would be very much obliged to you for a copy.[2]

1. A Boston firm that supplied books for the University of Virginia Library See *Jefferson's Ideas on A University Library* (Charlottesville, 1950) edited by Elizabeth Cometti, for TJ's correspondence with William Hilliard.

2. It was not printed until 1828. See *1828 Catalogue of the Library of the University of Virginia, Reproduced in Facsimile with an Introduction by William Harwood Peden* . . . (Charlottesville, 1945).

TO FRANCIS WAYLES EPPES

Monto. Apr. [1825]

DEAR FRANCIS

The difficulty with which I write, my aversion to it, and the satiating dose which is forced upon me by an overwhelming correspondence have occasioned me to be thus late in acknoleging the rect of your letter of Feb. 24. I was glad to learn the damage to your house by the fire was less considerable than I had supposed. John Heming and his two aids have been engaged in covering this house with tin which is not yet finished. They shall repair to your assistance as soon as I can accompany them,[1] which shall be as soon as the roads become practicable. I would rather you should do nothing more than shelter by slabs or other temporary covering the uncovered parts of the house, any want of sawing which you can foresee had better be obtained while Captn. Martin's sawmill has waters for the terras, joists of the length and breadth of the former will be needed, but they may be 3.I. thick only as we can make the gutters in a different way which will for ever protect the joists from decay, pine would be the best timber, heart poplar will do. Oak is too springy. I will desire Colo. Peyton to send up tin for covering the dwelling house.

I will bring with me a plat of the land as you desire; but Mr. Yancey[2] knows so well the line between Cobb and myself, that I am sure he can point it out. So also can the surveyor who run the lines. The Catalogue of our library is not printed. Mr. Hilliard is now here and has brought on a collection of about 1000.D's worth of books, but chiefly of those called for by the schools. He will be able in abt. 3. months to furnish us with 30. copies of Thomas's Co.Lit. and his selling price will be 35.D. Your copy with all costs of importations cost me 30.91 and at that price I charged it to your father. If you prefer it's value in other books I would allow you the price which Hilliard will furnish it at, 35.D.

But could you not sell it for more in your n'bhood? In this do as best suits you. It would be indiff't. to me to take your copy or one of Hilliard's. Ever and affectionately your's,   TH: J.

1. John Hemings arrived and completed the work of repairing the house, but TJ did not supervise it. There are a number of interesting letters between him and TJ relative to the progress of this work. See John Hemings to TJ, July 23, August 11, September 18 and 28, 1825, and TJ to Hemings, August 17, 1825 (MHi), and Hemings to Septimia Anne Randolph, August 28, 1825 (ViU).

2. Joel Yancey was the overseer at Poplar Forest.

FROM ELLEN RANDOLPH COOLIDGE

Boston. August.1.25.

Having reached Boston[1] in safety, my dearest grandfather, one of my first cares is to write to you, to thank you for all the kindness I have received from you, and for all the affection you have shewn me, from my infancy and childhood, throughout the course of my maturer years: the only return I can make is by gratitude the deepest and most enduring; and love the most devoted; and although removed by fortune to a distance from you, yet my heart is always with you; I shall write as often as the fear of troubling you, (who are already so much troubled by numerous letters from others,) will permit; and return to see you whenever I possibly can and this I hope will not be unfrequently. The facility of travelling is now such that I have myself passed over about 1000 miles in 12 days; for, of the five weeks that elapsed between my leaving Monticello and reaching Boston, we have stopped more than three in the different great cities on the road. Mr. Coolidge wished to give me an idea of the beauty and prosperity of the New England States; and, instead of taking me from New York to Boston, by sea, he planned a tour, which we have accordingly made, up the Hudson as far as Albany; from thence to Saratoga, Lakes George and Champlain; as far north as Burlington in Vermont; from Burlington across the country to the Connecticut River; and down this river to Springfield; from whence, through the interior of Massachusetts to Boston: the journey has been long and somewhat fatiguing; but it has made me acquainted with probably the fairest and most flourishing portion of New England, and I do not regret having taken it: it has given me an idea of prosperity and improvement, such as I fear our Southern States cannot hope for, whilst the canker of slavery eats into their hearts, and diseases the whole body by this ulcer at the core. When I consider the im-

mense advantages of soil and climate which we possess over these
people, it grieves me to think that such great gifts of Nature
should have failed to produce any thing like the wealth and improvement which the New-Englanders have wrung from the hard
bosom of a stubborn and ungrateful land, and amid the gloom
and desolation of their wintry skies. I should judge from appearances that they are at least a century in advance of us in all
the arts and embellishments of life; and they are pressing forward
in their course with a zeal and activity which I think must ensure
success. It is certainly a pleasing sight, this flourishing state of
things: the country is covered with a multitude of beautiful villages; the fields are cultivated and forced into fertility; the roads
kept in the most exact order; the inns numerous, affording good
accommodations; and travelling facilitated by the ease with which
post carriages and horses are always to be obtained. Along the
banks of the Connecticut there are rich meadow lands, and here
New might, I should think, almost challenge *Old* England, in
beauty of landscape. From the top of Mount Holyoke which commands perhaps one of the most extensive views in these States,
the whole country as you look down upon it, resembles one vast
garden divided into it's parterns. There are upwards of twenty
villages in sight at once, and the windings of the Connecticut are
every where marked, not only by it's own clear and bright waters,
but by the richness and beauty of the fields and meadows, and the
density of population on it's banks. The villages themselves have
an air of neatness and comfort that is delightful. The houses have
no architectural pretensions, but they are pleasing to look at, for
they are almost all painted white, with vines about the windows
and doors, and grass plats in front decorated with flowers and
shrubs; a neat paling separates each little domain from it's neighbour; and the out-houses are uniformly excellent, especially the
wood-house, which is a prominent feature in every establishment,
and is, even at this season, well nigh filled with the stock for
winter's use. The school houses are comfortable-looking buildings,
and the Churches with their white steeples, add not a little to the
beauty of the landscape. It is common also to find the larger of
these country towns, the seats of colleges which are numerous
throughout the country.

The appearance of the people generally is much in their favor;
the men seem sober, orderly, and industrious: I have seen but one
drunken man since I entered New England, and he was a south
carolinian! The women are modest, tidy, and well-looking; the

children, even, are more quiet and civil than you generally find them elsewhere; they are almost all taught to curtsy, or bow to passers-by; and it is an amusing and not unpleasing sight, to see a group of these little urchins returning from school with their books in their hands, draw up by the side of the road and gravely salute the traveller, who rewards their courtesy only by a smile and a nod. I have visited one only of the great cotton factories which are beginning to abound in the country; and, although it was a flourishing establishment, and excited my astonishment by it's powers of machinery, and the immense saving of time and labor, yet I could not get reconciled to it. The manufacturer grows rich, whilst the farmer plods on in comparative poverty; but the pure air of heaven, and the liberty of the fields in summer, with a quiet and comfortable fire-side in winter, certainly strikes the imagination more favorably, than the confinement of the large but close, heated, and crowded rooms of a factory; the constant whirl and deafening roar of machinery; and the close, sour and greasy smells emitted by the different ingredients employed in the different processes of manufacturing cotton, and woollen cloths: also, I fancied the farmers and labourers looked more cheerful and healthy than the persons employed in the factories, and their wives and daughters prettier, and neater, than the women and girls I saw before the looms and spinning jennies. There are two little spectacles I liked much to look out upon from the windows of the carriage; the one was, the frequent waggons laden high above their tops with hay (the country through which I have passed being principally a grass-growing one) and drawn by the largest, finest and handsomest oxen I have ever seen, and driven by a hail ruddy farmer's lad; the other was, a country girl driving home her cow, for the girls as I have said before, are well looking, healthy and modest, and the cows laden with their milky treasures might, any one of them, serve as a study for a painter who desired to express this sort of abundance.

I have written badly, I fear almost illegibly, for I am not yet recovered from the fatigue of my journey, and my hand trembles; after this long letter then, my dearest grandfather, I will bid you adieu. I have been received with great kindness by my new relations, but my heart turns towards those who love me so much better than any others can ever do; I am anxious, however, to conciliate those with whom I am hereafter to reside; and shall strive to make friends, particularly as I have every reason to believe that my husband's family and circle of immediate friends are persons of uncommon merit. Mr. Coolidge prays to be permitted to express his regard and veneration for you, and will attend immediately to your memorandum. Once more adieu my dear grandpapa, love to all and for yourself the assurance of my devoted love.

ELLEN W. COOLIDGE

1. She married Joseph Coolidge, Jr., of Boston, May 27, 1825, in the parlour at Monticello. See *The Annual Report of the Monticello Association Nineteen Hundred and Thirty-two*, page 11, for additional information on the wedding. For the story of their extended wedding trip, see Harold J. Coolidge, "An American Wedding Journey in 1825," *Atlantic Monthly* (March, 1929). They resided in Boston, where Coolidge was a successful merchant whose trade was chiefly with the Far East. Ellen died April 21, 1876, and her husband December 15, 1879.

To ELLEN RANDOLPH COOLIDGE

Monticello Aug. 27. 25

Your affectionate letter, my dear Ellen, of the 1st. inst. came to hand in due time. The assurances of your love, so feelingly expressed, were truly soothing to my soul, and none were ever met with warmer sympathies. We did not know, until you left us, what a void it would make in our family. Imagination had illy sketched it's full measure to us: and, at this moment, every thing around serves but to remind us of our past happiness, only consoled by the addition it has made to yours. Of this we are abundantly assured by the most excellent and amiable character to which we have committed your future well-being, and by the kindness with which you have been recieved by the worthy family into which you are now engrafted. We have no fear but that their affections will grow with their growing knolege of you, and the assiduous cultivation of these becomes the first object in importance to you. I have no doubt you will find also the state of society there more congenial with your mind, than the rustic scenes you have left: altho these do not want their points of endearment. Nay, one single circumstance changed, and their scale would hardly be the lightest. One fatal stain deforms what nature had bestowed on us of her fairest gifts. I am glad you took the delightful tour which you describe in your letter. It is almost exactly that which Mr. Madison and myself pursued in May and June 1791. Setting out from Philadelphia, our course was to N. York, up the Hudson to Albany, Troy, Saratoga, Ft. Edward, Ft. George, L. George Ticonderoga, Crown point, penetrated into L. Champlain, returned the same way to Saratoga, thence crossed the mountains to Bennington, Northampton, along Connecticut river to it's mouth, crossed the Sound into Long-island, and along it's Northern margin to Brooklyn, re-crossed to N. York and returned. But, from Saratoga till we got back to Northampton, was then mostly desert. Now it is what 34. years of free and good government have made it. It shews how soon the labor of man would make a paradise of the whole earth, were it not for misgovernment, and a diversion of all his energies from their proper object, the happiness of man, to the selfish interests of kings, nobles and priests.

Our University goes on well. We have past the limit of 100. Students some time since. As yet it has been a model of order and good behavior, having never yet an occasion for the exercise of a single act of authority. We studiously avoid too much government. We treat them as men and gentlemen, under the guidance mainly of their own discretion. They so consider themselves, and make it their pride to acquire that character for their institution. In short we are as quiet on that head as the experience of 6. months only can justify. Our Professors too continue to be what we wish them. Mr. Gilmer accepts the Law-chair, and all is well.

My own health is what it was when you left me. I have not been out of the house since, except to take the turn of the Round-about twice; nor have I any definite prospect when it will be otherwise. I shall not venture into the region of small news, of which your other correspondents of the family are so much better informed. I am expecting to hear from Mr. Coolidge on the subject of the clock for the Rotunda. Assure him of my warmest affections, and respect, and pray him to give you ten thousand kisses for me, and they will still fall short of the measure of my love to you. If his parents and family can set any store by the esteem and respect of a stranger, mine are devoted to them.

TH: JEFFERSON

FROM ELLEN RANDOLPH COOLIDGE

Boston Oct. 10. 25.

MY DEAR GRANDPAPA

The Rev. Mr. Brazer,[1] a Unitarian Clergyman of Salem in this State, asks from Mr. Coolidge or myself a letter of introduction to you, as he proposed to make a tour through the middle states, and wishes to visit Monticello, and pay his respects to you there. Knowing, as we do, how much you are harassed and oppressed by the crowd of strangers who think themselves privileged to waste and misuse your time, intruding upon you at all hours, and sacrificing your comfort and even health without reflection and without remorse, we are always unwilling to add, by the introduction of new visitors, to the burthen which weighs so heavily upon you; but it is likewise difficult, sometimes almost impossible to refuse the recommendations which are asked of us. In this instance, I have yielded to the wishes of Mr. Brazer, taking care at the same time to let him know that your health is very feeble, and that his seeing you must depend upon your having a moment's respite from bodily suffering and extreme debility. Mama, or one of my sisters, will be so good as to receive him, and let him know whether you are well enough to admit of his visit to yourself. He is a man held in great esteem on account of the entire respectability of his character, and has a high reputation for talents and learning, being known among the literary men of Boston for his able articles in the North American Review and other periodical works of the day. He was formerly Latin Tutor in Cambridge University, and is the author of a criticism upon "Pickering on Greek pronunciation," and a review of Chalmers' "Christianity in connexion with modern Astronomy." Mr. Brazer tells me that he has had some correspondence with you upon the subject of his criticism on Pickering's Greek pronunciation, but as it was several years ago, he thinks you may have forgotten the circumstance.

Adieu my dearest grandfather. Mr. Coolidge offers his most respectful and affectionate regards, and from me you need no new assurance of my devoted love.   ELLEN: W: COOLIDGE

1. The Reverend Mr. John Brazer.

To Thomas Jefferson Randolph

Oct. 21. 25

DEAR JEFFERSON

I inclose you a letter from N. H. Lewis as Secretary of the Rivanna company,[1] as also a copy of the interlocutory decree of Chancellor Brown for the appointment of Commissioners, which is the object of this letter. I have informed Mr. Lewis that I leave all further proceedings in this matter to you, and shall confirm whatever you do in it. Affectionately yours,

TH: JEFFERSON

1. A company chartered in December, 1806, to improve the navigation

of the Rivanna River past Milton to Moore's Ford near Charlottesville. TJ had a few disagreements with the directors, but they in general enjoyed his cooperation, for which they extended him certain shipping considerations. The canal was completed in 1812 (it did not include TJ's canal), and its use contributed a great deal to the demise of Milton, then a thriving river port and a more important commercial center than Charlottesville.

To Ellen Randolph Coolidge

Monticello, Nov. 14. 1825.

My dear Ellen

In my letter of Oct. 13. to Mr. Coolidge, I gave an account of the riot[1] we had at the University, and of it's termination. You will both of course be under anxiety till you know how it has gone off? With the best effects in the world. Having let it be understood, from the beginning, that we wished to trust very much to the discretion of the Students themselves for their own government. With about four fifths of them, this did well, but there were about 15. or 20. bad subjects who were disposed to try whether our indulgence was without limit. Hence the licentious transaction of which I gave an account to Mr. Coolidge. But when the whole mass saw the serious way in which that experiment was met, the Faculty of Professors assembled, the Board of Visitors coming forward in support of that authority, a grand jury taking up the subject, four of the most guilty expelled, the rest reprimanded, severer laws enacted, and a rigorous execution of them declared in future, it gave them a shock and struck a terror, the most severe, as it was less expected. It determined the well disposed among them to frown upon every thing of the kind hereafter, and the ill-disposed returned to order from fear if not from better motives. A perfect subordination has succeeded, entire respect towards the Professors, and industry, order, and quiet the most exemplary, has prevailed ever since. Every one is sensible of the strength which the institution has derived from what appeared at first to threaten it's foundation. We have no further fear of any thing of the kind from the present set. But as at the next term their numbers will be more than doubled by the accession of an additional band, as unbroken as these were, we mean to be prepared, and to ask of the legislature a power to call in the civil authority in the first instant of disorder, and to quell it on the spot by imprisonment and the same legal coercions, provided against disorder generally, committed by other citizens, from whom, at their age, they have no right to distinction.

We have heard of the loss of your baggage, with the vessel carrying it, and sincerely condole with you on it. It is not to be estimated by it's pecuniary value, but by that it held in your affections. The documents of your childhood, your letters, correspondencies, notes, books, &c., &c., all gone! And your life cut in two, as it were, and a new one to begin, without any records of the former. John Hemmings was the first who brought me the news. He had caught it accidentally from those who first read the letter from Col. Peyton announcing it. He was au desespoir! That beautiful writing desk he had taken so much pains to make for you! Everything else seemed as nothing in his eye, and that loss was everything. Virgil could not have been more afflicted had his Aeneid fallen a prey to the flames. I asked him if he could not replace it by making another? No. His eyesight had failed him too much, and his recollection of it was too imperfect. It has occurred to me however, that I can replace it, not, indeed, to you, but to Mr. Coolidge, by a substitute, not claiming the same value from it's decorations, but from the part it has *borne* in our history and the events with which it has been associated. I recieved a letter from a friend in Philadelphia lately, asking information of the house, and room of the house there, in which the Declaration of Independence was written, with a view to future celebrations of the 4th. of July in it, another, enquiring whether a paper given to the Philosophical society there, as a rough draught of that Declaration was genuinely so? A society is formed there lately for an annual celebration of the advent of Penn to that place. It was held in his antient Mansion, and the chair in which he actually sat when at his writing table was presented by a lady owning it, and was occupied by the president of the celebration. Two other chairs were given them, made of the elm, under the shade of which Penn had made his first treaty with the Indians. If then things acquire a superstitious value because of their connection with particular persons, surely a connection with the great Charter of our Independence may give a value to what has been associated with that; and such was the idea of the enquirers after the room in which it was written. Now I happen still to possess the writing-box [2] on which it was written. It was made from a drawing of my own, by Ben. Randall, a cabinet maker in whose house I took my first lodgings on my arrival in Philadelphia in May 1776. And I have used it ever since. It claims no merit of particular beauty. It is plain, neat, convenient, and, taking no more room on the writing table than a moderate 4to. volume, it yet displays it self sufficiently for any writing. Mr. Coolidge must do me the favor of accepting this. Its imaginary value will increase with the years, and if he lives to my age, or another half century, he may see it carried in the procession of our nation's birthday, as the relics of the saints are in those of the church. I will send it thro' Colonel Peyton, and hope with better fortune than that for which it is to be a substitute.

I remark what you say in your letter to your mother, relative to Mr. Willard [3] and our University clock. Judging from that that he is the person whom Mr. Coolidge would recommend, and having recieved from Dr. Waterhouse a very strong recommendation of him, you may assure the old gentleman from me that he shall have the making of it. We have lately made an important purchase of lands amounting to 7000. D. and the government is taking from us, under their old and new Tariff, 2700. D. duty on the marble caps and bases of the Portico of our Rotunda, of 10 columns only. These things try our funds for the moment. At the end of the year we shall see how we stand, and I expect we may be able to give the final order for the clock by February.

I want to engage you, as my agent at Boston, for certain articles not to be had here, and for such only. But it will be on the indispensable condition that you keep as rigorous an account of Dollars and cents as old Yerragan our neighbor would do. This alone can induce friends to ask services freely, which would otherwise be the asking of presents and amount to a prohibition. We should be very glad occasionally to get small supplies of the fine dumb codfish to be had at Boston, and also of the tongues and sounds of the Cod. This selection of the articles I trouble you for is not of such as are better there than here; for on that ground we might ask for every thing from thence, but such only as are not to be had here at all. Perhaps I should trespass on Mr. Coolidge for one other article. We pay here 2. D. a gallon for bad French brandy. I think I have seen in Degrand's Price current Marseilles brandy, from Dodge and Oxnard,[4] advertised good at 1. Dollar; and another kind called Seignettes, which I am told is good Cognac at 1.25. D. I will ask of you then a supply of a kental of good dumb fish, and about 20 or 30 lbs. of tongues and sounds; and of Mr. Coolidge a 30 gallon cask of Dodge and Oxnard's Marseilles brandy, if tolerable good at 1.D. or thereabouts, but double cased to guard against spoliation. Knowing nothing of the prices of the fish, I will at a venture, desire Col. Peyton to remit 60. D. to Mr. Coolidge immediately, and any little difference between this and actual cost either way, may stand over to your next account. We should be the better perhaps of your recipe for dressing both articles.

I promised Mr. Ticknor[5] to inform him at times how our University goes on. I shall be glad if you will read to him that part of this letter which respects it, presuming Mr. Coolidge may have communicated to him the facts of my former letter to him. These facts may be used ad libitum, only keeping my name out of sight. Writing is so irksome to me, especially since I am obliged to do it in a recumbent posture, that I am sure Mr. Ticknor will excuse my economy in this exercise. To you perhaps I should apologize for the want of it on this occasion. The family is well. My own health changes little. I ride two or three miles in a carriage every day. With my affectionate salutations to Mr. Coolidge, be assured yourself of my tender and constant love.

TH: JEFFERSON

1. A spirit of insubordination among the students had cropped out on June 22, August 5, and September 19. About ten days later the disorders began in earnest. At first they seemed directed principally at the European professors, that is, at Long and Key in particular, but soon came to include all the faculty. See Bruce, *University of Virginia*, II, 298–301.

2. This lap desk is now in the National Museum. TJ misspelled the cabinetmaker's name; it was Benjamin Randolph. See Margaret W. Brown, *The Story of the Declaration of Independence Desk and How It came to the National Museum* (Washington, 1954).

3. Simon Willard, the famed Boston clockmaker.

4. Marseilles merchants.

5. George Ticknor.

TO ELLEN RANDOLPH COOLIDGE

Monticello Nov. 26.25.

MY DEAR ELLEN

The inclosed letter (Nov. 14th.) has been written near a fortnight and has laid by me awaiting a pacotille which your Mama was making up of some things omitted to be sent to you with those so unfortunately lost. That is now made up and will be immediately forwarded to Richmond to the care of Colo. Peyton.

FROM ELLEN RANDOLPH COOLIDGE

Boston.Dec.26.25.

Your letter of Nov.14. and 26. my dearest Grandpapa, gave me a degree of pleasure only to be understood by those, who, like me, are far separated from the best and kindest of friends; it is some compensation for the pains of absence, this increased sensibility to the pleasures left still within our reach whereby an occasional and limited intercourse with those dearest to us, acquires a value so great as to be a sort of equivalent for the temporary loss of their society. But joyful as the receipt of a letter from you makes my heart, I still look forward, with longing eyes, to the moment which shall again bring me into your presence, and count the months until the return of summer shall restore me to the beloved circle of native home and early friends. I have found great kindness where I am, and feel sincerely grateful for it, and anxious to give the most convincing proof of that gratitude by shewing myself sensible to the attentions that are paid me, and satisfied with my residence among those from whom I have received them. But all this is consistent with the most lively desire to revisit the scenes of my childhood and the friends who have loved me first and longest; and whose claims upon my devoted affection is one of my chief pleasures to feel and acknowledge.

The account contained in your letter of the transactions at the University, Mr. Coolidge and myself were very glad to receive, and he particularly, always respecting *your name,* has made considerable use of it, to place things in their true point of view, and counteract the effect of false or exaggerated statements. To Mr. Tichnor, we communicated portions of both your letters, not withholding your name, as we had your permission for doing so, and believed him entirely worthy of the confidence. He is, as you know, a strenuous advocate for reform in the Cambridge University, which has brought him into trouble with many of the most distinguished men of letters here; and I have no doubt the opposition he meets with strengthens his interest in an institution based upon more liberal principles, and animates his kind feelings for the University of Virginia. Your old friend Gen. Dearborn is always mindful of his former attachment to you, and has shewn it by kindness to me, for your sake, and many enquiries whenever we have met and relating to your health and well-being. Numerous engagements at first, and latterly the severities of a New England winter, have prevented me from paying more than one visit to Mr. Adams at Quincy. As soon as the weather moderates a little we shall go again. We found the old gentleman, just as he has been frequently described to you, afflicted with bodily infirmities, lame, and almost blind, but, as far as his mind is concerned, as full of life as he could have been fifty years ago; not only does he seem to have preserved the full vigor of his intellect, but all the sprightliness of his fancy, all the vivacity of his thoughts and opinions. He converses with fluency and cheerfulness and a visible interest upon almost any topic; his manners are kind and courteous, his countenance animated, and his hearing so little impaired as to require only distinctness of articulation and scarcely any raising of the voice in speaking to him. He is surrounded by grand-children exceedingly attached to him, and watching over him with great care and tenderness, and altogether presented an image so venerable, so august even amid the decay of his bodily powers, as sent us away penetrated with respect and admiration for the noble ruin which time-worn and shattered looks still so grand in comparison with what is offered to us by present times. Mr. Adams might say with Ossian, "the sons of feeble men shall behold me and admire the stature of the chiefs of old." I am afraid our revolutionary worthies have been succeeded by a race comparatively small.

The weather has been, here, cold beyond the season; the Bostonians do not generally calculate upon anything as severe before January. I have not suffered as much as I feared I should, because great precautions are taken to guard against the inclemency of the climate. The houses are well built, with double doors, small close rooms, stoves and whatever contributes to keep out the general enemy, the intense cold; great stores of wood and other fuel are timely laid in, and against the open air, the females particularly, defend themselves by warm clothing. I find that with the wrappings generally made use of, I can walk or ride without inconvenience, and that it is not at all necessary to confine myself to the house more than I should do in Virginia. The New Englanders are so reconciled by habit to their climate as really to prefer it to a more [word omitted] one, a degree of philosophy which I do not think I shall very readily attain to. I have written a long letter, and in great part by candle-light, but I cannot close without saying that the brandy &c. will be shipped in about a week along with a piano built for Virginia, in this town, a very beautiful piece of workmanship, and doing, I think, great credit to the young mechanic whom we employed, and whose zeal was much stimulated by the knowledge that his work would pass under your eye. The tones of the instrument are fine, and it's interior structure compares most advantageously with that of the English-built pianos, having, we think, a decided superiority. The manufacturer believes that it will be to his advantage to have it known that he was employed in such a work for you, or what amounts to the same thing, for one of your family, living under your roof. Willard the clock maker, is, as I mentioned before, very solicitous to have the making of the time-piece for the University, has already begun it, (*upon his own responsibility,* and knowing the circumstances of the case, as we have taken care to mislead or deceive him in nothing,) and wishes to be informed exactly as to the dimensions of the room in which the clock is to stand.

I shall attend to your wishes in respect to the recipes you mention. Mr. Coolidge will write to you soon, and in the mean time offers the assurance of his great respect and warm affection; the family hears from me so often, it is almost unnecessary to send any messages, I shall therefore add nothing farther to this unreasonably long letter, but what I feel to be the inadequate expression of my own devoted love for you my dearest, kindest, best grandfather. Adieu then, since I must say adieu, and believe me with the same heart always your own,   ELLEN: W: COOLIDGE.

M. Sales is quite satisfied with a message, instead of a letter in reply to his own, and very grateful for the kindness of your expressions.

FROM THOMAS JEFFERSON RANDOLPH

Jany 31 1826

MY DEAR GRANDFATHER

I hastened upon my first arrival here to deliver your letters and communi[cations] with your friends upon the subject of the lottery, the leading men have taken up the affair with zeal and are making their impressions upon others. We propose on thursday to ask leave to bring in the bill. Your friends are confident of success. The bill has been drawn in conformity to the opinions of the most zealous and most judicious of your friends. It is drawn with a preamble simply stating the length of your public services, the cause great embarrassment therefrom. To take away all ground of objection, as a scheme to raise money, valuers are appointed to set a fair and liberal value on the property on the usual credit and we are authorised to raise such a sum as will give us that valuation nett. I have named persons in whose character and feelings I could rely. I hope by next mail to give you more decisive information. I will purchase the negroe clothing and send it. As ever and affectionately yours,

TH: J. RANDOLPH

FROM THOMAS JEFFERSON RANDOLPH

Richmd Feb. 3d [1826]

[MY] DEAR GRANDFATHER

You will be disappointed in hearing [that] your bill[1] is not yet before the Legislature. Upon the [fact] being generally known that such an application would be made a panic seised the timid and indecisive among your friends as to the effect it might have upon your reputation which produced a reaction so powerfull that yesterday and the day before I almost dispaired of doing anything. But upon availing myself of the councils of Judges Brook, Cabell, Green and Carr[2] and their weight of character and soundness of views, to act upon gentlemen of less experience and decision. They have been again rallied to the charge and are now bold and determined, and assure me they will not again hesitate or look back and feel confident of success; they do not believe that the delay has been injurious. The policy of the state had been against lotteries as immoral and the first view of the subject was calculated to give alarm which it took time and reflection to remove.

We owe great obligations to the kindness and zeal of the Judges; particularly Brook whose tact and readiness and decision [letter torn] to us invaluable. The importance [letter torn] more urgent than ever. The Banks, with [letter torn] for us, without additional [illegible; letter torn] your friend; and which I properly [letter torn] ordered. If we fail I shall endeavor [to raise] money for pressing demands by pledging property [which will] give us time to sell ourselves. I do not anticipate [trouble, but] will not be unprepared to meet it. If you will preserve y[our health] and spirits and not suffer yourself to be affected by it; [your grandc]hildren will be so happy in that, that we shall never think of difficulties or loss of property as an evil. My own trials and struggles with the world have been so salutary, as to give me a decision of character and confidence in myself not to be dismayed at any difficulties which can arise. And if the worst happens we shall among us have a plenty for the comfort of my mother and yourself during your lives: and children that make the poverty of rich men, make the wealth of the poor ones. Peyton has been kind and true. He sees our difficulties and can wait for our crop Most devotedly yours, TH J RANDOLPH

1. Jefferson's financial plight in 1826 was almost beyond recovery: his debts amounted to something over $100,000; bankruptcy was impossible, for his lands were mortgaged to their limit. As disaster stared him in the face he snatched at a last straw: a lottery to dispose of his property. The consent of

the legislature was necessary, but this did not appear as a serious hurdle. Thomas J. Randolph was sent to Richmond to seek the needed authorization, and a bill was drafted for immediate introduction. After much haggling the bill passed, on February 20. In anticipation, tickets were printed, but their sale did not catch on despite heroic efforts by TJ's grandson; the plans for the lottery were called off. Instead, it was replaced by a public subscription plan that was only a partial help.

2. Judges Francis T. Brooke, William H. Cabell, John Williams Green, and Dabney Carr of the Supreme Court of Appeals of Virginia.

To Thomas Jefferson Randolph

Monticello Feb. 4. 26

DEAR JEFFERSON

Your letter of the 31st. was recieved yesterday and gave me a fine night's rest which I had not had before since you left us, as the failure to hear from you by the preceding mail had filled me with fearful forebodings. I am pleased with the train you are proceeding in, and particularly with the appointment of valuers. Under all circumstances I think I may expect a liberal valuation, an exaggerated one I should negative myself. I would not be stained with the suspicions of selfishness at this time of life, and this will protect me from them. I hope the paper I gave you will justify me in the eyes of all those who have been consulted.

Have you attended to the white lead mentioned in my former letter? I hope the negro-clothing is on it's way.

I mentioned to you my neighborhood debts, and you wished me not to draw on Colo. Peyton till you should be there. Their pressure, and particularly the University entrances, is such that I must draw the day after tomorrow for 250. D. I can put off some what longer the bills of Raphael and Heiskil for the last quarter's groceries. About 130. students had arrived at the University yesterday, of which ⅔ were new-comers. About 60 old ones are still to come and probably a like number at least of new ones. You know that Jane has brought you another daughter. All doing well. Affectionately yours,   TH: J

From Thomas Jefferson Randolph

Richmond Feb 7 1826

My DEAR GRANDFATHER

I am sorry I cannot announce to you any definitive result as to the object of my visit here. To-morrow however the bill will be brought in without fail; there will be opposition but wither by silent vote or active debate is not known; your friends are sanguine. There has been no pause or hesitation with them since I last wrote. By the next mail or by private conveyance if any offers earlier I can give you something decisive and certain. Ever affectionately yours,   TH: J. RANDOLPH

TO THOMAS JEFFERSON RANDOLPH

Monticello. Feb. 8. 26.

MY DEAR JEFFERSON

I duly received your affectionate letter of the third, and perceive there are greater doubts than I had apprehended whether the Legislature will indulge my request to them. It is a part of my mortification to perceive that I had so far overvalued myself as to have counted on it with too much confidence. I see, in the failure of this hope, a deadly blast of all my peace of mind, during my remaining days. You kindly encourage me to keep up my spirits but oppressed with disease, debility, age and embarrassed affairs, this is difficult. For myself, I should not regard a prostration of fortune. But I am over whelmed at the prospect of the situation in which I may leave my family. My dear and beloved daughter, the cherished companion of my early life, and nurse of my age, and her children, rendered as dear to me as if my own, from having lived with me from their cradle, left in a comfortless situation, hold up to me nothing but future gloom. And I should not care were life to end with the line I am writing, were it not that I may be of some avail to the family. Their affectionate devotion to me (in the unhappy state of mind which your father's misfortunes have brought upon him,) I may yet be of some avail to the family. Their affectionate devotion to me makes a willingness to endure life a duty, as long as it can be of any use to them. Yourself particularly, dear Jefferson, I consider as the greatest of the god-sends which heaven has granted to me. Without you, what could I do under the difficulties now environing me? These have been produced in some degree by my own unskillful management, and devoting my time to the service of my country, but much also by the unfortunate fluctuations in the value of our money, and the long continued depression of farming business. But for these last, I am confident my debts might be paid, leaving me Monticello and the Bedford estate. But where there are no bidders, property, however, great, is no resource for the payment of debts.

All may go for little or nothing. Perhaps however, even in this case, I may have no right to complain, as these misfortunes have been held back for my last days, when few remain to me. I duly acknoledge that I have gone through a long life, with fewer circumstances of affliction than are the lot of most men. Uninterrupted health, a competence for every reasonable want, usefulness to my fellow-citizens, a good portion of their esteem, no complaint against the world which has sufficiently honored me, and above all, a family which has blessed me by their affections, and never by their conduct given me a moment's pain. And should this my last request be granted, I may yet close with a cloudless sun a long and serene day of life. Be assured, my dear Jefferson, that I have a just sense of the part you have contributed to this, and that I bear you unmeasured affection.   TH: JEFFERSON

To Thomas Jefferson Randolph

Monticello, Feb.11th, '26.

Bad news, my dear Jefferson, as to your sister Anne. She expired about half an hour ago.[1] I have been so ill for several days that I could not go to see her till this morning, and found her speechless and insensible. She breathed her last about 11 o'clock. Heaven seems to be overwhelming us with every form of misfortune, and I expect your next will give me the *coup de grâce*. Your own family are all well. Affectionately adieu.   TH: JEFFERSON

1. Anne Cary Randolph Bankhead died at Monticello and was buried in the graveyard there. For the only account of her death, see Samuel X. Radbill, editor, "The Autobiographical Ana of Robley Dunglison, M.D.," *Transactions of the American Philosophical Society*, New Series, Vol. 58, Part 8 (1963).

From Francis Wayles Eppes

Poplar Forest. Feb. 23. 26.

It was with infinite pain My Dr. Grandfather, that I saw your application to the legislature; the first information which reached me, of the immediate pressure of your difficulties: and I write as well to express, My unfeigned grief, as to assure you, that I return to your funds with the utmost good will, the portion of property which you designed for me; and which I should always have considered as yours, even had it been, legally secured to me. As long as, I was able to consider, the gift, of no evil consequence to your-self, and as the equivalent of the land intended for my mother, the possession was grateful both to my feelings, and to My sense of propriety: but, now, when I learn that after the payment of your debts, but little of your property will be left, I hope that under such, or even better circumstances, you cannot do me the injustice to suppose, that I could even consent to retain the smallest portion. You have been to me ever, an affectionate, and tender Father, and you shall find me ever, a loving, and devoted son, what that son would do, I will, under all circumstances; and I now with the great-est allacrity relinquish, that competence which you so kindly gave and I do assure you, if there be sincerity in human nature, that it is with greatest satisfaction, and that I shall remain ever, as deeply indebted, as though your kind intentions had been completely fulfilled. As to myself it is sufficient to say, that I am still young, healthy, and strong, and so being feel able to provide for myself, and for those who depend upon me. In a few months more, with the knowledge already acquired, I feel confident of obtaining admittance to the bar, and in the time that intervenes between introduction and practice, of perfecting that knowledge suffi-ciently for after occasions. Having held you ever in the light of a Father, I could see no impropriety, while the gift was not preju-dicial to yourself, in accep[ting] and retaining, whatever you were pleased in your goodness, to give me; and deeming what you gave, amply sufficient for all My wants, a life of quiet independence, and of moderate but sure gains, suited my tastes better, than the all engrossing, and laborious, study and practice of law. It afforded too more leisure for the acquisition of general information, which has always appeared to me preferable to that which is confined, and particular: and the certainty of being always with my family was no small addition to the considerations which swayed me. But these views which may account for My want of immediate preparation, I can easily forego; and I shall feel happy in so doing only: and I am well assured that my attention once turned, and rivetted, on another object, interest will soon render that most agreable. Do not therefore, My dear Grandfather, from any ill founded fears on my account, or from any other motive oppose an act which setting aside its justice, is the necessary consequence, of the filial tenderness with which my heart is over-flowing, do not mortify me by refusing that which you own; and which if it were not, I should think the same feelings which prompt the son to offer, should compel the Father to accept. Forgive me if I have spoken too freely on a subject which, interests me so deeply. I feel your past kindness, that ought to excuse all. May God bless and long preserve you My dearest Grandfather, my best friend, with most sincere love your grandson,   FRANS. EPPES. P. S. Elizabeth is well and joins me in love to yourself and the family. May I ask, what your scheme is, for the lottery?

FROM THOMAS JEFFERSON RANDOLPH

Richmond February [26.] 1826

MY DEAREST GRANDFATHER

Last night I recieved yours of the 8th and 11th conveying the heart rending intelligence of the death of my beloved sister an event for which I had been in a manner prepared by previous letters from home, and adding another pang to your afflictions. Let me intreat you to restrain yourself and cheer up with the hope of better times. We have proceeded slowly but surely we hope in our business here. The vote given the other day was without debate on the reading of the bill; its enemies had been active against it and shuned discussion. We believe a reaction has taken place and that it will be carried by a large majority. The unanimous opinion of all its friends is that it is daily gaining ground. It would have been acted upon today but for the death of a member for which the house adjourned yesterday and a pageant in delivering a sword to Commodore Warrington to day; it will be certain to be taken up day after to morrow and by the next mail I hope to communicate its passage thro the lower house: It will pass the senate by a large vote. Preserve your self for our sakes. If the worst should happen which I again repeat I do not in the least suppose neither My Mother or Yourself can ever want comforts as long as you both live. I have property enough for us all and it shall ever be my pride and happiness to watch over you both with the warmest affection and guard you against the shafts of adversity. How wretched are those possessing large property and unfortunate in the vices and ingratitude of their children. How rich you are in the virtues and devoted attachment of yours, preserve your health and spirits and all other ills are but comparative and imaginery: under the worst possible circumstances we shall all be rich enough for our desires and on the passage of this bill (which is not doubted by its friends) our ills will vanish like smoke. Your devoted grandson,   TH J. RANDOLPH

FROM ELLEN RANDOLPH COOLIDGE

Boston March 8.26.

I enclose a bill for the brandy &c. my dearest Grandpapa, by which you will see that we save still a few dollars remaining of the sixty sent by Col. Peyton. There are also such receipts for dressing the fish and tongues and sounds as I could obtain, but these dishes, especially the latter, are scarcely ever brought upon table in Boston, owing, I suppose, to their being so easily obtained as to lose their value by their commonness. The salt cod is prepared the first day very much as we do our bacon and hams, soaked the over night and boiled a good deal to soften and freshen it; it is then eaten with hard boiled eggs melted butter, or oil, and various boiled vegetables as beets, carrots &c. Egg or anchovy sauce may be served with it and is prepared by some. The second day the fragments of the cold fish are minced very fine and mixed with boiled potatoes, and either eaten with a sauce or made into cakes and browned in a frying pan. With the tongues and sounds the principal care is to freshen them as much as possible by washing and soaking and they are oftenest boiled plain and served with a sauce. You will see that the brandy came to $1.30 by the gallon, it was the lowest price for which it could be obtained good. The merchant who supplied these articles exerted himself to get them of the best quality knowing for whom they were and anxious that they should give satisfaction. Any thing that we can do for you, my dearest grandpapa, will be so much gain for us, who look upon the power of serving you, ever in such trifles as these, as one of our great pleasures, and a privilege we would exercise wherever we may.

By the same mail with this letter I shall send a pamphlet directed to you but intended for Mr. Trist as the best answers to some questions of his concerning the schools of Boston. Having mentioned in one of my letters the circumstance that none but Bostonians were admitted to these schools, (a regulation so apparently illiberal,) I should have added that they are free schools, supported by a tax upon the townspeople, who of course would not be called upon to pay for the education of any children but their own and those of their fellow citizens. The sum of 70,000 Ds. is annually taken from the pockets of the Bostonians for the single purpose of maintaining the schools in their own city; and there is no tax paid with less reluctance, for not only does the public spirit and ambition, of the people generally, flow with it's greatest strength and vigour in this one of the channels of public improvement, but their zeal is kept alive by the success of their efforts; I am told that the schools are rising in character from year to year and that the scholars they turn out now are of much higher order than those of a few years back. The children of the rich and the poor indiscriminately attend them, and are educated gratis. There is no pride upon this subject; the rich man, to be sure, may say that there is nothing gratis for him but the name, since he is taxed in proportion to his property, and married or single, childless or with a numerous family he must still pay his quota for the good of the rising generation. Wealthy bachelors are thus compelled to educate the offspring of their neighbours, and Mr. Sears[1] with a wife and six children, and an annual income of 90,000 Ds, cannot shrink from contributing his proportion towards the proper training of the twenty one sons and daughters of his neighbor, an honest mechanic, whose yearly gains may not be more than twenty one hundred dollars. I have never however heard anything like a murmur upon the subject of this tax so beneficial in it's results.

As the winter wears away I am beginning to look with longing eyes towards the South, and the gloom which now overspreads my beloved family makes me but the more anxious to join them. I shall find the circle diminished by one of it's members whose misfortunes had only served to endear her to her friends, and draw her nearer to their hearts whilst they removed her from their eyes, and alienated her from their society. Would I could hope that he, whose vices embittered her life, might be touched by her death, with a tardy remorse, and bring forth the fruits of repentance, in such a degree of reformation, as will render our future intercourse with him supportable if not desirable. I hope to leave Boston for Monticello before the heats of summer make it unpleasant to travel, but this will depend, in a great degree, upon the state of Mr. Coolidge's business. He may be detained much later. With Virginia's piano, (which I hope is by this time near Monticello,) there is a book sent by Mr. Coolidge to my father, which has a high reputation, and you might perhaps take some pleasure in looking over; Russel's Tour in Germany. I have found it very interesting, and it is said to be the best book of travels through that country, which has been published for a long time.

I know not whether my sisters mentioned to you the wish of Mr. John Gray son of the late Lieutenant Governor Gray, to procure some slips of a cider apple which he understands you have and consider one of the best in the State. I presume it to be, not the Crab, for that is common in other parts of Virginia, but a red apple which I remember you prized for it's cider; and Horace Gray, who visited you some years ago, was the person who spoke of it to his brother in such a way as makes him anxious to obtain and propagate it here. Mr. Coolidge wrote to you about a week ago, and desires now to be affectionately remembered to you. With love to all my family circle I bid you adieu my dearest grandpapa, in the hope that no new assurance can be necessary of the unbounded veneration and affection of your devoted grand daughter.   ELLEN W. COOLIDGE

1. Probably Frederick R. Sears, whose son Frederick R., Jr., married Ellenora Randolph Coolidge, a great-great-granddaughter of TJ.

To Ellen Randolph Coolidge

Monticello Mar. 19. 26.

MY DEAR ELLEN

Your letter of the 8th. was recieved the day before yesterday, and as the season for engrafting is passing rapidly by I will not detain the applecuttings for Mr. Gray, (but until I may have other matter for writing a *big* letter to you) I send a dozen cuttings, as much as a letter can protect, by our 1st. mail, and wish they may retain their vitality until they reach him. They are called the Taliaferro apple, being from a seedling tree, discovered by a gentleman of that name near Williamsburg, and yield unquestionably the finest cyder we have ever known, and more like wine than any liquor I have ever tasted which was not wine. If it is worth reminding me of the ensuing winter, I may send a larger supply, and in better time through Colo. Peyton. Our brandy, fish, tongues and sounds are here and highly approved. The Piano forte is also in place, and Mrs. Carey *happening* to be here has exhibited to us it's full powers, which are indeed great. Nobody slept the 1st. night, nor is the tumult yet over on this the 3d day of it's emplacement. These things will draw trouble on you; for we shall no longer be able to drink Raphael's *Imitation brandy* at 2. D. the gallon, nor to be without the luxury of the fish, and especially the tongues and sounds, which we consider as a great delicacy. All here are well, and growing in their love to you, and none so much as the oldest, who embraces in it your other self, so worthy of all our affections, and so entirely identified in them with yourself.

TH: JEFFERSON

FROM THOMAS JEFFERSON RANDOLPH

Richmond April 3 1826

MY DEAR GRANDFATHER

Upon my arrival here I found no steps had been taken to prepare the tickets for the Lottery. Some difference of opinion existed as to the expediency of price proposed viz $10. I find no reason to alter and I believe none will exist: the ticket scheme &c. I propose to have prepared in New York to which place I shall hurry on without stopping in Washington or Philadelphia. After every thing is arranged I shall then return to Philadelphia and deliver my letters and proceed to the disposition of the tickets. No doubt is entertained of the immediate sale. John Randolph has written here to have $500. vested in tickets for him and Judge Marshall has requested Peyton to inform him as soon as he recieves them as he wishes to buy some. In tomorrows paper, (the idea I suggested i.e. communities instead of individuals buying the tickets) will be noticed and there is strong reason to believe that it will go down. Before the tickets can be prepared we shall be enabled to see more clearly what the result will be.

The distress of the money market is great beyond all former example. The Banks are curtailing and universal distrust prevails. Heavy failures are anticipated upon the arrival of the next packets from England. The first of which have [been] due since the first of March. Direct to me to the care of Mr. Coolidge Boston until further advised. If you see nothing wrong in it my wifes letters would reach me more certainly under cover from you.

Affectionately,   ThJ RANDOLPH

FROM THOMAS JEFFERSON RANDOLPH

New York April 25 1826

MY DEAR GRANDFATHER

I have returned thus far on my way home and can yet report nothing definitivly. Some feeble attempts have been made here and in Boston to raise money by subscription. They have neither succeeded or failed. The extreme pressure of the money market will I think prevent any thing being done at present in that way. Altho it will not prevent the sale of tickets. Persons do not like to subscribe ten dollars where others have subscribed $500. The prospectus of the lottery will be published in the course of next week and tickets offered every where at once for sale. I am told by every body they will sell rapidly. Persons will purchase one, two or three who would not like to subscribe so small a sum. Every [thing] is as favorable as I could expect. I will write from Philadelphia by the 5 or 6 of next month when I hope to report progress. Most affectionately yours,   THS J RANDOLPH

FROM THOMAS JEFFERSON RANDOLPH

Philadelphia April 30th 1826

MY DEAR GRANDFATHER

I arrived here this morning from New York. Every thing is now ready to commence the sale of the tickets. But a movement has taken place in New-York promising some thing more in its effects than any thing of the kind heretofore. A meeting has been called (in pursuance of the request of individuals) by the Mayor to be held to morrow to take the subject into consideration. I had an interview previous to my departure yesterday with the Mayor, several Aldermen and leading republicans at their instance to inform them what course would be most agreeable to you. Much zeal was expressed and much confidence of success. At their special request I agreed to assist. 15 days or to the 15th of May to see the result of their operations before any tickets shall be sold. I do not doubt a rapid sale, if the N York movement should fail. In my next I may hope to be more certain upon the subject. I propose to remain here this week and spend ten days or a fortnight in Baltimore and Washington. If I find my services can then be dispensed with I shall joyfully turn my steps towards home. It is however possible I may find it necessary to return to N. York for a few days. Most affectionately yours,   THJ RANDOLPH

TO ELLEN RANDOLPH COOLIDGE

Monticello June 5. 26.

A word to you, my dearest Ellen, under the cover of Mr. Coolidge's letter. I address you the less frequently, because I find it easier to write 10. letters of business, than one on the intangible affections of the mind. Were these to be indulged as calls for writing letters to express them, my love to you would engross the unremitting exercises of my pen. I hear of you regularly however, thro' your correspondents of the family, and also of Cornelia since she has joined you. She will find, on her return some changes in our neighborhood. The removal of the family of Ashton to New London will be felt by us all; and will scarcely be compensated by an increased intercourse with the house beyond them. Yesterday closed a visit of 6 weeks from the younger members of the latter, during which their attractions had kept us full of the homagers to their beauty. According to appearances they had many nibbles and bites, but whether the hooks took firm hold of any particular subject or not, is a secret not communicated to me. If not, we shall know it by a return to their angling grounds, for here they fix them until they catch something to their palate. The annual visit of the family en masse begins, you know, the next month. Our near relationship of blood interests me of course in their success. For by ascending to my great grandfather to their great, great, great grandfather, we come to a common ancestor. Shall I say anything to you of my health? It is as good as I ever expect it to be. At present tolerable, but subject to occasional relapses of sufferance. I am just now out of one of these. The pleasure of seeing yourself, Mr. Coolidge and Cornelia I begin to enjoy in anticipation; and am sure I shall feel it's sanative effects when the moment arrives. I commit my affections to Mr. Coolidge to my letter to him. Communicate those to Cornelia by a thousand kisses from me, and take to yourself those I impress on this paper for you.   TH: JEFFERSON

FROM FRANCIS WAYLES EPPES

P. F. June 23. 26.

MY DR. GRANDFATHER

Knowing that all of your pavilions at the university have tin coverings, I write to learn whether they have ever leaked, and if so what method of prevention had been used. Our roof here was perfectly close until about mid winter. It then began to leak not in one but a hundred places: and from that time I have endeavoured to discover the cause without effect. For some time I thought that the water found its way, between the sheeting and the bottom of the platform, just where the gutters vent their

water, but after removing the tin and making the sheeting perfectly tight, I found myself mistaken. A subsequent examination
immediately after a hard rain, showed me, on the lowest side of
every sheet of tin, spots of water on the sheeting plank. This water
must have been drawn upwards, as there were no traces above:
and that a few drops could be so drawn up, I could readily con-
ceive; but the quantity is really incridible. The plaistering of the
parlour is so entirely wet every rain, that I begin to fear it will
fall in. Large buckets of water pass through it. Your room is
nearly as bad and the others leak more and more every rain. The
hall is in fact, the only dry room in the house. I have been so completely baffled in every attempt to stop the leaking, that I really
feel quite at a loss; we have had here, in the last four weeks three
of the most destructive rains ever known in this neighbourhood.
The tobacco hills on flat land were entirely swept off. Mine were
hilled over twice, and the third swept off soil and all. I count my
loss equal to a good hogshead. Your loss would more than double
that in first rate tobacco; for the land was heavily Manured, and
nothing but the clay is left behind. The wheat is fairly buried in
the mud every where. My love to all, my tenderest love to you
My dear Grandfather.   F. EPPES

This is the last located Jefferson family letter, received less than
two weeks before TJ's death. The old patriarch had been in
noticeably failing health prior to the receipt of this letter, for on
June 24 he had yielded to the entreaties of his family and asked
Dr. Robley Dunglison, a professor at the University of Virginia
and trusted physician, to come to Monticello. Dr. Dunglison recalled this visit in his "Memoirs": "I immediately saw that the
affection was making a decided impression on his bodily powers
. . . [and] was apprehensive that the attack [probably dysentery]
would prove fatal. Nor did Mr. Jefferson indulge in any other
opinion. From this time his strength gradually diminished and
he had to remain in bed. The evacuations became less numerous,
but it was manifest that his powers were failing." (Randall, III,
548.)

Jefferson died of the infirmities of old age aggravated by a
severe visceral complaint at ten minutes before one o'clock on
July 4, 1826, at Monticello. Here, in Jefferson's bedroom, a small
group of family and servants had maintained a death vigil. Included were Jefferson Randolph, Nicholas P. Trist, and Martha

Jefferson Randolph, and the servants Burwell and possibly Joe Fosset and John Hemings. Alexander Garrett, a friend, wrote from Monticello of Jefferson's death: "Mr. Jefferson is no more, he breathed his last . . . almost without a struggle. . . . His remains will be buried tomorrow at 5 o'clock P.M. No invitations will be given, all coming will be welcome *at the grave*. (Garrett to Mrs. Alexander Garrett, July 4, 1826, Garrett Papers, Manuscripts Division, Alderman Library, University of Virginia.) On July 5 Thomas Jefferson was interred at Monticello by the Reverend Mr. Hatch according to the rites of the Episcopal Church.

Index